Queen's English

FRENCH-ENGLISH
ENGLISH-FRENCH
DICTIONARY

Queen's English

FRENCH–ENGLISH
ENGLISH–FRENCH
DICTIONARY

This is a Parragon Book
First published in 2002

Parragon
Queen Street House
4 Queen Street
Bath, BA1 1HE

Published for Parragon by Geddes & Grosset,
David Dale House, New Lanark, ML11 9DJ

ISBN 0-75259-366-8

Printed and bound in Europe

Contents

Abbreviations/Abréviations

abrev	abbreviation	abréviation
adj	adjective	adjectif
adv	adverb	adverbe
anat	anatomy	anatomie
art	article	article
auto	automobile	automobile
aux	auxiliary	auxiliaire
bot	botany	botanique
chem, chim	chemistry	chimie
cin	cinema	cinéma
col	colloquial term	expression familière
com	commerce	commerce
compd	compound	mot composé
comput	computers	informatique
conj	conjunction	conjonction
excl	exclamation	exclamation
f	feminine noun	substantif féminin
fam	colloquial term	expression familière
fig	figurative	figuré
geol	geology	géologie
gr	grammar	grammaire
imp	impersonal	impersonnel
inform	computers	informatique
interj	interjection	interjection
invar	invariable	invariable
irr	irregular	irrégulier
jur	law term	juridique
law	law term	droit
ling	linguistics	linguistique

m	masculine noun	substantif masculin
mar	marine term	vocabulaire marin
mat, math	mathematics	mathématiques
med	medicine	médecine
mil	military term	vocabulaire militaire
mus	music	musique
n	noun	substantif
orn	ornithology	ornithologie
o.s.	oneself	
pej	pejorative	péjoratif
pl	plural	pluriel
pn	pronoun	pronom
poet	poetical term	vocabulaire poétique
p.p.	past participle	participle passé
prep	preposition	préposition
qch		quelque chose
qn		quelqu'un
rad	radio	radio
rail	railway	chemin de fer
sb	somebody, someone	
sl	slang	argot
sth	something	
thea	theatre	théâtre
tec	technology	technologie
TV	television	télévision
vi	intransitive verb	verbe intransitif
vr	reflexive verb	verbe réfléchi
vt	transitive verb	verbe transitif
zool	zoology	zoologie

French–English Dictionary

A

à *prép* (in) to; at; on; by, per; aller ~ l'école to go to school; ~ neuf heures at nine o'clock; c'est ~ toi it's yours; it's your turn.

abaissement *m* fall, drop.

abaisser *vt* to lower; s'~ à faire qch to stoop to doing sth.

abandon *m* abandonment, desertion.

abandonné *adj* deserted.

abandonner *vt* to abandon, leave.

abasourdi *adj* stunned.

abasourdir *vt* to stun.

abats *mpl* giblets.

abat-jour *m* lampshade.

abattement *m* despondency; exhaustion.

abattoir *m* abattoir, slaughterhouse.

abattre *vt* to shoot; to slaughter.

abattu *adj* despondent; exhausted.

abbaye *f* abbey.

abbé *m* abbot.

abbesse *f* abbess.

abcès *m* abscess.

abdiquer *vt vi* to abdicate.

abdomen *m* abdomen.

abdominal *adj* abdominal.

abeille *f* bee.

aberrant *adj* aberrant; absurd.

aberration *f* aberration.

abêtissant *adj* mindless.

abêtissement *m* mindlessness.

abîme *m* chasm.

abîmer *vt* to spoil, damage; * s'~ *vr* to get spoiled *ou* damaged.

abject *adj* abject.

abjection *f* abjectness.

abjurer *vt* to abjure.

ablatif *m* ablative.

ablation *f* (*med*) removal.

abnégation *f* abnegation.

aboiement *m* bark.

abolir *vt* to abolish.

abolition f abolition.

abominable adj abominable;
~**ment** adv abominably.

abondamment adv abundantly.

abondance f abundance.

abondant adj abundant,
plentiful.

abonder vi to be abundant
ou plentiful.

abonné m -**ée** f subscriber.

abonnement m subscription.

abonner vt ~ **qn** to subscribe,
take out a subscription (à
to); * **s'**~ vr to subscribe,
take out a subscription (à
to).

abord m: **d'**~ first (of all).

abordable adj affordable.

aborder vt to approach.

aborigène mf aborigine; * adj
aboriginal.

aboutir vi to succeed.

aboutissement m outcome;
success.

abrasif adj abrasive.

abrégé m summary; **en** ~
briefly.

abréger vt to shorten; to
abridge.

abreuver vt to water.

abreuvoir m drinking trough.

abréviation f abbreviation.

abri m shelter.

abricot m apricot.

abriter vt to shelter; * **s'**~ vr
to shelter.

abroger vt to repeal.

abrupt adj abrupt; ~**ement**
adv abruptly.

abruti m -**e** f idiot; * adj idiotic.

abrutir vt to make stupid.

abrutissant adj stunning;
mind-numbing.

abscisse f (math) abscissa.

absence f absence.

absent adj absent.

absenter (s') vr to leave, go
out.

abside f apse.

absolu adj absolute; ~**ment**
adv   absolutely;
* m absolute.

absolution f absolution.

absolutisme m absolutism.

absorbant adj absorbent.

absorber vt to absorb.

absorption f absorption.

absoudre vt to absolve.

abstenir (s') vr to abstain
(from).

abstention f abstention.

abstentionniste mf abstainer.

abstinence f abstinence.

abstraction f abstraction.

abstrait *adj* abstract; ~ement *adv* in the abstract; * *m* abstract; abstract art.

absurde *adj* absurd; ~ment *adv* absurdly.

absurdité *f* absurdity.

abus *m* abuse.

abuser *vt* ~ de to exploit; to abuse.

abusif *adj* improper.

académicien *m* -ne *f* academician.

académie *f* academy; learned society.

académique *adj* academic.

acajou *m* mahogany.

acariâtre *adj* cantankerous.

accablant *adj* overwhelming.

accabler *vt* to overwhelm.

accalmie *f* lull, calm.

accéder *vi*: ~ à to reach.

accélérateur *m* accelerator.

accélération *f* acceleration.

accélérer *vi* to speed up, accelerate.

accent *m* accent.

accentuation *f* accentuation.

accentué *adj* pronounced.

accentuer *vt* to accentuate.

acceptable *adj* acceptable.

accepter *vt* to accept.

accès *m* access.

accessible *adj* accessible.

accessoire *adj* secondary; ~ment *adv* secondarily; if need be; * *m* accessory.

accident *m* accident.

accidentel *adj* accidental; ~lement *adv* accidentally.

acclamations *fpl* cheers; acclamation.

acclamer *vt* to acclaim, cheer.

acclimater *vt* to acclimatize; s'~ *vr* to become acclimatized.

accolade *f* embrace.

accommodant *adj* accommodating.

accommoder *vt* to prepare; to adapt.

accompagnateur *m* -trice *f* (*mus*) accompanist; guide.

accompagnement *m* accompaniment.

accompagner *vt* to accompany.

accomplir *vt* to achieve, accomplish.

accomplissement *m* accomplishment.

accord *m* agreement; d'~! okay!, all right!; être d'~ to agree.

accordéon *m* accordion.

accorder *vt* to grant; s'~ *vr* to agree.

accoster *vt* to accost.

accouchement *m* (*med*) delivery.

accoucher *vi* to give birth.

accoudoir *m* armrest.

accouplement *m* coupling; joining.

accourir *vi* to run up (*à, vers* to).

accoutrement *m* (*pej*) outfit, dress.

accréditer *vt* to accredit.

accroc *m* tear, breach.

accrocher *vt* to hang up (*à* on).

accroissement *m* increase.

accroître *vt* to increase.

accroupir (s') *vr* to crouch.

accueil *m* welcome, reception.

accueillant *adj* welcoming.

accueillir *vt* to welcome.

accumulateur *m* battery.

accumulation *f* accumulation.

accumuler *vt* to accumulate.

accusateur *m* -trice *f* accuser; * *adj* accusing.

accusatif *m* accusative (case).

accusation *f* accusation.

accusé *m* -e *f* (*jur*) accused, defendant.

accuser *vt* to accuse.

acerbe *adj* harsh; acrid.

acétate *m* acetate.

acétone *f* acetone.

acharné *adj* bitter, fierce; unrelenting.

acharnement *m* relentlessness; determination.

acharner (s') *vr* ~ à faire qch to try desperately to do sth; ~ contre qn to hound sb.

achat *m* purchase.

acheminer *vt* to convey.

acheter *vt* to buy.

acheteur *m* -euse *f* buyer, purchaser.

achèvement *m* completion.

achever *vt* to finish, complete.

acide *adj* acid, sour; * *m* acid.

acidité *f* acidity.

acidulé *adj* acid, acidulous.

acier *m* steel.

aciérie *f* steelworks.

acné *f* acne.

acompte *m* deposit, downpayment.

à-côté *m* side issue.

à-coup *m* jolt.

acoustique *adj* acoustic; * *f* acoustics.

acquéreur *m* buyer, purchaser.

acquérir *vt* to buy, purchase.

acquiescer *vi* to agree, acquiesce.

acquis *adj* acquired; * *m* experience.

acquisition *f* acquisition; purchase.

acquittement *m* payment; (*jur*) acquittal.

acquitter *vt* to acquit; to pay.

acre *f* acre.

âcre *adj* acrid.

acrobate *mf* acrobat.

acrobatie *f* acrobatics.

acrobatique *adj* acrobatic.

acrylique *m*, *adj* acrylic.

acte *m* act; deed.

acteur *m*, **actrice** *f* actor.

actif *adj* active; * *m* (*ling*) active (voice).

action *f* act, action; share.

actionnaire *mf* shareholder.

actionner *vt* to activate; to drive.

activement *adv* actively.

activer *vt* to speed up; s'~ *vr* to bustle about.

activité *f* activity; hustle and bustle.

actualité *f*: l'**actualité** current events.

actuel *adj* current, present; ~lement *adv* currently, at present.

acuité *f* acuteness; shrillness.

acuponcture *f* acupuncture.

adaptable *adj* adaptable.

adaptateur *m* adaptor.

adaptation *f* adaptation.

adapter *vt* to adapt (*à* to); s'~ *vr* to adapt o.s. (*à* to).

additif *m* additive.

addition *f* addition; bill.

additionnel *adj* additional.

additionner *vt* to add up.

adepte *mf* follower; enthusiast.

adéquat *adj* suitable, appropriate.

adhérence *f* adhesion.

adhérent *m* -e *f* member, adherent; * *adj* : ~ à which adheres *ou* sticks to.

adhérer *vi* to adhere, stick.

adhésif *adj* adhesive.

adhésion *f* adherence; membership.

adjacent *adj* adjacent (*à* to).

adjectif *m* adjective.

adjoint *m* -e *f* assistant, deputy.

adjudant *m* warrant officer.

adjudication *f* sale by auction.

adjuger *vt* to auction.

admettre *vt* to admit; to accept; to assume.

administrateur *m* -trice *f* administrator.

administratif *adj* administrative.

administration *f* management; administration.

administrer *vt* to run, administer.

admirable *adj* admirable; -ment *adv* admirably, brilliantly.

admiratif *adj* admiring.

admiration *f* admiration.

admirativement *adv* admiringly.

admirer *vt* to admire.

admissible *adj* allowable.

admission *f* admission.

adolescence *f* adolescence.

adolescent *m* -e *f* adolescent.

adopter *vt* to adopt; to pass.

adoption *f* adoption; passing.

adorable *adj* adorable; ~ment *adv* delightfully.

adorer *vt* to adore, worship.

adoucir *vt* to soften.

adrénaline *f* adrenalin.

adresse *f* address; skill.

adresser *vt* to address; to send; **s'~** *vr* **s'~ à** to apply to; to speak to.

adroit *adj* deft, skilful; ~ement *adv* deftly, skilfully.

aduler *vt* to flatter.

adulte *mf* adult, grown-up; *adj* adult, full-grown.

adultère *m* adultery.

adverbe *m* adverb.

adverbial *adj*, *f* -e adverbial; ~ement *adv* adverbially.

adversaire *mf* adversary, opponent.

adversité *f* adversity.

aération *f* ventilation.

aérer *vt* to air.

aérien *adj*, *f* -ne air, airy; aerial.

aérodrome *m* aerodrome, airfield.

aérodynamique *adj* aerodynamic; * *f* aerodynamics.

aérogare *f* (air) terminal.

aéroglisseur *m* hovercraft.

aéronautique *adj* aeronautic; * *f* aeronautics.

aéronaval *adj* air and sea.

aéroport *m* airport.

aérospatial *adj* aerospace.

affable *adj* affable.

affaiblir *vt* to weaken; **s'~** *vr* to weaken, grow weaker.

affaiblissement *m* weakening.

affaire *f* matter.

affaissement *m* subsidence.

affaisser *vt* to cause to subside *ou* cave in; **s'~** *vr* to subside; to cave in.

affamé *adj* starving.

affamer *vt* to starve.

affectation *f* allocation (*à* to); affectation.

affecté *adj* affected.

affecter *vt* to affect.

affectif *adj* emotional.

affection *f* affection.

affectueux *adj* affectionate.

affectueusement *adv* affectionately.

affermir *vt* to strengthen; to make firm.

affermissement *m* strengthening.

affichage *m* bill posting.

affiche *f* poster.

afficher *vt* to post *ou* put up.

affiner *vt* to refine.

affinité *f* affinity.

affirmatif *adj* affirmative.

affirmation *f* assertion.

affirmativement *adv* in the affirmative.

affirmer *vt* to assert.

affluent *m* tributary.

affluer *vi* to rush (*à* to).

afflux *m* influx, rush.

affolant *adj* alarming.

affolement *m* panic.

affoler *vt* to throw into a panic; **s'~** *vr* to get into a panic.

affranchir *vt* to frank, stamp; to free.

affranchissement *m* stamping, franking; freeing.

affréter *vt* to charter.

affreux *adj* horrible; awful.

affreusement *adv* horribly, dreadfully.

affrontement *m* confrontation.

affronter *vt* to confront; **s'~** *vr* to confront one another.

afin *prép*: ~ **de** (in order) to; ~ **que** in order that, so that.

africain *adj*, *mf* African.

Afrique *f* Africa.

agaçant *adj* annoying.

agacer *vt* to annoy, irritate.

âge *m* age; **quel ~ as-tu?** how old are you?

âgé *adj* old; ~ **de 10 ans** 10 years old.

agence *f* agency; branch; offices.

agencement *m* organization, arrangement; equipment.

agencer *vt* to arrange; to equip.

agenda *m* diary.

agenouiller (s') *vr* to kneel (down).

agent *m* agent; policeman.

agglomération *f* town, urban area.

aggravant *adj* aggravating.

aggravation *f* worsening, aggravation; increase.

aggraver *vt* to make worse; to increase; **s'~** *vr* to get worse, worsen; to increase.

agile *adj* agile, nimble; **~ment** *adv* nimbly.

agilité *f* agility.

agir *vi* to act.

agitateur *m* **-trice** *f* agitator.

agitation *f* agitation.

agiter *vt* to shake; to wave; **s'~** *vr* to move about; to fidget.

agneau *m* lamb.

agonie *f* death throes.

agrafe *f* staple; hook.

agrafer *vt* to staple (together); to fasten up.

agrafeuse *f* stapler.

agraire *adj* agrarian; land.

agrandir *vt* to make bigger; to widen; to expand; **s'~** *vr* to get bigger; to widen; to expand.

agrandissement *m* enlargement.

agréable *adj* agreeable, pleasant; **~ment** *adv* agreeably, pleasantly.

agresser *vt* to attack.

agresseur *m* attacker.

agressif *adj* aggressive.

agression *f* attack.

agressivement *adv* aggressively.

agressivité *f* aggressiveness.

agricole *adj* agricultural.

agriculteur *m* farmer.

agriculture *f* agriculture, farming.

agripper *vt* to grab (hold of); **s'~** **à** *vr* to grab on to.

agronome *m* agronomist.

agronomie *f* agronomy.

agrumes *mpl* citrus fruits.

ahuri *adj* stunned; stupefied.

ahurissant *adj* staggering.

aide *f* help; aid.

aider *vt* to help.

aigle *m* eagle.

aigre *adj* sour, bitter; **~ment** *adv* sourly.

aigreur *f* sourness; acidity.

aigri *adj* bitter, embittered.

aigu *adj*, *f* **aiguë** shrill; acute; sharp.

aiguillage *m* shunting.

aiguille *f* needle.

aiguiller *vt* to direct; to shunt.

aiguiser *vt* to sharpen.

ail *m* garlic.

ailé *adj* winged.

aileron *m* fin; aileron.

ailleurs *adv* elsewhere; **partout ~** everywhere else;

nulle part ~ nowhere else; **d'**~ moreover; by the way.

aimable *adj* kind; **~ment** *adv* kindly.

aimant *m* magnet.

aimanter *vt* to magnetize.

aimer *vt* to love.

aîné *m*, **aînée** *f* eldest *ou* oldest child; * *adj* elder, older; eldest, oldest.

ainsi *adv* so, thus; **puisque c'est** ~ since this is the way it is *ou* things are.

air *m* air; **avoir l'**~ content to look happy; **d'un** ~ **moqueur** in a mocking fashion.

aire *f* area.

aise *f* ease, comfort.

aisé *adj* easy; well-off; **~ment** *adv* easily.

aisselle *f* armpit.

ajournement *m* adjournment; postponement.

ajourner *vt* to adjourn; to defer, postpone.

ajout *m* addition.

ajouter *vt* to add.

ajuster *vt* to adjust.

alarmant *adj* alarming.

alarme *f* alarm.

alarmer *vt* to alarm; **s'**~ *vr* to get alarmed (*de* at, about).

albâtre *m* alabaster.

album *m* album.

albumine *f* albumen.

alcalin *adj* alkaline.

alcaloïde *m* alkaloid.

alchimie *f* alchemy.

alchimiste *m* alchemist.

alcool *m* alcohol.

alcoolique *adj* alcoholic; * *mf* drunkard.

alcoolisme *m* alcoholism.

aléatoire *adj* uncertain; risky.

alentours *mpl* surroundings, neighbourhood.

alerte *adj* alert; agile; * *f* alarm, alert.

alerter *vt* to alert; to notify; to warn.

algèbre *f* algebra.

algébrique *adj* algebraic; **~ment** *adv* algebraically.

algorithme *m* algorithm.

algue *f* seaweed.

alibi *m* alibi.

aliénation *f* alienation.

aliéner *vt* to alienate.

alignement *m* alignment; aligning.

aligner *vt* to align, line up.

aliment *m* food.

alimentaire *adj* alimentary, food.

alimentation *f* feeding; diet; food industry.

alimenter *vt* to feed; **s' ~** *vr* to eat.

alinéa *m* paragraph.

allée *f* avenue; path.

alléger *vt* to make lighter; to alleviate.

allégorie *f* allegory.

allégresse *f* cheerfulness.

alléguer *vt* to allege, put forward.

aller *vi* to go; **comment allez-vous?** how are you?; **allons-y** let's go; **s'en aller** to go away, leave; * *m* outward journey; single ticket.

allergie *f* allergy.

allergique *adj* allergic (*à* to).

alliage *m* alloy.

alliance *f* alliance; marriage; wedding ring.

allié *m* -e *f* ally; * *adj* allied.

allier *vt* to combine.

allô *excl* hello!

allocation *f* allocation; allowance.

allongé *adj* être allongé to be lying (down).

allonger *vt* to lengthen; **s' ~** *vr* to lengthen; to lie down.

allouer *vt* to allocate.

allumage *m* ignition.

allumer *vt* to light; to turn *ou* switch on.

allumette *f* match.

allure *f* speed; look.

allusion *f* allusion (*à* to).

alluvions *fpl* alluvium, alluvial deposits.

alors *adv* then; ~ **que** while; whereas.

alouette *f* lark.

alourdir *vt* to make heavy; to increase.

alphabet *m* alphabet.

alphabétique *adj* alphabetical; **~ment** *adv* alphabetically.

alpinisme *m* mountaineering.

alpiniste *mf* mountaineer.

altération *f* alteration, change.

altercation *f* altercation.

altérer *vt* to change, alter.

alternance *f* alternation.

alternatif *adj* alternate.

alternative *f* alternative.

alternativement *adv* in turn, alternately.

alterner *vt* *vi* to alternate (*avec* with).

altitude *f* altitude, height.

altruisme *m* altruism.

aluminium *m* aluminium.

alvéole *f* cell.

amabilité *f* kindness.

amaigrir *vt* to make thin(ner).

amaigrissant *adj* slimming.

amalgame *m* mixture, amalgam.

amalgamer *vt* to combine.

amande *f* almond.

amant *m* lover.

amarrer *vt* to moor.

amas *m* pile, heap.

amasser *vt* to amass, pile up.

amateur *m* amateur; connoisseur.

ambassade *f* embassy.

ambassadeur *m* -drice *f* ambassador.

ambiance *f* atmosphere.

ambigu *adj*, *f* **ambiguë** ambiguous.

ambiguïté *f* ambiguity.

ambitieux *adj* ambitious.

ambition *f* ambition.

ambivalence *f* ambivalence.

ambre *m* amber.

ambulance *f* ambulance.

ambulant *adj* travelling, mobile.

âme *f* soul.

amélioration *f* improvement.

améliorer *vt* to improve; **s'~** *vr* to improve.

aménagement *m* fitting out; adjustment; development.

aménager *vt* to fit out; to adjust; to develop.

amende *f* fine.

amendement *m* amendment.

amener *vt* to bring.

amer *adj* bitter.

amèrement *adv* bitterly.

Américain *m* -e *f* American.

américain *adj* American.

Amérique *f* America.

amertume *f* bitterness.

ameublement *m* furniture.

ami *m* -e *f* friend.

amiante *m* asbestos.

amibe *f* amoeba.

amical *adj* friendly; **~ement** *adv* in a friendly manner.

amincir *vt* to thin (down).

amiral *m* admiral.

amitié *f* friendship.

ammoniac *m* ammonia.

amnésie *f* amnesia.

amnistie *f* amnesty.

amnistier *vt* to grant an amnesty to.

amoindrir *vt* to weaken; to reduce.

amoindrissement *m* weakening; reduction.

amoncellement *m* pile; accumulation.

amorcer *vt* to bait; to begin.

amorphe *adj* apathetic.

amortir *vt* to soften; to deaden.

amortissement *m* paying off.

amour *m* love.

amoureux *adj* in love (*de* with).

amovible *adj* detachable.

ampère *m* ampere, amp.

amphibie *adj* amphibious.

amphithéâtre *m* amphitheatre.

ample *adj* roomy; wide; ~ment *adv* amply, fully.

ampleur *f* fullness; range.

amplifier *vt* to increase; to amplify.

amplitude *f* amplitude; magnitude.

ampoule *f* bulb; phial; blister.

amputation *f* amputation.

amputer *vt* to amputate.

amusant *adj* amusing.

amuser *vt* to amuse.

an *m* year; **avoir vingt ~s** to be 20 (years old).

anabolisant *m* anabolic steroid.

anachronisme *m* anachronism.

anagramme *m* anagram.

analgésique *adj* analgesic.

analogie *f* analogy.

analogique *adj* analogical.

analogue *adj* analogous (*à* to).

analphabète *adj* illiterate.

analyse *f* analysis; test.

analyser *vt* to analyse.

analyste *mf* analyst; psychoanalyst.

analytique *adj* analytical; ~ment *adv* analytically.

ananas *m* pineapple.

anarchie *f* anarchy.

anarchiste *mf* anarchist.

anathème *m* anathema.

anatomie *f* anatomy.

anatomique *adj* anatomical; ~ment *adv* anatomically.

ancestral *adj* ancestral.

ancêtre *m* ancestor.

anchois *m* anchovy.

ancien *adj* old; former; ~nement *adv* formerly.

ancienneté *f* (years of) service; seniority; age.

ancrage *m* anchorage.

ancre *f* anchor.

ancrer *vt* to anchor.

âne *m* ass, donkey.

anéantir *vt* to annihilate.

anéantissement *m* annihilation.

anecdote *f* anecdote.

anémie *f* anemia.

anémone *f* anemone.

anesthésie *f* anaesthetic; anaesthesia.

anesthésique *m* anaesthetic.

ange *m* angel.

angélique *adj* angelic; * *f* angelica.

angine *f* tonsillitis.

Anglais *m* -e *f* Englishman; Englishwoman.

anglais *adj* English; * *m* (*ling*) English.

angle *m* angle; corner.

Angleterre *f* England.

anglophone *adj* English-speaking; *mf* English speaker.

angoissant *adj* agonizing.

angoisse *f* anguish.

angoisser *vt* to cause anguish.

animal *m* animal.

animateur *m* -trice *f* host, compère; leader.

animation *f* animation; hustle and bustle.

animé *adj* busy; lively.

animer *vt* to lead; to host; to liven up; s'~ *vr* to liven up.

animisme *m* animism.

animosité *f* animosity.

annales *fpl* annals.

anneau *m* ring.

année *f* year; les ~s soixante the Sixties.

annexe *f* annexe; * *adj* subsidiary.

annexer *vt* to annex; to append.

annihiler *vt* to annihilate.

anniversaire *m* birthday; joyeux ~! happy birthday!

annonce *f* advertisement; announcement.

annoncer *vt* to announce (*à* to).

annoter *vt* to annotate.

annuaire *m* telephone directory, phone book.

annuel *adj* annual; ~lement *adv* annually.

annulation *f* cancellation; nullification.

annuler *vt* to cancel; to nullify.

anode *f* anode.

anodin *adj* insignificant.

anomalie *f* anomaly.

anonyme *adj* anonymous; impersonal; ~ment *adv* anonymously.

anorexie *f* anorexia.

anorexique *adj*, *mf* anorexic.

anormal *adj* abnormal; ~ement *adv* abnormally.

anse *f* handle.

antagonisme *m* antagonism.

antagoniste *adj* antagonistic.

antécédent *m* antecedent.

antenne *f* (*rad*, *TV*) aerial; (*zool*) feeler.

antérieur *adj* earlier, previous; **~ement** *adv* earlier, previously.

anthologie *f* anthology.

anthracite *m* anthracite.

anthropologie *f* anthropology.

anthropologue *m* anthropologist.

antiaérien *adj* antiaircraft.

anticancéreux *adj* cancer.

antichambre *f* antechamber.

anticipation *f* anticipation.

anticonceptionnel *adj* contraceptive.

anticonformiste *adj*, *mf* non-conformist.

anticorps *m* antibody.

anticyclone *m* anticyclone.

antidater *vt* to backdate.

antidépresseur *adj*, *m* antidepressant.

antidote *m* antidote.

antigel *m* antifreeze.

antimilitariste *adj*, *mf* antimilitarist.

antinucléaire *adj*, *mf* antinuclear.

antipathie *f* antipathy.

antipathique *adj* unpleasant.

antipode *m* antipodes; **aux ~s de** the polar opposite of.

antiquaire *mf* antique dealer.

antique *adj* ancient.

antiquité *f* antiquity; antique.

antirouille *adj invar* rustproof.

antisémite *mf* antisemite; *adj* antisemitic.

antiseptique *adj* antiseptic.

antisocial *adj* antisocial.

antitétanique *adj* (anti-)tetanus.

antithèse *f* antithesis.

antitoxine *f* antitoxin.

antivol *m invar* anti-theft *ou* security device; lock; * *adj invar* anti-theft.

antonyme *m* antonym.

antre *m* den.

anus *m* anus.

anxiété *f* anxiety.

anxieux *adj* anxious.

aorte *f* aorta.

août *m* August.

apaisant *adj* soothing.

apaisement *m* calm(ing down); relief.

apaiser *vt* to calm (down); to relieve.

apathie *f* apathy.

apathique *adj* apathetic.

apercevoir *vt* to see; to catch a glimpse of.

aperçu *m* (overall *ou* general) idea.

apéritif *m* aperitif.

apesanteur *f* weightlessness.

apeuré *adj* frightened.

aphone *adj* voiceless, hoarse.

aphrodisiaque *adj*, *m* aphro-
disiac.

apiculteur *m* beekeeper.

apitoyer *vt* to move to pity;
s'~ *vr* to feel pity (*sur* for).

aplanir *vt* to level (out); to
smooth away.

aplati *adj* flat.

aplatir *vt* to flatten (out).

apocalypse *f* apocalypse.

apocalyptique *adj* apocalyp-
tic.

apogée *m* apogee, peak.

apolitique *adj* apolitical; non-
political.

apologie *f* apology.

apoplexie *f* apoplexy.

apostrophe *f* apostrophe.

apothéose *f* apotheosis.

apôtre *m* apostle.

apparaître *vi* to appear.

appareil *m* device; appliance;
(tele)phone; ~-**photo** camera.

appareillage *m* casting off;
equipment.

appareiller *vi* (*mar*) to cast
off.

apparemment *adv* apparently.

apparence *f* appearance.

apparent *adj* apparent.

apparition *f* appearance; apparition.

appartement *m* flat, apartment.

appartenance *f* membership.

appartenir *vi*: ~ à to belong
to.

appât *m* bait.

appâter *vt* to lure; to bait.

appauvrir *vt* to impoverish;
s'~ *vr* to grow poorer.

appauvrissement *m* impoverishment.

appel *m* call; appeal.

appeler *vt* to call; to call out;
s'~ *vr* je m'appelle Léon my
name is Leon.

appellation *f* appellation;
name.

appendicite *f* appendicitis.

appesantir *vt* to weigh down;
to strengthen; s'~ *vr* to
grow heavier; to grow
stronger.

appétissant *adj* appetizing.

appétit *m* appetite (*de* for).

applaudir *vt vi* to applaud.

applaudissements *mpl* applause.

applicable *adj* applicable (*à*
to).

application *f* application; use.

appliqué *adj* thorough, industrious.

appliquer *vt* to apply (*à* to); **s'~** *vr* to apply o.s.

apport *m* supply.

apporter *vt* to bring.

apposer *vt* to append; to affix.

appréciable *adj* appreciable.

appréciatif *adj* evaluative; appreciative.

appréciation *f* estimation, assessment

apprécier *vt* to appreciate; to assess

appréhender *vt* to apprehend; to dread.

appréhension *f* apprehension.

apprendre *vt* to learn; ~ **à lire** to learn to read; ~ **à lire à un enfant** to teach a child to read.

apprenti *m* **-e** *f* apprentice.

apprentissage *m* apprenticeship.

apprêter *vt* to dress; to size; **s'~** *vr* to get ready.

apprivoiser *vt* to tame.

approbateur *adj*, *f* **-trice** approving.

approbation *f* approval.

approche *f* approach.

approcher *vt* to move near; to approach; **s'~** *vr* to approach.

approfondir *vt* to deepen.

approfondissement *m* deepening.

approprier (s') *vr* to appropriate.

approuver *vt* to approve of.

approvisionnement *m* supplying.

approvisionner *vt* to supply; **s'~** *vr* to stock up (*de, en* with).

approximatif *adj* approximate.

approximation *f* approximation.

approximativement *adv* approximately.

appui *m* support.

appuie-tête *m invar* headrest.

appuyer *vt* to press; to lean; to support; * *vi* to press; *vr* **s'~** to lean against; *vr* **s'~ sur** to lean on; to rely on.

âpre *adj* bitter, harsh; ~**ment** *adv* bitterly.

après *prép* after; **après tout** after all; **d'~ elle** according to her; **collé ~ la vitre** stuck

on the window; * *adv*
after(wards); **tout de suite**
~ immediately after *ou* afterwards.

après-demain *adv* the day after tomorrow.

après-midi *m/f invar* afternoon.

âpreté *f* bitterness.

a priori *m* apriorism; * *adv* a
priori.

apte *adj* capable (*à* of).

aptitude *f* aptitude; ability.

aquarium *m* aquarium.

aquatique *adj* aquatic.

aqueduc *m* aqueduct.

aqueux *adj* aqueous, watery.

arabesque *f* arabesque.

arable *adj* arable.

arachide *f* peanut, ground-
nut.

araignée *f* spider.

arbalète *f* crossbow.

arbitrage *m* arbitration.

arbitraire *adj* arbitrary;
~**ment** *adv* arbitrarily.

arbitre *m* arbiter; referee.

arbitrer *vt* to arbitrate; to referee.

arborer *vt* to wear; to bear.

arborescence *f* arborescence.

arboriculture *f* arboriculture,
tree cultivation.

arbre *m* tree.

arbrisseau *m* shrub.

arbuste *m* bush.

arc *m* bow; arc; arch.

arcade *f* arcade.

arc-bouter (s') *vr* to lean.

arc-en-ciel *m*, *pl* **arcs-en-ciel**
rainbow.

archaïque *adj* archaic.

archange *m* archangel.

arche *f* arch.

archéologie *f* archaeology.

archéologue *mf* archaeolo-
gist.

archétype *m* archetype.

archevêque *m* archbishop.

archipel *m* archipelago.

architecte *mf* architect.

architectonique   *adj*
architectonic

architectural *adj* architectural.

architecture *f* architecture.

archiver *vt* to file, archive.

archives *fpl* archives, records.

archiviste *mf* archivist.

ardemment *adv* ardently.

ardent *adj* ardent, burning.

ardeur *f* ardour.

ardoise *f* slate.

ardu *adj* difficult.

are *f* are, a hundred square
metres.

arène *f* arena.

arête *f* (fish)bone.

argent *m* silver; money.

argenté *adj* silver; silver-plated.

argenterie *f* silverware.

argile *f* clay.

argot *m* slang.

argument *m* argument.

argumentation *f* argumentation.

argumenter *vi* to argue (*sur* about).

aride *adj* arid.

aridité *f* aridity.

aristocrate *mf* aristocrat.

aristocratie *f* aristocracy.

aristocratique *adj* aristocratic.

arithmétique *f* arithmetic; * *adj* arithmetical; ~ment *adv* arithmetically.

armature *f* (frame)work.

arme *f* arm, weapon.

armée *f* army.

armement *m* arms, weapons; armaments.

armer *vt* to arm; s'~ *vr* to arm o.s.

armistice *m* armistice.

armoire *f* cupboard; wardrobe.

armure *f* armour.

aromate *m* herb; spice.

aromatique *adj* aromatic.

aromatiser *vt* to flavour.

arôme *m* aroma; flavour.

arpenteur *m* (land) surveyor.

arqué *adj* curved, arched.

arquebuse *f* arquebus.

arrachement *m* wrench; pulling *ou* tearing off.

arracher *vt* to pull (out); to tear off.

arrangeant *adj* obliging.

arrangement *m* arrangement.

arranger *vt* to arrange; to fix; cela m'arrangerait that would suit me; s'~ *vr* to come to an arrangement; to manage; to get better.

arrestation *f* arrest.

arrêt *m* stopping; stop (button).

arrêté *m* order.

arrêter *vt* to stop; s'~ *vr* to stop.

arrhes *fpl* deposit.

arrière *m invar* back; en ~ back(wards); à l'~ at the back; * *adj invar* back, rear.

arriéré *adj* backward.

arrière-goût *m* aftertaste.

arrière-grand-mère *f* great-grandmother.

arrière-grand-père *m* great-grandfather.

arrière-pays *m* hinterland.

arrière-pensée *f* ulterior motive.

arrière-petits-enfants *mpl* great grandchildren.

arrière-plan *m* background.

arrimer *vt* to stow.

arrivage *m* delivery.

arrivant *m* -e *f* newcomer.

arrivée *f* arrival, coming.

arriver *vi* to arrive, come.

arriviste *mf* careerist; social climber.

arrogance *f* arrogance.

arrogant *adj* arrogant.

arroger (s') *vr* to assume (without rights to).

arrondi *adj* round(ed).

arrondir *vt* to make round; to round off.

arrondissement *m* district.

arrosage *m* watering.

arroser *vt* to water.

arsenal *m* arsenal.

arsenic *m* arsenic.

art *m* art.

artère *f* artery; road.

artériel *adj* arterial.

arthrite *f* arthritis.

artichaut *m* artichoke.

article *m* article.

articulation *f* joint; knuckle.

articuler *vt* to articulate.

artifice *m* trick.

artificiel *adj* artificial; ~**lement** *adv* artificially.

artillerie *f* artillery.

artisan *m* artisan, craftsman.

artisanal *adj* craft.

artisanat *m* craft industry.

artiste *mf* artist.

artistique *adj* artistic; ~**ment** *adv* artistically.

as *m* ace.

ascendance *f* ancestry.

ascendant *adj* upward, rising; * *m* (strong) influence, ascendancy (*sur* over).

ascenseur *m* lift, elevator.

ascension *f* ascent.

ascète *mf* ascetic.

ascétique *adj* ascetic.

aseptiser *vt* to sterilize; to disinfect.

asexué *adj* asexual.

asiatique *adj* Asian.

asile *m* refuge; asylum.

aspect *m* appearance, look.

asperge *f* asparagus.

asperger *vt* to splash (*de* with).

aspérité *f* bump.

asphalte *m* asphalt.

asphyxie *f* asphyxiation, suffocation.

asphyxier *vt* to asphyxiate, suffocate.

aspirateur *m* vacuum cleaner.

aspiration *f* inhalation.

aspirer *vt* to inhale.

aspirine *f* aspirin.

assagir *vt* to quieten (down); **s'~** *vr* to quieten (down).

assaillant *m* assailant.

assaillir *vt* to assail.

assainir *vt* to clean up; to purify.

assainissement *m* cleaning up.

assaisonnement *m* seasoning.

assaisonner *vt* to season.

assassin *m* murderer; assassin.

assassinat *m* murder; assassination.

assassiner *vt* to assassinate.

assaut *m* assault, attack (*de* on).

assécher *vt* to drain; **s'~** *vr* to dry (up *ou* out).

assemblage *m* assembly; assembling.

assemblée *f* meeting.

assembler *vt* to assemble; **s'~** *vr* to assemble.

assentiment *m* assent.

asseoir (s') *vr* to sit down.

assermenté *adj* on oath.

assertion *f* assertion.

asservissement *m* enslavement; slavery.

assez *adv* enough; quite, rather; **avoir ~ d'argent** to have enough money; **~ bien** quite well; **j'en ai ~!** I've had enough!; I'm fed up.

assidu *adj* assiduous; regular.

assiduité *f* assiduity; regularity.

assiéger *vt* to besiege.

assiette *f* plate.

assigner *vt* to assign.

assimilation *f* assimilation; comparison; classification.

assimiler *vt* to assimilate.

assis *adj* seated, sitting (down).

assistance *f* audience; assistance.

assistant *m* **-e** *f* assistant.

assister *vt* to attend; to assist.

association *f* association.

associé *m* **-e** *f* associate, partner.

associer *vt* to associate (*à* with); **s'~** *vr* to join together.

assombrir *vt* to darken; **s'~** to darken.

assommer *vt* to stun.

Assomption *f*: **l'~** *the Assumption*.

assortiment *m* assortment.

assortir *vt* to match; **s'~** *vr* to go well together.

assoupir (s') *vr* to doze off.

assoupissement *m* doze.

assouplir *vt* to make supple; to relax.

assouplissement *m* softening; relaxing.

assourdir *vt* to deafen; to muffle.

assourdissant *adj* deafening.

assouvir *vt* to satisfy.

assouvissement *m* satisfying, satisfaction.

assujettir *vt* to subjugate.

assumer *vt* to assume.

assurance *f* (self-)assurance; assurance; insurance (policy).

assuré *m* **-e** *f* assured; * *adj* confident.

assurer *vt* to assure; **s'~** *vr* to insure o.s.

assureur *m* (insurance) agent; insurer(s), insurance company.

astérisque *m* asterisk.

asthmatique *adj*, *mf* asthmatic.

asthme *m* asthma.

asticot *m* maggot.

astigmate *adj* astigmatic.

astiquer *vt* to polish.

astre *m* star.

astreignant *adj* demanding.

astreindre *vt* to force, compel; **s'~** *vr* **s'~ à faire** to force ou compel o.s. to do.

astrologie *f* astrology.

astrologique *adj* astrological.

astrologue *m* astrologer.

astronaute *m* astronaut.

astronome *m* astronomer.

astronomie *f* astronomy.

astronomique *adj* astronomical.

astuce *f* shrewdness; (clever) trick; pun.

astucieux *adj* astute.

asymétrique *adj* asymmetric(al).

atelier *m* workshop; studio.

atermoyer *vi* to procrastinate.

athée *mf* atheist; *adj* atheistic.

athéisme *m* atheism.

athlète *mf* athlete.

athlétique *adj* athletic.

athlétisme *m* athletics.

atlas *m* atlas.

atmosphère *f* atmosphere.

atmosphérique *adj* atmospheric.

atome *m* atom.

atomique *adj* atomic.

atomiseur *m* spray; atomizer.

atout *m* trump; advantage, asset.

âtre *m* hearth.

atroce *adj* atrocious; dreadful; **~ment** *adv* atrociously; dreadfully.

atrocité *f* atrocity.

atrophié *adj* atrophied.

attachant *adj* endearing.

attache *f* fastener.

attaché *m* **-e** *f* attaché; assistant.

attachement *m* attachment (*à* to).

attacher *vt* to tie together; to tie up; to fasten; to attach (*à* to).

attaque *f* attack.

attaquer *vt* to attack; to tackle.

attarder (s') *vr* to linger.

atteindre *vt* to reach; to affect; to contact.

atteinte *f* attack (*à* on); **hors d'~** beyond *ou* out of reach.

attenant *adj* adjoining.

attendre *vt* to wait; **en attendant** meanwhile, in the meantime; **s'~** *vr* : **s'~ à qch** to expect sth.

attendrir *vt* to fill with pity, move; to soften; to tenderize; **s'~** *vr* to be moved (*sur* by).

attendrissant *adj* touching, moving.

attendrissement *m* emotion.

attendu *adj* expected; long-awaited.

attentat *m* attack (*contre* on); murder attempt.

attente *f* wait; expectation.

attentif *adj* attentive; careful.

attention *f* attention; care.

attentionné *adj* considerate, thoughtful (*pour* towards).

attentivement *adv* attentively; carefully.

atténuation *f* alleviation; easing.

atténuer *vt* to alleviate, ease; to appease; to lighten.

atterrir *vi* to land, touch down.

atterrissage *m* landing, touchdown.

attester *vt* to testify to.

attirail *m* gear.

attirant *adj* attractive.

attirer *vt* to attract; **~ des ennuis à qn** to cause sb trouble.

attiser *vt* to stir up.

attitude *f* attitude; bearing.

attraction *f* attraction.

attrait *m* attraction, appeal.

attraper *vt* to catch.

attrayant *adj* attractive.

attribuer *vt* to attribute; to award.

attribut *m* attribute.

attribution *f* attribution.

attrister *vt* to sadden.

attroupement *m* crowd, gathering.

au = à le.

aube *f* dawn, daybreak.

auberge *f* inn; ~ de jeunesse youth hostel.

aubergine *f* aubergine.

aucun *adj* no; not any; any; sans ~ doute without (any) doubt; ~ement *adv* in no way; not in the least; * *pn* none; not any; any (one); ~ d'entre eux none of them.

audace *f* audacity; daring.

audacieux *adj* audacious, bold; daring.

audience *f* audience; hearing.

audiovisuel *adj* audiovisual.

auditeur *m* -trice *f* listener; auditor.

auditoire *m* audience.

augmentation *f* increase, rise

(*de* in); increasing, raising (*de* of).

augmenter *vt* to increase, raise.

augure *f* omen; oracle.

aujourd'hui *adv* today.

aumône *f* alms; demander/ faire l'~ to beg for/give alms.

auparavant *adv* before, previously; before, first.

auprès *prép*: ~ de next to; (compared) with.

auquel = à lequel.

auréole *f* halo, aureole; ring (mark).

auriculaire *adj* auricular; * *m* little finger.

aurore *f* dawn, first light.

ausculter *vt* to auscultate.

aussi *adv* too, also; so; nous ~ us too; une ~ belle journée such a beautiful day; il est ~ petit qu'elle he is as small as she is.

aussitôt *adv* immediately; ~ dit, ~ fait no sooner said than done; ~ que as soon as.

austère *adj* austere; ~ment *adv* austerely.

austérité *f* austerity.

autant *adv* as much; as many;

so much; such; so many; such a lot of; the same; ~ que je sache as far as I know; ~ que possible as much as possible; elle n'est pas plus heureuse pour ~ she's not any happier for it *ou* for all that.

autel *m* altar.

auteur *m* author.

authenticité *f* authenticity.

authentifier *vt* to authenticate.

authentique *adj* authentic; ~ment *adv* authentically.

autobiographie *f* autobiography.

autobiographique *adj* autobiographical.

autocar *m* coach.

autocollant *adj* self-adhesive.

autocuiseur *m* pressure cooker.

autodéfense *f* self-defence.

autodestruction *f* self-destruction.

autodidacte *adj* self-taught.

auto-école *f* driving school.

automate *m* automaton.

automatique *adj* automatic; ~ment *adv* automatically.

automatiser *vt* to automate.

automatisme *m* automatism.

automne *m* autumn.

automobile *f* (motor) car.

automobiliste *mf* motorist.

autonome *adj* autonomous; self-governing.

autonomie *f* autonomy; self-government.

autoportrait *m* self-portrait.

autopsie *f* autopsy, post-mortem (examination).

autoradio *m* car radio.

autorisation *f* authorization, permission; permit.

autoriser *vt* to authorize, give permission for; to allow.

autoritaire *adj* authoritarian.

autorité *f* authority.

autoroute *f* motorway.

autosatisfaction *f* self-satisfaction.

auto-stop *m* hitch-hiking; faire de l'~ to hitch-hike.

auto-stoppeur *m* -euse *f* hitch-hiker.

autour *prép* ~ de (a)round; * *adv* (a)round; il y en a tout ~ there is/are some all around.

autre *adj* other; ~ chose something else *ou* different; ~ part somewhere else; d'~ part on the other hand; moreover; * *pn* another (one); **j'en veux un ~** I'd like another (one); **encore deux ~s** another two; **les cinq ~s** the five others; the other five.

autrefois *adv* in the past, in days gone by.

autrement *adv* differently; otherwise; **je n'ai pas pu faire ~** I couldn't do differently *ou* otherwise.

autruche *f* ostrich.

autrui *pn* others.

aux = à les.

auxiliaire *adj* auxiliary; * *m* auxiliary; * *mf* assistant.

avachir (s') *vr* to become *ou* grow limp.

avalanche *f* avalanche.

avaler *vt* to swallow.

avance *f* advance; lead; **arriver en ~** to arrive early; **payer d'~** to pay in advance; **réserver à l'~** to book in advance; **avoir de l'~ sur** to have the lead over.

avancement *m* promotion; progress; forward movement.

avancer *vt* to move forward; to bring forward; to put forward; **s'~** *vr* to advance, move forward; * *vi* to move

forward, advance; to make progress; to project, stick out.

avant *prép* before; **~ peu** shortly; **~ tout** above all; * *adv* before; **en ~** in front, ahead; * *m* front; (*mar*) bow; forward.

avantage *m* advantage.

avantager *vt* to favour; to flatter.

avantageux *adj* profitable, worthwhile; attractive; flattering.

avant-bras *m invar* forearm.

avant-coureur *adj* precursory.

avant-dernier *m* **-ière** *f*, *adj* next to last, second last, last but one.

avant-garde *f* avant-garde; vanguard.

avant-goût *m* foretaste.

avant-hier *adv* the day before yesterday.

avant-première *f* preview.

avare *mf* miser; *adj* miserly.

avarice *f* avarice, miserliness.

avarie *f* damage.

avarié *adj* rotting; damaged.

avec *prép* with; to.

avènement *m* accession (*à* to); advent.

avenir *m* future.

aventure f adventure; venture; experience; affair.

aventurer (s') vr to venture.

aventurier m **-ière** f adventurer.

avenue f avenue.

avérer (s') vr to turn out, prove to be.

averse f shower (of rain).

aversion f aversion (*pour* to); loathing (*pour* for).

avertir vt to warn; to inform (*de* of).

avertissement m warning.

aveu m admission, confession.

aveuglant adj blinding.

aveugle adj blind; * mf blind person.

aveuglement m blindness.

aveugler vt to blind.

aviateur m **-trice** f pilot, aviator.

aviation f flying; aviation.

avide adj greedy; eager; ~**ment** adv greedily; eagerly.

avidité f greed; eagerness.

avilir vt to degrade.

avilissant adj degrading.

avion m (air)plane, aircraft.

aviron m oar; rowing.

avis m opinion.

avisé adj wise, sensible.

aviser vt to advise, inform; to notice; s'~ vr s'**aviser de** to realize suddenly.

aviver vt to sharpen; to deepen; to arouse.

avocat m **-e** f lawyer, advocate; * m avocado (pear).

avoine f oats.

avoir vt to have; **il y a** there is/ are; **il y a deux mois** two months ago; **qu'as-tu?** what's wrong (with you)?; **il n'avait qu'à le dire** he only had to say (the word); * m resources; credit.

avortement m abortion.

avorter vi to abort; to fail.

avoué m solicitor.

avouer vt to admit (to); to confess (to).

avril m April.

axe m axis; axle; main road.

axial adj axial.

azote m nitrogen.

B

babines *fpl* chops.

babiole *f* trinket, trifle.

bâbord *m* (*mar*) port.

babouin *m* baboon.

bac *m* ferry.

bâche *f* tarpaulin, cover.

bâcler *vt* to botch.

bactérie *f* bacterium.

badaud *m* idle onlooker.

badge *m* badge.

bafouer *vt* to scorn.

bafouiller *vi* to stammer; to babble.

bagage *m* luggage; stock of knowledge.

bagarre *f* fight, brawl.

bagarrer (se) *vr* to fight; to riot.

bagatelle *f* trinket; trifling sum.

bagne *m* penal servitude; (*fig*) grind.

bague *f* ring.

baguette *f* stick; loaf of French bread.

baie *f* (*geog*) bay.

baigner *vt vi* to bathe; * se ~ *vr* to have a bath, swim.

baignoire *f* bath(tub).

bâiller *vi* to yawn.

bâillon *m* gag.

bâillonner *vt* to gag.

bain *m* bath; bathe; swim.

baiser *m* kiss; * *vt* to kiss.

baisse *f* fall, drop.

baisser *vi* to fall, drop; * *vt* to lower.

bal *m* dance.

balade *f* (*fam*) walk; drive.

balader (se) *vr* (*fam*) to go for a walk; to go for a drive.

balai *m* broom, brush.

balance *f* scales; balance.

balancement *m* sway; rocking.

balancer *vt* to swing; to balance.

balançoire *f* swing; seesaw.

balayer *vt* to sweep, brush.

balbutiement *m* stammering, babbling.

balbutier *vt* to stammer, babble.

balbuzard *m* osprey.

balcon *m* balcony.

baleine *f* whale.

balistique *f* ballistics.

ballast *m* ballast.

balle *f* bullet; ball.

ballet *m* ballet.

ballon *m* ball; balloon.

ballotter *vt* jolt, shake about.

balourd *adj* stupid; clumsy.

balustrade *f* balustrade; handrail.

bambou *m* bamboo.

banal *adj* banal, trite; ~ement *adv* tritely.

banalisation *f* vulgarizing; standardization.

banalité *f* banality, triteness.

banane *f* banana.

bancaire *adj* banking, bank.

bancal, *pl* **bancals** *adj* lame; rickety.

bandage *m* bandage.

bande *f* band; tape; ~ dessinée strip cartoon.

bandeau *m* headband; blindfold.

bander *vt* to bandage; to stretch.

banderole *f* banner streamer.

bandit *m* bandit.

banlieue *f* suburbs.

bannière *f* banner.

bannir *vt* to banish; to prohibit.

bannissement *m* banishment.

banque *f* bank; banking.

banqueroute *f* bankruptcy.

banquet *m* banquet.

banquette *f* seat, stool.

banquier *m* banker.

banquise *f* ice floe.

baptême *m* baptism.

baptiser *vt* to baptise.

bar *m* bar; (*zool*) bass.

barbare *adj* barbarian; barbaric.

barbarie *f* barbarism; barbarity.

barbarisme *m* (*gr*) barbarism.

barbe *f* beard.

barbelé *adj* barbed.

barbiturique *adj* barbituric; * *m* barbiturate.

barboter *vi* to dabble; to splash.

barbouillage *m* scribble; daub.

barbouiller *vt* to smear; to scrawl.

barbu *adj* bearded; * *m* bearded man.

barème *m* list, schedule.

baril *m* barrel, cask.

bariolé *adj* multicoloured, motley.

baromètre *m* barometer.

baron *m* baron **-ne** *f* baroness.

baroque *adj* baroque; * *m* baroque.

barque *f* small boat.

barrage *m* barrage, barrier, dam.

barre *f* bar, rod.

barré *adj* barred, blocked.

barreau *m* rung; bar (cage).

barrer *vt* to bar, block.

barrette *f* (hair) slide, brooch.

barricader *vt* to barricade; **se ~** *vr* to barricade o.s.

barrière *f* barrier; fence.

baryton *m* baritone.

bas *adj* low, base; * *n* stocking; sock; **~sement** *adv* basely, meanly.

basalte *m* basalt.

bas-côté *m* verge; aisle.

bascule *f* weighing machine, scales.

basculer *vi* to tip up, topple over.

base *f* base; basis.

baser *vt* to base; **se ~ sur** *vr* to depend on, rely on.

bas-fond *m* (*naut*) shallow, shoal.

basilic *m* (*bot*) basil.

basilique *f* basilica.

basket *m* basketball.

basketteur *m* **-euse** *f* basketball player.

bas-relief *m* bas-relief.

basse *f* (*mus*) bass.

basse-cour *f* poultry-yard.

bassesse *f* meanness; vulgarity.

bassin *m* pond, pool; dock.

bassine *f* bowl.

basson *m* bassoon.

bastion *m* bastion.

bas-ventre *m* lower abdomen.

bataille *f* battle.

batailler *vi* (*fig*) to fight, battle.

batailleur *adj* combative, aggressive.

bataillon *m* (*mil*) battalion.

bâtard *adj* bastard, illegitimate.

bateau *m* boat, ship.

batelier *m* boatman.

bâtiment *m* building; ship.

bâtir *vt* to build.

bâtisse *f* building, house.

bâton *m* stick, staff.

batracien *m* batrachian.

battant *m* clapper (bell); shutter.

batte *f* bat.

battement *m* banging; beating.

batterie *f* battery.

batteur *m* drummer; batsman.

battre *vt* to beat, defeat.

battu *adj* beaten.

baudet *m* donkey.

baume *m* balm, balsam.

bauxite *f* bauxite.

bavard *m* -e *f* chatterbox; * *adj* talkative, loquacious.

bavardage *m* chatting, gossiping.

bavarder *vi* to chat, gossip.

bave *f* dribble, slobber.

baver *vi* to dribble, drool.

bavure *f* smudge, blunder.

bazar *m* bazaar; general store.

B.D. *f* (bande dessinée) strip cartoon.

béant *adj* gaping, wide open.

béat *adj* blissful; ~ement *adv* rapturously.

béatitude *f* beatitude; bliss.

beau, *f* belle *adj* beautiful, lovely.

beaucoup *adv* a lot, a great deal; ~ de monde a lot of people; ~ de temps a great deal of time.

beau-fils *m* son-in-law; stepson.

beau-frère *m* brother-in-law.

beau-père *m* father-in-law; stepfather.

beauté *f* beauty, loveliness.

beaux-arts *mpl* fine arts.

beaux-parents *mpl* parents-in-law.

bébé *m* baby.

bec *m* beak, bill.

béchamel *f* béchamel (sauce).

bée *adj* open-mouthed, flabbergasted.

bégaiement *m* stammering, faltering.

bégayer *vi* to stammer, stutter.

bégonia *m* begonia.

beige *adj* beige; * *m* beige.

beignet *m* fritter; doughnut.

bêlement *m* bleating.

bêler *vi* to bleat.

Belge *mf* Belgian.

belge *adj* Belgian.

Belgique *f* Belgium.

belle-fille *f* daughter-in-law, stepdaughter.

belle-mère *f* mother-in-law, stepmother.

belle-sœur *f* sister-in-law.

belligérant *m* -e *f* belligerent; * *adj* belligerent.

belliqueux *adj* aggressive; warlike.

bémol *m* (*mus*) flat.

bénédictin *m* **-e** *f* Benedictine.

bénédiction *f* benediction, blessing.

bénéfice *m* profit; benefit.

bénéficiaire *mf* beneficiary.

bénéficier *vi* to benefit; to enjoy.

bénévole *adj* voluntary; unpaid; **~ment** *adv* voluntarily.

bénin, f bénigne *adj* benign; minor; harmless.

bénir *vt* to bless.

bénit *adj* consecrated, holy.

benne *f* skip; tipper.

benzène *m* benzene.

béquille *f* crutch; prop.

berceau *m* cradle.

bercement *m* rocking.

bercer *vt* to rock, cradle.

berceuse *f* lullaby; rocking chair.

béret *m* beret.

berge *f* riverbank.

berger *m* shepherd, **-ère** *f* shepherdess.

bergerie *f* sheepbarn.

berner *vt* to fool, hoax.

besogne *f* work; job.

besoin *m* need; want; **avoir ~ de** to need.

bestial *adj* bestial; **~ement** *adv* bestially.

bestialité *f* bestiality; brutishness.

bétail *m* livestock; cattle.

bête *adj* stupid, silly; **~ment** *adv* stupidly, foolishly; * *f* animal.

bêtifier *vt* to play the fool; to prattle stupidly.

bêtise *f* stupidity, foolishness.

béton *m* concrete.

betterave *f* beetroot, beet.

beurre *m* butter.

beurrer *vt* to butter.

bévue *f* blunder.

biais *m* slant; angle; bias.

biathlon *m* biathlon.

bibelot *m* curio.

biberon *m* baby's bottle.

bible *f* bible.

bibliographie *f* bibliography.

bibliothécaire *mf* librarian.

bibliothèque *f* library; bookcase.

bicarbonate *m* bicarbonate.

bicentenaire *m* bicentenary.

biceps *m* biceps.

biche *f* doe; darling, pet.

bicolore *adj* bi-coloured, two-tone.

bicyclette *f* bicycle.

bidon *m* tin, can; flask.

bidonville *m* shanty town.

bien *adv* well; properly; very; c'est ~ cela that's right; * *n* property, estate.

bien-être *m* well-being.

bienfaisant *adj* beneficial, kind.

bienfaiteur *m* benefactor, -trice *f* benefactress.

bienheureux *adj* blessed; lucky; happy.

bientôt *adv* soon.

bienveillant *adj* benevolent, kindly.

bienvenu *adj* welcome.

bienvenue *f* welcome.

bière *f* beer; coffin.

bifteck *m* steak.

bifurcation *f* bifurcation, fork.

bifurquer *vi* to fork, branch off.

bigot *adj* bigoted.

bihebdomadaire *adj* twice-weekly.

bijou *m* jewel.

bijouterie *f* jewellery.

bijoutier *m* -ière *f* jeweller.

bilan *m* balance sheet; assessment.

bilatéral *adj* bilateral.

bile *f* bile.

bilingue *adj* bilingual.

billard *m* billiards.

bille *f* marble; billiard ball.

billet *m* ticket; note.

billetterie *f* cash dispenser.

billion *m* billion.

bimensuel *adj* fortnightly.

bimestriel *adj* every two months.

binaire *adj* binary.

biochimie *f* biochemistry.

biochimiste *mf* biochemist.

biodégradable *adj* biodegradable.

bioéthique *f* bioethics.

biographie *f* biography.

biologie *f* biology.

biologique *adj* biological.

biologiste *mf* biologist.

biosphère *f* biosphere.

bioxyde *m* dioxide.

bipède *m* biped.

bipolaire *adj* bipolar.

bisannuel *adj* biennial.

biscornu *adj* crooked, misshapen; odd, outlandish.

biscuit *m* cake; biscuit.

bisexuel *adj* bisexual.

bissextile *adj* bissextile, leap (year).

bistouri *m* bistoury.

bitume *m* bitumen.

bitumer *vt* to asphalt, tarmac.

bizarre *adj* bizarre, strange; ~ment *adv* strangely, oddly.

bizarrerie *f* strangeness, singularity.

blafard *adj* pale, pallid.

blague *f* joke, trick.

blaguer *vi* to joke.

blagueur *m* -euse *f* joker, wag; * *adj* jokey, teasing.

blaireau *m* badger.

blâme *m* blame, rebuke.

blâmer *vt* to blame, rebuke.

blanc *adj*, *f* **blanche** white; * *m* white; blank; * *mf* white person; * *f* (*mus*) minim.

blancheur *f* whiteness.

blanchir *vi* to turn white; to become lighter; * *vt* to whiten; to lighten.

blanchissage *m* laundering; refining.

blanchisserie *f* laundry.

blasé *adj* blasé.

blason *m* blazon, coat of arms.

blasphème *m* blasphemy.

blasphémer *vi* to blaspheme.

blé *m* wheat.

blême *adj* pale, wan.

blêmir *vi* to turn pale.

blessant *adj* cutting, hurtful.

blessé *adj* injured, wounded.

blesser *vt* to injure, wound.

blessure *f* injury, wound.

bleu *adj* blue; * *m* blue; bruise.

bleuet *m* cornflower.

bleuir *vt* *vi* to turn blue.

bleuté *adj* bluish.

blindage *m* armour plating.

blindé *adj* armoured, reinforced.

bloc *m* block, group, unit.

blocage *m* blocking, freezing.

blocus *m* blockade.

blond *adj* blond, fair.

blondir *vi* to turn blond, turn golden; * *vt* to bleach.

bloquer *vt* to block, blockade.

blottir (se) *vr* to curl up, snuggle up.

blouse *f* blouse; overall.

blouson *m* windcheater, bomber jacket.

bobine *f* reel, bobbin.

bocal *m* jar; bowl.

bœuf *m* ox, bullock.

bohémien *m* -ne *f* Bohemian.

boire *vt* to drink; * *vi* to drink, tipple.

bois *m* wood.

boisé *adj* wooded.

boisson *f* drink.

boîte *f* box.

boiter *vi* to limp.

boiteux *adj* lame.

boîtier *m* case, body.

boitillant *adj* limping.

boitiller *vi* to hobble slightly.

bol *m* bowl.

bolet *m* boletus.

bombardement *m* bombardment, bombing.

bombarder *vt* to bombard, bomb.

bombe *f* bomb.

bombé *adj* rounded, domed.

bon *adj*, *f* **bonne** good; * *m* slip, coupon, bond.

bonbon *m* sweet, candy.

bond *m* leap; bounce.

bonde *f* stopper, plug.

bondé *adj* packed.

bondir *vi* to jump, leap; to bounce.

bonheur *m* happiness; luck.

bonhomme *m*, *pl* **bonshommes** chap, fellow.

bonification *f* improvement; bonus.

bonifier *vt* to improve; * **se ~** *vr* to improve.

bonjour *m* hello, good morning.

bonnet *m* bonnet, hat.

bonneterie *f* hosiery.

bonsoir *m* good evening.

bonté *f* goodness, kindness.

bon vivant *m* bon vivant.

bord *m* side, edge.

bordé *adj* edged, bordered.

bordée *f* broadside, volley.

border *vt* to edge, border.

bordereau *m* note; invoice.

bordure *f* frame, border.

borgne *adj* one-eyed.

borne *f* boundary; milestone.

borné *adj* narrow-minded.

borner *vt* to restrict, limit.

bosse *f* hump, knob.

bosseler *vt* to dent, emboss.

bossu *m* **-e** *f* hunchback; * *adj* hunchbacked.

botanique *f* botany; * *adj* botanical.

botaniste *f* botanist.

botte *f* boot.

bottine *f* ankle boot, bootee.

bouche *f* mouth.

bouché *adj* cloudy, overcast.

bouchée *f* mouthful.

bouche-à-bouche *m* kiss of life.

boucher *vt* to block, clog up; * **se ~** *vr* to become cloudy; * *m*, **-ère** *f* (woman) butcher.

boucherie *f* butcher's; butchery.

bouchon *m* cork.

boucle *f* curl; buckle.

boucler *vt* to buckle; to surround.

bouclier *m* shield.

bouddhisme *m* Buddhism.

boudeur *adj* sullen, sulky.

boudin *m* (black) pudding.

boue *f* mud.

bouée *f* buoy.

boueur *m* dustman.

bouffée *f* whiff, puff.

bouffi *adj* swollen, puffed up.

bouffon *m* buffoon, clown.

bougeoir *m* candlestick.

bouger *vi* to move; * *vt* to move, shift.

bougie *f* candle.

bouillant *adj* boiling.

bouillir *vi* to boil.

bouilloire *f* kettle.

bouillon *m* broth.

bouillonner *vi* to bubble, foam.

bouillotte *f* hot-water bottle.

boulanger *m* -ère *f* baker.

boulangerie *f* bakery.

boule *f* ball, bowl.

boulet *m* cannonball; (*fig*) millstone.

boulevard *m* boulevard.

bouleversant *adj* upsetting, confusing.

bouleversement *m* confusion, disruption.

bouleverser *vt* to confuse, disrupt.

boulimie *f* bulimia.

boulimique *adj* bulimic.

boulon *m* bolt.

bouquet *m* bouquet, posy.

bouquin *m* (*fam*) book.

bouquiniste *mf* second-hand book-seller.

bourbeux *adj* muddy.

bourbier *m* quagmire.

bourdon *m* bumblebee.

bourdonnement *m* buzz, buzzing.

bourdonner *vi* to buzz, hum.

bourg *m* market-town.

bourgeois *m* -e *f* bourgeois, middle-class person; * *adj* bourgeois, middle-class.

bourgeoisie *f* bourgeoisie, middle classes.

bourgeon *m* bud.

bourgeonner *vi* to bud.

bourrasque *f* squall, gust.

bourreau *m* torturer, executioner.

bourrelet *m* pad, cushion.

bourrer *vt* to stuff, cram.

bourse *f* purse; la **Bourse** stock exchange.

boursier *m* -ière *f* broker; speculator.

boursouflé *adj* bloated, swollen.

bousculade *f* hustle, scramble.

bousculer *vt* to jostle, hustle.

boussole *f* compass.

bout *m* end; piece, scrap.

boutade *f* whim, caprice; jest.

bouteille *f* bottle.

boutique *f* shop, store.

bouton *m* button.

boutonner *vt* to button.

boutonnière *f* buttonhole.

bouture *f* cutting.

bovin *adj* bovine.

boxe *f* boxing.

boxer *vi* to box.

boxeur *m* boxer.

boyau *m* guts, insides.

boycottage *m* boycotting.

boycotter *vt* to boycott.

bracelet *m* bracelet.

braconnier *m* poacher.

brader *vt* to sell at a discount.

braderie *f* discount sale.

braguette *f* fly (trousers).

braise *f* embers.

brancard *m* shaft, stretcher.

branche *f* branch.

branchement *m* branching; connection.

brancher *vt* to connect, link.

branchies *fpl* gills.

brandir *vt* to brandish, flourish.

branlant *adj* loose; shaky.

bras *m* arm.

brasier *m* brazier, furnace.

brasse *f* breaststroke.

brassée *f* armful.

brasser *vt* to brew; to mix.

brasserie *f* bar; brewery.

bravade *f* bravado.

brave *adj* brave, courageous; ~**ment** *adv* bravely, courageously.

braver *vt* to brave, defy.

bravoure *f* bravery, courage.

brebis *f* ewe.

brèche *f* breach, gap.

bredouillant *adj* mumbling.

bredouille *adj* empty-handed.

bredouiller *vi* to mumble.

bref *adj*, *f* **brève** brief, concise; en ~ *adv* in short.

bretelle *f* strap, sling.

brevet *m* licence, patent.

breveté *adj* patented.

bribe *f* bit, scrap.

bric-à-brac *m* bric-a-brac.

bricolage *m* DIY, odd jobs.

bricole *f* small job.

bricoler *vi* to do odd jobs.

bricoleur *m* handyman, -**euse** *f* handywoman.

bride *f* bridle.

bridé *adj* restrained, restricted.

brider *vt* to restrain, restrict.

brièvement *adv* briefly, concisely.

brièveté *f* brevity.

brigade *f* brigade.

brigadier *m* corporal, sergeant (police).

brillamment *adv* brilliantly.

brillant *adj* brilliant, shining.

briller *vi* to shine.

brin *m* stalk, strand.

brindille *f* twig.

brique *f* brick, slab.

briquet *m* lighter.

brise *f* breeze.

briser *vt* to smash, shatter.

brocante *f* second-hand dealing.

brocanteur *m* -euse *f* second-hand dealer.

broche *f* brooch.

brochure *f* brochure, booklet.

broder *vt* to embroider, *vi* to embellish, elaborate.

broderie *f* embroidery.

bronche *f* bronchus.

bronchite *f* bronchitis.

bronzage *m* tan.

bronze *m* bronze.

bronzer *vi* to get a tan.

brosse *f* brush.

brosser *vt* to brush.

brouette *f* wheelbarrow.

brouillard *m* fog, mist.

brouiller *vt* to blur, confuse.

brouillon *m* rough copy, draft; * *adj* untidy.

broussaille *f* brushwood, undergrowth.

broussailleux *adj* bushy, overgrown.

brousse *f* undergrowth, bush.

brouter *vt vi* to graze.

broyer *vt* to grind, pulverize.

broyeur *adj* crushing, grinding.

bruine *f* drizzle.

bruissement *m* rustle.

bruit *m* noise, sound.

bruitage *m* sound-effects.

brûlant *adj* burning, scorching.

brûler *vt vi* to burn.

brûlure *f* burn.

brume *f* haze, mist.

brumeux *adj* hazy, misty.

brun *m* dark-haired man, **brune** *f* brunette; * *adj* brown.

brusque *adj* brusque, abrupt; ~ment *adv* brusquely, abruptly.

brusquer *vt* to offend; to hasten.

brut *adj* crude, raw.

brutal *adj* brutal, rough;

~ement *adv* brutally, roughly.

brutaliser *vt* to brutalize; to bully.

brutalité *f* brutality.

brute *f* brute; beast.

bruyamment *adv* noisily.

bruyant *adj* noisy.

bruyère *f* heather.

bûche *f* log.

bûcheron *m* **-ne** *f* woodcutter, lumberjack.

budget *m* budget.

budgétaire *adj* budgetary.

buée *f* condensation; steam.

buffet *m* sideboard, buffet.

buisson *m* bush.

bulbe *m* bulb.

bulle *f* bubble; blister.

bulletin *m* bulletin.

buraliste *mf* tobacconist.

bureau *m* office; desk.

bureaucrate *mf* bureaucrat.

bureaucratie *f* bureaucracy.

bureaucratique *adj* bureaucratic.

burin *m* chisel.

bus *m* bus.

buste *m* bust, chest.

but *m* objective, goal.

butane *m* butane.

buté *adj* stubborn.

butin *m* booty, loot.

butte *f* knoll, mound.

buvable *adj* drinkable.

buvard *m* blotting paper.

buvette *f* refreshment-room.

buveur *m* **-euse** *f* drinker.

C

ça *pn* that; it; ~ **va?** How goes it?; ~ **y est** that's it; **qui** ~**?** who (do you mean)?; **comment** ~**?** how (do you mean)?; ~ **alors!** you don't say!

cabale *f* cabal, intrigue.

cabane *f* cabin, shed.

cabanon *m* cottage; chalet.

cabaret *m* cabaret; tavern.

cabine *f* cabin, cab; cockpit.

cabinet *m* surgery; office, study.

câble *m* cable.

câbler *vt* to cable.

cabosser *vt* to dent.

cabotage *m* coastal navigation.

cabriolet *m* convertible.

cacahuète *f* peanut.

cacao *m* cocoa.

cache *m* cache; mask; hiding place.

caché *adj* hidden, secluded.

cache-col *m invar* scarf.

cache-nez *m invar* scarf, muffler.

cacher *vt* to hide, conceal; **se** ~ *vr* to hide o.s.

cacheter *vt* to seal.

cachette *f* hideout, hiding place.

cachot *m* dungeon, prison cell.

cachottier *m* **-ière** *f* secretive.

cactus *m* cactus.

cadavre *m* corpse.

cadeau *m* present.

cadenas *m* padlock.

cadenasser *vt* to padlock.

cadence *f* rhythm, time, cadence.

cadet *m* **-te** *f* youngest child.

cadrage *m* framing.

cadran *m* dial, face.

cadre *m* frame; context; scope.

cadrer *vt* to centre; to fit with.

caduc *adj*, *f* **caduque** null and void; obsolete.

cafard *m* hypocrite; cockroach.

café *m* coffee.

cafétéria *f* cafeteria.

cafetière *f* coffeepot.

cage *f* cage.

cageot *m* crate.

cagoule *f* cowl; balaclava.

cahier *m* notebook.

cahot *m* jerk, jolt.

caillot *m* clot.

caillou *m* stone; pebble.

caisse *f* box; till; fund.

caissier *m* **-ière** *f* cashier.

cajoler *vt* to cajole, coax; to pet.

cajou *m* cashew.

calamité *f* calamity.

calcaire *m* calcareous, chalky.

calcination *f* calcination.

calciner *vt* to calcine; to char.

calcium *m* calcium.

calcul *m* sum, calculation.

calculateur *adj, f* **-trice** calculating.

calculatrice, calculette *f* calculator.

calculer *vt* to calculate, reckon; * *vi* to budget carefully.

cale *f* (*mar*) wedge, hold.

caleçon *m* shorts, pants.

calembour *m* pun.

calendrier *m* calendar.

calepin *m* notebook.

caler *vi* to stall; to give up; to wedge.

calfeutrer *vt* to make airtight, draughtproof.

calibre *m* calibre, bore.

calibrer *vt* to calibrate.

calice *m* chalice.

câlin *m* cuddle; * *adj* cuddly.

câliner *vt* to cuddle.

calligraphie *f* calligraphy.

callosité *f* callosity.

calmant *m* tranquillizer, sedative; * *adj* tranquillizing.

calmar *m* squid.

calme *m* calm, stillness; * *adj* calm, still; **~ment** *adv* calmly, quietly.

calmer *vt* calm, soothe, pacify.

calomnie *f* slander, calumny.

calomnier *vt* to slander; to libel.

calomnieux *adj* slanderous, calumnious.

calorie *f* calorie.

calorifique *adj* calorific.

calque *m* tracing; copy.

calquer *vt* to trace; to copy.

calvaire *m* calvary; ordeal.

calvitie *f* baldness.

camarade *mf* companion, friend.

camaraderie *f* camaraderie, friendship.

cambouis *m* dirty grease.

cambré *adj* arched.

cambriolage *m* burglary.

cambrioler *vt* to burgle.

cambrioleur *m* **-euse** *f* burglar.

caméléon *m* chameleon.

camélia *m* camellia.

caméra *f* camera.

camion *m* lorry.

camionneur *m* lorry driver, trucker.

camomille *f* camomile.

camouflage *m* camouflage.

camoufler *vt* to camouflage.

camp *m* camp.

campagnard *m* countryman, **-e** *f* countrywoman; * *adj* country, rustic.

campagne *f* country, countryside.

campement *m* camp, encampment.

camper *vi* to camp.

campeur *m* **-euse** *f* camper.

canal *m* canal, channel.

canalisation *f* canalization; mains.

canaliser *vt* to channel, funnel.

canapé *m* sofa, settee.

canard *m* duck.

cancer *m* cancer.

cancéreux *adj* cancerous.

candeur *f* ingeniousness.

candidat *m* **-e** *f* candidate.

candidature *f* candidature, candidacy.

candide *adj* guileless, ingenuous; **~ment** *adv* openly, ingenuously.

canevas *m* canvas; framework.

canicule *m* heatwave.

canif *m* penknife.

canine *f* eye tooth.

caniveau *m* gutter.

canne *f* cane, rod.

cannelle *f* cinnamon.

canoè *m* canoe.

canon *m* cannon, gun.

canot *m* boat, dinghy.

cantate *f* cantata.

cantatrice *f* opera singer.

cantine *f* canteen.

cantique *m* canticle, hymn.

canton *m* canton.

cantonner (se) *vr* to take up position in.

caoutchouc *m* rubber.

cap *f* cape; course.

capable *adj* capable, competent.

capacité *f* capacity.

cape *f* cloak.

capillaire *adj* capillary.

capitaine *m* captain.

capital *adj* capital, cardinal, major; * *m* capital, stock.

capitale *f* capital (letter, city).

capitalisme *m* capitalism.

capitaliste *mf* capitalist.

capiteux *adj* heady, strong.

capitonner *vt* to pad.

capitulation *f* capitulation.

capituler *vt* to capitulate.

caporal *m* corporal.

capot *m* bonnet, hood.

capote *f* great-coat, hood.

capoter *vt* to capsize, overturn.

câpre *m* caper.

caprice *m* caprice, whim.

capricieusement *adv* capriciously.

capricieux *adj* capricious.

capricorne *m* capricorn.

capsule *f* capsule.

capter *vt* to catch; to pick up.

capteur *m* captor; pick-up.

captif *m* **-ive** *f* captive; * *adj* captive.

captivant *adj* enthralling, captivating.

captiver *vt* to captivate, enthral.

captivité *f* captivity.

capture *f* capture.

capturer *vt* to capture.

capuche *f* hood.

car *conj* for; because; * *m* bus; van.

carabine *f* carbine, rifle.

caractère *m* character, disposition.

caractérisé *adj* marked, blatant.

caractériser *vt* to characterize.

caractéristique *f* characteristic, feature; * *adj* characteristic.

carafe *f* carafe.

carambolage *m* pile-up (car).

caramel *m* caramel.

caraméliser *vt* to caramelize.

carapace *f* carapace, shell.

carat *m* carat.

caravane *f* caravan.

caravelle *f* caravel.

carbonate *m* carbonate.

carbone *m* carbon.

carbonique *adj* carbonic.

carboniser *vt* to carbonize; to char.

carburant *m* motor-fuel.

carburateur *m* carburettor.

carburation *f* carburation.

carbure *m* carbide.

carcasse *f* carcass.

carcéral *adj* prison.

cardiaque *adj* cardiac.

cardigan *m* cardigan.

cardinal *m* cardinal; * *adj* cardinal.

cardiologie f cardiology.

cardiologue m cardiologist.

cardio-vasculaire adj cardio-vascular.

carême m fast, fasting.

carence f deficiency; insolvency.

caressant adj affectionate.

caresse f caress.

caresser vt to caress, fondle.

cargaison f cargo, freight.

cargo m cargo-boat.

caricatural adj caricatural; grotesque.

caricature f caricature.

caricaturer vt to caricature.

caricaturiste m caricaturist.

carie f decay; caries.

carié adj decayed.

carillon m carillon, chime, peal.

caritatif adj charitable.

carnage m carnage.

carnassier m carnivore, -ière f gamebag; * adj carnivorous.

carnaval m carnival.

carnet m notebook.

carnivore mf carnivore; adj carnivorous.

carotide f carotid.

carotte f carrot.

carpe f carp.

carpette f rug, doormat.

carré m square; * adj square; straightforward.

carreau m tile; pane.

carrefour m crossroads.

carrelage m tiling.

carrément adv bluntly, directly.

carrière f career.

carrosse m coach.

carrosserie f bodywork, coachwork.

carrossier m coachbuilder.

carrure f build, stature.

cartable m satchel.

carte f card; map.

cartel m cartel.

cartésien adj Cartesian.

cartilage m cartilage.

cartilagineux adj cartilaginous.

cartomancien m -ne f fortune-teller.

carton m cardboard.

cartonner vt to bind (book).

cartouche f cartridge.

cas m case; circumstance.

casanier m -ière f homebody.

cascade f waterfall; stunt.

cascadeur m -euse f acrobat, stuntman.

case f square; box.

caser vt (fam) to set up (job, marriage).

caserne f barracks.

casier m compartment; filing cabinet.

casino m casino.

casque m helmet.

casquette f peaked cap.

cassant adj brittle.

casse-croûte m invar snack.

casser vt to break; **se ~** vr to break.

casserole f saucepan.

casse-tête m invar puzzle, conundrum.

cassette f cassette; cash-box.

cassis m blackcurrant.

cassure f break, crack.

caste f caste.

castor m beaver.

castration f castration.

castrer vt to castrate.

cataclysme m cataclysm.

catacombe f catacomb.

catalogue m catalogue.

cataloguer vt to catalogue.

catalyseur m catalyst.

catalytique adj catalytic.

cataplasme m cataplasm.

catapulte f catapult.

cataracte f cataract.

catastrophe f catastrophe.

catastrophique adj catastrophic.

catéchisme m catechism.

catégorie f category.

catégorique adj categorical; **~ment** adv categorically.

cathédrale f cathedral.

cathode f cathode.

cathodique adj cathodic.

catholicisme m Catholicism.

catholique adj Catholic.

cauchemar m nightmare.

cause f cause, reason.

causer vt to cause; to chat; * vi to talk, chat.

caustique adj caustic.

caution f deposit; guarantee.

cautionner vt to guarantee.

cavalerie f cavalry.

cavalier m -ière f rider.

cave f cellar.

caveau m tomb; small cellar.

caverne f cave, cavern.

caverneux adj cavernous.

caviar m caviar.

cavité f cavity.

ce adj **cet** (before vowel and mute h), f **cette**, pl **ces** this, these; **cet homme-là** that man; * pn: **c'est le facteur** it's the postman; **~ sont mes lunettes** these are my glasses; **~ que tu veux** what you want; **c'est ~ dont je vous parle** that's what I am speaking to you about.

ceci *pn* this.

cécité *f* blindness.

céder *vi* to give in; * *vt* to give up, transfer.

ceindre *vt* to put round, encircle.

ceinture *f* belt, girdle.

ceinturer *vt* to surround.

ceinturon *m* belt.

cela *pn* that; *emphasis* qui ~? who? (do you mean)?; comment ~? how? (do you mean?).

célébration *f* celebration.

célèbre *adj* famous.

célébrer *vt* to celebrate.

célébrité *f* fame, celebrity.

célérité *f* celerity, speed.

céleste *adj* celestial.

célibat *m* celibacy.

célibataire *mf* single person; * *adj* single, unmarried.

cellulaire *adj* cellular.

cellule *f* cell, unit.

cellulite *f* cellulite.

celluloïd *m* celluloid.

cellulose *f* cellulose.

celui *pn*, *f* **celle** this one, *pl* **ceux** these ones.

cendre *f* ash.

cendrier *m* ashtray.

censé *adj* supposed; deemed.

censure *f* censorship.

censurer *vt* to censor.

cent *adj* a hundred; tu as ~ fois raison you are absolutely right; faire les ~ pas to walk up and down; * *m* a hundred; pour ~ per cent.

centaine *f* about a hundred, a hundred or so.

centenaire *m* centenarian; * *adj* a hundred years old.

centésimal *adj* centesimal.

centième *mf* hundredth; * *adj* hundredth.

centigrade *m* centigrade.

centigramme *m* centigram.

centime *m* centime.

centimètre *m* centimetre.

central *adj* central.

centraliser *vt* to centralize.

centre *m* centre.

centrer *vt* to centre, focus.

centrifuge *adj* centrifugal.

centuple *adj* centuple, hundredfold; * *mf* centuple.

cependant *conj* however.

céramique *f* ceramic.

cerceau *m* hoop.

cercle *m* circle, ring.

cercueil *m* coffin.

céréale *f* cereal.

cérébral *adj* cerebral.

cérémonial *adj* ceremonial.

cérémonie *f* ceremony.

cérémonieux *adj* ceremonious.

cerf-volant *m* kite.

cerise *f* cherry.

cerisier *m* cherry tree.

cerne *f* ring.

cerner *vt* to circle, encompass.

certain *adj* certain, sure; ~**ement** *adv* certainly, most probably; ~**s** *pn* some, certain people.

certificat *m* certificate.

certifier *vt* to certify; to guarantee.

certitude *f* certainty, certitude.

cerveau *m* brain.

cervelle *f* brains.

cervical *adj* cervical.

césarienne *f* Caesarean.

cesser *f* to cease, stop.

cessez-le-feu *m* cease-fire.

cet *adj*, *f* **cette** *see* **ce**.

cétacé *m* cetacean.

ceux *see* **ce**.

chacun *pn* each one; ~**e** d'entre elles each of them; ~ **son tour** each in turn.

chagrin *m* sorrow, grief.

chahut *m* row, uproar.

chahuter *vi* to make a row.

chaîne *f* chain.

chaînon *m* link.

chair *f* flesh.

chaise *f* chair.

châle *m* shawl.

châlet *m* chalet.

chaleur *f* heat.

chaleureusement *adv* warmly.

chaleureux *adj* warm, cordial.

chalumeau *m* blowlamp.

chalutier *m* trawler.

chambre *f* room.

chameau *m* camel.

champ *m* field.

champêtre *adj* rural, country.

champignon *m* mushroom.

champion *m* -**ne** *f* champion.

championnat *m* championship.

chance *f* luck.

chancelant *adj* staggering, tottering.

chanceler *vi* to stagger, totter.

chancelier *m* chancellor.

chanceux *adj* lucky, fortunate.

chandail *m* sweater.

chandeleur *f* Candlemas.

chandelier *m* candlestick.

chandelle *f* candle.

changeant *adj* changeable, variable.

changement *m* change, changing.

changer *vi* to change; * *vt* to change.

chanson *f* song.

chant *m* song; singing.

chantage *m* blackmail.

chanter *vt vi* to sing.

chanteur *m* -**euse** *f* singer.

chantier *m* building site.

chantonner *vt vi* to hum.

chanvre *m* hemp.

chaos *m* chaos.

chaotique *adj* chaotic.

chapeau *m* hat.

chapelet *m* rosary; string.

chapelle *f* chapel.

chapiteau *m* capital (column).

chapitre *m* chapter.

chaque *adj* each.

char *m* (*mil*) tank; chariot.

charabia *m* gibberish.

charbon *m* coal.

charcuterie *f* pork meat trade.

charcutier *m* -**ière** *f* pork butcher.

chardon *m* thistle.

charge *f* load; responsibility.

chargé *adj* loaded.

chargement *m* loading; freight.

charger *vt* to load; **se ~ de** to take responsibility for, attend to.

chariot *m* waggon; freight car.

charisme *m* charisma.

charitable *adj* charitable, kind; ~**ment** *adv* charitably.

charité *f* charity.

charlatan *m* charlatan.

charmant *adj* charming, delightful.

charme *m* charm.

charmer *vt* to charm, beguile.

charmeur *m* -**euse** *f* charmer; * *adj* winning, enchanting.

charnel *adj* carnal.

charnière *f* hinge, pivot.

charnu *adj* fleshy.

charogne *f* carrion.

charpente *f* structure, framework.

charpentier *m* carpenter.

charrette *f* cart.

charrier *vt* to cart, carry.

charrue *f* plough.

chasse *f* hunting; chase.

chasse-neige *m invar* snowplough.

chasser *vt* to hunt, chase.

chasseur *m* -**euse** *f* hunter.

châssis *m* chassis.

chaste *adj* chaste; ~**ment** *adv* chastely.

chasteté *f* chastity.

chat *m*, **chatte** *f* cat.

châtaigne *f* chestnut.

châtain *adj* chestnut brown.

château *m* castle.

châtiment *m* chastisement, punishment.

chaton *m* kitten.

chatouiller *vt* to tickle.

chatoyant *adj* shimmering.

châtrer *vt* to castrate.

chaud *adj* warm, hot; ~ement *adv* warmly, hotly.

chaudière *f* boiler.

chaudron *m* cauldron.

chauffage *m* heating.

chauffard *m* road-hog.

chauffe-eau *m invar* water-heater.

chauffer *vi* to heat; * *vt* to heat up.

chauffeur *m* driver.

chaumière *f* cottage.

chaussée *f* road, street.

chausse-pied *m* shoehorn.

chaussette *f* sock.

chausson *m* slipper.

chaussure *f* shoe.

chauve *adj* bald.

chauve-souris *f* bat.

chauvin *adj*, *f* chauvine chauvinistic.

chauvinisme *m* chauvinism.

chaux *f* lime.

chavirer *vi* to capsize, overturn.

chef *m* head, boss; chef.

chef-d'œuvre *m* masterpiece.

chemin *m* way, road; ~ de fer railway.

cheminée *f* chimney.

cheminement *m* progress; course.

chemise *f* shirt.

chemisier *m* shirtmaker.

chêne *m* oak.

chenil *m* kennel.

chenille *f* caterpillar.

chèque *m* cheque.

chéquier *m* chequebook.

cher *adj*, *f* **chère** dear; expensive.

chercher *vt* to look for.

chercheur *m* -euse *f* researcher; seeker.

chéri *m* -ie *f* darling, dearest; * *adj* beloved, cherished.

chétif *adj* puny, paltry.

cheval *m* horse.

chevalet *m* easel.

chevalier *m* knight.

chevelu *adj* long-haired.

chevelure *f* hair, head of hair.

chevet *m* chevet; bedside.

cheveu *m* hair.

cheville *f* ankle.

chèvre *f* goat.

chèvrefeuille *m* honeysuckle.

chevreuil *m* roe deer.

chez *prép* at home: je rentre ~ moi I'm going home; ~ ta tante at your aunt's.

chic *m* style, stylishness; avoir le ~ pour to have the knack for.

chicorée *f* chicory.

chien *m*, **chienne** *f* dog.

chiffon *m* rag, cloth.

chiffonné *adj* crumpled, rumpled.

chiffre *m* figure.

chignon *m* chignon, bun.

chimère *f* chimera.

chimérique *adj* chimerical, fanciful.

chimie *f* chemistry.

chimique *adj* chemical; ~ment *adv* chemically.

chimiste *mf* chemist.

chimpanzé *m* chimpanzee.

chiot *m* puppy.

chipoteur *m* -euse *f* haggler.

chirurgical *adj* surgical.

chirurgie *f* surgery.

chirurgien *m* surgeon.

chlore *m* chlorine.

chloroforme *m* chloroform.

chlorophyle *f* chlorophyll.

chlorure *m* chloride.

choc *m* shock, crash.

chocolat *m* chocolate.

chœur *m* choir, chorus.

choir *vi* to fall.

choisir *vt* to choose.

choix *m* choice.

choléra *m* cholera.

chômage *m* unemployment.

chômeur *m* -euse *f* unemployed person.

choquant *adj* shocking, appalling.

choquer *vt* to shock.

chorale *f* choral.

chorégraphe *mf* choreographer.

choréraphie *f* choreography.

choriste *mf* chorister.

chose *f* thing, matter, object.

chou *m* cabbage.

chouette *f* owl.

chou-fleur *m* cauliflower.

choyer *vt* to cherish.

chrétien *m* -ne *f* Christian, *adj* christian.

christianisme *m* Christianity.

chrome *m* chromium.

chromosome *m* chromosome.

chronique *adj* chronic; * *f* chronicle; column; page.

chronologie *f* chronology.

chronologique *adj* chronological; ~ment *adv* chronologically.

chronomètre *m* chronometer.

chronométrer *vt* to time.

chrysanthème *m* chrysanthemum.

chuchotement *m* whisper, rustling.

chuchoter *vi* to whisper.

chuintement *m* hissing.

chuinter *vi* to hiss.

chute *f* fall, drop.

chuter *vi* to fall.

ci *adv*: **ces fleurs-ci** these flowers; **ci-joint** enclosed; **ci-dessous** below; **ci-contre** opposite; in the margin; annexed.

cible *f* target.

cibler *vt* to target.

cicatrice *f* scar.

cicatrisation *f* cicatrization, healing.

cicatriser *vt* to heal; **se ~** *vr* to heal, form a scar.

cidre *m* cider.

ciel *m*, *pl* **cieux, ciels** sky.

cierge *m* candle.

cigale *f* cicada.

cigare *m* cigar.

cigarette *f* cigarette.

cil *m* eyelash.

ciller *vi* to blink.

cime *f* summit.

ciment *m* cement.

cimenter *vt* to cement.

cimetière *m* cemetery.

cinéaste *mf* film-maker.

cinéma *m* cinema.

cinémathèque *f* film library.

cinématographique *adj* film, cinema.

cinéphile *mf* film enthusiast.

cinétique *adj* kinetic.

cinglant *adj* bitter, lashing, cutting.

cingler *vt* to lash, sting.

cinq *m* five.

cinquantaine *f* about fifty.

cinquante *m* fifty.

cinquantenaire *m* fiftieth anniversary.

cinquantième *mf* fiftieth, *adj* fiftieth.

cinquième *mf* fifth, *adj* fifth; **~ment** *adv* in fifth place.

cintre *m* arch.

cirage *m* polish.

circonférence *f* circumference.

circonscription *f* division, constituency.

circonspect *adj* circumspect.

circonstance *f* circumstance.

circuit *m* circuit, tour.

circulaire *adj* circular; **~ment** *adv* circularly.

circulation *f* circulation; traffic.

circuler *vi* to circulate, move.

cire *f* wax.

cirer *vt* to polish.

cirque *m* circus.

ciseau *m* chisel; ~x *pl* scissors.

citadelle *f* citadel.

citadin *m* -e *f* city dweller; *
adj* town, urban.

citation *f* citation, summons.

cité *f* city.

citer *vt* to quote, cite.

citerne *f* water tank.

citoyen *m* -ne *f* citizen.

citron *m* lemon.

citrouille *f* pumpkin.

civière *f* stretcher.

civil *adj* civil; ~ement *adv*
civilly.

civilisation *f* civilization.

civilisé *adj* civilized.

civiliser *vt* to civilize.

civique *adj* civic.

clair *adj* clear, bright; ~ement
adv clearly.

clairière *f* clearing, glade.

clairsemé *adj* scattered.

clairvoyance *f* perspicacity;
clairvoyance.

clairvoyant *adj* perceptive;
clairvoyant.

clameur *f* clamour.

clan *m* clan.

clandestin *adj* clandestine;
~ement clandestinely.

clandestinité *f* secrecy.

clapoter *vi* to lap (water).

clapotis *m* lapping.

claque *f* slap, smack.

claquement *m* clapping,
slamming.

claquer *vi* to bang, slam.

clarifier *vt* to clarify; se ~ *vr*
to become clear.

clarinette *f* clarinet.

clarté *f* light, brightness.

classe *f* class, standing.

classement *m* filing; grading.

classer *vt* to file, classify.

classeur *m* filing cabinet.

classification *f* classification.

classique *adj* classical, standard; ~ment *adv* classically.

clause *f* clause.

claustrer *vt* to confine.

claustrophobie *f* claustropho-
bia.

clavecin *m* harpsichord.

clavicule *f* collarbone.

clavier *m* keyboard.

clé, clef *f* key.

clémence *f* clemency, mildness.

clergé *m* clergy.

cliché *m* cliché; negative.

client *m* -e *f* client.

clientèle *f* clientele; customers.

cligner *vi* to blink.

clignotant *adj* blinking, flickering; * *m* indicator.

clignotement *m* blinking, flickering.

clignoter *vi* to blink, flicker.

climat *m* climate.

climatique *adj* climatic.

climatisation *f* air-conditioning.

climatiser *vt* to air-condition.

clin d'œil *m* wink.

clinique *f* clinic.

cliqueter *vi* to jingle, clink.

clitoris *m* clitoris.

clochard *m* -e *f* tramp.

cloche *f* bell.

clocher *m* steeple, bell tower.

clochette *f* hand-bell.

cloison *f* partition.

cloîtrer (se) *vr* to enter the monastic life.

clore *vt* to close, conclude.

clos *adj* closed, enclosed.

clôture *f* fence, hedge.

clou *m* nail.

clouer *vt* to nail.

club *m* club.

coagulation *f* coagulation.

coaguler *vi* to coagulate.

coaliser *vt vi* to form a coalition.

coalition *f* coalition.

cobalt *m* cobalt.

cobaye *m* guinea-pig.

cobra *m* cobra.

cocaïne *f* cocaine.

coccinelle *f* ladybird.

coccyx *m* coccyx.

cocher *vt* to notch; to tick off.

cochon *m* -ne *f* pig.

code *m* code.

coder *vt* to code.

codifier *vt* to codify.

coefficient *m* coefficient.

coéquipier *m* -ière *f* team mate.

cœur *m* heart.

coexister *vi* to coexist.

coffre *m* chest; ~-fort safe.

coffret *m* casket.

cogner *vi* to hammer, bang.

cohabitation *f* cohabitation.

cohabiter *vi* to cohabit.

cohérence *f* coherence.

cohérent *adj* coherent.

cohésion *f* cohesion.

cohue *f* crowd.

coiffer *vt* to arrange sb's hair; se ~ *vr* to do one's hair.

coiffeur *m* -euse *f* hairdresser.

coiffure *f* hairstyle.

coin *m* corner.

coincer *vt* to wedge, jam.

coïncidence *f* coincidence.

coït *m* coitus.

col *m* collar; neck.

colère *f* anger.

colérique *adj* quick-tempered, irascible.

colibri *m* hummingbird.

colique *f* diarrhoea.

colis *m* parcel.

collaborateur *m* -trice *f* collaborator, colleague.

collaboration *f* collaboration.

collaborer *vi* to collaborate.

collant *adj* clinging, sticky; * *m* leotard.

collecte *f* collection.

collectif *adj* collective.

collection *f* collection.

collectionner *vt* to collect.

collectionneur *m* -euse *f* collector.

collectivement *adv* collectively.

collectivité *f* community; collective ownership.

collège *m* secondary school.

collègue *mf* colleague.

coller *vt* to stick, glue; * *vi* to stick, be sticky.

collier *m* necklace.

colline *f* hill.

collision *f* collision.

colloque *m* colloquium.

colocataire *mf* co-tenant.

colombe *f* dove.

colon *m* colonist.

colonel *m* colonel.

colonie *f* colony.

colonisation *f* colonization.

coloniser *vt* to colonize.

colonne *f* column.

colorant *m* colouring.

coloration *f* colouring, staining.

coloré *adj* coloured.

colorier *vt* to colour in.

coloris *m* colouring, shade.

colossal *adj* colossal.

colporter *vt* to peddle.

colza *m* rape seed.

coma *m* coma.

comateux *adj* comatose.

combat *m* combat, fight.

combatif *adj* combative.

combativité *f* combativeness.

combattant *adj* fighting, combatant.

combattre *vt* to fight, combat; * *vi* to fight.

combien *adv* how much, how many; ~ de temps? how much time?; ~ sont-ils? how many are they?

combinaison *f* combination.

combiner *vt* to combine.

comble *m* height, peak.

combler *vt* to fill; to fulfil.

combustible *m* fuel.

combustion *f* combustion.

comédie *f* comedy.

comédien *m* **-ne** *f* actor.

comestible *adj* edible.

comète *f* comet.

comique *adj* comic; ~**ment** *adv* comically.

comité *m* committee.

commandant *m* commander.

commande *f* command, order.

commandement *m* command, commandment.

commander *vt vi* to order, command.

commanditer *vt* to finance, sponsor.

commando *m* commando.

comme *conj* as, like; ~ **ci** ~ **ça** so-so; ~ **il faut** properly; * *adv* how.

commémoration *f* commemoration.

commémorer *vt* to commemorate.

commencement *m* beginning, start.

commencer *vt vi* to begin, start.

comment *adv* how; ~ **dire?** how shall we say?; ~ **cela?** what do you mean?

commentaire *m* comment; commentary.

commentateur *m* **-trice** *f* commentator.

commenter *vt* to comment.

commérage *m* piece of gossip.

commerçant *m* **-e** *f* merchant, trader.

commerce *m* business, commerce.

commercial *adj* commercial; ~**ement** *adv* commercially.

commercialiser *vt* to market.

commère *f* gossip.

commettre *vt* to commit.

commissaire *m* representative; commissioner.

commissariat *m* police station; commissionership; commissariat.

commission *f* commission, committee.

commissionnaire *m* messenger; agent.

commode *adj* convenient, comfortable.

commodité *f* convenience.

commun *adj* common, joint; ~**ément** *adv* commonly.

communal *adj* council; common, communal.

communautaire *adj* community.

communauté *f* community; joint estate.

commune *f* town, district.

communication *f* communication.

communier *vi* to receive communion.

communion *f* communion.

communiqué *m* communiqué.

communiquer *vt* to communicate, transmit; * *vi* to communicate.

communisme *m* communism.

communiste *mf* communist.

compact *adj* compact, dense.

compagne *f* companion.

compagnie *f* company.

compagnon *m* companion.

comparable *adj* comparable.

comparaison *f* comparison.

comparaître *vi* to appear.

comparativement *adv* comparatively.

comparer *vt* to compare.

compartiment *m* compartment.

compartimenter *vt* to compart, partition.

compas *m* compass.

compassion *f* compassion.

compatibilité *f* compatibility.

compatible *adj* compatible.

compatir *vi* to sympathize.

compatissant *adj* compassionate.

compatriote *mf* compatriot.

compensation *f* compensation.

compenser *vt* to compensate; to offset; **se ~** *vr* to balance each other, make up for.

compétence *f* competence.

compétent *adj* competent, capable.

compétitif *adj* competitive.

compétition *f* competition.

compétitivité *f* competitiveness.

complaisance *f* kindness; complacency.

complaisant *adj* kind; complacent.

complément *m* complement; extension.

complémentaire *adj* complementary, supplementary.

complet *adj* complete, full.

complètement *adv* completely, fully.

compléter *vt* to complete; **se ~** *vr* to complement one another.

complexe *adj* complex, complicated.

complexé *adj* mixed up.

complication *f* complication.

complice *mf* accomplice.

complicité *f* complicity, collusion.

compliment *m* compliment.

complimenter *vt* to compliment, congratulate.

compliqué *adj* complicated, intricate.

compliquer *vt* to complicate.

complot *m* plot.

comportement *m* behaviour; performance.

comporter *vt* to consist of, comprise; **se ~** *vr* to behave.

composant *m* component, constituent.

composante *f* component.

composer *vt* to compose, make up; **se ~** *vr*: **se ~ de** to be made up of.

compositeur *m* **-trice** *f* composer; typesetter.

composition *f* composition, formation.

compréhensible *adj* compréhensible.

compréhensif *adj* compréhensive, understanding.

compréhension *f* comprehension, understanding.

comprendre *vt* to understand; to consist of.

compresse *f* compress.

compresseur *m* compressor.

compression *f* compression; reduction.

comprimé *adj* compressed; restrained; * *m* tablet.

comprimer *vt* to compress; to restrain.

compromettant *adj* compromising.

compromettre *vt* to compromise.

compromis *m* compromise.

comptabilité *f* accountancy.

comptable *adj* accounting; * *mf* accountant.

compte *m* account.

compter *vt vi* to count.

compteur *m* meter.

comptoir *m* counter, bar.

comte *m* count, **comtesse** *f* countess.

concave *adj* concave.

concéder *vt* to grant, concede.

concentration *f* concentration.

concentré *adj* concentrated; reserved.

concentrer *vt* to concentrate; **se ~** *vr* to concentrate.

concept *m* concept.

conception *f* conception, design.

concerner *vt* to concern, regard.

concert *m* concert.

concertation *f* dialogue, consultation.

concession f concession; privilege.

concessionnaire mf concessionaire, grantee.

concevoir vt to imagine, conceive.

concierge mf caretaker, concierge.

conciliant adj conciliatory.

conciliation f conciliation; reconciliation.

concilier vt to reconcile; to attract.

concis adj concise.

concision f conciseness, brevity.

concluant adj conclusive, decisive.

conclure vt to conclude; to decide; se ~ vr to conclude, come to an end.

conclusion f conclusion.

concombre m cucumber.

concordance f agreement, accord.

concorder vi to agree, coincide.

concours m competition; conjuncture.

concret adj concrete, solid.

concrètement adv concretely.

concrétiser vt to put in concrete form.

concubin m -e f concubine; cohabitant.

concubinage m concubinage; cohabitation.

concurrence f competition.

concurrent m -e f concurrent; competitor.

condamnation f condemnation; sentencing.

condamné m -e f convict; sentenced person; * adj sentenced.

condamner vt to condemn; to sentence.

condensation f condensation.

condensé adj condensed, evaporated.

condenser vt to condense, compress.

condescendant adj condescending.

condiment m condiment.

condition f condition, term.

conditionné adj conditioned; packaged.

conditionnement m conditioning; packaging.

conditionner vt to condition; to package.

condoléances fpl condolences.

conducteur m -trice f driver; operator.

conduire vt vi to lead; to drive.

conduit *m* conduit, pipe.

conduite *f* conduct; driving; behaviour.

cône *m* cone.

confédération *f* confederation.

conférence *f* conference.

conférencier *m* **-ière** *f* speaker; lecturer.

confesser *vt* to confess; **se ~** *vr* to go to confession.

confession *f* confession.

confiance *f* confidence, trust.

confiant *adj* confident; confiding.

confidence *f* confidence; disclosure.

confident *m* **-e** *f* confidant.

confidentiel *adj* confidential; **~lement** *adv* confidentially.

confier *vt* to confide, entrust; **se ~** *vr* to confide in.

confiner *vt* to confine; **se ~** to be confined; *vr*: **se ~ à** to confine o.s. to.

confirmation *f* confirmation.

confirmer *vt* to confirm; **se ~** *vr* to be confirmed.

confiserie *f* confectionery.

confisquer *vt* to confiscate, impound.

confiture *f* jam.

conflictuel *adj* conflicting.

conflit *m* conflict, contention.

confondre *vt* to confuse, mingle.

conforme *adj* consistent; true.

conformément *adv* in accordance with.

conformer *vt* to model; **se ~** *vr* to conform.

conformiste *mf* conformist.

conformité *f* conformity; likeness.

confort *m* comfort.

confortable *adj* comfortable, cosy; **~ment** *adv* comfortably.

confrère *m* colleague.

confrontation *f* confrontation; comparison.

confronter *vt* to confront.

confus *adj* confused, indistinct; **~ément** *adv* confusedly, vaguely.

confusion *f* confusion, disorder.

congé *m* leave; holiday.

congédier *vt* to dismiss.

congélateur *m* freezer.

congeler *vt* to freeze.

congestion *f* congestion; stroke.

congratulation *f* congratulation.

congratuler *vt* to congratulate.

congrégation f congregation.

congrès m congress, conference.

conifère m conifer.

conjoint m -e f spouse; * adj joint; linked; ~ement adv jointly.

conjonctivite f conjunctivitis.

conjoncture f conjuncture; situation.

conjugaison f conjugation.

conjugal adj conjugal.

conjuguer vt to conjugate; to combine.

conjuration f conspiracy, plot.

conjurer vt to conspire; to implore; to ward off.

connaissance f knowledge; consciousness.

connaisseur m -euse f connoisseur; expert.

connaître vt to know, be acquainted with.

connecter vt to connect.

connecteur m connective.

connexion f connection, link.

connivence f connivance.

connotation f connotation.

connu adj known; famous.

conquérant m -e f conqueror; * adj conquering.

conquérir vt to conquer.

conquête f conquest.

conquis adj conquered, vanquished.

consacrer vt to devote, dedicate; se ~ vr to dedicate o.s. to.

consciemment adv consciously, knowingly.

conscience f consciousness; conscience.

consciencieusement adv conscientiously.

consciencieux adv conscientious.

conscient adj conscious, aware.

consécration f consecration.

consécutif adj consecutive.

consécutivement adv consecutively.

conseil m advice, counsel.

conseiller m -ère f counsellor, adviser; * vt to advise, counsel.

consentant adj consenting, willing.

consentement m consent.

consentir vi to consent, acquiesce.

conséquence f consequence, result.

conséquent adj consequent; substantial.

conservateur m -trice f conservative; curator.

conservation f conservation.

conservatoire m conservatory; academy.

conserve f canned food.

conserver vt to keep, preserve; **se ~** vr to keep.

considérable adj considerable; notable; **~ment** adv considerably.

considération f consideration, respect.

considérer vt to consider, regard.

consigne f orders, instructions.

consistance f consistency; strength.

consister vi: **~ en** to consist of; **cela consiste à** that consists in doing.

consolation f consolation, solace.

console f console.

consoler vt to console, comfort.

consolidation f consolidation, reinforcement.

consolider vt to consolidate, reinforce.

consommateur m **-trice** f consumer.

consommation f consumption; accomplishment.

consommé adj consummate, accomplished; ***** m consommé.

consommer vt to consume, use.

consonne f consonant.

conspirateur m **-trice** f conspirator.

conspiration f conspiracy, plot.

conspirer vi to conspire, plot.

constamment adv constantly, continually.

constant adj constant, continuous.

constante f constancy.

constat m report; acknowledgement.

constatation f authentication, verification.

constater vt to record; to verify.

constellation f constellation, galaxy.

consternation f consternation, dismay.

consterner vt to dismay.

constipation f constipation.

constituer vt to constitute, form.

constitution f constitution, formation.

constitutionnel adj constitutional; **~lement** adv constitutionally.

constructeur *m* **-trice** *f* builder, maker.

constructif *adj* constructive.

construction *f* building, construction.

construire *vt* to construct, build.

consul *m* consul.

consulaire *adj* consular.

consulat *m* consulate.

consultant *m* **-e** *f* consultant; * *adj* consulting.

consultation *f* consultation, advice.

consulter *vt* to consult, take advice from.

consumer *vt* to consume, spend; **se ~** *vr* to be burning, waste away.

contact *m* contact, touch.

contacter *vt* to contact, approach.

contagieux *adj* contagious, infectious.

contamination *f* contamination, pollution.

contaminer *vt* to contaminate, pollute.

conte *m* story, tale.

contemplation *f* contemplation, meditation.

contempler *vt* to contemplate, meditate.

contemporain *adj* contemporary.

contenance *f* capacity, volume.

contenir *vt* to contain.

contentement *m* contentment, satisfaction.

contenter *vt* to please, satisfy; **se ~** *vr*: **se ~ de** to content o.s. with.

contenu *m* contents, enclosure.

contestation *f* dispute, controversy.

contester *vt* to contest, dispute.

contexte *m* context.

contigu *adj*, *f* **contiguè** contiguous, adjacent.

continent *m* continent.

continental *adj* continental.

contingent *m* quota; (*mil*) draft.

continu *adj* continuous, incessant.

continuation *f* continuation.

continuel *adj* continual, continuous; **~lement** *adv* continuously, continually.

continuer *vt* to continue, proceed with; * *vi* to continue, go on.

contour *m* contour, outline.

contourner *vt* to bypass, skirt.

contraceptif *adj* contraceptive.

contraception *f* contraception.

contracter *vt* to contract, acquire; **se ~** *vr* to contract, shrink.

contraction *f* contraction.

contradiction *f* contradiction, discrepancy.

contradictoire *adj* contradictory, conflicting.

contraindre *vt* to constrain, compel.

contrainte *f* constraint, compulsion.

contraire *m* opposite, contrary; * *adj* opposite, contrary; **~ment** *adv* contrarily.

contrariant *adj* contrary; perverse.

contrarier *vt* to annoy; to oppose.

contrariété *f* annoyance, disappointment.

contraste *m* contrast.

contrat *m* contract, agreement.

contre *prép* against; **parier à 10 ~ 1** to bet at 10 to 1; **~ toute attente** contrary to all expectations; **par ~** on the other hand.

contre-attaque *f* counter-attack.

contre-attaquer *vi* to counter-attack.

contrebalancer *vt* to counterbalance.

contrebande *f* contraband, smuggling.

contrebandier *m* -**ière** *f* smuggler.

contrebasse *f* double bass.

contrecarrer *vt* to thwart, oppose.

contrecœur: **à ~** reluctantly.

contrecoup *m* rebound, repercussion.

contredire *vt* to contradict, refute.

contrefaçon *f* counterfeit, forgery.

contrefaire *vt* to counterfeit, forge.

contre-indication *f* contraindication.

contremaître *m* foreman.

contre-offensive *f* counter-offensive.

contrepartie *f* compensation; consideration.

contre-plaqué *m* plywood.

contrepoison *m* antidote, counter-poison.

contresens *m* nonsense; misunderstanding; mistranslation.

contretemps *m* mishap; contretemps; (*mus*) syncopation.

contribuable *mf* taxpayer.

contribuer *vt vi* to contribute.

contribution *f* contribution; tax.

contrôle *m* control, check.

contrôler *vt* to control, check.

contrôleur *m* -**euse** *f* inspector; auditor.

controverse *f* controversy.

controversé *adj* disputed.

contusion *f* bruise, contusion.

convaincant *adj* convincing.

convaincre *vt* to convince, persuade.

convaincu *adj* convinced, persuaded.

convalescence *f* convalescence.

convenable *adj* fitting, suitable; ~**ment** *adv* suitably, fitly.

convenir *vi* to agree, accord.

convention *f* convention, agreement.

conventionnel *adj* conventional; contractual; ~**lement** *adv* conventionally.

convenu *adj* agreed; stipulated.

convergent *adj* convergent.

converger *vi* to converge.

conversation *f* conversation, talk.

conversion *f* conversion.

convertir *vt* to convert; **se ~** *vr* to be converted.

convexe *adj* convex.

conviction *f* conviction.

convier *vt* to invite; to urge.

convivial *adj* convivial; user-friendly.

convocation *f* convocation, summoning.

convoi *m* convoy; train.

convoiter *vt* to covet.

convoquer *vt* to convoke, convene.

convulsion *f* convulsion.

coopératif *adj* cooperative.

coopération *f* cooperation.

coopérative *f* cooperative.

coopérer *vi* to cooperate, collaborate.

coordinateur *m* -**trice** *f* coordinator.

coordination *f* coordination; committee.

coordonnées *fpl* coordinates.

coordonner *vt* to coordinate.

copain *m* friend, pal.

copeau *m* shaving, chip.

copie *f* copy, reproduction.

copier *vt* to copy, reproduce.

copieusement *adv* copiously, abundantly.

copieux *adj* copious, abundant.

copilote *m* co-pilot.

copine *f* friend, mate.

coproduction *f* coproduction.

copropriété *f* co-ownership, joint ownership.

coq *m* cock, rooster.

coque *f* (*mar*) hull; shell.

coquelicot *m* poppy.

coquet *adj* stylish, smart; ~**tement** *adv* stylishly, smartly.

coquetterie *f* smartness, stylishness.

coquillage *m* shellfish.

coquille *f* shell, scallop.

coquin *m* -e *f* naughty, mischievous.

cor *m* (*mus*) horn; corn.

corail *m* coral.

coran *m* Koran.

corbeau *m* crow.

corbeille *f* basket.

corbillard *m* hearse.

cordage *m* rope; rigging.

corde *f* rope; string.

cordée *f* roped mountaineering party.

cordial *adj* cordial, warm; ~**ement** *adv* cordially, warmly.

cordialité *f* cordiality, warmth.

cordon *m* cord, string; cordon.

cordonnerie *f* shoemending.

cordonnier *m* -ière *f* shoemender, cobbler.

coriace *adj* tough; tight.

coriandre *m* coriander.

corne *f* horn, antler.

cornée *f* cornea.

corneille *f* crow.

cornemuse *f* bagpipes.

cornet *m* cone, cornet.

corniche *f* cornice; ledge.

cornichon *m* gherkin; greenhorn.

corporatif *adj* corporative, corporate.

corporation *f* corporation, guild.

corporatisme *m* corporatism.

corporel *adj* corporal, bodily.

corps *m* body, corpse.

corpulence *f* corpulence.

corpulent *adj* corpulent.

corpus *m* corpus.

correct *adj* correct, accurate; ~**ement** *adv* correctly, accurately.

correcteur *m* **-trice** *f* examiner; proofreader.

correction *f* correction; proofreading.

corrélation *f* correlation.

correspondance *f* correspondence, communication.

correspondant *m* **-e** *f* correspondent; * *adj* corresponding.

correspondre *vi* to correspond, communicate.

corridor *m* corridor, passage.

corrigé *m* corrected version, fair copy.

corriger *vt* to correct.

corroborer *vt* to corroborate.

corroder *vt* to corrode.

corrompre *vt* to corrupt, debase.

corrompu *adj* corrupt.

corrosif *adj* corrosive.

corrosion *f* corrosion.

corruption *f* corruption, debasement.

corsage *m* blouse, bodice.

corsaire *m* corsair.

corsé *adj* rich, full-bodied.

corset *m* corset.

cortège *m* cortège, procession.

cortex *m* cortex.

cortical *adj* cortical.

cortisone *f* cortisone.

corvée *f* fatigue duty; forced labour.

cosmétique *m* cosmetic.

cosmique *adj* cosmic.

cosmonaute *mf* cosmonaut.

cosmopolite *adj* cosmopolitan.

cosmos *m* cosmos.

costume *m* costume, dress.

cotation *f* quotation, valuation.

côte *f* coast; rib; slope.

côté *m* side; point.

coteau *m* hill.

côtelé *adj* ribbed.

côtelette *f* cutlet.

coter *vt* to quote; to classify.

côtier *adj* coastal, inshore.

coton *m* cotton.

cotonneux *adj* fleecy, fluffy.

côtoyer *vt* to mix with, skirt.

cou *m* neck.

couchant *adj* setting.

couche *f* layer, coat.

coucher *vt* to put to bed; se ~ *vr* to go to bed.

coucou *m* cuckoo.

coude *m* elbow.

coudé *adj* angled, bent.

coudoyer *vt* mix with, rub shoulders with.

coudre *vt vi* to sew.

couette *f* duvet.

coulant *adj* flowing; smooth.

couler *vi* to flow, run.

couleur *f* colour, shade.

couleuvre *f* grass snake.

coulis *m* sauce, purée.

coulissant *adj* sliding.

coulisse *f* groove; (*thea*) wings.

coulisser *vi* to slide, run.

couloir *m* corridor, passage.

coup *m* blow; shot; ~ sur ~ one after another, incessantly; tout à ~ suddenly; après ~ afterwards, after the event; ~ de feu shot; jeter un ~ d'œil to glance; ~ de coude nudge; ~ de téléphone phone call; ~ de soleil sunstroke.

coupable *mf* culprit; * *adj* guilty.

coupant *adj* cutting, sharp.

coupe *f* cut; cutting.

coupe-papier *m invar* paper knife.

couper *vt* to cut, slice.

couple *m* couple, pair.

couplet *m* couplet, verse.

coupole *f* dome.

coupon *m* coupon, voucher, ticket.

coupure *f* cut; break.

cour *f* court, yard, courtyard.

courage *m* courage, daring.

courageusement *adv* courageously.

courageux *adj* courageous.

couramment *adv* fluently; commonly.

courant *adj* current; present; * *m* stream, current.

courbature *f* stiffness; ache.

courbaturé *adj* aching.

courbe *f* curve; contour.

courbé *adj* curved, stooped.

courber *vt* to curve, bend.

coureur *m* -euse *f* runner.

courgette *f* courgette.

courir *vi* to run, race.

couronne *f* crown, wreath.

couronnement *m* coronation.

couronner *vt* to crown.

courrier *m* mail, post.

courroie *f* strap, belt.

cours *m* course; flow; path.

course *f* running; race; flight; journey.

coursier *m* -ière *f* courier, messenger.

court *adj* short, brief.

court-bouillon *m* court-bouillon, wine sauce.

court-circuit *m* short-circuit.

court-circuiter *vt* to short-circuit.

courtier *m* **-ière** *f* broker, agent.

courtiser *vt* to court.

courtois *adj* courteous; **~ement** *adv* courteously.

courtoisie *f* courtesy, courteousness.

cousin *m* **-e** *f* cousin.

coussin *m* cushion, pillow.

coussinet *m* pad; bearing.

coût *m* cost, charge.

couteau *m* knife.

coûter *vt vi* to cost.

coûteusement *adv* expensively.

coûteux *adj* costly, expensive.

coutume *f* custom, habit.

coutumier *adj* customary, usual.

couture *f* sewing, needlework.

couturier *m* couturier, fashion designer.

couturière *f* dressmaker.

couvent *m* convent.

couver *vt* to hatch, incubate; * *vi* to smoulder, lurk.

couvercle *m* lid, cap.

couvert *m* shelter; cover; pretext; * *adj* covered; secret; obscure.

couverture *f* blanket; cover; roofing.

couvre-feu *m* curfew.

couvreur *m* roofer.

couvrir *vt* to cover; **se ~** *vr* to cover up; to become overcast.

crabe *m* crab.

crachement *m* spitting.

cracher *vt* to spit.

crachin *m* drizzle.

craie *f* chalk.

craindre *vt* to fear.

crainte *f* fear, dread.

craintif *adj* timid, cowardly.

crampe *f* cramp.

crampon *m* stud, spike, crampon.

cramponner *vt* to cramp, clamp; **se ~** *vr* to cling, hang on.

cran *m* notch, cog.

crâne *m* cranium, skull.

crânien *adj* cranial.

crapaud *m* toad.

crapule *f* villain.

crapuleux *adj* villainous, vicious.

craquellement *m* cracking.

craquement *m* crack, creaking, snap.

craquer *vi* to creak, squeak, crack.

crasseux *adj* grimy, filthy.

cratère *m* crater.

cravate *f* tie.

créancier *m* **-ière** *f* creditor.

créateur *m* **-trice** *f* creator, author.

créatif *adj* creative.

création *f* creation.

créativité *f* creativity.

créature *f* creature.

crèche *f* crèche; crib.

crédibilité *f* credibility.

crédible *adj* credible.

crédit *m* credit, trust.

crédit-bail *m* lease; leasing.

crédule *adj* credulous, gullible.

crédulité *f* credulity, gullibility.

créer *vt* to create, produce.

crémaillère *f* rack, chimney hook.

crème *f* cream.

crémerie *f* dairy.

crémeux *adj* creamy.

crémier *m* dairyman, **-ière** *f* dairywoman.

créneau *m* battlement.

crêpe *f* pancake; * *m* crepe, crape.

crêperie *f* pancake restaurant.

crépitement *m* crackling; rattling.

crépiter *vi* to crackle; to rattle.

crépu *adj* frizzy, woolly.

crépuscule *m* twilight, dusk.

cresson *m* watercress.

crête *f* crest, comb.

crétin *m* **-e** *f* cretin, idiot.

creuser *vi* to dig, burrow; * *vt* to dig, hollow.

creuset *m* crucible.

creux *adj* hollow, empty.

crevaison *f* puncture, flat.

crevé *adj* burst, punctured.

crever *vt* to burst; to gouge; * *vi* to burst; to split.

crevette *f* prawn.

cri *m* cry, howl, yell.

criant *adj* crying; striking; glaring.

criard *adj* yelling; scolding.

crible *m* riddle, sieve; **passer au ~** to riddle; to examine closely.

cribler *vt* to sift, riddle.

cric *m* (*auto*) jack.

crier *vi* to cry, shout.

crime *m* crime, offence.

criminel *m* **-le** *f* criminal; * *adj* criminal.

crin *m* horsehair.

crinière *f* mane.

criquet *m* locust.

crise *f* crisis, attack.

crisper *vt* to shrivel; to clench.

cristal *m* crystal, glassware.

cristallin *adj* crystalline.

cristallisation *f* crystallization.

cristalliser *vt* to crystallize.

critère *m* criterion, standard.

critiquable *adj* censurable, open to criticism.

critique *adj* critical, censorious; * *f* criticism; critique.

critiquer *vt* to criticize, censure.

croc *m* fang; hook.

croche *f* quaver.

crochet *m* hook, clasp.

crochu *adj* hooked, claw-like.

crocodile *m* crocodile.

croire *vt* to believe, think.

croisade *f* crusade.

croisement *m* crossing, junction.

croiser *vt* to cross; to fold; se ~ *vr* to cross, intersect.

croisière *f* cruise.

croissance *f* growth, increase.

croissant *adj* growing, increasing; * *m* croissant; crescent.

croître *vi* to grow, rise.

croix *f* cross.

croque-monsieur *m* toasted cheese and ham sandwich.

croquer *vt* to crunch.

croquette *f* croquette.

croquis *m* sketch, outline.

crosse *f* (*rel*) crozier; butt, grip.

crotte *f* manure, dung.

croupir *vi* to stagnate, wallow.

croustillant *adj* crusty, crisp.

croustiller *vi* to be crusty, crispy.

croûte *f* crust.

croûton *m* crust, crouton.

croyance *f* belief.

croyant *adj* believing.

cru *adj* raw, uncooked; * *m* vineyard; wine.

cruauté *f* cruelty, inhumanity.

cruche *f* pitcher.

crucial *adj* crucial, decisive.

crucifix *m* crucifix.

crucifixion *f* crucifixion.

crudité *f* crudity, coarseness.

crue *f* flood.

cruel *adj* cruel; ~lement *adv* cruelly.

crustacé *m* crustacean, shellfish.

crypte *m* crypt.

crypter *vt* to encode, scramble.

cube *m* cube, block.

cubique *adj* cubic.

cubisme *m* cubism.

cueillette *f* picking, gathering.

cueillir *vt* to pick, gather.

cuiller, cuillère f spoon, spoonful.

cuir m leather, hide.

cuirasse f (zool) cuirass, breastplate.

cuirassé adj armoured; * m battleship.

cuire vi to cook.

cuisine f kitchen; cookery.

cuisiner vt vi to cook.

cuisinier m -ière f cook.

cuisinière f cooker, stove.

cuisse f thigh.

cuisson f cooking, baking.

cuit adj cooked.

cuivre m copper.

cul m (col) bottom, ass.

culasse f cylinder-head; breech.

cul-de-jatte mf legless cripple.

cul-de-sac m blind alley, cul-de-sac.

culinaire adj culinary.

culminer vi to culminate, tower.

culot m cheek, nerve.

culotte f knickers; underpants; shorts.

culpabiliser vt to make sb feel guilty; se ~ vr to feel guilty.

culpabilité f guilt, culpability.

culte m cult, veneration.

cultivable adj cultivable.

cultivateur m -trice f farmer.

cultivé adj cultured.

cultiver vt to cultivate; se ~ vr to improve o.s.

culture f culture; cultivation.

culturel adj cultural.

culturisme m body-building.

cumin m cumin.

cumul m pluralism; accumulation.

cumuler vt to accumulate; to hold concurrently.

cupide adj greedy; ~ment adv greedily.

cupidité f greed, cupidity.

cure f cure; treatment.

curé m parish priest, parson.

cure-dents m toothpick.

curieusement adv curiously.

curieux m -euse f inquisitive person; onlooker; * adj curious, inquisitive.

curiosité f curiosity, inquisitiveness.

cursus m degree course.

cutané adj skin, cutaneous.

cuve f vat, tank.

cuvette f basin, bowl.

cyanure m cyanide.

cybernétique f cybernetics.

cyclable adj cycle, for cycling.

cyclamen *m* cyclamen.

cycle *m* cycle; stage.

cyclique *adj* cyclical.

cyclisme *m* cycling.

cycliste *mf* cyclist; * *adj* cycle.

cyclomoteur *m* moped.

cyclone *m* cyclone.

cyclope *m* Cyclops.

cygne *m* swan.

cylindre *m* cylinder.

cylindrée *f* capacity (engine).

cylindrique *adj* cylindrical.

cymbale *f* cymbal.

cynique *adj* cynical; ~ment *adv* cynically.

cynisme *m* cynicism.

cytologie *f* cytology.

cytoplasme *m* cytoplasm.

D

dactylographe *mf* typist.

dactylographie *f* typing, typewriting.

dactylographier *vt* to type.

dada *m* (*fam*) hobbyhorse; gee-gee.

dahlia *m* dahlia.

daigner *vt* to deign, condescend.

daim *m* deer.

dalle *f* flagstone, slab.

dalmatien *m* Dalmatian.

daltonien *adj* colour-blind.

dame *f* lady; dame.

damier *m* draughtboard.

damnation *f* damnation.

damné *adj* damned.

damner *vt* to damn.

danger *m* danger, risk.

dangereusement *adv* dangerously.

dangereux *adj* dangerous, risky.

dans *prép* in; into; il a ~ les trente ans he's thirty or so.

dansant *adj* dancing.

danse *f* dance; dancing.

danser *vi* to dance.

danseur *m* **-euse** *f* dancer.

dard *m* sting.

datation *f* dating.

date *f* date.

dater *vt* to date.

datif *m* dative.

datte *f* (*bot*) date.

dattier *m* date palm.

dauphin *m* dolphin.

daurade *f* sea bream.

davantage *adv* more.

de *prép* of; from; **une femme ~ quarante ans** a forty-year-old woman; **~ bonne heure** early; **deux ~ plus** two more; * *art* some, any.

dé *m* dice; thimble.

déambuler *vi* to stroll.

débâcle *f* disaster; collapse.

déballage *m* unpacking; display.

déballer *vt* to unpack; to display.

débandade *f* rout, stampede.

débarbouiller *vt* to wash; **se ~** *vr* to wash o.s.

débarcadère *m* landing; wharf.

débardeur *m* docker, stevedore.

débarquement *m* landing, disembarkment.

débarquer *vt* to land, unship; * *vi* to disembark, land.

débarrasser *vt* to clear, rid; **se ~** *vr*: **se ~ de** to rid o.s. of.

débat *m* debate; dispute, contest.

débattre *vi* to debate, discuss.

débauche *f* debauchery, dissoluteness.

débaucher *vt* to debauch, corrupt.

débile *adj* weak, feeble.

débilitant *adj* debilitating, weakening.

débit *m* debit; turnover; flow.

débiter *vt* to debit; to produce.

débiteur *m* **-trice** *f* debtor.

déblayer *vt* to clear away, remove.

déblocage *m* unblocking; freeing, releasing.

débloquer *vt* to release, unlock.

déboisement *m* deforestation.

déboiser *vt* to deforest.

déboîtement *m* dislocation.

débordant *adj* exuberant, overflowing.

débordé *adj* overwhelmed.

débordement *m* overflowing; outflanking.

déborder *vi* to overflow; to outflank.

débouché *m* outlet; issue.

déboucher *vt* to open, uncork; * *vi* to pass out, emerge.

debout *adv* upright, standing; **être ~** to stand.

déboutonner *vt* to unbutton.

débraillé *adj* untidy, disordered.

débrancher *vt* to disconnect.

débrayer *vi* to declutch; to stop work.

débris *m* debris, waste.

débrouiller *vt* to disentangle, unravel; **se ~** *vr* to cope, manage.

début *m* beginning, outset.

débutant *adj* novice.

débuter *vi* to start, begin; * *vt* to lead, start.

décadence *f* decadence, decline.

décadent *adj* decadent.

décaféiné *adj* decaffeinated.

décagone *m* decagon.

décalage *m* gap, interval; discrepancy.

décalcifier *vt* to decalcify.

décaler *vt* to shift; to stagger.

décalitre *m* decalitre.

décamètre *m* decametre.

décaper *vt* to clean, scour.

décapotable *adj* convertible; * *f* convertible.

décapsuler *vt* to take the lid off.

décapsuleur *m* bottle-opener.

décathlon *m* decathlon.

décéder *vi* to die.

décelable *adj* detectable.

déceler *vt* to detect; to disclose.

décembre *m* December.

décemment *adv* decently.

décence *f* decency.

décennal *adj* decennial.

décennie *f* decade.

décent *adj* decent, proper.

décentralisation *f* decentralization.

décentraliser *vt* to decentralize.

déception *f* disappointment; deceit.

décerner *vt* to award, confer.

décès *m* death, decease.

décevant *adj* disappointing; deceptive.

décevoir *vt* to disappoint; to deceive.

déchaîné *adj* wild, unbridled.

déchaîner *vt* to unleash; **se ~** *vr* to break loose, run wild.

décharge *f* discharge; receipt.

déchargement *m* unloading.

décharger *vt* to unload, discharge.

décharné *adj* lean, emaciated.

déchausser *vt* to take off footwear; **se ~** *vr* to take one's shoes off.

déchéance *f* decay, decline.

déchet *m* loss, waste.

déchiffrer *vt* to decipher, decode.

déchiqueter *vt* to tear; to slash; to shred.

déchirant *adj* harrowing, excruciating.

déchirement *m* tearing, ripping.

déchirer *vt* to tear, rip.

déchirure *f* tear, rip.

déchoir *vi* to decline; to sink.

déchu *adj* fallen; declined; deposed.

décibel *m* decibel.

décidé *adj* decided; determined; ~**ment** *adv* positively; resolutely; certainly.

décigramme *m* decigram.

décilitre *m* decilitre.

décimal *adj* decimal.

décimètre *m* decimetre.

décisif *adj* decisive, conclusive.

décision *f* decision.

déclamation *f* declamation.

déclamer *vt* to declaim.

déclaré *adj* professed, avowed.

déclarer *vt* to declare, announce; **se ~** *vr* to speak one's mind.

déclenchement *m* release, setting off.

déclencher *vt* to release, set off; **se ~** *vr* to release itself, go off.

déclic *m* click; trigger.

déclin *m* decline, deterioration.

déclinaison *f* declension; declination.

déclinant *adj* declining.

décliner *vi* to decline, refuse.

déclivité *f* declivity, slope.

décloisonner *vt* to decompartmentalize.

décoder *vt* to decode, decipher.

décodeur *m* decoder, decipherer.

décoiffer *vt* to disarrange sb's hair.

décoincer *vt* to loose, release.

décollage *m* take-off, lift-off.

décoller *vi* to unpaste, steam off; to take off; * *vt*: **se ~** *vr* to come unstuck, become detached.

décolleté *adj* low-necked, low-cut; *m* decolletage, low neckline.

décolorant *adj* bleaching, decolorizing; * *m* bleaching substance.

décolorer *vt* to decolour, bleach.

décombres *mpl* rubble, debris.

décomposer *vt* to decompose; to break up; to dissect; **se ~** *vr* to decompose, decay.

décomposition *f* decomposition, breaking up.

décompression *f* decompression.

décomprimer *vt* to decompress.

décompte *m* discount; deduction.

déconcentrer *vt* to devolve;

to disperse; **se ~** *vr* to lose concentration.

déconcertant *adj* disconcerting.

déconcerter *vt* to disconcert.

décongeler *vt* to thaw, defrost.

déconnecter *vt* to disconnect.

déconnexion *f* disconnection.

décontenancé *adj* embarrassed; disconcerted.

décontracté *adj* relaxed.

décontracter *vt* to relax; **se ~** *vr* to relax.

décontraction *f* relaxation.

décor *m* scenery; setting.

décorateur *m* **-trice** *f* decorator; set designer.

décoratif *adj* decorative, ornamental.

décoration *f* decoration, embellishment.

décorer *vt* to decorate, adorn.

décortiquer *vt* to husk, shell.

découler *vi* to flow; to ensue.

découpage *m* cutting up, carving.

découper *vt* to carve, cut up.

décourageant *adj* discouraging, disheartening.

découragement *m* discouragement.

décourager *vt* to discourage, dishearten; **se ~** *vr* to become discouraged.

décousu *adj* unsewn; loose; disconnected.

découvert *adj* uncovered; open; * *m* overdraft.

découverte *f* discovery.

découvrir *vt* to discover.

décret *m* decree, enactment.

décréter *vt* to decree, enact.

décrire *vt* to describe.

décrocher *vt* to take down; to unhook.

décroissant *adj* decreasing, lessening.

décroître *vi* to decrease, diminish.

déçu *adj* disappointed.

décupler *vi* to increase tenfold.

dédaigner *vt* to disdain, scorn.

dédaigneusement *adv* disdainfully.

dédaigneux *adj* disdainful, scornful.

dédain *m* disdain, scorn.

dedans *adv* inside, indoors; * *m* inside; **au ~** inside.

dédicace *f* dedication.

dédier *vt* to consecrate, dedicate to.

dédommagement *m* compensation, damages.

dédommager *vt* to compensate, indemnify.

dédouanement *m* customs clearance.

dédoubler *vt* to divide in two; to remove lining.

déduction *f* deduction.

déduire *vt* to deduct; to deduce.

déesse *f* goddess.

défaillance *f* faintness; exhaustion; blackout.

défaillant *adj* faint; weakening.

défaillir *vi* to faint; to weaken.

défaire *vt* to undo, dismantle.

défaite *m* defeat, overthrow.

défaitiste *adj*, *mf* defeatist.

défaut *m* defect, fault.

défavorable *adj* unfavourable; **~ment** *adv* unfavourably.

défavoriser *vt* to penalize, treat unfairly.

défection *f* defection.

défectueux *adj* defective, faulty.

défendeur *m* -**eresse** *f* defendant.

défendre *vt* to defend, protect; to prohibit; **se ~** *vr* to defend o.s.

défense *f* defence; prohibition.

défenseur *m* defender.

défensif *adj* defensive.

défi *m* defiance; challenge.

défiant *adj* mistrustful, distrustful.

déficience *f* deficiency.

déficient *adj* deficient; weak.

déficit *m* deficit, shortfall.

déficitaire *adj* deficient, in deficit.

défier *vt* to challenge, defy.

défilé *m* procession, parade.

défiler *vi* to parade, march.

défini *adj* definite, precise.

définir *vt* to define, specify.

définitif *adj* definitive, final.

définition *f* definition.

définitivement *adv* definitively, finally.

déflagration *f* deflagration, explosion.

déflation *f* deflation.

défoncer *vt* to smash in; to dig deeply.

déformation *f* deformation, distortion.

déformer *vt* to deform, distort; **se ~** *vr* to bend; to lose its shape.

défoulement *m* outlet; release.

défouler *vt* to unwind, relax; **se ~** *vr* to get rid of one's inhibitions.

défricher *vt* to clear; to reclaim.

défunt *m* -e *f* deceased; * *adj* late, deceased.

dégagé *adj* clear; open.

dégagement *m* freeing, clearance.

dégager *vt* to free, clear; **se ~** *vr* to free o.s., extricate o.s.

dégarnir *vt* to empty; to clear.

dégât *m* havoc, damage.

dégel *m* thaw.

dégeler *vt vi* to thaw, melt.

dégénérer *vi* to degenerate, decline.

dégivrer *vt* to de-ice, defrost.

dégonfler *vt* to deflate, empty.

dégourdir *vt* to warm up, revive.

dégourdissement *m* reviving, return of circulation.

dégoût *m* disgust, distaste.

dégoûter *vt* to disgust.

dégradant *adj* degrading.

dégradation *f* degradation, debasement.

dégradé *m* shading off; gradation.

dégrader *vt* to degrade, debase; **se ~** *vr* to become degraded, debased.

dégrafer *vt* to unfasten, unhook.

dégraisser *vt* to remove grease.

degré *m* degree; grade.

dégrèvement *m* reduction; redemption.

dégripper *vt* to unblock; to unchoke.

déguisement *m* disguise.

déguiser *vt* to disguise; **se ~** *vr* to disguise o.s.

dégustation *f* tasting, sampling.

dehors *adv* outside, outdoors; **au ~** outwardly; **en ~ de** outside; apart from; * *m* outside, exterior.

déjà *adv* already.

déjeuner *vi* to lunch; * *m* lunch.

déjouer *vt* to elude; to thwart.

delà *adv*: **au ~ de** beyond; **par ~** beyond.

délabré *adj* dilapidated, ramshackle.

délacer *vt* to unlace, undo.

délai *m* delay; respite; time limit.

délaisser *vt* to abandon, quit.

délassant *adj* relaxing, refreshing.

délasser *vt* to refresh, relax; **se ~** *vr* to rest, relax.

délateur *m* **-trice** *f* informer.

délation *f* denouncement; informing.

délavé *adj* diluted; faded.

délayage *m* dragging-out, spinning-out.

délayer *vt* to thin; to drag out.

délectation *f* delectation, delight.

délecter (se) *vr* to delight, revel.

délégation *f* delegation.

délégué *m* -e *f* delegate, representative; * *adj* delegate, delegated.

déléguer *vt* to delegate.

délibération *f* deliberation; resolution.

délibéré *adj* deliberate; resolute; ~ment *adv* deliberately.

délicat *adj* delicate, dainty; ~ment *adv* delicately.

délicatesse *f* delicacy, daintiness.

délice *m* delight, pleasure.

délicieux *adj* delicious, delightful.

délier *vt* to unbind, untie.

délimitation *f* delimitation.

délimiter *vt* to delimit, demarcate.

délinquance *f* delinquency.

délinquant *m* -e *f* delinquent, offender; * *adj* delinquent.

délirant *adj* delirious, frenzied.

délire *m* delirium, frenzy.

délirer *vi* to be delirious.

délit *m* offence, misdemeanour.

délivrance *f* deliverance; release; delivery.

délivrer *vt* to deliver; to release; **se ~** *vr* to free o.s.

déloger *vt* to evict, dislodge.

déloyal *adj* disloyal, unfaithful; ~ement *adv* disloyally.

déloyauté *f* disloyalty, treachery.

delta *m* delta.

deltaplane *m* hang-glider.

démagogie *f* demagogy.

démagogique *adj* demagogic.

démagogue *m* demagogue.

demain *adv* tomorrow.

demande *f* request, petition; question.

demander *vt* to ask, request; **se ~** *vr* to wonder.

démangeaison *f* itch; longing.

démaquillant *m* make-up remover; * *adj* make-up removing.

démaquiller *vt* to remove make-up; **se ~** *vr* to take one's make-up off.

démarche *f* gait, walk, step.

démarrage *m* moving off, casting off.

démarrer *vi* to start up, move off; * *vt* to start, get started.

démarreur *m* starter.

démasquer *vt* to unmask, uncover.

démêlage *m* disentangling; combing.

démêler *vt* to disentangle, unravel; comb.

déménagement *m* removal; moving (house).

déménager *vi* to move house.

déménageur *m* removal man.

démener (se) *vr* to struggle, strive.

dément *adj* mad, insane, crazy.

démenti *m* denial, refutation.

démentir *vt* to deny, refute.

démesuré *adj* excessive, inordinate; **~ment** *adv* excessively, inordinately.

démettre *vt* to dislocate; to dismiss.

demeure *f* residence, dwelling place.

demeurer *vi* to live at, reside, stay.

demi *adj* half; **à ~** halfway; * *m* half.

demi-cercle *m* semicircle.

demi-douzaine *f* half-dozen.

demi-droite *f* half-line.

demi-finale *f* semi-final.

demi-frère *m* half-brother.

demi-heure *f* half-hour.

demi-jour *m* half-light.

démilitariser *vt* to demilitarize.

demi-litre *m* half-litre.

demi-lune *f* half-moon.

demi-mesure *f* half-measure.

demi-mot *m*: **à ~** without spelling out.

demi-pension *f* half-board.

demi-sœur *f* half-sister.

démission *f* resignation.

démissionner *vi* to resign.

demi-tarif *m* half-fare.

demi-tour *m* half-turn.

démocrate *mf* democrat.

démocratie *f* democracy.

démocratique *adj* democratic; **~ment** *adv* democratically.

démocratiser *vt* to democratize.

démodé *adj* old-fashioned, out-of-date.

démographie *f* demography.

démographique *adj* demographic.

demoiselle f young lady; spinster; damsel.

démolir vt to demolish, knock down.

démolition f demolition.

démon m demon, fiend.

démoniaque adj demoniac, fiendish.

démonstrateur m -**trice** f demonstrator.

démonstratif adj demonstrative.

démonstration f demonstration; proof.

démontable adj collapsible, that can be dismantled.

démonte-pneu m tyre lever.

démonter vt to dismantle, take down, dismount; se ~ vr to come apart, be nonplussed.

démontrer vt demonstrate; to prove.

démoralisant adj demoralizing.

démoraliser vt to demoralize; se ~ vr to become demoralized.

démouler vt to take out of a mould.

démunir vt to deprive; to divest.

démystifier vt to demystify, disabuse.

dénaturé adj denatured, disfigured.

dénégation f denial.

déneiger vt to clear snow from.

déni m denial, refusal.

dénicher vt to dislodge; to unearth.

dénier vt to deny, disclaim.

dénigrer vt to denigrate, disparage.

dénivellation f difference in level, unevenness.

dénombrer vt to number, enumerate.

dénomination f denomination, designation.

dénoncer vt to denounce; to inform against.

dénonciation f denunciation.

dénouement m dénouement; unravelling; outcome.

dénouer vt to unravel, untie, undo.

dénoyauter vt to stone (fruit).

denrée f commodity, provisions, foodstuff.

dense adj dense, thick.

densité f density, denseness.

dent f tooth.

dentaire adj dental.

dentelé adj jagged, perforated.

dentelle *f* lace.

dentier *m* denture, dental plate.

dentifrice *m* toothpaste.

dentiste *mf* dentist.

dentition *f* dentition, teething.

dénuder *vt* to bare, denude; **se ~** *vr* to strip off.

dénué *adj* devoid, bereft.

dénuement *m* destitution; deprivation.

déodorant *m* deodorant.

déontologie *f* deontology.

dépannage *m* repairing, fixing.

dépanner *vt* to repair, fix.

dépanneur *m* **-euse** *f* breakdown mechanic.

dépanneuse *f* breakdown lorry.

dépareillé *adj* unmatched; odd.

déparer *vt* to spoil; to disfigure.

départ *m* departure; start.

département *m* department.

dépasser *vt* to exceed; to go past.

dépaysé *adj* disoriented, out of one's element.

dépaysement *m* disorientation.

dépêcher *vt* to dispatch, send; **se ~** *vr* to hurry, rush.

dépendance *f* dependence; dependency.

dépendant *adj* dependent.

dépendre *vi* to depend on, be dependent on.

dépens *mpl*: **aux ~ de** at the expense of.

dépense *f* expenditure, outlay.

dépenser *vt* to expend, spend; **se ~** *vr* to exert o.s.

dépérir *vi* to decline, waste away.

dépeupler *vt* to depopulate; to clear.

dépistage *m* tracking; detection.

dépister *vt* to track.

dépit *m* spite; grudge; **en ~ de** in spite of.

dépité *adj* vexed; frustrated.

déplacé *adj* misplaced; ill-timed.

déplacement *m* displacement; removal.

déplacer *vt* to displace; to move; **se ~** *vr* to change residence.

déplaire *vi* to displease; to offend.

déplaisant *adj* disagreeable, unpleasant.

dépliant *m* prospectus, leaflet; * *adj* extendible; folding.

déplier *vt* to unfold; to open out.

déploiement *m* (*mil*) deployment; display.

déplorable *adj* deplorable, disgraceful.

déplorer *vt* to deplore, bewail.

déployer *vt* to deploy; to display.

dépopulation *f* depopulation.

déportation *f* deportation, transportation.

déporté *m* **-e** *f* deportee.

déporter *vt* to deport, transport.

déposer *vt* to lodge, deposit.

dépositaire *mf* depository; trustee.

déposition *f* deposition; evidence.

dépôt *m* deposit; warehouse.

dépouillement *m* scrutiny, perusal; despoiling.

dépouiller *vt* to strip; to despoil; to peruse.

dépourvu *adj* lacking, wanting; **au ~** off guard.

dépoussiérer *vt* to dust.

dépravation *f* depravity, corruption.

dépravé *adj* depraved, corrupt.

dépréciation *f* depreciation.

déprécier *vt* to depreciate; to disparage; **se ~** *vr* to depreciate, fall in value.

dépressif *adj* depressive.

dépression *f* depression, slump; dejection.

déprimant *adj* depressing.

déprimer *vt* to depress; to discourage.

depuis *prép* since, from; after.

député *m* deputy, delegate.

déracinement *m* uprooting.

déraciner *vt* to uproot.

déraillement *m* derailment.

dérailler *vi* to be derailed, run off the rails.

dérailleur *m* (*rail*) derailleur, derailer.

déraisonner *vi* to talk irrationally, rave.

dérangement *m* derangement; inconvenience.

déranger *vt* to upset, unsettle; **se ~** *vr* to move; to put o.s. out.

dérapage *m* skid.

déraper *vi* to skid, slip.

déréglé *adj* out of order; irregular; unruly.

dérèglement *m* disturbance; irregularity; dissoluteness.

dérégler *vt* to disturb; to put out of order; to upset.

dérision *f* derision, mockery.

dérisoire *adj* derisory; pathetic.

dérivation *f* derivation; diversion.

dérive *f* drift; aller à la ~ to drift away.

dériver *vi* to drift.

dermatologie *f* dermatology.

dermatologue *mf* dermatologist.

derme *m* dermis.

dernier *adj* last; latest; back; * *m* -ière *f* last one; latter.

dernièrement *adv* recently; lately.

dérobade *f* sidestepping; evasion.

dérober *vt* to steal; to hide; se ~ *vr* to steal away, escape.

dérogation *f* derogation; dispensation.

déroger *vi* to derogate; to detract.

déroulement *m* unfolding; pro-gress, development.

dérouler *vt* to unwind, uncoil; se ~ *vr* to develop; to unfold.

déroutant *adj* disconcerting.

déroute *f* rout, overthrow.

dérouter *vt* to rout, overthrow.

derrière *prép* behind; * *adv*; par ~ at the back; * *m* bottom; back; de ~ back, rear.

des *art* = de les; *see* un, une.

dès *prép* from, since; ~ que when; as soon as.

désabusé *adj* disenchanted; disabused.

désaccord *m* disagreement, discord.

désaffecté *adj* disused.

désagréable *adj* disagreeable, unpleasant; ~ment *adv* disagreeably, unpleasantly.

désagréger *vt* to break up, disintegrate; se ~ *vr* to break up, disintegrate.

désagrément *m* displeasure, annoyance.

désaltérant *adj* thirstquenching.

désaltérer *vt* to refresh; se ~ *vi* to quench one's thirst.

désamorcer *vt* to unprime, defuse.

désapprobateur *adj* disapproving.

désapprobation *f* disapproval.

désapprouver *vt* to disapprove, object.

désarçonner *vt* to unsaddle; to nonplus, baffle.

désarmant *adj* disarming.

désarmement *m* disarmament.

désarmer *vt* to disarm; to unload.

désarroi *m* disarray, confusion.

désarticuler *vt* to dislocate; to upset.

désastre *m* disaster.

désastreux *adj* disastrous, unfortunate.

désavantage *m* disadvantage; prejudice.

désavantager *vt* to disadvantage, handicap.

désaveu *m* disavowal, retraction.

désavouer *vt* to disavow, retract.

descendance *f* descent, lineage.

descendant *m* -e *f* descendant; * *adj* falling, descending.

descendre *vi* to descend, go down; * *vt* to take down, bring down.

descente *f* descent, way down.

descriptif *adj* descriptive, explanatory.

description *f* description.

désemparé *adj* helpless; distraught.

désenchantement *m* disenchantment; disillusion.

désenfler *vi* to become less swollen.

désensibiliser *vt* to desensitize.

déséquilibre *m* imbalance, unbalance.

déséquilibré *adj* unbalanced, unhinged.

déséquilibrer *vt* to unbalance, throw off balance.

désert *m* desert, wilderness; * *adj* deserted.

déserter *vt* to desert.

déserteur *m* deserter.

désertification   *f* desertification.

désertion *f* desertion.

désertique *adj* desert; barren.

désespérant *adj* desperate, hopeless; discouraging.

désespéré *adj* desperate, hopeless; ~ment *adv* desperately.

désespérer *vi* to despair, give up hope.

désespoir *m* despair, despondency.

déshabiller *vt* to undress; se ~ *vr* to undress.

désherbage *m* weeding.

désherbant *m* weed killer.

désherber *vt* to weed.

déshériter *vt* to disinherit.

déshonorant *adj* dishonourable, disgraceful.

déshonorer *vt* to dishonour, disgrace.

déshydraté *adj* dehydrated.

déshydrater *vt* to dehydrate; se ~ *vr* to become dehydrated.

désignation *f* designation, nomination; name.

désigner *vt* to designate, indicate.

désillusion *f* disillusion; disappointment.

désillusionner *vt* to disillusion; to disappoint.

désincarné *adj* disincarnate, disembodied.

désinfectant *m* disinfectant; * *adj* disinfectant.

désinfecter *vt* to disinfect.

désinfection *f* disinfection.

désinformation *f* disinformation.

désintégration *f* disintegration.

désintégrer *vt* to split, break up; se ~ *vr* to disintegrate.

désintéressé *adj* disinterested, unselfish.

désintéressement *m* disinterestedness, unselfishness.

désintéresser (se) *vr* to lose interest in.

désintoxiquer *vt* to detoxify; to dry out; se faire ~ *vr* to dry out.

désinvolte *adj* easy, offhand, casual.

désinvolture *f* casualness, offhandedness.

désir *m* desire, wish, longing.

désirable *adj* desirable.

désirer *vt* to desire, wish, long.

désobéir *vi* to disobey.

désobéissance *f* disobedience.

désobéissant *adj* disobedient.

désobligeant *adj* disobliging; uncivil.

désodorisant *m* deodorant; * *adj* deodorizing, deodorant.

désodoriser *vt* to deodorize.

désœuvré *adj* unoccupied, idle.

désœuvrement *m* idleness.

désolation *f* desolation; ruin; grief.

désolé *adj* desolate; disconsolate, grieved.

désordonné *adj* untidy; inordinate; reckless.

désordre *m* disorder, confusion, disturbance.

désorganisation *f* disorganization.

désorienté *adj* disorientated.

désormais *adv* from now on, henceforth.

désossé *adj* boned.

despote *m* despot.

despotique *adj* despotic; ~ment *adv* despotically.

dessèchement *m* dryness, drying up, withering.

dessécher *vt* to dry, parch, wither; se ~ *vr* to dry out, become parched.

dessein *m* design, plan, scheme; à ~ *adv* intentionally.

desserrer *vt* to loosen; to unscrew; to slacken; se ~ *vr* to work loose, come undone.

dessert *m* dessert, sweet.

desservir *vt* to clear (table); to do a disservice to.

dessin *m* drawing, sketch; draft.

dessinateur *m* -trice *f* drawer, draughtsman.

dessiner *vt* to draw, sketch; to design.

dessous *adv* under, beneath; * *m* underside, bottom.

dessus *adv* over, above; * *m*; prendre le ~ to gain the upper hand; le ~ du panier the upper crust, the pick of the bunch.

destabiliser *vt* to destabilize.

destin *m* destiny, fate, doom.

destinataire *mf* addressee, consignee.

destination *f* destination; purpose.

destinée *f* destiny, fate.

destiner *vt* to determine; to intend, destine, aim.

destituer *vt* to dismiss, depose.

destructeur *adj* destructive, ruinous.

destruction *f* destruction.

désuétude *f* disuse **tomber en ~** to fall into disuse.

détachable *adj* detachable.

détachant *m* cleaner, stain remover.

détaché *m* (*mus*) detached.

détachement *m* detachment, indifference.

détacher *vt* (*mus*) to detach; to unfasten; se ~ *vr* to become detached.

détail *m* detail, particular.

détaillant *m* -**e** *f* retailer.

détailler *vt* to detail; to sell retail.

détartrage *m* descaling.

détartrant *m* descaling substance; * *adj* descaling.

détartrer *vt* to descale.

détaxe *f* reduction in tax.

détecter *vt* to detect.

détecteur *m* detector.

détection *f* detection.

détective *m* detective.

déteindre *vi* to lose colour, fade.

détendre *vt* to release, loosen; se ~ to relax, calm down.

détendu *adj* slack; relaxed.

détenir *vt* to detain; to hold.

détente *f* relaxation, easing.

détenteur *m* -**trice** *f* holder, possessor.

détergent *m* detergent.

détérioration *f* deterioration.

détériorer *vt* to damage, impair; se ~ *vr* to deteriorate, worsen.

déterminant *adj* determining, deciding.

détermination *f* determination; resolution.

déterminé *adj* determined, resolute.

déterminer *vt* to determine, decide.

déterrer *vt* to dig up, disinter.

détestable *adj* detestable, odious; ~**ment** *adv* detestably.

détester *vt* to detest, hate.

détonateur *m* detonator.

détonation *f* detonation, explosion.

détonner *vi* to clash (colour); to go out of tune.

détour *m* detour; curve; evasion.

détourné *adj* indirect, oblique.

détournement *m* diversion, rerouting.

détourner *vt* to divert, reroute.

détracteur *m* -**trice** *f* detractor, disparager.

détraquer *vt* to upset; to disorder; se ~ *vr* to become upset; to go wrong.

détresse *f* distress, trouble.

détriment *m*: au ~ de to the detriment of.

détritus *m* refuse, rubbish.

détroit *m* strait.

détrôner *vt* to dethrone, depose.

detruire *vt* to destroy, demolish.

dette *f* debt.

deuil *m* mourning, bereavement, grief.

deux *adj* two; * *m* two; entre les ~ so-so, fair to middling; en moins de ~ in a jiffy.

deuxième *adj* second; ~ment *adv* secondly; * *mf* second.

deux-points *m* colon.

deux-roues *m* two-wheeled vehicle.

dévaler *vt vi* to hurry down, tear down.

dévaliser *vt* to burgle; to rifle.

dévalorisation *f* depreciation.

dévaloriser *vt* to depreciate, reduce the value of.

dévaluation *f* devaluation.

devancer *vt* to outstrip, outrun; to precede.

devant *prép* in front of, before; * *adv* in front; * *m* front; prendre les ~s to make the first move, pre-empt; aller au-~ de to anticipate.

devanture *f* display; shopfront.

dévaster *vt* to devastate, lay waste.

développement *m* development; growth; progress.

développer *vt* to develop, expand; se ~ *vr* to develop, grow.

devenir *vi* to become, grow.

déverrouiller *vt* to unbolt, unlock.

déverser *vt* to pour; to dump.

dévêtir *vt* to undress; se ~ *vr* to get undressed.

déviation *f* deviation; diversion.

dévier *vi* to deviate; to turn aside; to swerve.

devin *m* -eresse *f* seer, soothsayer.

deviner *vt* to guess; to solve; to foretell.

devinette *f* riddle.

devis *m* estimate, quotation.

dévisager *vt* to stare at.

devise *f* currency.

dévisser *vt* to unscrew, undo.

dévoiler *vt* to unveil, disclose.

devoir *m* duty; homework; * *vt* to owe; to have to.

dévorer *vt* to devour, consume.

dévot *adj* devout, pious.

dévotion *f* devotion, piety.

dévoué *adj* devoted, dedicated.

dévouement *m* devotion, dedication.

dévouer (se) *vr* to devote o.s., sacrifice o.s.

dextérité *f* dexterity, adroitness.

diabète *m* diabetes.

diabétique *adj* diabetic.

diable *m* devil.

diablotin *m* imp; cracker (Christmas).

diabolique *adj* diabolical, devilish; ~**ment** *adv* diabolically.

diagnostic *m* diagnosis.

diagnostiquer *vt* to diagnose.

diagonale *f* diagonal.

diagramme *m* diagram; graph.

dialecte *m* dialect.

dialectique *f* dialectic; * *adj* dialectic.

dialogue *m* dialogue, conversation.

dialoguer *vt* to write in dialogue form; *vi* to have talks (with).

dialyse *f* dialysis.

diamant *m* diamond.

diamètre *m* diameter.

diaphragme *m* diaphragm.

diarrhée *f* diarrhoea.

dictaphone *m* dictaphone.

dictateur *m* **-trice** *f* dictator.

dictatorial *adj* dictatorial.

dictature *f* dictatorship.

dictée *f* dictating; dictation.

dicter *vt* to dictate, impose.

dictionnaire *m* dictionary.

dicton *m* saying, dictum.

didactique *adj* didactic.

dièse *f* (*mus*) sharp.

diesel *m* diesel.

diète *f* light diet.

diététicien *m* **-ne** *f* dietician.

diététique *adj* dietary.

dieu *m* god.

diffamation *f* defamation, slandering.

diffamer *vt* to defame, slander.

différé *adj* postponed; (*rad*, *TV*) pre-recorded.

différemment *adv* differently.

différence *f* difference.

différenciation *f* differentiation.

différencier *vt* to differentiate.

différend *m* disagreement, difference of opinion.

différent *adj* different; various.

différer *vt* to differ; to vary.

difficile *adj* difficult; awkward, tricky; ~**ment** *adv* with difficulty.

difficulté *f* difficulty; problem.

difforme *adj* deformed, misshapen.

difformité *f* deformity.

diffuser *vt* to diffuse, circulate, broadcast.

diffusion *f* diffusion, circulation, broadcasting.

digérer *vt* to digest.

digeste *adj* easily digestible.

digestif *adj* digestive.

digestion *f* digestion.

digital *adj* digital.

digne *adj* worthy; dignified; ~**ment** *adv* worthily, deservedly.

dignité *f* dignity.

digression *f* digression.

digue *f* dyke; sea wall.

dilapider *vt* to squander; to embezzle.

dilatation *f* dilation, distension.

dilater *vt* to dilate, distend; **se ~** *vr* to dilate, distend.

dilemme *m* dilemma.

dilettante *mf* dilettante.

diluer *vt* to dilute.

dilution *f* dilution.

dimanche *m* Sunday.

dimension *f* dimension, size.

diminuer *vt* to diminish, reduce; * *vi* to diminish, lessen.

diminutif *m* diminutive.

diminution *f* reduction, lessening.

dinde *f* turkey hen.

dindon *m* turkey cock.

dindonneau *m* young turkey.

dîner *vi* to dine; * *m* dinner.

dinosaure *m* dinosaur.

diocèse *m* diocese.

diode *f* diode.

dioxyde *m* dioxide.

diphtérie *f* diphtheria.

diphtongue *f* diphthong.

diplomate *mf* diplomat.

diplomatie *f* diplomacy.

diplomatique *adj* diplomatic; ~**ment** *adv* diplomatically.

diplôme *m* diploma, certificate.

diplômé *m* -**e** *f* graduate; * *adj* qualified.

dire *vt* to say; to tell; **se ~** to say to o.s.; to call o.s.; *vr*: **se ~ que** to tell o.s. that.

direct *adj* direct; ~**ement** *adv* directly; * *m* (*rail*) express.

directeur *m* -**trice** *f* director.

direction f direction, management.

directive f directive, order.

dirigeant m -e f leader, ruler; * adj ruling, executive.

diriger vt to run, direct; se ~ vr: se ~ vers to head for, make for.

discernement m discernment, judgment.

discerner vt to discern, distinguish.

disciple m disciple.

disciplinaire adj disciplinary.

discipline f discipline.

discipliné adj disciplined.

discontinu adj discontinuous.

discordant adj discordant, conflicting.

discorde f discord, dissension.

discothèque f discotheque.

discours m speech, talking.

discourtois adj discourteous.

discréditer vt to discredit.

discret adj discreet.

discrétion f discretion, prudence.

discrétionnaire adj discretionary.

discrimination f discrimination.

discriminer vt to distinguish; to discriminate.

disculper vt to excuse, exonerate; se ~ vr to justify o.s., excuse o.s.

discussion f discussion, debate.

discutable adj debatable, questionable.

discuter vt vi to discuss, debate.

disgrâce f disgrace.

disgracieux adj awkward, ungraceful.

disjoncter vi to cut off, disconnect.

disjoncteur m cutout, circuit breaker.

disparaître vi to disappear, vanish.

disparate adj disparate, incongruous.

disparité f disparity, incongruity.

disparition f disappearance; death; extinction.

disparu adj vanished; bygone; missing.

dispensaire m dispensary.

dispense f dispensation, exemption.

dispenser vt to dispense, exempt; se ~ vr: se ~ de to dispense with; to avoid.

disperser *vt* to spread, scatter; **se ~** *vr* to disperse, scatter.

dispersion *f* dispersal, scattering.

disponibilité *f* availability.

disponible *adj* available; transferable.

dispos *adj* refreshed; alert; in form.

disposer *vt* to arrange, dispose; **se ~** *vr*: **se ~ à** to prepare to do; ** vi* to leave.

dispositif *m* device, mechanism.

disposition *f* arrangement, layout.

disproportionné *adj* disproportionate.

dispute *f* dispute, argument.

disputer *vt* to dispute, rival; **se ~** *vr* to quarrel, argue.

disquaire *mf* record-dealer.

disqualifier *vt* to disqualify.

disque *m* disk; record.

disquette *f* diskette.

dissection *f* dissection.

dissemblable *adj* dissimilar; different.

disséminer *vt* to disseminate, scatter.

dissentiment *m* disagreement, dissent.

disséquer *vt* to dissect.

dissertation *f* dissertation.

dissidence *f* dissidence, dissent.

dissident *adj* dissident.

dissimulation *f* dissimulation, double-dealing.

dissimulé *adj* double-faced, dissembling.

dissimuler *vt* to dissemble, conceal; **se ~** *vr* to conceal o.s.

dissipation *f* dissipation, waste.

dissipé *adj* dissipated, undisciplined.

dissiper *vt* to dispel; to dissipate; **se ~** *vr* to disperse, become undisciplined.

dissociation *f* dissociation.

dissocier *vt* to dissociate.

dissolution *f* dissolution.

dissolvant *m* solvent, dissolvent.

dissonant *adj* dissonant; discordant.

dissoudre *vt* to dissolve.

dissuader *vt* to dissuade.

dissuasif *adj* dissuasive, deterrent.

dissuasion *f* dissuasion.

distance *f* distance, interval.

distancier (se) *vr* to distance o.s. from.

distant *adj* distant.

distendre *vt* to distend, strain; se ~ *vr* to slacken.

distillation *f* distillation.

distiller *vt* to distil.

distillerie *f* distillery.

distinct *adj* distinct, different; ~ement *adv* distinctly.

distinctif *adj* distinctive.

distinction *f* distinction.

distingué *adj* distinguished.

distinguer *vt* to distinguish; to discern; se ~ *vr* to distinguish o.s.

distorsion *f* distortion.

distraction *f* inattention; absentmindedness; abstraction.

distraire *vt* to distract; to amuse; se ~ *vr* to enjoy o.s.

distrait *adj* inattentive, absent-minded; ~ement *adv* absent–mindedly.

distrayant *adj* entertaining, diverting.

distribuer *vt* to distribute.

distributeur *m* distributor.

distribution *f* distribution.

district *m* district.

diurétique *adj* diuretic; * *m* diuretic.

divagation *f* wandering, rambling.

divaguer *vi* to ramble, rave.

divan *m* divan.

divergence *f* divergence.

divergent *adj* divergent.

diverger *vi* to diverge, differ.

divers *adj* diverse, varied; ~ement *adv* diversely.

diversification *f* diversification.

diversifier *vt* to vary, diversify; se ~ *vr* to diversify.

diversion *f* diversion.

diversité *f* diversity, variety.

divertir *vt* to amuse, entertain; se ~ *vr* to amuse o.s.

divertissant *adj* amusing, entertaining.

divertissement *m* entertainment, recreation.

dividende *m* dividend.

divin *adj* divine, exquisite; ~ement *adv* divinely.

divination *f* divination.

divinité *f* divinity.

diviser *vt* to divide, split; se ~ *vr* to split up, divide into.

division *f* division.

divorce *m* divorce.

divorcé *m* -e *f* divorcee; * *adj* divorced.

divorcer *vi* to divorce.

divulgation *f* disclosure, divulgence.

divulguer *vt* to divulge, disclose.

dix *adj, m* ten.

dix-huit *adj, m* eighteen.

dix-huitième *adj, mf* eighteenth.

dixième *adj* tenth; ~ment *adv* tenthly; * *mf* tenth.

dix-neuf *adj, m* nineteen.

dix-neuvième *adj, mf* nineteenth.

dix-sept *adj, m* seventeen.

dix-septième *adj, mf* seventeenth.

dizaine *f* ten, ten or so.

docile *adj* docile, submissive; ~ment *adv* docilely.

docilité *f* docility, submissiveness.

dock *m* dock, dockyard.

docteur *m* doctor.

doctorat *m* doctorate.

doctrine *f* doctrine.

document *m* document.

documentaire *adj* documentary.

documentaliste *mf* researcher.

documentation *f* documentation; information.

documenter *vt* to document; **se ~** *vr* to gather information on.

dogmatique *adj* dogmatic.

dogme *m* dogma.

doigt *m* finger; **être à deux ~s de** to come very close to doing; **obéir au ~ et à l'œil** to obey (sb) slavishly.

doigté *m* touch; fingering technique.

domaine *m* domain, estate; sphere.

domanial *adj* state-owned.

dôme *m* dome, vault.

domestique *adj* domestic, household.

domestiquer *vt* to domesticate, tame.

domicile *m* domicile, address.

domicilié *adj* domiciled.

dominant *adj* dominant, prevailing.

dominante *f* dominant characteristic.

dominateur *adj* governing; domineering.

domination *f* domination.

dominer *vt* to dominate; to prevail; **se ~** to control o.s.

dominical *adj* Sunday.

dommage *m* damage; harm; **c'est ~** it's a pity.

dompter *vt* to tame, train.

dompteur *m* **-euse** *f* trainer, tamer.

don *m* gift; talent.

donateur *m* **-trice** *f* donor.

donation *f* donation.

donc *conj* so, therefore, thus; **pourquoi ~?** why was that?

donné *adj* given; fixed; **étant ~** seeing that, in view of.

donnée *f* datum.

donner *vt* to give; * *vi* to yield (crop).

donneur *m* **-euse** *f* giver, donor; dealer.

dont *pn* whose, of which.

dopage *m* doping.

doper *vt* to dope; **se ~** *vr* to take drugs, dope o.s.

doré *adj* gilded; tanned.

dorénavant *adv* from now on, henceforth.

dorer *vt* to gild; to tan.

dorloter *vt* to pamper, pet.

dormir *vi* to sleep, be asleep; to be still.

dortoir *m* dormitory.

dos *m* back; top; ridge.

dosage *m* mixture; balance; proportioning.

dose *f* dose; amount; quantity.

doser *vt* to measure out, proportion; to strike a balance.

dossier *m* dossier, file; case.

dot *f* dowry.

doter *vt* to provide with a dowry; to endow.

douane *f* customs.

douanier *m* customs officer.

double *adj* double, duplicate, dual; **~ment** *adv* doubly; * *m* copy, double, replica; twice as much.

doubler *vt* *vi* to double, duplicate.

doublure *f* lining; (*thea*) understudy.

doucement *adv* softly, gently.

doucereux *adj* sugary; mawkish; suave.

douceur *f* softness, gentleness.

douche *f* shower.

doucher *vt* to give a shower to; **se ~** *vr* to take a shower.

doué *adj* gifted, endowed with.

douille *f* case; cartridge.

douillet *adj* delicate, tender; soft.

douleur *f* pain, ache; anguish.

douloureusement *adv* painfully, grievously.

douloureux *adj* painful, grievous.

doute *m* doubt; **sans ~** without doubt.

douter *vi* to doubt, question; se ~ *vr* se ~ de to suspect sb; se ~ que to suspect that, expect that.

douteux *adj* doubtful, dubious.

doux *adj*, *f* **douce** soft; sweet; mild.

douzaine *f* dozen.

douze *adj*, *m* twelve.

douzième *adj* twelfth; ~**ment** *adv* twelfthly; * *mf* twelfth.

doyen *m* -**ne** *f* dean; doyen.

draconien *adj* draconian, drastic.

dragée *f* bonbon, sugared almond.

dragon *m* dragon.

dramatique *adj* dramatic, tragic; ~**ment** *adv* dramatically.

dramatiser *vt* to dramatize.

dramaturge *mf* playwright.

drame *m* drama.

drap *m* sheet; ~-**housse** fitted sheet; être dans de beaux ~s to be in a fine mess.

drapeau *m* flag.

draper *vt* to drape.

dressage *m* taming; pitching.

dresser *vt* to draw up; to put up; se ~ *vr* to stand up; to rear up.

dresseur *m* -**euse** *f* trainer, tamer.

dribbler *vi* to dribble.

drogue *f* drug.

drogué *m* -**e** *f* drug addict; * *adj* drugged.

droguer *vt* to drug, administer drugs; se ~ *vr* to dose up; to take drugs.

droguerie *f* hardware trade.

droguiste *mf* hardware storekeeper.

droit *adj* right; straight; sound; honest; ~**ement** *adv* uprightly, honestly; * *adv* straight, straight ahead; * *m* right; law; tax.

droite *f* right side; right (wing); straight line.

droitier *adj* right-handed.

droiture *f* uprightness, honesty.

drôle *adj* funny, amusing; peculiar; ~**ment** *adv* funnily, peculiarly.

dromadaire *m* dromedary.

dru *adj* thick, dense; sturdy.

du *art* of the.

dû *adj* owed; due; ~**ment** *adv* duly.

dualité *f* duality.

dubitatif *adj* doubtful, dubious.

dubitativement *adv* doubtfully, dubiously.

duc *m* duke, **duchesse** *f* duchess.

duché *m* duchy.

duel *m* duel; dual.

duettiste *mf* duettist.

dune *f* dune.

duo *m* duo; duet.

duodénum *m* duodenum.

dupe *adj* easily duped; * *f* dupe.

duper *vt* to dupe, take in.

duplex *m* duplex, two-way.

dupliquer *vt* to duplicate.

dur *adj* hard, tough; difficult; ~**ement** *adv* harshly, severely.

durable *adj* durable, lasting; ~**ment** *adv* durably.

duralumin *m* duralumin.

durant *prép* during, for.

durcir *vt vi* to harden; **se ~** *vr* to become hardened.

durcissement *m* hardening.

durée *f* duration, length.

durer *vi* to last.

dureté *f* hardness; austerity, harshness.

durillon *m* callus, corn.

duvet *m* down.

duveté *adj* downy.

dynamique *f* dynamic; dynamics; * *adj* dynamic; ~**ment** *adv* dynamically.

dynamiser *vt* to energize; to potentiate.

dynamisme *m* dynamism.

dynamitage *m* dynamiting.

dynamite *f* dynamite.

dynamiter *vt* to dynamite.

dynamo *f* dynamo.

dynastie *f* dynasty.

dynastique *adj* dynastic.

dysenterie *f* dysentery.

dyslexie *f* dyslexia.

dyslexique *adj* dyslexic.

E

eau *f* water; rain.

eau-de-vie *f* brandy.

ébahir *vt* to astonish, stupefy, dumbfound.

ébahissement *m* astonishment, amazement.

ébauche *f* rough draft, rough outline.

ébaucher *vt* to sketch; to roughcast.

ébène *f* ebony.

ébéniste *m* cabinetmaker.

éblouir *vt* to dazzle; to fascinate.

éblouissant *adj* dazzling; amazing.

éblouissement *m* dazzle; bedazzlement.

ébouillanter *vt* to scald; to blanch; s'~ *vr* to scald o.s.

éboulement *m* collapse, caving in; fall.

ébouriffé *adj* tousled, ruffled.

ébranler *vt* to shake; to unsettle, disturb.

ébrécher *vt* to chip, indent; to break into (fortune).

ébriété *f* intoxication.

ébrouer (s') *vr* to shake o.s.

ébruiter *vt* to disclose, divulge; s'~ *vr* to spread, be noised abroad.

ébullition *f* boiling; effervescence; turmoil.

écaille *f* scale; shell.

écailler *vt* to scale; to chip; s'~ *vr* to flake off, peel off.

écarlate *adj* scarlet.

écart *m* distance; interval; discrepancy; rester à l'~ to steer clear of.

écarteler *vt* to tear apart; to quarter.

écarter *vt* to separate; to avert; to dismiss; s'~ *vr* to make way; to swerve.

ecchymose *f* bruise, ecchymosis.

ecclésiastique *adj* ecclesiastical; * *m* ecclesiastic, clergyman.

échafaud *m* scaffold.

échafaudage *m* scaffolding.

échange *m* exchange, barter, trade.

échanger *vt* to exchange.

échantillon *m* sample.

échappée *f* breakaway; glimpse.

échappement *m* exhaust; release.

échapper *vi* to escape, avoid, elude; **s'~** *vr* to escape from; to leak.

écharde *f* splinter, sliver.

écharpe *f* scarf; arm-sling.

échassier *m* wader.

échauffement *m* heating; warm-up; constipation.

échauffer *vt* to heat, over-heat; to excite; **s'~** *vr* to warm up; to get worked up.

échéance *f* expiry; maturity date.

échec *m* failure, defeat; chess.

échelle *f* ladder; scale.

échelon *m* rung; grade.

échelonner *vt* to grade; to stagger, set at intervals; **s'~** *vr* to be graduated, staggered.

échine *f* backbone, spine; **courber l'~** to submit.

échiquier *m* chessboard.

écho *m* echo; rumour.

échographie *f* ultrasound scan.

échoir *vi* to fall due; to befall, fall to sb's lot.

échouer *vi* to fail; to end up; to run aground.

éclabousser *vt* to splash, spatter.

éclair *m* flash; lightning flash; spark.

éclairage *m* lighting, light.

éclairagiste *m* electrician; lighting engineer.

éclaircie *f* clear interval, bright spot; glade.

éclaircir *vt* to lighten; to thin down; to brighten up; **s'~** *vr* to clear (up).

éclaircissement *m* clearing up, explanation, elucidation.

éclairer *vt* to light, illuminate; clarify, explain.

éclat *m* brightness, glare; splinter; splendour.

éclatant *adj* bright, blazing; resounding; blatant.

éclatement *m* explosion, bursting, rupture.

éclater *vi* to explode; to break out; to exclaim.

éclectique *adj* eclectic.

éclipse *f* eclipse.

éclipser *vt* to eclipse, overshadow; **s'~** *vr* to disappear, vanish.

éclore *vi* to hatch out; to blossom.

éclosion *f* hatching; blooming; birth.

écluse *f* lock.

écœurant *adj* disgusting, nauseating.

écœurement *m* nausea, disgust; discouragement.

écœurer *vt* to nauseate, disgust.

école *f* school, schooling; sect, doctrine.

écolier *m* schoolgirl, **-ière** *f* schoolgirl.

écologie *f* ecology.

écologique *adj* ecological.

écologiste *mf* ecologist.

économe *adj* thrifty; * *mf* steward, treasurer; (*mar*) bursar.

économie *f* economy, thrift; economics.

économique *adj* economic; **~ment** *adv* economically.

économiser *vt* to economize, save.

écorce *f* bark, peel, skin.

écorchure *f* scratch; graze.

Écossais *m* Scotsman, **-e** *f* Scotswoman.

écossais *adj* Scottish.

Écosse *f* Scotland.

écoulement *m* flow, discharge, outlet; disposal, selling.

écouler *vt* to flow, discharge; to sell; **s'~** *vr* to leak, flow out; to pass by; to sell.

écoute *f* listening, audience.

écouter *vt* to listen to.

écran *m* screen.

écrasant *adj* crushing; overwhelming.

écraser *vt* to crush; to overwhelm; to run over; **s'~** *vr* to crash; to get crushed.

écrémer *vt* to skim, cream.

écrevisse *f* crayfish.

écrin *m* box, casket.

écrire *vt* to write; to spell.

écrit *adj* written; * *m* document; piece of writing.

écriteau *m* notice, sign.

écriture *f* writing; handwriting; script.

écrivain *m* writer.

écrou *m* nut.

écroulement *m* collapse, caving in.

écrouler (s') *vr* to collapse, crumble.

écru *adj* raw; unbleached; untreated.

ectoplasme *m* ectoplasm.

écueil *m* reef, shelf; peril.

écume *f* foam, froth; scum.

écureuil *m* squirrel.

écurie *f* stable.

écusson *m* badge, shield.

eczéma *m* eczema.

édification *f* erection, construction.

édifice *m* edifice, building.

édifier *vt* to build, construct; to edify.

éditer *vt* to publish, produce; to edit.

éditeur *m* **-trice** *f* publisher; editor.

édition *f* publishing; edition; editing.

éditorial *m* leading article, editorial.

éducatif *adj* educational.

éducation *f* education; upbringing.

édulcorant *m* sweetener; * *adj* sweetening.

éduquer *vt* to educate; to bring up, raise.

effacer *vt* to delete, erase, wipe off; **s'~** *vr* to wear away, become obliterated.

effaré *adj* alarmed, bewildered.

effaroucher *vt* to frighten off; to alarm.

effectif *m* staff; size, complement; * *adj* effective, positive.

effectivement *adv* effectively, positively.

effectuer *vt* to effect, execute, carry out.

effervescence *f* effervescence; excitement, ferment.

effervescent *adj* effervescent; excited.

effet *m* effect, impression; spin; bill, note.

efficace *adj* effective; efficient; **~ment** *adv* effectively, efficiently.

efficacité *f* effectiveness, efficiency.

effleurer *vt* to touch lightly, skim across.

effondrement *m* collapse, caving in.

effondrer (s') *vr* to collapse, cave in.

efforcer (s') *vr* to endeavour, do one's best.

effort *m* effort, exertion; stress, strain.

effraction *f* breaking and entering.

effrayant *adj* frightening, fearsome.

effrayer *vt* to frighten, scare.

effriter *vt* to crumble; to exhaust (land); **s'~** *vr* to crumble away, disintegrate.

effroi *m* terror, dismay.

effronté *adj* shameless, impudent, cheeky; **~ment** *adv* shamelessly, impudently.

effroyable *adj* horrifying, appalling; **~ment** *adv* horrifyingly, appallingly.

égal *adj* equal; even, level; equable; **~ement** *adv* evenly; equally; also, as well.

égaler *vt* to equal, match.

égalisation *f* equalization; levelling.

égaliser *vt* to equalize; to level out.

égalitaire *adj* egalitarian.

égalité *f* equality; equableness; evenness.

égard *m* consideration, respect; **à l'~ de** concerning, regarding; **à tous ~s** in all respects.

égarer *vt* to mislead, lead astray; **s'~** *vr* to get lost; to wander from the point.

égayer *vt* to enliven, cheer up.

églantine *f* dog-rose, wild rose.

église *f* church.

égocentrique *adj* egocentric, self-centred.

égoïsme *m* selfishness, egoism.

égoïste *mf* egotist; * *adj* egotistic; **~ment** *adv* egotistically.

égout *m* sewer.

égoutter *vt* to strain; to wring out.

égratignure *f* scratch, scrape.

éjecter *vt* to eject, throw out.

élaboration *f* elaboration, development.

élaborer *vt* to elaborate, develop.

élan *m* surge, momentum, speed; spirit, elan.

élancer (s') *vr* to rush, spring, hurl o.s.

élargir *vt* to widen, stretch; **s'~** *vr* to get wider.

élargissement *m* widening, stretching, enlarging.

élastique *adj* elastic; flexible; * *m* elastic, elastic band.

électeur *m* **-trice** *f* voter, elector.

élection *f* election; choice.

électoral *adj* electoral.

électorat *m* electorate; constituency; franchise.

électricien *m* electrician.

électricité *f* electricity.

électrique *adj* electric.

électrocardiogramme *m* electrocardiogram.

électrode *f* electrode.

électrolyse *f* electrolysis.

électroménager *m* household appliance; * *adj* electrical (household).

électron *m* electron.

électronicien *m* electronics engineer.

électronique *f* electronics; * *adj* electronic.

élégance *f* elegance, stylishness.

élégant *adj* smart, elegant, stylish.

élément *m* element, component; cell; fact.

élémentaire *adj* elementary; basic.

éléphant *m* elephant.

élevage *m* rearing, breeding.

élève *mf* pupil, student.

élevé *adj* high; heavy; lofty, exalted.

élever *vt* to bring up, raise; to put up, lift up; **s'~** *vr* to rise, go up.

éleveur *m* **-euse** *f* stockbreeder.

éligible *adj* eligible.

élimination *f* elimination.

éliminatoire *adj* eliminatory; * *f* preliminary heat.

éliminer *vt* to eliminate, discard.

élire *vt* to elect.

élite *f* elite.

élitisme *m* elitism.

elle *pn* she; it; her; **c'est à ~** it's up to her; it's hers; **~-même** herself.

elliptique *adj* elliptic; **~ment** *adv* elliptically.

élocution *f* elocution, diction.

éloge *m* praise; eulogy.

élogieux *adj* laudatory, eulogistic.

éloigné *adj* distant, remote.

éloigner *vt* to move away, take away; **s'~** *vr* to go away; to grow distant.

éloquence *f* eloquence.

éloquent *adj* eloquent.

élu *adj* chosen, elected.

élucider *vt* to elucidate, clear up.

émacié *adj* emaciated, wasted.

émail *m* enamel.

émailler *vt* to enamel.

émancipation *f* emancipation, liberation.

émanciper *vt* to emancipate, liberate; **s'~** *vr* to become emancipated, liberated.

émaner *vi* to emanate, issue.

emballage *m* packing paper, wrapping paper.

emballer *vt* to pack up, wrap up.

embarcadère *m* landing stage, pier.

embarcation *f* boat, craft.

embargo *m* embargo.

embarquement *m* loading; embarkation.

embarquer *vt* to embark; to load; * *vi* to embark, go aboard.

embarras *m* embarrassment, confusion; trouble.

embarrassant *adj* embarrassing, uncomfortable.

embarrassé *adj* embarrassed, self-conscious.

embarrasser *vt* to embarrass; to hinder, hamper; **s'~** *vr* to burden o.s. with; to be troubled by.

embaucher *vt* to take on, hire.

embellir *vt* to beautify, make more attractive.

embellissement *m* embellishment, improvement.

embêter *vt* (*fam*) to bore; to get on one's nerves; **s'~** *vr* to be bored, fed up.

emblème *m* symbol, emblem.

emboîter *vt* to fit together; **s'~** *vr* to fit together; to fit into each other.

embonpoint *m* stoutness, plumpness.

embouchure *f* mouth (river); mouthpiece.

embouteillage *m* traffic jam; bottling.

embranchement *m* junction; side road.

embrasser *vt* to kiss, embrace.

embrayage *m* clutch.

embrayer *vi* to engage the clutch.

embrouiller *vt* to tangle up, mix up; **s'~** *vr* to become muddled, confused.

embryon *m* embryo.

embryonnaire *adj* embryonic.

embuscade *f* ambush.

émeraude *f* emerald.

émerger *vi* to emerge; to stand out.

émeri *m* emery.

émerveiller *vt* to astonish, amaze; **s'~** *vr* to marvel at.

émetteur *adj*, *f* **-trice** transmitting.

émettre *vt* to send out, emit, transmit.

émeute *f* riot.

émietter *vt* to crumble; to disperse, break up; **s'~** *vr* to crumble; to disperse, break up.

émigration *f* emigration.

émigré *m* **-e** *f* émigré, expatriate.

émigrer *vi* to emigrate.

éminence *f* hill, elevation; eminence, distinction.

éminent *adj* eminent, distinguished.

émir *m* emir.

émission *f* sending out; transmission; broadcast; emission.

emmêler *vt* to entangle; confuse; **s'~** *vr* to tangle.

emménager *vi* to move in.

emmener *vt* to take away; to lead.

émoi *m* agitation, emotion.

émotif *adj* emotional; emotive.

émotion *f* emotion; commotion.

émotivité *f* emotionalism.

émouvant *adj* moving, touching.

émouvoir *vt* to move, disturb, upset; **s'~** *vr* to be moved; to get worried, upset.

empailler *vt* to stuff.

empaqueter *vt* to parcel up, pack.

emparer (s') *vr* to seize, grab; to take possession of.

empêchement *m* obstacle, hitch; impediment.

empêcher *vt* to prevent, stop; **s'~** *vr*: **s'~ de** to refrain from doing something.

empereur *m* emperor.

empester *vt* to stink out; to poison, infect.

empêtrer *vt* to entangle,; **s'~** *vr* to get involved in, get mixed up in.

emphase *f* pomposity; emphasis, stress.

empiéter *vi* to encroach, overlap.

empiler *vt* to pile up, stack.

empire *m* empire; influence. ascendancy.

empirer *vi* to get worse, deteriorate.

empirique *adj* empirical; **~ment** *adv* empirically.

emplacement *m* site, location.

emploi *m* use; job, employment.

employé *m* **-e** *f* employee.

employer *vt* to use, spend; to employ.

employeur *m*, **euse** *f* employer.

empoisonner *vt* to poison; to annoy.

emporter *vt* to take; to carry off; to involve; **s'~** *vr* to lose one's temper.

empreinte *f* imprint, impression, stamp.

empresser (s') *vi* to rush to; to press around, fuss around.

emprise *f* hold, ascendancy.

emprisonner *vt* to imprison, trap.

emprunt *m* borrowing, loan.

emprunter *vt* to borrow; to assume; to derive.

ému *adj* moved, touched, excited.

émulsion *f* emulsion.

en *prép* in; to; by; on; **~ tant que** as; ***** *pn* from there; of it, of them; **je n'~ veux plus** I don't want any more of them; **s'~ faire** to worry; **il**

~ va de même pour the same goes for.

encadré *m* box; framed text.

encadrement *m* framing; training; managerial staff.

encadrer *vt* to frame; to train; to surround.

encaissement *m* collection; receipt; cashing.

encaisser *vt* to collect, receive; to cash.

encastrer *vt* to embed, fit in, encase.

enceinte *adj* pregnant.

encens *m* incense.

encenser *vt* (*rel*) to cense; to shower praise on.

encercler *vt* to encircle, surround.

enchaînement *m* linking; link; sequence.

enchaîner *vt* to chain.

enchanté *adj* enchanted, delighted.

enchantement *m* enchantment, delight.

enchanter *vt* to enchant, delight.

enchâsser *vt* to set, imbed.

enchère *f* bid, offer.

enchevêtrement *m* entanglement, confusion.

enclave *f* enclave.

enclencher *vt* to engage; to set in motion.

enclin *adj* inclined, prone.

enclore *vt* to enclose, shut in.

enclume *f* anvil; engine block.

encoder *vt* to encode.

encolure *f* neck; collar size.

encombrant *adj* unwieldy, cumbersome.

encombrement *m* congestion; jumble; obstruction.

encombrer *vt* to clutter, obstruct; **s'~** *vr* to burden o.s.

encore *adv* still; only; again; more; **~ que** even though.

encourageant *adj* encouraging, heartening.

encouragement *m* encouragement.

encourager *vt* to encourage; to incite.

encre *f* ink.

encyclopédie *f* encyclopaedia.

endettement *m* indebtedness; debt.

endetter *vt* to get sb into debt; **s'~** *vr* to get into debt.

endive *f* chicory.

endoctrinement *m* indoctrination.

endoctriner *vt* to indoctrinate.

endommager *vt* to damage.

endormir *vt* to put to sleep; **s'~** *vr* to fall asleep.

endossement *m* endorsement.

endosser *vt* to put on; to shoulder; to endorse.

endroit *m* place; side part; à l'~ regarding.

enduire *vt* to coat, smear.

enduit *m* coating.

endurance *f* endurance, stamina.

endurci *adj* hardened; hardhearted.

endurcir *vt* to harden; **s'~** *vr* to become hardened.

endurer *vt* to endure, bear.

énergétique *adj* energy; energising.

énergie *f* energy; spirit, vigour.

énergique *adj* energetic, vigorous; **~ment** *adv* energetically.

énervant *adj* enervating; irritating.

énervement *m* irritation; nervousness.

énerver *vt* to irritate, annoy; to get on one's nerves; **s'~** *vr* to get excited, worked up.

enfance *f* childhood; infancy.

enfant *mf* child; native.

enfanter *vt* to give birth to.

enfantillage *m* childishness.

enfantin *adj* childish, infantile.

enfer *m* hell.

enfermer *vt* to lock up; to confine; to box in.

enfiévrer *vt* to stir up, inflame.

enfiler *vt* to string, thread; to put on.

enfin *adv* at last; in short; after all.

enflammer *vt* to set on fire; to inflame, kindle; **s'~** *vr* to catch fire, ignite.

enflé *adj* swollen; bombastic, turgid.

enfler *vi* to swell up, inflate.

enfoncer *vt* to stick in, thrust; to break open; **s'~** *vr* to sink into, disappear into.

enfouir *vt* to bury.

enfuir (s') *vr* to run away, flee.

engagement *m* agreement, commitment, undertaking; engaging; opening.

engager *vt* to bind; to involve; to insert; to open; **s'~** *vr* to undertake to; to take a job.

engelure *f* chilblain.

engendrer *vt* to create, engender; to father.

engin *m* machine; instrument; contraption.

englober *vt* to include, encompass.

engloutir *vt* to wolf down; to engulf.

engorgement *m* obstruction, clogging; glut.

engouement *m* infatuation; fad, craze.

engouffrer *vt* to devour, swallow up, engulf; **s'~** *vr* to rush into, sweep, surge.

engourdi *adj* numb; dull.

engourdir *vt* to numb; to dull, blunt; **s'~** *vr* to become numb, to grow sluggish.

engourdissement *m* numbness; sleepiness.

engrais *m* fertilizer; manure.

engraisser *vi* to get fatter; * *vt* to fatten; to fertilize.

engrenage *m* gears, gearing.

énigmatique *adj* enigmatic; **~ment** *adv* enigmatically.

énigme *f* enigma, riddle.

enivrer *vt* to intoxicate, make drunk; **s'~** *vr* to get drunk.

enjeu *m* stake.

enjoliver *vt* to ornament; to embroider (truth).

enlacer *vt* to embrace, intertwine.

enlaidir *vt* to make ugly; **s'~** *vr* to become ugly.

enlèvement *m* abduction, kidnapping; removal.

enlever *vt* to remove; to take off; to deprive; to abduct.

enliser *vt* to get stuck (car); **s'~** *vr* to get bogged down, get sucked into.

enneigé *adj* snowy, snowbound.

enneigement *m* snow coverage.

ennemi *m* **-e** *f* enemy.

ennui *m* boredom, tedium, weariness.

ennuyer *vt* to bore, bother; **s'~** *vr* to get bored.

ennuyeux *adj* boring, tedious.

énorme *adj* enormous, huge.

énormément *adv* enormously.

énormité *f* enormity, hugeness; howler.

enquête *f* inquiry, investigation; survey.

enquêter *vi* to hold an inquiry; to investigate.

enraciner *vt* to implant, root; **s'~** *vr* to take root; to settle down somewhere.

enragé *adj* furious; keen.

enregistrement *m* recording; registration.

enregistrer *vt* to record; to register.

enrichi *adj* improved, enriched; nouveau riche.

enrichir *vt* to enrich, expand; **s'~** *vr* to get rich.

enrichissant *adj* enriching.

enrichissement *m* enrichment.

enrober *vt* to wrap, cover, coat.

enrôler *vt* to enlist, enrol.

enrouement *m* hoarseness.

enrouer *vt* to make hoarse.

enrouler *vt* to roll up, wind up.

enseignant *m* **-e** *f* teacher.

enseigne *f* sign; (*mil*) ensign.

enseignement *m* education, training, instruction.

enseigner *vt* to teach.

ensemble *adv* together, at the same time; * *m* unity; whole.

ensoleillé *adj* sunny.

ensorceler *vt* to bewitch, enchant.

ensuite *adv* then, next, afterwards.

entaille *f* cut, gash.

entamer *vt* to start, open, make a hole in.

entassement *m* piling up, heaping up.

entasser *vt* to pile up, heap up.

entendement *m* understanding, comprehension.

entendre *vt* to hear; to intend, mean; to understand; **s'~** *vr* to agree; to know how to.

entendu *adj* agreed; **bien ~** of course.

entente *f* harmony, understanding; accord.

enterrement *m* burial; funeral.

enterrer *vt* to bury, inter.

en-tête *m* heading, header.

entêté *adj* stubborn, obstinate.

entêtement *m* stubbornness, obstinacy.

entêter *vt* to go to the head of; **s'~** *vr* to persist in.

enthousiasme *m* enthusiasm.

enthousiasmer *vt* to fill with enthusiasm; **s'~** *vr* to be enthusiastic about.

enthousiaste *adj* enthusiastic; * *mf* enthusiast.

entier *adj* entire, whole; intact.

entièrement *adv* entirely, wholly, completely.

entité *f* entity.

entonnoir *m* funnel; swallow hole; shell-hole.

entorse *f* sprain.

entortiller *vt* to twist, twine; to hoodwink, wheedle.

entourage *m* set, circle; entourage.

entourer *vt* to surround, frame, encircle; **s'~** *vr*: **s'~ de** to surround o.s. with.

entracte *m* interval, intermission.

entraide *f* mutual aid.

entraider (s') *vr* to help one another.

entrailles *fpl* entrails, guts; womb.

entrain *m* spirit, liveliness.

entraînement *m* training, coaching; force, impetus.

entraîner *vt* to drag; to lead; to train; **s'~** *vr* to train o.s.

entraîneur *m* trainer, coach.

entrave *f* hindrance, obstacle; shackle.

entraver *vt* to hold up; to shackle.

entre *prép* between, among, into.

entrebâiller *vt* to half-open; s'~ *vr* to be half-open.

entrecôte *f* rib steak.

entrecouper *vt* to intersperse, interrupt with.

entrée *f* entry, entrance; admission; insertion; ~ en matière introduction; d'~ de jeu from the outset.

entrejambes *m* crotch.

entrelacer *vt* to intertwine, interlace.

entremêler *vt* to intermingle, intermix.

entremets *m* sweet, dessert.

entreposer *vt* to store, put into storage.

entrepôt *m* warehouse, bonded warehouse.

entreprenant *adj* enterprising.

entreprendre *vt* to embark upon, undertake.

entrepreneur *m* -euse *f* contractor; entrepreneur.

entreprise *f* company; venture, business.

entrer *vi* to enter, go in.

entresol *m* entresol, mezzanine.

entretemps *adv* meanwhile.

entretenir *vt* to maintain, look after; to speak with.

entretien *m* upkeep, maintenance; conversation.

entrevoir *vt* to make out; to glimpse; to anticipate.

entrevue *f* meeting, interview.

entrouvert *adj* half-open.

entrouvrir *vt* to half-open; s'~ *vr* to half-open; to gape.

énumération *f* enumeration, listing.

énumérer *vt* to enumerate, list.

envahir *vt* to invade, overrun.

envahissant *adj* invasive; intrusive; pervasive.

enveloppe *f* envelope; covering; exterior.

envelopper *vt* to envelop; to wrap up; to veil.

envergure *f* breadth, scope, scale.

envers *prép* towards, to; * *m*; à l'~ inside out, upside down.

envie *f* desire, longing, inclination; envy.

envier *vt* to envy.

envieux *adj* envious.

environ *adv* about, around;

~s *mpl* vicinity, neighbourhood.

environnant *adj* surrounding.

environnement *m* environment.

environnemental *adj* environmental.

environner *vt* to surround, encircle.

envisager *vt* to view, envisage.

envoi *m* dispatch, remittance; kick-off.

envol *m* takeoff, flight.

envoler (s') *vr* to fly away; to disappear.

envoûtant *adj* bewitching, entrancing.

envoûter *vt* to bewitch.

envoyé *m* **-e** *f* messenger, envoy.

envoyer *vt* to send, dispatch; hurl, fire.

enzyme *m* enzyme.

épais *adj* thick; deep.

épaisseur *f* thickness; depth.

épaissir *vi* to thicken; to deepen; * *vt:* **s'~** *vr* to thicken, get thicker.

épanoui *adj* radiant, beaming.

épanouir *vt* to brighten, light

up; open out; **s'~** *vr* to bloom.

épanouissement *m* blooming; lighting up; opening out.

épargne *f* saving, savings.

épargner *vt* to save; to spare.

éparpiller *vt* to scatter, distribute; **s'~** *vr* to scatter.

épaule *f* shoulder.

épauler *vt* to support, back up.

épave *f* wreck; derelict; ruin.

épée *f* sword.

épeler *vt* to spell.

éperdu *adj* distraught, overcome; **~ment** *adv* frantically, desperately.

éperon *m* spur; *(mar)* ram.

épervier *m* sparrowhawk.

éphémère *adj* ephemeral, fleeting.

épi *m* ear; tuft.

épice *m* spice.

épicé *adj* spicy; juicy.

épicerie *f* grocery trade; grocer's shop.

épicier *m* **-ière** *f* grocer; greengrocer.

épidémie *f* epidemic.

épidémique *adj* epidemic; contagious.

épiderme *m* epidermis; skin.

épier *vt* to spy on.

épiglotte *f* epiglottis.

épilation *f* removal of hair.

épilepsie *f* epilepsy.

épileptique *adj* epileptic.

épiler *vt* to remove hair, pluck.

épilogue *m* epilogue; conclusion.

épinard *m* spinach.

épine *f* spine; thorn.

épineux *adj* thorny, prickly; tricky.

épingle *f* pin.

Épiphanie *f* Epiphany.

épique *adj* epic.

épiscopal *adj* episcopal.

épiscopat *m* episcopate.

épisode *m* episode.

épisodique *adj* occasional; transitory; ~**ment** *adv* occasionally.

épitaphe *f* epitaph.

épithète *f* epithet.

éplucher *vt* to clean; to peel; to sift.

épluchure *f* peeling, paring.

éponge *f* sponge.

éponger *vt* to sponge, mop.

épopée *f* epic.

époque *f* time, epoch, age, period.

épouser *vt* to marry, wed; espouse.

épousseter *vt* to dust.

épouvantable *adj* terrible, appalling; ~**ment** *adv* terribly, appallingly.

épouvantail *m* scarecrow.

épouvante *f* terror, dread.

épouvanter *vt* to terrify, appall.

époux *m* **épouse** *f* spouse.

éprendre *vr*: s'~ **de** to fall in love with.

épreuve *f* test; ordeal, trial; proof.

éprouvant *adj* trying, testing.

éprouver *vt* to feel, experience.

éprouvette *f* test tube.

épuisé *adj* exhausted; sold out.

épuisement *m* exhaustion.

épuiser *vt* to exhaust, wear out; s'~ *vr* to run out; to exhaust o.s.

épuisette *f* landing net.

épurer *vt* to purify, refine.

équateur *m* equator.

équation *f* equation.

équatorial *adj* equatorial.

équerre *f* square; bracket.

équestre *adj* equestrian.

équilibre *m* balance, equilibrium; harmony.

équilibrer *vt* to balance; s'~ *vr* to balance each other.

équipage *m* crew; gear, equipment.

équipe *f* team, crew, gang, staff.

équipement *m* equipment; fitting out, fittings.

équiper *vt* to equip, fit out.

équipier *m* **-ière** *f* team member.

équitable *adj* equitable, fair; ~**ment** *adv* equitably, fairly.

équitation *f* equitation, riding.

équivalence *f* equivalence.

équivalent *adj* equivalent, same; * *m* equivalent.

équivoque *adj* equivocal, questionable.

érable *m* maple.

érafler *vt* to scratch, scrape.

ère *f* era.

érection *f* erection; establishment.

éreintant *adj* exhausting, backbreaking.

ergot *m* spur; (*tec*) lug.

ériger *vt* to erect; to establish.

ermite *m* hermit.

éroder *vt* to erode.

érosion *f* erosion.

érotique *adj* erotic.

érotisme *m* eroticism.

errant *adj* wandering, stray.

errer *vi* to wander, roam.

erreur *f* error, mistake, fault.

erroné *adj* erroneous.

éructation *f* eructation.

érudit *adj* erudite, learned; * *m* scholar.

érudition *f* erudition, learning.

éruptif *adj* eruptive.

éruption *f* eruption.

escabeau *m* stool; stepladder.

escadron *m* squadron, platoon.

escalade *f* climbing; escalation.

escalader *vt* to climb, scale.

escale *f* port of call, touchdown.

escalier *m* stairs, steps.

escalope *f* escalope.

escamoter *vt* to dodge, evade; to pilfer.

escapade *f* escapade; prank, jaunt.

escargot *m* snail.

escarpement *m* escarpment; steepness.

esclavage *m* slavery, bondage.

esclavagisme *m* proslavery.

esclave *mf* slave.

escompte *m* discount.

escompter *vt* to discount.

escorte *f* escort; retinue.

escorter *vt* to escort.

escrime *f* fencing.

escrimeur *m* **-euse** *f* fencer.

escroc *m* crook, con man.

escroquer *vt* to swindle, con.

ésotérique *adj* esoteric.

espace *m* space, interval.

espacement *m* spacing, interval.

espacer *vt* to space out.

espadon *m* swordfish.

espadrille *f* espadrille, rope-soled sandal.

espèce *f* sort, kind; species.

espérance *f* hope, expectation.

espérer *vt* to hope.

espion *m* **-ne** *f* spy.

espionnage *m* espionage, spying.

espionner *vt* to spy.

esplanade *f* esplanade.

espoir *m* hope.

esprit *m* mind, intellect; spirit; wit.

esquimau *m* **-de** *f* Eskimo.

esquisse *f* sketch, outline.

esquisser *vt* to sketch, outline.

esquiver *vt* to dodge; to shirk.

essai *m* test, trial; attempt; essay.

essaim *m* swarm.

essayage *m* fitting, trying on.

essayer *vt* to test, try, try on.

essence *f* petrol; essential oil.

essentiel *adj* essential, basic; **-lement** *adv* essentially, basically.

essieu *m* axle.

essorage *m* wringing, mangling.

essorer *vt* to wring, mangle.

essouffler *vt* to wind; s'~ *vr* to get out of breath.

essuyer *vt* to wipe, mop; s'~ *vr* to wipe o.s.

est *m* east.

esthète *mf* aesthete.

esthéticien *m* **-ne** *f* beautician.

esthétique *adj* aesthetic; ~ment *adv* aesthetically; * *f* aesthetics.

estimation *f* valuation; estimation, reckoning.

estime *f* esteem, respect, regard.

estimer *vt* to value, assess, estimate.

estival *adj* summer; summery.

estivant *m* **-e** *f* holidaymaker, summer visitor.

estomac *m* stomach.

estomper *vt* to blur, dim; **s'~** *vr* to become blurred.

estrade *f* platform, rostrum.

estragon *m* tarragon.

et *conj* and.

étable *f* cowshed.

établi *adj* established; * *m* workbench.

établir *vt* to establish, set up; **s'~** *vr* to settle; to set o.s. up as; to become established.

établissement *m* establishing, building; establishment.

étage *m* floor, storey; stage, level.

étagère *f* shelf.

étalage *m* display, display window; stall.

étalagiste *mf* window dresser.

étaler *vt* to spread, strew; to stagger; to display.

étalon *m* stallion.

étanche *adj* waterproof.

étanchéité *f* waterproofness.

étang *m* pond.

étape *f* stage, leg; staging point.

état *m* state, condition; statement.

étatique *adj* under state control.

étatiser *vt* to bring under state control, nationalize.

état-major *m* (*mil*) staff; staff headquarters.

étau *m* vice.

étayer *vt* to prop up, support.

été *m* summer.

éteindre *vt* to put out, extinguish; **s'~** *vr* to go out; to die; to evaporate.

éteint *adj* faded; extinct.

étendard *m* standard, flag.

étendre *vt* to spread, extend; to floor; **s'~** *vr* to spread; to stretch out; to increase.

étendu *adj* extensive, sprawling, wide.

étendue *f* expanse, area; duration.

éternel *adj* eternal, everlasting; **~lement** *adv* eternally.

éterniser *vt* to draw out; to immortalize; **s'~** *vr* to drag on, linger on.

éternité *f* eternity; ages.

éternuer *vi* to sneeze.

éthane *m* ethane.

éther *m* ether.

ethnie *f* ethnic unit.

ethnique *adj* ethnic.

ethnologie *f* ethnology.

ethnologue *mf* ethnologist.

étincelant *adj* sparkling; gleaming.

étinceler *vi* to sparkle, gleam.

étincelle *f* spark; gleam, glimmer.

étiqueter *vt* to label, mark.

étiquette *f* label, tag; etiquette.

étirement *m* stretching.

étirer *vt* to stretch, draw out; **s'~** *vr* to stretch out.

étoffe *f* material, fabric; stuff.

étoile *f* star.

étoilé *adj* starry.

étonnant *adj* astonishing, surprising.

étonné *adj* astonished, surprised.

étonnement *m* surprise, astonishment.

étonner *vt* to astonish, surprise; **s'~** *vr* to be astonished.

étouffant *adj* stifling.

étouffer *vt* to suffocate; to muffle; **s'~** *vr* to be suffocated, to swelter.

étourderie *f* absentmindedness.

étourdi *adj* absentminded; **~ment** *adv* absentmindedly.

étourdir *vt* to stun, daze; to deafen.

étourdissant *adj* deafening; stunning.

étourdissement *m* blackout, dizzy spell; surprise.

étourneau *m* starling.

étrange *adj* strange, funny; **~ment** *adv* strangely, oddly.

étranger *m* **-ère** *f* foreigner, stranger, alien; * *adj* foreign, strange, unknown.

étrangeté *f* strangeness, oddness.

étranglement *m* strangulation; bottleneck.

étrangler *vt* to strangle, stifle; **s'~** *vr* to strangle o.s., choke.

être *vi* to be; **c'est-à-dire** namely, that is to say; * *m* being, person, soul.

étreindre *vt* to embrace, hug; to seize.

étreinte *f* embrace; stranglehold.

étrier *m* stirrup.

étroit *adj* narrow; strict; **~ement** *adv* closely; strictly.

étude *f* study; survey; office.

étudier *vt* to study, examine.

étui *m* case; holster.

étymologie *f* etymology.

étymologique *adj* etymological.

eu = *p.p.* avoir had.

eucalyptus *m* eucalyptus.

eucharistie *f* eucharist.

euphémisme *m* euphemism.

euphorie *f* euphoria.

euphorique *adj* euphoric.

européen *m* **-ne** *f* European;
* *adj* European.

euthanasie *f* euthanasia.

eux *pn* they, them; **c'est à ~**
it's up to them; it's theirs;
~-mêmes themselves.

évacuation *f* evacuation;
emptying.

évacuer *vt* to evacuate, clear.

évader (s') *vr* to escape.

évaluation *f* evaluation, appraisal.

évaluer *vt* to evaluate, appraise.

évangélique *adj* evangelical.

évangéliser *vt* to evangelize.

évangile *m* gospel.

évanouir (s') *vr* to faint, pass
out.

évanouissement *m* faint,
blackout.

évaporation *f* evaporation.

évaporer (s') *vr* to evaporate.

évasif *adj* evasive.

évasion *f* escape; escapism.

évasivement *adv* evasively.

évêché *m* bishopric.

éveil *m* awakening; dawn-
ing.

éveiller *vt* to waken, arouse;
s'~ *vr* to wake up.

événement *m* event, incident.

éventail *m* fan; range.

éventaire *m* tray; stall.

éventualité *f* eventuality, possibility.

éventuel *adj* possible;
~lement *adv* possibly.

évêque *m* bishop.

évertuer (s') *vr* to strive to.

évidemment *adv* obviously,
evidently.

évidence *f* evidence, proof.

évident *adj* obvious, evident.

évier *m* sink.

évincer *vt* to oust; to evict.

éviter *vt* to avoid; to spare.

évocation *f* evocation, recall.

évolué *adj* developed, advanced; enlightened.

évoluer *vi* to evolve, develop.

évolution *f* evolution, development.

évoquer *vt* to evoke, recall.

exacerber *vt* to exacerbate,
aggravate.

exact *adj* exact, accurate;
~ement *adv* exactly.

exactitude *f* exactness, accuracy.

exagération *f* exaggeration.

exagéré *adj* exaggerated, excessive; ~**ment** *adv* exaggeratedly.

exagérer *vt* to exaggerate.

exaltation *f* elation; extolling, praising.

exalter *vt* to exalt, glorify; to elate.

examen *m* examination, survey, investigation.

examinateur *m* **-trice** *f* examiner.

examiner *vt* to examine, survey.

exaspération *f* exasperation.

exaspérer *vt* to exasperate.

exaucer *vt* to fulfil, grant.

excédent *m* surplus, excess.

excédentaire *adj* surplus, excess.

excellent *adj* excellent.

exceller *vi* to excel.

excentricité *f* eccentricity.

excentrique *adj* eccentric; ~**ment** *adv* eccentrically.

excepté *adj* apart, aside; * *prép* except, but for.

exception *f* exception.

exceptionnel *adj* exceptional; ~**lement** *adv* exceptionally.

excès *m* excess, surplus.

excessivement *adv* excessively.

excitant *m* stimulant; * *adj* exciting, stimulating.

excitation *f* excitation, stimulation; incitement.

exciter *vt* to excite, stimulate; **s'~** *vr* to become excited.

exclamation *f* exclamation.

exclamer (s') *vr* to exclaim.

exclu *adj* excluded, outcast.

exclure *vt* to exclude, oust, expel.

exclusif *adj* exclusive.

exclusion *f* exclusion, suspension.

exclusivement *adv* exclusively.

exclusivité *f* exclusive rights.

excrément *m* excrement.

excroissance *f* (*med*) excrescence, outgrowth.

excursion *f* excursion, trip.

excursionniste *mf* tripper; walker.

excuse *f* excuse, pretext.

excuser *vt* to excuse, forgive; **s'~** *vr* to apologize for.

exécrable *adj* execrable, atrocious; ~**ment** *adv* atrociously, execrably.

exécration *f* execration, loathing.

exécrer *vt* to execrate, loathe.

exécuter *vt* to execute, carry out, perform; to produce.

exécution *f* execution, carrying out, performance.

exemplaire *m* copy, archetype; * *adj* model, exemplary; ~**ment** *adv* exemplarily.

exemple *m* example, model, instance.

exempt *adj* exempt, free from.

exercer *vt* to exercise, perform, fulfil; **s'**~ *vr* to practise.

exercice *m* exercise, practice, use; financial year.

exhaustif *adj* exhaustive.

exhaustivement *adv* exhaustively.

exhiber *vt* to exhibit, show; to produce; **s'**~ *vr* to show off; to expose o.s.

exhibition *f* exhibition, show; display.

exhibitionniste *mf* exhibitionist.

exhortation *f* exhortation.

exhorter *vt* to exhort, urge.

exigeant *adj* demanding, exacting.

exigence *f* demand, requirement; exigency.

exiger *vt* to demand, require.

exigu *adj*, *f* **exiguë** scanty, exiguous.

exiguïté *f* exiguity, scantiness.

exil *m* exile.

exilé *m* -**e** *f* exile;* *adj* exiled.

exiler *vt* to exile, banish; **s'**~ *vr* to go into exile.

existant *adj* existing.

existence *f* existence, life.

exister *vi* to exist; to be.

exode *m* exodus; drift, loss.

exonération *f* exemption.

exonérer *vt* to exempt.

exorbitant *adj* exorbitant, outrageous.

exorciser *vt* to exorcise.

exotique *adj* exotic.

exotisme *m* exoticism.

expansif *adj* expansive, outgoing.

expansion *f* expansion, development.

expatrié *m* -**e** *f* expatriate; * *adj* expatriate.

expatrier *vt* to expatriate; **s'**~ *vr* to expatriate o.s.

expectative *f* expectation, hope; **être dans l'**~ to be waiting (to see, to hear).

expédier *vt* to send, dispatch; to dispose of.

expéditeur *m* -**trice** *f* sender; shipper, consignor.

expéditif *adj* quick, expeditious.

expédition *f* dispatch; consignment.

expérience *f* experience; experiment.

expérimental *adj* experimental; ~**ement** *adv* experimentally.

expérimentateur *m* -**trice** *f* experimenter.

expérimentation *f* experimentation.

expérimenté *adj* experienced.

expérimenter *vt* to test; to experiment with.

expert *adj* expert, skilled in; * *m* expert; connoisseur; assessor.

expertise *f* expertise; expert appraisal.

expiation *f* expiation, atonement.

expier *vi* to expiate, atone for.

expiration *f* expiry; expiration, exhalation.

expirer *vi* to breathe out, expire.

explicatif *adj* explanatory.

explication *f* explanation, analysis.

explicite *adj* explicit ~**ment** *adv* explicitly.

expliquer *vt* to explain, account for; to analyse.

exploitant *m* -**e** *f* farmer, smallholder.

exploitation *f* working; exploitation; operating; concern; smallholding.

exploiter *vt* to work, exploit; run, operate.

explorateur *m* -**trice** *f* explorer.

exploration *f* exploration.

explorer *vt* to explore.

exploser *vi* to explode.

explosif *adj* explosive; * *m* explosive.

explosion *f* explosion.

exportateur *m* -**trice** *f* exporter.

exportation *f* export, exportation.

exporter *vt* to export.

exposé *m* exposition, overview, statement.

exposer *vt* to display; to explain, state; to expose; s'~ *vr* to expose o.s. to, run the risk of.

exposition *f* display; exposition; exposure.

exprès *adj* express.

express *adj* fast; ** m* fast train.

expressif *adj* expressive.

expression *f* expression.

expressionnisme *m* expressionism.

expressionniste *mf* expressionist; ** adj* expressionist, expressionistic.

exprimer *vt* to express, voice; **s'~** *vr* to express o.s.

expropriation *f* expropriation.

expulser *vt* to expel; to evict.

expulsion *f* expulsion; eviction.

exquis *adj* exquisite; **~ément** *adv* exquisitely.

extase *f* ecstasy; rapture.

extasier (s') *vr* to go into ecstasies.

extensible *adj* extensible, extendable.

extension *f* extension; stretching; expansion.

exténuant *adj* exhausting.

exténuer *vt* to exhaust; **s'~** *vr* to exhaust o.s.

extérieur *m* exterior, outside; ** adj* outer, external, exterior; **~ement** *adv* externally, outwardly.

extérioriser *vt* to show, express; to exteriorize.

extermination *f* extermination.

exterminer *vt* exterminate.

externe *adj* external, outer.

extincteur *m* extinguisher.

extinction *f* extinction, extinguishing.

extraction *f* extraction; mining.

extradition *f* extradition.

extraire *vt* to extract; to mine.

extrait *m* extract; (*jur*) abstract.

extraordinaire *adj* extraordinary; **~ment** *adv* extraordinarily.

extraterrestre *mf* extraterrestrial; ** adj* extraterrestrial.

extravagant *adj* extravagant, wild.

extraverti *m* **-e** *f* extrovert; ** adj* extrovert.

extrême *adj* extreme; **~ment** *adv* extremely.

extrémiste *mf, adj* extremist.

extrémité *f* end, extremity, limit.

exubérance *f* exuberance.

exubérant *adj* exuberant.

exulter *vi* to exult.

F

fable *f* fable, story, tale.

fabricant *m* **-e** *f* manufacturer, maker.

fabrication *f* manufacture, production.

fabrique *f* factory.

fabriquer *vt* to manufacture; to forge; to fabricate.

fabuleux *adj* fabulous, mythical, legendary.

façade *f* façade, front.

face *f* face, side, surface, aspect; **en ~** opposite, over the road; **~ à** facing; **faire ~ à** to confront, face up to; **de ~** fullface, frontal; **~ à ~** face to face.

face à face *m* encounter, interview.

facette *f* facet.

fâché *adj* angry; sorry.

fâcher *vt* to anger, make angry; to grieve; **se ~** *vr* to get angry.

fâcheux *adj* deplorable, regrettable.

facile *adj* easy; facile; **~ment** *adv* easily.

facilité *f* easiness, ease; ability; facility.

faciliter *vt* to make easier, facilitate.

façon *f* way, fashion; make; imitation; **de toute ~** at any rate; **non merci, sans ~** no thanks, honestly; **de ~ à** so that, so as to.

façonner *vt* to shape, fashion, model; to till.

fac-similé *m* facsimile.

facteur *m* postman.

factice *adj* artificial, imitation.

faction *f* faction; sentry-duty.

facturation *f* invoicing.

facture *f* bill, invoice; construction, technique.

facturer *vt* to invoice, charge for.

facultatif *adj* optional.

faculté *f* faculty; power, ability; right.

fade *adj* insipid, bland, dull.

fagot *m* faggot, bundle of firewood.

faible *adj* weak, feeble; slight, poor; ~**ment** *adv* weakly, faintly, feebly.

faiblesse *f* weakness, feebleness, faintness.

faiblir *vi* to fail, flag, weaken; to wane.

faïence *f* earthenware, crockery.

faille *f* fault; flaw; weakness.

faillir *vi*: to come close to; to fail **j'ai failli tomber** I almost fell.

faillite *f* bankruptcy; collapse.

faim *f* hunger; appetite; famine.

fainéant *m* -**e** *f* idler, loafer.

faire *vt* to do; to make; **rien à ~!** nothing doing!; **se ~ à** to get used to; **s'en ~** to worry.

faire-part *m* announcement (birth, marriage, death).

faisable *adj* feasible.

faisan *m* pheasant.

faisceau *m* bundle, stack; beam.

fait *m* event; fact; act.

faîte *m* summit; rooftop.

falaise *f* cliff.

falloir *vi*: to be necessary; **il faut, que tu partes** you must leave.

falsifier *vt* to falsify, alter.

famélique *adj* starving, scrawny.

fameux *adj* famous; excellent.

familial *adj* family, domestic.

familiariser *vt* to familiarize; **se ~** *vr* to familiarize o.s.

familiarité *f* familiarity.

familier *adj* familiar; colloquial; informal.

familièrement *adv* familiarly, informally.

famille *f* family.

famine *f* famine.

fanatique *adj* fanatic; ~**ment** *adv* fanatically; * *mf* fanatic; zealot.

fanatisme *m* fanaticism.

fané *adj* faded, withered.

faner *vt* to turn (hay); to fade; **se ~** *vr* to wither, fade.

fanfare *f* fanfare, flourish; brass band.

fantaisie *f* whim, extravagance; imagination.

fantasme *m* fantasy.

fantasmer *vi* to fantasize.

fantastique *adj* fantastic;

~ment *adv* fantastically; eerily.

fantôme *m* ghost, phantom.

faon *m* fawn.

farce *f* joke, prank; farce.

farceur *m* -euse *f* joker; clown.

farci *adj* stuffed, crammed, packed.

farcir *vt* to stuff, cram.

fard *m* make-up.

fardeau *m* load, burden.

farder *vt* to make up; to disguise; se ~ *vr* to make o.s. up.

farine *f* flour.

farineux *adj* floury, powdery; * *m* starchy food.

farouche *adj* shy, timid; unsociable; fierce; ~ment *adv* fiercely.

fascicule *m* booklet, fascicule, part, instalment.

fascinant *adj* fascinating.

fascination *f* fascination.

fasciner *vt* to fascinate, bewitch.

fascisme *m* fascism.

fasciste *mf, adj* fascist.

faste *m* pomp, ostentation.

fastidieux *adj* tedious, boring.

fastueux *adj* sumptuous, luxurious.

fatal *adj* fatal, deadly; fateful; ~ement *adv* inevitably, unavoidably.

fataliste *mf* fatalist; * *adj* fatalistic.

fatalité *f* fatality; inevitability.

fatidique *adj* fateful; fatal.

fatigant *adj* tiring, fatiguing.

fatigue *f* fatigue, tiredness.

fatigué *adj* tired, weary; overworked, strained.

fatiguer *vt* to tire; to overwork, strain; se ~ *vr* to get tired.

faubourg *m* suburb.

faucher *vt* to reap; to flatten, knock down.

faucille *f* sickle.

faucon *m* falcon, hawk.

faufiler *vt* to tack; to insinuate, introduce; se ~ *vr* to worm one's way in.

faune *f* wildlife, fauna.

faussaire *mf* forger.

faussement *adv* wrongly; falsely.

fausser *vt* to distort, alter; to warp.

fausseté *f* falseness; deceitfulness.

faute *f* mistake, foul, fault; ~ de mieux for lack of anything better.

fauteuil *m* armchair.

fautif *m* -ive *f* culprit, guilty party; * *adj* at fault, guilty; faulty, incorrect.

fauve *m* wild animal; fawn (colour).

faux *adj* false, forged, fake; wrong; bogus.

faux-filet *m* sirloin.

faux-fuyant *m* evasion, equivocation.

faux-semblant *m* sham, pretence.

faveur *f* favour.

favorable *adj* favourable, sympathetic; ~ment *adv* favourably.

favori *m* -te *f* favourite; * *adj* favourite.

favoriser *vt* to favour, further.

fébrile *adj* feverish, febrile; ~ment *adv* feverishly.

fébrilité *f* feverishness.

fécond *adj* fertile; prolific, fruitful; creative.

fécondation *f* impregnation, fertilization.

féconder *vt* to impregnate; to fertilize, pollinate.

fécondité *f* fertility, fecundity.

fécule *f* starch.

féculent *adj* starchy; * *m* starchy food.

fédéral *adj* federal.

fédération *f* federation.

fée *f* fairy.

féerique *adj* magical, fairy.

feindre *vt* to feign, pretend.

feinte *f* dummy, feint.

fêlé *adj* cracked, harebrained.

félicitation *f* congratulation.

féliciter *vt* to congratulate.

félin *adj* feline; * *m* feline.

femelle *f* female.

féminin *adj* feminine, female.

féminisme *m* feminism.

féministe *mf* feminist; * *adj* feminist.

féminité *f* femininity.

femme *f* woman; wife; ~ de ménage cleaning woman; ~ de chambre chambermaid.

fémur *m* femur.

fendiller *vt* to chink, crack, craze; se ~ *vr* to be covered in small cracks.

fendre *vt* to split, cleave, crack; se ~ *vr* to crack.

fenêtre *f* window.

fenouil *m* fennel.

fente *f* crack, fissure; slot.

féodal *adj* feudal.

fer *m* iron, point, blade; ~ à cheval horseshoe.

férié *adj* public holiday.

ferme *adj* firm, steady; definite; ~**ment** *adv* firmly; * *f* farm.

fermé *adj* closed; exclusive; inscrutable.

ferment *m* ferment, leaven.

fermentation *f* fermentation, fermenting.

fermenter *vi* to ferment, work.

fermer *vt* to close; block; turn off; **se** ~ *vr* to close, shut up; to close one's mind to.

fermeté *f* firmness, steadiness.

fermeture *f* closing, shutting; latch; fastener.

fermier *m* -**ière** *f* farmer.

féroce *adj* ferocious, savage; ~**ment** *adv* ferociously, savagely.

férocité *f* ferocity, fierceness.

ferraille *f* scrap iron.

ferronnerie *f* ironworks; ironwork.

ferroviaire *adj* railway.

fertile *adj* fertile, productive.

fertilisation *f* fertilization.

fertiliser *vt* to fertilize.

fertilité *f* fertility.

fervent *adj* fervent, ardent.

ferveur *f* fervour, ardour.

fesse *f* buttock.

festin *m* feast.

festival *m* festival.

fête *f* feast, holiday.

fêter *vt* to celebrate, fête.

fétichisme *m* fetishism.

fétichiste *mf*; * *adj* fetishist.

fétide *adj* fetid.

feu *m* fire; light; hearth; **en** ~ on fire.

feuillage *m* foliage, greenery.

feuille *f* leaf.

feuillet *m* leaf, page, layer.

feuilleté *adj* foliated; laminated.

feuilleter *vt* to leaf through.

feuilleton *m* serial, series.

feutre *m* felt; felt hat.

fève *f* broad bean.

fiabilité *f* accuracy; dependability.

fiable *adj* reliable; dependable.

fiançailles *fpl* engagement, betrothal.

fiancer (se) *vr* to become engaged.

fiasco *m* fiasco.

fibre *f* fibre.

fibreux *adj* fibrous, stringy.

fibrome *m* fibroid, fibroma.

ficeler *vt* to tie up.

ficelle *f* string; stick (bread).

fiche *f* card; sheet; certificate.

ficher *vt* to file, put on file.

fichier *m* catalogue; file.

fictif *adj* fictitious; imaginary.

fiction *f* imagination, fiction.

fidèle *adj* faithful, loyal; ~ment *adv* faithfully; * *mf* believer.

fidélité *f* fidelity, loyalty.

fief *m* fief; stronghold, preserve.

fier (se) *vr* to trust, rely on.

fier *adj* proud, haughty; noble.

fièrement *adv* proudly.

fierté *f* pride; arrogance.

fièvre *f* fever, temperature; excitement.

fiévreux *adj* feverish.

figer *vt* to congeal, freeze; to clot; **se** ~ *vr* to congeal, freeze; to clot.

figue *f* fig.

figuier *m* fig tree.

figurant *m* -e *f* extra, walk-on; stooge.

figuratif *adj* figurative, representational.

figure *f* face; figure; illustration, diagram.

figuré *adj* figurative, metaphorical, diagrammatic; * *m*: **au** ~ in the figurative sense.

figurer *vt* to represent; * *vi* to appear, feature; **se** ~ *vr* to imagine.

figurine *f* figurine.

fil *m* thread; wire; cord; ~ **de fer** wire; ~ **à plomb** plumb line; **au** ~ **des jours** with the passing days.

filament *m* filament, strand, thread.

filature *f* spinning; mill; tailing.

file *f* line, queue; **à la** ~ in line, in succession; **stationner en double** ~ to double-park.

filer *vt* to spin; to tail; to draw out; * *vi* to run, trickle; to fly by; to make off.

filet *m* dribble, trickle; fillet; net.

filiation *f* filiation; relation.

filière *f* path; procedures; network.

fille *f* daughter, girl.

fillette *f* (small) girl.

filleul *m* -e *f* godson, godchild.

film *m* film, picture.

filmer *vt* to film.

filon *m* vein, seam.

fils *m* son.

filtre *m* filter.

filtrer *vt* to filter; to screen.

fin *f* end, finish; **prendre ~ to** terminate, come to an end; * *adj* thin, fine; delicate; **~ement** *adv* finely, delicately.

final *adj* final; **~ement** *adv* finally.

finale *f* finale.

finance *f* finance.

financement *m* financing.

financer *vt* to finance.

financier *m* **-ière** *f* financier.

financièrement *adv* financially.

finesse *f* fineness; sharpness; neatness; delicacy.

fini *adj* finished, over, complete.

finir *vt* to finish, complete; * *vi* to finish, end; to die.

finition *f* finish, finishing.

fisc *m* tax department.

fiscal *adj* fiscal, tax.

fissure *f* crack, fissure.

fixation *f* fixation; fixing, fastening.

fixe *adj* fixed, permanent, set; **~ment** *adv* fixedly, steadily.

fixer *vt* to fix, fasten; to arrange; **se ~** *vr* to settle.

flacon *m* bottle, flask.

flageolant *adj* shaky.

flageolet *m* flageolet.

flagrant *adj* flagrant, blatant.

flair *m* sense of smell, nose; intuition.

flairer *vt* to smell, sniff; to scent.

flambeau *m* torch; candlestick.

flamboyant *adj* blazing; flamboyant.

flamboyer *vi* to blaze, flash, gleam.

flamme *f* flame; fervour; ardour.

flan *m* custard tart; mould.

flanc *m* flank, side.

flanelle *f* flannel.

flâner *vi* to stroll; to lounge about.

flasque *adj* flaccid; spineless.

flatter *vt* to flatter, gratify; to pander; to delight.

flatterie *f* flattery.

flatteur *m* **-euse** *f* flatterer.

fléau *m* scourge; plague.

flèche *f* arrow.

fléchir *vi* to bend, yield, weaken; * *vt* to bend, sway.

fléchissement *m* bending; flexing; bowing.

flegmatique *adj* phlegmatic.

flegme *m* composure, phlegm.

flétrir *vt* to wither, fade; to stigmatize; **se ~** *vr* to wither, wilt.

fleur *f* flower.

fleuri *adj* in bloom; flowery.

fleurir *vi* to blossom, flower; * *vt* to decorate with flowers.

fleuriste *mf* florist.

fleuve *m* river.

flexibilité *f* flexibility.

flexible *adj* flexible, pliant.

flic *m* (*fam*) cop, policeman.

flocon *m* fleck, flake.

floraison *f* flowering, blossoming.

floral *adj* floral, flower.

flore *f* flora.

florissant *adj* flourishing, blooming.

flot *m* stream, flood; floodtide; wave.

flotte *f* fleet; (*col*) rain.

flottement *m* wavering; vagueness, imprecision.

flotter *vi* to float; to drift; to wander; to waver.

flotteur *m* float.

flou *adj* blurred, hazy.

fluctuant *adj* fluctuating.

fluctuation *f* fluctuation.

fluide *adj* fluid, flowing.

fluidité *f* fluidity.

fluor *m* fluorine.

fluorescent *adj* fluorescent.

fluorure *m* fluoride.

flûte *f* flute; French stick (bread).

flûtiste *mf* flautist.

flux *m* flood; flow; flux.

focaliser *vt* to focus; **se ~** *vr* to be focused on.

foetus *m* foetus.

foi *f* faith, trust.

foie *m* liver.

foin *m* hay.

foire *f* fair, trade fair.

fois *f* time, occasion.

folie *f* madness, insanity; extravagance.

folklore *m* folklore.

folklorique *adj* folk.

follement *adv* madly, wildly.

foncé *adj* dark, deep (colours).

foncer *vi* to hammer along, rush at; * *vt* to make darker; (*tec*) to sink, bore.

foncier *adj* land, landed, property.

foncièrement *adv* fundamentally, basically.

fonction *f* post, duty; function.

fonctionnaire *mf* civil servant.

fonctionnement *m* working, functioning, operation.

fonctionner *vi* to work, function, operate.

fond *m* bottom, back; **au ~** basically, in fact; **à ~** thoroughly, in depth; **dans le ~** in reality, basically; **~ de teint** foundation.

fondamental *adj* fundamental, basic; **~ement** *adv* fundamentally.

fondamentalisme *m* fundamentalism.

fondamentaliste *mf*; * *adj* fundamentalist.

fondant *adj* thawing, melting.

fondateur *m* -**trice** *f* founder.

fondation *f* foundation.

fondement *m* foundation; ground.

fonder *vt* to found; to base.

fondre *vi* to melt; to vanish; to slim; * *vt* to melt; to cast; to merge.

fonds *m* business; fund; money; stock.

fondu *adj* melted; molten; cast.

fontaine *f* fountain, spring.

fonte *f* melting; casting; smelting.

football *m* football, soccer.

forage *m* drilling, boring.

forain *m* -**e** *f* stallholder; fairground entertainer; * *adj* fairground.

force *f* strength, force, violence, energy; **à ~ de** by dint of.

forcé *adj* forced; emergency; **~ment** *adv* inevitably.

forcené *adj* deranged, frenzied.

forcer *vt* to force, compel; track down; * *vi* to overdo, strain; **se ~** *vr* to force o.s. to.

forestier *adj* forest; forestry.

forêt *f* forest.

forfait *m* set price, package; (*sport*) withdrawal.

forfaitaire *adj* fixed, set, inclusive.

forge *f* forge, smithy.

forger *vt* to forge, form, mould.

forgeron *m* blacksmith, smith.

formaliser (se) *vr* to take offence at.

formalité *f* formality.

format *m* format, size.

formation *f* formation; training.

forme *f* form, shape; mould,

fitness; **être en ~** to be on form; **en ~ de** forming.

formel *adj* definite, positive; formal; **~lement** *adv* positively, definitely; formally.

former *vt* to form, make up; to train; **se ~** *vr* to form, gather; to train o.s.

formidable *adj* tremendous; fantastic; **~ment** *adv* tremendously, fantastically.

formulaire *m* form.

formule *f* formula; phrase; system.

formuler *vt* to formulate; express.

fort *adj* strong; high; loud; pronounced; **~ement** *adv* strongly; highly; very much; * *adv* loudly; greatly; most; * *m* fort; strong point; (*mus*) forte.

forteresse *f* fortress.

fortifiant *m* tonic; * *adj* fortifying; invigorating.

fortification *f* fortification.

fortifier *vt* to fortify, strengthen; **se ~** *vr* to grow stronger.

fortuit *adj* fortuitous, chance; **~ement** *adv* fortuitously.

fortune *f* fortune, luck.

fortuné *adj* wealthy; fortunate.

fosse *f* pit; grave.

fossé *m* ditch; gulf.

fossette *f* dimple.

fossile *m* fossil.

fou *adj*, *f* **folle** mad, wild; tremendous; erratic.

foudre *f* lightning, thunderbolt.

foudroyant *adj* lightning; thundering; violent.

foudroyer *vt* to strike (lightning).

fouet *m* whip; whisk.

fouetter *vt* to whip, flog.

fougère *f* fern.

fougue *f* ardour, spirit.

fougueux *adj* fiery, ardent.

fouille *f* frisking; excavations.

fouiller *vt* to search, scour.

foulard *m* scarf.

foule *f* crowd; masses, heaps.

four *m* oven; furnace; fiasco.

fourbe *adj* deceitful, two-faced.

fourbu *adj* exhausted.

fourche *f* pitchfork; crotch.

fourchette *f* fork.

fourchu *adj* forked; cloven.

fourgon *m* coach, wagon, van.

fourmi *f* ant.

fourmilière *f* anthill.

fourmillement *m* swarming, milling.

fourmiller *vi* to swarm, teem.

fourneau *m* stove.

fournir *vt* to supply, provide.

fournisseur *m* -euse *f* purveyor, supplier.

fourniture *f* supplying, provision.

fourrage *m* fodder, forage.

fourré *adj* filled; fur-lined; * *m* thicket.

fourrer *vt* to stuff; to line.

fourrière *f* pound (car).

fourrure *f* coat, fur.

foutu *adj* bloody, damned; lousy.

foyer *m* home; fireplace; club; focus.

fracas *m* crash; roar, din.

fraction *f* fraction, part.

fractionnement *m* splitting up, division.

fracture *f* fracture.

fracturer *vt* to fracture, break open.

fragile *adj* fragile, delicate.

fragilité *f* fragility, flimsiness.

fragment *m* fragment.

fragmentation *f* fragmentation; splitting up.

fragmenter *vt* to break up,

fragment; **se ~** *vr* to fragment, break up.

fraîcheur *f* freshness, coolness.

frais *mpl* expenses; * *adj, f* **fraîche** fresh, cool.

fraise *f* strawberry.

framboise *f* raspberry.

franc *adj, f* **franche** frank, open; clear; absolute.

Français *m* Frenchman, -e *f* Frenchwoman.

français *adj* French; * *m* French (language).

France *f* France.

franchement *adv* frankly, openly; boldly; clearly.

franchir *vt* to clear, get over, cross.

franchise *f* frankness, openness; exemption; franchise.

francophone *mf* Frenchspeaker, *adj* French-speaking.

francophonie *f* French-speaking communities.

frange *f* fringe; threshold.

frappant *adj* striking.

frapper *vt* to hit; to strike down; to infringe; * *vi* to strike, knock.

fraternel *adj* fraternal; **~lement** *adv* fraternally.

fraterniser *vi* to fraternize.

fraternité *f* fraternity.

fraude *f* fraud, cheating.

frauduleux *adj* fraudulent.

frayeur *f* fright.

frein *m* brake; check.

freinage *m* braking; slowing down.

freiner *vi* to brake, slow down; * *vt* to slow down; to curb, check.

frêle *adj* flimsy, fragile.

frémir *vi* to quiver, tremble.

frémissant *adj* quivering, trembling.

frémissement *m* shudder, quiver.

frénétique *adj* frenetic; ~ment *adv* frenetically.

fréquemment *adv* frequently.

fréquence *f* frequency.

fréquent *adj* frequent.

frère *m* brother.

fresque *f* fresco.

friand *adj* partial to, fond of.

friandise *f* delicacy, sweetmeat.

fric *m* (*fam*) cash, lolly.

friction *f* friction.

frigidaire *m* refrigerator.

frigide *adj* frigid.

frileux *adj* susceptible to cold; chilly.

frire *vt* to fry.

frisé *adj* curly, curly-haired.

friser *vi* to curl, be curly; * *vt* to curl; to graze, skim.

frisson *m* shiver, shudder.

frissonnant *adj* shivering, shuddering.

frissonnement *m* shuddering, shivering.

frissonner *vi* to shudder, tremble, shiver.

frite *f* chip.

friteuse *f* chip pan.

friture *f* frying; frying fat.

frivole *adj* frivolous, shallow.

frivolité *f* frivolity.

froid *adj* cold, cool; ~ement *adv* coldly, coolly; * *m* cold; coolness; refrigeration.

froideur *f* coldness, chilliness.

froissement *m* creasing; rustling, rustle.

froisser *vt* to crease; to offend; **se ~** *vr* to crease; to take offence.

frôler *vt* to brush against; to verge on.

fromage *m* cheese.

front *m* forehead; face; front.

frontal *adj* frontal.

frontalier *adj* border, frontier.

frontière *f* border, frontier.

frottement *m* rubbing, scraping.

frotter *vt* to rub, scrape.

fructifier *vi* to bear fruit.

fructueux *adj* fruitful, profitable.

frugal *adj* frugal; ~**ement** *adv* frugally.

frugalité *f* frugality.

fruit *m* fruit, result.

fruité *adj* fruity.

frustration *f* frustration.

frustrer *vt* to frustrate, deprive.

fugace *adj* fleeting, transient.

fugitif *m* -**ive** *f* fugitive; * *adj* fugitive, runaway.

fugue *f* running away.

fuir *vi* to avoid; to flee; to leak.

fuite *f* flight, escape; leak.

fulgurant *adj* lightning; dazzling.

fumant *adj* smoking, fuming.

fumé *adj* smoked.

fumée *f* smoke; vapour.

fumer *vi* to smoke, steam, give off smoke; * *vt* to smoke.

fumet *m* aroma.

fumeur *m* -**euse** *f* smoker.

fumier *m* dung, manure.

funèbre *adj* funeral; funerary.

funérailles *fpl* funeral.

funéraire *adj* funeral, funerary.

funeste *adj* disastrous; harmful.

fureur *f* fury; violence.

furie *f* fury, rage.

furieusement *adv* furiously.

furieux *adj* furious, violent.

furtif *adj* furtive; stealthy.

furtivement *adv* furtively.

fusée *f* rocket, missile.

fusible *m* fuse.

fusil *m* rifle, gun.

fusillade *f* fusillade; gunfire; shoot-out.

fusiller *vt* to shoot.

fusion *f* fusion; melting; merger; blending.

fusionner *vt* to merge, combine.

fût *m* trunk; shaft; barrel.

futé *adj* crafty, cunning.

futile *adj* futile; ~**ment** *adv* futilely.

futilité *f* futility.

futur *adj* future; * *m* intended, fiancé; future.

fuyant *adj* fleeting; evasive.

fuyard *m* -**e** *f*; * *adj* runaway.

G

gabarit *m* size, build; calibre.

gâcher *vt* to mix; to waste.

gachette *f* trigger.

gâchis *m* mess.

gadget *m* gadget; gimmick.

gaffe *f* blunder; boat hook.

gage *m* security; pledge; proof.

gagnant *m* -e *f* winner; * *adj* winning.

gagner *vt* to earn, to win, beat; to gain; * *vi* to win; to spread.

gai *adj* cheerful, happy, gay; ~ement *adv* cheerfully, happily.

gaieté *f* cheerfulness, gaiety.

gain *m* earnings; gain, profit, benefit; saving.

gaine *f* girdle; sheath.

gala *m* official reception; gala.

galamment *adv* courteously, gallantly.

galant *adj* gallant, courteous.

galanterie *f* gallantry.

galaxie *f* galaxy.

galère *f* galley.

galerie *f* gallery; tunnel.

galet *m* pebble.

galette *f* pancake.

Gallois *m* Welshman, -e *f* Welshwoman.

gallois *adj* Welsh; * *m* Welsh (language).

galon *m* braid; stripe.

galop *m* gallop; canter.

galoper *vi* to gallop; to run wild.

galvaniser *vt* to galvanize.

gamba *f* large prawn.

gamin *m* -e *f* kid, street urchin.

gaminerie *f* playfulness; childishness.

gamme *f* range; scale.

ganglion *m* ganglion.

gangrène *f* gangrene.

gant *m* glove.

garage *m* garage.

garagiste *mf* garage owner.

garant *m* -e *f* (*jur*) guarantor.

garantie *f* guarantee, surety.

garantir *vt* to guarantee, secure.

garçon *m* boy; assistant; waiter.

garde *f* custody; guard; surveillance; * *m* guard, warder.

garde-à-vous *m* standing to attention.

garde-boue *m* mudguard.

garde-chasse *m* gamekeeper.

garde-fou *m* railing, parapet; safeguard.

garder *vt* to look after; to stay in; to keep on.

garderie *f* day nursery.

garde-robe *f* wardrobe.

gardien *m* -ne *f* guard, guardian, warden; protector.

gare *f* rail station; (*mar*) basin; depot.

garer *vt* to park; to dock; se ~ *vr* to avoid, steer clear of.

gargariser (se) *vr* to gargle; to crow about.

gargarisme *m* gargle.

gargouillement *m* gurgling; rumbling.

gargouiller *vi* to gurgle; to rumble.

garnir *vt* to fit with; to trim, decorate.

garnison *f* (*mil*) garrison.

garniture *f* trimming, lining; garnish.

garrot *m* garrotte; (*med*) tourniquet.

gars *m* (*fam*) lad; bloke.

gaspillage *m* waste; squandering.

gaspiller *vt* to waste, squander.

gastrique *adj* gastric.

gastronome *m* gourmet, gastronome.

gastronomie *f* gastronomy.

gâté *adj* ruined; spoiled.

gâteau *m* cake.

gâter *vt* to ruin; to spoil; se ~ *vr* to go bad, go off.

gâteux *adj* senile; (*fam*) doddering.

gauche *adj* left; awkward, clumsy; ~ment *adv* awkwardly; * *f* left; left wing.

gaucher *adj* left-handed.

gauchisant *m* -e *f* leftist; * *adj* of leftist tendencies.

gauchiste *mf*; * *adj* leftist.

gaufre *f* waffle.

gaver *vt* to force-feed, fill up; se ~ *vr* to stuff o.s.; to devour.

gaz *m invar* gas; fizz; wind.

gaze *f* gauze.

gazelle *f* gazelle.

gazeux *adj* gaseous; fizzy.

gazon *m* lawn; turf.

gazouiller *vi* to chirp, warble.

géant *m* giant, **-e** *f* giantess.

geindre *vi* to groan; to whine.

gel *m* frost; gel.

gélatine *f* gelatine.

gelé *adj* frozen; cold, unresponsive.

gelée *f* frost; jelly.

geler *vi* to freeze, be frozen; * *vt* to freeze, turn to ice; to suspend.

gélule *f* capsule.

Gémeaux *mpl* Gemini.

gémir *vi* to groan, moan.

gémissement *m* groan, moan; groaning.

gênant *adj* annoying; awkward.

gencive *f* gum.

gendarme *m* policeman; gendarme.

gendarmerie *f* police force, constabulary.

gendre *m* son-in-law.

gêne *f* discomfort; trouble; embarrassment; **être sans** ~ to be inconsiderate.

généalogie *f* genealogy.

généalogique *adj* genealogical.

gêner *vt* to bother; to hinder; to make uneasy; **se** ~ *vr* to get in each other's way.

général *adj* general, broad; common; ~**ement** *adv* generally; * *m* general, **-e** *f* general's wife; (*thea*) dress rehearsal.

généralisation *f* generalization.

généraliser *vt* to generalize; **se** ~ *vr* to become widespread.

généraliste *m* general practitioner; * *adj* general-interest; non-specialized.

généralité *f* majority; general points.

générateur *m* generator.

génération *f* generation.

générer *vt* to generate

généreusement *adv* generously; nobly.

généreux *adj*, *f* **-euse** generous; noble; magnanimous.

générosité *f* generosity; nobility; magnanimity.

génétique *adj* genetic; ~**ment** *adv* genetically.

génial *adj* inspired, of genius.

génie *m* genius; spirit; genie.

génital *adj* genital.

génocide *m* genocide.

genou *m* knee.

genre *m* kind, type; gender; genre.

gens *mpl* people, folk.

gentil *adj*, *f* **-le** kind; good; pleasant.

gentillesse *f* kindness; favour.

gentiment *adv* kindly; nicely.

géographe *mf* geographer.

géographie *f* geography.

géographique *adj* geographic.

géologie *f* geology.

géologue *mf* geologist.

géomètre *m* land surveyor.

géométrie *f* geometry.

géométrique *adj* geometric; ~**ment** *adv* geometrically.

géranium *m* geranium.

gérant *m* **-e** *f* manager.

gerbe *f* sheaf, bundle; collection.

gercer *vt* to chap, crack; **se ~** *vr* to chap, crack.

gerçure *f* (small) crack.

gérer *vt* to manage, administer.

germe *m* germ; seed.

germer *vi* to sprout, germinate.

gérondif *m* gerundive; gerund.

gésier *m* gizzard.

gestation *f* gestation.

geste *m* gesture; act, deed.

gesticuler *vi* to gesticulate.

gestion *f* management, administration.

gestionnaire *adj* administrative, management.

ghetto *m* ghetto.

gibier *m* game; prey.

gicler *vi* to spurt, squirt.

gicleur *m* jet.

gifle *f* slap, smack.

gifler *vt* to slap, smack.

gigantesque *adj* gigantic, immense.

gigot *m* leg (mutton/lamb), haunch.

gilet *m* waistcoat.

gingembre *m* ginger.

girafe *f* giraffe.

giratoire *adj* gyrating, gyratory.

girouette *f* weather vane.

gisement *m* deposit; mine; pool.

gitan *m* **-e** *f* gipsy.

gîte *m* shelter; home.

givre *m* frost, rime.

givré *adj* covered in frost.

glace *f* ice; ice cream; mirror.

glacé *adj* icy; frozen; glazed; chilly.

glacer *vt* to freeze; to chill; to glaze.

glacial *adj* icy; freezing.

glacier *m* glacier; ice cream maker.

glacière *f* icebox.

glaçon *m* icicle; ice cube.

glaïeul *m* gladiola.

glaise *f* clay.

gland *m* acorn.

glande *f* gland.

glaner *vt* to glean.

glauque *adj* murky; shabby, run-down.

glissade *f* slide, skid.

glissant *adj* slippery.

glissement *m* sliding; gliding; downturn, downswing.

glisser *vi* to slide, slip, skid.

glissière *f* slide; runner.

global *adj* global, overall; ~ement *adv* globally.

globe *m* globe, sphere; earth.

globulaire *adj* global; (*med*) corpuscular.

globule *m* globule; corpuscle.

globuleux *adj* globular; protruding.

gloire *f* glory; distinction; celebrity.

glorieux *adj* glorious.

glorifier *vt* to glory, honour; se ~ *vr* to glory in; to boast.

glossaire *m* glossary.

glouton *m* -ne *f* glutton; * *adj* gluttonous, ravenous; ~nement *adv* gluttonously.

gluant *adj* sticky, slimy.

glucide *m* glucide.

glucose *m* glucose.

glycérine *f* glycerine.

gobelet *m* beaker, tumbler.

gober *vt* to swallow; to fall for.

goéland *m* gull.

goinfre *m* pig; * *adj* piggish.

golf *m* golf.

golfeur *m* -euse *f* golfer.

gomme *f* gum; rubber, eraser.

gommer *vt* to rub out; to gum.

gond *m* hinge.

gondole *f* gondola.

gondoler *vi* to crinkle, warp, buckle; se ~ *vr* to crinkle; to split one's sides laughing.

gonflable *adj* inflatable.

gonflement *m* inflation, swelling.

gonfler *vt* to pump up, inflate; se ~ *vr* to swell; to be puffed up.

gong *m* gong; bell.

gorge *f* throat.

gorgée *f* sip, gulp.

gorille *m* gorilla.

gosier *m* throat, gullet.

gosse *mf* (*fam*) kid.

gothique *m, adj* Gothic.

goudron *m* tar.

goudronner *vt* to tar.

gouffre *m* gulf, chasm, abyss.

goulu *adj* greedy, gluttonous.

goulûment *adv* greedily, gluttonously.

goupille *f* pin.

gourd *adj* numb (with cold).

gourde *f* gourd; flask.

gourdin *m* club, cudgel.

gourmand *adj* greedy.

gourmandise *f* greed, greediness.

gourmet *m* gourmet.

gourmette *f* chain bracelet.

gousse *f* pod.

goût *m* taste; liking; style.

goûter *vt* to taste; to appreciate; * *vi* to have a snack; to taste good; * *m* snack.

goutte *f* drop; dram; gout.

gouttière *f* gutter; drainpipe.

gouvernail *m* rudder; helm.

gouvernement *m* government.

gouvernemental *adj* government, governmental.

gouverner *vt* to govern, rule; to control; to steer.

gouverneur *m* governor.

goyave *f* guava.

grâce *f* grace; favour; mercy; pardon; ~ à thanks to.

gracier *vt* to pardon.

gracieusement *adv* gracefully; kindly.

gracieux *adj* gracious.

grade *m* rank; grade; degree.

gradé *m* officer; * *adj* promoted.

gradin *m* tier; step; terrace.

graduel *adj* gradual; progressive; ~lement *adv* gradually.

graduer *vt* to step up; to graduate.

graffiti *mpl* graffiti.

grain *m* grain, seed; bead.

graine *f* seed.

graissage *m* greasing, lubricating.

graisse *f* grease, fat.

graisser *vt* to grease, lubricate.

grammaire *f* grammar.

grammairien *m* -ne *f* grammarian.

grammatical *adj* grammatical; ~ement *adv* grammatically.

gramme *m* gram.

grand *adj* big; tall; great; leading; pas ~-chose not a lot, not up to much; ~ement *adv* greatly; a great deal; nobly.

grandeur *f* size; greatness; magnitude.

grandiose *adj* imposing, grandiose.

grandir *vi* to grow bigger, increase; * *vt* to magnify; exaggerate.

grand-mère *f* grandmother.

grand-père *m* grandfather.

grand-parents *mpl* grandparents

granit(e) *m* granite.

granulé *m* granule; * *adj* granular.

granuleux *adj* granular; grainy.

graphique *m* graph; * *adj* graphic; ~ment *adv* graphically.

graphite *m* graphite.

grappe *f* cluster, bunch.

gras *adj*, *f*-**se** fatty; fat; greasy; crude.

gratification *f* gratuity; bonus.

gratin *m* cheese dish, gratin.

gratis *adv* free, gratis.

gratitude *f* gratitude, gratefulness.

gratter *vt* to scratch, scrape.

gratuit *adj* free, gratuitous; disinterested; ~ement *adv* free; gratuitously.

grave *adj* grave, solemn; ~ment *adv* gravely, solemnly.

graver *vt* to engrave, imprint.

graveur *m* engraver, woodcutter.

gravier *m* gravel.

gravir *vt* to climb.

gravitation *f* gravitation.

gravité *f* gravity.

gravure *f* engraving, carving.

gré *m*: liking, taste; au ~ de depending on, at the mercy of; **bon ~ mal ~** like it or not, willy-nilly; **savoir ~** to be grateful.

greffe *f* transplant, graft.

greffer *vt* to transplant, graft.

grégaire *adj* gregarious.

grêle *f* hail.

grêlon *m* hailstone.

grelotter *vi* to shiver.

grenade *f* pomegranate; grenade.

grenat *m* garnet.

grenier *m* attic, garret.

grenouille *f* frog.

grès *m* sandstone; stoneware.

grésiller *vi* to sizzle; splutter.

grève f strike; shore.

gribouillage m scrawl, scribble.

gribouiller vi to doodle; * vt to scribble, scrawl.

grièvement adv seriously.

griffe f claw.

griffer vt to scratch.

griffonner vt to scribble, jot down.

grignoter vi to nibble at, pick at; * vt to nibble at; to eat away.

gril m grill pan; rack.

grillade f grilled meat.

grillage m toasting; grilling.

grille f railings; gate; grill.

grille-pain m invar toaster.

griller vt to toast, scorch; to put bars on; * vi to toast, grill.

grillon m cricket.

grimace f grimace; funny face.

grimper vi to climb up.

grincement m grating, creaking.

grincer vi to grate, creak.

grincheux adj grumpy.

griotte f Morello cherry; marble.

grippe f flu, influenza.

grippé adj suffering from flu.

gris adj grey.

grisant adj exhilarating; intoxicating.

griser vt to intoxicate; se ~ vr to get drunk.

grisonnant adj greying.

grive f thrush.

grog m grog.

grognement m grunt, grunting.

grogner vi to grumble, moan.

grognon m grumbler, moaner, adj grumpy, surly.

grommeler vi to mutter; to grumble; * vt to mutter.

grondement m rumbling, growling.

gronder vt to scold; * vi to rumble, growl.

gros adj, f -se big; fat; thick; serious; heavy; coarse; en ~ in bulk; * m bulk; wholesale; fat man.

groseille f currant.

grossesse f pregnancy.

grosseur f thickness; lump; fatness.

grossier adj coarse; unrefined; base.

grossièrement adv roughly; coarsely.

grossièreté f rudeness; coarseness.

grossir vi to get fatter; to swell, grow; * vt to magnify; to exaggerate.

grossiste mf wholesaler.

grotesque *adj* grotesque, ludicrous; ~**ment** *adv* grotesquely.

grotte *f* cave; grotto.

grouiller *vi* to mill about; to swarm; **se** ~ *vr* (*fam*) to get a move on.

groupe *m* group; party; cluster.

groupement *m* grouping; group.

grouper *vt* to group together; to bulk; **se** ~ *vr* to gather.

grue *f* crane.

grumeau *m* lump.

gruyère *m* gruyère (cheese).

guenon *f* female monkey; hag.

guépard *m* cheetah.

guêpe *f* wasp.

guêpier *m* trap; wasp's nest.

guère *adv* hardly, scarcely.

guéri *adj* cured.

guéridon *m* pedestal table.

guérir *vi* to get better; to heal; * *vt* to cure, heal; **se** ~ *vr* to get better; to recover from.

guérison *f* recovery; curing.

guérisseur *m* -**euse** *f* healer.

guerre *f* war; warfare.

guerrier *m* -**ière** *f* warrior.

guet *m* watch; **faire le** ~ to be on the watch.

guetter *vt* to watch; to lie in wait for.

gueule *f* (*fam*) mouth; face; muzzle.

gueuler *vi* (*fam*) to bawl; bellow.

guichet *m* counter; ticket office, booking office.

guichetier *m* -**ière** *f* counter clerk.

guidage *m* guides; guidance.

guide *m* guide.

guider *vt* to guide; **se** ~ *vr* to be guided by.

guidon *m* handlebars.

guignol *m* puppet; puppet show.

guillemet *m* inverted comma; quotation mark.

guillotine *f* guillotine.

guimauve *f* marshmallow.

guindé *adj* stiff, uptight.

guirlande *f* garland.

guise *f* manner, way; **en** ~ **de** by way of; **à ta** ~ as you please.

guitare *f* guitar.

guitariste *mf* guitarist.

guttural *adj* guttural

gymnase *m* gymnasium.

gymnastique *f* gymnastics.

gynécologie *f* gynaecology.

gynécologue, gynécologiste *mf* gynaecologist.

gyrophare *m* revolving light.

H

habile *adj* skilful, skilled; clever; ~**ment** *adv* skilfully.

habileté *f* skill, skilfulness; clever move.

habiliter *vt* to qualify; to authorize.

habillement *m* clothing, dress, outfit.

habiller *vt* to dress, clothe; s'~ *vr* to get dressed.

habit *m* clothes; apparel; dresscoat; outfit

habitable *adj* inhabitable.

habitant *m* -e *f* inhabitant; occupant; dweller.

habitat *m* habitat; housing conditions.

habitation *f* dwelling; residence; house.

habité *adj* manned.

habiter *vi* to live; * *vt* to live in; occupy.

habitude *f* habit, custom, routine.

habituel *adj* usual, customary; ~**lement** *adv* usually, generally.

habituer *vt* to accustom; to teach; s'~ *vr* to get used to.

hache *f* axe, hatchet.

hacher *vt* to chop, mince.

hachoir *m* chopper, cleaver.

hachure *f* hatching.

hagard *adj* wild; haggard; distraught.

haie *f* hedge.

haine *f* hatred.

haineux *adj* full of hatred; malevolent.

haïr *vt* to hate, detest.

hâle *m* tan, sunburn.

hâlé *adj* tanned, sunburnt.

haleine *f* breath, breathing.

haletant *adj* panting, gasping.

haleter *vi* to pant, gasp for breath.

hall *m* hall, foyer.

halle *f* covered market; hall.

hallucination *f* hallucination.

halo *m* halo.

halte *f* stop, break; stopping place.

haltère f dumbbell.

hamac m hammock.

hameçon m fish-hook.

hamster m hamster.

hanche f hip; haunch.

handball m handball.

handballeur m **-euse** f handball player.

handicap m handicap.

handicaper vt to handicap

hangar m shed, barn; hangar.

hanneton m maybug.

hanter vt to haunt.

happer vt to snap up, snatch.

harassant adj exhausting, wearing.

harcèlement m harassment; pestering.

harceler vt to harass; to pester; to plague.

hardi adj bold, daring; brazen; **~ment** adv boldly, daringly; brazenly.

hareng m herring.

hargne f spite.

hargneux adj aggressive, belligerent.

haricot m bean.

harmonica m harmonica.

harmonie f harmony; wind section.

harmonieusement adv harmoniously.

harmonieux adj harmonious; well-matched.

harmoniser vt to harmonize; **s'~** vr to be in harmony.

harnacher m to harness.

harnais m harness; equipment.

harpe f harp.

harpiste mf harpist.

harpon m harpoon.

hasard m chance; accident; hazard; risk.

hasardeux adj hazardous, risky.

hâte f haste; impatience.

hâter vt to hasten; to quicken; **se ~** vr to hurry.

hâtif adj precocious; early; hasty.

hâtivement adv hastily.

hausse f rise, increase.

hausser vt to raise; to heighten.

haut adj high, tall; upper; superior; **~ement** adv highly.

hautain adj haughty, lofty.

hautbois m oboe.

hauteur f height; elevation; haughtiness; bearing.

haut-parleur m loudspeaker.

hebdomadaire adj; * m weekly.

hébergement *m* accommodation; lodging.

héberger *vt* to accommodate, lodge.

hectare *m* hectare.

hectogramme *m* hectogram.

hectolitre *m* hectolitre.

hectomètre *m* hectometre.

hélice *f* propeller; helix.

hélicoptère *m* helicopter.

hélium *m* helium.

hématome *m* severe bruise, haematoma.

hémicycle *m* semicircle, hemicycle; amphitheatre.

hémiplégique *mf* person paralysed on one side, hemiplegic; * *adj* hemiplegic.

hémisphère *m* hemisphere.

hémoglobine *f* haemoglobin.

hémophile *adj* haemophiliac.

hémophilie *f* haemophilia.

hémorragie *f* bleeding, haemorrhage.

hémorroïde *f* haemorrhoid, pile.

henné *m* henna.

hépatique *adj* hepatic.

hépatite *f* hepatitis.

herbe *f* grass; **en ~** in the blade.

herbivore *m* herbivore; *adj* herbivorous.

herboriste *mf* herbalist.

héréditaire *adj* hereditary.

hérédité *f* heredity; heritage; right of inheritance.

hérésie *f* heresy.

hérétique *adj* heretical.

hérissé *adj* bristling; spiked.

hérisser *vt* to bristle; to spike; * **se ~** *vr* to stand on end; to bristle.

hérisson *m* hedgehog.

héritage *m* inheritance; heritage, legacy.

hériter *vi* to inherit.

héritier *m* heir -**ière** *f* heiress.

hermaphrodite *m* hermaphrodite; * *adj* hermaphrodite.

hermétique *adj* airtight, watertight, hermetic; **~ment** *adv* hermetically.

hermine *f* ermine; stoat.

hernie *f* hernia, rupture.

héroïne *f* heroine; heroin.

héroïque *adj* heroic; **~ment** *adv* heroically.

héroïsme *m* heroism.

héron *m* heron.

héros *m* hero.

herpès *m* herpes; cold sore.

hésitant *adj* hesitant.

hésitation *f* hesitation.

hésiter *vi* to hesitate.

hétéroclite *adj* heterogeneous; sundry; eccentric.

hétérogène *adj* heterogeneous.

hétérosexuel *adj* heterosexual.

hêtre *m* beech.

heure *f* hour; time of day; **de bonne ~** early; **tout à l'~** a short time ago, just now.

heureusement *adv* luckily; happily.

heureux *adj* lucky; happy.

heurter *vt* to strike, hit; to jostle.

hexagone *m* hexagon.

hibernation *f* hibernation.

hibou *m* owl.

hideux *adj* hideous.

hier *adv* yesterday.

hiérarchie *f* hierarchy.

hiérarchique *adj* hierarchical; **~ment** *adv* hierarchically

hilarant *adj* hilarious, side-splitting.

hilarité *f* hilarity, laughter.

hindouisme *m* Hinduism.

hippisme *m* riding, equestrianism.

hippocampe *m* sea horse.

hippodrome *m* racecourse.

hippopotame *m* hippopotamus.

hirondelle *f* swallow.

hirsute *adj* dishevelled, tousled.

hisser *vt* to hoist, haul up.

histoire *f* history; story; business; **~ de dire** just to say.

historien *m* **-ne** *f* historian.

historique *adj* historic; historical; **~ment** *adv* historically.

hiver *m* winter.

hivernal *adj* winter; wintry.

HLM (habitation à loyer modéré) *f/m* public sector housing.

hocher *vt* to nod; to shake one's head.

hochet *m* rattle; toy.

holocauste *m* holocaust.

homard *m* lobster.

homéopathe *mf* homeopath.

homéopathie *f* homeopathy.

homicide *m* homicide.

hommage *m* homage, tribute; **rendre ~ à** to pay homage to.

homme *m* man.

homme-grenouille *m* frogman.

homogène *adj* homogeneous.

homogénéiser *vt* to homogenize.

homogénéité *f* homogeneity.

homologue *adj* homologous; equivalent.

homologuer *vt* to ratify; to approve.

homonyme *m* homonym; * *adj* homonymous.

homosexualité *f* homosexuality.

homosexuel *m* **-le** *f* homosexual.

honnête *adj* honest; decent; honourable; ~**ment** *adv* honestly, decently.

honnêteté *f* honesty, decency.

honneur *m* honour; integrity; credit; **en l'~ de** in honour of.

honorable *adj* honourable; reputable; ~**ment** *adv* honourably.

honoraire *adj* honorary.

honoraires *mpl* fees.

honorer *vt* to honour; to esteem; to do credit to; **s'~** *vr*: **s'~ de** to pride o.s. on.

honte *f* shame, disgrace.

honteusement *adv* shamefully; disgracefully.

honteux *adj* shameful; disgraceful.

hôpital *m* hospital.

hoquet *m* hiccough, hiccup.

horaire *m* timetable; * *adj* hourly.

horizon *m* horizon.

horizontal *adj* horizontal; ~**ement** *adv* horizontally.

horloge *f* clock.

horloger *m* **-ère** *f* watchmaker, clockmaker.

hormone *f* hormone.

horoscope *m* horoscope.

horreur *f* horror.

horrible *adj* horrible; dreadful; ~**ment** *adv* horribly

horrifier *vt* to horrify.

hors *prép* outside; beyond; save; except; ~ **série** incomparable, outstanding; special issue.

hors-bord *m invar* speedboat.

hors-d'œuvre *m invar* hors d'œuvre, starter.

hors-jeu *m invar* offside.

hors-piste *m invar* off-piste.

hortensia *m* hydrangea.

horticulteur *m* horticulturist.

horticulture *f* horticulture.

hospice *m* home, asylum; hospice.

hospitalier *adj* hospital; hospitable.

hospitalisation *f* hospitalization.

hospitaliser *vt* to hospitalize.

hospitalité *f* hospitality.

hostie *f* host.

hostile *adj* hostile; **~ment** *adv* hostilely.

hostilité *f* hostility.

hôte *m* **hôtesse** *f* host; landlord.

hôtel *m* hotel.

hôtelier *m* **-ière** *f* hotelier; * *adj* hotel.

hôtellerie *f* inn; hotel business.

hotte *f* basket.

houblon *m* hop.

houille *f* coal.

houle *f* swell.

houleux *adj* stormy; turbulent.

houppe *f* tuft; tassel.

housse *f* cover, dust-sheet.

houx *m* holly.

hublot *m* porthole.

huer *vt* to boo.

huile *f* oil; petroleum.

huissier *m* bailiff; usher.

huit *adj*, *m* eight.

huitaine *f* eight or so.

huitième *adj* eighth; **~ment** *adv* eighthly; * *mf* eighth.

huître *f* oyster.

humain *adj* human; humane; **~ement** *adv* humanly; humanely; * *m* human.

humanisme *m* humanism.

humaniste *m* humanist; * *adj* humanist.

humanitaire *adj* humanitarian.

humanité *f* humanity.

humble *adj* humble; modest; **~ment** *adv* humbly.

humecter *vt* to dampen, moisten.

humeur *f* mood, humour; temper.

humide *adj* humid.

humidité *f* humidity.

humiliant *adj* humiliating.

humiliation *f* humiliation.

humilier *vt* to humiliate.

humilité *f* humility.

humoristique *adj* humorous.

humour *m* humour.

hurlement *m* roar, yell; howl.

hurler *vi*; * *vt* to roar, yell.

hutte *f* hut.

hybride *adj* hybrid; * *m* hybrid.

hydratant *adj* moisturizing.

hydratation *f* hydration; moisturizing.

hydrater *vt* to hydrate; to moisturize.

hydraulique *adj* hydraulic.

hydravion *m* seaplane.

hydrocarbure *m* hydrocarbon.

hydrogène *m* hydrogen.

hydrolyse *f* hydrolysis.

hydrophile *adj* absorbent.

hydroxyde *m* hydroxide.

hyène *f* hyena.

hygiène *f* hygienics; hygiene.

hygiénique *adj* hygienic; ~ment *adv* hygienically.

hymne *m* hymn.

hyperbole *f* hyperbole; hyperbola.

hypermarché *m* hypermarket.

hypermétrope *adj* long-sighted; * *mf* long-sighted person.

hypertension *f* hypertension.

hypertrophié *adj* (*med*) enlarged; overdeveloped.

hypnose *f* hypnosis

hypnotique *adj* hypnotic.

hypnotiser *vt* to hypnotize.

hypocondriaque *mf* hypochondriac; * *adj* hypochondriac.

hypocrisie *f* hypocrisy.

hypocrite *mf* hypocrite; * *adj* hypocritical; ~ment *adv* hypocritically.

hypophyse *f* pituitary gland, hypophysis.

hypothalamus *m* hypothalamus.

hypothèque *f* mortgage.

hypothéquer *vt* to mortgage.

hypothèse *f* hypothesis; assumption.

hypothétique *adj* hypothetical; ~ment *adv* hypothetically.

hystérie *f* hysteria.

hystérique *mf* hysterical; * *adj* hysteric.

I

ibis *m* ibis.

iceberg *m* iceberg.

idéal *adj*; * *m* ideal.

idéaliser *vt* to idealize.

idéaliste *adj* idealistic; * *mf* idealist.

idée *f* idea.

identifier *vt* to identify; s'~ *vr* to identify with.

identique *adj* identical; ~ment *adv* identically.

identité *f* identity; similarity.

idéologie *f* ideology.

idiot *m* -e *f* idiot, fool; * *adj* idiotic, stupid; ~ement *adv* idiotically.

idole *f* idol.

igloo *m* igloo.

ignoble *adj* ignoble, mean, base.

ignorance *f* ignorance.

ignorant *adj* ignorant; unacquainted; uninformed.

ignorer *vt* to be ignorant of; to be unaware of; to ignore.

iguane *m* iguana.

il *pn* he, it.

île *f* island, isle.

illégal *adj* illegal; unlawful; ~ement *adv* illegally.

illégalité *f* illegality.

illégitime *adj* illegitimate; unwarranted.

illettré *adj* illiterate.

illicite *adj* illicit; ~ment *adv* illicitly.

illimité *adj* unlimited; limitless.

illisible *adj* illegible, unreadable.

illogique *adj* illogical.

illumination *f* illumination, lighting.

illuminer *vt* to light up, illuminate; to enlighten.

illusion *f* illusion

illusoire *adj* illusory; illusive; ~ment *adv* illusorily.

illustration *f* illustration.

illustre *adj* illustrious, renowned.

illustrer *vt* to illustrate.

îlot *m* islet; block (flats).

image *f* image, picture; reflection.

imagé *adj* colourful; full of imagery.

imaginaire *adj* imaginary.

imagination *f* imagination.

imaginer *vt* to imagine; to suppose; to devise; **s'~** *vr* to imagine o.s.; to think.

imbattable *adj* unbeatable.

imbécile *mf* idiot, imbecile; * *adj* stupid, idiotic.

imbiber *vt* to soak, moisten.

imbriquer *vt* to fit into; to overlap; **s'~** *vr* to be linked.

imbuvable *adj* undrinkable; unbearable.

imitation *f* imitation; mimicry; forgery.

imiter *vt* to imitate.

immaculé *adj* spotless, immaculate.

immangeable *adj* inedible.

immatriculation *f* registration.

immatriculer *vt* to register.

immédiat *adj* immediate; instant; **~ement** *adv* immediately, instantly.

immense *adj* immense, boundless.

immensément *adv* immensely; hugely.

immensité *f* immensity; immenseness.

immergé *adj* submerged.

immersion *f* immersion; submersion.

immeuble *m* building; block of flats; real estate.

immigrant *m* -e *f* immigrant.

immigration *f* immigration.

immigré *m* -e *f* immigrant.

imminent *adj* imminent, impending.

immobile *adj* motionless, still.

immobilier *adj* property; * *m* property business.

immobiliser *vt* to immobilize; to bring to a standstill; **s'~** *vr* to stop, stand still.

immobilité *f* stillness; immobility; permanence.

immonde *adj* squalid; base, vile.

immoral *adj* immoral.

immoralité *f* immorality.

immortaliser *vt* to immortalize.

immortel *adj* immortal.

immuable *adj* unchanging, immutable; **~ment** *adv* immutably.

immuniser *vt* to immunize.

immunité *f* immunity.

impact *m* impact.

impair *adj* odd, uneven.

impalpable *adj* impalpable.

impardonnable *adj* unforgivable, unpardonable.

imparfait *adj* imperfect; ~ement *adv* imperfectly.

impartial *adj* impartial; ~ement *adv* impartially.

impartialité *f* impartiality.

impasse *f* dead end, cul-de-sac; impasse.

impassible *adj* impassive.

impatiemment *adv* impatiently.

impatience *f* impatience.

impatient *adj* impatient.

impatienter *vt* to irritate, annoy; s'~ *vr* to grow, get impatient.

impeccable *adj* perfect; faultless, impeccable; ~ment *adv* perfectly, impeccably.

impénétrable *adj* impenetrable; inscrutable.

impensable *adj* unthinkable.

impératif *adj* imperative; mandatory; * *m* requirement; demand; constraint.

impératrice *f* empress.

imperceptible *adj* imperceptible; ~ment *adv* imperceptibly.

imperfection *f* imperfection.

impérial *adj* imperial.

impérialisme *m* imperialism.

imperméable *adj* impermeable, waterproof; ~ à impervious to.

impersonnel *adj* impersonal.

impertinence *f* impertinence.

impertinent *adj* impertinent.

imperturbable *adj* unshakeable; imperturbable; ~ment *adv* imperturbably.

impétueux *adj* impetuous.

impitoyable *adj* merciless, pitiless; ~ment *adv* mercilessly, pitilessly.

implacable *adj* implacable; ~ment *adv* implacably.

implantation *f* implantation; establishment; introduction.

implanter *vt* to introduce; to establish; to implant; s'~ *vr* to be established; to become implanted.

implication *f* implication; involvement.

implicite *adj* implicit; ~ment *adv* implicitly.

impliquer *vt* to imply; to necessitate; to implicate; s'~ *vr* to get involved in one's work.

impoli *adj* impolite, rude.

impolitesse *f* impoliteness, rudeness.

impopulaire *adj* unpopular.

importance *f* importance, significance; size.

important *adj* important, significant; sizeable.

importateur *m* **-trice** *f* importer; * *adj* importing.

importation *f* import, importation.

importer *vt* to import; * *vi* to matter; **que m'importe que** what does it matter to me that; **peu importe** whatever; **n'importe qui** anybody; **n'importe quoi** anything; **n'importe comment** anyhow; **n'importe quel** any.

importuner *vt* to importune, bother.

imposant *adj* imposing; stately.

imposer *vt* to impose, lay down; **s'~** *vr* to be essential; to assert o.s.

impossibilité *f* impossibility.

impossible *adj* impossible.

imposteur *m* impostor.

impôt *m* tax, duty.

impotent *adj* disabled, crippled.

imprégner *vt* impregnate; to permeate; to imbue; **s'~** *vr* to become impregnated with; to become imbued with.

impresario *m* manager, impresario.

impression *f* feeling, impression.

impressionnant *adj* impressive; upsetting.

impressionner *vt* to impress; to upset.

impressionisme *m* impressionism.

impressioniste *mf*; * *adj* impressionist.

imprévisible *adj* unforeseeable; unpredictable.

imprévoyant *adj* improvident.

imprévu *adj* unforeseen, unexpected.

imprimante *f* printer.

imprimé *adj* printed; * *m* printed form; printed material.

imprimer *vt* to print.

imprimerie *f* printing works; printing house.

imprimeur *m* printer.

improbable *adj* improbable, unlikely.

improductif *adj* unproductive.

improvisation *f* improvisation.

improviser *vt* to improvise.

improviste *adv*: à l'~ unexpectedly.

imprudence *f* carelessness, imprudence.

imprudent *adj* careless, imprudent.

impudence *f* impudence; shamelessness.

impudique *adj* immodest, shameless.

impuissance *f* powerlessness, helplessness.

impuissant *adj* powerless, helpless.

impulsif *adj* impulsive.

impulsion *f* impulse; impetus.

impulsivement *adv* impulsively.

impunément *adv* with impunity.

impur *adj* impure; mixed.

impureté *f* impurity.

inacceptable *adj* unacceptable.

inaccessible *adj* inaccessible; obscure; incomprehensible.

inaccoutumé *adj* unusual.

inachevé *adj* unfinished, uncompleted.

inactif *adj* inactive, idle.

inaction *f* inactivity, idleness.

inactivité *f* inactivity.

inadapté *adj* unsuitable; maladjusted.

inadéquat *adj* inadequate.

inadmissible *adj* (*jur*) inadmissible.

inaltérable *adj* stable; unchanging, permanent.

inamovible *adj* irremovable; fixed.

inanimé *adj* inanimate; unconscious.

inaperçu *adj*: unnoticed **passer** ~ to go unnoticed.

inappréciable *adj* invaluable, inestimable.

inapte *adj* unfit.

inattaquable *adj* unassailable; irrefutable.

inattendu *adj* unexpected, unforeseen.

inattention *f* inattention, lack of attention.

inauguration *f* inauguration, opening.

inaugurer *vt* to inaugurate, open.

inavouable *adj* shameful; undisclosable.

incapable *adj* incapable; incompetent.

incapacité *f* incompetence;

disability; être dans l'~ de to be unable to do.

incarcérer *vt* to incarcerate.

incarnation *f* incarnation.

incarner *vt* to incarnate, embody.

incendiaire *adj* incendiary; inflammatory; * *mf* arsonist.

incendie *m* fire, blaze.

incendier *vt* to set alight; to kindle.

incertain *adj* uncertain, unsure.

incertitude *f* uncertainty; être dans l'~ to feel uncertain.

incessant *adj* incessant, ceaseless.

inceste *m* incest.

incident *m* incident, point of law.

incinération *f* incineration; cremation.

inciser *vt* to incise; (*med*) to lance.

incisive *f* incisive; piercing.

incitation *f* incitement; incentive.

inciter *vt* to incite, urge.

inclinaison *f* incline; gradient.

incliner *vt* to bend; to slope; to bow.

inclure *vt* to include; to insert.

inclus *adj* enclosed; included; ci-~ herein enclosed.

incohérence *f* incoherence; inconsistency.

incohérent *adj* incoherent; inconsistent.

incolore *adj* colourless; clear.

incommode *adj* inconvenient; awkward.

incommoder *vt* to disturb, bother.

incomparable *adj* incomparable; ~**ment** *adv* incomparably.

incompatibilité *f* incompatibility.

incompatible *adj* incompatible.

incompétence *f* incompetence.

incompétent *adj* incompetent; inexpert.

incomplet *adj* incomplete.

incompréhensible *adj* incomprehensible.

incompréhension *f* lack of understanding.

inconcevable *adj* inconceivable.

inconciliable *adj* irreconcilable.

inconditionnel *adj* unconditional; unreserved; unquestioning.

inconfortable *adj* uncomfortable; awkward; ~**ment** *adv* uncomfortably.

incongru *adj* unseemly; incongruous.

inconnu *m* -e *f* stranger, unknown person; * *m* unknown; * *adj* unknown.

inconsciemment *adv* unconsciously; thoughtlessly.

inconscience *f* unconsciousness; thoughtlessness.

inconscient *adj* unconscious; thoughtless, reckless; * *m* subconscious, unconscious.

inconsidéré *adj* inconsiderate; thoughtless; ~ment *adv* inconsiderately.

inconsistant *adj* flimsy; colourless; watery.

inconsolable *adj* disconsolate; inconsolable.

inconstant *adj* fickle; variable, inconstant.

incontestable *adj* incontestable, unquestionable; ~ment *adv* incontestably, unquestionably.

inconvénient *m* drawback, inconvenience.

incorporation *f* incorporation; integration; blending.

incorporer *vt* to incorporate, integrate.

incorrect *adj* faulty, incorrect; ~ement *adv* incorrectly.

incorrigible *adj* incorrigible.

incorruptible *adj* incorruptible.

incrédule *adj* incredulous; * *mf* unbeliever, non-believer.

incrédulité *f* incredulity, lack of belief.

incroyable *adj* incredible; unbelievable; ~ment *adv* incredibly, unbelievably.

incruster *vt* to inlay; to superimpose; s'~ *vr* to become imbedded in; to become rooted in.

inculpation *f* inculcation, instilling.

inculpé *m* -e *f* accused; * *adj* accused.

incurable *adj* incurable; ~ment *adv* incurably, hopelessly.

indécent *adj* indecent, improper.

indéchiffrable *adj* indecipherable; incomprehensible.

indécis *adj* indecisive; unsettled; undefined.

indéfini *adj* undefined; indefinite; ~ment *adv* indefinitely.

indéfinissable *adj* indefinable.

indemne *adj* unharmed, unhurt.

indemniser *vt* to indemnify; to compensate.

indemnité *f* compensation; indemnity.

indéniable *adj* undeniable, indisputable; **~ment** *adv* undeniably.

indépendance *f* independence.

indépendant *adj* independent.

indestructible *adj* indestructible.

indéterminé *adj* undetermined; unspecified; undecided.

index *m* index; index finger.

indexer *vt* to index.

indicatif *m* signature tune; dialling code; * *adj* indicative.

indication *f* indication; piece of information; instruction.

indice *m* indication; clue; sign.

indifféremment *adv* indiscriminately, equally.

indifférence *f* indifference.

indifférent *adj* indifferent; immaterial.

indigène *mf* native; local; * *adj* indigenous, native.

indigeste *adj* indigestible.

indigestion *f* indigestion.

indigne *adj* unworthy; undeserving.

indigner *vt* to annoy, make indignant; **s'~** *vr* to be indignant.

indiquer *vt* to indicate, point out; to tell.

indirect *adj* indirect; circumstantial; collateral; **~ement** *adv* indirectly.

indiscipliné *adj* undisciplined.

indiscret *adj* indiscreet; inquisitive.

indiscrétion *f* indiscretion; inquisitiveness.

indiscutable *adj* indisputable; unquestionable; **~ment** *adv* indisputably.

indispensable *adj* indispensable; essential.

indisponible *adj* unavailable.

indistinct *adj* indistinct, vague; **~ement** *adv* indistinctly.

individu *m* individual.

individuel *adj* individual; **~lement** *adv* individually.

indolore *adj* painless.

indubitable *adj* indubitable; certain; **~ment** *adv* indubitably.

indulgence *f* indulgence; leniency.

indulgent *adj* indulgent; lenient.

industrialisation *f* industrialization.

industrie *f* industry; dexterity, ingenuity.

industriel *m* **-le** *f* industrialist, manufacturer; * *adj* industrial.

inébranlable *adj* steadfast, unwavering.

inédit *adj* unpublished; original.

inefficace *adj* ineffective; inefficient.

inefficacité *f* ineffectiveness; inefficiency.

inégal *adj* unequal; uneven; irregular; ~**ement** *adv* unequally.

inégalité *f* inequality; difference, disparity.

inéluctable *adj* ineluctable, unavoidable; ~**ment** *adv* ineluctably.

inépuisable *adj* inexhaustible.

inerte *adj* inert; lifeless.

inertie *f* inertia, apathy.

inespéré *adj* unexpected.

inestimable *adj* inestimable, invaluable.

inévitable *adj* inevitable, unavoidable.

inexact *adj* inexact, inaccurate.

inexactitude *f* inaccuracy.

inexistant *adj* nonexistent.

inexorable *adj* inexorable; ~**ment** *adv* inexorably.

inexpérimenté *adj* inexperienced; inexpert.

inexplicable *adj* inexplicable; ~**ment** *adv* inexplicably.

inexprimable *adj* inexpressible.

infaillible *adj* infallible.

infâme *adj* infamous; base, vile.

infantile *adj* infantile, childish.

infatigable *adj* indefatigable, tireless; ~**ment** *adv* indefatigably.

infect *adj* vile; revolting; filthy.

infecter *vt* to infect; to contaminate; **s'**~ *vr* to become infected.

infection *f* infection.

inférieur *adj* inferior; lower.

infériorité *f* inferiority.

infernal *adj* infernal, diabolical.

infester *vt* to infest, overrun.

infidèle *adj* unfaithful, disloyal.

infidélité *f* infidelity.

infiltration *f* infiltration.

infini *adj* infinite; interminable; **~ment** *adv* infinitely.

infinitif *m* infinitive.

infirme *adj* feeble; crippled, disabled.

infirmerie *f* infirmary; sick bay.

infirmier *m* **-ière** *f* nurse.

infirmité *f* disability; infirmity.

inflammation *f* inflammation.

inflation *f* inflation.

inflexible *adj* inflexible, rigid.

infliger *vt* to inflict; to impose.

influence *f* influence.

influencer *vt* to influence, sway.

informaticien *m* **-ne** *f* computer scientist.

information *f* piece of information; information; inquiry.

informatique *f* computing; data processing; * *adj* computer.

informer *vt* to inform, tell; **s'~** *vr* to find out, inquire.

infraction *f* infraction, infringement; offence.

infranchissable *adj* impassable; insuperable.

infrarouge *adj* infrared.

infrastructure *f* infrastructure; substructure.

infructueux *adj* fruitless, unsuccessful.

infusion *f* infusion, herb tea.

ingénieur *m* engineer.

ingénieux *adj* ingenious, clever.

ingénu *adj* ingenuous, naive.

ingrat *adj* ungrateful; unprofitable.

ingratitude *f* ingratitude.

ingrédient *m* ingredient; component.

inhabité *adj* uninhabited, unoccupied.

inhabituel *adj* unusual, unaccustomed.

inhumain *adj* inhuman.

inimaginable *adj* unimaginable.

inimitable *adj* inimitable.

ininterrompu *adj* uninterrupted; unbroken.

initial *adj* initial; **~ement** *adv* initially.

initiation *f* initiation.

initiative *f* initiative; enterprise.

initier *vt* to initiate.

injecter *vt* to inject.

injection *f* injection.

injure *f* injury; insult.

injurier *vt* to abuse; insult.

injuste *adj* unjust, unfair; ~**ment** *adv* unjustly.

injustice *f* injustice.

injustifié *adj* unjustified.

inné *adj* innate, inborn.

innocence *f* innocence.

innocent *m* -*e f* innocent person; simpleton; * *adj* innocent.

innocenter *vt* to clear, prove innocent.

innovation *f* innovation.

innover *vi* to innovate, make innovations.

inodore *adj* odourless, scentless.

inoffensif *adj* inoffensive, harmless.

inondation *f* flood.

inonder *vt* to flood, inundate.

inopportun *adj* ill-timed, inopportune.

inoubliable *adj* unforgettable.

inouï *adj* unprecedented, unheard of.

inox *m* stainless steel.

inqualifiable *adj* unspeakable.

inquiet *adj* worried, anxious, uneasy.

inquiéter *vt* to worry, disturb; **s'~** *vr* to get worried.

inquiétude *f* restlessness, uneasiness.

insaisissable *adj* elusive; imperceptible.

insalubre *adj* insalubrious; unhealthy.

insatiable *adj* insatiable; ~**ment** *adv* insatiably.

insatisfaction *f* dissatisfaction.

inscription *f* inscription; registration; matriculation.

inscrire *vt* to inscribe; to enter; to set down; to register; **s'~** *vr* to join; to register, enrol.

insecte *m* insect.

insecticide *m* insecticide.

insémination *f* insemination.

insensé *adj* insane, demented.

insensible *adj* insensible, unfeeling, insensitive; imperceptible; ~**ment** *adv* imperceptibly; insensibly.

inséparable *adj* inseparable.

insérer *vt* to insert.

insertion *f* insertion, inserting.

insidieux *adj* insidious

insignifiant *adj* insignificant, trifling.

insinuation *f* insinuation.

insinuer *vt* to insinuate, imply; **s'~** *vr* to insinuate o.s. into; to creep into.

insipide *adj* insipid, tasteless.

insister *vi* to insist, be insistent; to stress.

insolence *f* insolence.

insolent *adj* insolent; brazen.

insolite *adj* unusual; strange.

insomnie *f* insomnia.

insouciance *f* unconcern; carelessness.

insouciant *adj* carefree; careless.

insoutenable *adj* unbearable; untenable.

inspecter *vt* to inspect, examine.

inspecteur *m* **-trice** *f* inspector

inspection *f* inspection.

inspiration *f* inspiration; suggestion.

inspirer *vt* to inspire; to breathe in; **s'~** *vr*: **s'~ de** to be inspired by.

instable *adj* unstable; unsettled.

installation *f* installation; installing.

installer *vt* to install; to fit out; **s'~** *vr* to set o.s. up; to settle down.

instant *m* moment, instant.

instantané *adj* instant, instantaneous; **~ment** *adv* instantly.

instaurer *vt* to institute; to impose.

instinct *m* instinct.

instinctif *adj* instinctive.

instinctivement *adv* instinctively.

institut *m* institute; school.

instituteur *m* **-trice** *f* teacher.

institution *f* institution; establishment.

instructif *adj* instructive.

instruction *f* instruction; education; inquiry.

instruire *vt* to instruct; to teach; to conduct an inquiry; **s'~** *vr* to educate o.s.; to obtain information.

instrument *m* instrument, implement.

insuffisance *f* insufficiency, inadequacy.

insuffisant *adj* insufficient, inadequate.

insuline *f* insulin.

insulte *f* insult.

insulter *vt* to insult, affront.

insupportable *adj* unbearable, intolerable; **~ment** *adv* unbearably, intolerably.

insurrection *f* insurrection, revolt.

intact *adj* intact.

intégral *adj* integral; uncut; complete; **~ement** *adv* integrally; in full.

intégralité *f* whole; entirety.

intégrer *vt* to integrate; **s'~** *vr* to become integrated; to fit in.

intégrité *f* integrity.

intellectuel *m* **-le** *f* intellectual; * *adj* intellectual, mental.

intelligence *f* intelligence; understanding.

intelligent *adj* intelligent, shrewd, bright.

intelligible *adj* intelligible.

intempéries *fpl* bad weather.

intendant *m* **-e** *f* bursar; steward, stewardess.

intense *adj* intense; severe.

intensément *adv* intensely.

intensif *adj* intensive.

intensifier *vt* to intensify; **s'~** *vr* to intensify.

intensité *f* intensity; severity.

intention *f* intention; purpose, intent.

interaction *f* interaction.

intercaler *vt* to intercalate; to interpolate.

intercepter *vt* to intercept.

interchangeable *adj* interchangeable.

interdiction *f* interdiction, prohibition, ban.

interdire *vt* to forbid, ban, prohibit.

interdit *adj* forbidden, prohibited; dumbfounded.

intéressant *adj* interesting; attractive, worthwhile.

intéresser *vt* to interest; to concern; *vr:* **s'~** **à** to be interested in.

intérêt *m* interest; significance, importance.

interférence *f* interference; conjunction.

intérieur *adj* interior, internal, inland; **à l'~** inside; within; **~ement** *adv* inwardly.

intérimaire *adj* interim; acting; temporary.

interligne *m* line space; interlining; lead.

interlocuteur *m* **-trice** *f* interlocutor, speaker.

intermède *m* interlude.

intermédiaire *adj* intermediate; intermediary.

interminable *adj* interminable; endless; **~ment** *adv* interminably, endlessly.

intermittent *adj* intermittent, sporadic.

international *adj* international.

interne *adj* internal; * *mf* boarder; house doctor.

interpeller *vt* to call out to; (*police*) to interpellate.

interphone *m* intercom, entryphone.

interposer *vt* to interpose; s'~ *vr* to intervene.

interprétation *f* interpretation, rendering.

interprète *mf* interpreter.

interpréter *vt* to interpret; to perform.

interrogation *f* interrogation, questioning; question.

interrogatoire *m* questioning; cross-examination.

interroger *vt* to question; to interrogate; s'~ *vr* to wonder.

interrompre *vt* to interrupt, break; s'~ *vr* to break off, interrupt o.s.

interrupteur *m* switch.

interruption *f* interruption, break.

intervalle *m* interval; space, distance.

intervenir *vi* to intervene; to take part in.

intervention *f* intervention; operation.

intestinal *adj* intestinal

intestin *m* intestine.

intime *adj* intimate; private; ~ment *adv* intimately; * *mf* close friend.

intimider *vt* to intimidate.

intimité *f* intimacy; privacy.

intituler *vt* to call, entitle; s'~ *vr* to be called; to call o.s.

intolérable *adj* intolerable.

intolérance *f* intolerance.

intolérant *adj* intolerant.

intonation *f* intonation.

intoxication *f* poisoning; indoctrination.

intransigeant *adj* intransigent, uncompromising.

intransitif *adj* intransitive.

intrépide *adj* intrepid, fearless; ~ment *adv* intrepidly.

intrigant *adj* scheming.

introduction *f* introduction; launching; (*jur*) institution.

introduire *vt* to introduce, insert; to present; s'~ *vr* to find one's way in; to be introduced.

introuvable   *adj* undiscoverable; not to be found.

introverti *m* **-e** *f* introvert; *
adj introverted.

intrus *m* **-e** *f* intruder; * *adj*
intruding, intrusive.

intuitif *adj* intuitive.

intuition *f* intuition.

inutile *adj* useless; unavail-
ing; pointless; ~**ment** *adv*
uselessly, needlessly.

inutilisable *adj* unusable.

invalide *adj* disabled; (*jur*)
invalid.

invariable *adj* invariable; un-
varying; ~**ment** *adv* invariably.

invasion *f* invasion.

inventaire *m* inventory;
stocklist.

inventer *vt* to invent; to devise; to make up.

inventeur *m* **-trice** *f* inventor.

invention *f* invention; inven-
tiveness.

inverse *adj* opposite; * *m* opposite, reverse.

inverser *vt* to reverse, invert.

inversion *f* inversion; reversal.

investir *vt* to invest; to surround.

investissement *m* investment;
investing.

invincible *adj* invincible, indomitable.

invisible *adj* invisible; unseen.

invitation *f* invitation.

invité *m* **-e** *f* guest.

inviter *vt* to invite, ask.

involontaire *adj* involuntary;
unintentional; ~**ment** *adv*
involuntarily.

invoquer *vt* to invoke; to call
up; to plead.

invraisemblable *adj* unlikely,
improbable; ~**ment** *adv*
improbably.

invulnérable *adj* invulnerable.

iode *m* iodine.

ion *m* ion.

iris *m* iris.

Irlandais *m* Irishman, **-e** *f*
Irishwoman

irlandais *adj* Irish.

Irlande *f* Ireland.

ironie *f* irony.

ironique *adj* ironic; ~**ment**
adv ironically.

irradiation *f* irradiation; radiation.

irrationnel *adj* irrational.

irrécupérable *adj* irretrievable.

irréel *adj* unreal.

irréfléchi *adj* unconsidered;
hasty.

irrégularité *f* irregularity; variation; unevenness.

irrégulier *adj* irregular; varying; uneven.

irrégulièrement *adv* irregularly; unevenly.

irrémédiable *adj* irreparable; incurable; **~ment** *adv* irreparably.

irremplaçable *adj* irreplaceable.

irréparable *adj* irreparable; irretrievable; **~ment** *adv* irreparably.

irrésistible *adj* irresistible; **~ment** *adv* irresistibly.

irresponsable *adj* irresponsible

irréversible *adj* irreversible; **~ment** *adv* irreversibly.

irrigation *f* irrigation.

irriguer *vt* to irrigate.

irriter *vt* to irritate; to provoke.

irruption *f* irruption.

Islam *m* Islam.

isolement *m* loneliness; isolation; insulation.

isoler *vt* to isolate; to insulate; **s'~** *vr* to cut o.s. off.

issu *adj* descended from; stemming from.

issue *f* outlet; solution; outcome.

ivoire *m* ivory.

ivre *adj* drunk, inebriated.

ivresse *f* drunkenness.

ivrogne *mf* drunkard.

J

jachère *f* fallow; leaving land lying fallow.

jade *m* jade.

jadis *adv* formerly, long ago.

jaguar *m* jaguar.

jaillir *vi* to spout, gush; to spring.

jalon *m* staff; landmark, milestone.

jalonner *vt* to mark out.

jalousie *f* jealousy, envy.

jaloux *m* **-ouse** *f* jealous person; * *adj* jealous, envious.

jamais *adv* never, not ever; à ~ for ever.

jambe *f* leg.

jambon *m* ham.

janvier *m* January.

jardin *m* garden.

jardinage *m* gardening.

jardiner *vi* to garden.

jardinier *m* **-ière** *f* gardener.

jargon *m* jargon, slang; gibberish.

jarret *m* hock; (*zool*) hollow of the knee.

jaser *vi* to chatter; to twitter; to babble.

jasmin *m* jasmine.

jauge *f* gauge; capacity; tonnage.

jauger *vt* to gauge the capacity of; to size up.

jaunâtre *adj* yellowish.

jaune *adj* yellow; * *m* yellow.

jaunir *vi* to yellow, turn yellow; * *vt* to make yellow.

jaunisse *f* jaundice.

jazz *m* jazz.

je, j' *pn* I.

jésuite *m* Jesuit.

jet *m* jet, spurt; throwing.

jetable *adj* disposable.

jetée *f* pier.

jeter *vt* to throw; to discard; to give out; **se ~** *vr* to throw o.s.; to rush at.

jeton *m* token; counter.

jeu *m* play; game; gambling; ~ **de jambes** footwork; ~ **de mots** pun, play on words;

cacher son ~ to conceal one's intentions.

jeudi *m* Thursday.

jeun *adv*: à ~ on an empty stomach.

jeune *adj* young; junior; new; youthful; * *m* youth, young man; *f* young girl.

jeûne *m* fast.

jeûner *vi* to fast.

jeunesse *f* youth, youthfulness.

joaillerie *f* jewellery.

joaillier *m* -ière *f* jeweller.

joie *f* joy, happiness; pleasure.

joindre *vt* to join, link; to attach; se ~ *vr* to join, join in.

joint *m* joint; join.

jointure *f* (*anat*) joint.

joli *adj* pretty; good, handsome; ~ment *adv* nicely, attractively.

jonc *m* rush; cane.

joncher *vt* to strew with.

jonction *f* junction. ·

jongler *vi* to juggle.

jongleur *m* -euse *f* juggler.

jonquille *f* daffodil, jonquil.

joue *f* cheek

jouer *vi* to play; to gamble; to act.

jouet *m* toy.

joueur *m* -euse *f* player; gambler.

joufflu *adj* chubby; round-faced.

joug *m* yoke.

jouir *vi* to enjoy; to delight in.

jouissance *f* enjoyment; use.

jour *m* day; daylight; tous les ~s every day; à ~ up to date; vivre au ~ le ~ to live from day to day; ~ férié public holiday; mise à ~ updating; update; du ~ au lendemain overnight.

journal *m* newspaper; bulletin, journal; ~ de bord logbook; ~ télévisé television news.

journalisme *m* journalism.

journaliste *mf* journalist.

journée *f* day; day's work.

jovial *adj* jovial, jolly.

jovialité *f* joviality.

joyau *m* jewel, gem.

joyeusement *adv* joyfully, cheerfully.

joyeux *adj* joyful, cheerful.

jubiler *vi* to be jubilant, exult.

judaïsme *m* Judaism.

judiciaire *adj* judicial, legal.

judicieusement *adv* judiciously.

judicieux *adj* judicious.

judo *m* judo

judoka *mf* judoka.

juge *m* judge.

jugement *m* judgment; sentence; opinion.

juger *vt* to judge; to decide; to consider.

juif *m* Jew; Jewish; **juive** *f* Jewess; * *adj* Jewish.

juillet *m* July.

juin *m* June.

jumeau *m* **-elle** *f* twin; * *adj* twin; double.

jumelage *m* twinning.

jumelé *adj* twinned, twin.

jumelle(s) *f(pl)* binoculars.

jument *f* mare.

jungle *f* jungle.

jupe *f* skirt.

jurer *vt* to swear, pledge.

juridiction *f* jurisdiction; court of law.

juridique *adj* legal, juridical; **~ment** *adv* juridically, legally.

jurisprudence *f* case law, jurisprudence.

juriste *m* lawyer; jurist.

juron *m* oath, curse.

jury *m* jury; board of examiners.

jus *m* juice.

jusque, jusqu' *prép* to, as far as; until.

justaucorps *m* jerkin; leotard.

juste *adj* just, fair; exact; sound; **~ment** *adv* exactly, precisely.

justesse *f* accuracy; aptness; soundness.

justice *f* justice, fairness.

justicier *m* **-ière** *f* justiciary; dispenser of justice.

justificatif *adj* supporting, justificatory.

justification *f* justification; proof.

justifier *vt* to justify, prove; **se ~** *vr* to justify o.s.

jute *m* jute.

juteux *adj* juicy; lucrative.

juvénile *adj* young, youthful.

juxtaposer *vt* to juxtapose.

juxtaposition *f* juxtaposition.

K

kaki *adj* khaki.

kaléidoscope *m* kaleidoscope.

kangourou *m* kangaroo.

karaté *m* karate.

kayac, kayak *m* kayak.

képi *m* kepi.

kermesse *f* fair; bazaar.

kérosène *m* kerosene, aviation fuel.

kidnapper *vt* to kidnap, abduct.

kidnappeur *m* -euse *f* kidnapper.

kilogramme *m* kilogram.

kilohertz *m* kilohertz.

kilométrage *m* total kilome-
tres travelled (mileage).

kilomètre *m* kilometre.

kimono *m* kimono.

kinésithérapeute *mf* physi-
otherapist.

kiosque *m* kiosk, stall.

kiwi *m* kiwi, Chinese gooseberry.

klaxon *m* horn.

klaxonner *vi* to sound one's
horn.

kleptomane *mf* kleptomaniac.

kleptomanie *f* kleptomania.

koala *m* koala.

kyste *m* cyst.

L

la *art pn: see* **le.**

là *adv* there; over there; then; **par ~** that way; **~-dedans** inside, in there; **~-dessous** underneath, under there; **~-dessus** on that; thereupon; **~-haut** up there, up on top; **celui-~** that one.

label *m* label; seal.

labeur *m* labour, toil.

laboratoire *m* laboratory.

laborieux *adj* laborious, toilsome.

labourer *vt* to plough; to dig over; to rip open.

labyrinthe *m* labyrinth.

lac *m* lake.

lacer *vt* to lace up; to tie up.

lacérer *vt* to lacerate; to tear.

lacet *m* lace.

lâche *adj* slack; loose; lax; cowardly; **~ment** *adv* loosely; in a cowardly manner; * *mf* coward.

lâcher *vt* to loosen; to release.

lâcheté *f* cowardice; meanness.

laconique *adj* laconic; **~ment** *adv* laconically.

lacté *adj* milky, lacteal.

lactique *adj* lactic.

lacune *f* lacuna; gap.

lagon *m* lagoon.

lagune *f* lagoon.

laïc *m* layman, **laïque** *f* laywoman; * **laïque** *adj* lay, civil.

laid *adj* ugly, unsightly.

laideur *f* ugliness, unsightliness.

lainage *m* woollen article.

laine *f* wool.

laisse *f* leash, string, lead.

laisser *vt* to leave; to let; **~ tomber** to drop; **se ~ aller** to let o.s. go.

laisser-passer *m invar* pass, permit.

lait *m* milk

laitage *m* milk; milk products.

laiton *m* brass.

laitue *f* lettuce.

lama *m* (*zool*) llama; lama.

lambeau *m* shred; tatter.

lambris *m* plastering; panelling.

lame *f* blade; strip; metal plate.

lamelle *f* slide; small strip.

lamentable *adj* lamentable, distressing; **~ment** *adv* lamentably.

lamentation *f* lamentation; wailing.

lamenter (se) *vr* to lament, bewail.

laminer *vt* to laminate.

lampadaire *m* standard-lamp; street lamp.

lampe *f* lamp, light; bulb.

lance *f* lance, spear.

lance-flammes *m invar* flamethrower.

lancement *m* launching; starting up; throwing.

lance-pierres *m invar* catapult.

lancer *vt* to throw; to launch; **se ~** *vr* to leap, jump; to embark on.

lancinant *adj* nagging; haunting.

lande *f* moor.

langage *m* language, speech.

langoureux *adj* languid, languorous.

langouste *f* spiny lobster.

langoustine *f* Dublin bay prawn.

langue *f* tongue; language.

languette *f* tongue; tongue-like strip.

langueur *f* languor.

languir *vi* to languish; to linger.

lanière *f* thong; lash.

lanoline *f* lanolin.

lanterne *f* lantern; lamp.

lapin *m* **-e** *f* rabbit.

lapsus *m* slip, mistake.

laque *f* hairspray; lacquer; * *m* lacquer ware.

lard *m* fat; bacon.

lardon *m* bacon cube.

large *adj* wide; generous; lax; great; **~ment** *adv* widely; greatly.

largeur *f* width, breadth.

larguer *vt* to loose, release; cast off.

larme *f* tear.

larmoyant *adj* tearful, weeping.

larve *f* larva, grub.

laryngite *f* laryngitis.

larynx *m* larynx.

las *adj*, *f* **-se** weary, tired.

lasagne *f* lasagne.

laser *m* laser.

lasser *vt* to tire; **se ~** *vr* to grow tired.

lassitude *f* tiredness, weariness.

latent *adj* latent.

latéral *adj* lateral, side; **~ement** *adv* laterally.

latex *m* latex.

latin *adj* Latin; * *m* Latin.

latitude *f* latitude; margin.

latte *f* lath.

lauréat *m* **-e** *f* prize winner.

laurier *m* bay-tree, laurel.

lavabo *m* washbasin.

lavage *m* washing; bathing.

lavande *f* lavender.

lave *f* lava.

lavement *m* enema.

laver *vt* to wash; to cleanse; **se ~** *vr* to wash o.s.

laverie *f* laundry.

lave-vaisselle *m invar* dishwasher.

laxatif *adj* laxative; * *m* laxative.

laxisme *m* laxness.

layette *f* baby clothes.

le *art*, *f* **la**, *devant voyelle* **l'**, *pl* **les** the; * *pn* him, her, them.

lécher *vt* to lick.

leçon *f* lesson; reading; class.

lecteur *m* **-trice** *f* reader.

lecture *f* reading; perusal.

légal *adj* legal, lawful; **~ement** *adv* legally.

légaliser *vt* to legalize.

légalité *f* legality, lawfulness.

légendaire *adj* legendary.

légende *f* legend; inscription.

léger *adj* light; slight; faint; inconsiderate.

légèrement *adv* lightly; thoughtlessly.

légèreté *f* lightness; nimbleness; thoughtlessness.

légion *f* legion.

législatif *adj* legislative; * *m* legislature.

législation *f* legislation, laws.

légitime *adj* legitimate, lawful; **~ment** *adv* legitimately.

légitimité *f* legitimacy.

legs *m* legacy, bequest.

léguer *vt* to bequeath; (*jur*) to devise.

légume *m* vegetable.

lendemain *m* next day, day after.

lent *adj* slow; tardy; sluggish; **~ement** *adv* slowly.

lente *f* (*zool*) nit.

lenteur *f* slowness.

lentille *f* lentil; lens.

léopard *m* leopard.

lèpre *f* leprosy.

lépreux *m* **-euse** *f* leper; * *adj* leprous.

lequel *pn*, *f* **laquelle**, *pl* **lesquels**, **lesquelles** who, whom, which.

lesbienne *f* lesbian.

léser *vt* to wrong; to damage.

lésion *f* wrong; lesion, wound.

lessive *f* washing powder.

leste *adj* nimble, agile; ~**ment** *adv* nimbly.

lester *vt* to fill; to ballast.

léthargie *f* lethargy.

léthargique *adj* lethargic.

lettre *f* letter, note; literature; **en toutes** ~**s** in black and white; **suivre à la** ~ to carry out to the letter; **avant la** ~ in advance, premature.

leucémie *f* leukaemia.

leucocyte *m* leucocyte.

leur *pn* them; **le** ~, **la** ~, **les** ~**s** theirs.

leurrer *vt* to deceive; to lure; **se** ~ *vr* to delude o.s.

levain *m* leaven.

lever *vt* to lift, raise; to levy; **se** ~ *vr* to get up; * *m* rising; getting up.

levier *m* lever.

lèvre *f* lip.

lévrier *m* greyhound.

levure *f* yeast.

lexique *m* vocabulary, lexis.

lézard *m* lizard.

lézarde *f* crack.

liaison *f* affair; connection; liaison, link.

liasse *f* bundle.

libellule *f* dragonfly.

libéral *adj* liberal; ~**ement** *adv* liberally; * *m* liberal.

libéraliser *vt* to liberalize.

libéralisme *m* liberalism.

libéralité *f* liberality, generosity.

libération *f* release, liberation.

libérer *vt* to release; to liberate; **se** ~ *vr* to free o.s.

liberté *f* liberty, freedom.

libido *f* libido.

libraire *mf* bookseller.

librairie *f* bookshop; bookselling.

libre *adj* free; independent; ~**ment** *adv* freely.

licence *f* degree; permit; licentiousness.

licenciement *m* redundancy; dismissal.

licencier *vt* to make redundant; to dismiss.

lichen *m* lichen.

licorne *f* unicorn.

lie *f* dregs, sediment.

liège *m* cork.

lien *m* bond; link, connection; tie.

lier *vt* to bind; to link; **se ~** *vr*: **se ~ avec** to make friends.

lierre *m* ivy.

lieu *m* place, position; cause; occasion; **avoir ~** to take place; **en premier ~** in the first place; **au ~ de** instead of.

lieutenant *m* (*mil*) lieutenant.

lièvre *m* hare.

ligament *m* ligament

ligature *f* ligature; tying up.

ligne *f* line; row; range.

lignée *f* lineage; offspring.

lignite *m* lignite.

ligoter *vt* to bind hand and foot.

ligue *f* league.

lilas *m* lilac; * *adj* lilac.

limace *f* slug.

limande *f* dab.

lime *f* file.

limer *vt* to file down.

limitation *f* limitation, restriction.

limite *f* boundary, limit; **à la ~** ultimately.

limiter *vt* to limit, restrict; **se ~** *vr* to limit o.s. to.

limitrophe *adj* border.

limon *m* silt.

limonade *f* lemonade.

limpide *adj* limpid, clear.

limpidité *f* limpidity, clearness.

lin *m* flax; linen.

linceul *m* shroud.

linéaire *adj* linear.

linge *m* linen; washing.

lingerie *f* linen room; underwear, lingerie.

lingot *m* ingot.

linguiste *mf* linguist.

linguistique *f* linguistics; * *adj* linguistic.

lion *m* lion, **lionne** *f* lioness.

lionceau *m* lion cub.

lipide *m* lipid.

liquéfier *vt* to liquefy; **se ~** *vr* to liquefy.

liqueur *f* liqueur; liquid.

liquidation *f* liquidation; winding up; elimination.

liquide *m* liquid.

liquider *vt* to settle; to wind up; to eliminate

lire *vt* to read.

lis *m* lily.

lisible *adj* legible; readable; **~ment** *adv* legibly.

lisière *f* edge; border; outskirts.

lisse *adj* smooth, glossy.

lisser *vt* to smooth, gloss.

liste *f* list; (*jur*) schedule.

lit *m* bed; layer.

litanie *f* litany.

literie *f* bedding.

lithographie *f* lithography.

litière *f* litter.

litige *m* lawsuit; dispute.

litigieux *adj* litigious.

litre *m* litre.

littéraire *adj* literary.

littéral *adj* literal; ~ement *adv* literally.

littérature *f* literature; writing.

littoral *m* coast; * *adj* coastal, littoral.

liturgie *f* liturgy.

livide *adj* livid, pale.

livraison *f* delivery; number, issue.

livre *m* book; * *f* pound (weight, currency).

livrer *vt* to deliver, hand over; to give away; **se ~** *vr* to abandon o.s.

livret *m* (*mus*) libretto; booklet.

livreur *m* delivery man, -euse *f* delivery woman.

lobe *m* lobe.

lobotomie *f* lobotomy.

local *adj* local; ~ement *adv* locally.

localisation *f* localization.

localiser *vt* to localize.

localité *f* locality; town.

locataire *mf* tenant; lodger.

location *f* renting; lease, leasing.

locomotion *f* locomotion.

locomotive *f* locomotive, engine; dynamo.

locution *f* locution, idiom.

logarithme *m* logarithm.

loge *f* lodge; dressing room; box.

logement *m* housing; accommodation.

loger *vt* to accommodate; to billet; * *vi* to live in.

logiciel *m* software.

logique *f* logic; * *adj* logical; ~ment *adv* logically.

logistique *f* logistics.

logo *m* logo.

loi *f* law; act, statute; rule.

loin *adv* far, a long way; * *m*: distance; background **au ~** in the distance; **de ~** from a distance.

lointain *adj* distant, remote; * *m* distance; background.

loir *m* dormouse.

loisir *m* leisure, spare time.

lombaire *adj* lumbar; * *f* lumbar vertebra.

lombric *m* earthworm.

long *adj, f* -**ue** long, lengthy; ~**uement** *adv* at length.

longer *vt* to border; to walk along.

longévité *f* longevity.

longitude *f* longitude.

longtemps *adv* for a long time.

longueur *f* length.

longue-vue *f* telescope.

loquace *adj* loquacious, talkative.

loque *f* rag.

loquet *m* latch; clasp.

lorgner *vt* to leer, ogle.

lors *adv* then; ~ **de** at the time of; **dès** ~ from that time.

lorsque *conj* when.

losange *m* lozenge, diamond.

lot *m* prize; lot; portion.

loterie *f* lottery; raffle.

lotion *f* lotion.

lotissement *m* allotment; site, housing development.

lotus *m* lotus.

louange *f* praise, commendation.

louche *adj* dubious; suspicious, shady.

loucher *vi* to squint; to ogle.

louer *vt* to rent, lease; to book.

loup *m* wolf.

loupe *f* magnifying glass.

louper *vt* (*fam*) to botch, bungle; to flunk.

lourd *adj* heavy; sultry; unwieldy; ~**ement** *adv* heavily.

lourdeur *f* heaviness.

loutre *f* otter.

louve *f* she-wolf.

louveteau *m* wolf-cub.

loyal *adj* loyal, faithful; ~**ement** *adv* loyally.

loyauté *f* loyalty.

loyer *m* rent.

lubrifiant *m* lubricant; * *adj* lubricating.

lubrifier *vt* to lubricate.

lubrique *adj* lustful, lecherous; ~**ment** *adv* lustfully.

lucarne *f* skylight.

lucide *adj* lucid, clear; ~**ment** *adv* lucidly.

lucidité *f* lucidity, clearness.

lucratif *adj* lucrative.

ludique *adj* play.

lueur *f* glimmer, gleam; glimpse.

luge *f* sledge, toboggan.

lugubre *adj* lugubrious, gloomy; **~ment** *adv* lugubriously.

lui *pn* him, her, it; **c'est à ~** it is his; **~-même** himself, itself.

luire *vt* to shine, gleam.

luisant *adj* gleaming, shining.

lumbago *m* lumbago.

lumière *f* light; daylight; lamp; insight.

lumineux *adj* luminous; illuminated.

lunaire *adj* lunar, moon.

lunatique *adj* fantastical, whimsical, quirky.

lundi *m* Monday.

lune *f* moon.

lunette *f* telescope; **~s** glasses.

lustré *adj* glossy; shiny.

luth *m* lute.

luthérien *adj* Lutheran.

luthiste *mf* lutanist.

lutin *m* imp; goblin.

lutte *f* struggle; contest; strife.

lutter *vi* to struggle, fight.

lutteur *m* **-euse** *f* wrestler, fighter.

luxation *f* dislocation, luxation.

luxe *m* luxury, excess.

luxueusement *adv* luxuriously.

luxueux *adj* luxurious.

luxure *f* lust.

luxuriance *f* luxuriance.

luxuriant *adj* luxuriant.

luzerne *f* lucerne, alfalfa.

lycée *m* secondary school.

lycéen *m* secondary school boy, **-ne** *f* secondary school girl.

lymphatique *adj* lymphatic.

lymphe *f* lymph.

lymphocyte *m* lymphocyte.

lyncher *vt* to lynch.

lynx *m* lynx.

lyre *f* lyre.

lyrique *adj* lyric; **~ment** *adv* lyrically.

lyrisme *m* lyricism.

M

macabre *adj* macabre.

macadam *m* tarmac.

macaque *m* macaque.

macédoine *f* medley, hotch-potch; macedoine.

macérer *vt* to macerate; to mortify o.s.; * *vi* to macerate, steep.

mâche *f* corn-salad.

mâcher *vt* to chew.

machiavélique *adj* Machiavellian.

machin *m* (*fam*) gadget; thingamajig.

machinal *adj* mechanical, automatic; ~ement *adv* mechanically.

machination *f* machination, plot.

machine *f* machine; engine; apparatus.

machinerie *f* machinery, plant.

machiniste *m* machinist; driver; stagehand.

mâchoire *f* jaw.

maçon *m* builder, mason.

maçonnerie *f* masonry; building.

macrobiotique *adj* macrobiotic; * *f* macrobiotics

madame *f* Madam; Mrs; lady.

madeleine *f* madeleine.

mademoiselle *f* Miss; young lady.

magasin *m* shop, store; warehouse.

magazine *m* magazine.

mage *m* magus; seer.

magicien *m* -ne *f* magician.

magie *f* magic

magique *adj* magic; magical; ~ment *adv* magically.

magistral *adj* masterly; authoritative; ~ement *adv* in a masterly fashion.

magistrat *m* magistrate.

magistrature *f* magistracy; magistrature.

magnanime *adj* magnanimous; ~ment *adv* magnanimously.

magnanimité *f* magnanimity.

magnat *m* magnate.

magnésium *m* magnesium.

magnétique *adj* magnetic.

magnétiser *vt* to magnetize; to hypnotize.

magnétisme *m* magnetism; hypnotism.

magnétophone *m* tape recorder.

magnétoscope *m* video recorder; videotape.

magnifique *adj* magnificent; sumptuous; ~**ment** *adv* magnificently.

magnolia *m* magnolia.

magot *m* (*fam*) savings, hoard, nest egg.

magouille *f* (*fam*) fiddle, scam; scheming.

mai *m* May.

maigre *adj* thin; meagre, scarce; ~**ment** *adv* meagrely.

maigreur *f* thinness; meagreness; sparseness.

maigrir *vi* to get thinner; to waste away.

maille *f* stitch; mesh; link.

maillet *m* mallet.

maillon *m* link; shackle.

maillot *m* jersey; leotard.

main *f* hand; **avoir la ~** to have the lead; **passer la ~** to make way for sb.

main-d'œuvre *f* workforce.

maintenance *f* maintenance, servicing.

maintenant *adv* now; **à partir de ~** from now on.

maintenir *vt* to keep, maintain; preserve; **se ~** *vr* to persist; to hold one's own.

maintien *m* maintenance; preservation; keeping up.

maire *m* mayor, *f* mayoress.

mairie *f* mayoralty; town hall.

mais *conj* but.

maïs *m* maize; corn.

maison *f* house; home; building; premises.

maître *m* -**esse** *f* master; ruler; lord; proprietor.

maîtresse *f* mistress; teacher.

maîtrise *f* mastery; control; expertise.

maîtriser *vt* to control; to master; **se ~** *vr* to control o.s.

majesté *f* majesty, grandeur.

majestueusement *adv* majestically.

majestueux *adj* majestic.

majeur *adj* major; main; chief; superior; * *m* major *mf* adult.

majoration *f* increased charge; overestimation.

majordome *m* majordomo, butler.

majorer *vt* to increase, raise.

majorette *f* majorette.

majoritaire *adj* majority.

majorité *f* majority.

majuscule *f* capital letter.

mal *adv* wrong, badly; * *m* evil, wrong; harm; pain.

malachite *f* malachite.

malade *adj* sick, ill; diseased; * *mf* invalid, sick person.

maladie *f* illness; malady, complaint; disorder.

maladresse *f* clumsiness; awkwardness.

maladroit *adj* clumsy, awkward; ~ement *adv* clumsily.

malaise *m* uneasiness, discomfort; indisposition.

malchance *f* ill luck; misfortune; mishap.

malchanceux *adj* unlucky, unfortunate.

mâle *m* male; * *adj* male; manly, virile.

malédiction *f* malediction, curse.

maléfique *adj* hurtful; malignant; baleful.

malencontreux *adj* unfortunate, untoward.

malentendu *m* misunderstanding.

malfaisant *adj* malevolent; harmful; wicked.

malfaiteur *m* criminal; malefactor.

malgré *prép* in spite of; despite.

malheur *m* misfortune; calamity.

malheureusement *adv* unfortunately.

malheureux *adj* unfortunate; unlucky; unhappy.

malhonnête *adj* dishonest, crooked; uncivil; ~ment *adv* dishonestly.

malhonnêteté *f* dishonesty; incivility.

malice *f* malice, spite; mischievousness.

malicieux *adj* malicious, spiteful; mischievous.

malin *adj* shrewd, cunning, crafty; malignant.

malintentionné *adj* ill-disposed, spiteful.

malle *f* trunk.

malléable *adj* malleable.

malmener *vt* to ill-treat, maltreat.

malnutrition *f* malnutrition.

malsain *adj* unhealthy, unwholesome; immoral.

malt *m* malt.

maltraiter *vt* to abuse; to handle roughly.

malveillance *f* malevolence, spite.

malveillant *adj* malevolent, spiteful.

maman *f* mother, mummy, mum.

mamelle *f* breast; udder.

mamelon *m* nipple, teat.

mammifère *m* mammal.

manche *f* sleeve; game, round; * *m* handle, shaft.

manchot *m* **-e** *f* one-armed person; * *adj* one-armed; * *m* penguin.

mandarin *m* mandarin; Mandarin.

mandarine *f* tangerine.

mandat *m* mandate; money order; proxy.

mandataire *mf* proxy; representative.

mandibule *f* mandible, jaw.

mandoline *f* mandolin.

manège *m* roundabout, merry-go-round.

manette *f* lever, tap.

manganèse *m* manganese.

mangeable *adj* edible.

manger *vt* to eat; to consume.

mangeur *m* **-euse** *f* eater.

mangouste *f* mongoose.

mangue *f* mango.

maniable *adj* handy, workable, tractable; amenable.

maniaque *adj* eccentric; fussy.; * *mf* maniac; fusspot; fanatic.

manie *f* mania.

maniement *m* handling; management, use.

manier *vt* to handle; to manipulate.

manière *f* manner, way, style.

maniéré *adj* affected.

manifestation *f* demonstration; expression, manifestation.

manifeste *adj* manifest, evident, obvious; ~**ment** *adv* manifestly, obviously; * *m* manifesto.

manifester *vt* to display, make known; to demonstrate; se ~ *vr* to make o.s. known; to appear; to express o.s.

manigancer *vt* to contrive; to scheme.

manipulation *f* handling; manipulation.

manipuler *vt* to handle; to manipulate

manivelle *f* crank.

mannequin *m* model; dummy.

manœuvre *f* manoeuvre, operation; scheme; * *m* labourer.

manœuvrer *vt* to manoeuvre; to operate; * *vi* to manoeuvre, move.

manoir *m* manor.

manomètre *m* manometer.

manquant *adj* missing.

manque *m* lack, shortage; shortcoming, deficiency.

manquer *vt* to miss; to fail; to be absent.

mansarde *f* attic, garret.

manteau *m* coat; mantle, blanket; cloak.

manuel *m* manual, handbook; * *adj* manual; ~lement *adv* manually.

manufacture *f* factory; manufacture.

manufacturier *m* -ière *f* factory owner; manufacturer; * *adj* manufacturing.

manuscrit *m* manuscript; typescript; * *adj* handwritten.

manutention *f* handling.

mappemonde *f* map of the world.

maquereau *m* mackerel.

maquette *f* model; mock-up; dummy; sketch.

maquillage *m* make-up.

maquiller *vt* to make up; to fake; to fiddle; **se ~** *vr* to put make-up on.

marais *m* marsh, swamp.

marasme *m* stagnation; depression, slump.

marathon *m* marathon.

marbre *m* marble; marble statue.

marbré *adj* marbled; mottled, blotchy.

marbrier *m* marble-cutter; monumental mason.

marchand *m* -e *f* shopkeeper; dealer; merchant; * *adj* market, trade.

marchandage *m* bargaining, haggling.

marchander *vi* to bargain over, haggle.

marchandise *f* merchandise, commodity; goods.

marche *f* walk; journey; progress; movement; **mettre en ~** to start up; to turn on.

marché *m* market; transaction, contract.

marcher *vi* to walk, march; to progress; to work.

marcheur *m* **-euse** *f* walker, pedestrian.

mardi *m* Tuesday.

mare *f* pool, pond.

marécage *m* marsh, swamp.

maréchal *m* marshal.

marée *f* tide.

margarine *f* margarine.

marge *f* margin; latitude, freedom; mark-up.

marginal *adj* marginal.

marginaliser *vt* to marginalize.

marguerite *f* daisy.

mari *m* husband.

mariage *m* marriage.

marié *m* bridegroom; * *adj* married.

marier *vt* to marry; blend, harmonize; se ~ *vr* to get married.

marin *m* sailor.

marine *f* navy; seascape; marine.

mariner *vi* to marinate; to hang about; * *vt* to marinate.

marionnette *f* puppet; puppet show.

maritime *adj* maritime; seaboard.

marjolaine *f* marjoram.

marmelade *f* stewed fruit; marmalade.

marmite *f* pot.

marmonner *vt* to mumble, mutter.

marmotte *f* marmot.

maroquinerie *f* tannery; fine leather craft.

maroquinier *m* leather craftsman; dealer in fine leather.

marquant *adj* outstanding, vivid.

marque *f* mark, sign; brand; make.

marquer *vt* to mark; to note down; to score.

marquis *m* marquis, **-e** *f* marchioness.

marraine *f* godmother; sponsor.

marron *m* chestnut; brown; * *adj* brown.

marronnier *m* chestnut tree.

mars *m* March.

marsouin *m* porpoise.

marteau *m* hammer; knocker.

marteler *vt* to hammer; to beat.

martial *adj* martial, warlike.

martin-pêcheur *m* kingfisher.

martyr *m* **-e** *f* martyr; * *adj* martyred.

martyre *m* martyrdom.

martyriser *vt* to torture, martyrize.

mascarade *f* farce, mascarade.

masculin *adj* masculine.

masochisme *m* masochism.

masochiste *mf* masochist; * *adj* masochistic.

masque *m* mask; facade, front.

masquer *vt* to mask, conceal; to disguise.

massacre *m* massacre; slaughter.

massacrer *vt* to massacre, slaughter.

massage *m* massage.

masse *f* mass, heap; bulk; mob.

masser *vt* to mass, assemble; to massage.

masseur *m* masseur, **-euse** *f* masseuse.

massif *adj* massive, solid, heavy; * *m* massif; clump.

massivement *adv* en masse, massively, heavily.

massue *f* club.

mastic *m* mastic; cement; putty.

mastiquer *vt* to chew, masticate.

masturbation *f* masturbation.

masturber *vi* se ~ *vr* to masturbate.

mat *adj* matt, dull; dead, dull-sounding.

mât *m* mast; pole.

match *m* match; game.

matelas *m* mattress.

matelassé *adj* stuffed; padded, cushioned.

matelot *m* sailor; seaman.

mater *vt* to subdue; to control, curb; to spy on; to ogle.

matérialiser *vt* to embody; se ~ *vr* to materialize.

matériaux *mpl* material, materials.

matériel *adj* material, physical; practical; ~lement *adv* materially, practically.

maternel *adj* maternal, motherly; ~lement *adv* maternally.

maternité *f* motherhood; pregnancy; maternity hospital.

mathématicien *m* **-ne** *f* mathematician.

mathématique *adj* mathematical; ~ment *adv* mathematically; * *f* mathematics.

matière *f* material, matter; subject; ~ **première** raw material.

matin *m* morning; dawn.

matinal *adj* morning.

matinée *f* morning; matinée.

matraque *f* truncheon; cosh.

matrice *f* womb; mould; matrix.

matricule *m* reference number; ** f* roll, register.

matrimonial *adj* matrimonial, marriage.

maturation *f* maturing; maturation.

maturité *f* maturity; prime.

maudire *vt* to curse.

maudit *adj* cursed; blasted, damned.

maussade *adj* sulky, sullen; ~ment *adv* sulkily, sullenly.

mauvais *adj* bad; wicked; faulty; hurtful; poor.

mauve *adj* mauve; ** f* mallow.

maximal *adj* maximal.

maxime *f* maxim.

maximum *m* maximum.

mayonnaise *f* mayonnaise.

me, m' *pn* me; myself.

mécanicien *m* -ne *f* mechanic; engineer.

mécanique *f* mechanics; mechanical engineering; ** adj* mechanical; ~ment *adv* mechanically.

mécanisme *m* mechanism, working.

mécène *m* patron.

méchamment *adv* spitefully; wickedly.

méchanceté *f* spitefulness; wickedness; mischievousness.

méchant *adj* spiteful; wicked; mischievous.

mèche *f* wick, fuse; tuft.

méconnaissable *adj* unrecognizable.

méconnu *adj* unrecognized; misunderstood.

mécontent *adj* discontent, displeased.

mécontentement *m* discontent; displeasure.

médaille *f* medal; stain, mark.

médaillon *m* medallion; locket.

médecin *m* doctor, physician.

médecine *f* medicine

médiateur *m* -trice *f* mediator; arbitrator.

médiatique *adj* media.

médical *adj* medical; ~ement *adv* medically.

médicament *m* medicine, drug.

médicinal *adj* medicinal.

médiéval *adj* medieval.

médiocre *adj* mediocre; passable; indifferent; ~ment

adv indifferently; poorly.

médisant *adj* slanderous.

méditation *f* meditation.

méditer *vi* to meditate; * *vt* to contemplate, have in mind.

médium *m* medium.

méduse *f* jellyfish.

méfiance *f* distrust, mistrust.

méfiant *adj* distrustful, mistrustful.

méfier (se) *vr* to mistrust, distrust; to be suspicious.

mégalomane *adj* megalomaniac; * *mf* megalomaniac.

mégaphone *m* megaphone.

mégot *m* cigarette-end, stub.

meilleur *adj* better, preferable; le ~, la ~e the best.

mélancolie *f* melancholy, gloom.

mélancolique *adj* melancholy; melancholic; ~ment *adv* melancholically.

mélange *m* mixing, blending; mixture.

mélanger *vt* to mix, blend; to muddle.

mêlée *f* melee, fray; scrum.

mêler *vt* to mix; to combine; se ~ *vr* to mix, mingle; se ~ à to join; se ~ de to meddle in.

mélisse *f* lemon balm.

mélodie *f* melody, tune.

mélodieusement *adv* melodiously, tunefully.

mélodieux *adj* melodious, tuneful.

mélomane *mf* music lover.

melon *m* melon.

membrane *f* membrane.

membre *m* member; limb.

même *adv* even; **tout de ~** nevertheless, all the same; * *adj* same, identical; * *pn*: le ~, la ~, les ~s the same, the same ones.

mémoire *f* memory; * *m* memorandum, report.

mémorable *adj* memorable.

mémoriser *vt* to memorize.

menaçant *adj* menacing, threatening.

menace *f* threat; intimidation; danger.

menacer *vt* to threaten, menace; to impend.

ménage *m* housework, housekeeping; household.

ménager *vt* to treat with caution; to manage; to arrange.; se ~ *vr* to take care of o.s.; * *adj* household, domestic.

ménagère *f* housewife.

ménagerie *f* menagerie.

mendiant *m* -e *f* beggar.

mendier *vt* to beg; to implore.

mener *vt* to lead, guide; to steer; to manage.

meneur *m* -euse *f* leader; agitator.

menhir *m* menhir, standing stone.

méningite *f* meningitis.

ménopause *f* menopause.

menottes *fpl* handcuffs.

mensonge *m* lie, falsehood; error, illusion.

menstruation *f* menstruation.

mensuel *adj* monthly.

mental *adj* mental; ~ement *adv* mentally.

mentalité *f* mentality.

menteur *m* -euse *f* liar; * *adj* lying, deceitful.

menthe *f* mint.

menthol *m* menthol.

mention *f* mention; comment; grade.

mentionner *vt* to mention.

mentir *vi* to lie; to be deceptive.

menton *m* chin.

menu *m* menu; meal; * *adj* slender, thin; petty, minor.

menuiserie *f* joinery, carpentry.

menuisier *m* joiner, carpenter.

mépris *m* contempt, scorn.

méprisant *adj* contemptuous, scornful.

mépriser *vt* to scorn, despise.

mer *f* sea; tide.

mercenaire *m* mercenary.

mercerie *f* haberdashery.

merci *m* thank you; * *f* mercy; **sans ~** merciless; **être à la ~ de** to be at the mercy of.

mercredi *m* Wednesday.

mercure *m* mercury.

mère *f* mother.

méridien *m* meridian; midday.

méridional *adj* southern.

meringue *f* meringue.

merisier *m* wild cherry.

mérite *m* merit, worth; quality.

mériter *vt* to deserve, merit.

merlan *m* whiting.

merle *m* blackbird.

merveille *f* marvel, wonder.

merveilleusement *adv* marvellously, wonderfully.

merveilleux *adj* marvellous, wonderful.

mésange *f* (*orn*) tit.

mésentente *f* misunderstanding.

mesquin *adj* mean, niggardly; petty; **~ement** *adv* meanly, pettily.

message *m* message.

messager *m* **-ère** *f* messenger.

messagerie *f* parcels office, parcels service.

messe *f* mass.

messie *m* messiah.

mesure *f* measure; gauge; measurement; moderation; step; **au fur et à ~** as; one by one; **sans commune ~ avec** there is no possible comparison with; **dans la mesure où** insofar as; **en ~** in time.

mesurer *vt* to measure; to assess; to limit; **se ~** *vr* to try one's strength; **se ~ à** to pit o.s. against, measure one's strength against.

métabolisme *m* metabolism.

métal *m* metal.

métallique *adj* metallic.

métallisé *adj* metallic, metallized.

métallurgie *f* metallurgy.

métallurgiste *m* steelworker, metalworker.

métamorphose *f* metamorphosis.

métamorphoser *vt* to transform, metamorphose; **se ~** *vr* to be metamorphosed.

métaphore *f* metaphor.

métaphorique *adj* metaphorical; **~ment** *adv* metaphorically.

métaphysique *adj* metaphysical; * *f* metaphysics.

météore *m* meteor.

météorite *m/f* meteorite.

météorologue, météorologiste *mf* meteorologist.

méthane *m* methane.

méthode *f* method, way.

méthodique *adj* methodical; **~ment** *adv* methodically.

méthylène *m* methyl alcohol; methylene.

méticuleusement *adv* meticulously.

méticuleux *adj* meticulous.

métier *m* job; occupation; **~ à tricoter** knitting machine; **~ à tisser** weaving loom.

métis *m* **-se** *f* half-caste; hybrid; mongrel; * *adj* half-caste; hybrid, mongrel.

mètre *m* metre.

métro *m* underground, metro.

métronome *m* metronome.

métropole *f* metropolis.

métropolitain *adj* metropolitan; underground.

mets *m* dish.

metteur en scène *m* (*cin*) director.

mettre *vt* to put, place; to put on; ~ **en marche** to start up; **se ~** *vr* to place o.s.; to sit down; **se ~ à** to begin to; **se ~ en route** to start off.

meuble *m* piece of furniture.

meubler *vt* to furnish.

meule *f* millstone; grindstone.

meurtrier *m* murderer, -ière *f* murderess.

meurtrir *vt* to bruise.

meute *f* pack.

mezzanine *f* mezzanine.

mi- *adj* half; **à ~chemin** halfway; **~clos** half-closed; **à ~jambe** up to the knees; **à ~voix** in a low voice.

miauler *vi* to mew.

miche *f* round loaf.

microbe *m* germ, microbe.

microbien *adj* microbial, microbic.

microclimat *m* microclimate.

microfilm *m* microfilm.

micro-informatique *f* microcomputing.

micro-onde *f* microwave; * *m* **micro-ondes** microwave oven.

micro-ordinateur *m* microcomputer.

microphone *m* microphone.

microprocesseur *m* microprocessor.

microscope *m* microscope.

microscopique *adj* microscopic.

midi *m* midday, noon.

mie *f* crumb, soft part of a loaf.

miel *m* honey.

mien *pn*, *f* **mienne**: **le ~, la mienne, les ~s, les miennes** mine, my own.

miette *f* crumb; remnant; morsel.

mieux *m* improvement; **le ~** the best; **de ~ en ~** better and better.

mignon *adj* sweet, pretty.

migraine *f* headache; migraine.

migrateur *m* migrant.

migration *f* migration.

mijoter *vi* to simmer, be brewing; * *vt* to simmer; to scheme, plot.

milice *f* militia.

milieu *m* middle, centre; medium; environment.

militaire *m* serviceman; * *adj* military, army.

militant *m* -e *f* militant; * *adj* militant.

militer *vi* to militate; to be a militant.

mille *m* one thousand; * *adj* one thousand.

millénaire *m* millennium, a thousand years; thousandth anniversary; * *adj* thousand-year-old; millennial.

mille-pattes *m* millipede, centipede.

millésime *m* year, date; vintage.

millet *m* millet.

milliard *m* thousand million; billion.

milliardaire *adj* worth (many) millions; * *mf* multimillionaire.

milliardième *adj* thousand millionth; * *m* thousand millionth.

millième *adj* thousandth; * *m* thousandth.

millier *m* thousand.

milligramme *m* milligram.

millilitre *m* millilitre.

millimètre *m* millimetre.

million *m* million.

millionième *adj* millionth; * *m* millionth.

millionnaire *adj* millionaire; worth millions; * *mf* millionaire.

mime *m* mime; * *mf* mimic.

mimer *vt* to mime; to mimic, imitate.

mimétisme *m* mimicry; mimetism.

mimosa *m* mimosa.

minable *adj* seedy, shabby; ~**ment** *adv* shabbily.

mince *adj* thin, slender; meagre, trivial.

mincir *vi* to get slimmer, get thinner.

mine *f* expression; appearance; mine; **avoir bonne** ~ to look good.

minerai *m* ore.

minéral *adj* mineral; inorganic; * *m* mineral.

minéralogique *adj* mineralogical.

mineur *m* -e *f* minor; * *adj* minor; * *m* miner.

miniature *f* miniature.

mini-jupe *f* miniskirt.

minimal *adj* minimal, minimum.

minime *adj* minor, minimal.

minimum *m* minimum.

ministère *m* ministry; agency.

ministériel *adj* ministerial.

ministre *m* minister; clergyman.

minoritaire *adj* minority.

minorité *f* minority.

minuit *m* midnight.

minuscule *adj* minuscule, tiny, minute.

minute *f* minute, moment.

minuterie *f* time switch; regulator.

minutieux *adj* meticulous.

mirabelle *f* mirabelle.

miracle *m* miracle, wonder.

miraculeux *adj* miraculous.

mirage *m* mirage.

miroir *m* mirror, reflection.

misanthrope *mf* misanthrope; misanthropist; * *adj* misanthropic.

mise *f* putting, placing; stake; deposit; investment; ~ en scène production, staging; ~ en liberté release; ~ en ordre ordering, arrangement; ~ en œuvre implementation.

miser *vt* to stake, to bet.

misérable *adj* miserable; destitute; pitiable; ~ment *adv* miserably.

misère *f* misery; poverty; destitution.

miséricorde *f* mercy, forgiveness.

misogyne *mf* misogynist; * *adj* misogynous.

missile *m* missile.

mission *f* mission, assignment.

missionnaire *m* missionary.

mi-temps *f* half-time; half.

miteux *adj* dingy, shabby, poverty-stricken.

mitigé *adj* mitigated; lukewarm.

mitoyen *adj* common; semi-detached.

mitrailler *vt* to machine-gun.

mitraillette *f* submachine gun.

mitrailleuse *f* machine gun.

mixer *vt* to mix; to blend.

mixte *adj* mixed; joint; combined.

mixture *f* mixture, concoction.

mobile *adj* moving; movable; mobile; nimble; * *m* motive; moving body.

mobilier *m* furniture; * *adj* movable; personal; transferable.

mobilisation *f* mobilization, calling up.

mobilité *f* mobility.

mobylette f moped.

moche adj (fam) ugly, lousy.

mode f fashion; custom; * m form, mode; way.

modèle m model; pattern; design; example.

modeler vt to model; to shape; se ~ vr: se ~ sur to model o.s. on.

modem m modem.

modération f moderation; diminution.

modéré adj moderate; ~ment adv in moderation.

modérer vt moderate, restrained; se ~ vr to control o.s., keep one's temper.

moderne adj modern, up-to-date.

moderniser vt to modernize.

modeste adj modest, simple; unassuming; ~ment adv modestly.

modestie f modesty.

modification f modification.

modifier vt to modify, alter; se ~ vr to be modified.

modulation f modulation; adjustment.

moelle f marrow; core.

moelleux adj mellow; soft; smooth.

mœurs fpl morals; customs.

moi pn me, I; **c'est à** ~ it is mine, it is my turn; ~-**même** myself.

mois m month.

moisi adj mouldy, mildewed; * m mould.

moisir vi to go mouldy.

moisissure f mould, mildew.

moisson f harvest.

moissonner vt to reap, harvest.

moite adj moist, damp.

moitié f half.

molaire f molar.

molécule f molecule.

mollement adv softly; gently.

mollusque m mollusc.

moment m moment, instant, while; time; opportunity.

momentané adj momentary; brief; ~ment adv momentarily.

momie f mummy.

mon pn, f **ma**, pl **mes** my, my own.

monarchie f monarchy.

monastère m monastery.

mondain adj worldly, mundane; society, fashionable.

monde m world, earth; society, company; **il y a du** ~ there are some people there.

mondial *adj* world, world-wide; ~**ement** *adv* the world over.

monétaire *adj* monetary.

moniteur *m* -**trice** *f* instructor, coach; supervisor.

monnaie *f* currency; coin; change.

monoculture *f* single-crop farming, monoculture.

monologue *m* monologue.

monopole *f* monopoly.

monopoliser *vt* to monopolize.

monotone *adj* monotonous.

monotonie *f* monotony, sameness.

monseigneur *m* my lord, your grace.

monsieur *m* sir, gentleman, Mr, *pl* **messieurs** gentlemen, Messrs.

monstre *m* monster.

monstrueux *adj* monstrous.

mont *m* mountain; mount.

montage *m* assembly; setting up; editing.

montagnard *m* -**e** *f* mountain dweller.

montagne *f* mountain.

montagneux *adj* mountainous.

montant *m* upright; total, to-tal sum; * *adj* upward, ris-ing; upstream.

montée *f* climb, climbing; as-cent; rise.

monter *vi* to go up, ascend; get into (vehicle); * *vt* to go up; to carry/bring up.

monteur *m* -**euse** *f* fitter; edi-tor.

montre *f* watch.

montrer *vt* to show, point to; to prove; **se ~** *vr* to appear; to prove o.s.

monture *f* mount; setting; frame.

monument *m* monument, memorial.

monumental *adj* monumen-tal, colossal.

moquer (se) *vr* to make fun, jeer, laugh at.

moqueur *m* -**euse** *f* mocker, scoffer; * *adj* mocking.

moral *adj* moral, ethical; in-tellectual; ~**ement** *adv* morally.

moralité *f* morals, morality.

morbide *adj* morbid, un-healthy.

morceau *m* piece, morsel, fragment; extract.

mordant *adj* cutting, mor-dant; * *m* mordant.

mordre *vt* to bite, gnaw; to grip.

morgue f morgue; mortuary.

morille f morel.

morne adj gloomy, dismal.

morose adj sullen, morose.

morphine f morphine.

morphologie f morphology.

morse m Morse; walrus.

morsure f bite.

mort m dead man, -e f dead woman; * adj dead; * f death.

mortalité f mortality; death rate.

mortel adj mortal; fatal; ~lement adv mortally.

mortier m mortar.

mortuaire adj mortuary; funeral.

morue f cod.

mosaïque f mosaic.

mosquée f mosque.

mot m word; saying; ~s croisés crossword.

moteur m engine, motor; * adj motor, driving.

motif m motive, grounds; motif, design.

motion f motion; ~ de censure censure motion.

motivation f motivation.

motiver vt to justify; to motivate.

moto f motorbike.

moto-cross m motocross, scrambling.

motte f clod, lump; slab.

mou adj, f molle soft; gentle; muffled.

mouche f fly.

moucher vt to wipe sb's nose; se ~ vr to blow one's nose.

moucheron m midge, gnat.

moucheté adj speckled; flecked.

mouchoir m handkerchief.

moudre vt to mill, grind.

moue f pout; faire la ~ to pout.

mouette f gull.

moufle f mitten.

mouillé adj wet, soaked.

mouiller vt to wet; to water down; se ~ vr to get wet.

moulage m moulding, casting.

moule m mould; * f mussel.

mouler vt to mould; to model.

moulin m mill.

moulu adj ground; bruised.

mourant m dying man, -e f dying woman; * adj dying.

mourir vi to die.

mousse f moss; foam, froth.

mousser vi to froth, foam.

mousseux adj sparkling; frothy; * m sparkling wine.

moustache f moustache; whiskers.

moustachu adj moustached; * m moustached man.

moustiquaire f mosquito net.

moustique m mosquito.

moutarde f mustard.

mouton m sheep; mutton.

mouvement m movement, motion; animation.

mouvementé adj eventful; turbulent.

mouvoir vt to drive, power; se ~ vr to move.

moyen m means; way; * adj average, medium, moderate; ~nement adv fairly, moderately; ~ âge Middle Ages.

moyenne f average.

moyeu m hub; boss.

mue f moulting; shedding.

muer vi to moult; to slough.

muet m mute (man), **muette** f mute (woman); * adj dumb; silent, mute.

mufle m muffle; muzzle.

muguet m lily-of-the-valley; (med) thrush.

mule f she-mule.

mulet m mule.

multicolore adj multicoloured.

multinationale f multinational.

multiple adj numerous, multiple; * m multiple.

multiplication f multiplication.

multiplier vt se ~ vr to multiply, increase.

multitude f multitude, crowd.

municipal adj municipal; local.

municipalité f town, municipality.

munir vt to provide, equip with; se ~ vr to equip o.s.

munition f munition, ammunition.

mur m wall.

mûr adj ripe, mature; worn out.

muraille f city wall, rampart.

mûre f blackberry.

mûrir vi to ripen, mature.

murmure m murmur; muttering; grumbling.

murmurer vi to murmur; to whisper; grumble; to babble * vt to murmur.

muscle m muscle.

musclé adj muscular, brawny.

musculaire adj muscular.

muse f muse.

museau m muzzle, snout.

musée m art gallery, museum.

musicien *m* **-ne** *f* musician; *
  adj musical.

musique *f* music.

musulman *m* **-e** *f* Muslim; *
  adj Muslim.

mutant *m* **-e** *f* mutant; * *adj*
  mutant.

mutation *f* transfer; transformation; mutation.

muter *vt* to transfer, move.

mutilation *f* mutilation,
  maiming.

mutiler *vt* to mutilate; **se ~** *vr*
  to injure o.s.

mutisme *m* silence; dumb-
  ness, muteness.

mutuel *adj* mutual; **~lement**
  adv mutually.

mutuelle *f* mutual insurance
  company.

mycose *f* mycosis.

mygale *f* tarantula.

myope *mf* short-sighted person; * *adj* short-sighted.

myopie *f* short-sightedness,
  myopia.

myosotis *m* forget-me-not.

myrtille *f* bilberry, blueberry.

mystère *m* mystery.

mystérieusement *adv* myste-
  riously.

mystérieux *adj* mysterious.

mystifier *vt* to mystify; to
  hoax.

mystique *adj* mystical; * *mf*
  mystic.

mythe *m* myth.

mythique *adj* mythical.

mythologie *f* mythology.

N

nacre *f* mother-of-pearl.

nacré *adj* nacreous, pearly, iridescent.

nageoire *f* fin, flipper.

nager *vi* to swim.

nageur *m* **-euse** *f* swimmer; rower.

naïf *adj* naïve, artless, ingenuous.

nain *m* **-e** *f* dwarf; * *adj* dwarfish, dwarf.

naissance *f* birth, extraction; dawn, beginning.

naître *vi* to be born; to arise, spring up.

naïvement *adv* naïvely.

naïveté *f* naïvety, artlessness, gullibility.

nanti *m* rich man, *adj* rich, well-to-do.

nappe *f* tablecloth; layer; sheet, expanse.

napper *vt* to top with.

napperon *m* tablemat.

narcisse *m* narcissus.

narcotique *m* drug, narcotic; * *adj* narcotic.

narguer *vt* to flout, defy; to cheek.

narine *f* nostril.

narrateur *m* **-trice** *f* narrator.

narration *f* narration, narrative.

nasal *adj* nasal.

naseau *m* nostril.

natalité *f* birth rate.

natation *f* swimming.

nation *f* nation.

national *adj* national; domestic.

nationaliser *vt* to nationalize.

nationaliste *mf* nationalist; * *adj* nationalist.

nationalité *f* nationality.

natte *f* plait, braid.

naturalisation *f* nationalization.

naturaliste *mf* naturalist; taxidermist; * *adj* naturalistic.

nature *f* nature; kind, sort; temperament.

naturel *adj* natural; native;

unsophisticated; **~lement** *adv* naturally; of course.

naufrage *m* shipwreck; ruin, foundering.

nausée *f* nausea.

nautique *adj* nautical, water.

naval *adj* naval, shipbuilding.

navet *m* turnip.

navette *f* shuttle; **faire la ~ to** shuttle between.

navigateur *m* navigator, sailor.

navigation *f* sailing, navigation.

navire *m* ship, vessel.

navrant *adj* distressing, upsetting.

ne *adv* no, not.

né *adj* born.

néanmoins *adv* nevertheless.

néant *m* nothing, nothingness, emptiness.

nécessaire *adj* necessary; requisite; indispensable; **~ment** *adv* necessarily.

nécessité *f* necessity; need; inevitability.

nécessiter *vt* to require, necessitate.

nécropole *f* necropolis.

nectar *m* nectar.

nectarine *f* nectarine.

néfaste *adj* harmful; unlucky; ill-fated.

négatif *adj* negative.

négation *f* negation; negative.

négativement *adv* negatively.

négligemment *adv* negligently; carelessly; nonchalantly.

négligence *f* negligence, carelessness.

négligent *adj* negligent, careless; nonchalant.

négliger *vt* to neglect; to be negligent about.

négociant *m* **-e** *f* merchant.

négociation *f* negotiation.

négocier *vi* to negotiate; to trade; * *vt* to negotiate.

neige *f* snow.

neiger *vi* to snow, be snowing.

nénuphar *m* water-lily.

néophyte *mf* neophyte; novice; * *adj* newly converted.

nerf *m* nerve.

nerveusement *adv* nervously; irritably.

nerveux *adj* nervous; vigorous; excitable.

nervosité *f* nervousness; excitability.

nervure *f* nervure, vein; rib.

net *adj*, *f* **-te** clean; clear; plain; sharp; net; **~tement** *adv* cleanly; clearly; plainly.

netteté *f* neatness; clearness; sharpness.

nettoyage *m* cleaning; clearing up.

nettoyer *vt* to clean; to ruin, clean out.

neuf *adj* nine; * *m* nine.

neurologie *f* neurology.

neurone *m* neurone.

neutraliser *vt* to neutralize.

neutralité *f* neutrality.

neutre *adj* neutral; neuter.

neutron *m* neutron.

neuvième *adj* ninth; **~ment** *adv* ninthly; * *mf* ninth.

neveu *m* nephew.

névralgie *f* neuralgia.

névrose *f* neurosis.

nez *m* nose; flair; **avoir du ~** to have flair.

niais *adj* silly, simple, inane; **~ement** *adv* inanely.

niche *f* niche, nook; kennel; trick.

nickel *m* nickel.

nicotine *f* nicotine.

nid *m* nest; den; berth.

nièce *f* niece.

nier *vt* to deny; to repudiate.

nigaud *m* **-e** *f* simpleton.

nitrate *m* nitrate.

nitroglycérine *f* nitroglycerine.

niveau *m* level; standard; par; gauge.

niveler *vt* to level; to even out, equalize.

noble *adj* noble, dignified; **~ment** *adv* nobly.

noblesse *f* nobleness, nobility.

noce *f* wedding, wedding feast; marriage ceremony.

nocif *adj* noxious, harmful.

noctambule *mf* night reveller, night owl; sleepwalker; * *adj* enjoying night life; noctambulant.

nocturne *adj* nocturnal, night; * *f* evening fixture; late night opening.

nodule *m* nodule.

Noël *m* Christmas.

nœud *m* knot, bow; crux.

noir *adj* black; dark; * *m* black; darkness; black man.

noircir *vt* to blacken; to dirty; **se ~** *vr* to darken, grow black.

noire *f* black woman.

noisetier *m* hazel tree.

noisette *f* hazel.

noix *f* walnut.

nom *m* name; fame; noun.

nomade *mf* nomad.

nombre *m* number, quantity.

nombreux *adj* numerous, frequent.

nombril *m* navel.

nomenclature *f* list, catalogue; nomenclature.

nominal *adj* nominal; noun; ~ement *adv* nominally.

nominatif *m* nominative.

nomination *f* appointment; nomination.

nommer *vt* to appoint; nominate.

non *adv* no; not.

nonchalance *f* nonchalance.

nonchalant *adj* nonchalant.

non-conformiste *mf* nonconformist; * *adj* nonconformist.

non-lieu *m* (*jur*) no ground for prosecution.

non-sens *m* nonsense.

non-violence *f* non-violence.

nord *m* north, northerly (wind).

nordique *adj* Nordic; Scandinavian.

normal *adj* normal, usual; standard-sized; ~ement *adv* normally, usually.

norme *f* norm; standard.

nostalgie *f* nostalgia.

nostalgique *adj* nostalgic.

notable *adj* notable; noteworthy; ~ment *adv* notably.

notaire *m* notary; solicitor.

notamment *adv* notably; in particular.

note *f* note; minute; mark; bill.

noter *vt* to note down; to notice; to mark.

notice *f* note; directions; instructions.

notion *f* notion, idea.

notoire *adj* notorious; well-known, acknowledged; ~ment *adv* notoriously.

notoriété *f* notoriety; fame.

notre *adj*, *pl* **nos** ours, our own.

nôtre *pn*: **le ~, la ~, les ~s** ours, our own.

nouer *vt* to tie, knot; **se ~** *vr* to join together.

nouille *f* (piece of) pasta.

nourrice *f* child-minder, nanny.

nourrir *vt* to feed, provide for; to stoke; **se ~** *vr* to feed o.s.

nourrissant *adj* nourishing, nutritious.

nourrisson *m* infant, nursling.

nourriture f food; sustenance.

nous pn we; us; **c'est à ~** it's ours; it's our turn; **~-mêmes** ourselves.

nouveau adj new; recent; additional.

nouveau-né m **-e** f new-born child.

nouveauté f novelty; newness.

nouvelle f piece of news; short story.

novembre m November.

novice mf novice, beginner; * adj novice, unpractised, inexperienced.

noyade f drowning, drowning incident.

noyau m stone, pit; core; nucleus.

noyer vt to drown; to flood; **se ~** vr to drown, drown o.s.; * m walnut (tree).

nu adj naked, nude; plain, unadorned.

nuage m cloud.

nuageux adj cloudy, overcast.

nuance f shade, hue; faint difference, nuance.

nucléaire adj nuclear; * m nuclear energy.

nudiste mf nudist; * adj nudist.

nudité f nakedness, nudity.

nuée f dense cloud; horde, swarm.

nuire vi to harm, injure; to prejudice.

nuisible adj harmful; noxious; **~ment** adv harmfully.

nuit f night, darkness.

nul adj no; nil; null and void; nonexistent; **~lement** adv not at all, not in the least.

nullité f nullity; uselessness.

numéral adj numeral; * m numeral.

numérique adj numerical; digital.

numéro m number; issue.

numérotation f numbering, numeration.

numéroter vt to number.

nuptial adj nuptial, wedding.

nuque f nape (of the neck).

nutritif adj nutritious, nourishing.

nutrition f nutrition.

nylon m nylon.

nymphe f nymph.

O

oasis *m* oasis.

obéir *vt* to obey, be obedient; to comply.

obéissance *f* obedience; compliance.

obéissant *adj* obedient.

obèse *adj* obese.

obésité *f* obesity.

objecter *vt* to object.

objectif *adj* objective, unbiased; * *m* objective, target.

objection *f* objection.

objectivement *adv* objectively.

objet *m* object, thing; purpose; matter.

obligation *f* obligation, duty; bond.

obligatoire *adj* obligatory, compulsory; ~ment *adv* obligatorily.

obligé *adj* obliged, compelled; inevitable; necessary.

obliger *vt* to oblige, require; (*jur*) to bind.

oblique *adj* oblique, sidelong.

oblitérer *vt* to obliterate; to cancel (stamp).

obscène *adj* obscene.

obscénité *f* obscenity.

obscur *adj* obscure, dark, gloomy; ~ément *adv* obscurely.

obscurcir *vt* to darken; to obscure; s'~ *vr* to get dark.

obscurité *f* obscurity; darkness.

obséder *vt* to obsess, haunt.

obsèques *fpl* funeral.

observateur *m* -trice *f* observer; * *adj* observant.

observation *f* observation; remark.

observatoire *m* observatory.

observer *vt* to observe, watch; to notice; to comply with.

obsession *f* obsession.

obstacle *m* obstacle, hindrance.

obstétrique *f* obstetrics.

obstination *f* obstinacy, stubbornness.

obstiné *adj* obstinate, stubborn; **~ment** *adv* obstinately.

obstiner (s') *vr* to insist, persist.

obtenir *vt* to obtain, procure, get; to achieve.

obturation *f* stopping, closing up, obturation.

obus *m* shell.

occasion *f* occasion, opportunity; cause; bargain; **d'~** second-hand.

occident *m* west.

occidental *adj* western; Occidental.

occulte *adj* occult.

occupant *m* -e *f* occupant, occupier.

occupation *f* occupation, pursuit; work; occupancy.

occuper *vt* to occupy; to employ; to inhabit; **s'~** *vr* to keep busy.

océan *m* ocean.

ocre *m* ochre; * *adj* ochre.

octane *m* octane.

octave *f* octave.

octet *m* byte.

octobre *m* October.

octroyer *vt* to grant, bestow; **s'~** *vr* to allow o.s.

oculaire *adj* ocular.

odeur *f* smell, odour.

odieux *adj* hateful, obnoxious.

odorat *m* smell (sense).

oedème *m* oedema.

œil *m*, *pl* yeux eye; look; bud.

œillet *m* carnation.

œsophage *m* oesophagus.

œuf *m* egg.

œuvre *f* work; action, deed; production.

offense *f* offence; injury, wrong.

offenser *vt* to offend; to injure, shock; **s'~** *vr* to take offence.

offensif *adj* offensive; forceful, aggressive.

offensive *f* offensive, attack.

office *m* office, bureau; duty; function.

officiel *adj* official; **~lement** *adv* officially.

officier *m* officer.

officieusement *adv* officiously; unofficially.

officieux *adj* officious, over-obliging; unofficial.

offrande *f* offering.

offre *f* offer, tender, bid.

offrir *vt* to offer.

offusquer *vt* to offend; *s'~ vr* to take offence; to be offended.

ogive *f* ogive, pointed arch.

ogre *m* ogre, -**sse** *f* ogress.

ohm *m* ohm.

oie *f* goose.

oignon *m* onion; bulb.

oiseau *m* bird.

oisif *adj* idle.

oisiveté *f* idleness.

oléagineux *adj* oleaginous, oily.

oléoduc *m* oil pipeline.

olfactif *adj* olfactory.

oligarchie *f* oligarchy.

oligo-élément *m* trace element.

olive *f* olive.

olivier *m* olive tree.

olympique *adj* Olympic.

ombilical *adj* umbilical.

ombragé *adj* shaded, shady.

ombre *f* shade, shadow.

omelette *f* omelette.

omettre *vt* to leave out, miss out.

omission *f* omission.

omnibus *m* local train; omnibus.

omnipotent *adj* omnipotent.

omniprésent *adj* omnipresent.

omoplate *f* shoulder blade.

on *pn* one; someone, anyone.

once *f* ounce.

oncle *m* uncle.

onctueux *adj* smooth, creamy.

onde *f* wave.

ondoyant *adj* undulating, flowing; changeable.

ondulation *f* undulation; wave.

onduler *vi* to undulate; to ripple.

onéreux *adj* onerous; expensive, costly.

ongle *m* nail; claw, talon; hoof.

onomatopée *f* onomatopoeia.

onyx *m* onyx.

onze *adj* eleven; * *m* eleven.

onzième *adj* eleventh; ~**ment** *adv* in eleventh place; * *mf* eleventh.

opale *f* opal.

opaque *adj* opaque; impenetrable.

opéra *m* opera.

opération *f* operation, performance; transaction, deal.

opérationnel *adj* operational.

opératoire *adj* operating; operative, surgical.

opérer *vt* to operate; to carry out, implement.

opérette *f* operetta, light opera.

ophtalmie *f* ophthalmia.

opiniâtre *adj* stubborn; persistent; ~**ment** *adv* stubbornly; persistently.

opinion *f* opinion, view.

opium *m* opium.

opportun *adj* timely, opportune; ~**ément** *adv* opportunely.

opportuniste *mf* opportunist; * *adj* opportunist.

opportunité *f* opportuneness, expediency, timeliness.

opposant *m* -e *f* opponent; * *adj* opposing.

opposé *adj* opposite, contrary; facing; * *m* opposite; à l'~ contrary to.

opposer *vt* to oppose; to contrast; to object; s'~ *vr* to be opposed to; to clash, conflict.

opposition *f* opposition; conflict.

oppresser *vt* to oppress, weigh down.

oppressif *adj* oppressive.

oppression *f* oppression.

opprimer *vt* to oppress, crush.

opticien *m* -ne *f* optician.

optimisme *m* optimism.

optimiste *mf* optimist; * *adj* optimistic.

option *f* option, choice.

optionnel *adj* optional.

optique *adj* optical; * *f* optics.

opulence *f* opulence, wealth.

opulent *adj* opulent, wealthy.

or *m* gold; * *conj* now.

oracle *m* oracle.

orage *m* storm, tempest, thunderstorm.

orageux *adj* stormy.

oral *adj* oral, verbal; ~**ement** *adv* orally.

orange *f* orange; * *adj invar* orange.

oranger *m* orange tree.

orang-outan(g) *m* orang-utang.

orateur *m* -trice *f* orator.

orbite *f* orbit; socket; sphere.

orchestral *adj* orchestral.

orchestre *m* orchestra.

orchestrer *vt* to orchestrate, score.

orchidée *f* orchid.

ordinaire *adj* ordinary, common, usual; **~ment** *adv* ordinarily, usually; * *m* custom, usual routine; **d'~**, **à l'~** ordinarily, usually.

ordinateur *m* computer.

ordonnance *f* prescription, order, edict.

ordonner *vt* to arrange; to order; to prescribe.

ordre *m* order, command; class.

ordure *f* filth, dirt; excrement; rubbish.

oreille *f* ear; hearing; wing; handle.

oreiller *m* pillow.

oreillons *mpl* mumps.

orfèvre *m* silversmith, goldsmith.

orfèvrerie *f* silversmith's (goldsmith's) craft.

organe *m* organ; instrument; medium.

organigramme *m* organizational chart.

organique *adj* organic.

organisateur *m* -**trice** *f* organizer.

organisation *f* organization.

organiser *vt* to organize, arrange; **s'~** *vr* to organize o.s.

organisme *m* organism.

organiste *mf* organist.

orgasme *m* orgasm.

orge *f* barley.

orgie *f* orgy.

orgue *m* (*mus*) organ.

orgueil *m* pride, arrogance.

orgueilleux *adj* proud, arrogant.

orient *m* orient, east.

oriental *adj* eastern, oriental.

orientation *f* orientation; positioning; directing; trend.

orienter *vt* to orientate; to position; to direct; **s'~** *vr* to ascertain one's position; to turn towards.

orifice *m* orifice; aperture, opening.

originaire *adj* originating from, native to; **~ment** *adv* originally, primitively.

original *adj* original, novel; peculiar, bizarre; * *m* original; top copy.

originalité *f* originality; oddness.

origine *f* origin, source, derivation; **à l'~** originally.

originel *adj* original, primitive.

orme *m* elm.

ornement *m* ornament, embellishment.

ornemental *adj* ornamental.

orner *vt* to adorn, decorate.

ornière *f* rut.

ornithologie *f* ornithology.

ornithologiste, ornithologue *mf* ornithologist.

orphelin *m* **-e** *f* orphan.

orphelinat *m* orphanage.

orteil *m* toe.

orthodoxe *adj* orthodox; * *mf* orthodox.

orthogonal *adj* orthogonal.

orthographe *f* spelling.

orthopédie *f* orthopaedics.

orthopédique *adj* orthopaedic.

ortie *f* nettle.

orvet *m* slow-worm.

os *m* bone.

oscillation *f* oscillation, swinging.

osciller *vi* to oscillate, swing.

oseille *f* sorrel.

oser *vt* to dare.

osier *m* osier, willow, wicker.

osmose *f* osmosis.

ossature *f* skeleton; framework.

ossements *mpl* bones.

ostensible *adj* open, conspicuous; **~ment** *adv* openly; conspicuously.

ostentation *f* ostentation.

ostéopathe *mf* osteopath.

ostracisme *m* ostracism.

otage *m* hostage.

otarie *f* sea-lion.

ôter *vt* to take away, remove; to deprive, deduct.

otite *f* ear infection.

oto-rhino-laryngologie *f* oto-rhinolaryngology.

oto-rhino(-laryngologiste) *mf* ear, nose and throat specialist.

ou *conj* or.

où *adv* where, in which; * *pn* where.

ouate *f* cotton wool.

oubli *m* forgetfulness; oblivion; oversight, omission.

oublier *vt* to forget; to omit, neglect.

oubliette *f* oubliette.

ouest *m* west; *adj* west.

oui *adv* yes.

ouïe *f* hearing (sense).

ouragan *m* hurricane, whirlwind.

ourlet *m* hem.

ours *m* **-e** *f* bear.

oursin *m* sea urchin.

ourson *m* bear cub.

outil *m* tool, implement.

outillage *m* (set of) tools; equipment.

outiller *vt* to equip; to provide with tools.

outrage *m* outrage, insult, wrong.

outrageant *adj* outrageous, insulting.

outre *prép* as well as, besides; **en ~** moreover; **~ mesure** to excess, inordinately; **passer ~** to go on, to take no notice; * *f* goatskin, leather bottle.

outré *adj* excessive, exaggerated.

outremer *m* ultramarine.

outrepasser *vt* to exceed; to transgress.

ouvert *adj* open; exposed; frank; **~ement** *adv* openly, overtly.

ouverture *f* opening; mouth; overture; means, way.

ouvrable *adj* working, business.

ouvrage *m* work; piece of work.

ouvre-boîte *m* tin-opener.

ouvre-bouteille *m* bottle-opener.

ouvrier *m* **-ière** *f* worker; * *adj* working-class; industrial; labour.

ouvrir *vt* to open; to unlock; to broach; **s'~** *vr* to open; to open one's mind; to cut o.s.

ovaire *m* ovary.

ovale *adj* oval; * *m* oval.

ovation *f* ovation.

ovni *m* UFO.

ovulation *f* ovulation.

ovule *m* ovum; ovule.

oxydation *f* oxidation.

oxyde *m* oxide.

oxyder *vt* to oxidize; **s'~** *vr* to become oxidized.

oxygène *m* oxygen.

ozone *f* ozone.

P

pacifier *vt* to pacify.

pacifique *adj* peaceful, pacific; **~ment** *adv* peacefully, pacifically.

pacifiste *mf* pacifist; * *adj* pacifist.

pacte *m* pact, treaty.

pactiser *vt* to treat with sb; to come to terms with.

pagaie *f* paddle.

pagayer *vi* to paddle.

page *f* page; passage.

pagne *m* loincloth.

paiement *m* payment.

païen *m* **-ne** *f* pagan; * *adj* pagan.

paillasse *f* straw mattress.

paillasson *m* doormat.

paille *f* straw.

paillette *f* sequin; spangle.

pain *m* bread; loaf; bar.

pair *adj* even; * *m* peer; par; **hors ~** outstanding, matchless.

paire *f* pair; yoke; brace.

paisible *adj* peaceful; calm; **~ment** *adv* peacefully; calmly.

paître *vi* to graze.

paix *f* peace; quiet; stillness; tranquillity.

palais *m* palace; law courts; palate.

palan *m* hoist.

pâle *adj* pale, pallid.

palette *f* palette; pallet; paddle.

pâleur *f* paleness, pallor.

palier *m* landing; level; degree.

pâlir *vi* to turn pale; to dim; to fade.

palissade *f* fence; boarding; stockade.

palliatif *m* palliative; * *adj* palliative.

pallier *vt* to palliate; to offset.

palmarès *m* prize list; medal record.

palme *f* palm leaf; palm.

palmé *adj* palmate; webbed.

palmeraie *f* palm grove.

palmier *m* palm tree.

palmipède *m* palmiped.

palpable *adj* palpable.

palper *vt* to feel, touch; to palpate.

palpitation *f* palpitation; throbbing; quivering.

palpiter *vi* to palpitate; to beat; to race.

paludisme *m* malaria.

pamplemousse *m* grapefruit.

panache *m* panache; gallantry.

panaché *adj* variegated; motley.

pancarte *f* sign, notice; placard.

pancréas *m* pancreas.

panda *m* panda.

pané *adj* covered in breadcrumbs.

panier *m* basket; pannier (mode).

panique *f* panic.

paniquer *vi* to panic, get panicky.

panne *f* breakdown; fault, problem.

panneau *m* panel; sign, notice.

panoplie *f* outfit; display.

panorama *m* panorama.

panoramique *adj* panoramic.

pansement *m* dressing, bandage.

panser *vt* to dress, bandage.

pantalon *m* trousers; pants; knickers.

panthéon *m* pantheon.

panthère *f* panther.

pantin *m* jumping-jack; puppet.

pantomime *f* pantomime; mime.

pantoufle *f* slipper.

paon *m* peacock.

papa *m* dad; daddy.

papauté *f* papacy.

papaye *f* papaya.

pape *m* pope.

papeterie *f* stationery; stationer's shop; paper mill.

papetier *m* -ière *f* stationer; paper-maker.

papier *m* paper; article; wrapper.

papillon *m* butterfly.

papillote *f* sweet wrapper.

papoter *vi* to chatter.

Pâques *fpl* Easter.

paquebot *m* liner, steamer.

pâquerette *f* daisy.

paquet *m* packet, pack; bag; parcel.

par *prép* by, with, through; from; along; **~-ci, ~-là**

here and there, now and then; **~-derrière** round the back; **~-dessous** underneath; **~-dessus** over, above.

parabole f (*math*) parabola; parable.

parachever vt to perfect; to complete.

parachute m parachute.

parachuter vt to parachute.

parachutiste mf parachutist.

parade f parade, show; parry.

paradis m paradise; (*thea*) gallery.

paradoxal adj paradoxical; **~ement** adv paradoxically.

paradoxe m paradox.

paraffine f paraffin.

parages mpl vicinity; **dans les ~** in the area.

paragraphe m paragraph; section.

paraître vi to appear; to be published; to look, seem; **il paraît que** apparently.

parallèle adj parallel; **~ment** adv parallel; at the same time.

paralyser vt to paralyse.

paralysie f paralysis.

paralytique mf paralytic; * adj paralytic.

paramètre m parameter.

paranoïa f paranoia.

paranoïaque adj paranoiac, paranoid; * mf paranoiac, paranoid.

paraphraser vt to paraphrase.

parapluie m umbrella.

parasite m parasite, sponger.

parasol m parasol; sunshade.

paratonnerre m lightning conductor.

paravent m folding screen, partition.

parc m park; grounds; depot.

parcelle f fragment, particle; parcel.

parce que conj because.

parchemin m parchment.

parcimonie f parsimony.

parcmètre m meter (parking).

parcourir vt to travel through; to scour; to traverse.

pardon m pardon, forgiveness.

pardonner vt to pardon; to excuse, overlook.

pare-brise m invar windscreen.

pare-chocs m invar bumper.

pareil m **-le** f equal; match; **sans ~** unparalleled, unequalled; * adj like, equal,

similar; identical; ~**lement**
adv likewise, equally.

parent *m* **-e** *f* relative, relation; ~**s** (*pl*) parents.

parental *adj* parental.

parenté *f* relationship, kin-
ship.

parenthèse *f* parenthesis, digression.

parer *vt* to adorn, deck out;
to ward off; to parry; ~ **à** to
deal with, overcome.

paresse *f* laziness; sluggishness.

paresseux *m* **-euse** *f* lazy person, loafer; * *adj* lazy.

parfaire *vt* to perfect, bring
to perfection.

parfait *adj* perfect, flawless;
~**ement** *adv* perfectly;
completely, absolutely.

parfois *adv* sometimes, occasionally.

parfumer *vt* to perfume,
scent; **se** ~ *vr* to put perfume on.

parfumerie *f* perfumery.

parfumeur *m* **-euse** *f* per-
fumer.

pari *m* bet, wager.

parier *vt* to bet, wager.

parking *m* car park; parking.

parlement *m* Parliament.

parlementaire *adj* parliamentary; * *mf* member of parliament.

parler *vi* to talk, speak; * *vt*
to speak.

parmesan *m* parmesan.

parmi *prép* among.

parodie *f* parody.

paroi *f* wall; surface.

paroisse *f* parish.

parole *f* word; speech; voice;
lyrics.

paroxysme *m* paroxysm; crisis.

parquer *vt* to park; to enclose, pen.

parquet *m* floor, floorboards.

parrain *m* godfather; patron;
promoter.

parrainage *m* sponsorship;
promoting; patronage.

parrainer *vt* to sponsor; propose.

parsemer *vt* to sprinkle,
strew.

part *f* part; share; portion;
prendre ~ **à** to participate
in; **faire** ~ **de** to announce;
de sa part for his part; **autre**
~ elsewhere; **nulle** ~ nowhere; **d'autre** ~ moreover.

partage *m* sharing, distribution; portion.

partager *vt* to divide up, share out.

partenaire *mf* partner.

parti *m* party; option; match.

partial *adj* partial, biased; ~ement *adv* in a biased way.

participant *m* -e *f* participant, member; * *adj* participant, participating.

participation *f* participation; involvement.

participe *m* participle.

participer *vi* to take part in, participate.

particularité *f* particularity, characteristic.

particule *f* particle.

particulier *adj* particular, specific; peculiar, characteristic; * *m* person, private individual; character.

particulièrement *adv* particularly, especially.

partie *f* part; subject; game; party; faire ~ de to be a part of.

partiel *adj* part, partial; ~lement *adv* partially, in part.

partir *vi* to leave, set off; to start up; à ~ de from.

partisan *m* -e *f* partisan, supporter, proponent.

partition *f* partition; score.

partout *adv* everywhere.

parvenir *vi*: ~ à to reach; to achieve.

pas *m* step; pace; footprint; gait; * *adv* no, not.

passable *adj* passable, tolerable; ~ment *adv* tolerably; reasonably.

passage *m* passage, passing by; transit.

passager *m* -ère *f* passenger; * *adj* passing, transitory.

passant *m* -e *f* passer-by, wayfarer; * *adj* much-frequented, busy.

passe *f* pass; permit; channel.

passé *m* past.

passeport *m* passport.

passer *vi* to pass; to elapse; to disappear, fade; se ~ *vr* to pass; to take place; se ~ de to do without.

passerelle *f* footbridge; bridge; gangway.

passe-temps *m invar* pastime.

passif *adj* passive; * *m* passive.

passion *f* passion; fondness.

passionnant *adj* fascinating; exciting.

passionné *adj* passionate, impassioned; **~ment** *adv* passionately.

passionner *vt* to fascinate; to interest deeply, impassion; **se ~** *vr* to be fascinated by, have a passion for.

passivement *adv* passively.

passivité *f* passivity, passiveness.

pastel *m* pastel.

pastèque *f* watermelon.

pasteur *m* minister, pastor.

pasteuriser *vt* to pasteurize.

pastiche *m* pastiche.

pastille *f* pastille, lozenge.

patate *f* (*fam*) spud; sweet potato.

patauger *vi* to wade about, splash about.

pâte *f* pastry, pasta, dough, batter.

pâté *m* pâté.

paternel *adj* paternal, fatherly; **~lement** *adv* paternally.

paternité *f* paternity; fatherhood.

pathétique *adj* pathetic.

patiemment *adv* patiently.

patience *f* patience, endurance.

patient *adj* patient, enduring.

patienter *vi* to wait.

patin *m* skate; **~ à glace** ice skate; **~ à roulettes** roller skate.

patinage *m* skating; slipping; spinning.

patiner *vi* to skate; to slip; to spin.

patineur *m* **-euse** *f* skater.

patinoire *f* ice rink.

pâtisserie *f* cake shop, confectioner's.

pâtissier *m* **-ière** *f* pastry cook, confectioner.

patois *m* patois, provincial dialect.

patrie *f* homeland, country.

patrimoine *m* inheritance, patrimony.

patriote *mf* patriot; * *adj* patriotic.

patriotisme *m* patriotism.

patron *m* **-ne** *f* owner, boss, proprietor.

patronat *m* employers.

patronner *vt* to patronize, sponsor.

patrouille *f* patrol.

patte *f* leg, paw, foot.

pâturage *m* pasture, pasturage, grazing.

pâture *f* pasture; food.

paume *f* palm.

paumer *vt* (*fam*) to lose; se ~ *vr* to get lost.

paupière *f* eyelid.

paupiette *f* stuffed slice of meat.

pause *f* pause; half-time.

pauvre *adj* poor; indigent; scanty; weak; ~ment *adv* poorly; * *mf* poor person, pauper.

pavé *m* cobblestone, paving stone.

pavillon *m* house; pavilion; flag.

pavot *m* poppy.

paye *f* pay, wages.

payer *vt* to pay, settle; to reward.

pays *m* country; region; village; land.

paysage *m* landscape; scenery.

paysan *m* countryman, farmer; -ne *f* countrywoman.

PDG (président-directeur général) *m* chairman and managing director.

péage *m* toll; tollgate.

peau *f* skin; hide, pelt.

pêche *f* peach; fishing.

pécher *vi* to sin.

pêcher *vt* to fish; to catch; * *m* peach tree.

pécheur *m* -eresse *f* sinner.

pêcheur *m* fisherman, -euse *f* fisherwoman.

pectoral *adj* pectoral; cough.

pectoraux *mpl* pectorals.

pédagogie *f* education; educational methods.

pédagogue *mf* teacher; educationalist; * *adj* pedagogic.

pédale *f* pedal; treadle.

pédaler *vi* to pedal.

pédalier *m* pedal-board, crank-gear.

pédestre *adj* pedestrian.

pédiatre *mf* paediatrician.

pédicure *mf* chiropodist.

peigne *m* comb.

peigner *vt* to comb; to card; se ~ *vr* to comb one's hair.

peignoir *m* dressing gown.

peindre *vt* to paint; to depict, portray.

peine *f* effort; sadness; pain; punishment; difficulty.

peiner *vi* to toil; to struggle.

peintre *m* painter; portrayer.

peinture *f* painting, picture; paintwork.

péjoratif *adj* pejorative.

pelage *m* coat, fur.

peler *vi* to peel.

pèlerin *m* pilgrim; peregrine falcon.

pèlerinage *m* pilgrimage.

pélican *m* pelican.

pelle *f* shovel; spade.

pellicule *f* film; thin layer.

pelote *f* ball; pelota ball.

peloton *m* pack; squad; platoon.

pelouse *f* lawn, field; ground.

pelure *f* peeling, piece of peel.

pénal *adj* penal; criminal.

pénaliser *vt* to penalize.

pénalité *f* penalty.

penalty *m* penalty (kick).

pencher *vi* to lean; to tilt; (*mar*) to list; * *vt* to tip up; tilt; se ~ *vr* to bend down; to study, look at.

pendant *prép* during; for; ~ que while, whilst; * *adj* hanging, drooping; pending.

pendentif *m* pendant; pendentive.

pendre *vi* to hang, dangle; * *vt* to hang; se ~ *vr* to hang o.s.

pendule *f* clock; * *m* pendulum.

pénétrant *adj* penetrating, piercing; searching; acute.

pénétration *f* penetration; perception.

pénétrer *vi* to enter, penetrate; * *vt* to penetrate, pierce; to pervade.

pénible *adj* hard, tiresome; difficult; laborious; ~ment *adv* painfully; with difficulty.

péniche *f* barge.

péniciline *f* penicillin.

péninsule *f* peninsula.

pénis *m* penis.

pénitence *f* penitence, penance; punishment.

pénitencier *m* prison, penitentiary.

pénitent *m* -e *f* penitent; * *adj* penitent.

pénombre *f* half-light; penumbra (astronomy).

pensée *f* thought; thinking; mind.

penser *vt* to think, suppose, believe; * *vi* to think.

pensif *adj* pensive, thoughtful.

pension *f* pension; boarding house.

pensionnaire *mf* boarder; lodger.

pensionnat *m* boarding school.

pensivement *adv* pensively, thoughtfully.

pentagone *m* pentagon.

pentathlon *m* pentathlon.

pente *f* slope; gradient.

Pentecôte *f* Pentecost, Whitsun.

pénurie *f* shortage, scarcity; penury.

pépère *m* granddad, grandpa.

pépin *m* pip; snag, hitch.

pépinière *f* tree nursery; breeding-ground.

pépite *f* nugget.

perçant *adj* piercing, shrill.

percée *f* opening, clearing; breach; breakthrough.

perce-oreille *m* earwig.

perception *f* perception; collection.

percer *vt* to pierce; to drill; to see through.

percevoir *vt* to perceive, detect; to collect.

percher *vt* to stick; to place on; **se ~** *vr* to perch.

percussion *f* percussion.

percussionniste *mf* percussionist.

percuter *vt* to strike; to crash into.

perdant *m* **-e** *f* loser; * *adj* losing.

perdre *vt* to lose; to waste; to miss; * *vi* to lose; **se ~** *vr* to lose one's way.

perdrix *f* partridge.

perdu *adj* lost; wasted; missed.

père *m* father; sire.

péremptoire *adj* peremptory.

perfection *f* perfection.

perfectionnement *m* perfection, perfecting; improvement.

perfectionner *vt* to improve, perfect; **se ~** *vr* to improve, improve o.s.

perfectionniste *mf* perfectionist; * *adj* perfectionist.

perfide *adj* perfidious, treacherous; **~ment** *adv* perfidiously.

perforation *f* perforation.

perforer *vt* to perforate; to pierce.

performance *f* result, performance.

performant *adj* outstanding; high-performance, high-return.

péricliter *vi* to collapse; to be in jeopardy.

péril *m* peril, danger.

périlleux *adj* perilous.

périmé *adj* out-of-date; expired.

périmètre *m* perimeter.

période *f* period; epoch, era; wave, spell.

périodique *adj* periodic; **~ment** *adv* periodically.

péripétie *f* event, episode.

périphérie *f* periphery.

périphérique *adj* peripheral, outlying; * *m* ring road; peripheral.

périple *m* voyage; journey.

périr *vi* to perish, die.

périscope *m* periscope.

périssable *adj* perishable.

perle *f* pearl; bead; gem.

permanence *f* permanence; permanency.

permanent *adj* permanent, continuous.

permanente *f* perm.

permanenter *vt* to perm.

perméable *adj* permeable; pervious.

permettre *vt* to allow, permit; **se ~** *vr* to allow o.s.

permis *adj* permitted; * *m* permit, licence.

permission *f* permission; leave.

permutation *f* permutation.

permuter *vt* to change, switch round; to permutate.

pernicieux *adj* pernicious.

perpendiculaire *adj* perpendicular; **~ment** *adv* perpendicularly.

perpétuel *adj* perpetual; permanent; **~lement** *adv* perpetually.

perpétuer *vt* to perpetuate, carry on; **se ~** *vr* to be perpetuated; to survive.

perpétuité *f* perpetuity.

perplexe *adj* perplexed, confused.

perplexité *f* perplexity, confusion.

perquisition *f* search.

perquisitionner *vt* to make a search.

perron *m* flight of steps.

perroquet *m* parrot.

perruche *f* budgerigar; chatterbox.

perruque *f* wig.

persécuter *vt* to persecute; to harass.

persécution *f* persecution.

persévérance *f* perseverance.

persévérant *adj* persevering.

persévérer *vi* to persevere; to persist in.

persil *m* parsley.

persistance *f* persistence.

persistant *adj* persistent; evergreen.

persister *vi* to persist, keep up.

personnage *m* character, individual.

personnaliser *vt* to personalize.

personnalité *f* personality.

personne *f* person; self; appearance; en ~ in person; * *pn* anyone, anybody; nobody.

personnel *adj* personal; selfish; ~lement *adv* personally.

personnifier *vt* to personify.

perspective *f* perspective; view; angle.

perspicace *adj* shrewd, perspicacious.

perspicacité *f* insight, perspicacity.

persuader *vt* to persuade; to convince.

persuasif *adj* persuasive; convincing.

persuasion *f* persuasion; conviction.

perte *f* loss, losing; ruin.

pertinent *adj* pertinent.

perturbation *f* disruption; perturbation.

perturber *vt* to disrupt, disturb.

pervenche *f* periwinkle.

pervers *adj* perverse; perverted.

perversité *f* perversity.

pesant *adj* heavy, weighty.

pesanteur *f* gravity; heaviness.

pèse-personne *m* scales.

peser *vt* to weigh; to press; to evaluate; * *vi* to weigh, weigh down; to hang over; se ~ to weigh o.s.

pessimisme *m* pessimism.

pessimiste *mf* pessimist; * *adj* pessimistic.

peste *f* pest, nuisance; plague.

pesticide *m* pesticide.

pétale *f* petal.

pétanque *f* petanque.

pétard *m* firecracker; detonator; charge; racket, row.

pétillant *adj* bubbly, fizzy.

pétiller *vi* to crackle; to bubble; to sparkle.

petit *adj* small, tiny; slim; young.

petitesse *f* smallness, modesty; meanness.

petit-fils *m* grandson.

petite-fille *f* granddaughter.

pétition *f* petition.

petits-enfants *mpl* grandchildren.

pétrifié *adj* petrified; transfixed; fossilized.

pétrin m kneading trough; scrape, mess, tight spot.

pétrir vt to knead; to mould, shape.

pétrole m oil, petroleum.

pétrolier m oil tanker; * adj petroleum, oil, oil-producing.

pétrolifère adj oil-bearing.

pétunia m petunia.

peu adv little, not much, few; **un petit ~** a little bit; **quelque ~** a little; **pour ~ que** however little; **~ de** little, few.

peuplade f tribe, people.

peuple m people, nation; crowd.

peuplement m populating; stocking.

peupler vt to populate, stock; to plant.

peuplier m poplar.

peur f fear, terror, apprehension; **avoir ~** to be afraid.

peureux adj fearful, timorous.

peut-être adv perhaps.

phalange f phalanx.

phallocrate m male chauvinist.

pharaon m pharaoh.

phare m lighthouse; headlight.

pharmaceutique adj pharmaceutical.

pharmacie f pharmacy; pharmacology.

pharmacien m **-ne** f pharmacist; chemist.

pharynx m pharynx.

phase f phase, stage.

phénoménal adj phenomenal.

phénomène m phenomenon; freak; character.

philanthrope mf philanthropist.

philatélie f philately, stamp collecting.

philologie f philology.

philosophe mf philosopher; * adj philosophical.

philosopher vi to philosophize.

philosophie f philosophy.

philosophique adj philosophical; **~ment** adv philosophically.

phobie f phobia.

phonétique f phonetics; * adj phonetic; **~ment** adv phonetically.

phoque m seal; sealskin.

phosphate m phosphate.

phosphore m phosphorus.

phosphorescent adj luminous, phosphorescent.

photo *f* photo.

photocopie *f* photocopy.

photocopier *vt* to photocopy.

photocopieur *m*, **-euse** *f* photocopier.

photogénique *adj* photogenic.

photographe *mf* photograph.

photographie *f* photography.

photographier *vt* to photograph.

photographique *adj* photographic.

phrase *f* sentence; phrase.

physicien *m* **-ne** *f* physicist.

physiologie *f* physiology.

physiologique *adj* physiological.

physionomie *f* countenance, physiognomy.

physionomiste *adj* good at remembering faces.

physiothérapie *f* physiotherapy.

physique *f* physics; * *adj* physical; ~**ment** *adv* physically.

pianiste *mf* pianist.

piano *m* piano.

pic *m* peak; à ~ vertically, sheer.

pichet *m* pitcher, jug.

picorer *vt* to peck; to nibble.

picot *m* picot; (*bot*) burr; (*tec*) tooth.

picotement *m* tickle; prickling.

picoter *vt* to tickle; to prickle; to smart, sting.

pictural *adj* pictorial.

pie *f* magpie; chatterbox.

pièce *f* piece; object; component; room; paper, document.

pied *m* foot; track; hoof; bottom; à ~ on foot; **être sur ~** to be underway.

pied-à-terre *m invar* pied-à-terre.

piédestal *m* pedestal.

piège *m* trap; pit; snare.

piéger *vt* to trap, set a trap.

pierre *f* stone.

piété *f* piety.

piétiner *vi* to stamp (one's foot); * *vt* to trample on.

piéton *m* pedestrian; * *adj* pedestrian.

pieu *m* post, stake, pile.

pieusement *adv* piously, devoutly.

pieux *adj* pious, devout.

pigeon *m* pigeon; dupe, mug.

pigment *m* pigment.

pigmentation *f* pigmentation.

pignon *m* gable; cogwheel.

pile *f* pile; pier; battery; *
   adv dead; just, right, exactly.

piler *vt* to crush, pound.

pilier *m* pillar.

pillage *m* pillaging, looting.

piller *vt* to pillage, loot.

pilon *m* pestle; wooden leg.

pilote *m* pilot; driver.

piloter *vt* to pilot, fly; to drive.

pilotis *m* stilts; pilotis.

pilule *f* pill.

piment *m* hot pepper, capsicum.

pimenter *vt* to add spice.

pin *m* pine.

pince *f* pliers, crowbar; pincer; dart.

pinceau *m* brush, paintbrush.

pincée *f* pinch.

pincer *vt* to pinch, nip; to
   grip.

pinède *f* pine forest.

pingouin *m* penguin.

ping-pong *m* table tennis.

pintade *f* guinea-fowl.

pinte *f* pint.

pioche *f* pick, pickaxe.

piocher *vt* to use a pick; to
   swot.

piolet *m* ice axe.

pion *m* pawn; draught.

pionnier *m* pioneer.

pipe *f* pipe.

pipette *f* pipette.

piquant *adj* prickly; pungent;
   piquant; * *m* quill, spine;
   prickle.

pique *f* pike, lance.

pique-nique *m* picnic.

pique-niquer *vi* to picnic.

piquer *vt* to sting, bite; to
   goad; to puncture.

piquet *m* post, picket.

piqûre *f* prick; sting; bite.

pirate *m* pirate.

pire *adj* worse; le ~, la ~, les
   ~s the worst.

pirogue *f* pirogue, dugout canoe.

pirouette *f* pirouette; about-
   turn.

pis *m* udder.

pis-aller *m invar* last resort,
   stopgap.

piscine *f* swimming pool.

pissenlit *m* dandelion.

pistache *f* pistachio.

piste *f* track, trail; course;
   runway; lead, clue.

pistolet *m* pistol, gun.

piston *m* piston.

pistonner *vt* to pull strings
   for, recommend.

piteux *adj* pitiful, pathetic.

pitié *f* pity, mercy.

pitoyable *adj* pitiful, pitiable.

pittoresque *adj* picturesque.

pivoine *f* peony.

pivot *m* pivot; mainspring.

pivoter *vi* to revolve, pivot.

placard *m* cupboard; poster, notice.

place *f* place; square; seat; space; position; **à la ~ de** instead of.

placebo *m* placebo.

placement *m* placing; investment.

placenta *m* placenta; afterbirth.

placer *vt* to place, put; to fit; to seat; to sell; to invest; **se ~ vr** to take up position; to stand; to find a job.

placide *adj* placid, calm.

placidité *f* placidity, calmness.

plafond *m* ceiling; roof.

plafonner *vi* to reach a ceiling/maximum.

plage *f* beach.

plagiat *m* plagiarism, plagiary.

plagier *vt* to plagiarize.

plaider *vt* to plead; to defend; * *vi* to plead for, go to court.

plaidoirie *f* defence speech; plea.

plaidoyer *m* defence speech; plea.

plaie *f* wound, cut; scourge.

plaignant *m* **-e** *f* plaintiff.

plaindre *vt* to pity; to begrudge; **se ~ vr** to complain.

plaine *f* plain.

plainte *f* complaint; moan, groan.

plaintif *adj* plaintive, complaining.

plaire *vi* to please, be pleasant; **se ~ vr** to enjoy, take pleasure in.

plaisant *adj* pleasant, agreeable.

plaisanter *vi* to joke, jest.

plaisanterie *f* joking; pleasantry; humour.

plaisir *m* pleasure; delight; entertainment; **faire ~** to please.

plan *m* plan, scheme, project; plane, level.

planche *f* plank, board; plate; shelf.

plancher *m* floor.

planchette *f* small board, small shelf.

plancton *m* plankton.

planer *vi* to glide, soar; to hover over.

planétaire *adj* planetary.

planète *f* planet.

planeur *m* glider.

planifier *vt* to plan.

planisphère *m* planisphere.

planning *m* programme, schedule.

plantation *f* plantation; planting.

plante *f* plant.

planter *vt* to plant; to hammer in; to stick, dump.

plantureux *adj* copious, ample.

plaque *f* sheet, plate; plaque; slab.

plaqué *adj* plated.

plaquer *vt* to plate, veneer; to jilt; to tackle.

plaquette *f* plaque; tablet; slab.

plasma *m* plasma.

plastifier *vt* to coat with plastic.

plastique *m* plastic; * *adj* plastic.

plat *adj* flat; straight; dull, insipid; ~ement *adv* dully, insipidly; * *m* plate, dish; course.

platane *m* plane tree.

plateau *m* tray; turntable; plateau; stage.

plate-bande *f* border, flower-bed.

plate-forme *f* platform.

platine *m* platinum; * *f* deck; turntable; stage.

platitude *f* platitude; flatness, dullness.

platonique *adj* platonic.

plâtre *m* plaster.

plâtrer *vt* to plaster; to set in plaster.

plâtrier *m* plasterer.

plausible *adj* plausible.

plébiscite *m* plebiscite.

plébisciter *vt* to elect by plebiscite.

plein *adj* full; entire, whole; busy; ~ement *adv* fully, in full; wholly; * *m* filling up; full house; height, middle.

plénitude *f* plenitude, fullness.

pléonasme *m* pleonasm.

pleur *m* tear, sob; **en ~s** in tears.

pleurer *vi* to cry, weep; * *vt* to mourn for, lament.

pleurésie *f* pleurisy.

pleuvoir *vi* to rain; to shower down, rain down.

plexus *m* plexus.

pli *m* fold; crease; wrinkle; envelope.

pliant *adj* collapsible, folding.

plier *vt* to fold; to bend; * *vi* to bend; to yield; **se ~ vr** to fold up; to submit.

plinthe *f* plinth; skirting board.

plissement *m* creasing, folding; puckering.

plisser *vt* to pleat, fold; to pucker; * *vi* to become creased.

pliure *f* fold; bend.

plomb *m* lead; sinker; fuse.

plombage *m* weighting; leading; filling.

plomber *vt* to weight; to fill.

plomberie *f* plumbing.

plombier *m* plumber.

plongée *f* diving, dive.

plongeoir *m* diving board.

plongeon *m* dive.

plonger *vi* to dive; to plunge, dip sharply.

plongeur *m* **-euse** *f* diver; washer-up.

ployer *vi* to bend, to sag.

pluie *f* rain; shower.

plumage *m* plumage, feathers.

plume *f* feather.

plumeau *m* feather duster.

plumer *vt* to pluck.

plupart *f* most, most part, majority; **la ~ de** most of.

pluriel *m* plural; * *adj* plural.

plus *adv* more, most; **~ grand que** bigger than; **de ~ en ~** more and more; **de ~ be-** sides, moreover; **non ~** neither, not either.

plusieurs *adj* several.

plus-que-parfait *m* pluperfect.

plus-value *f* appreciation; increase in value.

plutonium *m* plutonium.

plutôt *adv* rather, quite, fairly; sooner.

pluvieux *adj* rainy, wet.

pneu *m* tyre.

pneumatique *adj* pneumatic; * *m* tyre.

pneumonie *f* pneumonia.

poche *f* pocket; pouch; bag.

pocher *vt* to poach.

pochette *f* pocket handkerchief; wallet; envelope.

pochoir *m* stencil.

podium *m* podium.

poêle *m* stove; * *f* frying pan.

poème *m* poem.

poésie *f* poetry.

poète *m* poet.

poétique *adj* poetic; **~ment** *adv* poetically.

poids *m* weight, influence; ~ lourd heavyweight; ~ **plume** featherweight.

poignant *adj* poignant.

poignard *m* dagger.

poignarder *vt* to stab.

poigne *f* grip; hand.

poignée *f* handful; ~ **de mains** handshake.

poignet *m* wrist; cuff.

poil *m* hair; coat; bristle.

poilu *adj* hairy.

poinçon *m* hallmark, style; awl.

poinçonner *vt* to stamp; to hallmark.

poindre *vi* to break, dawn.

poing *m* fist; **coup de ~** punch.

point *m* point, spot; stage; full stop; **mettre au ~** to finalize; to perfect; **faire le ~** (*mar*) to take bearings; **être sur le ~ de** to be about to; **à~** medium, just right, when due; **~-virgule** semicolon; **~ de vue** point of view.

pointage *m* checking off; sighting; scrutiny.

pointe *f* point, head; spike; tack; **tailler en ~** to cut to a point; **sur la ~ des pieds** on tiptoe.

pointer *vi* to clock in; to soar up; to peep out; * *vt* to check off; to clock in; to stick into.

pointillé *m* stipple engraving; dotted line.

pointilleux *adj* particular, fastidious.

pointu *adj* pointed, sharp; subtle.

pointure *f* size, number.

poire *f* pear.

poireau *m* leek.

poirier *m* pear tree.

pois *m* pea; ~ **chiche** chickpea; **petits ~** garden peas.

poison *m* poison.

poisseux *adj* sticky.

poisson *m* fish.

poissonnerie *f* fishmonger's, fish shop.

poissonnier *m* **-ière** *f* fishmonger.

poitrail *m* breast, chest.

poitrine *f* chest, breast; bosom.

poivre *m* pepper.

poivrer *vt* to pepper, put pepper in.

poivrière *f* pepperpot.

poivron *m* green pepper, capsicum.

polaire *adj* polar.

polariser *vt* to polarize; to attract.

polarité *f* polarity.

polaroïd *m* polaroid; * *adj* polaroid.

pôle *m* pole; centre.

polémique *f* controversy, polemic; * *adj* controversial, polemic.

poli *adj* polite; polished, smooth; ~**ment** *adv* politely.

police *f* police; policing; regulations.

polichinelle *m* buffoon.

policier *m* policeman, -**ière** *f* policewoman.

poliomyélite *f* poliomyelitis.

polir *vt* to polish; to refine.

politesse *f* politeness, courtesy.

politicien *m* -**ne** *f* politician; * *adj* (*pej*) politicking.

politique *f* politics; policy; * *adj* political; ~**ment** *adv* politically.

politiser *vt* to politicize; to make a political issue of.

pollen *m* pollen.

polluant *adj* polluting; * *m* pollutant.

polluer *vt* to pollute.

pollution *f* pollution.

polo *m* polo.

poltron *m* -**ne** *f* coward; * *adj* cowardly, craven.

polyamide *m* polyamide.

polycopier *vt* to duplicate, stencil.

polyester *m* polyester.

polygame *m* polygamist.

polygamie *f* polygamy.

polyglotte *adj* polyglot; * *mf* polyglot.

polygone *m* polygon.

polymère *m* polymer; * *adj* polymeric.

polyvalent *adj* polyvalent; varied; versatile.

pommade *f* ointment.

pomme *f* apple.

pomme de terre *f* potato.

pommette *f* cheekbone.

pommier *m* apple tree.

pompe *f* pump.

pomper *vt* to pump.

pompeux *adj* pompous; pretentious.

pompier *m* fireman.

pompiste *mf* pump attendant.

poncer *vt* to sand down, rub down.

ponction *f* (*med*) puncture.

ponctualité *f* punctuality.

ponctuation *f* punctuation.

ponctuel *adj* punctual; ~**lement** *adv* punctually.

ponctuer *vt* to punctuate; to phrase.

pondéré *adj* weighted; levelheaded.

pondre *vt* to lay; to produce.

poney *m* pony.

pont *m* bridge; deck; axle.

ponte *f* laying; clutch.

pontifical *adj* pontifical.

ponton *m* pontoon; landing stage.

populaire *adj* popular; working-class; vernacular.

populariser *vt* to popularize.

popularité *f* popularity.

population *f* population.

porc *m* pig; pork.

porcelaine *f* porcelain, china.

porc-épic *m* porcupine.

porche *m* porch.

porcherie *f* pigsty.

pore *m* pore.

poreux *adj* porous.

pornographique *adj* pornographic.

port *m* port, harbour; carrying, wearing.

portail *m* portal, gate.

portatif *adj* portable.

porte *f* door; gate; threshold.

porte-avions *m invar* aircraft carrier.

porte-bagages *m invar* luggage rack.

porte-bonheur *m invar* lucky charm.

porte-clefs, porte-clés *m invar* key ring.

porte-documents *m invar* briefcase.

portée *f* reach, range; capacity; impact, significance; **à la ~ de** within reach; **hors de ~** out of reach.

portefeuille *m* wallet; portfolio.

porte-jarretelles *m invar* suspender belt.

portemanteau *m* coat hanger; hat stand.

porte-parole *m invar* spokesperson.

porte-plume *m invar* penholder.

porter *vt* to carry; to take; to wear; to hold, keep; **se ~** *vr* to put o.s. forward; to go.

porteur *m* **-euse** *f* porter; carrier; * *adj* booster; strong, buoyant.

portier *m* commissionaire.

portière *f* door.

portillon *m* gate, barrier.

portion *f* portion, share.

portique *m* portico.

portrait *m* portrait.

portraitiste *mf* portraitist.

pose *f* pose, posture; laying, fitting, setting.

poser *vt* to put; to install; to set out; to ask; **se ~** *vr* to land, settle; to come up, arise.

positif *adj* positive, definite.

position *f* position; situation; state; stance.

positionner *vt* to position, locate.

positivement *adv* positively.

posologie *f* posology.

posséder *vt* to possess, have; to know inside out.

possesseur *m* possessor, owner.

possessif *adj* possessive.

possession *f* possession, ownership.

possibilité *f* possibility; potential.

possible *adj* possible, feasible; potential; * *m*: **faire son ~** to do one's best.

postal *adj* postal, mail.

poste *f* post office, post; * *m* post, position; station; job.

poster *vt* to post, mail; to station; **se ~** *vr* to take up a position.

postérieur *adj* later, subsequent; back, posterior.

postérité *f* posterity; descendants.

posthume *adj* posthumous.

postiche *adj* false; postiche; pretended; * *m* hairpiece; toupee.

postier *m* **-ière** *f* post office worker.

postillon *m* postilion.

postulant *m* **-e** *f* applicant.

postuler *vt* to apply for; to postulate.

posture *f* posture, position.

pot *m* jar; pot; can.

potable *adj* drinkable; passable.

potage *m* soup.

potager *m* kitchen garden; * *adj* vegetable, edible.

potassium *m* potassium.

pot-au-feu *m invar* stew.

pot-de-vin *m* bribe.

poteau *m* post, stake.

potée *f* hotpot.

potelé *adj* plump, chubby.

potence *f* gallows; bracket.

potentiel *adj* potential; * *m* potential.

poterie f pottery, piece of pottery.

potiche f vase, mere, puppet.

potier m potter.

potion f potion.

potiron m pumpkin.

pou m louse.

poubelle f dustbin.

pouce m thumb; big toe; inch.

poudre f powder, dust.

poudrer vt to powder.

poudrière f powder magazine.

poulailler m henhouse.

poulain m foal; protegé.

poule f hen, fowl.

poulet m chicken.

poulie f pulley.

poulpe m octopus.

pouls m pulse.

poumon m lung.

poupe f stern.

poupée f doll.

poupon m baby.

pouponnière f day nursery, crèche.

pour prép for; to; in favour of; on account of; in order; ~ que so that, in order that; être ~ to be in favour of.

pourboire m tip.

pourceau m pig, swine.

pourcentage m percentage.

pourchasser vt to pursue; to harry.

pourparlers mpl talks, negotiations.

pourpre adj crimson; * m crimson.

pourquoi adv why; ~ pas? why not?; * m reason, question.

pourri adj rotten, decayed; corrupt; * m rotten part, rottenness.

pourrir vi to rot, go rotten; to deteriorate.

pourriture f rot, rottenness.

poursuite f pursuit; prosecution.

poursuivant m -e f pursuer; plaintiff.

poursuivre vt to pursue; to seek; to prosecute.

pourtant adv however, yet, nevertheless.

pourtour m circumference, perimeter.

pourvoir vt to provide, equip.

pourvu conj: ~ que provided that.

pousse f shoot; sprouting.

poussée f pressure, pushing; thrust; upsurge.

pousser vt to push; to drive; to incite; * vi to push; to grow, expand; se ~ *vr* to move, shift.

poussette *f* pushchair.

poussière *f* dust.

poussiéreux *adj* dusty.

poussin *m* chick; junior.

poutre *f* beam.

pouvoir *vi* can, be able; may, be allowed; * *m* power, ability; authority; proxy.

pragmatique *adj* pragmatic.

prairie *f* meadow, prairie.

pralin *m* praline.

praline *f* sugared almond.

praticable *adj* practicable; passable.

pratiquant *m* -e *f* churchgoer; * *adj* practising.

pratique *f* practice; exercise; observance; * *adj* practical; ~ment *adv* practically.

pratiquer *vt* to practise, exercise; to carry out.

pré *m* meadow.

préalable *adj* preliminary; previous; ~ment *adv* previously, first.

préambule *m* preamble, prelude.

préau *m* covered playground; inner yard.

préavis *m* notice, advance warning.

précaire *adj* precarious.

précarité *f* precariousness.

précaution *f* precaution; care.

précautionneux *adj* cautious, careful.

précédent *adj* previous, preceding; * *m* precedent.

précéder *vt* to precede, go before.

précepte *m* precept.

prêcher *vt* to preach; * *vi* to preach, sermonize.

prêcheur *m* -euse *f* preacher.

précieux *adj* precious; invaluable.

précipice *m* precipice; abyss.

précipitamment *adv* hurriedly, hastily.

précipitation *f* haste, violent hurry.

précipiter *vt* to throw, push down; to hasten, precipitate; se ~ *vr* to rush forward; to speed up.

précis *adj* precise, exact; ~ément *adv* precisely.

préciser *vt* to specify; to clarify; se ~ *vr* to become clear.

précision *f* precision, preciseness.

précoce *adj* precocious, premature.

préconçu *adj* preconceived.

préconiser *vt* to recommend; to advocate.

précurseur *m* forerunner, precursor; * *adj* precursory, preceding.

prédateur *m* predator.

prédécesseur *m* predecessor.

prédestiné *adj* predestined, fated.

prédiction *f* prediction.

prédire *vt* to predict, foretell.

prédisposition *f* predisposition.

prédominance *f* predominance.

prédominant *adj* predominant.

prédominer *vi* to predominate.

préfabriqué *adj* prefabricated.

préface *f* preface, prelude.

préfecture *f* prefecture.

préférable *adj* preferable; better; ~**ment** *adv* preferably.

préféré *m* -**e** *f* favourite; *adj* favourite, preferred.

préférence *f* preference.

préférer *vt* to prefer.

préfet *m* prefect.

préfigurer *vt* to prefigure.

préhistoire *f* prehistory.

préhistorique *adj* prehistoric.

préjudice *m* loss; harm; wrong; damage.

préjudiciable *adj* prejudicial, detrimental.

préjudicier *vt* to be prejudicial.

préjugé *m* prejudice.

prélasser (se) *vr* to sprawl, lounge.

prélèvement *m* taking; levying; imposition.

prélever *vt* to take; to levy; to deduct.

préliminaire *m* preliminary; * *adj* preliminary.

prélude *m* prelude; warm-up.

prématuré *adj* premature; untimely; ~**ment** *adv* prematurely.

préméditation *f* premeditation.

prémédité *adj* premeditated.

premier *m* first, first floor, -**ière** *f* first, first gear; * *adj* first; former; chief; early; primary.

première *f* première.

premièrement *adv* firstly, in first place.

prémonition *f* premonition.

prémonitoire *adj* premonitory.

prénatal *adj* prenatal.

prendre *vt* to take; to pick up; to catch; * *vi* to take root; to harden; to start; **se ~** *vr* to consider o.s.; **s'y ~ mal** to set about the wrong way; **s'en ~ à** to set upon, take it out on.

prénom *m* first name, forename.

préoccuper *vt* to worry; to preoccupy; **se ~** *vr* to concern o.s.

préparatif *m* preparation.

préparation *f* preparation; making up; training.

préparatoire *adj* preparatory.

préparer *vt* to prepare, get ready; to train; **se ~** *vr* to prepare o.s.

prépondérant *adj* preponderant, dominating.

préposition *f* preposition.

prérogative *f* prerogative.

près *adv* near, close; nearly, almost; **de ~** closely; **à peu ~** just about, near enough; **à peu de choses ~** more or less.

présage *m* omen; harbinger.

presbytère *m* presbytery.

presbytie *f* long-sightedness, presbyopia.

prescrire *vt* to prescribe; to stipulate.

présélection *f* preselection.

présence *f* presence.

présent *m* present, gift; **-e** *f* this letter, the present letter; * *adj* present; * *m* present; **à ~** just now.

présentable *adj* presentable.

présentateur *m* **-trice** *f* host, compère; presenter.

présentation *f* presentation; introduction; **faire les ~s** to make the introductions.

présenter *vt* to introduce; to present; to explain; **se ~** *vr* to appear; to come forward; to introduce o.s.

présentoir *m* display shelf.

préservatif *m* condom.

préserver *vt* to preserve; to protect; **se ~** *vr* to protect o.s.

présidence *f* presidency; chairmanship.

président *m* **-e** *f* president.

présidentiel *adj* presidential.

présider *vt* to preside, chair; to direct.

présomption *f* presumption, assumption.

présomptueux *adj* presumptuous.

presque *adv* almost, nearly; hardly, scarcely.

presqu'île *f* peninsula.

pressant *adj* urgent, pressing.

presse *f* press, newspapers; throng.

pressé *adj* hurried, urgent.

presse-citron *m invar* lemon squeezer.

pressentiment *m* presentiment, foreboding, premonition.

pressentir *vt* to have a presentiment of.

presse-papiers *m invar* paperweight.

presser *vt* to press; to squeeze; to hurry up; **se ~** *vr* to hurry; to crowd around.

pression *f* pressure.

pressoir *m* press (wine, cider).

prestation *f* benefit; service; payment; allowance.

prestidigitateur *m* **-trice** *f* conjurer; magician.

prestige *m* prestige.

prestigieux *adj* prestigious.

présumer *vt* to presume, assume.

prêt *adj* ready; prepared, willing; * *m* loan, lending.

prêt-à-porter *m* ready-to-wear.

prétendant *m* **-e** *f* candidate.

prétendre *vt* to claim, maintain; to want; to intend, mean.

prétendu *adj* so-called, supposed; **~ment** *adv* supposedly, allegedly.

prétentieux *adj* pretentious.

prétention *f* pretension, claim; pretentiousness.

prêter *vt* to lend; to attribute; to give.

prétérit *m* preterite tense.

prétexte *m* pretext, excuse.

prêtre *m* priest.

preuve *f* proof, evidence.

prévaloir *vi* to prevail.

prévenant *adj* considerate, thoughtful.

prévenir *vt* to prevent; to warn, inform; to anticipate.

préventif *adj* preventive.

prévention *f* prevention.

prévisible *adj* foreseeable.

prévision *f* prediction; forecast.

prévoir *vt* to anticipate; to plan; to provide for.

prévoyance *f* foresight, forethought.

prévoyant *adj* provident.

prévu *adj* provided for.

prier *vi* to pray; * *vt* to pray to; to beg; to invite.

prière *f* prayer; entreaty.

primaire *adj* primary; elementary.

primate *m* primate.

primauté *f* primacy.

prime *f* premium, subsidy; free gift.

primer *vi* to dominate; to take first place; * *vt* to outdo, prevail.

primeurs *fpl* early fruit and vegetable.

primevère *f* primrose.

primitif *adj* primitive.

primordial *adj* primordial, essential.

prince *m* prince.

princesse *f* princess.

principal *m* principal; headmaster; * *adj* main, principal; ~ement *adv* principally.

principe *m* principle; origin; element; en ~ in principle.

printanier *adj* spring.

printemps *m* spring.

prioritaire *adj* having priority, priority.

priorité *f* priority.

pris *adj* taken; busy, engaged.

prise *f* hold, grip; catch; plug; dose; lâcher ~ to let go one's hold; ~ **de sang** blood sample; ~ **de courant** plug, power point; ~ **de conscience** awareness, realization.

prisme *m* prism.

prison *f* prison; jail.

prisonnier *m* **-ière** *f* prisoner; * *adj* captive.

privation *f* deprivation; forfeiture.

privatiser *vt* to privatize.

privé *adj* private; unofficial; independent.

priver *vt* to deprive; se ~ *vr* to go without.

privilège *m* privilege.

privilégié *m* **-e** *f* privileged person; * *adj* privileged, favoured.

privilégier *vt* to favour.

prix *m* price, cost; prize.

probabilité *f* probability, likelihood.

probable *adj* probable, likely; ~ment *adv* probably.

problématique *adj* problematical; * *f* problem; problematics.

problème *m* problem, issue.

procédé *m* process; behaviour.

procéder *vi* to proceed.

procédure *f* procedure; proceedings.

procès *m* proceedings; lawsuit, trial.

procession *f* procession.

processus *m* process; progress.

procès-verbal *m* minutes; report.

prochain *adj* next; imminent; ~**ement** *adv* soon, shortly; * *m* neighbour.

proche *adj* nearby; close, imminent.

proclamation *f* proclamation.

proclamer *vt* to proclaim, declare.

procuration *f* proxy, power of attorney.

procurer *vt* to procure, provide; se ~ *vr* to procure, obtain for o.s.

procureur *m* prosecutor.

prodige *m* marvel, wonder.

prodigieusement *adv* prodigiously, incredibly.

prodigieux *adj* prodigious.

prodiguer *vt* to be lavish, be unsparing; to squander.

producteur *m* -**trice** *f* producer; * *adj* producing, growing.

productif *adj* productive.

production *f* production; generation; output.

productivité *f* productivity.

produire *vt* to produce; to grow; to generate; se ~ *vr* to happen, take place.

produit *m* product; goods; yield, profit.

proéminent *adj* prominent.

profane *adj* secular, profane; * *mf* layman, lay person.

profaner *vt* to profane; to defile.

proférer *vt* to utter, pronounce.

professeur *m* teacher, professor.

profession *f* profession; occupation, trade.

professionnel *m* -**le** *f* professional; skilled worker; * *adj* professional; occupational; technical; ~**lement** *adv* professionally.

profil *m* profile, outline.

profiler *vt* to profile; to streamline; se ~ *vr* to stand out, be profiled.

profit *m* profit; advantage, benefit.

profitable *adj* profitable; ~**ment** *adv* profitably.

profiter *vi* to profit; to thrive.

profiteur *m* **-euse** *f* profiteer.

profond *adj* deep, profound; heavy; **~ément** *adv* deeply, profoundly.

profondeur *f* depth; profundity.

profusion *f* profusion, wealth; à ~ plenty, in profusion.

programme *m* program; syllabus; schedule.

programmer *vt* to program; to schedule.

progrès *m* progress; improvement; advance.

progresser *vi* to progress; to advance.

progression *f* progress; progression, spread.

progressivement *adv* progressively.

prohiber *vt* to prohibit, ban.

proie *f* prey, victim.

projecteur *m* projector; spotlight, floodlight.

projectile *m* projectile; missile.

projection *f* projection, casting; showing.

projet *m* plan; draft.

projeter *vt* to plan; to throw out; to cast, project.

prolétaire *mf* proletarian.

prolétariat *m* proletariat.

prolifération *f* proliferation.

proliférer *vi* to proliferate.

prologue *m* prologue.

prolongation *f* prolongation, extension.

prolongement *m* continuation, extension.

prolonger *vt* to prolong, extend; **se ~** *vr* to go on, persist.

promenade *f* walk, stroll; drive, spin.

promener *vt* to take out for a walk; **se ~** *vr* to go for a walk.

promeneur *m* **-euse** *f* walker.

promesse *f* promise.

prometteur *adj* promising.

promettre *vt* to promise.

promontoire *m* promontory, headland.

promoteur *m* **-trice** *f* promoter, instigator.

promotion *f* promotion; advancement.

promouvoir *vt* to promote, upgrade.

prompt *adj* prompt; swift; ready; **~ement** *adv* promptly; swiftly.

promptitude *f* promptness; swiftness.

promulgation f promulgation.

promulguer vt to promulgate.

prôner vt to advocate.

pronom m pronoun.

prononcer vt to pronounce, utter; **se ~** vr to reach a verdict.

prononciation f pronunciation.

pronostic m forecast; prognosis; tip.

pronostiquer vt to forecast, prognosticate.

propagande f propaganda.

propagation f propagation; spreading.

propager vt to propagate, spread; **se ~** vr to spread, be propagated.

propane m propane.

prophète m prophet.

prophétie f prophecy.

prophétique adj prophetic.

prophétiser vt to prophesy.

propice adj propitious, favourable.

proportion f proportion, ratio.

proportionné adj proportional; proportionate.

proportionnel adj proportional; **~lement** adv proportionally.

propos m talk, remarks; intention; **à ~ de** about, on the subject of; **hors de ~** irrelevant.

proposer vt to propose, suggest; **se ~** vr to offer one's services; to intend to.

proposition f proposition, suggestion.

propre adj clean, neat; honest; own; peculiar; suitable; **~ment** adv cleanly; exactly; specifically.

propreté f cleanliness; tidiness.

propriétaire mf owner; landlord.

propriété f ownership, property; appropriateness, suitability.

propulser vt to propel, power.

propulsion f propulsion.

prorogation f prorogation; deferment; extension.

proroger vt to prorogue; to defer; to extend.

prosaïque adj mundane, prosaic.

proscrire vt to proscribe; to prohibit.

prose f prose.

prospecter vt to prospect; to canvass.

prospecteur *m* -**trice** *f* prospector.

prospection *f* prospecting; canvassing.

prospectus *m* leaflet; prospectus.

prospère *adj* prosperous, flourishing.

prospérer *vi* to prosper, flourish.

prospérité *f* prosperity.

prostate *f* prostate.

prosterner (se) *vr* to prostrate o.s.

prostituée *f* prostitute.

prostitution *f* prostitution.

prostré *adj* prostrate, prostrated.

protagoniste *m* protagonist.

protecteur *m* -**trice** *f* protector; patron; * *adj* protective; patronizing.

protection *f* protection; patronage.

protectionnisme *m* protectionism.

protégé *m* -**e** *f* favourite, protégé; * *adj* protected, sheltered.

protéger *vt* to protect; to patronize; **se** ~ *vr* to protect o.s.

protéine *f* protein.

protestant *m* -**e** *f* Protestant; * *adj* Protestant.

protestantisme *m* Protestantism.

protestation *f* protest, protestation.

protester *vi* to protest; to affirm.

prothèse *f* prosthesis; prosthetics.

protocole *m* protocol; etiquette.

prototype *m* prototype.

protubérance *f* protuberance, bulge.

proue *f* prow; bows.

prouesse *f* prowess.

prouver *vt* to prove; to demonstrate.

provenir *vi* to come from; to be due to.

proverbe *m* proverb.

proverbial *adj* proverbial.

providence *f* providence.

providentiel *adj* providential.

province *f* province.

provincial *m* -**e** *f* provincial; * *adj* provincial.

provision *f* provision; supply, stock.

provisoire *adj* provisional, temporary; ~**ment** *adv* provisionally.

provocant *adj* provocative.

provocation *f* provocation.

provoquer *vt* to provoke; to cause.

proximité *f* proximity, closeness; imminence.

prudemment *adv* prudently, carefully.

prudence *f* prudence, care.

prudent *adj* prudent, careful.

prune *f* plum.

pruneau *m* prune.

prunelle *f* sloe; pupil, eye.

prunier *m* plum tree.

psaume *m* psalm.

pseudonyme *m* pseudonym; pen name; alias.

psoriasis *m* psoriasis.

psychanalyse *f* psychoanalysis.

psychanalyser *vt* to psychoanalyse.

psychanalyste *mf* psychoanalyst.

psychédélique *adj* psychedelic.

psychiatre *mf* psychiatrist.

psychiatrie *f* psychiatry.

psychiatrique *adj* psychiatric.

psychique *adj* psychic, mental.

psychisme *m* psyche, mind.

psychologie *f* psychology.

psychologique *adj* psychological; ~ment *adv* psychologically.

psychologue *mf* psychologist; * *adj* psychological.

psychopathe *mf* psychopath; mentally ill person.

psychose *f* psychosis; obsessive fear.

psychosomatique *adj* psychosomatic.

psychothérapie *f* psychotherapy.

puberté *f* puberty.

pubis *m* pubis.

public *adj*, *f* **publique** public, state; * *m* public, audience; public sector.

publication *f* publication, publishing.

publicité *f* publicity.

publier *vt* to publish; to make public.

publiquement *adv* publicly.

puce *f* flea.

puceron *m* aphid, greenfly.

pudeur *f* modesty, decency.

pudique *adj* modest; chaste; ~ment *adv* modestly.

puer *vi* to stink; * *vt* to stink.

puéricultrice *f* paediatric nurse.

puéril *adj* puerile, childish; ~ement *adv* puerilely, childishly.

puérilité *f* puerility, childishness.

puis *adv* then, next.

puiser *vt* to draw from, extract.

puisque *conj* since; as, seeing that.

puissance *f* power, strength; output; force.

puissant *adj* powerful; potent.

puits *m* well; shaft.

pull-over *m* pullover, sweater.

pulluler *vi* to swarm, pullulate.

pulmonaire *adj* pulmonary, lung.

pulpe *f* pulp.

pulsation *f* beat; beating; pulsation.

pulsion *f* drive, urge.

pulvériser *vt* to pulverize; to powder.

puma *m* puma.

punaise *f* bug; drawing pin.

punir *vt* to punish.

punition *f* punishment.

pupille *f* pupil; ward.

pupitre *m* desk; console; lectern.

pur *adj* pure; neat; clear; ~ement *adv* purely.

purée *f* mashed potatoes; purée.

pureté *f* purity, pureness.

purge *f* purge; purgative; draining.

purger *vt* to purge; to drain.

purifier *vt* to purify, cleanse.

purin *m* liquid manure, slurry.

puritain *m* -e *f* puritan; * *adj* puritan.

puritanisme *m* puritanism.

pur-sang *m invar* thoroughbred.

purulent *adj* purulent.

pus *m* pus.

putois *m* polecat; skunk.

putréfaction *f* putrefaction.

putréfier *vt* to putrefy, rot.

pyjama *m* pyjamas.

pylône *m* pylon.

pyramide *f* pyramid.

pyrex *m* Pyrex.

pyromane *mf* pyromaniac; arsonist.

python *m* python.

Q

quadragénaire *adj mf* forty-year-old.

quadrangle *m* quadrangle.

quadrature *f* quadrature.

quadriceps *m* quadriceps.

quadrilatère *m* quadrilateral.

quadrillage *m* covering, control; check pattern.

quadriller *vt* to mark out in squares; to cover, control.

quadrupède *adj m* quadruped.

quadruple *adj m* quadruple.

quai *m* quay, wharf; platform.

qualificatif *adj* qualifying.

qualification *f* qualification.

qualifier *vt* to describe; to qualify; **se ~** *vr* to qualify for; to call o.s.

qualitatif *adj* qualitative.

qualitativement *adv* qualitatively.

qualité *f* quality; skill; position.

quand *conj* when, whenever, while.

quant *prép*: **~ à lui** as for him/it.

quantifier *vt* to quantify.

quantitatif *adj* quantitative.

quantitativement *adv* quantitatively.

quantité *f* quantity, amount.

quarantaine *f* about forty; **avoir la ~** to be in one's forties.

quarante *adj, m inv* forty.

quarantième *adj, mf* fortieth.

quart *m* quarter; beaker; watch.

quartette *m* quartet.

quartier *m* district, neighbourhood; quarters; quarter.

quartz *m* quartz.

quasi *adv* almost, nearly.

quasiment *adv* almost, nearly.

quaternaire *adj* quaternary. ***** *m* Quaternary.

quatorze *adj, m* fourteen.

quatorzième *adj, mf* fourteenth; **~ment** *adv* in fourteenth place.

quatre *adj, m* four.

quatre-vingt(s) *adj, m* eighty.

quatre-vingt-dix *adj, m* ninety.

quatre-vingtième *adj, mf* eightieth.

quatrième *adj, mf* fourth; ~ment *adv* in fourth place.

quatuor *m* quartet.

que *conj* that; than; * *pn* that; whom; what; which.

quel, *f* **quelle** *adj* who, what, which.

quelconque *adj* some, any; least, slight; poor, indifferent.

quelque *adj* some; ~ part somewhere.

quelque chose *pn* something.

quelquefois *adv* sometimes

quelqu'un, *f* -une someone, somebody, *pl* **quelques-uns**, -unes *pn* some, a few; **il y a** ~? is there someone there?

quémander *vt* to beg for.

querelle *f* quarrel; row; debate.

quereller (se) *vr* to quarrel, squabble.

question *f* question; matter, issue.

questionnaire *m* questionnaire.

questionner *vt* to question.

quête *m* quest, search; collection; **en** ~ **de** in search of.

quêter *vi* to seek; to collect money.

queue *f* tail; stalk; queue; **faire la** ~ to queue.

qui *pn* who, whom; which.

quiche *f* quiche.

quiconque *pn* whoever, whosoever.

quiétude *f* quiet; peace; tranquillity.

quille *f* skittle; (*mar*) keel.

quincaillerie *f* hardware, ironmongery.

quinine *f* quinine.

quinquagénaire *adj mf* fifty-year-old.

quinquennal *adj* five-year, quinquennial.

quinquina *m* cinchona.

quinte *f* (*mus*) fifth; coughing fit.

quintette *m* quintet.

quintuple *adj* quintuple; * *m* quintuple.

quintupler *vt* to multiply by five; * *vi* to quintuple, increase fivefold.

quintuplés *mpl* -ées *fpl* quintuplets.

quinzaine *f* about fifteen; fortnight.

quinze *adj, m* fifteen.

quinzième *adj, mf* fifteenth; ~**ment** *adv* in fifteenth place.

quiproquo *m* mistake; misunderstanding.

quittance *f* receipt; bill.

quitte *adj* even, quits; être ~ envers to be quits, all square with; ~ à even if it means, although it may mean; ~ ou double double or quits.

quitter *vt* to leave; to give up; se ~ *vr* to part company, separate.

quoi *pn* what; ~ que whatever.

quoique *conj* although, though.

quolibet *m* gibe, jeer.

quote-part *f* share.

quotidien *adj* daily, everyday; ~**nement** *adv* daily, every day; * *m* everyday life.

quotient *m* quotient; quota.

R

rabâcher *vi* to harp on, keep on; * *vt* to rehearse, harp on.

rabais *m* reduction, discount; **au ~** at a reduced price.

rabaisser *vt* to humble, disparage; to reduce; **se ~** *vr* to belittle o.s.

rabattre *vt* to close; to pull down; to reduce; **se ~** *vr* to cut across, pull in front of; **se ~ sur** to fall back on.

rabbin *m* rabbi.

rabot *m* plane.

raboter *vt* to plane; to scrape.

rabougri *adj* stunted, puny.

racaille *f* rabble, scum.

raccommodage *m* mending, repairing.

raccommoder *vt* to mend, repair.

raccompagner *vt* to see back to; to accompany home.

raccord *m* join; link; pointing.

raccordement *m* linking; joining; connecting.

raccorder *vt* to link up, join up; **se ~** *vr* to link, join up.

raccourci *m* shortcut; **en ~** in short.

raccourcir *vt* to shorten, curtail; * *vi* to shrink; to grow shorter.

raccrocher *vt* to ring off; to hang up; to grab; **se ~** *vr* to catch; to cling to.

race *f* race; stock; breed.

rachat *m* repurchase, purchase.

racheter *vt* to repurchase; to redeem; to ransom.

rachitique *adj* rachitic; scrawny.

racial *adj* racial.

racine *f* root; **~ carrée** square root.

racisme *m* racism.

raciste *mf* racist; * *adj* racist.

racler *vt* to scrape; to rake.

racoler *vt* to accost; to solicit.

raconter *vt* to tell, recount.

radar *m* radar.

rade *f* (*mar*) harbour, roads.

radeau *m* raft.

radiateur *m* radiator; heater.

radiation *f* radiation.

radical *adj* radical; ~**ement** *adv* radically.

radieux *adj* radiant, dazzling.

radin *m* -**e** *f* skinflint; * *adj* mean, stingy.

radio *f* radio; X-ray.

radioactif *adj* radioactive.

radioactivité *f* radioactivity.

radiodiffuser *vt* to broadcast (radio).

radiodiffusion *f* broadcasting (radio).

radiographie *f* radiography; X-ray photography.

radiologie *f* radiology.

radiologue *mf* radiologist.

radiophonique *adj* radio.

radioscopie *f* radioscopy.

radio-taxi *m* radio taxi.

radis *m* radish.

radium *m* radium.

radoter *vi* to ramble; to dote.

radoucir *vt* to soften; se ~ *vr* to calm down; to mellow.

rafale *f* gust, blast; flurry.

raffermir *vt* to harden; to strengthen; se ~ *vr* to become strengthened.

raffinage *m* refining.

raffiné *adj* refined, sophisticated.

raffinement *m* refinement, sophistication.

raffiner *vt* to refine.

raffoler *vi*: ~ **de** to be crazy about.

rafle *f* raid, round-up.

rafraîchir *vt* to cool, freshen, chill; se ~ *vr* to freshen up; to get colder.

rafraîchissant *adj* refreshing, cooling.

rafraîchissement *m* cooling; cold drink.

rage *f* rage, fury; mania; rabies.

rageur *adj* quick-tempered; bad-tempered.

ragot *m* (*fam*) malicious gossip.

ragoût *m* ragout; stew.

raid *m* raid; trek.

raide *adj* stiff; steep; rough; (*col*) broke.

raideur *f* stiffness; steepness; roughness.

raidir *vt* to stiffen; to tighten; to harden.

raie *f* line; furrow; scratch.

raifort *m* horseradish.

rail *m* rail; railway.

railler *vt* to scoff at, mock.

raillerie *f* mockery, scoffing.

railleur *adj* mocking, scoffing.

rainette *f* tree frog.

raisin *m* grape.

raison *f* reason; motive; sense; ground; ratio; **avoir ~** to be right; **en ~ de** because of.

raisonnable *adj* reasonable, sensible; **~ment** *adv* reasonably.

raisonnement *m* reasoning; argument.

raisonner *vi* to reason; to argue.

rajeunir *vi* to feel younger; to be modernized; * *vt* to rejuvenate.

rajouter *vt* to put in; to add; **en ~** to exaggerate.

rajuster *vt* to readjust, rearrange; to tidy up.

râle *m* groan; death rattle.

ralenti *adj* slow; slackened; * *m* slow motion; **au ~** ticking over, idling.

ralentir *vi* to slow down, let up; * *vt* to slow down, check.

ralentissement *m* slowing down; slowing up.

râler *vi* to groan, moan.

ralliement *m* rallying, winning over; uniting.

rallier *vt* to rally; to win over; **se ~** *vr* to join; to side with.

rallonge *f* extension, lengthening; extension lead.

rallumer *vt* to relight; to switch on again; to revive.

ramadan *m* Ramadan.

ramage *m* song; foliage.

ramassage *m* collection; gathering.

ramasser *vt* to pick up; to collect, gather.

rambarde *f* guardrail.

rame *f* oar; underground train; stake.

rameau *m* branch; ramification.

ramener *vt* to bring back, restore.

ramer *vi* to row.

rameur *m* **-euse** *f* rower.

ramification *f* ramification.

ramifier (se) *vr* to ramify; to branch out.

ramollir *vt* to soften; to weaken; **se ~** *vr* to go soft.

ramoner *vt* to sweep.

ramoneur *m* chimney sweep.

rampant *adj* crawling, creeping.

rampe *f* ramp, slope; gradient.

ramper *vi* to crawl, slither.

rance *adj* rancid, rank.

rancœur *f* rancour, resentment.

rançon *f* ransom.

rancune *f* grudge, resentment.

rancunier *adj* rancorous, spiteful.

randonnée *f* drive; ride; ramble.

randonneur *m* **-euse** *f* hiker, rambler.

rang *m* row, line; rank; class.

rangée *f* row, range, tier.

rangement *m* arranging, putting in order.

ranger *vt* to arrange, array; to put in order; se ~ *vr* to line up; to make room; to park.

ranimer *vt* to reanimate, revive; to rekindle.

rapace *m* bird of prey.

rapatrié *m* **-e** *f* repatriate; * *adj* repatriated.

rapatriement *m* repatriation.

rapatrier *vt* to repatriate.

râpe *f* rasp, rough file.

râper *vt* to grate; to rasp.

râpeux *adj* rough.

rapide *adj* rapid, quick; steep; ~**ment** *adv* rapidly, quickly.

rapidité *f* rapidity, quickness.

rapiécer *vt* to patch up.

rappel *m* recall; reminder.

rappeler *vt* to recall; to remind; se ~ *vr* to remember.

rapport *m* report; relation; reference; profit; en ~ avec in touch with.

rapporter *vt* to report; to bring back; to yield; se ~ *vr*: se ~ à to relate to.

rapporteur *m* **-euse** *f* reporter; tell-tale; * *adj* tell-tale; * *m* (*math*) protractor.

rapprochement *m* drawing closer; reconciliation.

rapprocher *vt* to bring nearer; to reconcile; se ~ *vr* to approach; to come together, be reconciled.

rapt *m* abduction.

raquette *f* racket.

rare *adj* rare; few, odd; exceptional; ~**ment** *adv* rarely, seldom.

raréfier (**se**) *vr* to rarefy; become scarce.

rareté *f* rarity; scarcity; infrequency.

rarissime *adj* extremely rare.

ras *adj* close-shaven, shorn; à ~ short; level with; à ~ bords to the brim; en avoir ~ le bol (*fam*) to be fed up.

rasage *m* shaving; shearing.

raser *vt* to shave off; to scrape; to raze; **se ~** *vr* to have a shave.

rasoir *m* razor.

rassasier *vt* to fill sb up.

rassemblement *m* assembling, mustering; crowd; political group.

rassembler *vt* to rally, gather together; **se ~** *vr* to gather, assemble.

rasseoir (se) *vr* to sit down again.

rasséréner *vt* to clear up, restore serenity to.

rassis *adj* settled; calm; stale.

rassurant *adj* reassuring, comforting.

rassurer *vt* to reassure; to comfort; **se ~** *vr* to be reassured.

rat *m* rat.

ratatiner *vt* to shrivel; to wrinkle; **se ~** *vr* to become wrinkled.

ratatouille *f* ratatouille.

rate *f* spleen.

raté *m* -e *f* failure; * *m* misfire.

râteau *m* rake.

râtelier *m* rack; denture.

rater *vt* to miss; to spoil; to fail; * *vi* to misfire; to miss.

ratification *f* ratification.

ratifier *vt* to ratify, confirm.

ration *f* ration, allowance.

rationnel *adj* rational.

rationnement *m* rationing.

rationner *vt* to ration, put on rations; **se ~** *vr* to ration o.s.

ratisser *vt* to rake; to comb.

rattacher *vt* to refasten; to attach; to link.

rattraper *vt* to catch again, retake; to recover; **se ~** *vr* to catch hold of; to make up for.

rature *f* crossing-out.

raturer *vt* to cross out.

rauque *adj* hoarse, raucous.

ravage *m* havoc; ravaging, laying waste.

ravager *vt* to ravage; devastate.

ravaler *vt* to swallow again; to restore.

ravi *adj* delighted.

ravin *m* ravine, gully.

ravir *vt* to delight.

raviser (se) *vr* to think better of it, change one's mind.

ravissant *adj* ravishing, delightful.

ravitaillement *m* supplies; refuelling.

ravitailler *vt* to resupply; **se ~** *vr* to be resupplied; to refuel.

raviver *vt* to revive, reanimate; **se ~** *vr* to be revived.

rayer *vt* to scratch; to cross out.

rayon *m* ray, beam; spoke; shelf.

rayonnant *adj* radiant, beaming.

rayonnement *m* radiance, effulgence; influence.

rayonner *vi* to radiate, shine; to be influential.

rayure *f* stripe; streak; groove.

réaccoutumer *vt* to reaccustom; **se ~** *vr* to become reaccustomed.

réacteur *m* reactor; jet-engine.

réaction *f* reaction.

réactionnaire *adj* reactionary; * *mf* reactionary.

réactiver *vt* to reactivate.

réadaptation *f* rehabilitation; readjustment.

réadapter *vt* to readjust; to rehabilitate.

réagir *vi* to react.

réalisateur *m* -**trice** *f* director, film-maker.

réalisation *f* realization; achievement.

réaliser *vt* to realize; to carry out; to achieve; **se ~** *vr* to be realized, come true.

réalisme *m* realism.

réaliste *adj* realistic; * *mf* realist.

réalité *f* reality; **en ~** in fact, in reality.

réanimation *f* resuscitation.

réanimer *vt* to reanimate; to resuscitate.

réapparaître *vi* to reappear.

rébarbatif *adj* stern, grim, forbidding.

rebattu *adj* hackneyed.

rebelle *mf* rebel; * *adj* rebel, rebellious.

rebeller (se) *vr* to rebel.

rébellion *f* rebellion.

reboisement *m* reafforestation.

reboiser *vt* to reafforest.

rebondir *vi* to bounce; to rebound.

rebondissement *m* rebound; bouncing.

rebord *m* rim, edge; hem.

rebrousser *vt* to brush back; **~ chemin** to turn back.

rébus *m* rebus, puzzle.

rebut *m* scrap; repulse, rebuff.

récalcitrant *adj* recalcitrant, stubborn.

récapituler *vt* to recapitulate, sum up.

receler *vt* to receive; to harbour.

récemment *adv* recently.

recensement *m* census, inventory.

recenser *vt* to make a census of; to record.

récent *adj* recent; new.

récépissé *m* receipt.

récepteur *m* receiver.

réceptif *adj* receptive.

réception *f* reception, welcome; receipt.

réceptionniste *mf* receptionist.

récession *f* recession.

recette *f* recipe; formula; receipt.

receveur *m* -euse *f* recipient; collector.

recevoir *vt* to receive, welcome; to take, collect.

rechange *m*: change; spare; de ~ spare.

recharge *f* recharging; reloading.

rechargeable *adj* rechargeable; reloadable; refillable.

recharger *vt* to recharge; to reload; to refill.

réchaud *m* stove; dish-warmer.

réchauffer *vt* to reheat; to warm up; se ~ *vr* to get warmer.

rêche *adj* rough, harsh.

recherche *f* search; inquiry; investigation; research; être à la ~ de to be in search of.

recherché *adj* sought after, in demand; choice, exquisite.

rechercher *vt* to seek; to investigate.

rechigner *vt* to balk; to grumble.

rechute *f* relapse; lapse.

récidive *f* second offence, relapse into crime; (med) recurrence.

récidiver *vi* to reoffend; to recur.

récidiviste *mf* recidivist, habitual criminal.

récif *m* reef.

récipient *m* container, receptacle.

réciproque *adj* reciprocal, mutual; ~ment *adv* reciprocally.

récit *m* account, story.

récital *m*, *pl* -als recital.

récitation f recitation; recital.

réciter vt to recite.

réclamation f complaint; demand; claim.

réclame f advertisement; publicity; **en ~** on offer.

réclamer vt to claim, demand, ask for; * vi to complain.

reclus adj shut up, secluded.

réclusion f reclusion; confinement.

recoiffer vt to do sb's hair; **se ~** vr to do one's hair.

recoin m corner, nook.

recoller vt to restick.

récolte f harvest; collection; result.

récolter vt to harvest; to collect.

recommandation f recommendation, reference.

recommander vt to recommend; to commend; to register (letter).

recommencement m renewal; fresh beginning.

recommencer vi to begin again; * vt to begin again, resume.

récompense f reward; award.

réconciliation f reconciliation.

réconcilier vt to reconcile; **se ~** vr to become reconciled.

reconduire vt to bring back; to see home, escort.

réconfort m comfort.

réconfortant adj comforting; tonic.

réconforter vt to comfort; to fortify; **se ~** vr to take some refreshment.

reconnaissance f recognition; acknowledgement; gratitude.

reconnaissant adj grateful.

reconnaître vt to recognize; to acknowledge; to be grateful.

reconnu adj recognized, accepted.

reconquérir vt to reconquer; to recover.

reconsidérer vt to reconsider.

reconstituer vt to reconstitute; rebuild, restore.

reconstitution f reconstitution; rebuilding, restoration.

reconstruire vt to reconstruct, rebuild.

reconversion f reconversion, redeployment.

recopier vt to copy out.

record m record.

recoudre vt to sew up.

recoupement m crosscheck.

recourbé *adj* curved, hooked.

recourir *vi* to run again; ~ à to resort to.

recours *m* recourse; redress; (*jur*) appeal.

recouvrir *vt* to cover again; to cover up.

récréatif *adj* recreative; entertaining.

récréation *f* recreation; break.

récrimination *f* recrimination, remonstration.

récriminer *vi* to recriminate, remonstrate.

recroqueviller (se) *vr* to shrivel up.

recrudescence *f* recrudescence; upsurge; further outbreak.

recrue *f* recruit.

recrutement *m* recruiting, recruitment.

recruter *vt* to recruit.

rectal *adj* rectal.

rectangle *m* rectangle.

rectangulaire *adj* rectangular.

recteur *m* priest, rector.

rectificatif *m* correction; * *adj* corrected, rectified.

rectification *f* rectification; correction.

rectifier *vt* to rectify, correct; to adjust.

rectiligne *adj* straight; rectilinear.

recto *m* recto, first side; front.

rectum *m* rectum.

reçu *pp* recevoir accepted, successful; * *m* receipt.

recueil *m* collection, miscellany.

recueillement *m* meditation.

recueillir *vt* to gather, collect; to record; se ~ *vr* to collect one's thoughts.

recul *m* retreat; recession; decline.

reculer *vi* to fall back, retreat; * *vt* to move back; to defer.

récupération *f* recovery; retrieval.

récupérer *vt* to recover, retrieve; to recuperate; * *vi* to recover.

récurer *vt* to scour.

recycler *vt* to recycle.

rédacteur *m* -trice *f* editor, compiler; drafter; writer; sub-editor.

rédaction *f* drafting, drawing up.

rédemption *f* redemption.

redescendre *vi* to go down again; * *vt* to bring down again.

redevable *adj* indebted, owing; liable.

redevance *f* rent; tax; fees.

rediffusion *f* repeat, reshowing.

rédiger *vt* to write; to compile; to draft.

redire *vt* to repeat, say again; **trouver à ~ à** to find fault with.

redoubler *vt* to increase, intensify; * *vi* to increase, intensify; **~ de** to redouble.

redoutable *adj* redoubtable, formidable.

redouter *vt* to dread, fear.

redresser *vt* to rectify; to true; to set up again; **se ~** *vr* to stand up; to right o.s.

réduction *f* reduction; discount; mitigation.

réduire *vt* to reduce, diminish; **se ~** *vr*: **se ~ à** to boil down to.

réduit *adj* reduced, limited; miniature; * *m* retreat; recess; small room.

rééducation *f* re-education; rehabilitation.

rééduquer *vt* to re-educate; to rehabilitate.

réel *adj* real, genuine; **~lement** *adv* really.

réélire *vt* to re-elect.

rééquilibrer *vt* to restabilize.

réévaluer *vt* to revalue.

refaire *vt* to redo; to remake; to renew.

réfectoire *m* canteen, refectory.

référence *f* reference.

référendum *m* referendum.

refermer *vt* to close again.

réfléchi *adj* well-considered; reflective, thoughtful.

réfléchir *vi* to think, reflect; * *vt* to realize; to mirror.

reflet *m* reflection; reflex.

refléter *vt* to reflect, mirror.

réflexe *m* reflex.

réflexion *f* thought, reflection; remark; **à la ~** on reflection; **~ faite** all things considered.

reflux *m* reflux, ebb.

réforme *f* reform, amendment; discharge.

réformer *vt* to reform, correct; to invalid out; to scrap.

refouler *vt* to drive back, repel.

réfraction *f* refraction.

refrain *m* refrain, chorus.

réfréner *vt* to curb, hold in check.

réfrigérateur *m* refrigerator.

réfrigérer *vt* to refrigerate.

refroidir *vt* to cool; * *vi* to cool down, get cold.

refroidissement *m* cooling; chill.

refuge *m* refuge, shelter; lay-by.

réfugié *m* **-e** *f* refugee; * *adj* refugee.

réfugier (se) *vr* to take refuge.

refus *m* refusal.

refuser *vt* to refuse; to reject; to deny; **se ~** *vr* to deny o.s.; **se ~ à** to reject.

réfuter *vt* to refute.

regagner *vt* to regain, win back.

regain *m* renewal; revival.

régal *m* delight, treat.

régaler *vt* to regale; to treat; **se ~** *vr* to treat o.s.

regard *m* look; glance; expression; peephole.

regardant *adj* particular, meticulous; stingy.

regarder *vt* to look at; to glance; to be opposite; to concern; **~ à** to think about.

régates *fpl* regattas.

régénération *f* regeneration.

régénérer *vt* to regenerate, revive.

régent *m* **-e** *f* regent.

régenter *vt* to rule over, domineer.

régie *f* administration; state control.

régime *m* system, régime; scheme; diet; rate, speed.

régiment *m* regiment.

région *f* region, area.

régional *adj* regional.

régir *vt* to govern, rule.

régisseur *m* manager; steward; bailiff.

registre *m* register, record; style; compass.

réglable *adj* adjustable.

réglage *m* regulation, adjustment; tuning.

règle *f* rule; order; regularity; period.

règlement *m* regulation, rules; settlement.

réglementaire *adj* regulation; statutory.

réglementation *f* regulations; control.

réglementer *vt* to regulate, control.

régler *vt* to settle, pay; to regulate.

réglisse *f* liquorice.

règne *m* reign.

régner *vi* to reign; to prevail.

regorger *vi*: **~ de** to overflow with, abound in.

régresser *vi* to regress; to recede.

régression *f* regression.

regret *m* regret, yearning; à ~ regretfully.

regrettable *adj* regrettable.

regretter *vt* to regret, be sorry; to miss.

regroupement *m* gathering together; merger.

regrouper *vt* to group together; to reassemble; **se ~** *vr* to gather together.

régulariser *vt* to regularize; straighten out.

régularité *f* regularity; consistency.

régulier *adj* regular; consistent; steady; even; legitimate.

régulièrement *adv* regularly; consistently; lawfully.

réhabilitation *f* rehabilitation; discharge; reinstatement.

réhabiliter *vt* to rehabilitate; to discharge; to reinstate.

réhabituer *vt* to reaccustom sb to; **se ~** *vr* to reaccustom o.s. to.

rehausser *vt* to heighten, raise.

rein *m* kidney.

réincarnation *f* reincarnation.

reine *f* queen.

reine-claude *f* greengage.

réinsertion *f* reinsertion, reintegration.

réintégrer *vt* to reinstate; to return to.

réitérer *vt* to reiterate, repeat.

rejaillir *vi* to gush out; to rebound on.

rejet *m* rejection, dismissal; throwing up.

rejeter *vt* to reject, dismiss; throw up.

rejoindre *vt* to rejoin; to catch up with.

rejouer *vt* to replay; to perform again; * *vi* to play again.

réjouir *vt* to delight; to entertain; **se ~** *vr* to rejoice, be delighted.

réjouissance *f* rejoicing, merry-making.

relâche *f* intermission, respite; **faire ~** to be closed; **sans ~** relentlessly.

relâchement *m* relaxation, loosening; laxity.

relâcher *vt* to relax, slacken; **se ~** *vr* to relax; to become lax.

relais *m* relay; shift; staging post.

relatif *adj* relative; relating to.

relation *f* relation, relationship; reference; acquaintance; account; **être en ~ avec** to be in contact with.

relativement *adv* relatively.

relativisme *m* relativism.

relativité *f* relativity.

relaxant *adj* relaxing.

relaxation *f* relaxation.

relaxer *vt* to relax; to acquit; to release; **se ~** *vr* to relax.

relayer *vt* to relieve, take the place of; to relay; **se ~** *vr* to take turns.

relecture *f* rereading.

reléguer *vt* to relegate; to banish.

relève *f* relief; relief party.

relevé *m* statement; list; bill; * *adj* turned up, rolled up; elevated.

relever *vt* to set up again, raise again; to rebuild; to relieve; **se ~** *vr* to stand up again; to get up.

relief *m* relief; contours; depth.

relier *vt* to link up, connect; to bind.

religieux *m* monk, **-euse** *f* nun; * *adj* religious.

religion *f* religion.

relique *f* relic.

relire *vt* to reread.

reliure *f* binding; bookbinding.

reluire *vi* to gleam, shine.

remaniement *m* recasting; al-tering; revision; amendment.

remanier *vt* to recast, revise; to amend.

remarquable *adj* remarkable, notable; **~ment** *adv* remarkably.

remarque *f* remark, comment.

remarquer *vt* to remark; to notice.

rembourrer *vt* to stuff; to pad.

remboursement *m* reimbursement, repayment.

rembourser *vt* to reimburse, pay back.

remède *m* remedy, cure.

remédier *vi*: **~ à** to remedy, cure.

remerciement *m* thanks; thanking.

remercier *vt* to thank.

remettre *vt* to put back; to replace; to restart; to revive; **se ~** *vr* to recover, get better; **se ~ à** to start doing sth again; **se ~ de** to get over sth.

réminiscence *f* reminiscence.

remise *f* delivery; remittance; discount; deferment; **~ en état** repairing; **~ à neuf** restoration; **~ en jeu** throwin; ~ **en question** calling into question; ~ **en cause** calling into question; ~ **de peine** remission.

remmener *vt* to take back.

remontant *m* tonic; * *adj* invigorating, fortifying.

remonte-pente *m* ski tow.

remonter *vi* to go up again; to rise, increase; to return; * *vt* to go up; to take up.

remontrance *f* remonstrance.

remords *m* remorse.

remorque *f* trailer; towrope.

remorquer *vt* to tow.

remorqueur *m* tug.

rémouleur *m* knife-grinder.

remous *m* back-wash; eddy, swirl.

rempailler *vt* to reseat (chair).

rempart *m* rampart; defence.

remplaçant *m* -e *f* substitute.

remplacement *m* replacing; substitution.

remplacer *vt* to replace, stand in for.

remplir *vt* to fill; to fill in; to fulfil; se ~ *vr* to fill up.

remplissage *m* filling up; padding.

remporter *vt* to take away.

remuant *adj* restless, fidgety.

remue-ménage *m invar* commotion; hullabaloo.

remuer *vi* to move; to fidget; * *vt* to move, shift; to stir; se ~ *vr* to move; to shift o.s.

rémunération *f* remuneration, payment.

rémunérer *vt* to remunerate, pay.

renaissance *f* rebirth, Renaissance.

renaître *vi* to be reborn; to be revived; to reappear.

renard *m* fox.

renchérir *vi* to go further, go one better; to bid higher.

renchérissement *m* increase in price.

rencontre *f* meeting, encounter; conjuncture; collision.

rencontrer *vt* to meet; to find; to strike; se ~ *vr* to meet each other.

rendement *m* yield; output.

rendez-vous *m* appointment; date; meeting place.

rendormir *vt* to put to sleep again; se ~ *vr* to go back to sleep.

rendre *vt* to render; to give back, return; to yield; se ~ *vr* to surrender; to give way.

rêne *f* rein.

renfermé *adj* withdrawn, close; * *m* fusty/close smell.

renfermer *vt* to contain, hold.

renflement *m* bulge.

renflouer *vt* to refloat; to bail out.

renfoncement *m* recess.

renfoncer *vt* to drive further in; to recess.

renforcer *vt* to strengthen, reinforce.

renfort *m* reinforcement; help.

renfrogné *adj* frowning, glum.

renier *vt* to repudiate, disown.

renifler *vt* to sniff, snuffle.

renne *m* reindeer.

renom *m* renown, fame.

renommée *f* renowned, famed.

renoncement *m* renouncement; renunciation.

renoncer *vi* to renounce, give up.

renonciation *f* renunciation; waiver.

renouer *vt* to retie; to renew.

renouveau *m* spring; renewal.

renouveler *vt* to renew; to revive; **se ~** *vr* to be renewed.

renouvellement *m* renewal; revival.

rénovation *f* renovation; renewal.

rénover *vt* to renovate.

renseignement *m* information; intelligence.

renseigner *vt* to inform, give information to; **se ~** *vr* to ask for information.

rentabiliser *vt* to make profitable.

rentable *adj* profitable.

rente *f* rent; profit; annuity.

rentier *m* **-ière** *f* stockholder, fundholder; rentier.

rentrée *f* reopening; reassembly; reappearance.

rentrer *vi* to re-enter; to return home; to begin again; * *vt* to bring in.

renversement *m* inversion; reversal; overturning.

renverser *vt* to turn upside down; to reverse; to overturn.

renvoi *m* sending back; returning; dismissal.

renvoyer *vt* to send back; to return; to dismiss.

réorganisation *f* reorganization.

réorganiser *vt* to reorganize.

réouverture *f* reopening.

repaire *m* den, lair.

répandre *vt* to pour out; to scatter, spread; **se ~** *vr* to spread; to be spilled.

répandu *adj* widespread.

réparateur *m* **-trice** *f* repairer.

réparation *f* repairing; restoration.

réparer *vt* to repair; to restore; to make up for.

repartie *f* retort; **avoir de la ~** to have a quick wit.

repartir *vi* to set off again; to start up again.

répartir *vt* to share out; to distribute; **se ~** *vr* to share out.

répartition *f* sharing out; allocation.

repas *m* meal.

repassage *m* ironing; grinding, sharpening.

repasser *vt* to iron; to cross again; to resit; * *vi* to go past again.

repêcher *vt* to fish out, retrieve.

repeindre *vt* to repaint.

repenti *adj* repentant.

repentir *m* repentance, contrition.

repentir (se) *vr* to repent, rue.

répercussion *f* repercussion.

répercuter *vt* to reverberate; to echo; **se ~** *vr* to reverberate; to echo.

repère *m* line, mark; **point de ~** indication, reference mark.

repérer *vt* to spot, pick out; to mark out.

répertoire *m* index, catalogue; repertory.

répertorier *vt* to itemize; to index.

répéter *vt* to repeat; to rehearse; **se ~** *vr* to repeat o.s.; to reoccur.

répétitif *adj* repetitive.

répétition *f* repetition; rehearsal.

repiquer *vt* to plant out, transplant.

répit *m* respite, rest.

repli *m* fold, coil, meander; withdrawal; downturn.

replier *vt* to fold up; to withdraw; **se ~** *vr* to coil up, curl up.

réplique *f* reply, retort; counterattack.

répliquer *vt* to reply; to retaliate.

répondant *m* **-e** *f* guarantor; bail, surety.

répondeur *m* answering machine.

répondre *vt* to answer, reply.

réponse *f* response, reply.

report *m* postponement, deferment; carrying forward.

reportage *m* report; commentary; reporting.

reporter *vt* to postpone; to carry forward; to transfer; * *m* reporter.

repos *m* rest; tranquillity; landing.

reposant *adj* restful, refreshing.

reposer *vt* to put back; to rest; to ask again; se ~ *vr* to rest.

repoussant *adj* repulsive; repellent.

repousser *vt* to push back; to repel.

reprendre *vt* to retake, recapture; to resume; se ~ *vr* to correct o.s.; to pull o.s. together.

représailles *fpl* reprisals; retaliation.

représentant *m* representative.

représentatif *adj* representative.

représentation *f* representation; performance.

représenter *vt* to represent, depict; to perform; to symbolize.

répressif *adj* repressive.

répression *f* repression.

réprimande *f* reprimand, rebuke.

réprimander *vt* to reprimand, rebuke.

réprimer *vt* to repress; to quell.

reprise *f* resumption; recapture, taking back; à plusieurs ~s several times.

repriser *vt* to darn.

réprobation *f* reprobation.

reproche *m* reproach; objection.

reprocher *vt* to reproach, blame.

reproduction *f* reproduction; copy; duplicate.

reproduire *vt* to reproduce, copy; to repeat; se ~ *vr* to reproduce, breed.

reptile *m* reptile.

repu *adj* full, satiated.

républicain *m* -e *f* republican; * *adj* republican.

république *f* republic.

répudier *vt* to repudiate; to renounce.

répugnance *f* repugnance, disgust.

répugnant *adj* repugnant, disgusting, revolting.

répulsion *f* repulsion, repugnance.

réputation *f* reputation; character; fame.

réputé *adj* reputable, renowned; supposed, reputed.

requérir *vt* to call for, request.

requête *f* petition, request.

requin *m* shark.

requis *adj* required, requisite.

réquisition *f* requisition; conscription.

réquisitionner *vt* to requisition; to conscript.

rescapé *m* -e *f* survivor.

réseau *m* network, net.

réservation *f* reservation, booking.

réserve *f* reserve; reservation, caution.

réservé *f* reserved.

réserver *vt* to reserve, save; to book; to lay by.

réservoir *m* tank; reservoir.

résidence *f* residence; apartment block.

résidentiel *adj* residential.

résider *vi* to reside, dwell.

résidu *m* residue.

résignation *f* resignation.

résigner (se) *vr* to resign o.s.

résilier *vt* to terminate; to annul.

résine *f* resin.

résistance *f* resistance.

résistant *adj* resistant; tough, unyielding.

résister *vi* to resist, withstand.

résolu *adj* resolved, determined; **~ment** *adv* resolutely.

résolution *f* resolution, determination.

résonner *vi* to resound, resonate.

résorber *vt* to reduce; to absorb; **se ~** *vr* to be reduced.

résoudre *vt* to solve; to resolve; to annul; **se ~** *vr*: **se ~ à** to decide to do.

respect *m* respect, regard, deference.

respectable *adj* respectable; sizeable.

respecter *vt* to respect; to comply with.

respectif *adj* respective.

respectivement *adv* respectively.

respectueusement *adv* respectfully.

respectueux *adj* respectful.

respirable *adj* breathable.

respiration *f* breathing, respiration.

respiratoire *adj* respiratory.

respirer *vi* to breathe, respire; to rest; * *vt* to breathe in.

resplendissant *adj* shining, radiant.

responsabilité *f* responsibility; liability.

responsable *adj* responsible; liable; * *mf* official, manager.

resquiller *vi* to sneak in; to take a free ride.

ressaisir (se) *vr* to regain one's self-control.

ressemblance *f* resemblance, likeness; similarity.

ressemblant *adj* lifelike.

ressembler *vi* to resemble, be like; **se ~** *vr* to be alike.

ressemelage *m* soling, resoling.

ressentiment *m* resentment.

ressentir *vt* to feel, experience; **se ~** *vr*: **se ~ de** to feel the effects of.

resserrement *m* contraction, tightening; narrowing.

resserrer *vt* to tighten; to strengthen; **se ~** *vr* to grow tighter.

ressort *m* spring; motivation.

ressortir *vi* to go out again; to stand out.

ressortissant *m* **-e** *f* national.

ressource *f* resource, resort, expedient.

ressusciter *vi* to revive, reawaken; to come back to life; * *vt* to resuscitate; to revive.

restant *adj* remaining; * *m* rest, remainder.

restaurant *m* restaurant.

restaurateur *m* **-trice** *f* restaurateur; restorer.

restauration *f* restoration, rehabilitation; catering.

restaurer *vt* to restore; to feed; **se ~** *vr* to eat.

reste *m* rest, left-over, remainder; **du ~** besides; **être en ~** to be outdone.

rester *vi* to remain, stay; to be left; to continue; to pause.

restituer *vt* to return, restore; to refund.

restitution *f* restoration; restitution.

restreindre *vt* to restrict, curtail; **se ~** *vr* to restrain o.s.

restreint *adj* restricted, limited.

restrictif *adj* restrictive.

restriction *f* restriction, limitation; reserve.

restructurer *vt* to restructure.

résultat *m* result, outcome; profit.

résulter *vi*: ~ **de** to result, follow from, ensue.

résumé *m* summary, recapitulation; **en** ~ in brief.

résumer *vt* to sum up; **se** ~ *vr*: **se** ~ **à** to amount to.

résurrection *f* resurrection.

rétablir *vt* to re-establish, restore; **se** ~ *vr* to recover, get well again.

rétablissement *m* re-establishment, restoring.

retard *m* lateness; delay; **être en** ~ to be late; to be behind; to be backward.

retardataire *mf* latecomer; * *adj* obsolete.

retardé *adj* backward, slow.

retarder *vt* to delay; to hinder; to put back; * *vi* to be out of touch.

retenir *vt* to hold back, retain; to remember; **se** ~ *vr* to control o.s.

rétention *f* retention; withholding.

retentir *vi* to resound; to ring.

retentissant *adj* resounding; ringing.

retenue *f* discretion; deduction, stoppage; reservoir.

réticence *f* reticence.

réticent *adj* reticent.

rétine *f* retina.

retiré *adj* remote, isolated.

retirer *vt* to take off; to take out, withdraw; to redeem; **se** ~ *vr* to retire, withdraw; to stand down.

retombée *f* fallout; repercussions.

retomber *vi* to fall again; to have a relapse; ~ **sur** to come across again.

rétorquer *vt* to retort.

retouche *f* touching up; alteration.

retoucher *vt* to touch up; to alter.

retour *m* return; recurrence; vicissitude, reversal; **être de** ~ to be back.

retournement *m* reversal; turnaround.

retourner *vt* to reverse, turn over; to return; * *vi* to return, go back; **se** ~ *vr* to turn over; to overturn.

rétracter *vt* to retract, take back; **se** ~ *vr* to retract, withdraw one's evidence.

retrait *m* ebb; retreat; withdrawal; **être en** ~ to be set back.

retraite f retreat; retirement; refuge; à la ~ retired.

retraité m -e f pensioner; * adj retired.

retranchement m curtailment; entrenchment.

retrancher vt to curtail; to entrench.

retransmettre vt to retransmit.

retransmission f retransmission.

rétrécir vi to narrow; to shrink; * vt to take in, make narrower; se ~ vr to narrow; to shrink.

rétrécissement m narrowing; shrinking.

rétribuer vt to remunerate.

rétribution f retribution.

rétroactif adj retrospective; retroactive.

rétroaction f retroaction; retrospective action.

rétrograde adj reactionary, backward.

rétrograder vi to go backward, regress.

rétroprojecteur m overhead projector.

rétrospectif adj retrospective.

rétrospective f retrospective.

rétrospectivement adv retrospectively.

retrousser vt to roll up, hitch up.

retrouvailles fpl reunion.

retrouver vt to find again, to regain; to recover; to recognize; se ~ vr to meet up; to end up in.

rétroviseur m rear-view mirror.

réunifier vt to reunify.

réunion f reunion, gathering.

réunir vt to unite; to collect, gather; to combine; se ~ vr to meet; to assemble.

réussir vi to succeed, be a success; * vt to make a success of.

réussite f success, successful outcome.

revanche f revenge; en ~ on the other hand.

rêvasser vi to daydream.

rêve m dream, dreaming; illusion.

réveil m waking, awaking; alarm clock.

réveiller vt to wake; se ~ vr to awaken.

réveillon m midnight feast.

révélation f revelation, disclosure; developing.

révéler vt to reveal, disclose; se ~ vr to be revealed; to prove to be.

revenant *m* **-e** *f* ghost.

revendeur *m* **-euse** *f* retailer; dealer.

revendication *f* claiming; claim; demand.

revendiquer *vt* to claim; to demand.

revendre *vt* to resell.

revenir *vi* to come back, reappear; to happen again; **ne pas en ~** to not recover from, not pull through; **~ à soi** to come round.

revenu *m* income, revenue.

rêver *vi* to dream; to muse; * *vt* to dream of.

réverbération *f* reverberation.

réverbère *m* street lamp.

révérence *f* bow, curtsey.

révérend *adj* reverend.

révérer *vt* to revere.

rêverie *f* reverie, musing.

revers *m* back, reverse; counterpart.

réversible *adj* reversible.

revêtement *m* coating, surface.

revêtir *vt* to don; to assume.

rêveur *m* **-euse** *f* dreamer; * *adj* dreamy.

revigorer *vt* to invigorate; to revive.

revirement *m* change of mind; reversal; turnaround.

réviser *vt* to review; to revise.

révision *f* review; auditing; revision.

revivre *vt* to relive; * *vi* to live again, come alive again.

révocation *f* removal; dismissal; revocation.

revoir *vt* to see again; **se ~** *vr* to meet each other again.

révoltant *adj* revolting, appalling.

révolte *f* revolt, rebellion.

révolter *vt* to revolt, outrage; **se ~** *vr* to rebel, revolt.

révolu *adj* past, bygone.

révolution *f* revolution.

révolutionnaire *mf* revolutionary; * *adj* revolutionary.

révolutionner *vt* to revolutionize; to upset.

revolver *m* revolver.

révoquer *vt* to revoke; to dismiss.

revue *f* review; inspection.

rez-de-chaussée *m invar* ground floor.

rhabiller *vt* to dress (sb) again; to fit (sb) out again; **se ~** *vr* to get dressed again.

rhésus *m* rhesus.

rhétorique f rhetoric; * adj rhetorical.

rhinocéros m rhinoceros.

rhododendron m rhododendron.

rhubarbe f rhubarb.

rhum m rum.

rhumatisme m rheumatism.

rhume m cold.

riant adj smiling; cheerful.

ribambelle f swarm, herd.

ricanement m snigger, sniggering.

ricaner vi to snigger, giggle.

riche adj rich, wealthy; abundant; ~ment adv richly; * mf rich person.

richesse f richness; wealth; abundance.

ricochet m ricochet; rebound.

rictus m grin; grimace.

ride f wrinkle; ripple; ridge.

ridé adj wrinkled.

rideau m curtain.

ridicule adj ridiculous; * m ridiculousness; absurdity; ridicule.

ridiculiser vt to ridicule.

rien pn nothing; de ~ don't mention it; il n'en est ~ it's nothing of the sort; * m nothingness; mere nothing; pinch, shade; en un ~ de temps in no time; pour un ~ at the slightest little thing.

rieur adj cheerful; laughing.

rigide adj rigid; ~ment adv rigidly.

rigidité f rigidity, stiffness.

rigole f channel; rivulet.

rigoler vi (fam) to have a good laugh.

rigoureusement adv harshly, rigorously.

rigoureux adj rigorous, harsh.

rigueur f rigour; harshness, severity.

rime f rhyme.

rimer vi to rhyme (with).

rince-doigts m invar fingerbowl.

rincer vt to rinse out; to rinse.

ring m boxing ring.

riposte f riposte, retort.

riposter vi to answer back, retaliate.

rire vi to laugh; to smile; to joke; * m laughter, laugh.

risée f laugh; ridicule; mockery, derision.

risible adj laughable, ridiculous.

risque m risk, hazard.

risqué adj risky, hazardous; risqué.

risquer *vt* to risk; to venture; se ~ *vr* to venture, dare.

ristourne *f* discount, rebate.

rite *m* rite.

rituel *adj* ritual.

rivage *m* shore.

rival *m* -e *f* rival; sans ~ unrivalled; * *adj* rival.

rivaliser *vi* to rival, compete with; ~ de to vie with.

rivalité *f* rivalry.

rive *f* shore, bank.

river *vt* to clinch; to rivet.

riverain *m* -e *f* lakeside resident; riverside resident; * *adj* lakeside, riverside.

rivière *f* river.

riz *m* rice.

robe *f* dress; gown; ~ de chambre dressing gown.

robinet *m* tap.

robot *m* robot.

robotique *f* robotics.

robuste *adj* robust.

robustesse *f* robustness.

roc *m* rock.

rocaille *f* loose stones; rocky ground.

rocailleux *adj* rocky.

roche *f* rock.

rocher *m* rock, boulder.

rodage *m* grinding; running in, breaking in.

roder *vt* to grind; to run in.

rôder *vi* to roam; to prowl about.

rôdeur *m* -euse *f* prowler.

rogner *vt* to pare, prune, clip.

rognon *m* kidney.

roi *m* king.

rôle *m* role, character; roll, catalogue.

roman *m* novel; romance.

romancier *m* -ière *f* novelist.

romanesque *adj* fabulous; storybook; fictional.

romantique *adj* romantic.

romantisme *m* romanticism.

rompre *vt* to break; to snap; to dissolve; * *vi* to break; to burst.

ronce *f* bramble.

rond *m* circle, ring; slice, round; * *adj* round; chubby, plump; frank, ~ement *adv* briskly, frankly.

ronde *f* patrol; round; beat.

rondelle *f* slice, round; disc.

rondeur *f* plumpness; roundness.

rondin *m* log.

rond-point *m* roundabout.

ronflement *m* snore, snoring; humming; roaring.

ronfler *vi* to snore; to hum; to roar.

ronger *vt* to gnaw.

ronronner *vi* to purr; to hum.

rosbif *m* roast beef.

rose *f* rose; * *adj* pink; * *m* pink.

roseau *m* reed.

rosée *f* dew.

rosier *m* rosebush.

rossignol *m* nightingale.

rot *m* belch, burp.

roter *vi* to belch, burp.

rotation *f* rotation; turnover.

rôti *m* joint, roast.

rotin *m* rattan.

rôtir *vt* to roast.

rôtisserie *f* rotisserie, steak-house.

rotonde *f* rotunda; round-house.

rotule *f* kneecap, patella.

rouage *m* cog; gearwheel.

roucouler *vi* to coo; to bill.

roue *f* wheel.

rouge *adj* red; * *m* red; ~ à lèvres lipstick.

rouge-gorge *m* robin.

rougeole *f* measles.

rougeur *f* redness, blushing.

rougir *vi* to blush, go red; * *vt* to make red, redden.

rouille *f* rust.

rouiller *vi* to rust; * *vt* to make rusty.

roulant *adj* on wheels; moving.

rouleau *m* roll; roller.

roulement *m* rotation; movement; rumble, rumbling.

rouler *vt* to wheel, roll along; * *vi* to go, run (train); to drive.

roulette *f* castor; trundle; roulette.

roulis *m* rolling.

roulotte *f* caravan.

rouquin *m* -e *f* redhead; * *adj* red-haired.

route *f* road; way; course, direction.

routier *adj* road; * *m* lorry driver; transport café.

routine *f* routine.

routinier *adj* humdrum, routine.

roux *m*, **rousse** *f* redhead; * *adj* red, auburn.

royal *adj* royal, regal; ~ement *adv* royally.

royaliste *mf* royalist; * *adj* royalist.

royaume *m* kingdom.

royauté *f* monarchy.

ruade *f* kick (horse).

ruban *m* ribbon; tape, band.

rubéole *f* rubella.

rubis *m* ruby.

rubrique *f* column; heading, rubric.

ruche *f* hive.

rude *adj* rough; hard; unrefined; **~ment** *adv* roughly, harshly.

rudesse *f* roughness; harshness.

rudiment *m* rudiment; principle.

rudimentaire *adj* rudimentary.

rudoyer *vt* to treat harshly.

rue *f* street.

ruée *f* rush, stampede.

ruelle *f* alley.

ruer *vi* to kick (horse); **se ~** *vr* to pounce on.

rugby *m* rugby.

rugbyman *m* rugby player.

rugir *vi* to roar.

rugissement *m* roar, roaring.

rugueux *adj* rough; coarse.

ruine *f* ruin; wreck.

ruiner *vt* to ruin.

ruineux *adj* ruinous; extravagant.

ruisseau *m* stream, brook.

ruisseler *vi* to stream, flow.

ruissellement *m* streaming; cascading.

rumeur *f* rumour; murmur; hum.

ruminer *vt* to ruminate; to brood over.

rupture *f* break, rupture; breach; split.

rural *adj* rural, country.

ruse *f* cunning, slyness.

rusé *adj* cunning, crafty.

rustine ® *f* rubber repair patch.

rustique *adj* rustic.

rutilant *adj* gleaming, rutilant.

rythme *m* rhythm; rate, speed.

rythmique *adj* rhythmic.

S

sabbatique *adj* sabbatical.

sable *m* sand.

sablé *m* shortbread biscuit; * *adj* sandy, sanded.

sablier *m* hourglass, sandglass.

sabot *m* clog; hoof.

sabotage *m* sabotage.

saboter *vt* to sabotage; to mess up.

saboteur *m* -euse *f* saboteur; bungler.

sabre *m* sabre

sac *m* bag, sack; ~ à main handbag; ~ de voyage travelling bag.

saccade *f* jerk, jolt.

saccadé *adj* jerky, broken, staccato.

saccager *vt* to sack; to wreck, devastate.

saccharine *f* saccharin.

sacerdoce *m* priesthood.

sacerdotal *adj* priestly, sacerdotal.

sachet *m* bag; sachet; packet.

sacoche *f* saddlebag, satchel.

sacre *m* coronation; consécration.

sacré *adj* sacred, holy; damned, confounded.

Sacré-Cœur *m* Sacred Heart.

sacrer *vt* to crown; to consecrate.

sacrifice *m* sacrifice.

sacrifier *vt* to sacrifice; to give up; se ~ *vr* to sacrifice o.s.

sacrilège *m* sacrilege.

sacristie *f* sacristy.

sacrum *m* sacrum.

sadique *adj* sadistic; * *mf* sadist.

sadisme *m* sadism.

sadomasochiste *adj* sadomasochistic; * *mf* sadomasochist.

safari *m* safari.

safran *m* saffron.

saga *f* saga.

sagace *adj* sagacious, shrewd.

sagacité *f* sagacity, shrewdness.

sage *adj* wise, sensible; well-behaved; **~ment** *adv* wisely, sensibly; * *m* sage, wise man.

sage-femme *f* midwife.

sagesse *f* wisdom, sense; good behaviour.

sagittaire *m* archer; Sagittarius.

saignant *adj* bleeding; underdone.

saignement *m* bleeding.

saigner *vi* to bleed; * *vt* to bleed; to stick.

saillant *adj* prominent, protruding.

saillie *f* projection; sally; flash of wit.

saillir *vi* to gush out; to project, jut.

sain *adj* healthy; sound; sane; **~ement** *adv* healthily; soundly.

saindoux *m* lard.

saint *m* -e *f* saint; * *adj* holy, saintly; **Saint-Sylvestre** New Year's Eve; **Saint-Esprit** Holy Spirit.

saint-bernard *m* St Bernard.

sainteté *f* saintliness; holiness.

saisie *f* (*jur*) seizure, distraint; capture.

saisir *vt* to take hold of; (*jur*) to seize, distrain; to capture.

saisissant *adj* gripping, startling, striking.

saison *f* season.

saisonnier *adj* seasonal.

salade *f* salad; jumble, miscellany.

saladier *m* salad bowl.

salaire *m* salary, pay; reward.

salamandre *f* salamander.

salarié *m* -e *f* salaried employee; * *adj* salaried.

sale *adj* dirty, filthy; obscene; nasty; **~ment** *adv* dirtily.

salé *adj* salty, salted; savoury.

saler *vt* to salt, add salt.

saleté *f* dirtiness, dirt; rubbish; obscenity.

salière *f* saltcellar.

salin *adj* saline.

salir *vt* to make dirty, soil; **se ~** *vr* to get dirty.

salissant *adj* dirty; that gets dirty easily.

salive *f* saliva.

saliver *vi* to salivate; to drool.

salle *f* room; hall; theatre; audience; **~ de séjour** living room; **~ à manger** dining room; **~ de bain** bathroom; **~ de cinéma** cinema; **~ des ventes** saleroom.

salon *m* lounge, sitting room; exhibition.

salopette *f* overalls.

salpêtre *m* saltpetre.

salsifis *m* salsify.

salubre *adj* healthy, salubrious.

saluer *vt* to greet; to salute.

salut *m* safety, salvation; welfare; wave (hand); salute.

salutaire *adj* salutary; profitable; healthy.

salutation *f* salutation, greeting.

samedi *m* Saturday.

sanatorium *m* sanatorium.

sanctifier *vt* to sanctify, bless.

sanction *f* sanction, penalty; approval.

sanctionner *vt* to punish; to sanction, approve.

sanctuaire *m* sanctuary.

sandale *f* sandal.

sandwich *m* sandwich.

sang *m* blood; race; kindred.

sang-froid *m* sangfroid, cool, calm.

sanglant *adj* bloody, gory; bloodshot; blood-red.

sangle *f* strap; girth.

sanglier *m* wild boar.

sanglot *m* sob.

sangloter *vi* to sob.

sangsue *f* leech.

sanguinaire *adj* sanguinary, bloodthirsty.

sanitaire *adj* health, sanitary.

sans-abris *mf invar* homeless person.

sans-gêne *adj* inconsiderate; * *m invar* inconsiderate type.

santal *m* sandalwood.

santé *f* health, healthiness.

saper *vt* to undermine, sap.

sapeur-pompier *m* fireman.

saphir *m* sapphire.

sapin *m* fir tree, fir.

sarcasme *m* sarcasm.

sarcastique *adj* sarcastic.

sarcler *vt* to weed; to hoe.

sarcophage *m* sarcophagus.

sardine *f* sardine.

sardonique *adj* sardonic

SARL (société à responsabilité limitée) *f* limited liability company.

sarrasin *m* buckwheat.

sas *m* airlock; sieve.

satanique *adj* satanic, diabolical.

satellite *m* satellite.

satiété *f* satiety, satiation; à ~ ad nauseam.

satin *m* satin.

satiné *adj* satiny, satin-smooth; glazed.

satire *f* satire, lampoon.

satirique *adj* satirical.

satisfaction *f* satisfaction; gratification; appeasement.

satisfaire *vt* to satisfy; to gratify; to appease.

satisfaisant *adj* satisfactory; satisfying.

satisfait *adj* satisfied.

saturation *f* saturation.

saturé *adj* saturated; overloaded, jammed.

saturer *vt* to saturate; to surfeit; to congest.

satyre *m* satyr.

sauce *f* sauce, dressing.

saucière *f* sauceboat.

saucisse *f* sausage.

saucisson *m* large sausage; salami.

sauf *prép* save, except; unless; * *adj* safe, unhurt.

sauge *f* sage.

saugrenu *adj* preposterous, absurd.

saule *m* willow.

saumon *m* salmon.

sauna *m* sauna.

saupoudrer *vt* to sprinkle; to dust.

saut *m* jump, bound; waterfall.

sauté *adj* sauté.

sauter *vi* to jump, leap; to blow up; to get sacked.

sauterelle *f* grasshopper.

sautiller *vi* to hop, skip.

sauvage *adj* savage, wild; unsociable; ~ment *adv* savagely.

sauvegarde *f* safeguard; backup.

sauvegarder *vt* to safeguard.

sauver *vt* to save, rescue; to preserve; se ~ *vr* to save o.s.; to escape.

sauvetage *m* rescue; salvage.

sauveteur *m* rescuer.

savant *adj* learned; expert; skilled; * *m* scientist, scholar.

savate *f* old shoe.

saveur *f* flavour; savour.

savoir *vt* to know; to be aware; to understand; to be able; * *m* learning, knowledge.

savoir-faire *m* know-how.

savoir-vivre *m* good manners, good breeding.

savon *m* soap.

savonner *vt* to soap, lather.

savonnette *f* bar of soap.

savoureux *adj* tasty, savoury.

saxophone *m* saxophone.

saxophoniste *mf* saxophonist.

scabreux *adj* scabrous; dangerous; improper.

scalpel *m* scalpel.

scandale *m* scandal.

scandaleux *adj* scandalous.

scandaliser *vt* to scandalize, shock deeply; **se ~** *vr* to be scandalized.

scanner *m* scanner.

scaphandre *m* diving suit.

scarabée *m* beetle, scarab.

scarlatine *f* scarlet fever.

sceau *m* seal.

scélérat *m* -e *f* villain, rascal; * *adj* villainous, wicked.

sceller *vt* to seal.

scénario *m* scenario; screenplay.

scénariste *mf* scriptwriter.

scène *f* stage; scenery, scene.

scepticisme *m* scepticism.

sceptique *adj* sceptical; * *mf* sceptic.

sceptre *m* sceptre.

schéma *m* diagram, sketch; outline.

schématique *adj* diagrammatic, schematic; ~**ment** *adv* diagrammatically.

schématiser *vt* to schematize.

schisme *m* schism; split.

schiste *m* schist, shale.

schizophrène *mf* schizophrenic; * *adj* schizophrenic.

schizophrénie *f* schizophrenia.

sciatique *f* sciatica.

scie *f* saw; bore.

sciemment *adv* knowingly, on purpose.

science *f* science; skill; knowledge.

science-fiction *f* science fiction.

scientifique *adj* scientific; ~**ment** *adv* scientifically.

scierie *f* sawmill.

scinder *vt* to split, divide up.

scintillant *adj* sparkling, glistening.

scintillement *m* sparkling, glistening.

scintiller *vi* to sparkle, glisten.

scission *f* split, scission.

sciure *f* sawdust.

sclérose *f* sclerosis.

scléroser (se) *vr* to become sclerotic.

scolaire *adj* school; academic.

scolariser *vt* to send to school; to provide schools.

scolarité *f* schooling.

scoliose *f* scoliosis, curvature of the spine.

scooter *m* scooter.

score *m* score.

scorie *f* slag, scoria.

scorpion *m* scorpion.

scout *m* scout, boy scout.

script *m* printing; script.

scrupule *m* scruple, qualm, doubt.

scrupuleusement *adv* scrupulously.

scrupuleux *adj* scrupulous.

scruter *vt* to scrutinize, scan.

scrutin *m* ballot, poll.

sculpter *vt* to sculpt; to carve.

sculpteur *m* sculptor.

sculpture *f* sculpture.

se *pn* oneself, himself, herself, itself, themselves.

séance *f* meeting, sitting, session; seat.

seau *m* bucket, pail.

sec *adj, f* **sèche** dry, arid; barren; unfeeling; curt; neat.

sécateur *m* secateurs.

séchage *m* drying; seasoning.

sèche-cheveux *m invar* hairdrier

sèchement *adv* dryly; curtly.

sécher *vi* to dry, dry out; * *vt* to dry, wipe.

sécheresse *f* drought; dryness.

séchoir *m* drying room; ~ à linge clothes horse.

second *adj* second, in second place; * *m* second; second floor; second in command; * *f* second.

secondaire *adj* secondary.

seconder *vt* to assist, help.

secouer *vt* to shake, toss; se ~ *vr* to shake o.s.

secourir *vt* to help, assist.

secouriste *mf* first-aid worker.

secours *m* help, assistance; relief; rescue.

secousse *f* jolt, bump.

secret *m* secret; privacy; mystery; * *adj* secret; private; discreet.

secrétaire *mf* secretary; * *m* writing desk.

secrétariat *m* office of secretary; secretariat.

secrètement *adv* secretly.

secréter *vt* to secrete, exude.

sécrétion *f* secretion.

secte *f* sect.

secteur *m* sector, section, district.

section *f* section, division; branch.

sectionner *vt* to sever; to divide into sections.

séculaire *adj* secular, century-old, once a century.

sécurisant *adj* reassuring, lending security.

sécuriser *vt* to make sb feel secure.

sécuritaire *adj* security.

sécurité *f* security; safety.

sédatif *m* sedative; * *adj* sedative.

sédentaire *adj* sedentary; * *m* sedentary.

sédiment *m* sediment.

sédimentation *f* sedimentation.

séducteur *m* seducer -trice *f* seductress.

séduction *f* seduction; captivation.

séduire *vt* to seduce; to charm, captivate.

séduisant *adj* seductive; enticing, attractive.

segment *m* segment.

segmenter *vt* to segment.

ségrégation *f* segregation.

seigle *m* rye.

seigneur *m* lord, nobleman; master.

sein *m* breast, bosom; womb; au ~ de within.

séisme *m* earthquake, seism.

seize *adj*, *m* sixteen.

seizième *adj*, *mf* sixteenth; ~**ment** *adv* in sixteenth place.

séjour *m* stay, sojourn; abode; **salle de ~** living room.

séjourner *vi* to stay, sojourn.

sel *m* salt; wit.

sélecteur *m* selector; gear lever.

sélectif *adj* selective.

sélection *f* choosing, selection.

sélectionner *vt* to select, pick.

sélectivement *adv* selectively.

self-service *m* self-service restaurant.

selle *f* saddle.

selon *prép* according to; pursuant to.

semaine *f* week.

semblable *adj* like, similar, alike; such.

semblant *m* appearance, look; pretence; **faire ~ (de)** to pretend to.

sembler *vi* to seem, appear.

semelle *f* sole.

semence *f* seed; semen.

semer *vt* to sow; to scatter, strew.

semestre *m* half-year; semester.

semestriel *adj* half-yearly; semestral.

semi-conducteur *m* semiconductor.

séminaire *m* seminary; seminar.

semi-remorque *f* trailer, semitrailer.

semis *m* seedling; sowing; seedbed.

semoule *f* semolina.

sénat *m* senate.

sénateur *m* senator.

sénile *adj* senile.

sénilité *f* senility.

sens *m* sense; judgement; consciousness; meaning; direction; **bon** ~ good sense.

sensation *f* sensation, feeling.

sensationnel *adj* fantastic, sensational.

sensé *adj* sensible.

sensibiliser *vt* to make sensitive to, heighten awareness of.

sensibilité *f* sensitivity, sensitiveness.

sensible *adj* sensitive; perceptive; appreciable; ~**ment** *adv* approximately; noticeably.

sensoriel *adj* sensory.

sensualité *f* sensuality.

sensuel *adj* sensual.

sentence *f* sentence; maxim.

sentencieux *adj* sententious.

sentier *m* path, track.

sentiment *m* feeling, sentiment; emotion.

sentimental *adj* sentimental.

sentimentalisme *m* sentimentalism.

sentinelle *f* sentry, sentinel.

sentir *vt* to feel; to perceive, guess; to smell.

séparation *f* separation; division; pulling apart.

séparatiste *mf* separatist.

séparément *adv* separately.

séparer *vt* to separate, divide; to pull off; to split; **se** ~ *vr* to separate, divide; to part with.

sept *adj, m* seven.

septembre *m* September

septième *adj, mf* seventh; ~**ment** *adv* in seventh place.

sépulture *f* sepulture, burial.

séquelle *f* after-effect.

séquence *f* sequence.

séquestre *m* sequestration, confiscation.

séquestrer *vt* to sequester, impound.

serein *adj* serene, calm; ~**ement** *adv* serenely.

sérénade *f* serenade.

sérénité *f* serenity, calmness.

sergent *m* sergeant; ~ de ville police constable.

série *f* series, string; class; rank.

sérieusement *adv* seriously, responsibly.

sérieux *adj* serious; responsible; * *m* seriousness, reliability.

seringue *f* syringe.

serment *m* oath; pledge.

sermon *m* sermon.

sermonner *vt* to lecture, reprimand.

séropositif *adj* HIV positive, seropositive.

serpe *f* billhook, bill.

serpent *m* serpent, snake.

serpenter *vi* to meander, wind.

serpentin *m* coil; streamer.

serre *f* greenhouse; claw.

serré *adj* tight; close, compact.

serrer *vt* to tighten, fasten; to clench; se ~ *vr* to crowd, huddle.

serrure *f* lock.

serrurerie *f* locksmithing.

serrurier *m* locksmith.

sérum *m* serum.

servante *f* servant, maidservant.

serveur *m* waiter, -euse *f* waitress.

serviable *adj* obliging, helpful.

service *m* service; function; department; operation; rendre ~ to do a favour; ~ militaire national service.

serviette *f* towel; serviette, napkin.

servile *adj* servile, slavish; ~ment *adv* servilely, slavishly.

servilité *f* servility.

servir *vi* to be of use, be useful; * *vt* to serve, attend to; se ~ *vr* to help o.s.; se ~ de to use, make use of.

servitude *f* servitude; (*jur*) easement.

sésame *m* sesame.

session *f* session, sitting.

seuil *m* threshold.

seul *adj* alone; single; sole; ~ement *adv* only; but; solely.

sève *f* sap; pith, vigour.

sévère *adj* severe, austere; ~ment *adv* severely; strictly.

sévérité *f* severity; strictness.

sévir *vi* to deal severely; to rage, hold sway.

sevrer *vt* to wean; to deprive.

sexe *m* sex; genitals.

sexiste *mf* sexist; * *adj* sexist.

sexualité *f* sexuality.

sexuel *adj* sexual, sex; ~**lement** *adv* sexually.

sexy *adj* sexy.

seyant *adj* becoming.

shampooing *m* shampoo.

shooter *vt* to shoot, make a shot.

shopping *m* shopping.

short *m* shorts.

si *adv* so, so much, however much; yes; * *conj* if; whether.

siamois *adj* Siamese.

sida *m* Aids.

sidéral *adj* sidereal.

sidérer *vt* to flabbergast, stagger.

sidérurgie *f* steel metallurgy

sidérurgique *adj* steel-making.

sidérurgiste *mf* steel maker.

siècle *m* century; period.

siège *m* seat, bench; head office.

siéger *vi* to sit; to be located.

sien *pn, f* **sienne**: **le ~** his, its, his own, its own, **la sienne** her, its, her own, its own, **les ~s, les siennes** their, their own.

sieste *f* nap, snooze; siesta.

sifflement *m* whistling; hissing.

siffler *vi* to whistle; to hiss; * *vt* to whistle for; to hiss, boo.

sifflet *m* whistle; catcall.

sigle *m* abbreviation; acronym.

signal *m* signal, sign.

signalement *m* description, particulars.

signaler *vt* to signal, indicate; to point out.

signalisation *f* signalling system; installing signs.

signature *f* signature; signing.

signe *m* sign; mark; indication; symptom.

signer *vt* to sign; to hallmark.

signet *m* bookmark.

significatif *adj* significant, revealing.

signification *f* significance; meaning.

signifier *vt* to mean, signify; to make known; to serve notice.

silence *m* silence; stillness.
silencieusement *adv* silently.
silencieux *adj* silent; still.
silhouette *f* silhouette, outline.
silice *f* silica.
silicone *f* silicone.
sillage *m* wake; slipstream; trail.
sillon *m* furrow; fissure.
sillonner *vt* to plough, furrow; to criss-cross.
silo *m* silo.
similaire *adj* similar.
similarité *f* similarity.
similitude *f* similitude.
simple *adj* simple; mere; single; common; ~**ment** *adv* simply, merely.
simplicité *f* simplicity; simpleness.
simplification *f* simplification.
simplifier *vt* to simplify.
simpliste *adj* simplistic.
simulation *f* simulation.
simuler *vt* to simulate, feign.
simultané *adj* simultaneous; ~**ment** *adv* simultaneously.
sincère *adj* sincere, honest; ~**ment** *adv* sincerely.
sincérité *f* sincerity, honesty.
singe *m* monkey.
singulariser *vt* to singularize;

make conspicuous; **se** ~ *vr* to make o.s. conspicuous.
singularité *f* singularity; peculiarity.
singulier *adj* singular; peculiar; remarkable.
singulièrement *adv* singularly; remarkably.
sinistre *m* disaster; accident; * *adj* sinister; ~**ment** *adv* in a sinister way.
sinistré *m* -e *f* disaster victim; * *adj* disaster-stricken.
sinon *conj* otherwise, if not; except.
sinueux *adj* sinuous, winding.
sinus *m* sinus; (*math*) sine.
sinusite *f* sinusitis.
siphon *m* siphon.
sirène *f* mermaid; siren, hooter.
sirop *m* syrup.
sirupeux *adj* syrupy.
sismique *adj* seismic.
site *m* setting, beauty spot.
sitôt *adv* so soon, as soon; **pas de** ~ not for a while; ~ **que** as soon as.
situation *f* situation, position; state of affairs.
situer *vt* to site, situate; **se** ~ *vr* to place o.s.; to be situated.

six *adj, m* six.

sixième *adj, mf* sixth; **~ment** *adv* in sixth place.

sketch *m* sketch.

ski *m* ski, skiing.

skier *vi* to ski.

skieur *m* **-euse** *f* skier.

slalom *m* slalom.

slip *m* briefs, panties, swimming trunks.

slogan *m* slogan.

snack(-bar) *m* snack bar.

snob *adj* snobbish.

snobisme *m* snobbery, snobbishness.

sobre *adj* sober, temperate; **~ment** *adv* soberly, temperately.

sobriété *f* sobriety, temperance.

sobriquet *m* nickname.

sociable *adj* sociable; social.

social *adj* social; **~ement** *adv* socially.

social-démocrate *mf* social democrat; * *adj* social democrat.

socialisme *m* socialism.

socialiste *mf* socialist; * *adj* socialist.

sociétaire *mf* member.

société *f* society; company; partnership.

socio-économique *adj* socio-economic.

sociologie *f* sociology.

sociologique *adj* sociological; **~ment** *adv* sociologically.

sociologue *mf* sociologist.

socle *m* pedestal, plinth; base.

socquette *f* ankle sock.

sodium *m* sodium.

sodomie *f* sodomy.

sœur *f* sister; nun.

sofa *m* sofa.

soi *pn* one(self); self; **~même** oneself, himself, herself, itself; **~-disant** so called.

soie *f* silk.

soif *f* thirst.

soigné *adj* neat, well-kept.

soigner *vt* to look after, care for; **se ~** *vr* to take care of o.s.

soigneusement *adv* neatly; carefully.

soigneux *adj* neat; careful.

soin *m* care; attention; trouble.

soir *m* evening; night.

soirée *f* evening; evening party.

soit *conj* either; or; whether; * *adv* granted; that is to say.

soixantaine *f* about sixty.

soixante *adj, m* sixty.

soixantième *adj, mf* sixtieth.

soja *m* soya.

sol *m* ground; floor; soil.

solaire *adj* solar.

soldat *m* soldier.

solde *f* pay; * *m* balance; clearance sale.

solder *vt* to pay; to settle, discharge; se ~ *vr*: se ~ par to show (profit, loss).

sole *f* sole; hearth.

soleil *m* sun, sunshine; sunflower.

solennel *adj* solemn; ~lement *adv* solemnly.

solfège *m* musical theory; solfa.

solidaire *adj* jointly liable; interdependent; ~ment *adv* jointly.

solidarité *f* solidarity.

solide *adj* solid; stable; sound; ~ment *adv* solidly; soundly.

solidifier *vt* se ~ *vr* to solidify.

solidité *f* solidity; soundness.

soliste *mf* soloist.

solitaire *mf* recluse, hermit; * *adj* solitary, lone; ~ment *adv* alone.

solitude *f* solitude; loneliness.

sollicitation *f* entreaty, appeal.

solliciter *vt* to seek, solicit; to appeal to.

sollicitude *f* solicitude, concern.

solo *m* solo.

solstice *m* solstice.

soluble *adj* soluble, solvable.

solution *f* solution; solving; answer.

solvable *adj* solvent; creditworthy.

solvant *m* solvent.

somatique *adj* somatic.

sombre *f* dark; gloomy, dismal.

sombrer *vi* to sink, founder.

sommaire *m* summary, argument; * *adj* basic, brief, summary; ~ment *adv* basically, summarily.

sommation *f* summons; demand.

somme *m* nap, snooze.

sommeil *m* sleep; sleepiness, drowsiness.

sommeiller *vi* to slumber, doze.

sommelier *m* wine waiter.

sommet *m* summit; top; crest; apex.

sommier *m* springs, divan base; ledger (construction).

sommité *f* leading light, eminent person.

somnambule *mf* sleepwalker; * *adj* sleepwalking.

somnifère *m* sleeping pill; * *adj* soporific.

somnolent *adj* sleepy, drowsy.

somnoler *vi* to doze, drowse.

somptueux *adj* sumptuous, lavish.

son *m* sound; * *adj*, *f* **sa**; *pl* **ses** his, her, its.

sonate *f* sonata.

sondage *m* drilling; probing; sounding.

sonde *f* sounding line; probe; drill.

sonder *vt* to sound; to probe; to drill.

songe *m* dream.

songer *vt* to dream; to imagine; to consider.

songeur *adj* pensive.

sonner *vi* to ring; to go off; * *vt* to ring, sound.

sonnerie *f* ringing, bells; chimes.

sonnette *f* small bell; housebell.

sonore *adj* resonant, deeptoned.

sonorisation *f* sound recording; sound system.

sonorité *f* sonority, tone; resonance.

sophistiqué *adj* sophisticated.

soporiphique *m* sleeping drug; soporific; * *adj* soporific.

soprano *mf* soprano.

sorbet *m* sorbet, water ice.

sorcellerie *f* witchcraft, sorcery.

sorcier *m* sorcerer.

sorcière *f* witch, sorceress.

sordide *adj* sordid, squalid; **~ment** *adv* sordidly, squalidly.

sort *m* fate, destiny, lot.

sortant *adj* outgoing, retiring.

sorte *f* sort, kind, manner.

sortie *f* exit, way out; trip; sortie; outburst; export.

sortilège *m* spell (magical).

sortir *vi* to go out, emerge; to result; to escape; **se ~** *vr* to get out of; to extricate o.s.; **s'en ~** to get over, pull through.

sosie *m* double, second self.

sot *adj*, *f* **-te** silly, foolish; **~tement** *adv* foolishly, stupidly.

sottise *f* stupidity; stupid remark, action.

sou *m* five centimes; cent.

soubresaut *m* jolt; start.

souche *f* stump; stock.

souci *m* worry; concern.

soucier (se) *vr*: **se ~ de** to care about.

soucieux *adj* concerned, worried.

soucoupe *f* saucer.

soudain *adj* sudden, unexpected; **~ement** *adv* suddenly.

soude *f* soda.

souder *vt* to solder; to weld.

soudeur *m* **-euse** *f* solderer; welder.

soudoyer *vt* to bribe, buy over.

soudure *f* soldering, welding.

souffle *m* blow, puff; breath.

soufflé *m* soufflé; * *adj* flabbergasted.

souffler *vi* to blow; to breathe; to puff.

soufflerie *f* bellows.

soufflet *m* slap in the face; affront; bellows.

souffrance *f* suffering; pain.

souffrant *adj* suffering; in pain.

souffrir *vi* to suffer, be in pain.

souhait *m* wish.

souhaitable *adj* desirable.

souhaiter *vt* to wish for, desire.

souiller *vt* to soil, dirty; to tarnish.

soulagement *m* relief.

soulager *vt* to relieve, soothe.

soulèvement *m* uprising.

soulever *vt* to lift, raise; to excite, stir up; **se ~** *vr* to rise; to revolt.

soulier *m* shoe.

souligner *vt* to underline.

soumettre *vt* to subdue, subjugate; to submit, deliver; **se ~** *vr* to subject o.s. to.

soumis *adj* submissive.

soumission *f* submission.

soupape *f* valve; safety valve.

soupçon *m* suspicion, conjecture; hint.

soupçonner *vt* to suspect, surmise.

soupçonneux *adj* suspicious.

soupe *f* soup.

soupeser *vt* to feel the weight of; to weigh up.

soupière *f* soup tureen.

soupir *m* sigh; gasp.

soupirail *m* basement window.

soupirer *vi* to sigh; to gasp.

souple *adj* supple; pliable; **~ment** *adv* supply, flexibly.

souplesse *f* suppleness; flexibility.

source *f* source; origin; spring.

sourcil *m* eyebrow.

sourd *m* **-e** *f* deaf person; * *adj* deaf; muted; veiled; ~ement *adv* dully; silently.

sourdine *f* mute.

sourd(e)-muet(te) *m*(*f*) deafmute; * *adj* deaf and dumb.

souriant *adj* smiling, cheerful.

sourire *m* smile, grin.

souris *f* mouse.

sournois *adj* deceitful; sly; ~ement *adv* deceitfully.

sous *prép* under, beneath, below.

sous-alimenté *adj* undernourished.

sous-bois *m* undergrowth.

sous-chef *m* second-in-command.

souscrire *vi* to subscribe.

sous-développé *adj* underdeveloped.

sous-directeur *m* **-trice** *f* submanager.

sous-entendre *vt* to imply, infer.

sous-entendu *m* innuendo, understood.

sous-estimer *vt* to underestimate.

sous-jacent *adj* subjacent, underlying.

sous-louer *vt* to sublet.

sous-marin *m* submarine; * *adj* underwater.

sous-multiple *m* submultiple.

sous-officier *m* non-commissioned officer.

sous-préfecture *f* sub-prefecture.

sous-préfet *m* sub-prefect.

soussigné *adj* undersigned.

sous-sol *m* subsoil; basement.

sous-titre *m* subtitle.

sous-titrer *vt* to subtitle.

soustraction *f* subtraction.

soustraire *vt* to subtract; to remove; **se** ~ *vr*: **se** ~ **à** to escape, elude.

sous-traitance *f* subcontracting.

sous-traitant *m* subcontractor.

sous-traiter *vi* to subcontract.

sous-vêtement *m* undergarment.

soutane *f* cassock, soutane.

soute *f* hold; baggage hold.

soutenir *vt* to hold up; to sustain; to endure.

souterrain *m* underground passage; * *adj* underground.

soutien *m* support.

soutien-gorge *m* bra.

soutirer *vt* to extract from.

souvenir *m* memory; recollection; reminder.

souvenir (se) *vr* to remember, recollect.

souvent *adv* often, frequently.

souverain *m* -e *f* sovereign; * *adj* sovereign; supreme; ~ement *adv* supremely.

soyeux *adj* silky.

spacieux *adj* spacious, roomy.

spaghetti *mpl* spaghetti.

sparadrap *m* sticking plaster.

spasme *m* spasm.

spasmophilie *f* spasmophilia.

spatial *adj* spatial; space.

spatule *f* spatula.

spécial *adj* special, particular; ~ement *adv* specially.

spécialisation *f* specialization.

spécialiser *vt* to specialize; se ~ *vr* to be a specialist in sth.

spécialiste *mf* specialist.

spécialité *f* speciality; specialism.

spécieux *adj* specious.

spécification *f* specification.

spécifier *vt* to specify, determine.

spécifique *adj* specific; ~ment *adv* specifically.

spécimen *m* specimen; sample.

spectacle *m* spectacle, scene.

spectaculaire *adj* spectacular.

spectateur *m* -trice *f* spectator.

spectre *m* ghost.

spéculateur *m* -trice *f* speculator.

spéculation *f* speculation.

spéculer *vi* to speculate.

spéléologie *f* speleology; caving.

spermatozoïde *m* sperm; spermatozoon.

sperme *m* sperm, semen.

sphère *f* sphere.

sphérique *adj* spherical.

sphinx *m* sphinx.

spirale *f* spiral.

spiritisme *m* spiritualism.

spiritualité *f* spirituality.

spirituel *adj* witty; spiritual; ~lement *adv* wittily; spiritually.

splendeur *f* splendour, brilliance.

splendide *adj* splendid, magnificent; ~ment *adv* splendidly.

spongieux *adj* spongy.

sponsoriser *vt* to sponsor.

spontané *adj* spontaneous; ~**ment** *adv* spontaneously.

sporadique *adj* sporadic.

sport *m* sport.

sportif *m* sportsman, **-ive** *f* sportswoman; * *adj* sports; competitive; athletic.

square *m* (public) square.

squatter *vi* to squat in.

squelette *m* skeleton.

squelettique *adj* skeleton-like, scrawny.

stabiliser *vt* to stabilize, consolidate; **se** ~ *vr* to stabilize, become stabilized.

stabilité *f* stability.

stable *adj* stable, steady.

stade *m* stadium; stage.

stage *m* training course; probation.

stagiaire *mf* trainee.

stagnation *f* stagnation.

stagner *vi* to stagnate.

standard *m* standard; switchboard; * *adj* standard.

standardiser *vt* to standardize.

standardiste *mf* switchboard operator.

starter *m* choke.

station *f* station; stage, stop; resort; posture.

stationnaire *adj* stationary.

stationnement *m* parking.

stationner *vi* to park.

station-service *f* service station.

statique *adj* static.

statistique *f* statistics; * *adj* statistical.

statue *f* statue.

statuer *vt* to rule, give a verdict.

statu quo *m* status quo.

statut *m* statute, ordinance; status.

statutaire *adj* statutory; ~**ment** *adv* statutorily.

stencil *m* stencil.

sténodactylo *mf* shorthand typist.

sténographie *f* shorthand.

stentor *m*: une voix de ~ stentorian voice.

steppe *f* steppe.

stère *m* stere.

stéréo(phonique) *adj* stereophonic.

stéréotype *m* stereotype.

stérile *adj* sterile, infertile.

stérilet *m* coil, IUD.

stériliser *vt* to sterilize.

stérilité *f* sterility.

sternum *m* breastbone, sternum.

stéroïde *adj* steroidal; * *m* steroid.

stigmate *m* mark, scar; stigmata.

stimulant *adj* stimulating; * *m* stimulant, stimulus.

stimulation *f* stimulation.

stimuler *vt* to stimulate, spur on.

stipuler *vt* to stipulate, specify.

stock *m* stock, supply.

stockage *m* stocking; stockpiling.

stocker *vt* to stock, stockpile.

stoïcisme *m* stoicism.

stoïque *adj* stoical; ~ment *adv* stoically; * *mf* stoic.

stop *m* stop; stop sign; brakelight.

stopper *vt* to stop, halt; * *vi* to stop, halt.

store *m* blind, shade.

strabisme *m* squinting; strabismus.

strapontin *m* foldaway seat; minor role.

stratégie *f* strategy.

stratégique *adj* strategic; ~ment *adv* strategically.

stratifié *adj* stratified.

stress *m* stress.

stressant *adj* stressful.

stresser *vt* to cause stress to.

strict *adj* strict, severe; ~ement *adv* strictly.

strident *adj* strident, shrill.

strié *adj* streaked, striped, ridged.

stroboscope *m* stroboscope.

strophe *f* verse, stanza.

structural *adj* structural.

structure *f* structure.

structurel *adj* structural.

structurer *vt* to structure; se ~ *vr* to develop a structure.

stuc *m* stucco.

studieux *adj* studious.

studio *m* studio; film theatre.

stupéfaction *f* stupefaction, amazement.

stupéfait *adj* astounded, dumbfounded.

stupéfiant *adj* astounding, amazing; drug, narcotic.

stupéfier *vt* to stupefy; to astound.

stupeur *f* amazement; stupor.

stupide *adj* stupid, foolish; ~ment *adv* stupidly.

stupidité *f* stupidity.

style *m* style; stylus.

stylet *m* stiletto.

styliste *mf* designer; stylist.

stylo *m* pen.

su *m* knowledge.

suave *adj* suave, smooth.

subalterne *mf* subordinate; * *adj* subordinate.

subconscient *m* subconscious; * *adj* subconscious.

subdiviser *vt* to subdivide.

subdivision *f* subdivision.

subir *vt* to sustain, support; to undergo, suffer.

subit *adj* sudden; ~ement *adv* suddenly.

subjectif *adj* subjective.

subjectivement *adv* subjectively.

subjectivité *f* subjectivity.

subjonctif *m* subjunctive; * *adj* subjunctive.

subjuguer *vt* to subjugate; to captivate.

sublime *adj* sublime; * *m* sublime.

sublimer *vt* to sublimate.

subliminal *adj* subliminal.

submerger *vt* to submerge, flood; to engulf.

submersible *m* submersible; * *adj* submersible.

subordination *f* subordination.

subordonné *m* -e *f* subordinate; * *adj* subordinate.

subordonner *vt* to subordinate.

subreptice *adj* surreptitious; ~ment *adv* surreptitiously.

subséquent *adj* subsequent.

subside *m* grant.

subsidiaire *adj* subsidiary.

subsistance *f* subsistence, maintenance, sustenance.

subsister *vi* to subsist; to live on.

substance *f* substance.

substantiel *adj* substantial; ~lement *adv* substantially.

substantif *m* noun, substantive; * *adj* substantival, nominal.

substituer *vt* to substitute, replace.

substitut *m* substitute.

substitution *f* substitution.

subterfuge *m* subterfuge.

subtil *adj* subtle; ~ement *adv* subtly.

subtiliser *vt* to steal, spirit away.

subtilité *f* subtlety.

subvenir *vi*: ~ à to provide for.

subvention *f* grant, subsidy.

subventionner *vt* to subsidize.

subversif *adj* subversive.

suc *m* sap; juice.

succéder *vi*: ~ à to succeed, follow; * se ~ *vr* to succeed one another.

succès *m* success; hit.

successeur *m* successor.

successif *adj* successive.

succession *f* succession; inheritance, estate.

successivement *adv* successively.

succinct *adj* succinct; ~**ement** *adv* succinctly.

succomber *vi* to succumb, give way.

succulent *adj* succulent, delicious.

succursale *f* branch.

sucer *vt* to suck.

sucette *f* lollipop; dummy.

suçon *m* love bite.

sucre *m* sugar.

sucrer *vt* to sugar, sweeten.

sucrerie *f* sugar refinery.

sucrier *m* sugar bowl; * *adj* sugar; sugar-producing.

sud *m* south.

suer *vi* to sweat, perspire.

sueur *f* sweat.

suffire *vi* to suffice, be sufficient; **il suffit de** it is enough to, it only takes.

suffisamment *adv* sufficiently, enough.

suffisant *adj* sufficient, adequate.

suffoquer *vi* to choke, suffocate; * *vt* to choke, stifle.

suffrage *m* suffrage; vote; commendation, approval.

suggérer *vt* to suggest, put forward.

suggestion *f* suggestion.

suicidaire *adj* suicidal; * *mf* person with suicidal tendencies.

suicide *m* suicide.

suicider (se) *vr* to commit suicide.

suie *f* soot.

suif *m* tallow.

suintement *m* oozing; sweating.

suinter *vi* to ooze; to sweat.

suite *f* rest; sequel; continuation; series; connection; progress; **tout de** ~ at once; **deux fois de** ~ two times in a row; **et ainsi de** ~ and so on; **à la suite de** after, behind; **par la** ~ afterwards; **donner** ~ **à** to follow up.

suivant *m* -**e** *f* next one; attendant; * *adj* following, next; * *prép* according to; ~ **que** according to whether.

suivi *adj* steady, regular; widely adopted; * *m* follow-up.

suivre *vt* to follow; to attend,

accompany; to exercise; ~ **son cours** to take its course; **à suivre** to be continued; **se ~ vr** to follow each other; to be continuous.

sujet *m* subject, topic; ground; reason; * *adj*: **être ~ à** to be subject to, liable to.

sujétion *f* subjection; constraint.

sulfate *m* sulphate.

sulfater *vt* to apply copper sulphate.

sulfure *m* sulphur.

sulfureux *adj* sulphurous.

sulfurique *adj* sulphuric.

sultan *m* sultan, **-e** *f* sultana.

summum *m* climax, height.

super *m* super, four-star petrol; * *adj* (*fam*) ultra, super.

superbe *adj* superb, splendid; ~**ment** *adv* superbly.

supercarburant *m* high-octane petrol.

supercherie *f* trick, trickery.

superficie *f* area, surface.

superficiel *adj* superficial; ~**lement** *adv* superficially.

superflu *adj* superfluous.

supérieur *adj* upper; superior; higher, greater;

~**ement** *adv* exceptionally well.

supériorité *f* superiority.

superlatif *m* superlative; * *adj* superlative.

superposer *vt* to superpose, stack; to superimpose; **se ~ vr** to be superimposed.

superposition *f* superposing; superimposition.

supersonique *adj* supersonic.

superstitieux *adj* superstitious.

superstition *f* superstition.

superviser *vt* to supervise.

supplanter *vt* to supplant, oust.

suppléant *m* **-e** *f* substitute, understudy; * *adj* substitute.

supplément *m* supplement; extra charge.

supplémentaire *adj* supplementary, additional.

suppliant *adj* beseeching, entreating.

supplication *f* supplication; entreaty.

supplice *m* corporal punishment; torture.

supplier *vt* to beseech, entreat.

support *m* support, prop; stand.

supporter *vt* to support; to endure, bear.

supporter *m* supporter.

supposer *vt* to suppose; to assume; to imply.

supposition *f* supposition, surmise.

suppositoire *m* suppository.

suppression *f* suppression; deletion; cancellation.

supprimer *vt* to suppress; to cancel.

suppurer *vi* to suppurate.

suprématie *f* supremacy.

suprême *adj* supreme.

sur *prép* on; over, above; into; out of, from.

sûr *adj* sure, certain; secure; ~ **de soi** self-assured; **bien** ~ of course; **à coup** ~ for sure; ~**ement** *adv* surely, certainly.

surabondance *f* overabundance.

suranné *adj* outmoded, outdated.

surcharge *f* overloading; excess; surcharge.

surcharger *vt* to overload.

surchauffe *f* overheating.

surcroît *m*: surplus, excess; **de** ~ in addition.

surdité *f* deafness.

sureau *m* elder (tree).

surélever *vt* to raise, heighten.

surenchérir *vi* to outbid.

surestimer *vt* to overestimate; to overvalue.

sûreté *f* safety; guarantee, surety; **être en** ~ to be safe.

surexcité *adj* overexcited.

surface *f* surface.

surgeler *vt* to deep-freeze.

surgir *vi* to rise, appear; to arise, crop up.

surhomme *m* superman.

surintendant *m* superintendent.

surlendemain *m* day after tomorrow.

surmenage *m* overwork; overtaxing.

surmener *vt* to overwork; **se** ~ *vr* to overwork.

surmonter *vt* to surmount, overcome.

surnager *vi* to float.

surnaturel *adj* supernatural.

surnom *m* nickname.

surnommer *vt* to nickname.

surpasser *vt* to surpass, outdo.

surplomb *m* overhang; **en** ~ overhanging.

surplomber *vt* to overhang.

surplus *m* surplus, remainder, excess.

surpopulation *f* overpopulation.

surprenant *adj* surprising, amazing.

surprendre *vt* to surprise, amaze.

surprise *f* surprise.

surproduction *f* overproduction.

surréalisme *m* surrealism.

surréaliste *mf* surrealist; * *adj* surrealistic.

sursaut *m* start, jump.

sursauter *vi* to start, jump.

sursis *m* reprieve; deferment.

sursitaire *adj* deferred; suspended.

surtaxe *f* surcharge.

surtout *adv* especially; above all.

surveillance *f* surveillance; supervision; inspection.

surveillant *m* -e *f* warder, guard.

surveiller *vt* to watch; to supervise; to inspect.

survenir *vi* to take place, occur.

survêtement *m* tracksuit.

survie *f* survival.

survivant *m* -e *f* survivor; * *adj* surviving.

survivre *vi* to survive.

survoler *vt* to fly over.

susceptible *adj* sensitive; susceptible; capable; likely; être ~ de to be liable to.

susciter *vt* to arouse, incite.

suspect *m* -e *f* suspect; * *adj* suspicious, suspect.

suspecter *vt* to suspect.

suspendre *vt* to hang up; to suspend, defer.

suspendu *adj* hanging; suspended.

suspens *m*: en ~ in abeyance; shelved.

suspense *m* suspense.

suspension *f* suspension; deferment; adjournment.

suspicieux *adj* suspicious.

suspicion *f* suspicion.

susurrer *vt* to whisper.

suture *f* suture; points de ~ stitches.

svelte *adj* svelte, slim.

SVP *abrév de* s'il vous plaît please.

syllabe *f* syllable.

sylvestre *adj* forest.

symbole *m* symbol.

symbolique *adj* symbolic; token; nominal; ~ment *adv* symbolically.

symboliser *vt* to symbolize.

symbolisme *m* symbolism.

symétrie *f* symmetry.

symétrique *adj* symmetrical;
~**ment** *adv* symmetrically.

sympa *adj invar* (*fam*) nice,
friendly.

sympathie *f* liking; fellow
feeling; sympathy.

sympathique *adj* likeable,
nice; friendly.

sympathisant *m* -e *f* sympa-
thizer; * *adj* sympathizing.

sympathiser *vi* to get on well
with.

symphonie *f* symphony.

symphonique *adj* symphonic.

symptomatique *adj* sympto-
matic.

symptôme *m* symptom.

synagogue *f* synagogue.

synchronisation *f* synchroni-
zation.

synchroniser *vt* to synchro-
nize.

syncope *f* blackout, syncope.

syncopé *adj* syncopated.

syndical *adj* trade-union.

syndicalisme *m* trade union-
ism.

syndicaliste *mf* trade unionist; * *adj* trade union.

syndicat *m* trade union; association.

syndiquer *vt* to unionize; se
~ *vr* to form a trade union.

syndrome *m* syndrome.

synonyme *m* synonym; * *adj*
synonymous.

syntaxe *f* syntax.

synthèse *f* synthesis.

synthétique *adj* synthetic.

synthétiser *vt* to synthesize.

synthétiseur *m* synthesizer.

syphilis *f* syphilis.

systématique *adj* systematic;
~**ment** *adv* systematically.

système *m* system.

T

tabac *m* tobacco.

tabagisme *m* nicotine addiction.

tabatière *f* snuffbox; skylight.

table *f* table; ~ **de nuit** bedside table; ~ **ronde** round-table conference.

tableau *m* table; chart; timetable; scene; ~ **de bord** dashboard.

tablette *f* bar; tablet; block.

tablier *m* apron; pinafore; overall.

tabou *m* taboo.

tabouret *m* stool.

tache *f* mark; stain; spot.

tâche *f* task, assignment; work.

taché *adj* stained, blemished.

tâcher *vi* to endeavour.

tacheté *adj* spotted; freckled.

tachycardie *f* tachycardia.

tacite *adj* tacit; ~**ment** *adv* tacitly.

taciturne *adj* taciturn, silent.

tact *m* tact; **avoir du** ~ to have tact, be tactful.

tactile *adj* tactile.

tactique *f* tactics; * *adj* tactical.

taffetas *m* taffeta.

tagliatelles *fpl* tagliatelli.

taillader *vt* to slash, gash.

taille *f* waist; height, stature, size; **de** ~ considerable, sizeable; **être de** ~ **à** to be up to it.

taille-crayons *m* pencil sharpener.

tailler *vt* to cut; to carve; to sharpen; **se** ~ *vr* (*fam*) to clear off, split.

tailleur *m* tailor; cutter, hewer.

taillis *m* copse, coppice.

taire *vt* to hush up; to conceal; **se** ~ *vr* to be quiet; to fall silent.

talc *m* talc, talcum powder.

talent *m* talent, ability.

talentueux *adj* talented.

talisman *m* talisman.

talon *m* heel; end; pile.

talonner *vt* to follow closely; to hound.

talquer *vt* to put talcum powder on.

talus *m* embankment.

tambour *m* drum; barrel.

tambourin *m* tambourine.

tambouriner *vi* to drum; to beat, hammer.

tamis *m* sieve; riddle.

tamiser *vt* to sieve; to sift.

tampon *m* stopper, plug; tampon; buffer.

tamponner *vt* to mop up; to stamp.

tam-tam *m* tom-tom; row.

tandem *m* tandem; duo.

tandis *conj*: ~ **que** while; whereas.

tangent *adj* tangent, tangential.

tangible *adj* tangible.

tango *m* tango.

tanguer *vi* to pitch (ship).

tanière *f* den, lair.

tank *m* tank.

tanné *adj* tanned; weathered.

tanner *vt* to tan, weather.

tanneur *m* tanner.

tant *adv* so much; ~ **que** as long as; ~ **soit peu** ever so slightly; ~ **mieux** so much the better; that's a good job; ~ **pis** too bad; ~ **bien que mal** as well as can be expected.

tante *f* aunt.

tantôt *adv* sometimes; this afternoon; shortly.

taon *m* horsefly, gadfly.

tapage *m* din, uproar, racket.

tapageur *adj* noisy, rowdy; showy.

tape *f* slap.

taper *vi* to hit, tap, stamp; to beat down; * *vt* to beat; to slap; to type.

tapioca *m* tapioca.

tapir (se) *vr* to crouch; to hide away.

tapir *m* tapir.

tapis *m* carpet; rug; cloth.

tapisser *vt* to wallpaper; to cover; to carpet.

tapisserie *f* tapestry; tapestry-making; **faire** ~ to be a wallflower.

tapoter *vt* to pat; to tap; to strum.

taquin *adj* teasing.

taquiner *vt* to tease; to plague.

tarauder *vt* to tap; to torment.

tard *adv* late.

tarder *vi* to delay, put off; to dally.

tardif *adj* late; tardy; slow; backward.

tardivement *adv* late; tardily.

tare *f* tare; defect, flaw.

taré *adj* tainted, corrupt; sickly.

tari *adj* dried up.

tarif *m* tariff; price-list.

tarir *vt* to dry up; to exhaust; se ~ *vr* to dry up.

tarot *m* tarot.

tartare *adj* Tartar.

tarte *f* tart, flan.

tartelette *f* tartlet, tart.

tartine *f* slice of buttered bread.

tartiner *vt* to spread with butter, jam, etc.

tartre *m* tartar; fur, scale.

tas *m* heap, pile; lot, set.

tasse *f* cup.

tassement *m* settling, sinking.

tasser *vt* to heap up; se ~ *vr* to sink; subside.

tata *f* auntie.

tâter *vt* to feel, try; se ~ *vr* to feel o.s.

tâtonnement *m* trial and error; experimentation.

tâtonner *vi* to feel one's way, grope along.

tatouage *m* tattooing; tattoo.

tatouer *vt* to tattoo.

taudis *m* hovel, slum.

taupe *f* mole.

taureau *m* bull.

tauromachie *f* bullfighting.

taux *m* rate; ratio; ~ de change exchange rate.

taverne *f* tavern.

taxation *f* taxation, taxing.

taxe *f* tax; duty; rate.

taxer *vt* to tax; to fix the price of.

taxi *m* taxi.

tchin-tchin! *interj* cheers!

te *pn* you, yourself.

technicien *m* -ne *f* technician.

technique *f* technique; * *adj* technical; ~ment *adv* technically.

technocrate *m* technocrat.

technocratie *f* technocracy.

technologie *f* technology.

technologique *adj* technological.

téflon *m* teflon.

teigne *f* moth; ringworm.

teindre *vt* to dye.

teint *m* complexion, colouring.

teinte *f* tint, colour, shade.

teinter *vt* to tint; to stain.

teinture *f* dye; dyeing.

teinturerie *f* dyeing; dye-works; dry cleaner's.

teinturier *m* **-ère** *f* dyer; dry cleaner.

tel *adj* such; like, similar; ~ **quel** such as it is; **en tant que** ~ as such, in such a capacity; **il n'y a rien de** ~ there's nothing like…

télé *f* TV, telly.

télécarte *f* phonecard.

télécommande *f* remote control.

télécommunication *f* telecommunication.

télécopie *f* facsimile transmission, fax.

télécopieur *m* fax machine.

télédiffusion *f* television broadcasting.

téléphérique *m* cableway; cable-car.

télégramme *m* telegram; cable.

télégraphier *vt* to telegraph, cable.

téléguider *vt* to radio-control.

télématique *f* telematics.

téléobjectif *m* telephoto lens.

télépathie *f* telepathy.

téléphone *m* telephone.

téléphoner *vi* to telephone.

téléphonique *adj* telephone; telephonic.

télescope *m* telescope.

télescopique *adj* telescopic.

télésiège *m* chairlift.

téléski *m* lift, ski tow.

téléspectateur *m* **-trice** *f* television viewer.

téléviseur *m* television set.

télévision *f* television.

télex *m* telex.

tellement *adv* so, so much; ~ **de** so many, so much.

téméraire *adj* rash, reckless; **~ment** *adv* rashly; recklessly.

témérité *f* rashness; recklessness.

témoignage *m* testimony; evidence; certificate.

témoigner *vi* to testify.

témoin *m* witness; evidence; proof.

tempérament *m* constitution; temperament; character.

tempérance *f* temperance.

température *f* temperature.

tempéré *adj* temperate; tempered.

tempérer *vt* to temper; to assuage, soothe.

tempête *f* tempest.

temple *m* temple.

tempo *m* tempo, pace.

temporaire *adj* temporary; ~**ment** *adv* temporarily.

temporel *adj* worldly, temporal.

temporiser *vi* to temporize, delay.

temps *m* time; while; tense; beat; weather; **de ~ en ~** from time to time; **entre ~** meanwhile.

tenace *adj* tenacious, stubborn, persistent.

ténacité *f* tenacity; stubbornness.

tenaille *f* pincers; tongs.

tenailler *vt* to torture; to rack.

tendance *f* tendency; leaning; trend.

tendancieux *adj* tendentious.

tendinite *f* tendinitis.

tendon *m* tendon, sinew.

tendre *adj* tender, soft; delicate; ~**ment** *adv* tenderly, affectionately.

tendresse *f* tenderness; fondness.

tendu *adj* tight; stretched; concentrated; delicate, fraught.

ténèbres *fpl* darkness, gloom.

ténébreux *adj* dark, gloomy.

teneur *f* terms; content; grade.

tenir *vt* to hold, keep; to stock; to run; * *vi* to hold, stay in place; ~ **à** to value, care about; ~ **de** to take after; **se ~** *vr* to hold on to; to behave; **s'en ~ à** to limit o.s. to, stick to.

tennis *m* tennis; ~ **de table** table tennis.

ténor *m* tenor; leading light.

tentacule *m* tentacle.

tentant *adj* tempting, inviting.

tentation *f* temptation.

tentative *f* attempt, bid.

tente *f* tent.

tenter *vt* to tempt.

tenture *f* hanging; curtain.

tenue *f* holding; session; deportment, good behaviour; dress, appearance.

tergal *m* terylene.

tergiverser *vi* to procrastinate, beat about the bush.

terme *m* term; termination, end; word, expression; **au ~ de** at the end of.

terminaison *f* ending.

terminal *adj* terminal; * *m* terminal.

terminer *vt* to terminate; to

finish off; **se ~** *vr* to terminate; to come to an end.

terminologie *f* terminology.

termite *m* termite.

terne *adj* colourless; lustreless, drab; spiritless.

ternir *vt* to tarnish, dull.

terrain *m* ground, soil, earth; plot; position; site; field.

terrasse *f* terrace.

terrasser *vt* to floor, knock down; to strike down, overcome.

terre *f* earth; world; ground, land; **mettre pied à ~** to land, alight.

terre à terre *adj* down to earth, commonplace.

terreau *m* compost.

terre-plein *m* (*mil*) terreplein; platform; central reservation.

terrer (se) *vr* to crouch down; to lie low, go to ground.

terrestre *adj* land; terrestrial.

terreur *f* terror, dread.

terreux *adj* earthy; dirty; ashen.

terrible *adj* terrible, dreadful; terrific, great; **~ment** *adv* terribly.

terrien *m* countryman; earthling; **-ne** *f* countrywoman; earthling.

terrier *m* burrow; earth; terrier.

terrifiant *adj* terrifying, fearsome.

terrifier *vt* to terrify.

terrine *f* earthenware dish, terrine.

territoire *m* territory, area.

territorial *adj* land, territorial.

terroir *m* land.

terroriser *vt* to terrorize.

terrorisme *m* terrorism.

terroriste *mf* terrorist; * *adj* terrorist.

tertiaire *adj* tertiary.

test *m* test.

testament *m* will, testament.

tester *vt* to test; to make out one's will.

testicule *m* testicle, testis.

tétanos *m* tetanus; lockjaw.

têtard *m* tadpole.

tête *f* head; face; front; top; sense, judgment; **tenir ~** to stand up to sb; **faire la ~** to pout, sulk; **~ de turc** whipping boy; **~ de mort** skull and crossbones; **être en ~** to head.

tête à tête *m* private conversation; **en ~** in the lead.

tétée *f* feeding; nursing.

téter *vt* to suck.

tétine *f* teat; udder; dummy.

téton *m* breast.

têtu *adj* headstrong, stubborn.

texte *m* text.

textile *adj* textile.

textuel *adj* textual, literal, exact; **~lement** *adv* literally; word for word.

texture *f* texture.

thé *m* tea.

théâtral *adj* theatrical, dramatic.

théâtre *m* theatre; drama.

théière *f* teapot.

thématique *adj* thematic.

thème *m* theme.

théologie *f* theology.

théorème *m* theorem.

théoricien *m* **-ne** *f* theoretician, theorist.

théorie *f* theory.

théorique *adj* theoretical; **~ment** *adv* theoretically.

thérapeute *mf* therapist.

thérapie *f* therapy.

thermal *adj* thermal; hydropathic.

thermique *adj* thermal; thermic.

thermomètre *m* thermometer.

thermos *f/m* thermos.

thermostat *m* thermostat.

thésaurus *m* thesaurus.

thèse *f* thesis.

thon *m* tuna.

thoracique *adj* thoracic; **cage** ~ ribcage.

thorax *m* thorax.

thrombose *f* thrombosis.

thym *m* thyme.

thyroïde *f* thyroid.

tibia *m* tibia.

tic *m* twitch, tic; mannerism.

ticket *m* ticket.

tiède *adj* lukewarm, tepid.

tien *pn*, *f* **tienne**: **le ~, la tienne, les ~s, les tiennes** yours, your own.

tiers *adj* third; **~-monde** Third World; * *m* third; third party.

tige *f* stem, stalk.

tigre *m* tiger.

tigresse *f* tigress.

tilleul *m* lime, linden.

timbale *f* kettledrum.

timbre *m* stamp; postmark; bell; tone, timbre.

timbré *adj* stamped; resonant.

timbrer *vt* to stamp; to postmark.

timide *adj* timid, shy; **~ment** *adv* timidly.

timidité *f* timidity, shyness.

timonier *m* (*mar*) helmsman.

tintamarre *m* hubbub, uproar.

tintement *m* ringing; chiming; toll.

tinter *vi* to ring, toll; to chime.

tique *f* tick.

tiquer *vi* to wince.

tir *m* shooting, firing, fire; shot; ~ à l'arc archery.

tirade *f* tirade; monologue.

tirage *m* drawing, drawing off; printing; circulation; friction.

tiraillement *m* tugging; pulling.

tirailler *vt* to tug; to plague; to pester.

tire-bouchon *m* corkscrew.

tire-fesses *m* ski tow.

tirelire *f* moneybox.

tirer *vt* to pull; to draw; to extract; **se** ~ *vr* (*fam*) to clear off; **bien s'en** ~ to make a good job of sth.

tiret *m* dash; hyphen.

tireur *m* -euse *f* gunner, sharpshooter; printer; drawer (cheque).

tiroir *m* drawer.

tison *m* brand.

tisonnier *m* poker.

tissage *m* weaving.

tisser *vt* to weave.

tissu *m* texture, fabric; tissue.

titan *m* titan.

titane *m* titanium.

titanesque *adj* titanic.

titre *m* title; heading; denomination; claim, right; deed; à ~ de by right of; à juste ~ deservedly, justly; en ~ titular, acknowledged.

tituber *vi* to stagger.

titulaire *mf* incumbent, holder; * *adj* titular; entitled.

toast *m* slice of toast; toast; **porter un** ~ to drink a toast.

toboggan *m* toboggan.

toc *m* tap, knock; sham jewellery etc.; **en** ~ imitation, fake.

toi *pn* you; ~-même yourself; **c'est à** ~ it's your's; it's your turn.

toile *f* cloth; canvas; sheet.

toilette *f* cleaning, grooming; washstand; **faire sa** ~ to wash o.s.; **cabinet de** ~ bathroom.

toiser *vt* to survey; to evaluate.

toison *f* fleece.

toit *m* roof; home.

toiture *f* roof, roofing.

tôle *f* sheet metal.

tolérable *adj* tolerable, bearable.

tolérance *f* tolerance.

tolérant *adj* tolerant.

tolérer *vt* to tolerate; to put up with.

tomate *f* tomato.

tombe *f* tomb; grave.

tombeau *m* tomb.

tomber *vi* to fall; to sink; to decay; **laisser ~** to drop; **~ malade** to fall sick; **~ amoureux** to fall in love; **~ sur** to come across; **bien/ mal ~** to be lucky/unlucky.

tombola *f* tombola.

tome *m* book; volume.

ton *adj, f* **ta,** *pl* **tes** your; * *m* tone; pitch; shade.

tonalité *f* tonality; key.

tondeuse *f* clippers, shears; mower.

tondre *vt* to shear, clip; mow.

tonifiant *m* tonic; * *adj* bracing; invigorating.

tonifier *vt* to tone up; to invigorate.

tonique *adj* tonic; fortifying; invigorating *m* tonic.

tonitruant *adj* thundering.

tonnage *m* tonnage; displacement.

tonne *f* ton.

tonneau *m* barrel, cask.

tonnelle *f* bower, arbour.

tonnerre *m* thunder.

tonton *m* (*fam*) uncle.

tonus *m* tone; energy.

top *m* pip, stroke.

topaze *f* topaz.

topographie *f* topography.

toquade *f* infatuation; fad, craze.

toque *f* fur hat; cap.

toquer *vi* to tap, rap.

torche *f* torch.

torcher *vt* to wipe, mop up; **se ~** *vr* to wipe o.s.

torchon *m* cloth; duster.

tordre *vt* to twist, contort; **se ~** *vr* to bend, twist; to sprain.

tordu *adj* twisted, crooked, bent.

tornade *f* tornado.

torpeur *f* torpor.

torpille *f* torpedo.

torpiller *vt* to torpedo.

torréfaction *f* roasting; toasting.

torrent *m* torrent.

torrentiel *adj* torrential.

torride *adj* torrid; scorching.

torsade *f* twist; cable moulding.

torse *m* chest; torso.

torsion *f* twisting; torsion.

tort *m* fault; wrong; prejudice; **avoir ~** to be wrong; **en ~** in the wrong; **à ~ ou à raison** wrongly or rightly; **faire du ~** to harm; **à ~ et à travers** wildly; here, there and everywhere.

torticolis *m* stiff neck; torticollis.

tortiller *vt* to twist; **se ~** *vr* to wriggle; to squirm.

tortionnaire *mf* torturer; * *adj* pertaining to torture.

tortue *f* tortoise.

tortueux *adj* tortuous, winding, meandering.

torture *f* torture.

torturer *vt* to torture.

tôt *adv* early; soon, quickly; **au plus ~** as soon as possible; **plus ~** sooner.

total *adj* total; absolute; **~ement** *adv* totally.

totaliser *vt* to totalize, add up.

totalitaire *adj* totalitarian.

totalitarisme *m* totalitarianism.

totalité *f* totality; whole.

totem *m* totem.

touchant *adj* touching, moving.

touche *f* touch; trial; stroke; key.

toucher *vt* to touch; to feel; * *m* touch, feeling.

touffe *f* tuft, clump.

touffu *adj* bushy, thick.

toujours *adv* always; still; all the same; **pour ~** for ever; **~ est-il que** the fact remains that.

toupet *m* quiff, tuft; cheek.

toupie *f* spinning top.

tour *f* tower; * *m* turn, round; circuit; tour; trick; **faire un ~** to take a stroll; **faire le tour de** to go around; **fermer à double ~** to double-lock; **jouer un ~** to play a trick; **~ à ~** by turns.

tourbe *f* peat.

tourbillon *m* whirlwind, whirlpool.

tourbillonner *vi* to whirl, eddy.

tourisme *m* tourism.

touriste *mf* tourist.

touristique *adj* tourist.

tourment *m* torment, agony.

tourmente *f* storm, tempest.

tourmenter *vt* to rack, torment; **se ~** *vr* to fret; to worry.

tournage *m* turning; (*cin*) shooting.

tournant *m* bend; turning point; * *adj* revolving, swivelling; winding.

tournedos *m* fillet steak.

tournée *f* tour; round.

tourner *vt* to turn; to round; * *vi* to turn; to work; to change; **se ~** *vr* to turn round; to change.

tournesol *m* sunflower.

tourneur *m* turner.

tournevis *m* screwdriver.

tourniquet *m* tourniquet; turnstile.

tournis *m* (*vet*) sturdy, staggers; **avoir le ~** to feel giddy.

tournoi *m* tournament.

tournoyer *vi* to whirl, swirl.

tournure *f* turn; turn of phrase.

tourte *f* pie.

tourerelle *f* turtledove.

tourtière *f* pie tin.

Toussaint *f* All Saints' Day.

tousser *vi* to cough.

tout *adj*, *pl* **tous**, **toutes** all; whole; every; **~ le monde** everybody; * *pn* everything; all; **c'est ~** that is all; * *m* whole, only thing; **pas du ~** not at all; **du ~ au ~**

completely; * *adv* entirely, quite; **~ droit** straight on; **~ à fait** completely, quite; **~ de suite** immediately.

toutefois *adv* however.

tout-puissant *adj* all-powerful.

toux *f* cough.

toxicomane *mf* drug addict; * *adj* drug addicted.

toxicomanie *f* drug addiction.

toxine *f* toxin.

toxique *adj* toxic.

trac *m* nerves, stage fright.

tracas *m* bustle, turmoil; worry.

tracasser *vt* to worry; to harass.

trace *f* track, impression; outline, sketch; vestige, trace.

tracé *m* layout, plan.

tracer *vt* to draw, trace; to open up.

trachée *f* trachea, windpipe.

tract *m* leaflet, tract.

tractation *f* transaction; bargaining.

tracteur *m* tractor.

traction *f* traction; pulling.

tradition *f* tradition.

traditionaliste *mf* traditionalist; * *adj* traditionalist.

traditionnel *adj* traditional;

usual; **~lement** *adv* traditionally.

traducteur *m* **-trice** *f* translator.

traduction *f* translation.

traduire *vt* to translate.

trafic *m* traffic; trading; dealings.

trafiquant *m* **-e** *f* trafficker.

trafiquer *vi* to fiddle, tamper with.

tragédie *f* tragedy.

tragédien *m* **-ne** *f* tragedian, tragic actor.

tragique *adj* tragic; **~ment** *adv* tragically.

trahir *vt* to betray.

trahison *f* betrayal, treason.

train *m* train; pace, rate; **être en ~ de** to be in the act of doing sth.

traînasser *vi* to dawdle; to loiter.

traîne *f* dragging; train; **être à la ~** to be in tow.

traîneau *m* sleigh, sledge.

traînée *f* trail, track; drag.

traîner *vi* to lag, dawdle; to drag on; * *vt* to drag, pull; to protract; **se ~** *vr* to drag o.s.; to crawl along.

train-train *m* humdrum routine.

traire *vt* to milk.

trait *m* trait, feature; deed; relation; **avoir ~ à** to have reference; **~ d'union** hyphen, connecting link.

traite *f* trade; draft, bill; milking.

traité *m* treaty; treatise, tract.

traitement *m* treatment; salary; processing.

traiter *vt* to treat; to process; * *vi* to treat, negotiate.

traiteur *m* caterer; trader.

traître *m* traitor **-sse** *f* traitress.

traîtrise *f* treachery, treacherousness.

trajectoire *f* trajectory.

trajet *m* distance; journey; course, path.

trame *f* framework; web.

tramer *vt* to plot; to weave.

trampoline *m* trampoline.

tramway *m* tram, tramway.

tranchant *adj* sharp, cutting.

tranche *f* slice; edge; section.

tranchée *f* trench; cutting.

trancher *vt* to cut, sever; to conclude; to settle; * *vi* to cut; to resolve; to stand out.

tranquille *adj* quiet, tranquil; **~ment** *adv* quietly, tranquilly.

tranquillisant *m* tranquillizer; * *adj* soothing, tranquillizing.

tranquilliser *vt* to reassure.

tranquillité *f* tranquillity.

transaction *f* transaction, arrangement.

transatlantique *m* transatlantic liner; * *adj* transatlantic.

transcendant *adj* transcendent; transcendental.

transcender *vt* to transcend.

transcription *f* transcription; copy.

transcrire *vt* to transcribe; copy out.

transe *f* trance.

transept *m* transept.

tranférer *vt* to transfer.

transfert *m* transfer; conveyance.

transfiguration *f* transfiguration.

transfigurer *vt* to transfigure.

transformateur *m* transformer.

transformation *f* transformation.

transformer *vt* to transform, change; **se ~** *vr* to be transformed; to change.

transfuge *mf* defector.

transfuser *vt* to transfuse.

transfusion *f* transfusion.

transgresser *vt* to transgress, infringe.

transgression *f* transgression, infringement.

transi *adj* numb, paralysed.

transiger *vi* to compromise, come to terms.

transistor *m* transistor.

transit *m* transit.

transiter *vi* to pass in transit.

transitif *adj* transitive.

transition *f* transition.

transitoire *adj* transitory.

translucide *adj* translucent.

transmettre *vt* to transmit; to pass on, hand down.

transmissible *adj* transmissible.

transmission *f* transmission; passing on; handing down.

transmuter *vt* to transmute.

transparaître *vi* to show through.

transparence *f* transparency.

transparent *adj* transparent.

transpercer *vt* to pierce; to penetrate.

transpiration *f* transpiration; perspiration.

transpirer *vi* to perspire; to come to light.

transplanter *vt* to transplant.

transport *m* carrying; transport; conveyance; transfer.

transportable *adj* transportable.

transporter *vt* to carry; to transport.

transporteur *m* haulier; carrier.

transposer *vt* to transpose.

transposition *f* transposition.

transsexuel *adj* transsexual.

transvaser *vt* to decant.

transversal *adj* transverse; ~ement *adv* crosswise; transversely.

transvider *vt* to pour into another container.

trapèze *m* trapeze.

trapéziste *mf* trapeze artist.

trappe *f* trap door.

trappeur *m* trapper.

trapu *adj* squat; thickset.

traquer *vt* to track; to hunt down.

traumatisant *adj* traumatizing.

traumatiser *vt* to traumatize.

traumatisme *m* traumatism.

travail *m* work; job, occupation; labour; *pl* travaux work, labour.

travailler *vi* to work; to endeavour; * *vt* to work, shape; to cultivate; to fatigue.

travailleur *m* -euse *f* worker; * *adj* diligent; hard-working.

travers *m* breadth; irregularity; fault; à ~ through, across; de ~ obliquely, askew; en ~ across, crosswise.

traversée *f* crossing, going through; traverse.

traverser *vt* to cross, traverse.

traversin *m* bolster.

travesti *m* drag artist; transvestite; * *adj* disguised.

trébucher *vi* to stumble, trip up.

trèfle *m* clover.

tréfonds *m* subsoil, bottom.

treille *f* climbing vine.

treillis *m* trellis; wire mesh.

treize *adj, m* thirteen.

treizième *adj, mf* thirteenth; ~ment *adv* in thirteenth place.

tréma *m* dieresis.

tremblant *adj* trembling, shaking.

tremblement *m* trembling; shiver; vibration; ~ de terre earthquake.

trembler *vi* to tremble, shake.

trembloter *vi* to tremble slightly, flicker.

trémousser (se) *vr* to wriggle.

tremper *vt* to soak; to dip; * *vi* to soak; to take part in.

tremplin *m* springboard; ski-jump.

trentaine *f* about thirty.

trente *adj, m* thirty.

trentième *adj, mf* thirtieth.

trépasser *vi* to pass away.

trépidant *adj* pulsating, quivering.

trépied *m* tripod.

trépigner *vi* to stamp one's feet.

très *adv* very; most; very much.

trésor *m* treasure.

trésorerie *f* treasury.

trésorier *m* **-ière** *f* treasurer.

tressaillir *vi* to thrill; to shudder.

tressauter *vi* to start, jump.

tresse *f* plait, braid.

tresser *vt* to plait, braid.

tréteau *m* trestle.

treuil *m* winch.

trêve *f* truce; respite, rest.

tri *m* sorting out; selection; grading.

triage *m* sorting out.

triangle *m* triangle.

triangulaire *adj* triangular.

triathlon *m* triathlon.

tribal *adj* tribal.

tribord *m* starboard.

tribu *f* tribe.

tribunal *m* court, tribunal.

tribune *f* gallery, stand; rostrum.

tribut *m* tribute.

tributaire *adj* dependent, tributary.

tricher *vi* to cheat.

tricheur *m* **-euse** *f* cheater.

trichloréthylène *m* trichlorethylene.

tricolore *adj* three-coloured, tricolour.

tricot *m* jumper; knitting.

tricoter *vt* to knit.

tridimensionnel *adj* three-dimensional.

triennal *adj* triennial; three-yearly.

trier *vt* to sort out; to pick over.

trifouiller *vi* (*fam*) to rummage about; * *vt* to rummage about in.

trigonométrie *f* trigonometry.

trilingue *adj* trilingual.

trilogie *f* trilogy.

trimer *vi* to slave away.

trimestre *m* quarter; term.

trimestriel *adj* quarterly; three-monthly.

tringle *f* rod.

trinité *f* trinity.

trinquer *vi* to toast; to booze.

trio *m* trio.

triomphal *adj* triumphal; ~ement *adv* triumphantly.

triomphant *adj* triumphant.

triomphe *m* triumph, victory.

triompher *vi* to triumph.

triparti, tripartite *adj* tripartite.

tripe *f* tripe; guts.

triple *adj* triple, treble.

tripler *vi* to triple, increase threefold; * *vt* to triple, treble.

tripoter *vt* to play with, speculate with.

trique *f* cudgel.

triste *adj* sad, melancholy; ~ment *adv* sadly.

tristesse *f* sadness; melancholy.

triton *m* triton; tritone.

triturer *vt* to grind up, triturate.

trivial *adj* mundane, trivial; coarse, crude.

trivialité *f* triviality; crudeness.

troc *m* exchange; barter.

troglodyte *m* cave dweller, troglodyte.

trognon *m* core; stalk.

trois *adj, m* three.

troisième *adj, mf* third; ~ment *adv* thirdly.

trombe *f*: ~ d'eau cloudburst, downpour; **entrer/sortir en** ~ to dash in/out.

trombone *m* trombone.

trompe *f* trumpet; trunk, snout.

trompe-l'œil *m invar* trompe-l'oeil.

tromper *vt* to deceive, trick; **se** ~ *vr* to be mistaken.

tromperie *f* deception, deceit.

trompette *f* trumpet.

trompettiste *mf* trumpet player.

trompeur *adj* deceitful; deceptive.

tronc *m* trunk, shaft.

tronçon *m* section, part.

tronçonner *vt* to cut up, cut into sections.

tronçonneuse *f* chain saw.

trône *m* throne.

trôner *vi* to sit on the throne.

tronquer *vt* to truncate, curtail.

trop *adv* too; too much, unduly; *m* ~ too much, too many.

trophée *m* trophy.

tropical *adj* tropical.

tropique *m* tropic.

trop-plein *m* overflow; excess.

troquer *vt* to barter, swap.

trot *m* trot.

trotter *vi* to trot; to run about; to toddle.

trottiner *vi* to jog along; to trot along.

trottinette *f* scooter.

trottoir *m* pavement.

trou *m* hole; gap; cavity.

troublant *adj* disturbing, disquieting.

trouble *adj* unclear; murky, suspicious; * *m* disturbance, confusion; disorder.

trouble-fête *mf* spoilsport, killjoy.

troubler *vt* to disturb, disconcert; to cloud, darken; se ~ *vr* to become cloudy; to become flustered.

trouer *vt* to make a hole in; to pierce.

trouille *f*: avoir la ~ to have the wind up.

troupe *f* troupé; troop, band.

troupeau *m* herd, drove.

trousse *f* case, kit; wallet.

trousseau *m* trousseau; outfit.

trouvaille *f* windfall; inspired idea.

trouver *vt* to find, detect; to think; se ~ *vr* to find o.s.; to be located; **il se trouve que** it happens that.

truand *m* (*fam*) gangster; tramp.

truc *m* (*fam*) trick; gadget, thingummy.

truculent *adj* truculent; colourful, vivid.

truelle *f* trowel.

truffe *f* truffle.

truie *f* sow.

truite *f* trout.

truquage *m* rigging, fixing; fiddling.

truquer *vt* to rig, fix; to fiddle.

tsar *m* tsar.

tu *pn* you.

tuant *adj* exhausting; exasperating.

tuba *m* tuba, snorkel.

tube *m* tube, pipe; duct.

tuberculose *f* tuberculosis.

tuer *vt* to kill; se ~ *vr* to be killed; to kill o.s.

tuerie *f* slaughter.

tueur *m* -euse *f* killer.

tuile *f* tile.

tulipe *f* tulip.

tulle *m* tulle.

tuméfié *adj* puffed-up, swollen.

tumeur *f* tumour.

tumulte *m* tumult, commotion.

tumultueux *adj* tumultuous, stormy.

tungstène *m* tungsten.

tunique *f* tunic; smock.

tunnel *m* tunnel.

turban *m* turban.

turbine *f* turbine.

turbo *m* turbo.

turbulence *f* turbulence; excitement.

turbulent *adj* turbulent.

turpitude *f* turpitude, baseness.

tutelle *f* guardianship, supervision.

tuteur *m* **-trice** *f* guardian; * *m* stake, prop.

tutoyer *vt* to address sb as '*tu*'.

tuyau *m* pipe.

tuyauterie *f* piping.

TVA (taxe à la valeur ajoutée) *f* VAT.

tympan *m* eardrum, tympanum.

type *m* type; model; sample; bloke, chap.

typé *adj* typical.

typhoïde *f* typhoid; * *adj* typhoid.

typhon *m* typhoon.

typhus *m* typhus.

typique *adj* typical; **~ment** *adv* typically.

tyran *m* tyrant.

tyrannie *f* tyranny.

tyrannique *adj* tyrannical.

tyranniser *vt* to tyrannize.

U

ulcère *m* ulcer.

ulcérer *vt* to sicken; to embitter.

ultérieur *adj* later, subsequent; **~ement** *adv* later, subsequently.

ultimatum *m* ultimatum.

ultime *adj* ultimate, final.

ultra-violet *m* ultraviolet ray; * *adj* ultraviolet.

un, une *art* a, an; (number) one; l'~ l'autre, les ~s les autres one another.

unanime *adj* unanimous; **~ment** *adv* unanimously.

uni *adj* plain, self-coloured; close; smooth; **~ment** *adv* plainly, smoothly.

unification *f* unification; standardization.

unifier *vt* to unify; to standardize.

uniforme *adj* uniform, regular; * *m* uniform.

uniformément *adv* uniformly, regularly.

uniformité *f* uniformity; regularity.

unilatéral *adj* unilateral.

union *f* union; combination, blending.

unique *adj* only, single; unique; **~ment** *adv* only, solely, exclusively; merely.

unir *vt* to unite; to join; to combine; **s'~** *vr* to unite; to be joined in marriage.

unisson *m* unison; à l'~ in unison.

unitaire *adj* unitary, unit.

unité *f* unity; unit.

univers *m* universe; world.

universalité *f* universality.

universel *adj* universal; all-purpose; **~lement** *adv* universally.

universitaire *adj* university; * *mf* academic.

université *f* university.

uranium *m* uranium.

urbain *adj* urban, city.

urbanisation *f* urbanization.

urbaniser *vt* to urbanize.

urbanisme *m* town planning.

urbaniste *mf* town planner.

urée *f* urea.

urgence *f* urgency; emergency.

urgent *adj* urgent.

urinaire *adj* urinary.

urine *f* urine.

uriner *vi* to urinate.

urne *f* ballot box; urn.

urticaire *f* hives, urticaria.

usage *m* use; custom; usage; practice; wear; **faire ~ de** to exercise; to make use of.

usagé *adj* worn, old.

usager *m* **-ère** *f* user.

usé *adj* worn; threadbare; banal, trite.

user *vt* to make use of, enjoy; to wear out; **~ de** to exercise; to employ; **s'~** *vr* to wear out.

usine *f* factory.

usiner *vt* to machine; to manufacture.

usité *adj* in common use, common.

ustensile *m* implement; utensil.

usuel *adj* ordinary; everyday; **~lement** *adv* ordinarily.

usufruit *m* (*jur*) usufruct.

usure *f* usury.

usurier *m* **-ière** *f* usurer.

usurper *vt* to usurp.

utérus *m* womb, uterus.

utile *adj* useful; **~ment** *adv* usefully.

utilisateur *m*, **-trice** *f* user.

utilisation *f* use, utilization.

utiliser *vt* to use, utilize; to make use of.

utilitaire *adj* utilitarian.

utilité *f* usefulness; use; profit.

utopie *f* utopia.

utopique *adj* utopian.

V

vacance *f* vacancy; ~s holiday, vacation.

vacancier *m* -**ière** *f* holidaymaker.

vacant *adj* vacant, unoccupied.

vacarme *m* racket, row.

vaccin *m* vaccine.

vaccination *f* vaccination.

vacciner *vt* to vaccinate.

vache *f* cow; cowhide.

vachement *adv* (*fam*) damned, bloody.

vacher *m* -**ère** *f* cowherd.

vacherie *f* (*fam*) rottenness, meanness; nasty remark/trick.

vaciller *vi* to sway, totter; to falter.

va-et-vient *m invar* comings and goings; to and fro.

vagabond *m* -**e** *f* tramp, vagabond.

vagabondage *m* wandering, roaming; (*jur*) vagrancy.

vagabonder *vi* to wander, roam.

vagin *f* vagina.

vaginal *adj* vaginal.

vague *adj* vague, hazy, indistinct; ~**ment** *adv* vaguely; * *m* vagueness; * *f* wave.

vaguer *vi* to wander, roam.

vaillamment *adv* bravely, courageously.

vaillant *adj* brave, courageous.

vain *adj* vain; empty, hollow; shallow; **en** ~ in vain; ~**ement** *adv* vainly.

vaincre *vt* to defeat, overcome.

vaincu *adj* defeated, beaten.

vainqueur *m* conqueror, victor.

vaisseau *m* vessel; ship.

vaisselle *f* crockery; dishes; **faire la** ~ to do the washing up.

valable *adj* valid, legitimate; worthwhile.

valet *m* valet; servant.

valeur *f* value, worth; security, share; meaning.

valide *adj* able, able-bodied; ~**ment** *adv* validly.

valider *vt* to validate.

validité *f* validity.

valise *f* suitcase.

vallée *f* valley.

vallon *m* vale, dale.

vallonné *adj* undulating, hilly.

valoir *vt* to be worth; to be valid; **il vaut mieux** it is better to; ~ **la peine** to be worth the trouble.

valoriser *vt* to valorize.

valse *f* waltz.

valser *vi* to waltz.

valve *f* valve.

vampire *m* vampire.

vandale *mf* vandal.

vandalisme *m* vandalism.

vanille *f* vanilla.

vanité *f* vanity, conceit.

vaniteux *adj* vain, conceited.

vanne *f* gate, sluice.

vannerie *f* basketry; wickerwork.

vantard *adj* boastful, bragging.

vantardise *f* boastfulness; boast.

vanter *vt* to praise, vaunt; **se** ~ *vr* to boast, brag.

vapeur *f* haze, vapour.

vaporeux *adj* filmy, vaporous.

vaporisateur *m* spray, atomizer.

vaporiser *vt* to spray; to vaporize.

varappe *f* rock-climbing.

variable *adj* variable, changeable.

variante *f* variant; variation.

variation *f* variation, change.

varice *f* varicose vein.

varicelle *f* chickenpox.

varié *adj* varied; variegated; various.

varier *vi* to vary, change; * *vt* to vary.

variété *f* variety, diversity.

variole *f* smallpox.

vasculaire *adj* vascular.

vase *m* vase, bowl; * *f* silt, mud.

vaseline *f* vaseline.

vaseux *adj* woolly, muddled; muddy, silty.

vasistas *m* fanlight.

vaste *adj* vast, huge.

vaudeville *m* vaudeville.

vaudou *m* voodoo.

vaurien *m* -**ne** *f* good-for-nothing.

vautour *m* vulture.

vautrer (se) *vr* to wallow in.

veau *m* calf; veal.

vecteur *m* vector.

vécu *adj* real, true-life; lived; * *m* real-life.

vedette *f* star; (*mar*) launch.

végétal *adj* vegetable.

végétarien *m* **-ne** *f* vegetarian; * *adj* vegetarian.

végétatif *adj* vegetative.

végétation *f* vegetation.

végéter *vi* to vegetate; to stagnate.

véhémence *f* vehemence.

véhément *adj* vehement.

véhicule *m* vehicle.

veille *f* wakefulness; watch; eve.

veillée *f* evening; evening meeting.

veiller *vi* to stay up, sit up.

veilleur *m* watchman.

veilleuse *f* night light; sidelight.

veinard *m* **-e** *f* lucky person; * *adj* lucky, jammy.

veine *f* vein, seam; inspiration; luck.

vêler *vi* to calve.

velléité *f* vague desire, vague impulse.

vélo *m* bike.

vélodrome *m* velodrome.

vélomoteur *m* moped.

velours *m* velvet.

velouté *adj* velvety, downy.

velu *adj* hairy.

vénal *adj* venal, mercenary.

vendange *f* wine harvest.

vendanger *vt* to harvest grapes from; * *vi* to harvest the grapes.

vendangeur *m* **-euse** *f* grape-picker.

vendetta *f* vendetta.

vendeur *m* **-euse** *f* seller, salesperson.

vendre *vt* to sell.

vendredi *m* Friday.

vénéneux *adj* poisonous.

vénérable *adj* venerable.

vénération *f* veneration.

vénérer *vt* to venerate.

vénérien *adj* venereal.

vengeance *f* vengeance, revenge.

venger *vt* to avenge; **se ~** *vr* to avenge o.s.

venimeux *adj* venomous, poisonous; vicious.

venin *m* venom; poison.

venir *vi* to come; to happen; to grow; **~ de** to come from; to derive from; **~ au monde** to be born.

vent *m* wind; breath; emptiness.

vente *f* sale; selling; auction; **en ~** for sale.

ventilateur *m* ventilator, fan.

ventiler *vt* to ventilate; to divide up.

ventouse *f* sucker; suction disc.

ventre *m* stomach, belly; womb.

ventricule *m* ventricle.

ventriloque *mf* ventriloquist; * *adj* ventriloquial.

venue *f* coming.

ver *m* worm; grub; ~ **de terre** earthworm.

véracité *f* veracity; truthfulness.

véranda *f* veranda.

verbal *adj* verbal; ~**ement** *adv* verbally.

verbe *m* verb; language, word.

verbiage *m* verbiage.

verdeur *f* vigour, vitality.

verdict *m* verdict.

verdir *vi* to go green; * *vt* to turn green.

verdure *f* greenery, verdure.

verge *f* stick, cane.

verger *m* orchard.

verglas *m* black ice.

véridique *adj* truthful, veracious; ~**ment** *adv* truthfully.

vérification *f* check; verification.

vérifier *vt* to verify, check; to audit.

véritable *adj* real, genuine; ~**ment** *adv* really, genuinely.

vérité *f* truth; truthfulness, sincerity; **en** ~ really, actually.

vermeil *adj* vermilion, ruby, cherry; * *m* vermeil.

vermicelle *m* vermicelli.

vermillon *m* vermilion; scarlet.

vermine *f* vermin.

vermisseau *m* small worm.

vermoulu *adj* worm-eaten.

verni *adj* varnished.

vernis *m* varnish; glaze; shine.

vernissage *m* varnishing; glazing.

verre *m* glass; lens; drink.

verrerie *f* glassworks; glassmaking.

verrière *f* window; glass roof.

verrou *m* bolt.

verrouillage *m* bolting; locking.

verrouiller *vt* to bolt; to lock.

verrue *f* wart, verruca.

vers *prép* towards; around; about; * *m* line, verse.

versatile *adj* versatile.

verse *f*: pleuvoir à ~ to pour down.

Verseau *m* Aquarius.

verser *vt* to pour, shed; to pay; (*mil*) to assign.

verset *m* verse.

version *f* version.

verso *m* back.

vert *m* green; * *adj* green; langue ~e slang; ~ement *adv* sharply, brusquely.

vertébral *adj* vertebral.

vertèbre *f* vertebra.

vertical *adj* vertical; ~ement *adv* vertically.

vertige *m* vertigo; dizziness.

vertigineux *adj* vertiginous, breathtaking.

vertu *f* virtue; courage; en ~ de in accordance with.

vertueux *adj* virtuous.

verve *f* verve, vigour.

verveine *f* verbena.

vésicule *f* vesicle; gall bladder.

vessie *f* bladder.

veste *f* jacket.

vestiaire *m* cloakroom; changing-room.

vestibule *m* hall, vestibule.

vestige *m* relic; trace, vestige.

veston *m* jacket.

vêtement *m* garment.

vétéran *m* veteran.

vétérinaire *mf* veterinary surgeon; * *adj* veterinary.

vêtir *vt* to clothe, dress; se ~ *vr* to dress o.s.

veto *m* veto.

vêtu *adj* dressed; clad, wearing.

vétuste *adj* dilapidated, ancient.

veuf *m* widower; * *adj* widowed.

veule *adj* spineless.

veuve *f* widow; * *adj* widowed.

vexant *adj* annoying, vexing.

vexer *vt* to annoy; to hurt.

viable *adj* viable.

viaduc *m* viaduct.

viande *f* meat.

vibration *f* vibration.

vibrer *vi* to vibrate; to quiver.

vibromasseur *m* vibrator.

vicaire *m* curate, vicar.

vice *m* vice; fault, defect.

vice-président *m* vice-president; deputy chairman.

vice-versa *adv* vice versa.

vicieux *adj* licentious; dissolute; incorrect.

vicissitude *f* vicissitude, change; trial.

vicomte *m* viscount, **-esse** *f* viscountess.

victime *f* victim, casualty; être ~ **de** to be the victim of.

victoire *f* victory.

victorieusement *adv* victoriously.

victorieux *adj* victorious.

vidange *f* emptying; waste outlet.

vidanger *vt* to empty; to drain off.

vide *adj* empty, vacant, devoid; * *m* vacuum; gap; void.

vidéo *f* video; * *adj invar* video.

vidéocassette *f* videocassette.

vide-ordures *m invar* rubbish chute.

vider *vt* to empty; to drain; to vacate; to gut.

videur *m* bouncer.

vie *f* life; living; être en ~ to be alive.

vieillard *m* old man.

vieillesse *f* old age; the elderly; oldness.

vieillir *vi* to get old; * *vt* to age; to put years on.

vieillissement *m* ageing; obsolescence.

vierge *f* virgin; * *adj* virgin; blank; unexposed.

vieux *adj*, *f* **vieille** old; ancient; obsolete.

vif *adj* alive, lively; quick; eager, passionate.

vigilance *f* vigilance.

vigilant *adj* vigilant.

vigile *m* vigil.

vigne *f* vine; vineyard.

vigneron *m* **-ne** *f* wine grower.

vignette *f* vignette; illustration; seal.

vignoble *m* vineyard.

vigoureusement *adv* vigorously, energetically.

vigoureux *adj* vigorous.

vigueur *f* vigour, strength, energy.

vil *adj* vile; lowly.

vilain *m* naughty boy, **-e** *f* naughty girl.

villa *f* villa, detached house.

village *m* village.

villageois *adj* village, rustic.

ville *f* town, city.

villégiature *f* holiday; vacation.

vin *m* wine.

vinaigre *m* vinegar.

vinaigrette *f* vinaigrette, oil and vinegar dressing, French dressing.

vindicatif *adj* vindictive.

vingt *adj*, *m* twenty.

vingtaine *f* about twenty; score.

vingtième *adj, mf* twentieth; ~**ment** *adv* in twentieth place.

vinicole *adj* wine, wine-growing.

vinyl *m* vinyl.

viol *m* rape.

violation *f* violation; transgression.

violemment *adv* violently.

violence *f* violence; force, duress.

violent *adj* violent; considerable, excessive.

violer *vt* to violate, desecrate; to rape.

violet *adj* purple, violet; * *m* purple, violet.

violette *f* (*bot*) violet.

violeur *m* rapist.

violon *m* violin.

violoncelle *m* cello, violoncello.

violoncelliste *mf* cello player.

violoniste *mf* violinist.

vipère *f* viper, adder.

virage *m* turn, bend; tacking.

viral *adj* viral.

virement *m* turning, tacking; transfer, clearance.

virer *vt* to transfer; * *vi* to turn, tack.

virevolter *vi* to spin round, pirouette.

virginité *f* virginity; purity.

virgule *f* comma; (*math*) point.

viril *adj* virile; male, masculine; ~**ement** *adv* in a virile way.

virilité *f* virility; masculinity.

virtuel *adj* virtual; potential; ~**lement** *adv* virtually.

virtuose *mf* virtuoso, master.

virulence *f* virulence, viciousness.

virulent *adj* virulent, vicious.

virus *m* virus.

vis *f* screw.

visa *m* stamp, visa.

visage *m* face; expression.

vis-à-vis *prép*: opposite; ~ **de** towards; as regards; * *m* encounter; person opposite; **en** ~ opposite each other.

viscéral *adj* visceral; deep-rooted.

viscère *f* viscera; intestines.

viser *vt* to aim, target; to visa.

viseur *m* sight; viewfinder.

visibilité *f* visibility.

visible *adj* visible; evident,

obvious; ~**ment** *adv* visibly; obviously.

visière *f* peak; eyeshade; visor.

vision *f* eyesight; vision.

visionnaire *mf* visionary; * *adj* visionary.

visite *f* visit; visiting, inspection; visitor.

visiter *vt* to visit; to examine, inspect.

visiteur *m* -**euse** *f* visitor; representative.

vison *m* mink.

visqueux *adj* viscous, thick.

visser *vt* to screw on.

visuel *adj* visual.

vital *adj* vital.

vitalité *f* energy, vitality.

vitamine *f* vitamin.

vite *adv* quickly, fast; soon; * *adj* swift; quick.

vitesse *f* speed, swiftness; gear.

viticole *adj* wine, wine-growing.

viticulteur *m* wine grower.

vitrage *m* glazing; windows.

vitrail *m* stained-glass window.

vitre *f* pane, window.

vitreux *adj* glassy, glazed, vitreous.

vitrier *m* glazier.

vitrine *f* shop window; display cabinet.

vitriol *m* vitriol.

vitupérer *vi* to vituperate, reprimand.

vivace *adj* hardy, perennial; enduring.

vivacité *f* vivacity, liveliness; vividness; acuteness.

vivant *adj* alive, living; lively.

vivement *adv* quickly, briskly; keenly, acutely.

vivier *m* fishpond.

vivifiant *adj* refreshing, invigorating.

vivifier *vt* to enliven, invigorate, refresh.

vivre *vi* to live, be alive; to last, endure; **vive la mariée!** three cheers for the bride; * *vt* to live, spend; to live through.

vivres *mpl* victuals, supplies.

VO (version originale) *f* original version.

vocabulaire *m* vocabulary.

vocal *adj* vocal; ~**ement** *adv* vocally.

vocalise *f* singing exercise.

vocation *f* vocation, calling.

vociférer *vi* to vociferate, bawl.

vœu *m* vow; wish.

vogue *f* fashion, vogue; **en ~** in fashion.

voici *prép* here is, here are; ago, past.

voie *f* way, road; means; process; **~ ferrée** railway; **~ d'eau** leak; **en ~ de** in the process of.

voilà *prép* there is, there are; ago; **et ~!** so there!

voile *f* sail; * *m* veil.

voilé *adj* veiled; hazy, blurred.

voiler *vt* to veil, shroud; **se ~ vr** to wear a veil; to mist over.

voilier *m* sailing boat, yacht.

voir *vt* to see; to deal with; to understand; **avoir à ~ avec** to have to do with; **se ~ vr** to find o.s.; to show.

voisin *m* **-e** *f* neighbour; fellow; * *adj* neighbouring, next.

voisinage *m* neighbourhood, vicinity.

voiture *f* car; carriage; cart.

voix *f* voice; vote; **parler à ~ basse/haute** to speak in a low/high voice.

vol *m* flight; flock; **à ~ d'oiseau** as the crow flies.

volaille *f* fowl, poultry.

volant *m* steering wheel; * *adj* flying.

volatile *adj* volatile.

volatiliser *vt* to volatilize; to extinguish; **se ~ vr** to volatilize; to vanish.

volcan *m* volcano.

volcanique *adj* volcanic.

volée *f* flight; volley; **à la ~** in mid-air; rashly, at random; **demi-~** half-volley.

voler *vi* to fly; **~ en éclats** to smash into pieces; * *vt* to steal; to rob.

volet *m* shutter; flap, paddle.

voleur *m* **-euse** *f* thief; * *adj* dishonest, thieving.

volley-ball *m* volleyball.

volleyeur *m* **-euse** *f* volleyball player.

volontaire *adj* voluntary; intentional; **~ment** *adv* voluntarily; intentionally.

volonté *f* will, wish; willingness; willpower.

volontiers *adv* willingly; gladly.

volt *m* volt.

volte-face *f invar* volte-face, about-turn; **faire ~** to turn round.

voltige *f* acrobatics; trick riding.

voltiger *vi* to flutter about.

volubile *adj* voluble.

volume *m* volume.

volumineux *adj* voluminous, bulky.

volupté *f* voluptuousness, sensual pleasure.

voluptueux *adj* voluptuous.

volute *f* volute, scroll; wreath.

vomir *vi* to vomit, be sick; * *vt* to vomit, bring up.

vomissement *m* vomiting.

vorace *adj* voracious; ~ment *adv* voraciously.

voracité *f* voracity, voraciousness.

vos = *pl* votre.

votant *m* -e *f* voter.

vote *m* vote; voting.

voter *vi* to vote.

votre *adj*, *pl* vos your, your own.

vôtre *pn*: le ~, la ~, les ~s yours, your own.

vouer *vt* to vow; to devote, dedicate.

vouloir *vt* to want, wish; to require; to try; ~ du mal à to wish sb harm; en ~ à to bear a grudge against sb; bien ~ to be happy that.

voulu *adj* required; deliberate.

vous *pn* you, yourself.

voûte *f* vault.

voûté *adj* vaulted.

vouvoyer *vt* to use the '*vous*' form.

voyage *m* journey, trip; travelling.

voyager *vi* to travel, journey.

voyageur *m* -euse *f* traveller, passenger.

voyant *m* -e *f* visionary, seer; * *m* signal light; * *adj* gaudy, showy.

voyelle *f* vowel.

voyeur *m* -euse *f* voyeur.

voyou *m* lout, loafer, hoodlum.

vrac *adv*: en ~ in bulk.

vrai *adj* true, genuine; ~ment *adv* truly, really.

vraisemblable *adj* likely, probable; ~ment *adv* probably.

vrille *f* tendril; spiral; descendre en ~ to come down in a spin.

vrombir *vi* to roar, hum.

vu *adj* seen; considered, regarded; être bien/mal ~ to be well/poorly thought of; ni ~ ni connu you won't discover anything; * *prép* in view of.

vue *f* sight, eyesight; **en ~ de** with a view to; **avoir des ~s sur** to have designs on.

vulgaire *adj* vulgar, crude; **~ment** *adv* vulgarly.

vulgariser *vt* to popularize; to coarsen.

vulgarité *f* vulgarity, coarseness.

vulnérable *adj* vulnerable.

vulve *f* vulva.

W

wagon *m* wagon, truck, freight car; wagonload.

wagon-citerne *m* tanker.

wagon-lit *m* sleeper.

wagon-restaurant *m* restaurant car.

water-polo *m* water polo.

watt *m* watt.

W-C (water-closet) *mpl* lavatory.

week-end *m* weekend.

western *m* western.

whisky *m* whisky.

XYZ

xénophobe *mf* xenophobe;
 * *adj* xenophobic.
xénophobie *f* xenophobia.
xylophone *m* xylophone.

yacht *m* yacht.
yang *m* yang.
yaourt *m* yoghurt.
yard *m* yard.
yeux *pl* = œil.
yin *m* yin.
yoga *m* yoga.
yogi *m* yogi.
yogourt *m* = yaourt.
yo-yo *m* yo-yo.
yucca *m* yucca.
yuppie *mf* yuppy.

zèbre *m* zebra.
zébu *m* zebu.
zèle *m* zeal.
zélé *adj* zealous.
zen *m* Zen.
zénith *m* zenith.

zéro *m* zero, nought, nothing.
zézayer *vi* to lisp.
zigzag *m* zigzag.
zigzaguer *vi* to zigzag.
zinc *m* zinc.
zizanie *f* ill-feeling.
zizi *m* (*fam*) willy.
zodiaque *m* zodiac.
zona *m* shingles.
zone *f* zone, area.
zoo *m* zoo.
zoologie *f* zoology.
zoologiste *mf* zoologist.
zoom *m* zoom; zoom lens.
zoophile *adj* zoophilic, zoo-
 philous.
zozoter *vi* (*fam*) to lisp.
ZUP (zone à urbaniser en
 priorité) *f* urban development zone.
zut *interj* damn! rubbish!
 shut up!

English–French Dictionary

A

a *art* un, une.

aback *adv* to be taken ~ *vi* être décontenancé.

abacus *n* abaque, boulier *m*.

abandon *vt* abandonner, laisser.

abandonment *n* abandon *m*.

abase *vt* avilir; humilier.

abasement *n* avilissement *m*; humiliation *f*.

abash *vt* couvrir de honte.

abate *vt* baisser; * *vi* baisser; se calmer.

abatement *n* baisse, réduction *f*.

abbess *n* abbesse *f*.

abbey *n* abbaye *f*.

abbot *n* abbé *m*.

abbreviate *vt* abréger, raccourcir.

abbreviation *n* abréviation *f*.

abdicate *vt* abdiquer; renoncer à.

abdication *n* abdication *f*; renonciation *f*.

abdomen *n* abdomen *m*.

abdominal *adj* abdominal.

abduct *vt* kidnapper, enlever.

abductor *n* abducteur *m*.

abed *adv* au lit.

aberrant *adj* aberrant.

aberration *n* aberration *f*.

abet *vt*: to aid and ~ être complice de.

abeyance *n* suspension *f*.

abhor *vt* abhorrer, exécrer.

abhorrence *n* exécration, horreur *f*.

abhorrent *adj* exécrable.

abide *vt* supporter, souffrir.

ability *n* capacité, aptitude *f*; abilities *pl* talents *mpl*.

abject *adj* misérable; abject, méprisable; ~ly *adv* misérablement.

abjure *vt* abjurer; renoncer à.

ablative *n* (*gr*) ablatif *m*.

ablaze *adj* enflammé.

able *adj* capable; to be ~ pouvoir.

able-bodied *adj* robuste.

ablution *n* ablution *f*.

ably *adv* habilement.

abnegation *n* renoncement *m*.

abnormal *adj* anormal.

abnormality *n* anomalie *f*.

aboard *adv* à bord.

abode *n* domicile *m*.

abolish *vt* abolir, supprimer.

abolition *n* abolition, suppression *f*.

abominable *adj* abominable; ~**bly** *adv* abominablement.

abomination *n* abomination *f*.

aboriginal *adj* aborigène.

aborigines *npl* aborigènes *mpl*.

abort *vi* avorter.

abortion *n* avortement *m*.

abortive *adj* raté.

abound *vi* abonder; ~ **with** abonder en.

about *prep* au sujet de; vers; **I carry no money** ~ me je n'ai pas d'argent sur moi; * *adv* çà et là; **to be** ~ **to** être sur le point de; **to go** ~ aller de- ci de- là; **to go** ~ **a thing** entreprendre qch; **all** ~ partout.

above *prep* au-dessus de; * *adv* au-dessus; ~ **all** surtout, principalement; ~ **mentioned** mentionné ci-dessus.

aboveboard *adj* franc.

abrasion *n* écorchure *f*.

abrasive *adj* abrasif.

abreast *adv* de front.

abridge *vt* abréger, raccourcir.

abridgment *n* abrégement *m*; version abrégée *f*.

abroad *adv* à l'étranger; **to go** ~ se rendre à l'étranger.

abrogate *vt* abroger.

abrogation *n* abrogation *f*.

abrupt *adj* abrupt; brusque; ~**ly** *adv* brusquement; rudement.

abscess *n* abcès *m*.

abscond *vi* s'enfuir.

absence *n* absence *f*.

absent *adj* absent; * *vi* s'absenter.

absentee *n* absent *m* -e *f*.

absenteeism *n* absentéisme *m*.

absent-minded *adj* distrait.

absolute *adj* absolu; ~**ly** *adv* absolument.

absolution *n* absolution *f*.

absolutism *n* absolutisme *m*.

absolve *vt* absoudre.

absorb *vt* absorber.

absorbent *adj* absorbant.

absorbent cotton *n* coton hydrophile *m*.

absorption *n* absorption *f*.

abstain *vi* s'abstenir.

abstemious *adj* sobre; ~ly *adv* sobrement.

abstemiousness *n* sobriété *f*.

abstinence *n* abstinence *f*.

abstinent *adj* abstinent.

abstract *adj* abstrait; * *n* abrégé *m*; in the ~ dans l'abstrait.

abstraction *n* abstraction *f*; extraction *f*.

abstractly *adv* abstraitement.

abstruse *adj* abstrus, obscur; ~ly *adv* obscurément.

absurd *adj* absurde; ~ly *adv* absurdement.

absurdity *n* absurdité *f*.

abundance *n* abondance *f*.

abundant *adj* abondant; ~ly *adv* abondamment.

abuse *vt* abuser de; insulter; maltraiter; * *n* abus *m*; injures *fpl*; mauvais traitements *mpl*.

abusive *adj* injurieux; ~ly *adv* injurieusement.

abut *vi* être contigu.

abysmal *adj* abominable.

abyss *n* abîme *m*.

acacia *n* acacia *m*.

academic *adj* universitaire; scolaire; théorique.

academician *n* académicien *m* -ne *f*.

academy *n* académie *f*.

accede *vi* accéder.

accelerate *vt* accélérer.

accelerator *n* accélérateur *m*.

acceleration *n* accélération *f*.

accent *n* accent *m*; * *vt* accentuer.

accentuate *vt* accentuer.

accentuation *n* accentuation *f*.

accept *vt* accepter.

acceptable *adj* acceptable.

acceptability *n* acceptabilité *f*.

acceptance *n* acceptation *f*.

access *n* accès *m*.

accessible *adj* accessible.

accession *n* augmentation *f*; accession *f*.

accessory *n* accessoire *m*; (*law*) complice *m*.

accident *n* accident *m*; hasard *m*.

accidental *adj* accidentel; ~ly *adv* par hasard.

acclaim *vt* acclamer.

acclamation *n* acclamation *f*.

acclimate *vt* (US) acclimater.

accommodate *vt* loger; accommoder.

accommodating *adj* obligeant.

accommodations *npl* logement *m*.

accompaniment *n* (*mus*) accompagnement *m*.

accompanist *n* (*mus*) accompagnateur *m* -trice *f*.

accompany *vt* accompagner.

accomplice *n* complice *mf*.

accomplish *vt* accomplir.

accomplished *adj* accompli.

accomplishment *n* accomplissement *m*; ~s *pl* talents *mpl*.

accord *n* accord *m*; with one ~ d'un commun accord; of one's own ~ de son propre chef.

accordance *n*: in ~ with conformément à.

according *prep* selon; ~ as selon que; ~ly *adv* en conséquence.

accordion *n* (*mus*) accordéon *m*.

accost *vt* accoster.

account *n* compte *m*; on no ~ en aucun cas; on ~ of en raison de; to call to ~ demander des comptes; to turn to ~ mettre à profit; * *vt* ~ for expliquer; représenter.

accountability *n* responsabilité *f*.

accountable *adj* responsable.

accountancy *n* comptabilité *f*.

accountant *n* comptable *mf*.

account book *n* livre *m* de comptes.

account number *n* numéro de compte *m*.

accrue *vi* s'accumuler; revenir.

accumulate *vt* accumuler; * *vi* s'accumuler.

accumulation *n* accumulation *f*.

accuracy *n* exactitude *f*.

accurate *adj* exact; ~ly *adv* exactement.

accursed *adj* maudit.

accusation *n* accusation *f*.

accusative *n* (*gr*) accusatif *m*.

accusatory *adj* accusateur.

accuse *vt* accuser.

accused *n* accusé *m* -e *f*.

accuser *n* accusateur *m* -trice *f*.

accustom *vt* accoutumer.

accustomed *adj* accoutumé.

ace *n* as *m*; within an ~ of à deux doigts de.

acerbic *adj* acerbe.

acetate *n* (*chem*) acétate *m*.

ache *n* douleur *f*; * *vi* faire mal.

achieve *vt* réaliser; obtenir.

achievement *n* réalisation *f*; exploit *m*.

acid *adj* acide; aigre; * *n* acide *m*.

acidity *n* acidité *f*.

acknowledge *vt* reconnaître, admettre.

acknowledgment *n* reconnaissance *f*.

acme *n* apogée *m*.

acne *n* acné *f*.

acorn *n* gland *m*.

acoustics *n* acoustique *f*.

acquaint *vt* informer, aviser.

acquaintance *n* connaissance *f*.

acquiesce *vi* acquiescer, consentir.

acquiescence *n* consentement *m*.

acquiescent *adj* consentant.

acquire *vt* acquérir.

acquisition *n* acquisition *f*.

acquit *vt* acquitter.

acquittal *n* acquittement *m*.

acre *n* acre *f*.

acrid *adj* âcre; acerbe.

acrimonious *adj* acrimonieux.

acrimony *n* acrimonie *f*.

across *adv* en travers, d'un côté à l'autre; * *prep* à travers; **to come** ~ tomber sur.

act *vt* jouer; * *vi* agir; jouer la comédie; * *n* acte *m*; ~**s of the apostles** Actes des Apôtres *mpl*.

acting *adj* intérimaire.

action *n* action *f*; combat *m*.

action replay *n* répétition *f*.

activate *vt* activer.

active *adj* actif; ~**ly** *adv* activement.

activity *n* activité *f*.

actor *n* acteur *m*.

actress *n* actrice *f*.

actual *adj* réel; concret; ~**ly** *adv* en fait; réellement.

actuary *n* actuaire *mf*.

acumen *n* perspicacité *f*.

acute *adj* aigu; perspicace; ~ **accent** *n* accent aigu *m*; ~ **angle** *n* angle aigu *m*; ~**ly** *adv* vivement; avec perspicacité.

acuteness *n* finesse *f*, intensité *f*.

ad *n* annonce *f*.

adage *n* adage *m*.

adamant *adj* inflexible.

adapt *vt* adapter, ajuster.

adaptability *n* adaptabilité *f*.

adaptable *adj* adaptable.

adaptation *n* adaptation *f*.

adaptor *n* adaptateur *m*.

add *vt* ajouter; ~ **up** additionner.

addendum *n* addendum *m*.

adder *n* vipère *f*.

addict *n* intoxiqué *m* -e *f*.

addiction *n* dépendance *f*.

addictive *adj* qui crée une dépendance.

addition *n* addition *f*.

additional *adj* additionnel; ~**ly** *adv* de plus.

additive n additif m.

address vt adresser; s'adresser à; * n adresse f; discours m.

adduce vt mentionner, citer.

adenoids npl végétations fpl.

adept adj expert.

adequacy n suffisance f; capacité f.

adequate adj adéquat; suffisant; ~ly adv convenablement; suffisamment.

adhere vi adhérer.

adherence n adhérence f.

adherent n adhérent, partisan m.

adhesion n adhérence f; adhésion f.

adhesive adj adhésif.

adhesive tape n (med) sparadrap m; papier m collant.

adhesiveness n adhérence f.

adieu adv adieu; * n adieux mpl.

adipose adj adipeux.

adjacent adj adjacent, contigu.

adjectival adj adjectival; ~ly adv adjectiva–lement.

adjective n adjectif m.

adjoin vi être contigu.

adjoining adj contigu.

adjourn vt reporter, remettre.

adjournment n ajournement m.

adjudicate vt décider; juger.

adjunct n subalterne mf; annexe f.

adjust vt ajuster, adapter.

adjustable adj ajustable, adaptable.

adjustment n ajustement m; réglage m.

adjutant n (mil) adjudant m.

ad lib vt improviser.

administer vt administrer; distribuer; ~ an oath faire prêter serment.

administration n administration f; gouvernement m.

administrative adj administratif.

administrator n administrateur m -trice f.

admirable adj admirable; ~bly adv admirablement.

admiral n amiral m.

admiralship n amirauté f.

admiralty n ministère de la Marine m.

admiration n admiration f.

admire vt admirer.

admirer n admirateur m -trice f.

admiringly *adv* avec admiration.

admissible *adj* admissible.

admission *n* admission, entrée *f*.

admit *vt* admettre; ~ to reconnaître, avouer.

admittance *n* admission *f*.

admittedly *adv* il est vrai (que).

admixture *n* mélange *m*.

admonish *vt* admonester, réprimander.

admonition *n* admonestation *f*; conseil *m*.

admonitory *adj* d'admonestation.

ad nauseam *adv* à saturation.

ado *n* agitation *f*.

adolescence *n* adolescence *f*.

adopt *vt* adopter.

adopted *adj* adoptif.

adoption *n* adoption *f*.

adoptive *adj* adoptif.

adorable *adj* adorable.

adorably *adv* adorablement.

adoration *n* adoration *f*.

adore *vt* adorer.

adorn *vt* orner.

adornment *n* ornement *m*.

adrift *adv* à la dérive.

adroit *adj* adroit, habile.

adroitness *n* adresse *f*.

adulation *n* adulation *f*.

adulatory *adj* adulateur.

adult *adj* adulte; * *n* adulte *mf*.

adulterate *vt* falsifier; * *adj* falsifié.

adulteration *n* falsification *f*.

adulterer *n* adultère *m*.

adulteress *n* adultère *f*.

adulterous *adj* adultère.

adultery *n* adultère *m*.

advance *vt* avancer; * *vi* avancer; faire des progrès; * *n* avance *f*.

advanced *adj* avancé.

advancement *n* avancement *m*.

advantage *n* avantage *m*; to take ~ of profiter de.

advantageous *adj* avantageux; ~ly *adv* avantageusement.

advantageousness *n* avantage *m*.

advent *n* venue *f*; Advent *n* Avent *m*.

adventitious *adj* accidentel.

adventure *n* aventure *f*.

adventurer *n* aventurier *m* -ière *f*.

adventurous *adj* aventureux; ~ly *adv* aventureusement.

adverb *n* adverbe *m*.

adverbial *adj* adverbial; ~ly *adv* adverbialement.

adversary n adversaire mf.

adverse adj défavorable, contraire.

adversity n adversité f; malheur m.

advertise vt faire de la publicité pour; mettre une annonce pour.

advertisement n publicité f; annonce f.

advertising n publicité f.

advice n conseil m; avis m.

advisability n opportunité f.

advisable adj prudent, conseillé.

advise vt conseiller; aviser.

advisedly adv de manière avisée.

advisory adj consultatif.

advocacy n défense f.

advocate n avocat m; * vt plaider pour.

aerial n antenne f.

aerobics npl aérobic m.

aerometer n aéromètre m.

aeroplane n avion m.

aerosol n aérosol m.

aerostat n aérostat m.

aesthetic adj esthétique; ~s npl esthétique f.

afar adv au loin; **from** ~ de loin.

affability n affabilité f.

affable adj affable; ~**bly** adv affablement.

affair n affaire f.

affect vt toucher; affecter.

affectation n affectation f.

affected adj affecté; ~**ly** adv avec affectation.

affectingly adv avec émotion.

affection n affection f.

affectionate adj affectueux; ~**ly** adv affectueusement.

affidavit n déclaration sous serment f.

affiliate vt affilier.

affiliation n affiliation f.

affinity n affinité f.

affirm vt affirmer, déclarer.

affirmation n affirmation f.

affirmative adj affirmatif; ~**ly** adv affirmativement.

affix vt coller; apposer; * n (gr) affixe m.

afflict vt affliger.

affliction n affliction f.

affluence n abondance f.

affluent adj riche; abondant.

afflux n afflux m, affluence f.

afford vt fournir; **to be able to** ~ avoir les moyens d'acheter.

affray n (law) rixe f.

affront n affront m, injure f; * vt affronter; insulter.

aflame *adv* en flammes.

afloat *adv* à flot.

afore *prep* avant; * *adv* d'abord.

afraid *adj* apeuré; I am ~ j'ai peur.

afresh *adv* à nouveau.

aft *adv* (*mar*) en poupe.

after *prep* après; * *adv* après; ~ all après tout.

afterbirth *n* placenta *m*.

after-crop *n* deuxième récolte *f*.

after-effects *npl* répercussions *fpl*.

afterlife *n* vie après la mort *f*.

aftermath *n* conséquences *fpl*.

afternoon *n* après-midi *mf*.

afterpains *npl* tranchées utérines *fpl*.

aftershave *n* après-rasage *m*.

aftertaste *n* arrière-goût *m*.

afterward(s) *adv* ensuite.

again *adv* à nouveau; ~ and ~ de nombreuses fois; as much ~ encore autant.

against *prep* contre; ~ the grain à contre fil; de mauvaise volonté.

agate *n* agate *f*.

age *n* âge *m*; vieillesse *f*; under ~ mineur; * *vt* vieillir.

aged *adj* âgé.

agency *n* agence *f*.

agenda *n* ordre du jour *m*.

agent *n* agent *m*.

agglomerate *vt* agglomérer.

agglomeration *n* agglomération *f*.

aggrandizement *n* avancement *m*.

aggravate *vt* aggraver; énerver.

aggravation *n* aggravation *f*; énervement *m*.

aggregate *n* agrégat *m*.

aggregation *n* agrégation *f*.

aggression *n* agression *f*.

aggressive *adj* agressif.

aggressor *n* agresseur *m*.

aggrieved *adj* offensé.

aghast *adj* horrifié.

agile *adj* agile; adroit.

agility *n* agilité *f*; adresse *f*.

agitate *vt* agiter.

agitation *n* agitation *f*.

agitator *n* agitateur *m* -trice *f*.

ago *adv*: how long ~? il y a combien de temps?

agog *adj* en émoi; impatient.

agonizing *adj* atroce, angoissant.

agony *n* douleur *f* atroce; angoisse *f*.

agrarian *adj* agraire.

agree *vt* convenir; * *vi* être d'accord.

agreeable *adj* agréable; ~bly *adv* agréablement; ~ with conforme à.

agreeableness *n* caractère agréable *m*.

agreed *adj* convenu; ~! *adv* d'accord!

agreement *n* accord *m*.

agricultural *adj* agricole.

agriculture *n* agriculture *f*.

agriculturist *n* agriculteur *m*.

aground *adv* (*mar*) échoué.

ah! *excl* ah!

ahead *adv* en avant; à l'avance; (*mar*) sur l'avant.

ahoy! *excl* (*mar*) ohé!

aid *vt* aider, secourir; ~ and abet être complice de; * *n* aide *f*, secours *m*; aide *mf*.

aide-de-camp *n* (*mil*) aide de camp *m*.

AIDS *n* SIDA *m*.

ail *vt* affliger.

ailing *adj* souffrant.

ailment *n* maladie *f*.

aim *vt* pointer; viser; aspirer à; * *n* but *m*; cible *f*.

aimless *adj* sans but; ~ly à la dérive, sans but.

air *n* air *m*; * *vt* aérer.

air balloon *n* ballon *m*.

airborne *adj* aéroporté.

air-conditioned *adj* climatisé.

air-conditioning *n* climatisation *f*.

aircraft *n* avion *m*.

air cushion *n* coussin d'air *m*.

air force *n* armée de l'air *f*.

air freshener *n* appareil de conditionnement d'air *m*.

air gun *n* carabine à air comprimé *f*.

air hole *n* trou d'aération *m*.

airiness *n* aération, ventilation *f*.

airless *adj* mal aéré, mal ventilé.

airlift *n* pont aérien *m*.

airline *n* ligne aérienne *f*.

airmail *n*: by ~ par avion.

airport *n* aéroport *m*.

air pump *n* compresseur *m*.

airsick *adj*: to be ~ avoir le mal de l'air.

airstrip *n* piste d'atterrissage *f*.

air terminal *n* aérogare *f*.

airtight *adj* hermétique.

airy *adj* aéré; léger.

aisle *n* nef d'église *f*.

ajar *adj* entrouvert.

akimbo *adj* les poings sur les hanches.

akin *adj* ressemblant.

alabaster *n* albâtre *m*; * *adj* d'albâtre.

alacrity *n* vivacité *f*.

alarm *n* alarme *f*; * *vt* alarmer; inquiéter.

alarm bell *n* sonnette d'alarme *f*.

alarmist *n* alarmiste *mf*.

alas *adv* hélas.

albeit *conj* bien que.

album *n* album *m*.

alchemist *n* alchimiste *m*.

alchemy *n* alchimie *f*.

alcohol *n* alcool *m*.

alcoholic *adj* alcoolisé; * *n* alcoolique *mf*.

alcove *n* alcôve *f*.

alder *n* aulne *m*.

ale *n* bière *f*.

alehouse *n* taverne, brasserie *f*.

alert *adj* vigilant; vif; * *n* alerte *f*.

alertness *n* vigilance *f*; vivacité *f*.

algae *npl* algues *fpl*.

algebra *n* algèbre *f*.

algebraic *adj* algébrique.

alias *adj* alias.

alibi *n* (*law*) alibi *m*.

alien *adj* étranger; * *n* étranger *m* -ère *f*; extra-terrestre *mf*.

alienate *vt* aliéner.

alienation *n* aliénation *f*.

alight *vi* mettre pied à terre; * *adj* en feu.

align *vt* aligner.

alike *adj* semblable, égal; * *adv* de la même façon.

alimentary *n* (*med*) digestif *m*.

alimony *n* (*law*) pension *f* alimentaire.

alive *adj* en vie, vivant; actif.

alkali *n* alcali *m*.

alkaline *adj* alcalin.

all *adj* tout; * *adv* totalement; ~ at once, ~ of a sudden soudain; ~ the same cependant; ~ the better tant mieux; not at ~! pas du tout!; il n'y a pas de quoi!; once and for ~ une fois pour toutes; * *n* tout *m*.

allay *vt* apaiser.

all clear *n* feu vert *m*.

allegation *n* allégation *f*.

allege *vt* alléguer.

allegiance *n* loyauté, fidélité *f*.

allegorical *adj* allégorique; ~ly *adv* allégoriquement.

allegory *n* allégorie *f*.

allegro *n* (*mus*) allegro *m*.

allergy *n* allergie *f*.

alleviate *vt* alléger.

alleviation n allègement m.

alley n ruelle f.

alliance n alliance f.

allied adj allié.

alligator n alligator m.

alliteration n allitération f.

all-night adj ouvert toute la nuit.

allocate vt allouer.

allocation n allocation f.

allot vt assigner.

allow vt permettre; accorder; ~ for tenir compte de.

allowable adj admissible, permis.

allowance n allocation f; concession f.

alloy n alliage m.

all right adv bien.

all-round adj complet.

allspice n piment m de la Jamaïque.

allude vi faire allusion à.

allure n charme, attrait m.

alluring adj attrayant; ~ly adv avec charme.

allurement n attrait m.

allusion n allusion f.

allusive adj allusif; ~ly adv par allusion.

alluvial adj alluvial.

ally n allié m -e f; * vt allier.

almanac n almanach m.

almighty adj omnipotent, tout-puissant.

almond n amande f.

almond-milk n lait d'amandes m.

almond tree n amandier m.

almost adv presque.

alms n aumône f.

aloft prep en l'air; en haut.

alone adj seul; * adv seul; to leave ~ laisser tranquille.

along adv le long (de); ~ side à côté.

aloof adj distant.

aloud adj à voix haute.

alphabet n alphabet m.

alphabetical adj alphabétique; ~ly adv par ordre alphabétique, alphabétiquement.

alpine adj alpin.

already adv déjà.

also adv aussi.

altar n autel m.

altarpiece n retable m.

alter vt modifier.

alteration n modification f.

altercation n altercation f.

alternate adj alterné; * vt alterner; ~ly adv alternativement.

alternating adj alterné.

alternation n alternance f.

alternator *n* alternateur *m*.

alternative *n* alternative *f*; * *adj* alternatif; ~ly *adv* sinon.

although *conj* bien que, malgré.

altitude *n* altitude *f*.

altogether *adv* complètement.

alum *n* alun *m*.

aluminium *n* aluminium *m*.

aluminous *adj* alumineux.

always *adv* toujours.

a.m. *adv* du matin.

amalgam *n* amalgame *m*.

amalgamate *vt* amalgamer; *vi* s'amalgamer.

amalgamation *n* amalgamation *f*.

amanuensis *n* copiste *mf*.

amaryllis *n* (*bot*) amaryllis *f*.

amass *vt* accumuler, amasser.

amateur *n* amateur *m*.

amateurish *adj* d'amateur.

amatory *adj* amoureux; galant.

amaze *vt* stupéfier.

amazement *n* stupéfaction *f*.

amazing *adj* stupéfiant; ~ly *adv* incroyablement.

amazon *n* amazone *f*.

ambassador *n* ambassadeur *m*.

ambassadress *n* ambassadrice *f*.

amber *n* ambre *m*; * *adj* ambré.

ambidextrous *adj* ambidextre.

ambient *adj* ambiant.

ambiguity *n* ambiguïté *f*.

ambiguous *adj* ambigu; ~ly *adv* de manière ambiguë.

ambition *n* ambition *f*.

ambitious *adj* ambitieux; ~ly *adv* ambitieusement.

amble *vi* marcher tranquillement.

ambulance *n* ambulance *f*.

ambush *n* embuscade *f*; to lie in ~ être embusqué; * *vt* tendre une embuscade à.

ameliorate *vt* améliorer.

amelioration *n* amélioration *f*.

amenable *adj* responsable.

amend *vt* modifier; amender.

amendable *adj* réparable, corrigible.

amendment *n* modification *f*; amendement *m*.

amends *npl* compensation *f*.

amenities *npl* commodités *fpl*.

America *n* Amérique *f*.

American *adj* américain.

amethyst *n* améthyste *f*.

amiability *n* amabilité *f*.

amiable *adj* aimable.

amiableness *n* amabilité *f*.

amiably *adv* aimablement.

amicable *adj* amical; ~**bly** *adv* amicalement.

amid(st) *prep* entre, parmi.

amiss *adv*: **something's** ~ quelque chose ne va pas.

ammonia *n* ammoniaque *m*.

ammunition *n* munitions *fpl*.

amnesia *n* amnésie *f*.

amnesty *n* amnistie *f*.

among(st) *prep* entre, parmi.

amoral *adj* amoral.

amorous *adj* amoureux; ~**ly** *adv* amoureusement.

amorphous *adj* informe.

amount *n* montant *m*; quantité *f*; * *vi* s'élever (à).

amp(ere) *n* ampère *m*.

amphibian *n* amphibie *m*.

amphibious *adj* amphibie.

amphitheatre *n* amphithéâtre *m*.

ample *adj* spacieux; abondant, gros.

ampleness *n* abondance *f*.

amplification *n* amplification *f*.

amplifier *n* amplificateur *m*.

amplify *vt* amplifier.

amplitude *n* amplitude *f*.

amply *adv* amplement.

amputate *vt* amputer.

amputation *n* amputation *f*.

amulet *n* amulette *f*.

amuse *vt* distraire, divertir.

amusement *n* distraction *f*, divertissement *m*.

amusing *adj* divertissant; ~**ly** *adv* de manière divertissante.

an *art* un, une.

anachronism *n* anachronisme *m*.

anaemia *n* anémie *f*.

anaemic *adj* (*med*) anémique.

anaesthetic *n* anesthésique *m*.

analog *adj* (*comput*) analogique.

analogous *adj* analogue.

analogy *n* analogie *f*.

analyse *vt* analyser.

analysis *n* analyse *f*.

analyst *n* analyste *mf*.

analytical *adj* analytique; ~**ly** *adv* analytiquement.

anarchic *adj* anarchique.

anarchist *n* anarchiste *mf*.

anarchy *n* anarchie *f*.

anatomical *adj* anatomique; ~**ly** *adv* anatomiquement.

anatomize *vt* disséquer.

anatomy *n* anatomie *f*.

ancestor *n* ancêtre *mf*.

ancestral *adj* ancestral.

ancestry *n* ascendance *f*.

anchor *n* ancre *f*; * *vi* jeter l'ancre.

anchorage *n* ancrage *m*.

anchovy *n* anchois *m*.

ancient *adj* ancien, antique; ~ly *adv* anciennement.

ancillary *adj* auxiliaire.

and *conj* et.

anecdotal *adj* anecdotique.

anecdote *n* anecdote *f*.

anemone *n* (*bot*) anémone *f*.

anew *adv* de nouveau.

angel *n* ange *m*.

angelic *adj* angélique.

anger *n* colère *f*; * *vt* mettre en colère, irriter.

angle *n* angle *m*; * *vi* pêcher à la ligne.

angled *adj* anguleux.

angler *n* pêcheur à la ligne *m*.

anglicism *n* anglicisme *m*.

angling *n* pêche à la ligne *f*.

angrily *adv* avec colère.

angry *adj* en colère, irrité.

anguish *n* angoisse *f*.

angular *adj* angulaire.

angularity *n* caractère anguleux *m*.

animal *n adj* animal *m*.

animate *vt* animer; * *adj* vivant.

animated *adj* animé.

animation *n* animation *f*.

animosity *n* animosité *f*.

animus *n* haine *f*.

anise *n* anis *m*.

aniseed *n* graine d'anis *f*.

ankle *n* cheville *f*; ~bone astragale *m*.

annals *n* annales *fpl*.

annex *vt* annexer; * *n* annexe *f*.

annexation *n* annexion *f*.

annihilate *vt* annihiler, anéantir.

annihilation *n* anéantissement *m*.

anniversary *n* anniversaire (de) *m*.

annotate *vt* annoter.

annotation *n* annotation *f*.

announce *vt* annoncer.

announcement *n* annonce *f*.

announcer *n* présentateur *m* -trice *f*.

annoy *vt* ennuyer.

annoyance *n* ennui *m*.

annoying *adj* ennuyeux.

annual *adj* annuel; ~ly *adv* annuellement.

annuity *n* rente viagère *f*.

annul *vt* annuler, abroger.

annulment *n* annulation *f*.

annunciation *n* annonciation *f*.

anodyne *adj* calmant.

anoint *vt* oindre.

anomalous *adj* anormal.

anomaly *n* anomalie, irrégularité *f*.

anon *adv* = **anonymous**.

anonymity *n* anonymat *m*.

anonymous *adj* anonyme; ~**ly** *adv* anonymement.

anorexia *n* anorexie *f*.

another *adj* un autre; **one** ~ l'un l'autre.

answer *vt* répondre à; ~ **for** répondre de; ~ **to** répondre à; * *n* réponse *f*.

answerable *adj* responsable.

answering machine *n* répondeur téléphonique *m*.

ant *n* fourmi *f*.

antagonism *n* antagonisme *m*; rivalité *f*.

antagonist *n* antagoniste *mf*.

antagonize *vt* provoquer.

antarctic *adj* antarctique.

anteater *n* fourmilier *m*.

antecedent *n*: ~**s** *pl* antécédents *mpl*.

antechamber *n* antichambre *f*.

antedate *vt* antidater.

antelope *n* antilope *f*.

antenna *n* antenne *f*.

anterior *adj* antérieur, précédent.

anthem *n* hymne *m*.

anthill *n* fourmilière *f*.

anthology *n* anthologie *f*.

anthracite *n* anthracite *m*.

anthropology *n* anthropologie *f*.

antiaircraft *adj* antiaérien.

antibiotic *n* antibiotique *m*.

antibody *n* anticorps *m*.

Antichrist *n* Antéchrist *m*.

anticipate *vt* prévoir.

anticipation *n* attente *f*; prévision *f*.

anticlockwise *adv* dans le sens contraire des aiguilles d'une montre.

antidote *n* antidote *m*.

antifreeze *n* antigel *m*.

antimony *n* antimoine *m*.

antipathy *n* antipathie *f*.

antipodes *npl* antipodes *fpl*.

antiquarian *n* antiquaire *mf*.

antiquated *adj* vieux; suranné.

antique *n* meuble *m* ancien.

antiquity *n* antiquité *f*.

antiseptic *adj* antiseptique.

antisocial *adj* antisocial.

antithesis *n* antithèse *f*.

antler *n* corne *f*.

anvil *n* enclume *f*.

anxiety *n* anxiété *f*; désir *m*.

anxious *adj* anxieux; ~**ly** *adv* anxieusement.

any *adj pn* n'importe quel,

n'importe quelle; un, une; tout; ~**body** quelqu'un; n'importe qui; personne; ~**how** de toute façon; de n'importe quelle manière; ~**more** plus; ~**place** n'importe où; nulle part; ~**thing** quelque chose; n'importe quoi; rien.

apace *adv* rapidement.

apart *adv* séparément.

apartment *n* appartement *m*.

apartment house *n* immeuble *m*.

apathetic *adj* apathique.

apathy *n* apathie *f*.

ape *n* singe *m*; * *vt* singer.

aperture *n* ouverture *f*.

apex *n* sommet *m*; apex *m*.

aphorism *n* aphorisme *m*.

apiary *n* rucher *m*.

apiece *adv* chacun, chacune.

aplomb *n* aplomb *m*.

Apocalypse *n* Apocalypse *f*.

apocrypha *npl* apocryphes *mpl*.

apocryphal *adj* apocryphe.

apologetic *adj* d'excuse.

apologist *n* apologiste *mf*.

apologize *vt* excuser.

apology *n* apologie, défense *f*.

apoplexy *n* apoplexie *f*.

apostle *n* apôtre *m*.

apostolic *adj* apostolique.

apostrophe *n* apostrophe *f*.

apotheosis *n* apothéose *f*.

appall *vt* horrifier, atterrer.

appalling *adj* horrible.

apparatus *n* appareil *m*.

apparel *n* vêtements *mpl*.

apparent *adj* évident, apparent; ~**ly** *adv* apparemment.

apparition *n* apparition, vision *f*.

appeal *vi* faire appel; * *n* (*law*) appel *m*.

appealing *adj* attrayant.

appear *vi* paraître.

appearance *n* apparence *f*.

appease *vt* apaiser.

appellant *n* (*law*) appelant *m*.

append *vt* annexer.

appendage *n* appendice *m*.

appendicitis *n* appendicite *f*.

appendix *n* appendice *m*.

appertain *vi* appartenir (à).

appetite *n* appétit *m*.

appetizing *adj* appétissant.

applaud *vt vi* applaudir.

applause *n* applaudissements *mpl*.

apple *n* pomme *f*.

apple pie *n* tourte aux pommes *f*; in ~ **order** parfaitement en ordre.

apple tree *n* pommier *m*.

appliance *n* appareil *m*.

applicability *n* applicabilité *f*.

applicable *adj* applicable.

applicant *n* candidat *m* -e *f*.

application *n* application *f*; candidature *f*.

applied *adj* appliqué.

apply *vt* appliquer; * *vi* s'adresser.

appoint *vt* nommer.

appointee *n* personne nommée *f*.

appointment *n* rendez-vous *m*; nomination *f*.

apportion *vt* répartir.

apportionment *n* répartition *f*.

apposite *adj* approprié, juste.

apposition *n* apposition *f*.

appraisal *n* estimation *f*.

appraise *vt* évaluer.

appreciable *adj* appréciable, sensible.

appreciably *adv* sensiblement.

appreciate *vt* apprécier; être conscient de.

appreciation *n* appréciation *f*.

appreciative *adj* reconnaissant.

apprehend *vt* appréhender.

apprehension *n* appréhension *f*; arrestation *f*.

apprehensive *adj* appréhensif.

apprentice *n* apprenti *m*; * *vt* mettre en apprentissage.

apprenticeship *n* apprentissage *m*.

apprise *vt* informer.

approach *vi* (s')approcher; * *vt* (s')approcher de; * *n* approche *f*.

approachable *adj* accessible, approchable.

approbation *n* approbation *f*.

appropriate *vt* s'approprier; * *adj* approprié, adéquat.

approval *n* approbation *f*.

approve (of) *vt* approuver.

approximate *vi* s'approcher; * *adj* approximatif; ~ly *adv* approximativement.

approximation *n* approximation *f*.

apricot *n* abricot *m*.

April *n* avril *m*.

apron *n* tablier *m*.

apse *n* abside *f*.

apt *adj* idéal; susceptible; ~ly *adv* opportunément.

aptitude *n* aptitude *f*.

aqualung *n* scaphandre autonome *m*.

aquarium *n* aquarium *m*.

Aquarius *n* Verseau *m* (signe du zodiaque).

aquatic *adj* aquatique.

aqueduct *n* aqueduc *m*.

aquiline *adj* aquilin.

arabesque *n* arabesque *f*.

arable *adj* arable.

arbiter *n* arbitre *m* (de la mode).

arbitrariness *n* caractère arbitraire *m*.

arbitrary *adj* arbitraire.

arbitrate *vt* arbitrer.

arbitration *n* arbitrage *m*.

arbitrator *n* arbitre *m*.

arbour *n* tonnelle *f*.

arcade *n* galerie *f*.

arch *n* arc *m*; * *adj* malicieux.

archaic *adj* archaïque.

archangel *n* archange *m*.

archbishop *n* archevêque *m*.

archbishopric *n* archevêché *m*.

archeological *adj* archéologique.

archeology *n* archéologie *f*.

archer *n* archer *m*.

archery *n* tir à l'arc *m*.

architect *n* architecte *mf*.

architectural *adj* architectural.

architecture *n* architecture *f*.

archives *npl* archives *fpl*.

archivist *n* archiviste *mf*.

archly *adv* malicieusement.

archway *n* arcade, voûte *f*.

arctic *adj* arctique.

ardent *adj* ardent; ~ly *adv* ardemment.

ardour *n* ardeur *f*.

arduous *adj* ardu, difficile.

area *n* région *f*; domaine *m*.

arena *n* arène *f*.

arguably *adv* peut-être, sans doute.

argue *vi* se disputer; * *vt* soutenir.

argument *n* argument *m*; dispute *f*.

argumentation *n* argumentation *f*.

argumentative *adj* raisonneur.

aria *n* (*mus*) aria *f*.

arid *adj* aride.

aridity *n* aridité *f*.

Aries *n* Bélier *m* (signe du zodiaque).

aright *adv* correctement; **to set ~** rectifier.

arise *vi* se lever; survenir.

aristocracy *n* aristocratie *f*.

aristocrat *n* aristocrate *mf*.

aristocratic *adj* aristocratique; ~ally *adv* aristocratiquement.

arithmetic *n* arithmétique *f*.

arithmetical *adj* arithmétique; ~ly *adv* arithmétiquement.

ark *n* arche *f*.

arm *n* bras *m*; arme *f*; * *vt* armer; * *vi* (s')armer.

armament *n* armement *m*.

armchair *n* fauteuil *m*.

armed *adj* armé.

armful *n* brassée *f*.

armhole *n* emmanchure *f*.

armistice *n* armistice *m*.

armour *n* armure *f*.

armoured car *n* voiture blindée *f*.

armoury *n* arsenal *m*.

armpit *n* aisselle *f*.

armrest *n* accoudoir *m*.

army *n* armée *f*.

aroma *n* arôme *m*.

aromatic *adj* aromatique.

around *prep* autour de; * *adv* autour.

arouse *vt* éveiller; exciter.

arraign *vt* traduire en justice.

arraignment *n* accusation *f*; procès criminel *m*.

arrange *vt* arranger, organiser.

arrangement *n* arrangement *m*.

arrant *adj* fieffé.

array *n* série *f*.

arrears *npl* arriéré *m*; retard *m*.

arrest *n* arrestation *f*; * *vt* arrêter.

arrival *n* arrivée *f*.

arrive *vi* arriver.

arrogance *n* arrogance *f*.

arrogant *adj* arrogant; ~ly *adv* avec arrogance.

arrogate *vt* s'arroger.

arrogation *n* usurpation *f*.

arrow *n* flèche *f*.

arsenal *n* (*mil*) arsenal *m*.

arsenic *n* arsenic *m*.

arson *n* incendie criminel *m*.

art *n* art *m*.

arterial *adj* artériel.

artery *n* artère *f*.

artesian well *n* puits artésien *m*.

artful *adj* malin, astucieux.

artfulness *n* astuce *f*; habileté *f*.

art gallery *n* musée d'art *m*.

arthritis *n* arthrite *f*.

artichoke *n* artichaut *m*.

article *n* article *m*.

articulate *vt* articuler.

articulated *adj* articulé.

articulation *n* articulation *f*.

artifice *n* artifice *m*.

artificial *adj* artificiel; ~ly *adv* artificiellement.

artificiality *n* caractère artificiel *m*.

artillery *n* artillerie *f*.

artisan *n* artisan *m*.

artist *n* artiste *mf*.

artistic *adj* artistique.

artistry *n* habileté *f*.

artless *adj* naturel, simple; ~ly *adv* naturellement, simplement.

artlessness *n* simplicité *f*, naturel *m*.

art school *n* école des beaux-arts *f*.

as *conj* comme; pendant que; aussi; ~ for, ~ to quant à.

asbestos *n* asbeste *m*, amiante *f*.

ascend *vi* monter.

ascendancy *n* ascendant *m*.

ascension *n* ascension *f*.

ascent *n* montée *f*.

ascertain *vt* établir.

ascetic *adj* ascétique; * *n* ascète *mf*.

ascribe *vt* attribuer.

ash *n* (*bot*) frêne *m*; cendre *f*.

ashamed *adj* honteux.

ashbin *n* poubelle *f*.

ashore *adv* à terre; to go ~ débarquer.

ashtray *n* cendrier *m*.

Ash Wednesday *n* mercredi des Cendres *m*.

aside *adv* de côté.

ask *vt* demander; ~ after demander des nouvelles de;

~ for demander; ~ out inviter à sortir.

askance *adv* avec méfiance.

askew *adv* de côté.

asleep *adj* endormi; to fall ~ s'endormir.

asparagus *n* asperge *f*.

aspect *n* aspect *m*.

aspen *n* (*bot*) tremble *m*.

aspersion *n* calomnie *f*.

asphalt *n* asphalte *m*.

asphyxia *n* (*med*) asphyxie *f*.

asphyxiate *vt* asphyxier.

asphyxiation *n* asphyxie *f*.

aspirant *n* aspirant *m* -e *f*.

aspirate *vt* aspirer; * *n* aspirée *f*.

aspiration *n* aspiration *f*.

aspire *vi* aspirer, désirer.

aspirin *n* aspirine *f*.

ass *n* âne *m*; she ~ ânesse *f*.

assail *vt* assaillir, attaquer.

assailant *n* assaillant, agresseur *m*.

assassin *n* assassin *m*.

assassinate *vt* assassiner.

assassination *n* assassinat *m*.

assault *n* assaut *m*; agression *f*; * *vt* agresser.

assemblage *n* assemblage *m*.

assemble *vt* assembler; * *vi* s'assembler.

assembly *n* assemblée *f*.

assembly line *n* chaîne de montage *f*.

assent *n* assentiment *m*; * *vi* donner son assentiment.

assert *vt* soutenir; affirmer.

assertion *n* assertion *f*.

assertive *adj* péremptoire.

assess *vt* évaluer.

assessment *n* évaluation *f*.

assessor *n* assesseur *m*.

assets *npl* biens *mpl*.

assiduous *adj* assidu; ~**ly** *adv* assidûment.

assign *vt* assigner.

assignation *n* rendez-vous *m*; (*law*) cession *f*.

assignment *n* (*law*) cession *f*; mission *f*.

assimilate *vt* assimiler.

assimilation *n* assimilation *f*.

assist *vt* assister, aider; secourir.

assistance *n* assistance, aide *f*; secours *m*.

assistant *n* aide *mf*, assistant *m* -e *f*.

associate *vt* associer; * *adj* associé; * *n* associé *m* -e *f*.

association *n* association *f*.

assonance *n* assonance *f*.

assorted *adj* assorti.

assortment *n* assortiment *m*.

assuage *vt* calmer, adoucir.

assume *vt* assumer; supposer.

assumption *n* supposition *f*; **Assumption** *n* Assomption *f*.

assurance *n* assurance *f*.

assure *vt* assurer.

assuredly *adv* assurément.

asterisk *n* astérisque *m*.

astern *adv* (*mar*) en poupe.

asthma *n* asthme *m*.

asthmatic *adj* asthmatique.

astonish *vt* surprendre, stupéfier.

astonishing *adj* stupéfiant; ~**ly** *adv* incroyablement.

astonishment *n* surprise, stupéfaction *f*.

astound *vt* ébahir.

astray *adv*: **to go** ~ s'égarer; **to lead** ~ détourner du droit chemin.

astride *adv* à califourchon.

astringent *adj* astringent.

astrologer *n* astrologue *mf*.

astrological *adj* astrologique.

astrology *n* astrologie *f*.

astronaut *n* astronaute *mf*.

astronomer *n* astronome *mf*.

astronomical *adj* astronomique.

astronomy *n* astronomie *f*.

astute *adj* malin.

asylum *n* asile, refuge *m*.

at *prep* à; en; ~ **once** tout de suite; ~ **all** du tout; ~ **all events** en tout cas; ~ **first** au début, d'abord; ~ **last** enfin.

atheism *n* athéisme *m*.

atheist *n* athée *mf*.

athlete *n* athlète *mf*.

athletic *adj* athlétique.

atlas *n* atlas *m*.

atmosphere *n* atmosphère *f*.

atmospheric *adj* atmosphérique.

atom *n* atome *m*.

atom bomb *n* bombe atomique *f*.

atomic *adj* atomique.

atone *vt* expier.

atonement *n* expiation *f*.

atop *adv* en haut.

atrocious *adj* atroce; ~**ly** *adv* atrocement.

atrocity *n* atrocité, énormité *f*.

atrophy *n* (*med*) atrophie *f*.

attach *vt* joindre.

attaché *n* attaché *m* -e *f*.

attachment *n* attachement *m*.

attack *vt* attaquer; * *n* attaque *f*.

attacker *n* attaquant *m* -e *f*.

attain *vt* atteindre, obtenir.

attainable *adj* accessible.

attempt *vt* essayer; * *n* essai *m*, tentative *f*.

attend *vt* servir; assister à; ~ **to** s'occuper de; * *vi* faire attention.

attendance *n* service *m*; assistance *f*; présence *f*.

attendant *n* serviteur *m*.

attention *n* attention *f*; soin *m*.

attentive *adj* attentif; ~**ly** *adv* attentivement.

attenuate *vt* atténuer.

attest *vt* attester.

attic *n* grenier *m*.

attire *n* atours *mpl*.

attitude *n* attitude *f*.

attorney *n* avocat *m*.

attract *vt* attirer.

attraction *n* attraction *f*; attrait *m*.

attractive *adj* attrayant.

attribute *vt* attribuer; * *n* attribut *m*.

attrition *n* usure *f*.

auburn *adj* auburn.

auction *n* vente aux enchères *f*.

auctioneer *n* commissaire-priseur *m*.

audacious *adj* audacieux, téméraire; ~**ly** *adv* audacieusement.

audacity *n* audace, témérité *f*.

audible *adj* audible; ~**ly** *adv* audiblement.

audience *n* audience *f*; auditoire *m*.

audit *n* audit *m*; * *vt* vérifier.

auditor *n* vérificateur(-trice) de comptes *m(f)*; auditeur *m* -trice *f*.

auditory *adj* auditif.

augment *vt vi* augmenter.

augmentation *n* augmentation *f*.

August *n* août *m*.

august *adj* auguste, majestueux.

aunt *n* tante *f*.

au pair *n* (jeune fille) au pair *f*.

aura *n* aura *f*.

auspices *npl* auspices *mpl*.

auspicious *adj* favorable, propice; ~ly *adv* favorablement.

austere *adj* austère, sévère; ~ly *adv* austèrement.

austerity *n* austérité *f*.

authentic *adj* authentique; ~ally *adv* authentiquement.

authenticate *vt* légaliser.

authenticity *n* authenticité *f*.

author *n* auteur *m*.

authoress *n* femme auteur *f*.

authoritarian *adj* autoritaire.

authoritative *adj* autoritaire; ~ly *adv* autoritairement.

authority *n* autorité *f*.

authorization *n* autorisation *f*.

authorize *vt* autoriser.

authorship *n* paternité *f* (d'un livre).

auto *n* voiture *f*.

autocrat *n* autocrate *mf*.

autocratic *adj* autocratique.

autograph *n* autographe *m*.

automated *adj* automatisé.

automatic *adj* automatique.

automaton *n* automate *m*.

autonomy *n* autonomie *f*.

autopsy *n* autopsie *f*.

autumn *n* automne *m*.

autumnal *adj* automnal.

auxiliary *adj* auxiliaire.

avail *vt*: to ~ oneself of profiter de; * *n*: to no ~ en vain.

available *adj* disponible.

avalanche *n* avalanche *f*.

avarice *n* avarice *f*.

avaricious *adj* avare.

avenge *vt* venger.

avenue *n* avenue *f*.

aver *vt* affirmer, déclarer.

average *vt* atteindre la moyenne de; * *n* moyenne *f*, moyen terme *m*.

aversion *n* aversion *f*, dégoût *m*.

avert *vt* détourner, écarter.

aviary *n* volière *f*.

avoid *vt* éviter; échapper à.

avoidable *adj* évitable.

await *vt* attendre.

awake *vt* réveiller; * *vi* se réveiller; * *adj* éveillé.

awakening *n* réveil *m*.

award *vt* attribuer; * *n* prix *m*; décision *f*.

aware *adj* conscient; au courant.

awareness *n* conscience *f*.

away *adv* absent; loin; ~! va-t-en!; allez-vous-en! **far and ~** de loin.

away game *n* match à l'extérieur *m*.

awe *n* peur, crainte *f*.

awe-inspiring, awesome *adj* terrifiant; imposant.

awful *adj* horrible, terrible; **~ly** *adv* horriblement, terriblement.

awhile *adv* un moment.

awkward *adj* gauche, maladroit; délicat; **~ly** *adv* maladroitement.

awkwardness *n* maladroitesse *f*; difficulté *f*.

awl *n* alêne *f*.

awning *n* (*mar*) taud *m*.

awry *adv* de travers.

axe *n* hache *f*; * *vt* licencier; supprimer.

axiom *n* axiome *m*.

axis *n* axe *m*.

axle *n* axe *m*.

ay(e) *excl* oui.

B

baa n bêlement m; * vi bêler.
babble vi bavarder, babiller;
~, **babbling** n bavardage,
babillage m.
babbler n bavard m.
babe, baby n bébé, enfant en
bas-âge m; nourrisson m.
baboon n babouin m.
baby carriage n voiture
d'enfant f.
babyhood n petite enfance f.
babyish adj enfantin; puéril.
baby linen n layette f.
bachelor n célibataire m;
(diplôme) licencié m -e f.
bachelorship n célibat m.
back n dos m; * adv en
arrière, à l'arrière; **a few
years** ~ il y a quelques
années, quelques années
en arrière; * vt soutenir,
appuyer, renforcer.
backbite vt médire de, sur.
backbiter n détracteur m
-trice f.
backbone n colonne vertébrale,
épine dorsale f.
backdate vt antidater.
backdoor n porte de derrière f.
backer n partisan m -e f.
backgammon n (jeu de)
jacquet m.
background n fond m.
backlash n réaction violente
f.
backlog n accumulation de
travail en retard f.
back number n vieux numéro
(magazine, journal) m.
backpack n sac à dos m.
back payment n rappel de
salaire m.
backside n derrière m.
back-up lights npl (auto) feux
de marche arrière mpl.
backward adj rétrograde;
retardé; lent; * adv en
arrière.
bacon n lard m.
bad adj mauvais, de
mauvaise qualité; méchant;
malade; ~ly adv mal.

badge n plaque f, insigne m, badge m; symbole m; signe m.

badger n blaireau m; * vt harceler.

badminton n badminton m.

badness n mauvaise qualité f; méchanceté f.

baffle vt déconcerter, confondre.

bag n sac m; valise f.

baggage n bagages mpl; équipement m.

bagpipe n cornemuse f.

bail n mise en liberté sous caution, caution f; * vt mettre en liberté sous caution; mettre en dépôt.

bailiff n huissier m; régisseur m.

bait vt tourmenter; appâter; * n appât m; amorce f.

baize n serge f.

bake vt faire cuire au four.

baker n boulanger m -ère f; ~'s **dozen** treize à la douzaine.

bakery n boulangerie f.

baking n cuisson f; fournée f.

baking powder n levure f.

balance n balance f; équilibre m; solde d'un compte m; to lose one's ~ perdre l'équilibre; * vt peser; peser le pour et le contre; solder; équilibrer.

balance sheet n bilan m.

balcony n balcon m.

bald adj chauve.

baldness n calvitie f.

bale n balle f; * vt emballer; écoper.

baleful adj sinistre, funeste, maléfique; ~ly adv sinistrement.

ball n balle f; boule f; ballon m.

ballad n ballade f.

ballast n lest m; * vt lester.

ballerina n ballerine f.

ballet n ballet m.

ballistic adj balistique.

balloon n montgolfière f, aérostat m.

ballot n scrutin m; vote m; * vi voter au scrutin.

ballpoint (pen) n stylo à bille m.

ballroom n salle de bal f.

balm, balsam n baume m.

balmy adj balsamique, parfumé; doux.

balustrade n balustrade f.

bamboo n bambou m.

bamboozle vt (fam) embobiner.

ban *n* interdiction *f*; * *vt* interdire.

banal *adj* banal.

banana *n* banane *f*.

band *n* bande *f*; reliure *f*; courroie de transmission *f*; orchestre *m*.

bandage *n* bande *f*, bandage *m*; * *vt* bander.

bandaid *n* pansement *m* adhésif.

bandit *n* bandit *m*.

bandstand *n* kiosque à musique *m*.

bandy *vt* avoir des mots.

bandy-legged *adj* aux jambes arquées.

bang *n* coup violent, claquement *m*, détonation *f*; * *vt* frapper violemment; claquer.

bangle *n* bracelet *m*.

bangs *npl* (US) frange (courte et droite) *f*.

banish *vt* bannir, exiler, chasser, expatrier.

banishment *n* exil, bannissement *m*.

banister(s) *n (pl)* rampe d'escalier *f*.

banjo *n* banjo *m*.

bank *n* rive *f*; remblai *m*; banque *f*; banc *m*; digue *f*;

* *vt* déposer de l'argent à la banque; ~ **on** compter sur.

bank account *n* compte en banque *m*.

bank card *n* carte bancaire *f*.

banker *n* banquier *m* -ière *f*.

banking *n* opérations bancaires *fpl*.

banknote *n* billet de banque *m*.

bankrupt *adj* failli; * *n* failli *m*.

bankruptcy *n* banqueroute, faillite *f*.

bank statement *n* relevé de compte *m*.

banner *n* bannière *f*; étendard *m*.

banquet *n* banquet *m*.

baptise *vt* baptiser.

baptism *n* baptême *m*.

baptismal *adj* de baptême, baptismal.

baptistery *n* baptistère *m*.

bar *n* bar *m*; barre *f*; obstacle *m*; (*law*) barreau *m*; * *vt* empêcher; interdire; exclure.

barbarian *n* barbare *mf*; * *adj* barbare, cruel.

barbaric *adj* barbare.

barbarism *n* (*gr*) barbarisme *m*; barbarie *f*.

barbarity *n* barbarie, atrocité *f*.

barbarous *adj* barbare, cruel.

barbecue *n* barbecue *m*.

barber *n* coiffeur (pour hommes) *m*.

bar code *n* code barres *m*.

bard *n* barde *m*; poète *m*.

bare *adj* nu, dépouillé; simple; pur; * *vt* dénuder, découvrir.

barefaced *adj* éhonté, impudent.

barefoot(ed) *adj* aux pieds nus.

bareheaded *adj* nu-tête.

barelegged *adj* aux jambes nues.

barely *adv* à peine, tout juste.

bareness *n* nudité *f*.

bargain *n* affaire *f*; contrat, marché *m*; occasion *f*; * *vi* conclure un marché; négocier; ~ **for** s'attendre à.

barge *n* péniche *f*.

baritone *n* (*mus*) baryton *m*.

bark *n* écorce *f*; aboiement *m*; * *vi* aboyer.

barley *n* orge *m*.

barmaid *n* serveuse *f*.

barman *n* barman *m*.

barn *n* grange *f*; étable *f*.

barnacle *n* anatife *m*, bernacle *f*.

barometer *n* baromètre *m*.

baron *n* baron *m*.

baroness *n* baronne *f*.

baronial *adj* de baron.

barracks *npl* caserne *f*.

barrage *n* barrage *m*; (*fig*) torrent *m*.

barrel *n* tonneau, fût *m*; canon de fusil *m*.

barrelled *adj* (firearms) à canons.

barrel organ *n* orgue de Barbarie *m*.

barren *adj* stérile, infertile, improductif.

barricade *n* barricade *f*; barrière *f*; * *vt* barricader, barrer.

barrier *n* barrière *f*; obstacle *m*.

barring *adv* excepté, sauf.

barrow *n* brouette *f*.

bartender *n* barman *m*.

barter *vi* faire du troc; * *vt* troquer, échanger.

base *n* base *f*; partie inférieure *f*; pied *m*; point de départ *m*; * *vt* fonder sur; * *adj* vil, abject.

baseball *n* baseball *m*.

baseless *adj* sans fondement, injustifié.

basement *n* sous-sol *m*.

baseness *n* bassesse, vilenie *f*.

bash *vt* frapper.

373

bashful *adj* timide, modeste;
~**ly** *adv* timidement.

basic *adj* fondamental, de
base; ~**ally** *adv*
fondamentalement.

basilisk *n* (*zool*) basilic *m*.

basin *n* cuvette *f*; lavabo *m*.

basis *n* base *f*; fondement *m*.

bask *vi* se prélasser.

basket *n* panier *m*, corbeille
f.

basketball *n* basket-ball *m*.

bass *n* (*mus*) contrebasse *f*.

bassoon *n* basson *m*.

bass viol *n* viole de gambe *f*.

bass voice *n* voix de basse *f*.

bastard *n, adj* bâtard *m*.

bastardy *n* bâtardise *f*.

baste *vt* arroser la viande de
son jus; bâtir.

basting *n* bâti *m*; jus (de
viande) *m*; rossée *f*.

bastion *n* (*mil*) bastion *m*.

bat *n* chauve-souris *f*.

batch *n* fournée *f*.

bath *n* bain *m*.

bathe *vt* (*vi*) (se) baigner.

bathing suit *n* maillot de bain
m.

bathos *n* platitudes (dans un
texte littéraire) *fpl*.

bathroom *n* salle de bain *f*.

baths *npl* piscine *f*.

bathtub *n* baignoire *f*.

baton *n* matraque *f*.

battalion *n* (*mil*) bataillon *m*.

batter *vt* battre; frapper,
martyriser; * *n* pâte à frire *f*.

battering ram *n* (*mil*) bélier
m.

battery *n* pile, batterie *f*.

battle *n* bataille *f*; combat *m*;
* *vi* se battre, combattre.

battle array *n* ordre de
bataille *m*.

battlefield *n* champ de
bataille *m*.

battlement *n* remparts *mpl*.

battleship *n* cuirassé *m*.

bawdy *adj* paillard.

bawl *vi* brailler, (*fam*)
gueuler.

bay *n* baie *f*; laurier *m*; * *vi*
aboyer, hurler; * *adj* bai.

bayonet *n* baïonnette *f*.

bay window *n* fenêtre en
saillie *f*.

bazaar *n* bazar *m*.

be *vi* être.

beach *n* plage *f*.

beacon *n* phare, signal
lumineux *m*.

bead *n* perle *f*; ~**s** *npl*
chapelet *m*.

beagle *n* beagle *m*.

beak *n* bec *m*.

beaker *n* gobelet *m*.

beam *n* rayon *m*; poutre *f*; * *vi* rayonner, resplendir.

bean *n* haricot *m*; **French ~** haricot *m* vert.

beansprouts *npl* germes de soja *mpl*.

bear *vt* porter, supporter, produire; * *vi* se diriger.

bear *n* ours *m*; **she ~** ourse *f*.

bearable *adj* supportable.

beard *n* barbe *f*.

bearded *adj* barbu.

bearer *n* porteur *m* -euse *f*; arbre fructifère *m*.

bearing *n* relation *f*; maintien, port *m*.

beast *n* bête *f*; brute *f*; **~ of burden** bête de somme *f*.

beastliness *n* bestialité, brutalité *f*.

beastly *adj* bestial, brutal; abominable; * *adv* terriblement.

beat *vt* battre; * *vi* battre, palpiter; * *n* battement *m*; pulsation *f*.

beatific *adj* béatifique; béat.

beatify *vt* béatifier, sanctifier.

beating *n* correction, raclée *f*; battement *m*.

beatitude *n* béatitude *f*.

beautiful *adj* beau, belle,

magnifique; **~ly** *adv* à la perfection, merveilleusement.

beautify *vt* embellir; décorer.

beauty *n* beauté *f*; **~ salon** *n* institut de beauté *m*; **~ spot** *n* site touristique *m*.

beaver *n* castor *m*.

because *conj* parce que; * *prép*: **~ of** en raison de.

beckon *vi* faire signe.

become *vt* convenir, aller à; * *vi* devenir, se faire.

becoming *adj* convenable, seyant.

bed *n* lit *m*.

bedclothes *npl* couvertures et draps *mpl*.

bedding *n* literie *f*.

bedecked *adj* orné.

bedlam *n* maison *f* de fous; chahut *m*.

bed-post *n* colonne de lit *f*.

bedridden *adj* cloué au lit; grabataire.

bedroom *n* chambre *f*.

bedspread *n* dessus-de-lit *m* invar.

bedtime *n* heure d'aller au lit *f*.

bee *n* abeille *f*.

beech *n* hêtre *m*.

beef *n* bœuf (viande) *m*.

beefburger *n* hamburger *m*.

beefsteak n bifteck m.

beehive n ruche f.

beeline n ligne droite f.

beer n bière f.

beeswax n cire f.

beet n betterave f.

beetle n scarabée m.

befall vi arriver, survenir; * vt arriver à.

befit vt convenir à.

before adv, prep avant; devant; * conj avant de, avant que.

beforehand adv à l'avance, au préalable.

befriend vt traiter en ami; aider.

beg vt mendier; solliciter; supplier; * vi demander la charité.

beget vt engendrer.

beggar n mendiant m -e f.

begin vt vi commencer.

beginner n débutant m -e f; novice mf.

beginning n commencement, début m, origine f.

begrudge vt donner à contrecœur; envier.

behalf n faveur f, intérêt m; nom m, part f.

behave vi se comporter, se conduire.

behaviour n conduite f; comportement m.

behead vt décapiter.

behind prep derrière; * adv derrière, par-derrière, en arrière.

behold vt voir; contempler; observer.

behove vi (impers) incomber à.

beige adj beige.

being n existence f; être m.

belated adj tardif.

belch vi éructer; * vt vomir; * n éructation f, rot m.

belfry n beffroi, clocher m.

belie vt démentir, tromper.

belief n foi, croyance f; conviction, opinion f, credo m.

believable adj croyable.

believe vt croire; * vi penser, croire.

believer n croyant m -e f; adepte mf, partisan m -e f.

belittle vt rabaisser.

bell n cloche f.

bellicose adj belliqueux.

belligerent adj belligérant.

bellow vi beugler, mugir; hurler; * n beuglement, mugissement m.

bellows npl soufflet m.

belly n ventre m.

bellyful *n* ventrée *f*; ras-le-bol *m*.

belong *vi* appartenir à.

belongings *npl* affaires *fpl*.

beloved *adj* chéri, bien-aimé.

below *adv* en dessous, en bas; * *prep* sous, au-dessous de, en dessous.

belt *n* ceinture *f*.

bemoan *vt* déplorer; pleurer.

bemused *adj* déconcerté.

bench *n* banc *m*.

bend *vt* courber, plier; incliner; * *vi* se courber, s'incliner; * *n* courbe *f*.

beneath *adv* au-dessous; * *prep* sous, au-dessous de.

benediction *n* bénédiction *f*.

benefactor *n* bienfaiteur *m* -trice *f*.

benefice *n* bénéfice *m*; bénéfice ecclésiastique *m*.

beneficent *adj* bienfaisant.

beneficial *adj* profitable, salutaire, utile.

beneficiary *n* bénéficiaire *mf*.

benefit *n* intérêt, avantage *m*; profit *m*; bienfait *m*; * *vt* profiter à; * *vi* bénéficier.

benefit night *n* soirée de bienfaisance *f*.

benevolence *n* bienveillance *f*; générosité *f*.

benevolent *adj* bienveillant; de bienfaisance.

benign *adj* bienveillant, doux, affable; bénin.

bent *n* penchant *m*.

benzine *n* (*chem*) benzine *f*.

bequeath *vt* léguer à.

bequest *n* legs *m*.

bereave *vt* priver.

bereavement *n* perte *f*; deuil *m*.

beret *n* béret *m*.

berry *n* baie *f*.

berserk *adj* fou furieux.

berth *n* (*mar*) couchette *f*.

beseech *vt* supplier, implorer, conjurer.

beset *vt* assaillir.

beside(s) *prep* à côté de; excepté; * *adv* de plus, en outre.

besiege *vt* assiéger, assaillir.

best *adj* le meilleur, la meilleure;
* *adv* le mieux; * *n* le meilleur, le mieux *m*.

bestial *adj* bestial, brutal; ~ly *adv* bestialement.

bestiality *n* bestialité, brutalité *f*.

bestow *vt* accorder, conférer; consacrer.

bestseller *n* best-seller *m*.

bet *n* pari *m*; * *vt* parier.

betray *vt* trahir.

betrayal *n* trahison *f*.

betroth *vt* promettre en mariage.

betrothal *n* fiançailles *fpl*.

better *adj adv* meilleur, mieux; **so much the ~** tant mieux; * *vt* améliorer.

betting *n* pari *m*.

between *prep* entre; * *adv* au milieu.

bevel *n* biseau *m*.

beverage *n* boisson *f*.

bevy *n* bande *f*, groupe *m*.

beware *vi* prendre garde.

bewilder *vt* déconcerter, dérouter.

bewilderment *n* perplexité *f*.

bewitch *vt* ensorceler, enchanter.

beyond *prep* au-delà de; au-dessus de; plus de; sauf; * *adv* au-delà, plus loin.

bias *n* préjugé *m*; tendance, inclination *f*.

bib *n* bavoir *m*.

Bible *n* Bible *f*.

biblical *adj* biblique.

bibliography *n* bibliographie *f*.

bicarbonate of soda *n* bicarbonate de soude *m*.

bicker *vi* se chamailler.

bicycle *n* bicyclette *f*.

bid *vt* ordonner, commander; offrir; * *n* offre, tentative *f*.

bidding *n* ordre *m*; enchère, offre *f*.

bide *vt* attendre, supporter.

biennial *adj* biennal, bisannuel.

bifocals *npl* verres à double foyer *mpl*.

bifurcated *adj* divisé en deux branches.

big *adj* grand, gros; important.

bigamist *n* bigame *mf*.

bigamy *n* bigamie *f*.

Big Dipper *n* Grande Ourse *f*.

bigheaded *adj* frimeur.

bigness *n* grandeur, grosseur *f*.

bigot *n* fanatique *mf*.

bigoted *adj* fanatique.

bike *n* vélo *m*.

bikini *n* bikini *m*.

bilberry *n* airelle *f*.

bile *n* bile *f*.

bilingual *adj* bilingue.

bilious *adj* bilieux.

bill *n* bec (d'oiseau) *m*; addition *f*; billet *m*.

billboard *n* panneau d'affichage *m*.

billet *n* logement *m*.

billiards *npl* billard *m*.

billiard table *n* table de billard *f*.

billion *n* milliard *m*.

bin *n* coffre *m*.

bind *vt* attacher; lier; entourer; relier.

binder *n* relieur *m* -euse *f*.

binding *n* reliure *f*, extra-fort *m*.

binge *n* beuverie, bringue *f*.

bingo *n* loto *m*.

binoculars *npl* jumelles *fpl*.

biochemistry *n* biochimie *f*.

biographer *n* biographe *mf*.

biographical *adj* biographique.

biography *n* biographie *f*.

biological *adj* biologique.

biology *n* biologie *f*.

biped *n* bipède *m*.

birch *n* bouleau *m*.

bird *n* oiseau *m*.

bird's-eye view *n* vue d'ensemble *f*.

bird-watcher *n* ornithologue *mf*.

birth *n* naissance *f*.

birth certificate *n* extrait de naissance *m*.

birth control *n* limitation des naissances *f*.

birthday *n* anniversaire *m*.

birthplace *n* lieu de naissance *m*.

birthright *n* droit de naissance *m*.

biscuit *n* biscuit *m*.

bisect *vt* coùper en deux.

bishop *n* évêque *m*.

bison *n* bison *m*.

bit *n* morceau *m*; peu *m*.

bitch *n* chienne *f*; (*fig*) plainte *f*.

bite *vt* mordre; ~ **the dust** (*fam*) mordre la poussière; * *n* morsure *f*.

bitter *adj* amer, âpre; cuisant, acerbe; glacial; ~**ly** *adv* amèrement; avec amertume; âprement.

bitterness *n* amertume *f*; rancœur *f*.

bitumen *n* bitume *m*.

bizarre *adj* étrange, bizarre.

blab *vi* jacasser; lâcher le morceau.

black *adj* noir, obscur; * *n* noir *m*.

blackberry *n* mûre *f*.

blackbird *n* merle *m*.

blackboard *n* tableau (noir) *m*.

blacken *vt* noircir, ternir.

black ice *n* verglas *m*.

blackjack *n* vingt-et-un *m*.

blackleg *n* jaune *m* (pendant une grève).

blacklist *n* liste noire *f*.

blackmail n chantage m; * vt faire chanter.

black market n marché noir m.

blackness n couleur noire f; obscurité f; noirceur f.

black pudding n boudin m.

black sheep n brebis galeuse f.

blacksmith n forgeron m.

blackthorn n épine noire f.

bladder n vessie f.

blade n lame f.

blame vt blâmer; * n faute f.

blameless adj irréprochable; ~ly adv irréprochablement.

blanch vt blanchir.

bland adj affable, suave; doux; apaisant.

blank adj blanc; vide, déconcerté; * n blanc m.

blank cheque n chèque en blanc m.

blanket n couverture f.

blare vi retentir.

blase adj blasé.

blaspheme vt blasphémer.

blasphemous adj blasphématoire.

blasphemy n blasphème m.

blast n souffle d'air m; explosion f; * vt faire sauter.

blast-off n lancement m, mise à feu f.

blatant adj flagrant.

blaze n flamme f; * vi flamber; resplendir.

bleach vt blanchir; décolorer; * vi blanchir; * n eau de Javel f.

bleached adj blanchi; décoloré.

bleachers npl gradins mpl.

bleak adj morne, lugubre, glacial, désolé.

bleakness n froid m; austérité f.

bleary(-eyed) adj larmoyant.

bleat n bêlement m; * vi bêler.

bleed vt vi saigner.

bleeding n saignement m.

bleeper n bip m.

blemish vt gâter; ternir; * n tache f; infamie f.

blend vt mélanger.

bless vt bénir.

blessing n bénédiction f; bienfait m.

blight vt détruire.

blind adj aveugle; ~ alley n impasse f; * vt aveugler; éblouir; * n aveugle mf; (Venetian) ~ store vénitien m.

blinders npl (US) œillères fpl.

blindfold vt bander les yeux de; ~ed adj les yeux bandés.

blindly *adv* à l'aveuglette, aveuglément.

blindness *n* cécité *f*.

blind side *n* côté faible de quelqu'un *m*.

blind spot *n* angle mort *m*.

blink *vi* clignoter.

blinkers *npl* clignotants *mpl*.

bliss *n* bonheur extrême *m*; félicité *f*.

blissful *adj* heureux; béat, bienheureux; **~ly** *adv* heureusement.

blissfulness *n* bonheur extrême *m*, félicité *f*.

blister *n* ampoule *f*, cloque *f*; * *vi* se couvrir de cloques.

blitz *n* bombardement aérien *m*.

blizzard *n* tempête de neige *f*.

bloated *adj* gonflé, boursouflé, bouffi.

blob *n* goutte, tache *f*.

bloc *n* bloc *m*.

block *n* bloc *m*; encombrement, blocage *m*; pâté de maisons *m*; **~ (up)** *vt* bloquer.

blockade *n* blocus *m*; * *vt* faire le blocus, bloquer.

blockage *n* obstruction *f*.

blockbuster *n* grand succès *m*.

blockhead *n* lourdaud, sot, crétin *m*.

blond *adj* blond; * *n* blond *m* -e *f*.

blood *n* sang *m*.

blood donor *n* donneur(-euse) de sang *m(f)*.

blood group *n* groupe sanguin *m*.

bloodhound *n* limier *m*.

bloodily *adv* cruellement.

bloodiness *n* (*fig*) cruauté *f*.

bloodless *adj* exangue, anémié; sans effusion de sang.

blood poisoning *n* empoisonnement du sang *m*.

blood pressure *n* pression artérielle *f*.

bloodshed *n* effusion de sang *f*; carnage *m*.

bloodshot *adj* injecté de sang.

bloodstream *n* système sanguin *m*.

bloodsucker *n* sangsue *f*; (*fig*) vampire *m*.

blood test *n* analyse de sang *f*.

bloodthirsty *adj* sanguinaire.

blood transfusion *n* transfusion sanguine *f*.

blood vessel *n* veine *f*; vaisseau sanguin *m*.

bloody *adj* sanglant,

ensanglanté; cruel; ~ minded *adj* pas commode, buté.

bloom *n* fleur *f* (*also fig*); * *vi* éclore, fleurir.

blossom *n* fleur *f*.

blot *vt* tacher; sécher; effacer; * *n* tache *f*.

blotchy *adj* marbré; couvert de taches.

blotting pad *n* buvard *m*.

blotting paper *n* papier buvard *m*.

blouse *n* chemisier *m*.

blow *vi* souffler; sonner; * *vt* souffler; faire voler; jouer de; ~ up exploser; * *n* coup *m*.

blowout *n* éclatement *m*.

blowpipe *n* sarbacane *f*.

blubber *n* blanc de baleine *m*; * *vi* pleurnicher.

bludgeon *n* gourdin *m*; matraque *f*.

blue *adj* bleu.

bluebell *n* campanule *f*.

bluebottle *n* (*bot*) bleuet *m*; mouche bleue *f*.

blueness *n* bleu *m*.

blueprint *n* (*fig*) projet *m*.

bluff *n* esbrouffe *f*; * *vt* faire de l'esbrouffe.

bluish *adj* bleuâtre.

blunder *n* gaffe *f*; * *vi* faire une gaffe.

blunt *adj* émoussé, obtus; direct; * *vt* émousser.

bluntly *adv* carrément; sans ménagements.

bluntness *n* brusquerie, rudesse *f*.

blur *n* image *f* floue; * *vt* brouiller.

blurt out *vt* laisser échapper.

blush *n* rougeur *f*; fard à joues *m*; * *vi* rougir.

blustery *adj* de tempête, violent.

boa *n* boa *m* (serpent).

boar *n* verrat *m*; wild ~ sanglier *m*.

board *n* planche *f*; table *f*; conseil *m*; * *vt* monter à bord de.

boarder *n* pensionnaire *mf*.

boarding card *n* carte d'embarquement *f*.

boarding house *n* internat *m*; pension (de famille) *f*.

boarding school *n* pensionnat *m*.

boast *vi* se vanter; * *n* vantardise *f*; rodomontade *f*.

boastful *adj* vantard.

boat *n* bateau *m*; canot *m*; barque *f*.

boating *n* canotage *m*; promenade en bateau *f*.

bobsleigh *n* bobsleigh *m*.

bode *vt* présager, augurer.

bodice *n* corsage *m*.

bodily *adj adv* physique(ment).

body *n* corps *m*; cadavre *m*; **any ~** n'importe qui; **every ~** tout le monde.

body-building *n* culturisme *m*.

bodyguard *n* garde du corps *m*.

bodywork *n* (*auto*) carrosserie *f*.

bog *n* marécage *m*.

boggy *adj* marécageux.

bogus *adj* faux.

boil *vi* bouillir; * *vt* faire bouillir; * *n* furoncle *m*; ébullition *f*.

boiled egg *n* œuf à la coque *m*.

boiled potatoes *npl* pommes de terre à l'eau *fpl*.

boiler *n* casserole *f*; chaudière *f*.

boiling point *n* point d'ébullition *m*.

boisterous *adj* bruyant; turbulent; tumultueux; **~ly** *adv* bruyamment, tumultueusement.

bold *adj* audacieux, téméraire, osé, hardi; **~ly** *adv* audacieusement, hardiment.

boldness *n* intrépidité *f*; audace *f*; effronterie *f*.

bolster *n* traversin *m*; * *vt* soutenir.

bolt *n* verrou *m*; * *vt* verrouiller, fermer au verrou.

bomb *n* bombe *f*; **~ disposal** déminage *m*.

bombard *vt* (*phys*) bombarder.

bombardier *n* bombardier *m*.

bombardment *n* bombardement *m*.

bombshell *n* (*fig*) bombe *f*.

bond *n* lien *m*; attache *f*; engagement *m*; obligation *f*.

bondage *n* esclavage, asservissement *m*.

bond holder *n* obligataire *mf*.

bone *n* os *m*; * *vt* désosser.

boneless *adj* désossé, sans os.

bonfire *n* feu (de joie) *m*.

bonnet *n* bonnet *m*.

bonny *adj* joli.

bonus *n* prime *f*.

bony *adj* osseux.

boo *vt* huer.

booby trap *n* mine *f*.

book *n* livre *m*; **to bring to ~** *vt* obliger à rendre des comptes.

bookbinder *n* relieur(-euse) de livres *m(f)*.

bookcase *n* bibliothèque *f*.

bookkeeper *n* comptable *mf*.

bookkeeping *n* comptabilité *f*.

bookmaking *n* prise des paris *f*.

bookmarker *n* signet *m*.

bookseller *n* libraire *mf*.

bookstore *n* librairie *f*.

bookworm *n* rat de bibliothèque *m*.

boom *n* grondement *m*; essor *m*; * *vi* gronder.

boon *n* bienfait *m*, aubaine *f*; faveur *f*.

boor *n* rustre *m*; brute *f*.

boorish *adj* rustre, rustique.

boost *n* stimulation *f*; * *vt* stimuler.

booster *n* propulseur *m*.

boot *n* botte *f*; coffre *m*; **to ~** *adv* de plus, de surcroît.

booth *n* cabine *f*; baraque *f*.

booty *n* butin *m*.

booze *vi* se saôuler; * *n* alcool *m*.

border *n* bord *m*; bordure *f*; lisière *f*; frontière *f*; * *vt* border, avoisiner.

borderline *n* limite *f*.

bore *vt* forer, percer; ennuyer; * *n* perceuse *f*; calibre *m*; raseur *m*.

boredom *n* ennui *m*.

boring *adj* ennuyeux.

born *adj* né; originaire.

borrow *vt* emprunter.

borrower *n* emprunteur *m* -euse *f*.

bosom *n* sein *m*, poitrine *f*.

bosom friend *n* ami(e) intime *m(f)*.

boss *n* chef *m*; patron(ne) *m(f)*.

botanic(al) *adj* botanique.

botanist *n* botaniste *mf*.

botany *n* botanique *f*.

botch *vt* cochonner.

both *pn* tou(te)s les deux, l'un(e) et l'autre; * *adj* les deux; * *conj* à la fois; autant que.

bother *vt* ennuyer, déranger; * *n* ennui, problème *m*.

bottle *n* bouteille *f*; * *vt* mettre en bouteille.

bottleneck *n* embouteillage *m*; goulot *m*.

bottle-opener *n* ouvre-bouteille *m invar*.

bottom *n* fond *m*; fondement *m*; * *adj* du bas; dernier.

bottomless *adj* sans fond, insondable; inépuisable.

bough *n* branche *f*; rameau *m*.

boulder *n* gros galet *m*.

bounce *vi* rebondir; bondir, faire des bonds; * *n* bond, rebond *m*.

bound *n* limite *f*; saut *m*; répercussion *f*; * *vi* bondir, sauter; * *adj* à destination de.

boundary *n* limite *f*; frontière *f*.

boundless *adj* illimité, infini.

bounteous, bountiful *adj* abondant; prodigue, généreux; bienfaisant.

bounty *n* libéralité, générosité *f*.

bouquet *n* bouquet *m*.

bourgeois *adj* bourgeois.

bout *n* attaque *f*; accès *m*; combat *m*.

bovine *adj* bovin.

bow *vt* incliner, baisser; * *vi* se courber; faire une révérence; * *n* salut *m*, révérence *f*.

bow *n* arc *m*; archet *m*; nœud *m*.

bowels *npl* intestins *mpl*; entrailles *fpl*.

bowl *n* bol, saladier *m*; boule *f*; * *vi* jouer aux boules.

bowling *n* boules *fpl*.

bowling alley *n* bowling *m*.

bowling green *n* terrain de boules *m*.

bowstring *n* corde (d'arc) *f*.

bow tie *n* nœud papillon *m*.

box *n* boîte, caisse *f*; loge *f*; ~ on the ear gifle *f*; * *vt* mettre en boîte; * *vi* boxer.

boxer *n* boxeur *m*.

boxing *n* boxe *f*.

boxing gloves *npl* gants de boxe *mpl*.

boxing ring *n* ring *m*.

box office *n* guichet *m*.

box-seat *n* place à côté du siège du cocher *f*.

boy *n* garçon *m*.

boycott *vt* boycotter; * *n* boycottage *m*.

boyfriend *n* petit ami *m*.

boyish *adj* d'enfant, puéril; de garçon.

bra *n* soutien-gorge *m*.

brace *n* attache *f*; bretelle *f*; appareil dentaire *m*.

bracelet *n* bracelet *m*

bracken *n* (*bot*) fougère *f*.

bracket *n* tranche *f*; parenthèse *f*; crochet *m*; * ~ with *vt* réunir par une accolade; mettre ensemble.

bracing *adj* vivifiant, tonifiant.

brag *n* fanfaronnade *f*; * *vi* se vanter, fanfaronner.

braid *n* tresse *f*; * *vt* tresser.

brain *n* cerveau *m*; tête *f*; * *vt* assommer, défoncer le crâne à.

brainchild *n* invention personnelle *f*.

brainless *adj* stupide.

brainwash *vt* faire un lavage de cerveau à.

brainwave *n* idée lumineuse *f*.

brainy *adj* intelligent.

brake *n* frein *m*; * *vi* freiner.

brake fluid *n* liquide de frein *m*.

brake light *n* feu de stop *m*.

bramble *n* ronce *f*.

bran *n* son *m*.

branch *n* branche *f*; ramification *f*; * *vi* se ramifier.

branch line *n* (*rail*) ligne d'embranchement *f*.

brand *n* marque *f*; marque au fer *f*; * *vt* marquer au fer.

brandish *vt* brandir.

brand-new *adj* flambant-neuf.

brandy *n* cognac *m*.

brash *adj* grossier; impertinent.

brass *n* cuivre *m*.

brassiere *n* soutien-gorge *m*.

brat *n* môme, gosse *mf*.

bravado *n* bravade *f*.

brave *adj* courageux, brave, vaillant; * *vt* braver; * *n* brave *m*; ~**ly** *adv* bravement, courageusement.

bravery *n* bravoure *f*; courage *m*; magnificence *f*.

brawl *n* bagarre, rixe *f*; * *vi* se bagarrer.

brawn *n* muscle *m*; fromage de tête *m*.

bray *vi* braire; * *n* braiment *m*.

braze *vt* souder au laiton.

brazen *adj* de cuivre; impudent, effronté; * *vi* crâner.

brazier *n* brasero *m*.

breach *n* rupture *f*; brèche *f*; violation *f*.

bread *n* pain *m* (*also fig*); brown ~ pain bis *m*.

breadbox *n* panière *f*.

breadcrumbs *npl* chapelure *f*.

breadth *n* largeur *f*.

breadwinner *n* soutien de famille *m*.

break *vt* casser; briser; violer; interrompre; * *vi* se casser; ~ **into** entrer par effraction;

~ **out** s'échapper; * *n* cassure, rupture *f*; interruption *f*; ~ **of day** point du jour *m*, aube *f*.

breakage *n* casse *f*.

breakdown *n* panne *f*; dépression nerveuse *f*.

breakfast *n* petit déjeuner *m*; * *vi* déjeuner.

breaking *n* bris *m*; violation *f*; fracture *f*.

breakthrough *n* percée, innovation *f*.

breakwater *n* digue *f*.

breast *n* poitrine *f*, sein *m*; cœur *m*.

breastbone *n* sternum *m*.

breastplate *n* pectoral *m*; plastron *m*.

breaststroke *n* brasse *f*.

breath *n* haleine *f*; respiration *f*; souffle *m*.

breathe *vt vi* respirer; exhaler.

breathing *n* respiration *f*; souffle *m*.

breathing space *n* moment de répit *m*.

breathless *adj* hors d'haleine.

breathtaking *adj* stupéfiant.

breed *n* race, espèce *f*; * *vt* élever, engendrer; produire; éduquer; * *vi* se reproduire.

breeder *n* éleveur *m* -euse *f*.

breeding *n* élevage *m*; éducation *f*.

breeze *n* brise *f*.

breezy *adj* frais.

brethren *npl* frères *mpl*.

breviary *n* bréviaire *m*.

brevity *n* brièveté *f*; concision *f*.

brew *vt* faire infuser; brasser; comploter * *vi* infuser; se tramer; * *n* infusion *f*.

brewer *n* brasseur *m*.

brewery *n* brasserie *f*.

briar, brier *n* ronce *f*; églantier *m*.

bribe *n* pot-de-vin *m*; * *vt* acheter, soudoyer.

bribery *n* corruption *f*.

bric-a-brac *n* bric-à-brac *m*.

brick *n* brique *f*; * *vt* bâtir en briques.

bricklayer *n* maçon *m*.

bridal *adj* de noces, nuptial.

bride *n* mariée *f*.

bridegroom *n* marié *m*.

bridesmaid *n* demoiselle d'honneur *f*.

bridge *n* pont *m*; arête du nez *f*; chevalet *m*; ~ **(over)** *vt* relier par un pont.

bridle *n* bride *f*; frein *m*; * *vt* brider; réfréner.

brief *adj* bref, concis, succinct;
* *n* affaire *f*; résumé *m*.

briefcase *n* serviette *f*.

briefly *adv* brièvement, en
peu de mots.

brigade *n* (*mil*) brigade *f*.

brigadier *n* (*mil*) général de
brigade *m*.

brigand *n* bandit, brigand *m*.

bright *adj* clair, brillant,
éclatant; ~ly *adv* avec éclat.

brighten *vt* faire briller; * *vi*
s'éclairer.

brightness *n* éclat, brillant *m*.

brilliance *n* éclat *m*.

brilliant *adj* éclatant; génial;
~ly *adv* avec éclat.

brim *n* bord *m*.

brimful *adj* plein jusqu'au
bord.

bring *vt* apporter; amener;
persuader; ~ about
entraîner, provoquer; ~
forth produire; provoquer;
~ up élever.

brink *n* bord *m*.

brisk *adj* vif, rapide, frais.

brisket *n* poitrine *f* (de bœuf).

briskly *adv* vivement;
rapidement.

bristle *n* poil *m*; soie *f*; * *vi* se
hérisser.

bristly *adj* hérissé.

brittle *adj* cassant, fragile.

broach *vt* aborder.

broad *adj* large.

broadbeans *npl* fèves *fpl*.

broadcast *n* émission *f*; * *vt*
vi diffuser, émettre.

broadcasting *n* radiodiffusion
f; émission de télévision *f*.

broaden *vt* élargir; * *vi*
s'élargir.

broadly *adv* généralement.

broad-minded *adj* tolérant,
aux idées larges.

broadness *n* largeur *f*.

broadside *n* flanc (d'un
navire) *m*; attaque *f*
cinglante.

broadways *adv* en large, dans
le sens de la largeur.

brocade *n* brocart *m*.

broccoli *n* brocoli *m*.

brochure *n* brochure *f*,
dépliant *m*.

brogue *n* accent *m* du terroir.

broil *vt* griller.

broken *adj* cassé; interrompu;
~ English mauvais anglais *m*.

broker *n* courtier *m*.

brokerage *n* courtage *m*.

bronchial *adj* des bronches.

bronchitis *n* bronchite *f*.

bronze *n* bronze *m*; * *vt*
bronzer, brunir.

brooch *n* broche *f*.

brood *vi* couver; ruminer; * *n* couvée *f*; nichée *f*.

brood-hen *n* couveuse *f*.

brook *n* ruisseau *m*.

broom *n* genêt *m*; balai *m*.

broomstick *n* manche à balai *m*.

broth *n* bouillon de viande et de légumes *m*.

brothel *n* bordel *m*.

brother *n* frère *m*.

brotherhood *n* fraternité *f*.

brother-in-law *n* beau-frère *m*.

brotherly *adj* fraternel; *adv* fraternellement.

brow *n* sourcil *m*; front *m*; sommet *m*.

browbeat *vt* intimider.

brown *adj* marron; brun; ~ paper *n* papier d'emballage *m*; ~ sugar *n* cassonade *f*; * *n* marron *m*; * *vt* brunir.

browse *vt* parcourir; * *vi* paître.

bruise *vt* faire un bleu à; * *n* bleu *m*, ecchymose *f*.

brunette *n* brune *f*.

brunt *n* choc *m*.

brush *n* brosse *f*; pinceau *m*; accrochage *m*; * *vt* brosser.

brushwood *n* broussailles *fpl*; brindilles *fpl*.

brusque *adj* brusque.

Brussels sprout *n* chou de Bruxelles *m*.

brutal *adj* brutal; ~ly *adv* brutalement.

brutality *n* brutalité *f*.

brutalize *vt* brutaliser.

brute *n* brute *f*; * *adj* bestial, féroce.

brutish *adj* brutal, bestial; féroce; ~ly *adv* brutalement.

bubble *n* bulle *f*; * *vi* faire des bulles, bouillonner; pétiller.

bubblegum *n* bubble-gum *m*.

bucket *n* seau *m*.

buckle *n* boucle *f*; * *vt* attacher, boucler; * *vi* se déformer.

bucolic *adj* bucolique.

bud *n* bourgeon, bouton *m*; * *vi* bourgeonner.

Buddhism *n* bouddhisme *m*.

budding *adj* en bouton.

buddy *n* copain *m*.

budge *vi* bouger, remuer; céder.

budgerigar *n* perruche *f*.

budget *n* budget *m*.

buff *n* mordu *m*.

buffalo *n* bison *m*.

buffers *npl* (*rail*) pare-chocs *m invar*.

buffet *n* buffet *m*; * *vt* gifler; frapper.

buffoon *n* bouffon *m*.

bug *n* punaise *f*.

bugbear *n* épouvantail, croquemitaine *m*.

bugle(horn) *n* clairon *m*.

build *vt* construire, bâtir.

builder *n* constructeur *m*; entrepreneur *m*.

building *n* bâtiment *m*; immeuble, édifice *m*.

building society *n* organisme de crédit immobilier *m*.

bulb *n* bulbe *m*; oignon *m*.

bulbous *adj* bulbeux.

bulge *vi* se renfler; * *n* gonflement, renflement *m*.

bulk *n* masse *f*; volume *m*; grosseur *f*; majeure partie *f*; in ~ en gros.

bulky *adj* volumineux; encombrant.

bull *n* taureau *m*.

bulldog *n* bouledogue *m*.

bulldozer *n* bulldozer *m*.

bullet *n* balle *f*.

bulletin board *n* panneau d'affichage *m*.

bulletproof *adj* pare-balles, blindé.

bullfight *n* corrida *f*.

bullfighter *n* torero *m*.

bullfighting *n* tauromachie *f*.

bullion *n* or en barre *m*.

bullock *n* bouvillon *m*.

bullring *n* arène *f*.

bull's-eye *n* centre de la cible *m*.

bully *n* tyran *m*; * *vt* tyraniser.

bulwark *n* rempart *m*.

bum *n* clochard *m*.

bumblebee *n* bourdon *m*.

bump *n* heurt *m*; secousse *f*; bosse *f*; * *vt* heurter.

bumpkin *n* rustre *m*; plouc *m*.

bumpy *adj* cahoteux, bosselé.

bun *n* petit pain *m*; chignon *m*.

bunch *n* botte *f*; groupe *m*.

bundle *n* paquet *m*, liasse *f*; ballot *m*; fagot *m*; * *vt* empaqueter, mettre en liasse.

bung *n* bonde *f*; * *vt* boucher.

bungalow *n* bungalow *m*.

bungle *vt* bousiller; * *vi* faire mal les choses.

bunion *n* (*med*) oignon *m*.

bunk *n* couchette *f*.

bunker *n* abri *m*; bunker *m*.

buoy *n* (*mar*) bouée *f*.

buoyancy *n* flottabilité *f*; optimisme *m*.

buoyant *adj* flottable; gai, enjoué.

burden n charge f; fardeau m; * vt charger.

bureau n commode f; bureau m.

bureaucracy n bureaucratie f.

bureaucrat n bureaucrate mf.

burglar n cambrioleur m -euse f.

burglar alarm n signal d'alarme, signal antivol m.

burglary n cambriolage m.

burial n enterrement m; obsèques fpl.

burial place n lieu de sépulture m.

burlesque n caricature, parodie f; * adj burlesque, caricatural.

burly adj robuste, de forte carrure.

burn vt brûler; incendier, mettre le feu à; * vi brûler; * n brûlure f.

burner n brûleur m.

burning adj brûlant.

burrow n terrier m; * vi se terrer.

bursar n intendant(e) m(f).

burst vi éclater; ~ into tears éclater en sanglots; ~ out laughing éclater de rire; * vt ~ into faire irruption dans; * n éclatement m; explosion f.

bury vt enterrer, inhumer.

bus n (auto)bus m.

bush n buisson, taillis m.

bushy adj touffu, plein de buissons.

busily adv activement, avec empressement.

business n entreprise f; commerce m; affaires fpl; activité f.

businesslike adj sérieux.

businessman n homme d'affaires m.

business trip n voyage d'affaires m.

businesswoman n femme d'affaires f.

bust n buste m.

bus-stop n arrêt d'autobus m.

bustle vi s'affairer; s'activer; * n remue-ménage m; animation f.

bustling adj animé.

busy adj occupé; actif.

busybody n mouche du coche f.

but conj mais; sauf, excepté, seulement.

butcher n boucher m -ère f; * vt abattre, massacrer.

butcher's (shop) n boucherie f.

butchery n boucherie f, carnage m.

butler n majordome m.

butt *n* butte *f*; mégot *m*; * *vt* donner un coup de tête à.

butter *n* beurre *m*; * *vt* beurrer.

buttercup *n* (*bot*) bouton d'or *m*.

butterfly *n* papillon *m*.

buttermilk *n* babeurre *m*.

buttocks *npl* fesses *fpl*.

button *n* bouton *m*; * *vt* boutonner.

buttonhole *n* boutonnière *f*.

buttress *n* contre-fort *m*; soutien *m*; * *vt* soutenir.

buxom *adj* bien en chair.

buy *vt* acheter.

buyer *n* acheteur *m* -euse *f*.

buzz *n* bourdonnement, murmure *m*; * *vi* bourdonner.

buzzard *n* buse *f*.

buzzer *n* interphone *m*.

by *prep* à côté de, près de; par; de; ~ **and** ~ bientôt; ~ **the** ~ à propos; ~ **much** de loin; ~ **all means** certainement; * *adv* près.

bygone *adj* passé.

by-law *n* arrêté municipal *m*.

bypass *n* route de contournement *f*.

by-product *n* sous-produit *m*.

by-road *n* chemin de traverse *m*.

bystander *n* spectateur *m* -trice *f*, badaud *m* -e *f*.

byte *n* (*comput*) octet *m*.

byword *n* proverbe, dicton *m*.

C

cab *n* taxi *m*.

cabbage *n* chou *m*.

cabin *n* cabine *f*; cabane *f*.

cabinet *n* conseil des ministres *m*; meuble de rangement *m*; console *f*.

cabinet-maker *n* ébéniste *m*.

cable *n* (*mar*) câble *m*.

cable car *n* téléphérique *m*.

cable television *n* télévision par câble *f*.

caboose *n* (*mar*) coquerie *f*.

cabstand *n* station de taxis *f*.

cache *n* cachette *f*.

cackle *vi* caqueter, jacasser; * *n* caquetage *m*; jacasserie *f*.

cactus *n* cactus *m*.

cadence *n* (*mus*) cadence *f*.

cadet *n* cadet *m*.

cadge *vt* taper (*fam*).

cafe *n* café *m*.

cafeteria *n* cafétéria *f*.

caffein(e) *n* caféine *f*.

cage *n* cage *f*; prison *f*; * *vt* mettre en cage; emprisonner.

cagey *adj* circonspect.

cajole *vt* cajoler pour amadouer.

cake *n* gâteau *m*.

calamitous *adj* calamiteux, catastrophique.

calamity *n* calamité *f*, désastre *m*.

calculable *adj* calculable.

calculate *vt* calculer, compter.

calculation *n* calcul *m*.

calculator *n* calculatrice *f*.

calculus *n* calcul *m*.

calendar *n* calendrier *m*.

calf *n* veau *m*; vachette *f*; mollet *m*.

calibre *n* calibre *m*.

calisthenics *npl* gymnastique rythmique *f*.

call *vt* appeler; appeler au téléphone; convoquer; to ~ for demander, nécessiter ; aller chercher quelqu'un; to ~ on rendre visite à; to ~ attention demander l'attention; to ~ names insulter; * *n* appel *m*; cri *m*;

visite f; nomination f; vocation f; profession f.

caller n visiteur m, -euse f.

calligraphy n calligraphie f.

calling n profession, vocation f.

callous adj dur ; insensible.

calm n calme m, tranquillité f; * adj calme, tranquille; * vt calmer; apaiser ; ~ly adv calmement.

calmness n calme m, tranquillité f.

calorie n calorie f.

calumny n calomnie f.

Calvary n Calvaire m.

calve vi vêler, mettre bas.

Calvinist n calviniste mf.

camel n chameau m.

cameo n camée m.

camera n appareil photographique m; caméra f.

cameraman n cameraman, cadreur m.

camomile n camomille f.

camouflage n camouflage m.

camp n camp m; * vi camper.

campaign n campagne f; * vi faire campagne.

campaigner n militant, candidat en campagne électorale m.

camper n campeur m -euse f.

camphor n camphre m.

campsite n camping m.

can v aux pouvoir; * n boîte de conserve f.

canal n conduit m; canal m.

cancel vt annuler.

cancellation n annulation f.

cancer n cancer m.

Cancer n Cancer m (signe du zodiaque).

cancerous adj cancéreux.

candid adj candide, simple, sincère; ~ly adv candidement, franchement.

candidate n candidat(e) m(f).

candied adj confit.

candle n bougie f; cierge m.

candlelight n lueur d'une bougie f.

candlestick n bougeoir m.

candour n candeur f; sincérité f.

candy n bonbon m.

cane n canne f; bâton m.

canine adj canin.

canister n boîte f métallique.

cannabis n cannabis m.

cannibal n cannibale mf; anthropophage mf.

cannibalism n cannibalisme m.

cannon n canon m.

cannonball n boulet de canon m.

canny *adj* rusé; prudent.

canoe *n* canoè *m*.

canon *n* canon *m*; règle *f*; ~law droit canon *m*.

canonization *n* canonisation *f*.

canonize *vt* canoniser.

can opener *n* ouvre-boîte *m*.

canopy *n* baldaquin *m*, marquise *f*.

cantankerous *adj* acariâtre, atrabilaire.

canteen *n* cantine *f*.

canter *n* petit galop *m*.

canvas *n* toile *f*.

canvass *vt* sonder, examiner; débattre; * *vi* solliciter des voix; faire du démarchage.

canvasser *n* prospecteur *m* -trice *f*, démarcheur *m* -euse *f*.

canyon *n* canyon *m*.

cap *n* casquette *f*.

capability *n* capacité, aptitude, faculté *f*; potentiel *m*.

capable *adj* capable.

capacitate *vt* rendre capable.

capacity *n* capacité, aptitude *f*; potentiel *m*.

cape *n* cap, promontoire *m*.

caper *n* cabriole *f*; gambade *f*; * *vi* cabrioler; gambader.

capillary *adj* capillaire.

capital *adj* capital; principal; * *n* capital *m*; capitale *f*; majuscule *f*.

capitalism *n* capitalisme *m*.

capitalist *n* capitaliste *mf*.

capitalize *vt* capitaliser; ~ **on** profiter de.

capital punishment *n* peine de mort, peine capitale *f*.

Capitol *n* Capitole *m*.

capitulate *vi* capituler.

capitulation *n* capitulation *f*.

caprice *n* caprice *m*.

capricious *adj* capricieux; ~ly *adv* capricieusement.

Capricorn *n* Capricorne *m* (signe du zodiaque).

capsize *vt* (*mar*) chavirer.

capsule *n* capsule *f*.

captain *n* capitaine *m*.

captaincy, captainship *n* grade de capitaine *m*; statut de capitaine *m*.

captivate *vt* captiver.

captivation *n* fascination *f*.

captive *n* captif *m* -ive *f*, prisonnier *m* -ière *f*.

captivity *n* captivité *f*.

capture *n* capture *f*; * *vt* prendre, capturer.

car *n* voiture *f*, automobile *f*; wagon *m*.

carafe *n* carafe *f*.

caramel n caramel m.

carat n carat m.

caravan n caravane f.

caraway n (bot) cumin m.

carbohydrates npl hydrates de carbone mpl.

carbon n carbone m.

carbon copy n copie carbone f, double carbone m.

carbonize vt carboniser.

carbon paper n papier carbone m.

carbuncle n escarboucle f; furoncle m, tumeur maligne f.

carburettor n carburateur m.

carcass n cadavre m.

card n carte f.

cardboard n carton m.

card game n jeu de cartes m.

cardiac adj cardiaque.

cardinal adj cardinal, principal; * n cardinal m.

card table n table de jeu f.

care n soin m; souci m; * vi se soucier de, être concerné par; **what do I ~?** qu'est-ce que cela peut me faire?; ~ **for** vt soigner; aimer.

career n carrière f; cours m; * vi aller à toute vitesse.

carefree n insouciant.

careful adj soigneux, consciencieux, prudent; ~ly adv soigneusement.

careless adj insouciant, négligent; indolent; ~ly adv négligemment.

carelessness n négligence, indifférence f.

caress n caresse f; * vt caresser.

caretaker n gardien m -ne f, concierge mf.

car-ferry n ferry m.

cargo n cargaison de navire f.

car hire n location de voiture f.

caricature n caricature f; * vt caricaturer.

caries n carie f.

caring adj aimant; humanitaire.

Carmelite n carmélite f.

carnage n carnage m.

carnal adj charnel; sensuel; ~ly adv charnellement.

carnation n œillet m.

carnival n carnaval m.

carnivorous adj carnivore.

carol n chant m (de Noël).

carpenter n charpentier m; ~'s **bench** banc de menuisier m.

carpentry n charpenterie f.

carpet n tapis m; * vt

recouvrir d'un tapis; moquetter.

carpeting n moquette f.

carriage n port m; voiture f; wagon m.

carriage-free adj franco de port.

carrier n porteur, transporteur m.

carrier pigeon n pigeon voyageur m.

carrion n charogne f.

carrot n carotte f.

carry vt porter; transporter; conduire; * vi porter; ~ the day être victorieux; ~ on continuer.

cart n charrette f; chariot m; * vt charrier.

cartel n cartel m.

carthorse n cheval de trait m.

Carthusian n chartreux m.

cartilage n cartilage m.

cartload n charretée f.

carton n pot m; boîte f.

cartoon n dessin animé m.

cartridge n cartouche f.

carve vt tailler, sculpter, ciseler.

carving n sculpture f.

carving knife n couteau à découper m.

car wash n station de nettoyage pour voitures f.

case n boîte f; valise f; cas m; étui m; enveloppe f; in ~ au cas où.

cash n espèces fpl; * vt encaisser.

cash card n carte bancaire f.

cash dispenser n distributeur automatique de billets m.

cashier n caissier m -ière f.

cashmere n cachemire m.

casing n chambranle m; enveloppe f.

casino n casino m.

cask n tonneau, fût m.

casket n cercueil m.

casserole n cocotte f.

cassette n cassette f.

cassette player, recorder n lecteur de cassettes, magnétophone m.

cassock n soutane f.

cast vt jeter, lancer; couler; * n coup m; moule m.

castanets npl castagnettes fpl.

castaway n réprouvé, paria m.

caste n caste f.

castigate vt punir sévèrement.

casting vote n voix prépondérante f.

cast iron n fonte f.

castle n château m.

castor oil *n* huile de ricin *f*.

castrate *vt* castrer.

castration *n* castration *f*.

cast steel *n* acier fondu *m*.

casual *adj* accidentel, fortuit; ~ly *adv* par hasard, fortuitement.

casualty *n* victime *f*, mort *m* -e *f*.

cat *n* chat *m*, chatte *f*.

catalogue *n* catalogue *m*.

catalyst *n* catalyseur *m*.

cataplasm *n* cataplasme *m*.

catapult *n* catapulte *f*.

cataract *n* cataracte *f*.

catarrh *n* rhume *m*; catarrhe *m*.

catastrophe *n* catastrophe *f*.

catcall *n* sifflet *m*.

catch *vt* attraper, saisir; prendre; surprendre; ~ **cold** attraper froid; ~ **fire** prendre feu; * *n* prise *f*; capture *f*; (*mus*) canon *m*; attrape *f*.

catching *adj* contagieux, communicatif.

catchphrase *n* rengaine *f*.

catchword *n* slogan *m*.

catchy *adj* qui attire l'attention; accrocheur.

catechism *n* catéchisme *m*.

catechize *vt* cathéchiser; interroger.

categorical *adj* catégorique; ~ly *adv* catégoriquement.

categorize *vt* classer par catégories.

category *n* catégorie *f*.

cater *vi* approvisionner en nourriture.

caterer *n* fournisseur, traiteur *m*.

catering *n* restauration *f*.

caterpillar *n* chenille *f*.

catgut *n* boyau de chat *m*.

cathedral *n* cathédrale *f*.

catholic *adj n* catholique *mf*.

Catholicism *n* catholicisme *m*.

cattle *n* bétail *m*.

cattle show *n* exposition bovine *f*.

caucus *n* réunion d'un comité électoral *f*.

cauliflower *n* chou-fleur *m*.

cause *n* cause *f*; raison *f*; motif *m*; procès *m*; * *vt* causer.

causeway *n* chaussée *f*.

caustic *adj n* caustique *m/f*.

cauterize *vt* cautériser.

caution *n* prudence, précaution *f*; avertissement *m*; * *vt* avertir.

cautionary *adj* d'avertissement.

cautious *adj* prudent, circonspect.

cavalier *adj* cavalier.

cavalry *n* cavalerie *f*.

cave *n* grotte *f*; caverne *f*.

caveat *n* avertissement *m*; mise en garde *f*; (*law*) notification *f*.

cavern *n* caverne *f*.

cavernous *adj* caverneux.

cavity *n* cavité *f*.

cease *vt* cesser, arrêter; * *vi* cesser.

ceasefire *n* cessez-le-feu *m*.

ceaseless *adj* incessant, continuel; ~ly *adv* continuellement.

cedar *n* cèdre *m*.

cede *vt* (*law*) céder.

ceiling *n* plafond *m*.

celebrate *vt* célébrer, fêter.

celebration *n* fête *f*.

celebrity *n* célébrité *f*.

celery *n* céleri *m*.

celestial *adj* céleste, divin.

celibacy *n* célibat *m*.

celibate *adj* célibataire.

cell *n* cellule *f*.

cellar *n* cave *f*; cellier *m*.

cello *n* violoncelle *m*.

cellophane *n* cellophane *f*.

cellular *adj* cellulaire.

cellulose *n* (*chem*) cellulose *f*.

cement *n* ciment *m* (*also fig*); * *vt* cimenter.

cemetery *n* cimetière *m*.

cenotaph *n* cénotaphe *m*.

censor *n* censeur *m*, critique *mf*.

censorious *adj* sévère, critique.

censorship *n* censure *f*.

censure *n* censure, critique *f*; * *vt* censurer, condamner; critiquer.

census *n* recensement *m*.

cent *n* centime *m*.

centenarian *n* centenaire *mf*.

centenary *n* centenaire *m*; * *adj* centenaire.

centennial *adj* centenaire.

centigrade *n* centigrade *m*.

centilitre *n* centilitre *m*.

centimetre *n* centimètre *m*.

centipede *n* mille-pattes *m invar*.

central *adj* central; ~ly *adv* de façon centralisée; dans le centre.

centralize *vt* centraliser.

centre *n* centre *m*; * *vt* centrer; concentrer; * *vi* se concentrer.

centrifugal *adj* centrifuge.

century *n* siècle *m*.

ceramic *adj* en céramique.

cereals *npl* céréales *fpl*.

cerebral *adj* cérébral.

ceremonial *adj n* cérémonial *m*; rituel *m*.

ceremonious *adj* cérémonieux; **~ly** *adv* solennellement.

ceremony *n* cérémonie *f*; cérémonies *fpl*.

certain *adj* certain, sûr; **~ly** *adv* certainement, sans aucun doute.

certainty, certitude *n* certitude, conviction *f*.

certificate *n* certificat, acte *m*.

certification *n* authentification *f*.

certified mail *n* envoi avec accusé de réception *m*.

certify *vt* certifier, assurer.

cervical *adj* cervical.

cessation *n* cessation *f*.

cesspool *n* cloaque *m*; fosse d'aisances *f*.

chafe *vt* irriter; frotter.

chaff *n* menue paille *f*.

chaffinch *n* pinson *m*.

chagrin *n* dépit *m*.

chain *n* chaîne *f*; série, suite *f*; * *vt* enchaîner; attacher avec une chaîne.

chain reaction *n* réaction en chaîne *f*.

chainstore *n* grand magasin à succursales *m*.

chair *n* chaise *f*; * *vt* présider.

chairman *n* président *m*.

chalice *n* calice *m*.

chalk *n* craie *f*.

challenge *n* défi *m*; * *vt* défier.

challenger *n* provocateur *m* -trice *f*.

challenging *adj* provocateur.

chamber *n* pièce *f*; chambre *f*.

chambermaid *n* femme de chambre *f*.

chameleon *n* caméléon *m*.

chamois leather *n* peau de chamois *f*.

champagne *n* champagne *m*.

champion *n* champion *m* -ne *f*; * *vt* défendre.

championship *n* championnat *m*.

chance *n* hasard *m*; chance *f*; occasion *f*; **by ~** par hasard; * *vt* faire par hasard.

chancellor *n* chancelier *m*.

chancery *n* chancellerie *f*.

chandelier *n* lustre *m*.

change *vt* changer; * *vi* changer, se transformer; * *n* changement *m*, modification *f*; variété *f*; change *m*.

changeable *adj* changeant, variable; inconstant.

changeless *adj* constant, immuable.

changing *adj* variable, changeant.

channel *n* canal *m*; chaîne *f*; * *vt* canaliser.

chant *n* chant *m* scandé; * *vt* scander.

chaos *n* chaos *m*.

chaotic *adj* chaotique.

chapel *n* chapelle *f*.

chaplain *n* chapelain *m*.

chapter *n* chapitre *m*.

char *vt* carboniser.

character *n* caractère *m*; personnage *m*.

characteristic *adj* caractéristique; ~ally *adv* typiquement.

characterize *vt* caractériser.

characterless *adj* sans caractère.

charade *n* charade *f*.

charcoal *n* charbon de bois *m*.

charge *vt* charger; accuser; * *n* fardeau *m*; accusation *f*; (*mil*) attaque *f*; prix *m*.

chargeable *adj* passible.

charge card *n* carte de crédit *f*.

charitable *adj* caritatif; charitable; ~**bly** *adv* charitablement.

charity *n* charité, bienfaisance *f*; aumône *f*.

charlatan *n* charlatan *m*.

charm *n* charme *m*; attrait *m*; * *vt* charmer, enchanter.

charming *adj* charmant.

chart *n* carte de navigation *f*; diagramme *m*.

charter *n* charte *f*; privilège *m*; * *vt* affréter.

charter flight *n* vol charter *m*.

chase *vt* donner la chasse à; poursuivre; * *n* chasse *f*.

chasm *n* abîme *m*.

chaste *adj* chaste; pur; sobre.

chasten *vt* châtier, corriger.

chastise *vt* châtier, punir, corriger.

chastisement *n* châtiment *m*.

chastity *n* chasteté, pureté *f*.

chat *vi* causer; * *n* petite conversation *f*, bavardage *m*.

chatter *vi* bavarder; jacasser; * *n* bavardage *m*; jacasserie *f*.

chatterbox *n* moulin à paroles *m*, pipelette *f*.

chatty *adj* bavard.

chauffeur *n* chauffeur *m*.

chauvinist *n* chauvin *m* -e *f*.

cheap *adj* bon marché, peu cher; ~**ly** *adv* bon marché.

cheapen *vt* baisser le prix de.

cheaper *adj* moins cher.

cheat *vt* tromper, frauder; *
n fraude, tricherie *f*;
tricheur *m* -euse *f*.

check *vt* vérifier; contrôler;
réprimer, enrayer; stopper;
enregistrer; * *n* contrôle
m.

checkmate *n* échec et mat *m*.

checkout *n* caisse *f*.

checkpoint *n* poste de
contrôle *m*.

checkup *n* bilan de santé *m*.

cheek *n* joue *f*; culot (*fam*) *m*.

cheekbone *n* pommette *f*.

cheer *n* gaieté *f*; joie *f*;
applaudissement *m*; * *vt*
réconforter, égayer.

cheerful *adj* gai, enjoué,
joyeux; ~ly *adv* gaiement.

cheerfulness, cheeriness *n*
gaieté *f*; bonne humeur *f*.

cheese *n* fromage *m*.

chef *n* chef (de cuisine) *m*.

chemical *adj* chimique.

chemist *n* chimiste *mf*;
pharmacien *m* -ne *f*.

chemistry *n* chimie *f*.

cheque *n* chèque *m*.

cheque account *n* compte
courant *m*.

chequerboard *n* échiquier *m*.

chequered *adj* à carreaux.

cherish *vt* chérir, aimer.

cheroot *n* petit cigare *m*.

cherry *n* cerise *f*; * *adj*
vermeil.

cherrytree *n* cerisier *m*.

cherub *n* chérubin *m*.

chess *n* échecs *mpl*.

chessboard *n* échiquier *m*.

chessman *n* pièce de jeu
d'échecs *f*.

chest *n* poitrine *f*; cage
thoracique *f*; ~ of drawers
commode *f*.

chestnut *n* châtaigne *f*.

chestnut tree *n* châtaigner *m*.

chew *vt* mâcher, mastiquer.

chewing gum *n* chewing-gum
m.

chic *adj* chic.

chicanery *n* chicane,
chicanerie *f*.

chick *n* poussin *m*; (*fig*)
poulette (*fam*) *f*, nana
(*fam*) *f*.

chicken *n* poulet *m*.

chickenpox *n* varicelle *f*.

chickpea *n* pois chiche *m*.

chicory *n* chicorée *f*.

chide *vt* gronder, réprimander.

chief *adj* principal, en chef;
~ly *adv* principalement; *
n chef *m*.

chief executive *n* directeur général *m*.

chieftain *n* chef *m* (de tribu).

chiffon *n* mousseline de soie *f*.

chilblain *n* engelure *f*.

child *n* enfant *m*; **from a ~** tout enfant; **with ~** enceinte.

childbirth *n* accouchement *m*.

childhood *n* enfance *f*.

childish *adj* enfantin, puéril; **~ly** *adv* puérilement.

childishness *n* enfantillage *m*, puérilité *f*.

childless *adj* sans enfants.

childlike *adj* d'enfant.

children *npl* de **child**: enfants *mpl*.

chill *adj* froid, frais, *f* fraîche; * *n* froid *m*; * *vt* refroidir; glacer.

chilly *adj* froid, très frais.

chime *n* carillon *m*; harmonie *f*; * *vi* sonner; s'accorder.

chimney *n* cheminée *f*.

chimpanzee *n* chimpanzé *m*.

chin *n* menton *m*.

china(ware) *n* porcelaine *f*.

chink *n* fente *f*; tintement *m*; * *vi* tinter.

chip *vt* ébrécher; * *vi* s'ébrécher; * *n* fragment, éclat *m*; puce *f*; frite *f*.

chiropodist *n* pédicure *mf*.

chirp *vi* pépier, gazouiller; * *n* pépiement, gazouillis *m*.

chirping *n* chant des oiseaux *m*.

chisel *n* ciseau *m*; * *vt* ciseler.

chitchat *n* bavardage, papotage *m*.

chivalrous *adj* chevaleresque.

chivalry *n* chevalerie *f*.

chives *npl* ciboulette *f*.

chlorine *n* chlore *m*.

chloroform *n* chloroforme *m*.

chock-full *adj* plein à craquer, comble.

chocolate *n* chocolat *m*.

choice *n* choix *m*, préférence *f*; assortiment *m*; sélection *f*; * *adj* de choix, de qualité.

choir *n* chœur *m*.

choke *vt* étrangler; étouffer.

cholera *n* choléra *m*.

choose *vt* choisir, élire.

chop *vt* trancher, couper, hacher; * *n* côtelette *f*; **~s** *pl* (*sl*) babines *fpl*.

chopper *n* hélicoptère *m*.

chopping block *n* billot *m*.

chopsticks *npl* baguettes *fpl*.

choral *adj* choral.

chord *n* corde *f*, (*mus*) accord *m*.

chore *n* corvée *f*; travail routinier *m*.

chorist, chorister *n* choriste *mf*.

chorus *n* chœur *m*.

Christ *n* Jésus-Christ.

christen *vt* baptiser.

Christendom *n* christianisme *m*; chrétienté *f*.

christening *n* baptême *m*.

Christian *adj n* chrétien *m* -ne *f*; ~ **name** prénom *m*.

Christianity *n* christianisme *m*; chrétienté *f*.

Christmas *n* Noël *f*.

Christmas card *n* carte de Noël *f*.

Christmas Eve *n* veille de Noël *f*.

chrome *n* chrome *m*.

chronic *adj* chronique.

chronicle *n* chronique *f*.

chronicler *n* chroniqueur *m*.

chronological *adj* chronologique; ~**ly** *adv* chronologiquement.

chronology *n* chronologie *f*.

chronometer *n* chronomètre *m*.

chubby *adj* potelé.

chuck *vt* lancer, jeter.

chuckle *vi* rire, glousser.

chug *vi* souffler, haleter.

chum *n* copain *m*, copine *f*.

chunk *n* gros morceau *m*.

church *n* église *f*.

churchyard *n* cimetière *m*.

churlish *adj* fruste, grossier; hargneux.

churn *n* baratte *f*; * *vt* baratter.

cider *n* cidre *m*.

cigar *n* cigare *m*.

cigarette *n* cigarette *f*.

cigarette case *n* étui à cigarettes *f*.

cigarette end *n* mégot *m*.

cigarette holder *n* fume-cigarette *m invar*.

cinder *n* braise *f*.

cinema *n* cinéma *m*.

cinnamon *n* cannelle *f*.

cipher *n* chiffre *m* (code).

circle *n* cercle *m*; groupe *m*; * *vt* encercler; tourner autour de; * *vi* décrire des cercles.

circuit *n* circuit *m*; tour *m*; tournée *f*.

circuitous *adj* détourné, indirect.

circular *adj* circulaire; * *n* circulaire *f*.

circulate *vi* circuler.

circulation *n* circulation *f*.

circumcise *vt* circoncire.

circumcision *n* circoncision *f*.

circumference *n* circonférence *f*. -

circumflex *n* accent circonflexe *m*.

circumlocution *n* circonlocution *f*.

circumnavigate *vt* contourner.

circumnavigation *n* circumnavigation *f*.

circumscribe *vt* circonscrire.

circumspect *adj* circonspect.

circumspection *n* circonspection *f*.

circumstance *n* circonstance, situation *f*.

circumstantial *adj* circonstancié; accessoire.

circumstantiate *vt* détailler.

circumvent *vt* circonvenir.

circumvention *n* évitement *m*; tricherie *f*.

circus *n* cirque *m*.

cistern *n* citerne *f*.

citadel *n* citadelle *f*.

citation *n* citation *f*.

cite *vt* citer.

citizen *n* citoyen *m* -ne *f*.

citizenship *n* citoyenneté *f*.

city *n* ville *f*.

civic *adj* civique.

civil *adj* civil, courtois; ~ly *adv* poliment.

civil defence *n* défense passive *f*.

civil engineer *n* ingénieur des travaux publics *m*.

civilian *n* civil *m* -e *f*.

civility *n* civilité, courtoisie *f*.

civilization *n* civilisation *f*.

civilize *vt* civiliser.

civil law *n* droit civil *m*.

civil war *n* guerre civile *f*.

clad *adj* vêtu, habillé.

claim *vt* revendiquer, réclamer; * *n* demande *f*; réclamation *f*.

claimant *n* demandeur *m*.

clairvoyant *n* voyant *m* -e *f*.

clam *n* palourde *f*.

clamber *vi* grimper (avec difficulté).

clammy *adj* moite.

clamour *n* clameur *f*, cris *mpl*; * *vi* vociférer, crier.

clamp *n* attache *f*; * *vt* serrer; imposer; ~ **down on** resserrer le contrôle.

clan *n* clan, groupe *m*.

clandestine *adj* clandestin.

clang *n* bruit métallique *m*; * *vi* faire un bruit métallique.

clap *vt vi* applaudir.

clapping *n* applaudissements *mpl*.

claret *n* vin rouge de Bordeaux *m*.

clarification *n* clarification *f*, éclaircissement *m*.

clarify *vt* clarifier, éclaircir.

clarinet *n* clarinette *f*.

clarity *n* clarté *f*.

clash *vi* se heurter; s'entrechoquer; * *n* choc *m*; affrontement *m*.

clasp *n* fermoir *m*; boucle *f*; étreinte *f*; * *vt* agrafer; étreindre.

class *n* classe *f*; catégorie *f*; * *vt* classer, classifier.

classic(al) *adj* classique; * *n* auteur classique *m*.

classification *n* classification *f*.

classified advertisement *n* petite annonce *f*.

classify *vt* classifier, classer.

classmate *n* camarade de classe *mf*.

classroom *n* salle de classe *f*.

clatter *vi* résonner; cliqueter; * *n* cliquetis *m*.

clause *n* (*gr*) proposition *f*; clause *f*.

claw *n* griffe *f*; serre *f*; pince *f*; * *vt* griffer; agripper.

clay *n* argile *m*.

clean *adj* propre; net; * *vt* nettoyer.

cleaning *n* nettoyage *m*.

cleanliness *n* propreté, pureté *f*.

cleanly *adj* propre; * *adv* proprement, nettement.

cleanness *n* propreté *f*.

cleanse *vt* nettoyer.

clear *adj* clair; net; transparent; évident; * *adv* distinctement; * *vt* clarifier, éclaircir; dégager; disculper; * *vi* s'éclaircir.

clearance *n* déblaiement *m*; autorisation *f*.

clear-cut *adj* net.

clearly *adv* clairement; manifestement.

cleaver *n* couperet *m*.

clef *n* (*mus*) clé *f*.

cleft *n* fissure, crevasse *f*.

clemency *n* clémence *f*.

clement *adj* clément.

clenched *adj* serré.

clergy *n* clergé *m*.

clergyman *n* ecclésiastique *m*.

clerical *adj* clérical, ecclésiastique.

clerk *n* ecclésiastique *m*; employé *m*.

clever *adj* intelligent; habile; astucieux; **~ly** *adv* intelligemment, habilement.

click *vt* claquer; * *vi* faire un bruit sec.

client *n* client *m* -e *f*.

cliff *n* falaise *f*.

climate *n* climat *m*.

climatic *adj* climatique.

climax n point culminant m, apogée m.

climb vt grimper, escalader; * vi grimper, escalader.

climber n alpiniste mf.

climbing n alpinisme m.

clinch vt serrer fort.

cling vi s'accrocher (à), se cramponner (à); adhérer, (se) coller.

clinic n clinique f.

clink vt faire tinter; * vi tinter, résonner; * n tintement m.

clip vt couper; * n clip m; pince f.

clipping n coupure f.

clique n clique f.

cloak n cape f; prétexte m; * vt masquer.

cloakroom n vestiaire m.

clock n horloge f.

clockwork n mécanisme d'horloge m; * adj précis.

clod n motte (de terre) f.

clog n sabot m; * vi se boucher.

cloister n cloître m.

close vt fermer; clore, conclure; terminer; * vi se fermer; * n fin f; conclusion f; * adj proche; étroit; ajusté; dense; réservé; * adv de près; ~ **by** tout près.

closed adj fermé.

closely adv étroitement; de près.

closeness n proximité f; fidélité, exactitude f; intimité f; minutie f.

closet n placard m.

close-up n gros plan m.

closure n fermeture f; clôture f.

clot n caillot m; grumeau m.

cloth n tissu m; chiffon m; toile f; clergé m.

clothe vt habiller, vêtir.

clothes npl vêtements mpl; linge m; **bed** ~ draps et couvertures mpl.

clothes basket n panière à linge f.

clotheshorse n séchoir à linge m.

clothesline n corde à linge f.

clothespin n pince à linge f.

clothing n vêtements mpl.

cloud n nuage m; nuée f; * vt rendre trouble; assombrir; * vi se couvrir; s'obscurcir.

cloudiness n nébulosité f; obscurité f.

cloudy adj nuageux, nébuleux; obscur; sombre, trouble.

clout n coup de poing m.

clove n clou de girofle m.

clover n trèfle m.

clown n clown m.

club n matraque f; club m.

club car n wagon-bar m (1ère classe).

clue n indice m, indication f; idée f.

clump n massif m.

clumsily adv gauchement.

clumsiness n gaucherie f.

clumsy adj gauche, maladroit; lourd.

cluster n bouquet m; grappe f; groupe m; * vt grouper; * vi se rassembler.

clutch n prise f; embrayage m; * vt empoigner, agripper.

clutter vt encombrer.

coach n autocar m; wagon m; entraîneur m; * vt entraîner, donner des cours particuliers à.

coach trip n excursion en car f.

coagulate vt coaguler; agglutiner; * vi se coaguler; s'agglutiner.

coal n charbon m.

coalesce vi s'unir, se fondre.

coalfield n gisement charbonnier m.

coalition n coalition f.

coalman n charbonnier m.

coalmine n mine de charbon, houillère f.

coarse adj rude; grossier; ~ly adv grossièrement.

coast n côte f.

coastal adj côtier.

coastguard n gendarmerie maritime f, garde-côte m.

coastline n littoral m.

coat n manteau m; pelage m; couche f; * vt enduire, revêtir.

coat hanger n cintre m.

coating n revêtement m.

coax vt cajôler.

cob n épi de maïs m.

cobbler n cordonnier m.

cobbles, cobblestones npl pavés ronds mpl.

cobweb n toile d'araignée f.

cocaine n cocaïne f.

cock n coq m; (zool) mâle m; * vt armer; dresser.

cock-a-doodle-doo n cocorico m.

cockcrow n chant du coq m.

cockerel n jeune coq m.

cockfight(ing) n combat de coqs m.

cockle n (zool) coque f.

cockpit n cabine de pilotage f.

cockroach n cafard m.

cocktail *n* cocktail *m*.

cocoa *n* cacao *m*.

coconut *n* noix de coco *f*.

cocoon *n* cocon *m*.

cod *n* morue *f*.

code *n* code *m*; indicatif *m*.

cod-liver oil *n* huile de foie de morue *f*.

coefficient *n* coefficient *m*.

coercion *n* coercition, contrainte *f*.

coexistence *n* coexistence *f*.

coffee *n* café *m*.

coffee break *n* pause-café *f*.

coffee house *n* café *m*.

coffeepot *n* cafetière *f*.

coffee table *n* table basse *f*.

coffer *n* coffre *m*; caisse *f*.

coffin *n* cercueil *m*.

cog *n* dent d'engrenage *f*.

cogency *n* puissance, force *f*.

cogent *adj* convaincant, puissant; ~**ly** *adv* d'une manière convaincante.

cognac *n* cognac *m*.

cognate *adj* apparenté.

cognisance *n* connaissance *f*; compétence *f*.

cognisant *adj* instruit; (*law*) compétent.

cognition *n* connaissance *f*; cognition *f*.

cogwheel *n* roue dentée *f*.

cohabit *vi* cohabiter.

cohabitation *n* cohabitation *f*.

cohere *vi* se tenir; être cohérent.

coherence *n* cohérence *f*.

coherent *adj* cohérent; logique.

cohesion *n* cohésion *f*.

cohesive *adj* cohésif.

coil *n* rouleau *m*; bobine *f*; * *vt* enrouler.

coin *n* pièce de monnaie *f*; * *vt* frapper.

coincide *vi* coïncider.

coincidence *n* coïncidence *f*.

coincident *adj* coïncident.

coke *n* coke *m*.

colander *n* passoire *f*.

cold *adj* froid; indifférent; ~**ly** *adv* froidement; avec froideur; * *n* froid *m*; rhume *m*.

cold-blooded *adj* insensible.

coldness *n* froideur *f*.

cold sore *n* bouton de fièvre *m*.

coleslaw *n* salade de chou cru *f*.

colic *n* coliques *fpl*.

collaborate *vi* collaborer.

collaboration *n* collaboration *f*.

collapse *vi* s'écrouler; * *n*

écroulement; (med)
évanouissement m.

collapsible adj pliant.

collar n col m.

collarbone n clavicule f.

collate vt collationner, confronter.

collateral adj concomitant; parallèle; * n nantissement m.

collation n collation f.

colleague n collègue mf, confrère m, consœur f.

collect vt rassembler; collectionner.

collection n collection f.

collective adj collectif; ~ly collectivement.

collector n collectionneur m -euse f.

college n faculté f.

collide vi entrer en collision, se heurter.

collision n collision f, heurt m.

colloquial adj familier; parlé; ~ly adv familièrement.

colloquialism n expression familière f.

collusion n collusion f.

colon n deux-points m invar; (med) colon m.

colonel n (mil) colonel m.

colonial adj colonial.

colonist n colon m.

colonize vt coloniser.

colony n colonie f.

colossal adj colossal.

colossus n colosse m.

colour n couleur f; prétexte m; ~s pl drapeau m; * vt colorer; * vi se colorer.

colour-blind adj daltonien.

colourful adj coloré.

colouring n teint m; coloris m.

colourless adj sans couleur, incolore.

colour television n télévision en couleur f.

colt n poulain m.

column n colonne f.

columnist n chroniqueur m.

coma n coma m.

comatose adj comateux.

comb n peigne m; * vt peigner.

combat n combat m; single ~ duel m; * vt combattre.

combatant n combattant m -e f.

combative adj combatif.

combination n combinaison, association f.

combine vt combiner; * vi s'unir.

combustion *n* combustion *f*.

come *vi* venir; ~ **across**, ~ **upon** *vt* rencontrer par hasard, tomber sur; ~ **by** *vt* obtenir; ~ **down** *vi* descendre; se résumer à, baisser (prices); ~ **from** *vt* provenir de; être originaire de; ~ **in for** *vt* être l'objet de; ~ **into** *vt* hériter de; ~ **round**, ~ **to** *vi* revenir à soi; ~ **up with** *vt* suggérer.

comedian *n* comédien *m*; comique *m*.

comedienne *n* comédienne *f*; comique *f*.

comedy *n* comédie *f*.

comet *n* comète *f*.

comfort *n* confort *m*; aises *fpl*; commodités *fpl*; consolation *f*; * *vt* réconforter; soulager; consoler.

comfortable *adj* confortable; réconfortant.

comfortably *adv* confortablement; agréablement.

comforter *n* personne qui réconforte *f*; édredon *m*.

comic(al) *adj* comique; ~ly *adv* comiquement.

coming *n* venue, arrivée *f*; * *adj* à venir.

comma *n* (*gr*) virgule *f*.

command *vt* ordonner, commander; * *n* ordre *m*.

commander *n* commandant *m*.

commandment *n* commandement *m*.

commando *n* commando *m*.

commemorate *vt* commémorer.

commemoration *n* commémoration *f*.

commence *vt* *vi* commencer.

commencement *n* commencement *m*.

commend *vt* recommander, confier à; louer.

commendable *adj* louable.

commendably *adv* élogieusement.

commendation *n* louange *f*; recommandation *f*.

commensurate *adj* proportionné.

comment *n* commentaire *m*; * *vt* commenter.

commentary *n* commentaire *m*; observation *f*.

commentator *n* commentateur *m* -trice *f*.

commerce *n* commerce *m*, affaires *fpl*; relations *fpl*.

commercial *adj* commercial.

commiserate *vt* compatir.

commiseration *n* commisération, pitié *f*.

commissariat *n* (*mil*) intendance *f*, ravitaillement *m*.

commission *n* commission *f*; * *vt* commissionner; commander.

commissioner *n* commissionnaire, coursier *m*.

commit *vt* commettre; confier à; engager.

commitment *n* engagement *m*.

committee *n* comité *m*.

commodity *n* produit *m*, denrée *f*.

common *adj* commun; ordinaire; in ~ en commun; * *n* terrain communal *m*.

commoner *n* roturier *m* -ière *f*.

common law *n* droit coutumier *m*.

commonly *adv* communément, généralement.

commonplace *n* lieux communs *mpl*; * *adj* banal.

common sense *n* bon sens *m*.

Commonwealth *n* Commonwealth *m*.

commotion *n* vacarme *m*; perturbation *f*.

commune *vi* discuter avec sincérité.

communicable *adj* communicable, transmissible.

communicate *vt* communiquer, transmettre; * *vi* communiquer.

communication *n* communication *f*.

communicative *adj* communicatif.

communion *n* communion *f*.

communiqué *n* communiqué *m*.

communism *n* communisme *m*.

communist *n* communiste *mf*.

community *n* communauté *f*.

community centre *n* centre social *m*.

community chest *n* fonds commun *m*.

commutable *adj* interchangeable, permutable.

commutation ticket *n* carte d'abonnement *f*.

commute *vt* échanger.

compact *adj* compact, serré, dense; * *n* accord, contrat *m*; ~ly *adv* de façon compacte; en peu de mots.

compact disc *n* disque compact *m*.

companion *n* compagnon *m*, compagne *f*.

companionship *n* camaraderie *f*; compagnie *f*.

company *n* compagnie, fréquentation *f*; société *f*.

comparable *adj* comparable.

comparative *adj* comparatif; ~ly *adv* comparativement.

compare *vt* comparer.

comparison *n* comparaison *f*.

compartment *n* compartiment *m*.

compass *n* boussole *f*.

compassion *n* compassion *f*.

compassionate *adj* compatissant.

compatibility *n* compatibilité *f*.

compatible *adj* compatible.

compatriot *n* compatriote *mf*.

compel *vt* contraindre, obliger, forcer.

compelling *adj* irrésistible.

compensate *vt* compenser.

compensation *n* compensation *f*; dédommagement *m*.

compère *n* animateur *m* -trice *f*.

compete *vi* rivaliser (avec), faire concurrence (à).

competence *n* compétence *f*; aptitude *f*.

competent *adj* compétent; suffisant; ~ly *adv* avec compétence.

competition *n* compétition *f*; concurrence *f*.

competitive *adj* concurrentiel, compétitif.

competitor *n* concurrent *m* -e *f*.

compilation *n* compilation *f*.

compile *vt* compiler.

complacency *n* suffisance *f*.

complacent *adj* suffisant.

complain *vi* se plaindre; déposer une plainte.

complaint *n* plainte *f*; réclamation *f*.

complement *n* complément *m*.

complementary *adj* complémentaire.

complete *adj* complet; achevé; ~ly *adv* complètement; * *vt* achever, mener à bien, compléter.

completion *n* achèvement *m*.

complex *adj* complexe.

complexion *n* teint *m*; aspect *m*.

complexity *n* complexité *f*.

compliance *n* conformité *f*; soumission *f*.

compliant *adj* docile, soumis.

complicate *vt* compliquer.

complication *n* complication *f*.

complicity *n* complicité *f*.

compliment *n* compliment *m*; * *vt* complimenter.

complimentary *adj* flatteur; à titre gracieux.

comply *vi* se soumettre, se plier, se conformer.

component *adj* composant.

compose *vt* composer; constituer.

composed *adj* calme, posé.

composer *n* auteur *m*; compositeur *m* -trice *f*.

composite *adj* composite, composé.

composition *n* composition *f*.

compositor *n* compositeur *m* -trice *f*.

compost *n* compost *m*.

composure *n* maîtrise de soi *f*, calme *m*, sang-froid *m*.

compound *vt* composer, combiner; * *adj n* composé *m*.

comprehend *vt* comprendre; englober.

comprehensible *adj* compréhensible; ~ly *adv* intelligiblement.

comprehension *n* compréhension *f*; inclusion *f*.

comprehensive *adj* global; complet; compréhensif; ~ly *adv* globalement.

compress *vt* comprimer, concentrer; * *n* compresse *f*.

comprise *vt* comprendre, embrasser.

compromise *n* compromis *m*; * *vt* compromettre; * *vi* adopter un compromis.

compulsion *n* contrainte *f*; compulsion *f*.

compulsive *adj* compulsif; ~ly *adv* compulsivement.

compulsory *adj* obligatoire.

compunction *n* remords, scrupule *m*.

computable *adj* computable, calculable.

computation *n* computation *f*, calcul *m*.

compute *vt* calculer.

computer *n* ordinateur *m*.

computerize *vt* traiter par ordinateur, informatiser.

computer programming *n* programmation *f*.

computer science *n* informatique *f*.

comrade *n* camarade *mf*,

compagnon *m*, compagne *f*.

comradeship *n* camaraderie
f.

con *vt* duper; * *n* duperie *f*.

concave *adj* concave.

concavity *n* concavité *f*.

conceal *vt* cacher, dissimuler.

concealment *n* dissimulation
f; recel *m*.

concede *vt* concéder,
accorder.

conceit *n* vanité *f*; trait
d'esprit *m*.

conceited *adj* vaniteux,
prétentieux.

conceivable *adj* concevable.

conceive *vt* concevoir; * *vi*
concevoir.

concentrate *vt* concentrer.

concentration *n* concentration *f*.

concentration camp *n* camp
de concentration *m*.

concentric *adj* concentrique.

concept *n* concept *m*.

conception *n* conception *f*.

concern *vt* concerner,
toucher; * *n* affaire *f*; souci
m.

concerning *prep* en ce qui
concerne, concernant.

concerto *n* concerto *m*.

concession *n* concession *f*.

conciliate *vt* concilier.

conciliation *n* conciliation *f*.

conciliatory *adj* conciliateur,
conciliant.

concise *adj* concis, succinct;
~ly *adv* avec concision.

conclude *vt* conclure;
décider; déduire.

conclusion *n* conclusion,
déduction *f*; fin *f*.

conclusive *adj* décisif,
concluant; ~ly *adv* de
façon concluante.

concoct *vt* confectionner,
fabriquer.

concoction *n* préparation *f*;
élaboration *f*.

concomitant *adj* concomitant.

concord *n* entente, harmonie *f*.

concordance *n* accord *m*.

concordant *adj* concordant.

concourse *n* rassemblement
m; carrefour *m*; foule *f*.

concrete *n* béton *m*; * *vt*
bétonner.

concubine *n* concubine *f*.

concur *vi* coïncider;
s'entendre.

concurrence *n* consentement
m, coïncidence *f*; union *f*.

concurrently *adv*
simultanément.

concussion *n* commotion *f*.

condemn *vt* condamner; désapprouver.

condemnation *n* condamnation *f*.

condensation *n* condensation *f*.

condense *vt* condenser.

condescend *vi* condescendre; daigner.

condescending *adj* condescendant.

condescension *n* condescendance *f*.

condiment *n* condiment *m*.

condition *vt* conditionner; * *n* condition, situation *f*; état *m*.

conditional *adj* conditionnel, hypothétique; ~ly *adv* conditionnellement.

conditioned *adj* conditionné.

conditioner *n* après-shampoing *m*.

condolences *npl* condoléances *fpl*.

condom *n* préservatif *m*.

condominium *n* condominium *m*, copropriété *f*.

condone *vt* pardonner, fermer les yeux sur.

conducive *adj* propice, opportun.

conduct *n* conduite *f*; comportement *m*; * *vt* conduire, mener.

conductor *n* receveur *m*; chef d'orchestre *m*; conducteur *m*.

conduit *n* conduit *m*; tuyau *m*.

cone *n* cône *m*.

confection *n* sucrerie, confiserie *f*; confection *f*.

confectioner *n* confiseur *m* -euse *f*.

confectioner's (shop) *n* confiserie *f*; pâtisserie *f*.

confederacy *n* confédération *f*.

confederate *vi* se confédérer; * *adj n* confédéré *m*.

confer *vt vi* conférer.

conference *n* conférence *f*.

confess *vt* confesser; * *vi* se confesser.

confession *n* confession *f*.

confessional *n* confessionnal *m*.

confessor *n* confesseur *m*.

confidant *n* confident *m* -e *f*.

confide *vt* confier; ~ in se confier à.

confidence *n* confiance *f*; assurance *f*.

confidence trick *n* abus de confiance *m*, escroquerie *f*.

confident *adj* confiant, assuré, sûr (de soi).

confidential *adj* confidentiel.

configuration *n* configuration *f*.

confine *vt* limiter; emprisonner.

confinement *n* détention *f*; alitement *m*.

confirm *vt* confirmer; ratifier.

confirmation *n* confirmation *f*; ratification *f*; corroboration *f*.

confirmed *adj* invétéré, endurci.

confiscate *vt* confisquer.

confiscation *n* confiscation *f*.

conflagration *n* incendie *m*; conflagration *f*.

conflict *n* conflit *m*; lutte *f*; dispute *f*.

conflicting *adj* contradictoire.

confluence *n* confluence *f*; rencontre *f*.

conform *vt* conformer, adapter; * *vi* se conformer (à), s'adapter (à).

conformity *n* conformité *f*, accord *m*.

confound *vt* confondre.

confront *vt* confronter; affronter.

confrontation *n* affrontement *m*, confrontation *f*.

confuse *vt* confondre; embarrasser; embrouiller.

confusing *adj* déroutant.

confusion *n* confusion *f*; désordre *m*.

congeal *vt* solidifier, congeler; * *vi* se solidifier, se congeler.

congenial *adj* sympathique; similaire.

congenital *adj* congénital.

congested *adj* encombré, congestionné.

congestion *n* encombrement *m*, congestion *f*.

conglomerate *vt* conglomérer, agglomérer; * *adj* aggloméré; * *n* (com) conglomérat *m*.

conglomeration *n* conglomération *f*.

congratulate *vt* complimenter, féliciter.

congratulations *npl* félicitations *fpl*.

congratulatory *adj* de félicitations.

congregate *vt* rassembler, réunir.

congregation *n* assemblée *f*, rassemblement *m*.

congress *n* congrès *m*; conférence *f*.

congressman *n* membre du Congrès *m*.

congruity *n* congruence *f*.

congruous *adj* congru, approprié.

conic(al) *adj* conique.

conifer *n* conifère *m*.

coniferous *adj* (*bot*) conifère.

conjecture *n* conjecture, supposition *f*; * *vt* conjecturer, supposer.

conjugal *adj* conjugal.

conjugate *vt* (*gr*) conjuguer.

conjugation *n* conjugaison *f*.

conjunction *n* conjonction *f*; union *f*.

conjuncture *n* conjoncture *f*; occasion *f*.

conjure *vt* conjurer; exorciser.

conjurer *n* magicien *m* -ne *f*, illusionniste *mf*.

con man *n* escroc *m*.

connect *vt* relier, joindre, rattacher.

connection *n* liaison, connexion *f*.

connivance *n* connivence *f*.

connive *vi* fermer les yeux (sur); être de connivence.

connoisseur *n* connaisseur *m* -euse *f*.

conquer *vt* conquérir; vaincre.

conqueror *n* vainqueur *m*; conquérant *m*.

conquest *n* conquête *f*.

conscience *n* conscience *f*.

conscientious *adj* consciencieux; de conscience; ~ly *adv* consciencieusement.

conscious *adj* conscient; intentionnel; ~ly *adv* consciemment, sciemment.

consciousness *n* conscience *f*.

conscript *n* conscrit *m*.

conscription *n* conscription *f*.

consecrate *vt* consacrer.

consecration *n* consécration *f*.

consecutive *adj* consécutif; ~ly *adv* consécutivement.

consensus *n* consensus *m*.

consent *n* consentement *m*; assentiment *m*; * *vi* consentir.

consequence *n* conséquence *f*; importance *f*.

consequent *adj* consécutif; ~ly *adv* par conséquent.

conservation *n* conservation *f*.

conservative *adj* conservateur.

conservatory *n* conservatoire *m*.

conserve *vt* conserver; * *n* conserve *f*.

consider *vt* considérer, examiner; * *vi* penser, délibérer.

considerable *adj* considérable; important; ~bly *adv* considérablement.

considerate *adj* prévenant, attentionné; prudent; ~ly *adv* avec prévenance; prudemment.

consideration *n* considération *f*; réflexion *f*; estime *f*; rémunération *f*.

considering *conj* étant donné que; ~ that vu que; étant donné que.

consign *vt* confier, remettre, expédier.

consignment *n* expédition *f*, envoi *m*.

consist *vi* consister (en).

consistency *n* consistance *f*; cohérence *f*; constance *f*.

consistent *adj* constant; cohérent; compatible; ~ly *adv* régulièrement.

consolable *adj* consolable.

consolation *n* consolation *f*; réconfort *m*.

consolatory *adj* consolateur.

console *vt* consoler.

consolidate *vt* consolider, grouper; * *vi* se consolider.

consolidation *n* consolidation *f*.

consonant *adj* en accord; * *n* (*gr*) consonne *f*.

consort *n* consort *m*; associé *m* -e *f*.

conspicuous *adj* voyant, manifeste; notable; ~ly *adv* manifestement.

conspiracy *n* conspiration *f*.

conspirator *n* conspirateur *m* -trice *f*.

conspire *vi* conspirer.

constancy *n* constance, fermeté d'âme *f*; persévérance *f*.

constant *adj* constant; persévérant; ~ly *adv* constamment.

constellation *n* constellation *f*.

consternation *n* consternation *f*.

constipated *adj* constipé.

constituency *n* électorat *m*; circonscription *f*.

constituent *n* composant *m*; * *adj* constituant.

constitute *vt* constituer; établir.

constitution *n* constitution *f*.

constitutional *adj* constitutionnel.

constrain *vt* contraindre, forcer, obliger.

constraint *n* contrainte *f*.
constrict *vt* serrer; gêner.
construct *vt* construire, bâtir.
construction *n* construction *f*.
construe *vt* interpréter, analyser.
consul *n* consul *m*.
consular *adj* consulaire.
consulate, consulship *n* consulat *m*.
consult *vt* consulter; * *vi* (se) consulter.
consultation *n* consultation, délibération *f*.
consume *vt* consommer; dissiper; consumer, brûler; * *vi* se consommer.
consumer *n* consommateur *m* -trice *f*.
consumer goods *npl* biens de consommation *mpl*.
consumerism *n* consumérisme *m*.
consumer society *n* société de consommation *f*.
consummate *vt* consommer, accomplir; perfectionner; * *adj* accompli, consommé.
consummation *n* consommation *f*; perfection *f*.
consumption *n* consommation *f*.
contact *n* contact *m*.

contact lenses *npl* lentilles de contact *fpl*.
contagious *adj* contagieux.
contain *vt* contenir, renfermer; refréner.
container *n* récipient *m*.
contaminate *vt* contaminer; ~d *adj* contaminé.
contamination *n* contamination *f*.
contemplate *vt* contempler.
contemplation *n* contemplation *f*.
contemplative *adj* contemplatif.
contemporaneous, contemporary *adj* contemporain.
contempt *n* mépris, dédain *m*.
contemptible *adj* méprisable, vil; ~bly *adv* vilement.
contemptuous *adj* méprisant, dédaigneux; ~ly *adv* dédaigneusement.
contend *vi* combattre, lutter; * *vt* affirmer.
content *adj* content, satisfait; * *vt* contenter, satisfaire; * *n* contentement *m*; ~s *pl* contenu *m*; table des matières *f*.
contentedly *adv* avec contentement.
contention *n* querelle, altercation *f*.

contentious *adj* litigieux; querelleur; ~ly *adv* en chicanant.

contentment *n* contentement *m*, satisfaction *f*.

contest *vt* contester, discuter, disputer; * *n* concours *m*; altercation *f*.

contestant *n* concurrent *m* -e *f*.

context *n* contexte *m*.

contiguous *adj* contigu, voisin.

continent *adj* continent, chaste; * *n* continent *m*.

continental *adj* continental.

contingency *n* contingence *f*; événement imprévu *m*; éventualité *f*.

contingent *n* contingent *m*; * *adj* contingent, éventuel; ~ly fortuitement.

continual *adj* continuel; ~ly *adv* continuellement.

continuation *n* continuation, reprise, suite *f*.

continue *vt* *vi* continuer.

continuity *n* continuité *f*.

continuous *adj* continu; ~ly *adv* sans interruption.

contort *vt* tordre, déformer.

contortion *n* contorsion *f*.

contour *n* contour *m*.

contraband *n* contrebande *f*; * *adj* de contrebande.

contraception *n* contraception *f*.

contraceptive *n* contraceptif *m*; * *adj* contraceptif.

contract *vt* contracter; * *vi* se contracter; * *n* contrat *m*.

contraction *n* contraction *f*.

contractor *n* entrepreneur *m*.

contradict *vt* contredire.

contradiction *n* contradiction *f*.

contradictory *adj* contradictoire.

contraption *n* gadget, bidule (*fam*) *m*.

contrariness *n* esprit de contradiction *m*.

contrary *adj* contraire, opposé; * *n* contraire *m*; on the ~ au contraire.

contrast *n* contraste *m*; * *vt* contraster, mettre en contraste.

contrasting *adj* contrasté, opposé.

contravention *n* infraction *f*.

contributary *adj* contributif.

contribute *vt* contribuer.

contribution *n* contribution *f*; cotisation *f*.

contributor *n* souscripteur(-trice), collaborateur(-trice) *m(f)*.

contributory *adj* contribuant.

contrite *adj* contrit, repentant.

contrition *n* contrition *f*, repentir *m*.

contrivance *n* dispositif *m*; invention *f*.

contrive *vt* inventer, combiner; trouver le moyen de.

control *n* contrôle *m*; maîtrise *f*; autorité *f*; * *vt* maîtriser; réguler; contrôler; gouverner.

control room *n* salle des commandes *f*.

control tower *n* tour de contrôle *f*.

controversial *adj* polémique.

controversy *n* polémique *f*.

contusion *n* contusion *f*.

conundrum *n* énigme *f*.

conurbation *n* conurbation *f*.

convalesce *vi* être en convalescence.

convalescence *n* convalescence *f*.

convalescent *adj* convalescent.

convene *vt* convoquer; réunir; * *vi* se réunir.

convenience *n* commodité, convenance *f*.

convenient *adj* commode, pratique; qui convient; ~ly *adv* commodément.

convent *n* couvent *m*.

convention *n* convention *f*; contrat *m*; assemblée *f*.

conventional *adj* conventionnel.

converge *vi* converger.

convergence *n* convergence *f*.

convergent *adj* convergent.

conversant *adj* au courant; compétent.

conversation *n* conversation *f*.

converse *vi* converser.

conversely *adv* inversement, réciproquement.

conversion *n* conversion; transformation *f*.

convert *vt* convertir; * *n* converti *m* -e *f*.

convertible *adj* convertible; * *n* décapotable *f*.

convex *adj* convexe.

convexity *n* convexité *f*.

convey *vt* transporter; transmettre, communiquer.

conveyance *n* transport *m*; transfert *m*; cession *f*.

conveyancer *n* notaire *m*.

convict *vt* déclarer coupable; * *n* détenu *m* -e *f*.

conviction *n* condamnation *f*; conviction *f*.

convince *vt* convaincre, persuader.

convincing *adj* convaincant.

convincingly *adv* de façon convaincante.

convivial *adj* jovial.

conviviality *n* jovialité *f*.

convoke *vt* convoquer.

convoy *n* convoi *m*.

convulse *vt* ébranler, convulser.

convulsion *n* convulsion *f*; bouleversement *m*; forte agitation *f*.

convulsive *adj* convulsif; ~ly *adv* convulsivement.

coo *vt vi* roucouler.

cook *n* cuisinier *m* -ière *f*; * *vt* cuire; falsifier; * *vi* faire la cuisine, cuisiner.

cookbook *n* livre de cuisine *m*.

cooker *n* cuisinière *f*.

cookery *n* cuisine *f*.

cookie *n* gâteau *m* sec.

cool *adj* frais; calme; * *n* fraîcheur *f*; * *vt* rafraîchir, refroidir.

coolly *adv* fraîchement; de sang-froid.

coolness *n* fraîcheur *f*; froideur *f*; sang-froid *m*.

cooperate *vi* coopérer.

cooperation *n* coopération *f*.

cooperative *adj* coopératif.

coordinate *vt* coordonner.

coordination *n* coordination *f*.

cop *n* (*fam*) flic *m*.

copartner *n* coassocié *m* -e *f*.

cope *vi* se débrouiller.

copier *n* photocopieuse *f*.

copious *adj* copieux, abondant; ~ly *adv* abondamment.

copper *n* cuivre *m*.

coppice, copse *n* taillis *m*.

copulate *vi* copuler.

copy *n* copie *f*; reproduction *f*; exemplaire *m*; * *vt* copier; imiter.

copybook *n* cahier *m*.

copying machine *n* photocopieuse *f*.

copyist *n* copiste *mf*.

copyright *n* droit d'auteur *m*.

coral *n* corail *m*.

coral reef *n* récif de corail *m*.

cord *n* cordon *m*, corde *f*.

cordial *adj* cordial, chaleureux; ~ly *adv* cordialement.

corduroy *n* velours côtelé *m*.

core *n* trognon *m*; noyau, centre, cœur *m*.

cork *n* liège *m*; bouchon *m*; * *vt* boucher.

corkscrew n tire-bouchon m.

corn n maïs m; grain m; blé m.

corncob n épi de maïs m.

cornea n cornée f.

corned beef n corned-beef m.

corner n coin m; angle m.

cornerstone n pierre angulaire f.

cornet n cornet m.

cornfield n champ de maïs m.

cornflakes npl flocons de maïs, cornflakes mpl.

cornice n corniche f.

cornstarch n (US) farine de maïs f.

corollary n corollaire m.

coronary n infarctus m.

coronation n couronnement m.

coroner n coroner m.

coronet n couronne f.

corporal n caporal m.

corporate adj en commun; d'entreprise.

corporation n corporation f; société par actions f.

corporeal adj corporel.

corps n (mil) corps m.

corpse n cadavre m.

corpulent adj corpulent.

corpuscle n corpuscule m; électron m.

corral n corral m.

correct vt corriger; rectifier; * adj correct, juste; ~ly adv correctement.

correction n correction f; rectification f.

corrective adj correcteur, correctif; * n rectificatif m.

correctness n correction f.

correlation n corrélation f.

correlative adj corrélatif.

correspond vi correspondre.

correspondence n correspondance f.

correspondent adj correspondant; * n correspondant m -e f.

corridor n couloir, corridor m.

corroborate vt corroborer.

corroboration n corroboration f.

corroborative adj qui corrobore.

corrode vt corroder.

corrosion n corrosion f.

corrosive adj n corrosif m.

corrugated iron n tôle ondulée f.

corrupt vt corrompre; * vi se corrompre, se pourrir; * adj corrompu; dépravé.

corruptible adj corruptible.

corruption n corruption f; dépravation f.

corruptive *adj* qui corrompt.

corset *n* corset *m*, gaine *f*.

cortege *n* cortège *m*.

cosily *adv* confortablement, douillettement.

cosmetic *adj* *n* cosmétique *m*.

cosmic *adj* cosmique.

cosmonaut *n* cosmonaute *mf*.

cosmopolitan *adj* cosmopolite.

cosset *vt* dorloter.

cost *n* prix, coût *m*; * *vi* coûter.

costly *adj* coûteux, cher.

costume *n* costume *m*.

cosy *adj* douillet.

cottage *n* cottage *m*.

cotton *n* coton *m*.

cotton candy *n* barbe à papa *f*.

cotton mill *n* filature de coton *f*.

cotton wool *n* coton hydrophile *m*.

couch *n* canapé, divan *m*.

couchette *n* couchette *f*.

cough *n* toux *f*; * *vi* tousser.

council *n* conseil *m*.

councillor *n* membre du conseil *m*; conseiller *m* -ère *f*.

counsel *n* conseil *m*; avocat *m*.

counsellor *n* conseiller *m* -ère *f*; avocat *m*.

count *vt* compter, dénombrer; calculer; ~ **on** compter sur; * *n* compte *m*; calcul *m*; chef d'accusation *m*; comte *m*.

countdown *n* compte à rebours *m*.

countenance *n* visage *m*; aspect *m*; mine *f*.

counter *n* comptoir *m*; pion *m*.

counteract *vt* contrecarrer; neutraliser; contrebalancer.

counterbalance *vt* contrebalancer; compenser; * *n* contrepoids *m*.

counterfeit *vt* contrefaire; * *adj* faux.

countermand *vt* annuler.

counterpart *n* contrepartie *f*; homologue *mf*.

counterproductive *adj* qui va à l'encontre du but visé.

countersign *vt* contresigner.

countess *n* comtesse *f*.

countless *adj* innombrable.

countrified *adj* rustique; campagnard.

country *n* pays *m*; patrie *f*; campagne *f*; région *f*; * *adj* rustique; campagnard.

country house *n* maison de campagne *f*.

countryman n campagnard m; compatriote m.

county n comté m.

coup n coup m d'État.

coupé n coupé m.

couple n couple m; a ~ of deux; * vt unir, associer.

couplet n distique m; couplet m.

coupon n coupon m, bon m.

courage n courage m.

courageous adj courageux; ~ly adv courageusement.

courier n messager m; guide m.

course n cours m; route f; chemin m; plat m; marche à suivre f; of ~ bien sûr, naturellement.

court n cour f; tribunal m; * vt courtiser; solliciter.

courteous adj courtois; poli; ~ly adv courtoisement.

courtesan n courtisane f.

courtesy n courtoisie f.

courthouse n palais de justice m.

courtly adj élégant, raffiné.

court-martial n conseil de guerre m.

courtroom n salle de tribunal f.

courtyard n cour f.

cousin n cousin m -e f; first ~ cousin(e) germain(e) m(f).

cove n (mar) crique, anse f.

covenant n contrat m; convention f; * vi convenir, stipuler par contrat.

cover n couverture f; abri m; prétexte m; * vt (re)couvrir; dissimuler; protéger.

coverage n reportage m, couverture f.

coveralls npl bleu de travail m.

covering n couverture f; couche f.

cover letter n lettre explicative f.

covert adj voilé; caché, secret; ~ly adv secrètement.

cover-up n dissimulation f.

covet vt convoiter.

covetous adj avide, cupide.

cow n vache f.

coward n lâche mf.

cowardice n lâcheté f.

cowardly adj lâche; adv lâchement.

cowboy n cowboy m.

cower vi se tapir.

cowherd n vacher m.

coy adj timide; coquet; évasif; ~ly adv évasivement.

coyness n timidité f; modestie f.

crab n crabe m.

crab-apple n pomme sauvage f; **crab-apple tree** n pommier sauvage m.

crack n craquement m; fente, fissure f; * vt fêler, craquer; ~ **down on** sévir; * vi se fêler; craquer.

cracker n pétard m; biscuit salé m.

crackle vi crépiter, pétiller.

crackling n crépitement m; friture f.

cradle n berceau m; * vt bercer.

craft n habileté f; métier manuel m; barque f.

craftily adv astucieusement.

craftiness n astuce, ruse f.

craftsman n artisan m.

craftsmanship n artisanat m.

crafty adj astucieux, rusé.

crag n rocher escarpé m.

cram vt bourrer; fourrer; * vi s'entasser.

crammed adj bourré.

cramp n crampe f; * vt entraver.

cramped adj à l'étroit.

crampon n crampon m.

cranberry n canneberge f.

crane n grue f.

crash vi s'écraser; * n fracas m; collision f.

crash helmet n casque m.

crash landing n atterrissage en catastrophe m.

crass adj grossier, crasse.

crate n caisse f; cageot m.

crater n cratère m.

cravat n foulard m, cravate f.

crave vt avoir extrêmement besoin de.

craving n désir extrême m, soif f.

crawfish n écrevisse f.

crawl vi ramper; ~ **with** grouiller de.

crayfish n écrevisse f.

crayon n crayon de couleur m.

craze n manie f, engouement m.

craziness n folie f.

crazy adj fou.

cream n crème f; * adj crème.

creamy adj crémeux.

crease n pli m; * vt froisser.

create vt créer; causer.

creation n création f.

creative adj créatif.

creator n créateur m -trice f.

creature n créature f.

credence n créance f; crédit m.

credentials npl lettres de créance fpl; preuves d'identité fpl.

credibility n crédibilité f.

credible adj crédible.

credit n crédit m; honneur m; reconnaissance f; * vt croire, reconnaître; créditer.

creditable adj estimable, honorable; ~bly adv honorablement.

credit card n carte de crédit f.

creditor n créancier m -ière f.

credulity n crédulité f.

credulous adj crédule; ~ly adv avec crédulité.

creed n credo m.

creek n ruisseau m.

creep vi ramper; avancer lentement.

creeper n (bot) plante grimpante f.

creepy adj terrifiant, qui donne la chair de poule.

cremate vt incinérer.

cremation n incinération, crémation f.

crematorium n crématoire m.

crescent adj croissant; * n croissant de lune m.

cress n cresson m.

crest n crête f.

crested adj à crête.

crestfallen adj découragé, abattu.

crevasse n crevasse f.

crevice n fissure, lézarde f.

crew n bande, équipe f; équipage m.

crib n berceau m; mangeoire f.

cricket n grillon m.

crime n crime m; délit m.

criminal adj criminel; ~ly adv criminellement; * n criminel m -le f.

criminality n criminalité f.

crimson adj n cramoisi m.

cripple n, adj invalide mf; * vt estropier; (fig) paralyser.

crisis n crise f.

crisp adj frais; croquant.

crispness n croquant m.

criss-cross adj entrecroisé.

criterion n critère m.

critic n critique m.

critical adj critique; exigeant, sévère; ~ly adv d'un œil critique; sévèrement.

criticism n critique f.

criticize vt critiquer.

croak vi coasser, croasser.

crochet n crochet m; * vt faire au crochet; vi faire du crochet.

crockery n poterie f.

crocodile n crocodile m.

crony n copain m (copine f) de longue date.

crook n escroc m; filou m.

crooked adj tordu; malhonnête.

crop n culture f; récolte f; * vt récolter.

cross n croix f; croisement m; * adj de mauvaise humeur, fâché; * vt traverser, croiser; ~ **over** traverser.

crossbar n barre transversale f.

crossbreed n hybride m.

cross-country n cross-country m.

cross-examine vt soumettre à un contre-interrogatoire.

crossfire n feux croisés mpl.

crossing n traversée f; passage pour piétons m.

cross-purpose n malentendu m; quiproquo m; **to be at** ~**s** comprendre (quelqu'un) de travers.

cross-reference n renvoi m, référence f.

crossroad n carrefour m.

crosswalk n (US) passage clouté m.

crotch n entre-jambes m.

crouch vi s'accroupir, se tapir.

crow n corbeau m; chant du coq m; * vi chanter victoire.

crowd n foule f; monde m; * vt entasser; * vi s'entasser.

crown n couronne f; sommet m; * vt couronner.

crown prince n prince héritier m.

crucial adj crucial.

crucible n creuset m.

crucifix n crucifix m.

crucifixion n crucifixion f.

crucify vt crucifier.

crude adj brut, grossier; ~**ly** adv crûment.

cruel adj cruel; ~**ly** adv cruellement.

cruelty n cruauté f.

cruet n huilier-vinaigrier m.

cruise n croisière f; * vi croiser.

cruiser n croiseur m.

crumb n miette f.

crumble vt émietter; effriter; * vi s'émietter; se désintégrer.

crumple vt froisser.

crunch vt croquer; * n (fig) crise f.

crunchy adj croquant.

crusade n croisade f.

crush vt écraser; opprimer; * n cohue f.

crust n croûte f.

crusty adj croustillant; hargneux, bourru.

crutch n béquille f.

crux *n* cœur *m* (d'une question).

cry *vt vi* crier; pleurer; * *n* cri *m*; sanglot *m*.

crypt *n* crypte *f*.

cryptic *adj* énigmatique.

crystal *n* cristal *m*.

crystal-clear *adj* clair comme de l'eau de roche.

crystalline *adj* cristallin; pur.

crystallize *vi* se cristalliser; * *vt* cristalliser.

cub *n* petit *m* (animal).

cube *n* cube *m*.

cubic *adj* cubique.

cuckoo *n* coucou *m*.

cucumber *n* concombre *m*.

cud *n*: to chew the ~ ruminer (*also fig*).

cuddle *vt* embrasser; * *vi* s'enlacer; * *n* étreinte *f*, câlin *m*.

cudgel *n* gourdin *m*, trique *f*.

cue *n* queue de billard *f*.

cuff *n* manchette *f*; revers de pantalon *m*.

culinary *adj* culinaire.

cull *vt* sélectionner; éliminer.

culminate *vi* culminer.

culmination *n* point culminant *m*.

culpability *n* culpabilité *f*.

culpable *adj* coupable; blâmable; ~bly *adv* coupablement.

culprit *n* coupable *mf*.

cult *n* culte *m*.

cultivate *vt* cultiver; améliorer, perfectionner.

cultivation *n* culture *f*.

cultural *adj* culturel.

culture *n* culture *f*.

cumbersome *adj* encombrant; lourd, pesant.

cumulative *adj* cumulatif.

cunning *adj* astucieux, rusé; ~ly *adv* astucieusement; habilement; * *n* astuce, finesse *f*.

cup *n* tasse, coupe *f*; (*bot*) corolle *f*.

cupboard *n* placard *m*.

curable *adj* guérissable.

curate *n* vicaire *m*.

curator *n* conservateur *m*; curateur *m*.

curb *n* frein *m*; bord du trottoir *m*; * *vt* freiner, juguler, modérer.

curd *n* lait caillé *m*.

curdle *vt* cailler, figer; *vi* se cailler, se figer.

cure *n* remède *m*; cure *f*; * *vt* guérir.

curfew *n* couvre-feu *m*.

curing *n* salaison *f*.

curiosity *n* curiosité *f*.

curious *adj* curieux; **~ly** *adv* avec curiosité; curieusement.

curl *n* boucle de cheveux *f*; * *vt* boucler; friser; * *vi* friser.

curling iron *n*, **curling tongs** *npl* fer à friser *m*.

curly *adj* frisé, bouclé.

currant *n* raisin *m* sec.

currency *n* monnaie *f*; circulation *f*; cours *m*.

current *adj* courant; actuel; * *n* cours *m*; tendance *f*; courant *m*.

current affairs *npl* actualité *f*; problèmes actuels *mpl*.

currently *adv* actuellement.

curriculum vitae *n* curriculum vitae *m*.

curry *n* curry *m*.

curse *vt* maudire; * *vi* jurer; * *n* malédiction *f*.

cursor *n* curseur *m*.

cursory *adj* superficiel; hâtif.

curt *adj* succinct; sec.

curtail *vt* réduire; écourter.

curtain *n* rideau *m*.

curtain rod *n* tringle à rideaux *f*.

curtsy *n* révérence *f*; * *vi* faire une révérence.

curvature *n* courbure *f*.

curve *vt* courber; * *n* courbe *f*.

cushion *n* coussin *m*.

custard *n* crème anglaise *f*.

custodian *n* gardien *m* -ne *f*.

custody *n* garde *f*; emprisonnement *m*.

custom *n* coutume *f*, usage *m*.

customary *adj* habituel, coutumier, ordinaire.

customer *n* client *m* -e *f*.

customs *npl* douane *f*.

customs duty *n* droits de douane *mpl*.

customs officer *n* douanier *m*.

cut *vt* découper; couper; tailler; réduire; blesser; **~ short** écourter; interrompre; **~ a tooth** percer une dent; * *vi* couper; se couper; * *n* coupe *f*; coupure *f*; réduction *f*; **~ and dried** *adj* arrangé.

cutback *n* réduction *f*.

cute *adj* mignon.

cutlery *n* couverts *mpl*.

cutlet *n* côtelette *f*.

cut-rate *adj* à prix réduit.

cut-throat *n* assassin *m*; * *adj* acharné.

cutting *n* coupure *f*; * *adj* coupant; tranchant.

cyanide *n* cyanure *m*.

cycle *n* cycle *m*; bicyclette *f*;
  * *vi* aller à bicyclette.
cycling *n* cyclisme *m*.
cyclist *n* cycliste *mf*.
cyclone *n* cyclone *m*.
cygnet *n* jeune cygne *m*.
cylinder *n* cylindre *m*;
  rouleau *m*.

cylindric(al) *adj* cylindrique.
cymbals *n* cymbale *f*.
cynic(al) *adj* cynique;
  sceptique; * *n* cynique *mf*.
cynicism *n* cynisme *m*.
cypress *n* cyprès *m*.
cyst *n* kyste *m*.
czar *n* tsar *m*.

D

dab *n* petit peu *m*; touche *f*.

dabble *vi* barboter.

Dacron *n* dacron *m*.

dad(dy) *n* papa *m*.

daddy-long-legs *n* (*zool*) cousin *m*.

daffodil *n* narcisse *m*, jonquille *f*.

dagger *n* poignard *m*.

daily *adj* quotidien; * *adv* quotidiennement, tous les jours; * *n* quotidien *m*.

daintily *adv* délicatement.

daintiness *n* élégance *f*; délicatesse *f*.

dainty *adj* délicat; élégant.

dairy *n* laiterie *f*.

dairy farm *n* laiterie *f*.

dairy produce *n* produits laitiers *mpl*.

daisy *n* marguerite *f*.

daisy wheel *n* marguerite *f*.

dale *n* vallée *f*.

dally *vi* traîner.

dam *n* barrage *m*; * *vt* endiguer.

damage *n* dommage *m*; tort *m*; * *vt* endommager; faire du tort à.

damask *n* damas *m*; * *adj* damassé.

dame *n* dame *f*; fille *f*.

damn *vt* condamner; * *adj* maudit.

damnable *adj* maudit; ~bly *adv* terriblement.

damnation *n* damnation *f*.

damning *adj* accablant.

damp *adj* humide; * *n* humidité *f*; * *vt* humidifier.

dampen *vt* humidifier.

dampness *n* humidité *f*.

damson *n* prune de Damas *f*.

dance *n* danse *f*; soirée dansante *f*; * *vt vi* danser.

dance hall *n* dancing *m*.

dancer *n* danseur *m* -euse *f*.

dandelion *n* pissenlit *m*.

dandruff *n* pellicules *fpl*.

dandy *adj* génial.

danger *n* danger *m*.

dangerous *adj* dangereux; ~ly *adv* dangereusement.

dangle *vi* pendre.

dank *adj* humide.

dapper *adj* soigné.

dappled *adj* tacheté.

dare *vi* oser; * *vt* défier.

daredevil *n* casse-cou *m invar*.

daring *n* audace *f*; * *adj* audacieux; ~**ly** *adv* audacieusement.

dark *adj* sombre, obscur; * *n* obscurité *f*; ignorance *f*.

darken *vt* assombrir, obscurcir; * *vi* s'assombrir, s'obscurcir.

dark glasses *npl* lunettes de soleil *fpl*.

darkness *n* obscurité *f*.

darkroom *n* chambre noire *f*.

darling *n*, *adj* chéri *m* -e *f*.

darn *vt* repriser.

dart *n* dard *m*.

darts *n* jeu de fléchettes *m*.

dash *vi* se dépêcher; * *n* goutte *f*; tiret, trait *m*; at one ~ tout d'un coup.

dashboard *n* tableau de bord *m*.

dashing *adj* impétueux; élégant.

dastardly *adj* infâme.

data *n* données *fpl*.

database *n* base de données *f*.

data processing *n* traitement de données *m*.

date *n* date *f*; rendez-vous *m*; (*bot*) datte *f*; * *vt* dater; sortir avec.

dated *adj* démodé.

dative *n* (*gr*) datif *m*.

daub *vt* barbouiller.

daughter *n* fille *f*; ~ **in-law** belle-fille *f*.

daunting *adj* décourageant.

dawdle *vi* traîner.

dawn *n* aube *f*; * *vi* se lever.

day *n* jour *m*, journée *f*; by ~ de jour; ~ **by** ~ de jour en jour.

daybreak *n* aube *f*.

day laborer *n* (US) journalier *m*.

daylight *n* lumière du jour, lumière naturelle *f*; ~ **saving time** *n* heure d'été *f*.

daytime *n* journée *f*, jour *m*.

daze *vt* étourdir.

dazed *adj* étourdi.

dazzle *vt* éblouir.

dazzling *adj* éblouissant.

deacon *n* diacre *m*.

dead *adj* mort; ~**wood** *n* bois mort *m*; ~ **silence** *n* silence de mort *m*; the ~ *npl* les morts *mpl*.

dead-drunk *adj* ivre-mort.

deaden *vt* amortir.

dead heat *n* arrivée ex-aequo *f*.

deadline *n* date limite *f*.

deadlock *n* impasse *f*.

deadly *adj* mortel; * *adv* terriblement.

dead march *n* marche funèbre *f*.

deadness *n* inertie *f*.

deaf *adj* sourd.

deafen *vt* assourdir.

deaf-mute *n* sourd(e)-muet(te) *mf*.

deafness *n* surdité *f*.

deal *n* accord *m*; marché *m*; a great ~ beaucoup; a good ~ pas mal; * *vt* distribuer, donner; * *vi* ~ **in** être dans le commerce de; ~ **with** avoir affaire à.

dealer *n* commerçant *m*; trafiquant *m*; donneur *m*.

dealings *npl* rapports *mpl*; transactions *fpl*.

dean *n* doyen *m*.

dear *adj* ~**ly** *adv* cher.

dearness *n* cherté *f*.

dearth *n* pénurie *f*.

death *n* mort *f*.

deathbed *n* lit de mort *m*.

deathblow *n* coup mortel *m*.

death certificate *n* acte de décès *m*.

death penalty *n* peine de mort *f*.

death throes *npl* agonie *f*.

death warrant *n* condamnation à mort *f*.

debacle *n* débâcle *f*.

debar *vt* exclure.

debase *vt* dégrader.

debasement *n* dégradation *f*.

debatable *adj* discutable.

debate *n* débat *m*; * *vt* discuter; examiner.

debauched *adj* débauché.

debauchery *n* débauche *f*.

debilitate *vt* débiliter.

debit *n* débit *m*; * *vt* (*com*) débiter.

debt *n* dette *f*; **to get into** ~ s'endetter.

debtor *n* débiteur *m* -trice *f*.

debunk *vt* démystifier.

decade *n* décennie *f*.

decadence *n* décadence *f*.

decaffeinated *adj* décaféiné.

decanter *n* carafe *f*.

decapitate *vt* décapiter.

decapitation *n* décapitation *f*.

decay *vi* décliner; pourrir; * *n* déclin *m*; pourrissement *m*; carie *f*.

deceased *adj* décédé.

deceit *n* tromperie *f*.

deceitful *adj* trompeur; **~ly** *adv* faussement.

deceive *vt* tromper.

December *n* décembre *m*.

decency *n* décence *f*; pudeur *f*.

decent *adj* décent; bien, bon; **~ly** *adv* décemment.

deception *n* tromperie *f*.

deceptive *adj* trompeur.

decibel *n* décibel *m*.

decide *vt* decider; * *vi* se décider.

decided *adj* décidé.

decidedly *adv* décidément.

deciduous *adj* (*bot*) à feuilles caduques.

decimal *adj* décimal.

decimate *vt* décimer.

decipher *vt* déchiffrer.

decision *n* décision, détermination *f*.

decisive *adj* décisif; **~ly** *adv* avec décision.

deck *n* pont *m*; * *vt* orner.

deckchair *n* chaise longue *f*.

declaim *vt* *vi* déclamer.

declamation *n* déclamation *f*.

declaration *n* déclaration *f*.

declare *vt* déclarer.

declension *n* déclinaison *f*.

decline *vt* (*gr*) décliner; refuser; * *vi* décliner; * *n* déclin *m*; décadence *f*.

declutch *vi* débrayer.

decode *vt* décoder.

decompose *vt* décomposer.

decomposition *n* décomposition *f*.

decor *n* décor *m*; décoration *f*.

decorate *vt* décorer, orner.

decoration *n* décoration *f*.

decorative *adj* décoratif.

decorator *n* décorateur *m* -trice *f*.

decorous *adj* bienséant, convenable; **~ly** *adv* convenablement.

decorum *n* décorum *m*.

decoy *n* leurre *m*.

decrease *vt* diminuer; * *n* diminution *f*.

decree *n* décret *m*; * *vt* décréter; ordonner.

decrepit *adj* décrépit.

decry *vt* décrier.

dedicate *vt* dédier; consacrer.

dedication *n* dédicace *f*; consacration *f*.

deduce *vt* déduire, conclure.

deduct *vt* déduire, soustraire.

deduction *n* déduction *f*.

deed *n* action *f*; exploit *m*.

deem *vt* juger, considérer.

deep *adj* profond.

deepen *vt* approfondir.

deep-freeze *n* congélateur *m*.

deeply *adv* profondément.

deepness *n* profondeur *f*.

deer *n* cerf *m*.

deface *vt* défigurer.

defacement *n* défiguration *f*.

defamation *n* diffamation *f*.

default *n* défaut *m*; manque *m*; * *vi* manquer à ses engagements.

defaulter *n* (*law*) défaillant *m* -e *f*.

defeat *n* défaite *f*; * *vt* vaincre; frustrer.

defect *n* défaut *m*.

defection *n* désertion *f*.

defective *adj* défectueux.

defend *vt* défendre; protéger.

defendant *n* accusé *m* -e *f*.

defense *n* défense *f*; protection *f*.

defenseless *adj* sans défense.

defensive *adj* défensif; ~ly *adv* défensivement.

defer *vt* déférer.

deference *n* déférence *f*.

deferential *adj* respectueux.

defiance *n* défi *m*.

defiant *adj* provocant.

deficiency *n* défaut *m*; manque *m*.

deficient *adj* insuffisant.

deficit *n* déficit *m*.

defile *vt* souiller.

definable *adj* définissable.

define *vt* définir.

definite *adj* sûr; précis; ~ly *adv* sans aucun doute.

definition *n* définition *f*.

definitive *adj* définitif; ~ly *adv* définitivement.

deflate *vt* dégonfler.

deflect *vt* dévier.

deflower *vt* déflorer.

deform *vt* déformer.

deformity *n* déformité *f*.

defraud *vt* escroquer.

defray *vt* payer.

defrost *vt* dégivrer; décongeler.

defroster *n* dégivreur *m*.

deft *adj* habile; ~ly *adv* habilement.

defunct *adj* défunt.

defuse *vt* désamorcer.

degenerate *vi* dégénérer; * *adj* dégénéré.

degeneration *n* dégénération *f*.

degradation *n* dégradation *f*.

degrade *vt* dégrader.

degree *n* degré *m*; diplôme *m*.

dehydrated *adj* déshydraté.

de-ice *vt* dégivrer.

deign *vi* daigner.

deity *n* divinité *f*.

dejected *adj* découragé.

dejection *n* découragement *m*.

delay *vt* retarder; * *n* retard *m*.

delectable *adj* délectable.

delegate *vt* déléguer; * *n* délégué *m* -e *f*.

delegation *n* délégation *f*.

delete *vt* effacer.

deliberate *vt* examiner; * *adj* délibéré; ~ly *adv* délibérément, exprès.

deliberation *n* délibération *f*.

deliberative *adj* délibérant.

delicacy *n* délicatesse *f*.

delicate *adj* délicat; ~ly *adv* délicatement.

delicious *adj* délicieux, exquis; ~ly *adv* délicieusement.

delight *n* délice *m*; enchantement *m*; * *vt* enchanter; * *vi* adorer.

delighted *adj* enchanté.

delightful *adj* charmant; ~ly *adv* merveilleusement.

delineate *vt* décrire; délimiter.

delineation *n* tracé *m*.

delinquency *n* délinquance *f*.

delinquent *n* délinquant *m* -e *f*.

delirious *adj* délirant.

delirium *n* délire *m*.

deliver *vt* livrer; délivrer; prononcer.

deliverance *n* libération *f*.

delivery *n* livraison *f*; accouchement *m*.

delude *vt* tromper.

deluge *n* déluge *m*.

delusion *n* tromperie *f*; illusion *f*.

delve *vi* creuser; chercher.

demagogue *n* démagogue *m*.

demand *n* demande *f*; * *vt* exiger; réclamer.

demanding *adj* exigeant.

demarcation *n* démarcation *f*.

demean *vi* s'abaisser.

demeanour *n* conduite *f*, comportement *m*.

demented *adj* dément.

demise *n* disparition *f*.

democracy *n* démocratie *f*.

democrat *n* démocrate *mf*.

democratic *adj* démocratique.

demolish *vt* démolir.

demolition *n* démolition *f*.

demon *n* démon, diable *m*.

demonstrable *adj* démontrable; ~bly *adv* manifestement.

demonstrate *vt* démontrer, prouver; * *vi* manifester.

demonstration *n* démonstration *f*; manifestation *f*.

demonstrative *adj* démonstratif.

demonstrator *n* manifestant *m* -e *f*.

demoralization *n* démoralisation *f*.

demoralize *vt* démoraliser.

demote *vt* rétrograder.

demur *vi* émettre une objection; rechigner.

demure *adj* réservé; ~ly *adv* avec réserve.

den *n* antre *m*.

denatured alcohol *n* alcool dénaturé *m*.

denial *n* dénégation *f*.

denims *npl* jean *m*.

denomination *n* valeur *f*; dénomination *f*.

denominator *n* (*math*) dénominateur *m*.

denote *vt* dénoter, indiquer.

denounce *vt* dénoncer.

dense *adj* dense, épais.

density *n* densité *f*.

dent *n* bosse *f*; * *vt* cabosser.

dental *adj* dentaire.

dentifrice *n* dentifrice *m*.

dentist *n* dentiste *mf*.

dentistry *n* dentisterie *f*.

denture *n* dentier *m*.

denude *vt* dénuder, dépouiller.

denunciation *n* dénonciation *f*.

deny *vt* nier.

deodorant *n* déodorant *m*.

deodorize *vt* déodoriser.

depart *vi* partir.

department *n* département *m*; service *m*.

department store *n* grand magasin *m*.

departure *n* départ *m*.

departure lounge *n* salle d'embarquement *f*.

depend *vi* dépendre; ~ on/ upon compter sur.

dependable *adj* fiable; sûr.

dependant *n* personne à charge *f*.

dependency *n* dépendance *f*.

dependent *adj* dépendant.

depict *vt* dépeindre, décrire.

depleted *adj* réduit.

deplorable *adj* déplorable, lamentable; ~bly *adv* déplorablement.

deplore *vt* déplorer, lamenter.

deploy *vt* (*mil*) déployer.

depopulated *adj* dépeuplé.

depopulation *n* dépopulation *f*.

deport *vt* déporter; expulser.

deportation *n* déportation *f*; expulsion *f*.

deportment *n* comportement *m*.

deposit *vt* déposer; * *n* dépôt *m*; caution *f*.

deposition *n* déposition *f*.

depositor *n* déposant *m* -e *f*.

depot *n* dépôt *m*.

deprave *vt* dépraver, corrompre.

depraved *adj* dépravé.

depravity *n* dépravation *f*.

deprecate *vt* désapprouver.

depreciate *vi* se déprécier.

depreciation *n* dépréciation *f*.

depredation *n* déprédation *f*.

depress *vt* déprimer.

depressed *adj* déprimé.

depression *n* dépression *f*.

deprivation *n* privation *f*.

deprive *vt* priver.

deprived *adj* défavorisé.

depth *n* profondeur *f*.

deputation *n* députation *f*.

depute *vt* députer, déléguer.

deputize *vi* remplacer.

deputy *n* remplaçant *m* -e *f*; député *m*; délégué *m* -e *f*.

derail *vt* faire dérailler.

deranged *adj* dérangé.

derby *n* chapeau melon *m*.

derelict *adj* abandonné, en ruines.

deride *vt* se moquer de.

derision *n* dérision *f*.

derisive *adj* ridicule; moqueur.

derivable *adj* déductible.

derivation *n* dérivation *f*.

derivative *n* dérivé *m*.

derive *vt vi* dériver.

derogatory *adj* désobligeant.

derrick *n* derrick *m*.

descant *n* (*mus*) déchant *m*.

descend *vi* descendre.

descendant *n* descendant *m* -e *f*.

descent *n* descente *f*.

describe *vt* décrire.

description *n* description *f*.

descriptive *adj* descriptif.

descry *vt* distinguer.

desecrate *vt* profaner.

desecration *n* profanation *f*.

desert *n* désert *m*; * *adj* désert; * *vt* abandonner; déserter.

deserter *n* déserteur *m*.

desertion *n* désertion *f*.

deserve *vt* mériter.

deservedly *adv* à juste titre.

deserving *adj* méritant.

déshabillé *n* déshabillé *m*.

desideratum *n* desideratum *m*.

design *vt* concevoir; dessiner; * *n* dessein *m*; design *m*; dessin *m*.

designate *vt* désigner.

designation *n* désignation *f*.

designedly *adv* exprès, délibérément.

designer *n* créateur *m* -trice *f*; styliste *mf*.

desirability *n* avantage *m*; attrait *m*.

desirable *adj* désirable.

desire *n* désir *m*; * *vt* désirer.

desirous *adj* désireux.

desist *vi* abandonner.

desk *n* bureau *m*.

desolate *adj* désert, désolé.

desolation *n* désolation *f*.

despair *n* désespoir *m*; * *vi* se désespérer.

despairingly *adv* désespérément.

despatch = dispatch.

desperado *n* bandit *m*.

desperate *adj* désespéré; ~ly *adv* désespérément; extrêmement.

desperation *n* désespoir *m*.

despicable *adj* méprisable.

despise *vt* mépriser.

despite *prep* malgré.

despoil *vt* dépouiller.

despondency *n* abattement *m*.

despondent *adj* abattu.

despot *n* despote *m*.

despotic *adj* despotique; ~ally *adv* despotiquement.

despotism *n* despotisme *m*.

dessert *n* dessert *m*.

destination *n* destination *f*.

destine *vt* destiner.

destiny *n* destin, sort *m*.

destitute *adj* indigent.

destitution *n* indigence *f*.

destroy *vt* détruire.

destruction *n* destruction *f*.

destructive *adj* destructeur.

desultory *adj* irrégulier; sans méthode.

detach *vt* séparer, détacher.

detachable *adj* détachable.

detachment *n* (*mil*) détachement *m*.

detail *n* détail *m*; in ~ en détail; * *vt* détailler.

detain *vt* retenir; détenir.

detect *vt* détecter.

detection *n* détection *f*; découverte *f*.

detective *n* détective *m*.

detector *n* détecteur *m*.

detention *n* détention *f*.

deter *vt* dissuader.

detergent *n* détergent *m*.

deteriorate *vt* détériorer.

deterioration *n* détérioration *f*.

determination *n* détermination *f*.

determine *vt* déterminer, décider.

determined *adj* déterminé.

deterrent *n* force de dissuasion *f*.

detest *vt* détester.

detestable *adj* détestable.

dethrone *vt* détrôner.

dethronement *n* détrônement *m*.

detonate *vi* détoner.

detonation *n* détonation *f*.

detour *n* déviation *f*.

detract *vi* nuire à.

detriment *n* détriment *m*.

detrimental *adj* préjudiciable.

deuce *n* deux *m*; égalité *f*.

devaluation *n* dévaluation *f*.

devastate *vt* dévaster.

devastating *adj* dévastateur.

devastation *n* dévastation *f*.

develop *vt* développer.

development *n* développement *m*.

deviate *vi* dévier.

deviation *n* déviation *f*.

device *n* mécanisme *m*.

devil *n* diable, démon *m*.

devilish *adj* diabolique; ~**ly** *adv* diaboliquement.

devious *adj* tortueux.

devise *vt* inventer; concevoir.

devoid *adj* dépourvu.

devolve *vt* déléguer.

devote *vt* consacrer.

devoted *adj* dévoué.

devotee *n* partisan *m* -e *f*.

devotion *n* dévotion *f*.

devotional *adj* dévot.

devour *vt* dévorer.

devout *adj* dévot, pieux; ~**ly** *adv* pieusement.

dew *n* rosée *f*.

dewy *adj* couvert de rosée; ingénu.

dexterity *n* dextérité *f*.

dexterous *adj* adroit, habile.

diabetes *n* diabète *m*.

diabetic *n* diabétique *mf*.

diabolic *adj* diabolique; ~**ally** *adv* diaboliquement.

diadem *n* diadème *m*.

diagnosis *n* (*med*) diagnostic *m*.

diagnostic *adj* diagnostique; * *npl* ~**s** diagnostic *m*.

diagonal *adj* diagonal; ~**ly** *adv* diagonalement; * *n* diagonale *f*.

diagram *n* diagramme *m*.

dial *n* cadrant *m*.

dial code *n* code *m*.

dialect *n* dialecte *m*.

dialogue *n* dialogue *m*.

dial tone *n* tonalité *f*.

diameter *n* diamètre *m*.

diametrical *adj* diamétral; ~**ly** *adv* diamétralement.

diamond *n* diamant *m*.

diamond-cutter *n* tailleur de diamant *m*.

diamonds *npl* (cards) carreaux *mpl*.

diaper *n* couche *f*.

diaphragm *n* diaphragme *m*.

diarrhoea *n* diarrhée *f*.

diary *n* journal *m*.

dice *npl* dés *mpl*.

dictate *vt* dicter; * *n* ordre *m*.

dictation *n* dictée *f*.

dictatorial *adj* dictatorial.

dictatorship *n* dictature *f*.

diction *n* diction *f*

dictionary *n* dictionnaire *m*.

didactic *adj* didactique.

die *vi* mourir; ~ away s'affaiblir; ~ down s'éteindre.

die *n* (*sing de* dice) dé *m*.

diehard *n* réactionnaire *mf*.

diesel *n* diesel *m*.

diet *n* diète *f*; régime *m*; * *vi* être au régime.

dietary *adj* diététique.

differ *vi* différer.

difference *n* différence *f*.

different *adj* différent; ~ly *adv* différemment.

differentiate *vt* différencier.

difficult *adj* difficile.

difficulty *n* difficulté *f*.

diffidence *n* timidité *f*; manque d'assurance *m*.

diffident *adj* timide; mal assuré; ~ly *adv* avec timidité.

diffraction *n* diffraction *f*.

diffuse *vt* diffuser, répandre; * *adj* diffus.

diffusion *n* diffusion *f*.

dig *vt* creuser; * *n* coup *m*.

digest *vt* digérer.

digestible *adj* digestible.

digestion *n* digestion *f*.

digestive *adj* digestif.

digger *n* excavatrice *f*.

digit *n* chiffre *m*.

digital *adj* digital; numérique.

dignified *adj* digne.

dignitary *n* dignitaire *m*.

dignity *n* dignité *f*.

digress *vi* faire une digression.

digression *n* digression *f*.

dike *n* digue *f*.

dilapidated *adj* délabré.

dilapidation *n* délabrement *m*.

dilate *vt* dilater; * *vi* se dilater.

dilemma *n* dilemme *m*.

diligence *n* assiduité *f*.

diligent *adj* assidu; ~**ly** *adv* avec assiduité.

dilute *vt* diluer.

dim *adj* indistinct; faible; sombre;

* *vt* affaiblir; troubler.

dime *n* pièce de dix cents *f*.

dimension *n* dimension *f*.

diminish *vt vi* diminuer.

diminution *n* diminution *f*.

diminutive *n* diminutif *m*.

dimly *adv* indistinctement; faiblement.

dimmer *n* interrupteur d'intensité *m*.

dimple *n* fossette *f*.

din *n* vacarme *m*.

dine *vi* dîner.

diner *n* restaurant (économique) *m*; dîneur *m* -euse *f*.

dinghy *n* canot pneumatique *f*.

dingy *adj* sale; miteux.

dinner *n* dîner *m*.

dinner time *n* heure du dîner *f*.

dinosaur *n* dinosaure *m*.

dint *n*: **by ~ of** à force de.

diocese *n* diocèse *m*.

dip *vt* tremper.

diphtheria *n* diphtérie *f*.

diphthong *n* diphtongue *f*.

diploma *n* diplôme *m*.

diplomacy *n* diplomatie *f*.

diplomat *n* diplomate *m*.

diplomatic *adj* diplomatique.

dipsomania *n* dipsomanie *f*.

dipstick *n* (*auto*) jauge *f*.

dire *adj* atroce, affreux.

direct *adj* direct; * *vt* diriger.

direction *n* direction *f*; instruction *f*.

directly *adv* directement; immédiatement.

director *n* directeur *m* -trice *f*.

directory *n* annuaire *m*.

dirt *n* saleté *f*.

dirtiness *n* saleté *f*.

dirty *adj* sale.

disability *n* incapacité *f*; infirmité *f*.

disabled *adj* infirme.

disabuse *vt* détromper.

disadvantage *n* désavantage *m*; * *vt* désavantager.

disadvantageous *adj* désavantageux.

disaffected *adj* mécontent.

disagree *vi* ne pas être d'accord.

disagreeable *adj* désagréable; ~**bly** *adv* désagréablement.

disagreement *n* désaccord *m*.

disallow *vt* rejeter.

disappear *vi* disparaître.

disappearance *n* disparition *f*.

disappoint *vt* décevoir.

disappointed *adj* déçu.

disappointing *adj* décevant.

disappointment *n* déception *f*.

disapproval *n* désapprobation *f*.

disapprove *vt* désapprouver.

disarm *vt* désarmer.

disarmament *n* désarmement *m*.

disarray *n* désordre *m*.

disaster *n* désastre *m*.

disastrous *adj* désastreux.

disband *vt* disperser.

disbelief *n* incrédulité *f*.

disbelieve *vt* ne pas croire.

disburse *vt* débourser.

discard *vt* jeter.

discern *vt* discerner, percevoir.

discernible *adj* perceptible.

discerning *adj* perspicace.

discernment *n* perspicacité *f*.

discharge *vt* décharger; régler (une dette); remplir; * *n* décharge *f*; règlement *m*.

disciple *n* disciple *m*.

discipline *n* discipline *f*; * *vt* discipliner.

disclaim *vt* nier.

disclaimer *n* dénégation *f*.

disclose *vt* révéler.

disclosure *n* révélation *f*.

disco *n* discothèque *f*.

discoloration *n* décoloration *f*.

discolour *vt* décolorer.

discomfort *n* incommodité *f*.

disconcert *vt* déconcerter.

disconnect *vt* débrancher.

disconsolate *adj* inconsolable; ~**ly** *adv* inconsolablement.

discontent *n* mécontentement *m*; * *adj* mécontent.

discontented *adj* mécontent.

discontinue *vt* interrompre.

discord *n* discorde *f*.

discordant *adj* discordant.

discount *n* escompte *m*; remise *f*; * *vt* escompter.

discourage *vt* décourager.

discouraged *adj* découragé.

discouragement *n* découragement *m*.

discouraging *adj* décourageant.

discourse *n* discours *m*.

discourteous *adj* discourtois; ~**ly** *adv* de manière discourtoise.

discourtesy *n* manque de courtoisie *m*.

discover *vt* découvrir.

discovery *n* découverte *f*.

discredit *vt* discréditer.

discreditable *adj* peu honorable.

discreet *adj* discret; ~ly *adv* discrètement.

discrepancy *n* contradiction *f*.

discretion *n* discrétion *f*.

discretionary *adj* discrétionnaire.

discriminate *vt* distinguer; discriminer.

discrimination *n* discrimination *f*.

discursive *adj* discursif.

discuss *vt* discuter.

discussion *n* discussion *f*.

disdain *vt* dédaigner; * *n* dédain, mépris *m*.

disdainful *adj* dédaigneux, méprisant; ~ly *adv* dédaigneusement, avec mépris.

disease *n* maladie *f*.

diseased *adj* malade.

disembark *vt vi* débarquer.

disembarkation *n* (*mil*) débarquement *m*.

disenchant *vt* désenchanter.

disenchanted *adj* désenchanté.

disenchantment *n* désenchantement *m*.

disengage *vt* dégager.

disentangle *vt* démêler.

disfigure *vt* défigurer.

disgrace *n* honte *f*; scandale *m*; * *vt* déshonorer.

disgraceful *adj* honteux; scandaleux; ~ly *adv* honteusement.

disgruntled *adj* mécontent.

disguise *vt* déguiser; * *n* déguisement *m*.

disgust *n* dégoût *m*; * *vt* dégoûter.

disgusting *adj* dégoûtant.

dish *n* plat *m*; assiette *f*; * *vt* servir dans un plat; ~ up servir.

dishcloth *n* torchon à vaisselle *m*.

dishearten *vt* démoraliser.

dishevelled *adj* ébouriffé.

dishonest *adj* malhonnête; ~ly *adv* malhonnêtement.

dishonesty *n* malhonnêteté *f*.

dishonour *n* déshonneur *m*; * *vt* déshonorer.

dishonourable *adj* déshonorable; ~bly *adv* de manière déshonorante.

dishtowel *n* torchon à vaisselle *m*.

dishwarmer *n* chauffe-plats *m*.

dishwasher *n* lave-vaisselle *m*; plongeur *m* -euse *f*.

disillusion *vt* désillusionner.

disillusioned *adj* désillusionné.

disincentive *n* élément dissuasif *m*.

disinclination *n* aversion *f*.

disinclined *adj* peu enclin.

disinfect *vt* désinfecter.

disinfectant *n* désinfectant *m*.

disinherit *vt* déshériter.

disintegrate *vi* se désintégrer.

disinterested *adj* désintéressé; ~ly *adv* de manière désintéressée.

disjointed *adj* déréglé; décousu.

disk *n* disque *m*; disquette *f*.

diskette *n* disque *m*, disquette *f*.

dislike *n* aversion *f*; * *vt* ne pas aimer.

dislocate *vt* disloquer.

dislocation *n* dislocation *f*.

dislodge *vt* déloger.

disloyal *adj* déloyal; ~ly *adv* déloyalement.

disloyalty *n* déloyauté *f*.

dismal *adj* triste, lugubre.

dismantle *vt* démonter.

dismay *n* consternation *f*.

dismember *vt* démembrer.

dismiss *vt* renvoyer; écarter.

dismissal *n* renvoi *m*; rejet *m*.

dismount *vt* désarçonner; * *vi* descendre.

disobedience *n* désobéissance *f*.

disobedient *adj* désobéissant.

disobey *vt* désobéir.

disorder *n* désordre *m*.

disorderly *adj* en désordre, confus.

disorganization *n* désorganisation *f*.

disorganized *adj* désorganisé.

disorientated *adj* désorienté.

disown *vt* renier.

disparage *vt* dénigrer.

disparaging *adj* désobligeant.

disparity *n* disparité *f*.

dispassionate *adj* impartial; calme.

dispatch *vt* envoyer; * *n* envoi *m*; dépêche *f*.

dispel *vt* dissiper.

dispensary *n* dispensaire *m*.

dispense *vt* dispenser; distribuer.

disperse *vt* disperser.

dispirited *adj* démoralisé.

displace *vt* déplacer.

display *vt* exposer; faire preuve de; * *n* exposition *f*; déploiement *m*.

displeased *adj* mécontent.

displeasure *n* mécontentement *m*.

disposable *adj* à jeter.

disposal *n* disposition *f*.

dispose *vt* disposer.

disposed *adj* disposé.

disposition *n* disposition *f*.

dispossess *vt* déposséder.

disproportionate *adj* disproportionné.

disprove *vt* réfuter.

dispute *n* dispute *f*; controverse *f*; * *vt* mettre en cause.

disqualify *vt* exclure; disqualifier.

disquiet *n* inquiétude *f*.

disquieting *adj* inquiétant.

disquisition *n* dissertation *f*.

disregard *vt* ne pas tenir compte de; mépriser; * *n* dédain *m*.

disreputable *adj* de mauvaise réputation.

disrespect *n* irrévérence *f*.

disrespectful *adj* irrespectueux; ~ly *adv* irrespectueusement.

disrobe *vt* dévêtir.

disrupt *vt* interrompre.

disruption *n* interruption *f*.

dissatisfaction *n* mécontentement *m*.

dissatisfied *adj* mécontent.

dissect *vt* disséquer.

dissection *n* dissection *f*.

disseminate *vt* disséminer.

dissension *n* dissension *f*.

dissent *vi* être en dissension; * *n* dissension *f*.

dissenter *n* dissident *m* -e *f*.

dissertation *n* thèse *f*.

dissident *n* dissident *m* -e *f*.

dissimilar *adj* dissemblable.

dissimilarity *n* dissemblance *f*.

dissimulation *n* dissimulation *f*.

dissipate *vt* dissiper.

dissipation *n* dissipation *f*.

dissociate *vt* dissocier.

dissolute *adj* dissolu.

dissolution *n* dissolution *f*.

dissolve *vt* dissoudre; * *vi* se dissoudre.

dissonance *n* dissonance *f*.

dissuade *vt* dissuader.

distance *n* distance *f*; at a ~ de loin; * *vt* distancer.

distant *adj* distant.

distaste *n* dégoût *m*.

distasteful *adj* désagréable.

distend *vt* distendre.

distil *vt* distiller.

distillation *n* distillation *f*.

distillery *n* distillerie *f*.

distinct *adj* distinct; ~ly *adv* distinctement.

distinction *n* distinction *f*.

distinctive *adj* distinctif.

distinctness *n* clarté *f*.

distinguish *vt* distinguer; discerner.

distort *vt* déformer.

distorted *adj* déformé.

distortion *n* distortion *f*.

distract *vt* distraire.

distracted *adj* distrait; ~ly *adv* distraitement.

distraction *n* distraction *f*; confusion *f*.

distraught *adj* éperdu.

distress *n* souffrance *f*; détresse *f*; * *vt* désoler; affliger.

distressing *adj* affligeant.

distribute *vt* distribuer, répartir.

distribution *n* distribution *f*.

distributor *n* distributeur *m*.

district *n* district *m*.

district attorney *n* procureur de la République *m*.

distrustful *adj* méfiant.

disturb *vt* déranger.

disturbance *n* dérangement *m*; trouble *m*.

disturbed *adj* troublé.

disturbing *adj* troublant.

disuse *n* désuétude *f*.

disused *adj* abandonné.

ditch *n* fossé *m*.

dither *vi* hésiter.

ditto *adv* idem.

ditty *n* chansonnette *f*.

diuretic *adj* (*med*) diurétique.

dive *vi* plonger.

diver *n* plongeur *m* -euse *f*.

diverge *vi* diverger.

divergence *n* divergence *f*.

divergent *adj* divergent.

diverse *adj* divers, différent; ~ly *adv* différemment.

diversion *n* diversion *f*.

diversity *n* diversité *f*.

divert *vt* dévier; divertir.

divest *vt* dénuder; dépouiller.

divide *vt* diviser; * *vi* se diviser.

dividend *n* dividende *m*.

dividers *npl* (*math*) compas à pointes sèches *m*.

divine *adj* divin.

divinity *n* divinité *f*.

diving *n* plongeon *m*.

diving board *n* plongeoir *m*.

divisible *adj* divisible.

division *n* (*math*) division *f*.

divisor *n* (*math*) diviseur *m*.

divorce *n* divorce *m*; * *vi* divorcer.

divorced *adj* divorcé.

divulge *vt* divulguer.

dizziness *n* vertige *m*.

dizzy *adj* pris de vertige.

DJ *n* disc-jockey, DJ *m*.

do *vt* faire.

docile *adj* docile.

dock *n* dock *m*; * *vi* entrer aux docks.

docker *n* docker *m*.

dockyard *n* chantier *m* naval.

doctor *n* docteur *m*.

doctrinal *adj* doctrinal.

doctrine *n* doctrine *f*.

document *n* document *m*.

documentary *adj* documentaire.

dodge *vt* esquiver.

doe *n* biche *f*; ~ **rabbit** lapine *f*.

dog *n* chien *m*.

dogged *adj* tenace; ~**ly** *adv* tenacement.

dog kennel *n* refuge pour chiens *m*.

dogmatic *adj* dogmatique; ~**ly** *adv* dogmatiquement.

doings *npl* faits *mpl*.

do-it-yourself *n* bricolage *m*.

doleful *adj* lugubre, triste.

doll *n* poupée *f*.

dollar *n* dollar *m*.

dolphin *n* dauphin *m*.

domain *n* domaine *m*.

dome *n* dôme *m*.

domestic *adj* domestique.

domesticate *vt* domestiquer.

domestication *n* domestication *f*.

domesticity *n* domesticité *f*.

domicile *n* domicile *m*.

dominant *adj* dominant.

dominate *vi* dominer.

domination *n* domination *f*.

domineer *vi* dominer.

domineering *adj* autoritaire.

dominion *n* domination *f*.

dominoes *npl* domino *m*.

donate *vt* donner, faire don de.

donation *n* donation *f*.

done *p, adj* fait; cuit.

donkey *n* âne *m*.

donor *n* donneur *m*; donateur *m*.

doodle *vi* gribouiller.

doom *n* sort *m*.

door *n* porte *f*.

doorbell *n* sonnette *f*.

door handle *n* poignée de porte *f*.

doorman *n* portier *m*.

doormat *n* paillasson *m*.

doorplate *n* plaque *f*.

doorstep *n* pas de porte *m*.

doorway *n* entrée *f*.

dormant *adj* latent; dormant.

dormer window *n* lucarne *f*.

dormitory *n* dortoir *m*.

dormouse *n* loir *m*.

dosage *n* dose *f*; dosage *m*.

dose *n* dose *f*; * *vt* doser; donner une dose à.

dossier *n* dossier *m*.

dot *n* point *m*.

dote *vi* adorer.

dotingly *adv* avec adoration.

double *adj* double; * *vt* doubler; * *n* double *m*.

double bed *n* lit *m* à deux places.

double-breasted *adj* croisé.

double chin *n* double menton *m*.

double-dealing *n* duplicité *f*.

double-edged *adj* à double tranchant.

double entry *n* (*com*) comptabilité en partie double *f*.

double-lock *vt* fermer à double tour.

double room *n* chambre pour deux *f*.

doubly *adv* doublement.

doubt *n* doute *m*; * *vt* douter de.

doubtful *adj* douteux.

doubtless *adv* indubitablement.

dough *n* pâte *f*.

douse *vt* éteindre.

dove *n* colombe *f*.

dovecot *n* colombier *m*.

dowdy *adj* mal habillé.

down *n* duvet *m*; * *prep* en bas; **to sit** ~ s'asseoir; **upside** ~ à l'envers.

downcast *adj* démoralisé; baissé.

downfall *n* ruine *f*.

downhearted *adj* découragé.

downhill *adv* en descendant, dans la descente.

down payment *n* acompte *m*.

downpour *n* grosse averse *f*.

downright *adj* manifeste.

downstairs *adv* en bas.

down-to-earth *adj* pratique; terre à terre.

downtown *adv* dans le centre, en ville.

downward(s) *adv* vers le bas.

dowry *n* dot *f*.

doze *vi* somnoler.

dozen *n* douzaine *f*.

dozy *adj* somnolent.

drab *adj* gris; morne.

draft *n* brouillon *m*; traite *f*.

drag *vt* tirer; * *n* drague *f*; ennui *m*.

dragnet *n* seine *f*; filet *m*.

dragon *n* dragon *m*.

dragonfly *n* libellule *f*.

drain *vt* drainer; vider; * *n* tuyau d'écoulement *m*.

drainage *n* drainage *m*.

drainboard *n* égouttoir *m*.

drainpipe *n* tuyau d'écoulement *m*.

drake *n* canard mâle *m*.

dram *n* petit verre *m*.

drama *n* drame *m*.

dramatic *adj* dramatique; ~ally *adv* dramatiquement.

dramatist *n* dramaturge *mf*.

dramatize *vt* dramatiser.

drape *vt* draper.

drapes *npl* tentures *fpl*.

drastic *adj* radical.

draught *n* courant d'air *m*.

draughts *npl* jeu de dames *m*.

draughty *adj* exposé aux courants d'air.

draw *vt* tirer; dessiner; ~ nigh s'approcher.

drawback *n* désavantage, inconvénient *m*.

drawer *n* tiroir *m*.

drawing *n* dessin *m*.

drawing board *n* planche à dessin *f*.

drawing room *n* salon *m*.

drawl *vi* parler d'une voix traînante.

dread *n* terreur *f*; * *vt* redouter, craindre.

dreadful *adj* horrible; ~ly *adv* horriblement.

dream *n* rêve *m*; * *vt vi* rêver.

dreary *adj* triste, morne.

dredge *vt* draguer.

dregs *npl* lie *fl*.

drench *vt* tremper.

dress *vt* habiller; panser; * *vi* s'habiller; * *n* robe *f*.

dresser *n* buffet *m*.

dressing *n* pansement *m*; sauce *f*.

dressing gown *n* peignoir *m*.

dressing room *n* loge *f*; garde-robe *f*.

dressing table *n* coiffeuse *f*.

dressmaker *n* couturier *m* -ière *f*.

dressy *adj* élégant.

dribble *vi* tomber goutte à goutte.

dried *adj* séché.

drift *n* amoncellement *m*; courant *m*; sens *m*; * *vi* aller à la dérive.

driftwood *n* bois flottant *m*.

drill *n* perceuse *f*; (*mil*) exercice *m*; * *vt* percer.

drink *vt vi* boire; * *n* boisson *f*.

drinkable *adj* potable; buvable.

drinker *n* buveur *m* -euse *f*.

drinking bout *n* beuverie *f*.

drinking water *n* eau potable *f*.

drip *vi* goutter; * *n* goutte *f*; goutte-à-goutte *m*.

dripping *n* graisse *f*.

drive *vt* conduire; pousser; * *vi* conduire; * *n* promenade en voiture *f*; allée, entrée *f*.

drivel *n* imbécilités *fpl*; * *vi* baver; dire des imbécilités.

driver n conducteur m -trice f; chauffeur m.

driveway n allée, entrée f.

driving n conduite f.

driving instructor n moniteur(-trice) d'auto-école m(f).

driving licence n permis m de conduire.

driving school n auto-école f.

driving test n examen m du permis de conduire.

drizzle vi bruiner.

droll adj drôle.

drone n bourdonnement m.

droop vi tomber.

drop n goutte f; * vt laisser tomber; * vi tomber; ~ out se retirer; abandonner.

drop-out n marginal m.

dropper n compte-gouttes m invar.

dross n scories fpl.

drought n sécheresse f.

drove n: in ~s en troupe.

drown vt noyer; * vi se noyer.

drowsiness n somnolence f.

drowsy adj somnolent.

drudgery n corvée f.

drug n drogue f; * vt droguer.

drug addict n drogué m -e f.

druggist n pharmacien m -ne f.

drugstore n pharmacie f.

drum n tambour m; * vi jouer du tambour.

drum majorette n majorette f.

drummer n batteur m.

drumstick n baguette de tambour f.

drunk adj ivre.

drunkard n ivrogne mf.

drunken adj ivre.

drunkenness n ivresse f.

dry adj sec; * vt faire sécher; * vi sécher.

dry-cleaning n nettoyage à sec m.

dry-goods store n (US) mercerie f.

dryness n sécheresse f.

dry rot n pourriture f.

dual adj double.

dual-purpose adj à double emploi.

dubbed adj doublé.

dubious adj douteux.

duck n canard m; * vt vi plonger.

duckling n caneton m.

dud adj nul; faux.

due adj dû, f due; * adv exactement; * n droit m; chose due f.

duel n duel m.

duet n (mus) duo m.

dull adj terne; insipide; gris; * vt ternir; atténuer.

duly *adv* dûment; en temps voulu.

dumb *adj* muet; ~**ly** *adv* sans dire un mot.

dumbbell *n* haltère *m*; (US) abruti *m*.

dumbfounded *adj* interloqué.

dummy *n* mannequin *m*; prête-nom *m*.

dump *n* tas *m*; * *vt* jeter; laisser tomber.

dumping *n* (com) dumping *m*.

dumpling *n* boulette de pâte *f*.

dumpy *adj* boulot, -te *f*.

dunce *n* cancre *m*.

dune *n* dune *f*.

dung *n* fumier *m*.

dungarees *npl* salopette *f*.

dungeon *n* donjon *m*; cachot *m*.

dupe *n* dupe *f*; * *vt* duper.

duplex *n* duplex *m*.

duplicate *n* duplicata *m*; copie *f*; * *vt* dupliquer.

duplicity *n* duplicité *f*.

durability *n* durabilité *f*.

durable *adj* durable.

duration *n* durée *f*.

during *prep* pendant.

dusk *n* crépuscule *m*.

dust *n* poussière *f*; * *vt* épousseter.

duster *n* chiffon *m*.

dusty *adj* poussiéreux.

Dutch courage *n* courage puisé dans la boisson *m*.

duteous *adj* fidèle, loyal.

dutiful *adj* obéissant, soumis; ~**ly** *adv* avec obéissance.

duty *n* devoir *m*; obligation *f*.

duty-free *adj* hors taxe.

dwarf *n* nain *m*, naine *f*; * *vt* rapetisser.

dwell *vi* habiter, vivre.

dwelling *n* habitation *f*; domicile *m*.

dwindle *vi* diminuer.

dye *vt* teindre; * *n* teinture *f*.

dyer *n* teinturier *m*.

dyeing *n* teinturerie *f*; teinture *f*.

dye-works *npl* teinturerie *f*.

dying *adj* mourant, agonisant; * *n* mort *f*.

dynamic *adj* dynamique.

dynamics *n* dynamique *f*.

dynamite *n* dynamite *f*.

dynamiter *n* dynamiteur *m* -euse *f*.

dynamo *n* dynamo *f*.

dynasty *n* dynastie *f*.

dysentery *n* dysenterie *f*.

dyspepsia *n* (med) dyspepsie *f*.

dyspeptic *adj* dyspeptique.

E

each *pn* chacun(e); ~ other les un(e)s les autres.

eager *adj* enthousiaste; ardent; ~ly *adv* avec enthousiasme; ardemment.

eagerness *n* enthousiasme *m*; ardeur *f*; désir *m*.

eagle *n* aigle *m*.

eagle-eyed *adj* aux yeux d'aigle.

eaglet *n* aiglon *m*.

ear *n* oreille *f*; ouïe *f*; by ~ en improvisant.

earache *n* mal d'oreille *m*.

eardrum *n* tympan *m*.

early *adj* premier; *adv* tôt, de bonne heure.

earmark *vt* (*fig*) désigner.

earn *vt* gagner.

earnest *adj* sérieux; ~ly *adv* sérieusement.

earnestness *n* sérieux *m*.

earnings *npl* revenus *mpl*.

earphones *npl* écouteurs *mpl*.

earring *n* boucle d'oreille *f*.

earth *n* terre *f*; * *vt* brancher à la terre.

earthen *adj* de terre.

earthenware *n* poterie *f*.

earthquake *n* tremblement de terre *m*.

earthworm *n* ver de terre *m*.

earthy *adj* terreux; truculent.

earwig *n* perce-oreille *m*.

ease *n* aise *f*; facilité *f*; at ~ à l'aise; * *vt* apaiser; soulager.

easel *n* chevalet *m*.

easily *adv* facilement.

easiness *n* facilité *f*.

east *n* est *m*; orient *m*.

Easter *n* Pâques *fpl*.

Easter egg *n* œuf de Pâques *m*.

easterly *adj* d'est.

eastern *adj* de l'est, oriental.

eastward(s) *adv* vers l'est.

easy *adj* facile; commode; ~ going décontracté.

easy chair *n* fauteuil *m*.

eat *vt vi* manger.

eatable *adj* comestible;

mangeable; * ~s *npl* vivres *mpl*.

eau de Cologne *n* eau *f* de Cologne.

eaves *npl* avant-toit *m*.

eavesdrop *vt* espionner; écouter discrètement.

ebb *n* reflux *m*; * *vi* refluer; décliner.

ebony *n* ébène *f*.

eccentric *adj* excentrique.

eccentricity *n* excentricité *f*.

ecclesiastic *adj* ecclésiastique.

echo *n* écho *m*; * *vi* résonner.

eclectic *adj* éclectique.

eclipse *n* éclipse *f*; * *vt* éclipser.

ecology *n* écologie *f*.

economic(al) *adj* économique; économe.

economics *npl* économie *f*.

economist *n* économiste *mf*.

economize *vt* économiser.

economy *n* économie *f*.

ecstasy *n* extase *f*.

ecstatic *adj* extatique; ~ally *adv* avec extase.

eczema *n* eczéma *m*.

eddy *n* tourbillon *m*; * *vi* tourbillonner.

edge *n* fil *m*; pointe *f*; bord *m*; acrimonie *f*; * *vt* border; affiler.

edgeways, edgewise *adv* de côté.

edging *n* bordure *f*.

edgy *adj* nerveux.

edible *adj* mangeable; comestible.

edict *n* édit *m*; décret *m*.

edification *n* édification *f*.

edifice *n* édifice *m*.

edify *vt* édifier.

edit *vt* diriger; rédiger; couper.

edition *n* édition *f*.

editor *n* directeur *m* -trice *f*; rédacteur *m* -trice *f*.

editorial *adj* rédactionnel; * *n* éditorial *m*.

educate *vt* éduquer; instruire.

education *n* éducation *f*; instruction *f*.

eel *n* anguille *f*.

eerie *adj* inquiétant; surnaturel.

efface *vt* effacer.

effect *n* effet *m*; réalité *f*; ~s *npl* biens *mpl*; * *vt* effectuer.

effective *adj* efficace; effectif; ~ly *adv* effectivement, en effet.

effectiveness *n* efficacité *f*.

effectual *adj* efficace; ~ly *adv* efficacement.

effeminacy *n* caractère efféminé *m*.

effeminate *adj* efféminé.

effervescence *n* effervescence *f*.

effete *adj* (*bot*) stérile; faible.

efficacy *n* efficacité *f*.

efficiency *n* efficacité *f*.

efficient *adj* efficace.

effigy *n* effigie *f*.

effort *n* effort *m*.

effortless *adj* sans effort.

effrontery *n* effronterie *f*.

effusive *adj* chaleureux; expansif.

egg *n* œuf *m*; * ~ **on** *vt* encourager.

eggcup *n* coquetier *m*.

eggplant *n* (US) aubergine *f*.

eggshell *n* coquille d'œuf *f*.

ego(t)ism *n* égoïsme *m*.

ego(t)ist *n* égoïste *mf*.

ego(t)istical *adj* égoïste.

eiderdown *n* édredon *m*.

eight *adj n* huit *m*.

eighteen *adj n* dix-huit *m*.

eighteenth *adj n* dix-huitième *mf*.

eighth *adj n* huitième *mf*.

eightieth *adj n* quatre-vingtième *mf*.

eighty *adj n* quatre-vingt.

either *pn* n'importe lequel, n'importe laquelle; * *conj* ou, soit.

ejaculate *vi* s'exclamer; éjaculer.

ejaculation *n* exclamation *f*; éjaculation *f*.

eject *vt* éjecter, expulser.

ejection *n* éjection, expulsion *f*.

ejector seat *n* siège éjectable *m*.

eke *vt* augmenter; prolonger.

elaborate *vt* élaborer; * *adj* élaboré; compliqué; ~**ly** *adv* avec soin.

elapse *vi* s'écouler.

elastic *adj* élastique.

elasticity *n* élasticité *f*.

elated *adj* exultant.

elation *n* exultation *f*.

elbow *n* coude *m*; * *vt* pousser du coude.

elbow-room *n* espace *m*; (*fig*) liberté, latitude *f*.

elder *n* sureau *m*; * *adj* aîné.

elderly *adj* d'un âge avancé.

elders *npl* anciens *mpl*.

eldest *adj* aîné.

elect *vt* élire; choisir; * *adj* élu; choisi.

election *n* élection *f*; choix *m*.

electioneering *n* propagande électorale *f*.

elective *adj* facultatif; électif.

elector *n* électeur *m* -trice *f*.

electoral *adj* électoral.

electorate *n* électorat *m*.

electric(al) *adj* électrique.

electric blanket *n* couverture électrique *f*.

electric cooker *n* cuisinière électrique *f*.

electric fire *n* radiateur électrique *m*.

electrician *n* électricien *m*.

electricity *n* électricité *f*.

electrify *vt* électriser.

electron *n* électron *m*.

electronic *adj* électronique; **~s** *npl* électronique *f*.

elegance *n* élégance *f*.

elegant *adj* élégant; **~ly** *adv* élégamment.

elegy *n* élégie *f*.

element *n* élément *m*.

elemental, elementary *adj* élémentaire.

elephant *n* éléphant *m*.

elephantine *adj* lourd.

elevate *vt* élever, hausser.

elevation *n* élévation *f*; hauteur *f*.

elevator *n* ascenseur *m*.

eleven *adj n* onze *m*.

eleventh *adj n* onzième *mf*.

elf *n* elfe *m*.

elicit *vt* tirer, obtenir.

eligibility *n* éligibilité *f*.

eligible *adj* éligible.

eliminate *vt* éliminer, écarter.

elk *n* élan *m*.

elliptic(al) *adj* elliptique.

elm *n* orme *m*.

elocution *n* élocution *f*.

elocutionist *n* professeur d'élocution *m*.

elongate *vt* allonger.

elope *vi* s'échapper, s'enfuir.

elopement *n* fugue, évasion *f*.

eloquence *n* éloquence *f*.

eloquent *adj* éloquent; **~ly** *adv* éloquemment.

else *pn* autre.

elsewhere *adv* ailleurs.

elucidate *vt* élucider, expliquer.

elucidation *n* élucidation, explication *f*.

elude *vt* éluder; éviter.

elusive, elusory *adj* insaisissable.

emaciated *adj* émacié.

emanate (from) *vi* émaner (de).

emancipate *vt* émanciper; affranchir.

emancipation *n* émancipation *f*; affranchissement *m*.

embalm *vt* embaumer.

embankment *n* talus *m*; quai *m*.

embargo *n* embargo *m*.

embark *vt* embarquer.

embarkation *n* embarcation *f*.

embarrass *vt* embarrasser.

embarrassed *adj* embarrassé.

embarrassing *adj* embarrassant.

embarrassment *n* embarras *m*.

embassy *n* ambassade *f*.

embed *vt* enchâsser; intégrer.

embellish *vt* embellir, orner.

embellishment *n* ornement *m*.

ember *n* braise *f*.

embezzle *vt* détourner.

embezzlement *n* détournement de fonds *m*.

embitter *vt* rendre amer.

emblem *n* emblème *m*.

emblematic(al) *adj* emblématique, symbolique.

embodiment *n* (*law*) incorporation *f*; incarnation *f*.

embody *vt* (*law*) incorporer; incarner.

embrace *vt* étreindre; comprendre; * *n* étreinte *f*.

embroider *vt* broder.

embroidery *n* broderie *f*.

embroil *vt* impliquer.

embryo *n* embryon *m*.

emendation *n* correction *f*.

emerald *n* émeraude *f*.

emerge *vi* émerger; apparaître.

emergency *n* urgence *f*.

emergency cord *n* sonnette d'alarme *f*.

emergency exit *n* sortie de secours *f*.

emergency landing *n* atterrissage forcé *m*.

emergency meeting *n* réunion extraordinaire *f*.

emery *n* émeri *m*.

emigrant *n* émigré *m* -e *f*.

emigrate *vi* émigrer.

emigration *n* émigration *f*.

eminence *n* hauteur *f*; éminence, excellence *f*.

eminent *adj* élevé; éminent, distingué; ~ly *adv* éminemment.

emission *n* émission *f*.

emit *vt* émettre.

emoluments *npl* émoluments *mpl*.

emotion *n* émotion *f*.

emotional *adj* émotionnel; ému.

emotive *adj* émotif.

emperor *n* empereur *m*.

emphasis *n* emphase *f*.

emphasize *vt* souligner, accentuer.

emphatic *adj* emphatique; ~ally *adv* avec emphase.

empire *n* empire *m*.

employ *vt* employer.

employee *n* employé *m* -e *f*.

employer *n* employeur *m*.

employment *n* emploi, travail *m*.

emporium *n* grand magasin *m*.

empress *n* impératrice *f*.

emptiness *n* vide *m*; futilité *f*.

empty *adj* vide; vain; * *vt* vider.

empty-handed *adj* les mains vides.

emulate *vt* imiter.

emulsion *n* émulsion *f*.

enable *vt* permettre.

enact *vt* promulguer; représenter.

enamel *n* émail *m*; * *vt* émailler.

enamour *vt* s'éprendre de.

encamp *vi* camper.

encampment *n* campement *m*.

encase *vt* entourer.

enchant *vt* enchanter.

enchanting *adj* enchanteur.

enchantment *n* enchantement *m*.

encircle *vt* encercler.

enclose *vt* entourer; inclure, joindre.

enclosure *n* clôture *f*; enceinte *f*.

encompass *vt* comprendre.

encore *adv* encore.

encounter *n* rencontre *f*; combat *m*; * *vt* rencontrer.

encourage *vt* encourager.

encouragement *n* encouragement *m*.

encroach *vi* empiéter (sur).

encroachment *n* empiètement *m*.

encrusted *adj* incrusté.

encumber *vt* embarrasser.

encumbrance *n* embarras *m*.

encyclical *adj* encyclique.

encyclopedia *n* encyclopédie *f*.

end *n* fin *f*; extrémité *f*; bout *m*; dessein *m*; to that ~ afin que; to no ~ en vain; on ~ debout; * *vt* terminer, conclure; * *vi* terminer.

endanger *vt* mettre en danger.

endear *vt* faire aimer.

endearing *adj* attachant.

endearment *n* expression de tendresse *f*.

endeavour *vi* s'efforcer, tenter; * *n* effort *m*.

endemic *adj* endémique.

ending *n* fin, conclusion *f*; dénouement *m*; terminaison *f*.

endive *n* (*bot*) endive *f*.

endless *adj* infini, perpétuel;
~ly *adv* sans fin,
perpétuellement.

endorse *vt* endosser;
approuver.

endorsement *n* endos *m*; approbation *f*.

endow *vt* doter.

endowment *n* dotation *f*.

endurable *adj* supportable.

endurance *n* endurance *f*; patience *f*.

endure *vt* supporter; * *vi*
durer.

endways, endwise *adv*
debout.

enemy *n* ennemi *mf*.

energetic *adj* énergique,
vigoureux.

energy *n* énergie, force *f*.

enervate *vt* débiliter.

enfeeble *vt* affaiblir.

enfold *vt* envelopper.

enforce *vt* mettre en vigueur.

enforced *adj* forcé.

enfranchise *vt* émanciper.

engage *vt* aborder; engager.

engaged *adj* fiancé; occupé.

engagement *n* engagement
m; combat *m*; fiançailles
fpl; ~ ring *n* bague de
fiançailles *f*.

engaging *adj* attrayant.

engender *vt* engendrer;
produire.

engine *n* moteur *m*; locomotive *f*.

engine driver *n* conducteur
m.

engineer *n* ingénieur *m*;
mécanicien *m*.

engineering *n* ingénierie *f*.

engrave *vt* graver.

engraving *n* gravure *f*.

engrossed *adj* absorbé.

engulf *vt* submerger.

enhance *vt* améliorer;
réhausser.

enigma *n* énigme *f*.

enjoy *vt* aimer; jouir de; ~
o.s. s'amuser.

enjoyable *adj* agréable;
amusant.

enjoyment *n* plaisir *m*;
jouissance *f*.

enlarge *vt* agrandir; étendre;
dilater.

enlargement *n* agrandissement
m; extension *f*; dilatation *f*.

enlighten *vt* éclairer.

enlightened *adj* éclairé.

Enlightenment *n*: the ~ le
Siècle des lumières *m*.

enlist *vt* recruter.

enlistment *n* recrutement *m*.

enliven *vt* animer; égayer.

enmity *n* inimitié *f*; haine *f*.

enormity *n* énormité *f*; atrocité *f*.

enormous *adj* énorme; ~ly *adv* énormément.

enough *adv* suffisamment; assez; * *n* assez *m*.

enounce *vt* déclarer.

enquire *vt* = inquire.

enrage *vt* rendre furieux.

enrapture *vt* enchanter, enthousiasmer.

enrich *vt* enrichir; orner.

enrichment *n* enrichissement *m*.

enrol *vt* enrôler; inscrire.

enrolment *n* inscription *f*.

en route *adv* en route.

ensign *n* (*mil*) drapeau *m*; porte-étendard *m*; (*mar*) pavillon *m*.

enslave *vt* asservir.

ensue *vi* s'ensuivre.

ensure *vt* assurer.

entail *vt* impliquer, entraîner.

entangle *vt* emmêler, embrouiller.

entanglement *n* emmêlement *m*.

enter *vt* entrer dans; inscrire; ~ for se présenter à; ~ into commencer; faire partie de.

enterprise *n* entreprise *f*.

enterprising *adj* entreprenant.

entertain *vt* divertir; recevoir; avoir.

entertainer *n* artiste *mf*.

entertaining *adj* divertissant, amusant.

entertainment *n* divertissement, passe-temps *m*.

enthralled *adj* captivé.

enthralling *adj* captivant.

enthrone *vt* introniser.

enthusiasm *n* enthousiasme *m*.

enthusiast *n* enthousiaste *mf*.

enthusiastic *adj* enthousiaste.

entice *vt* tenter; séduire.

entire *adj* entier, complet; parfait; ~ly *adv* entièrement.

entirety *n* intégralité *f*.

entitle *vt* intituler; conférer un droit à.

entitled *adj* intitulé; to be ~ to avoir le droit de.

entity *n* entité *f*.

entourage *n* entourage *m*.

entrails *npl* entrailles *fpl*.

entrance *n* entrée *f*; admission *f*.

entrance examination *n* examen d'entrée *m*.

entrance fee n droit d'inscription m.

entrance hall n vestibule m.

entrance ramp n bretelle d'accès f.

entrant n participant m -e f; candidat m -e f.

entrap vt piéger.

entreat vt implorer, supplier.

entreaty n supplication, prière f.

entrepreneur n entrepreneur m.

entrust vt confier.

entry n entrée f.

entry phone n interphone m.

entwine vt entrelacer.

enumerate vt énumérer.

enunciate vt énoncer.

enunciation n énonciation f.

envelop vt envelopper.

envelope n enveloppe f.

enviable adj enviable.

envious adj envieux; ~ly adv avec envie.

environment n environnement m.

environmental adj relatif à l'environnement.

environs npl environs mpl.

envisage vt envisager.

envoy n envoyé m -e f.

envy n envie f; * vt envier.

ephemeral adj éphémère.

epic adj épique; * n récit épique m.

epidemic adj épidémique; * n épidémie f.

epilepsy n épilepsie f.

epileptic adj épileptique.

epilogue n épilogue m.

Epiphany n Epiphanie f.

episcopacy n épiscopat m.

episcopal adj épiscopal.

episcopalian n épiscopalien m -ne f.

episode n épisode m.

epistle n épître f.

epistolary adj épistolaire.

epithet n épithète f.

epitome n modèle m; résumé m.

epitomize vt incarner; résumer.

epoch n époque f.

equable adj uniforme; ~bly adv uniformément.

equal adj égal; semblable; * n égal m -e f; * vt égaler.

equality n égalité f.

equalize vt égaliser.

equalizer n point égalisateur m.

equally adv également.

equanimity n équanimité f.

equate vt comparer; assimiler.

equation *n* équation *f*.

equator *n* équateur *m*.

equatorial *adj* équatorial.

equestrian *adj* équestre.

equilateral *adj* équilatéral.

equilibrium *n* équilibre *m*.

equinox *n* équinoxe *m*.

equip *vt* équiper.

equipment *n* équipement *m*.

equitable *adj* équitable, impartial; ~**ly** *adv* équitablement.

equity *n* équité, justice, impartialité *f*.

equivalent *adj n* équivalent *m*.

equivocal *adj* équivoque, ambigu; ~**ly** *adv* d'une manière équivoque.

equivocate *vt* équivoquer, user d'équivoques.

equivocation *n* faux-fuyants *mpl*.

era *n* ère *f*.

eradicate *vt* supprimer; extirper.

eradication *n* suppression *f*; extirpation *f*.

erase *vt* effacer; gommer.

eraser *n* gomme *f*.

erect *vt* ériger; élever; * *adj* droit, debout.

erection *n* érection *f*; structure *f*.

ermine *n* hermine *f*.

erode *vt* éroder; ronger.

erotic *adj* érotique.

err *vi* se tromper.

errand *n* message *m*; commission *f*.

errand boy *n* garçon de courses, messager *m*.

errata *npl* errata *m*.

erratic *adj* changeant; irrégulier.

erroneous *adj* erroné, faux; ~**ly** *adv* erronément, faussement.

error *n* erreur *f*.

erudite *adj* érudit.

erudition *n* érudition *f*.

erupt *vi* entrer en éruption; faire éruption.

eruption *n* éruption *f*.

escalate *vi* monter en flèche; s'intensifier.

escalation *n* montée en flèche *f*; intensification *f*.

escalator *n* escalier roulant *m*.

escapade *n* fredaine *f*.

escape *vt* éviter; échapper à; * *vi* s'évader, s'échapper; * *n* évasion, fuite *f*; **to make one's ~** prendre la fuite.

escapism *n* évasion de la réalité *f*.

eschew *vt* fuir; éviter.

escort *n* escorte *f*; * *vt* escorter.

esoteric *adj* ésotérique.

especial *adj* spécial; ~ly *adv* spécialement.

espionage *n* espionnage *m*.

esplanade *n* (*mil*) esplanade *f*.

espouse *vt* épouser.

essay *n* essai *m*.

essence *n* essence *f*.

essential *n* essentiel *m*; * *adj* essentiel, principal; ~ly *adv* essentiellement.

establish *vt* établir; fonder; démontrer.

establishment *n* établissement *m*; fondation *f*; institution *f*.

estate *n* état *m*; domaine *m*; biens *mpl*.

esteem *vt* estimer; apprécier; * *n* estime *f*; considération *f*.

esthetic *adj* (US) esthétique; ~s *npl* esthétique *f*.

estimate *vt* estimer; évaluer.

estimation *n* estimation, évaluation *f*; opinion *f*.

estrange *vt* éloigner, séparer.

estranged *adj* séparé.

estrangement *n* séparation *f*; distance *f*.

estuary *n* estuaire *m*.

etch *vt* graver à l'eau forte.

etching *n* gravure à l'eau forte *f*.

eternal *adj* éternel, perpétuel; ~ly *adv* éternellement.

eternity *n* éternité *f*.

ether *n* éther *m*.

ethical *adj* éthique, moral; ~ly *adv* éthiquement.

ethics *npl* éthique *f*.

ethnic *adj* ethnique.

ethos *n* génie *m*, esprit *m*.

etiquette *n* étiquette *f*.

etymological *adj* étymologique.

etymologist *n* étymologiste *mf*.

etymology *n* étymologie *f*.

Eucharist *n* Eucharistie *f*.

eulogy *n* éloge *m*.

eunuch *n* eunuque *m*.

euphemism *n* euphémisme *m*.

evacuate *vt* évacuer.

evacuation *n* évacuation *f*.

evade *vt* éviter; échapper à.

evaluate *vt* évaluer.

evangelic(al) *adj* évangélique.

evangelist *n* évangéliste *m*.

evaporate *vt* faire évaporer; * *vi* s'évaporer; se volatiliser.

evaporated milk *n* lait condensé *m*.

evaporation n évaporation f.

evasion n dérobade f.

evasive adj évasif; ~ly adv évasivement.

eve n veille f.

even adj égal; uni; pair; * adv même; encore; * vt égaliser; unir; * vi: ~ out s'égaliser.

even-handed adj impartial, équitable.

evening n soir m, soirée f.

evening class n cours du soir m.

evening dress n robe du soir f; tenue de soirée f.

evenly adv également; uniment.

evenness n égalité f; uniformité f; régularité f; impartialité f.

event n événement m; épreuve f.

eventful adj mouvementé.

eventual adj final ~ly adv finalement, en fin de comptes.

eventuality n éventualité f.

ever adv toujours; jamais; déjà; for ~ and ~ pour toujours; ~ since depuis.

evergreen adj à feuilles persistantes; * n arbre à feuilles persistantes m.

everlasting adj éternel.

evermore adv toujours.

every adj chacun, chacune; ~ where partout; ~ thing tout; ~ one, ~ body tout le monde.

evict vt expulser.

eviction n expulsion f.

evidence n évidence f; témoignage m; preuve f; * vt témoigner de.

evident adj évident; manifeste; ~ly adv manifestement, de toute évidence.

evil adj mauvais; malveillant; * n mal m.

evil-minded adj malintentionné.

evocative adj évocateur.

evoke vt évoquer.

evolution n évolution f.

evolve vt développer; * vi se développer, évoluer.

ewe n brebis f.

exacerbate vt exacerber.

exact adj exact; * vt exiger.

exacting adj exigeant.

exaction n exaction f; extorsion f.

exactly adv exactement.

exactness, exactitude n exactitude f.

exaggerate *vt* exagérer.

exaggeration *n* exagération *f*.

exalt *vt* exalter; élever.

exaltation *n* exaltation *f*; élévation *f*.

exalted *adj* exalté; élevé.

examination *n* examen *m*.

examine *vt* examiner.

examiner *n* examinateur *m* -trice *f*.

example *n* exemple *m*.

exasperate *vt* exaspérer, irriter.

exasperation *n* exaspération, irritation *f*.

excavate *vt* exhumer, creuser.

excavation *n* excavation *f*.

exceed *vt* excéder, dépasser.

exceedingly *adv* trop; extrêmement.

excel *vt* surpasser; *vi* exceller.

excellence *n* excellence *f*; supériorité *f*.

Excellency *n* Excellence (titre) *f*.

excellent *adj* excellent; ~ly *adv* excellemment, admirablement.

except *vt* excepter, exclure; ~(ing) *prep* excepté, à l'exception de.

exception *n* exception *f*.

exceptional *adj* exceptionnel.

excerpt *n* extrait *m*.

excess *n* excès *m*.

excessive *adj* excessif; ~ly *adv* excessivement.

exchange *vt* échanger; permuter; * *n* échange *m*; change *m*.

exchange rate *n* taux de change *m*.

excise *n* taxe *f*.

excitability *n* excitabilité *f*.

excitable *adj* excitable.

excite *vt* exciter; animer; enthousiasmer; stimuler.

excited *adj* animé, enthousiaste; excité.

excitement *n* animation *f*, enthousiasme *m*.

exciting *adj* passionnant; stimulant.

exclaim *vi* s'exclamer.

exclamation *n* exclamation *f*.

exclamation mark *n* point d'exclamation *m*.

exclamatory *adj* exclamatif.

exclude *vt* exclure.

exclusion *n* exclusion *f*; exception *f*.

exclusive *adj* exclusif; ~ly *adv* exclusivement.

excommunicate *vt* excommunier.

excommunication *n* excommunion *f*.

excrement *n* excrément *m*.

excruciating *adj* atroce, horrible.

exculpate *vt* disculper; justifier.

excursion *n* excursion *f*; digression *f*.

excusable *adj* excusable.

excuse *vt* excuser; pardonner; * *n* excuse *f*.

execute *vt* exécuter.

execution *n* exécution *f*.

executioner *n* bourreau *m*.

executive *adj* exécutif.

executor *n* exécuteur testamentaire *m*.

exemplary *adj* exemplaire.

exemplify *vt* exemplifier.

exempt *adj* exempt.

exemption *n* exemption *f*.

exercise *n* exercice *m*; * *vi* prendre de l'exercice; * *vt* exercer; montrer.

exercise book *n* cahier *m*.

exert *vt* employer, exercer; ~ o.s. s'efforcer.

exertion *n* effort *m*.

exhale *vt* exhaler; expirer.

exhaust *n* échappement *m*; * *vt* épuiser.

exhausted *adj* épuisé.

exhaustion *n* épuisement *m*.

exhaustive *adj* exhaustif, complet.

exhibit *vt* exhiber; montrer; * *n* (*law*) pièce à conviction *f*.

exhibition *n* exposition, présentation *f*.

exhilarating *adj* stimulant, grisant.

e.hilaration *n* joie *f* intense.

exhort *vt* exhorter.

exhortation *n* exhortation *f*.

exhume *vt* exhumer, déterrer.

exile *n* exil *m*; * *vt* exiler, déporter.

exist *vi* exister.

existence *n* existence *f*.

existent *adj* existant.

existing *adj* actuel, présent.

exit *n* sortie *f*; * *vi* sortir.

exit ramp *n* bretelle d'accès *f*.

exodus *n* exode *m*.

exonerate *vt* disculper; décharger.

exoneration *n* disculpation *f*; décharge *f*.

exorbitant *adj* exorbitant, excessif.

exorcise *vt* exorciser.

exorcism *n* exorcisme *m*.

exotic *adj* exotique.

expand *vt* étendre; dilater.

expanse *n* étendue *f*.

expansion *n* expansion *f*.

expansive *adj* expansif.

expatriate *vt* expatrier.

expect *vt* attendre; espérer; penser.

expectance, expectancy *n* attente *f*; espoir *m*.

expectant *adj* d'attente.

expectant mother *n* femme enceinte *f*.

expectation *n* expectative *f*; attente *f*.

expediency *n* convenance *f*; opportunité *f*.

expedient *adj* opportun; * *n* expédient *m*; ~ly *adv* de manière opportune.

expedite *vt* accélérer; expédier.

expedition *n* expédition *f*.

expeditious *adj* expéditif; ~ly *adv* de manière expéditive.

expel *vt* expulser.

expend *vt* dépenser; utiliser.

expendable *adj* jetable; consommable.

expenditure *n* dépense *f*.

expense *n* dépense *f*; coût *m*.

expense account *n* frais *mpl* de représentation.

expensive *adj* cher; coûteux; ~ly *adv* de manière coûteuse.

experience *n* expérience *f*; pratique *f*; * *vt* ressentir, éprouver; connaître.

experienced *adj* expérimenté.

experiment *n* expérience *f*; * *vi* expérimenter.

experimental *adj* expérimental; ~ly *adv* expérimentalement.

expert *adj* expert.

expertise *n* compétences *fpl*.

expiration *n* expiration *f*.

expire *vi* expirer.

explain *vt* expliquer.

explanation *n* explication *f*.

explanatory *adj* explicatif.

expletive *adj* explétif.

explicable *adj* explicable.

explicit *adj* explicite; ~ly *adv* explicitement.

explode *vt* faire exploser; *vi* exploser.

exploit *vt* exploiter; * *n* exploit *m*.

exploitation *n* exploitation *f*.

exploration *n* exploration *f*.

exploratory *adj* exploratoire.

explore *vt* explorer, examiner; sonder.

explorer *n* explorateur *m* -trice *f*.

explosion n explosion f.

explosive adj n explosif m.

exponent n (math) exposant m.

export vt exporter.

export, exportation n exportation f.

exporter n exportateur m -trice f.

expose vt exposer; dévoiler.

exposed adj exposé.

exposition n exposition f; interprétation f.

expostulate vi faire des remonstrances.

exposure n exposition f; temps de pose m; cliché m.

exposure meter n photomètre m.

expound vt exposer; interpréter.

express vt exprimer; * adj exprès; * n exprès m; (rail) rapide m.

expression n expression f; locution f.

expressionless adj inexpressif.

expressive adj expressif; ~ly adv d'une manière expressive.

expressly adv expressément.

expressway n autoroute f.

expropriate vt exproprier.

expropriation n (law) expropriation f.

expulsion n expulsion f.

expurgate vt expurger.

exquisite adj exquis; ~ly adv exquisément.

extant adj existant.

extempore adv à l'improviste.

extemporize vi improviser.

extend vt étendre; élargir; * vi s'étendre.

extension n extension f.

extensive adj étendu; important; ~ly adv considérablement.

extent n extension f.

extenuate vt atténuer.

extenuating adj atténuant.

exterior adj n extérieur m.

exterminate vt exterminer; supprimer.

extermination n extermination f; suppression f.

external adj externe; ~ly adv extérieurement; ~s npl apparence f.

extinct adj disparu; éteint.

extinction n extinction f.

extinguish vt éteindre; supprimer.

extinguisher n extincteur m.

extirpate vt extirper.

extol *vt* louer, exalter.

extort *vt* extorquer; arracher.

extortion *n* extorsion *f*.

extortionate *adj* exorbitant.

extra *adv* particulièrement; *n* supplément *m*.

extract *vt* extraire; * *n* extrait *m*.

extraction *n* extraction *f*; origine *f*.

extracurricular *adj* périscolaire.

extradite *vt* extrader.

extradition *n* (*law*) extradition *f*.

extramarital *adj* extérieur au mariage.

extramural *adj* extra-muros.

extraneous *adj* superflu; sans rapport.

extraordinarily *adv* extraordinairement.

extraordinary *adj* extraordinaire.

extravagance *n* extravagance *f*; gaspillage *m*.

extravagant *adj* extravagant; exorbitant; gaspilleur; ~ly *adv* de manière extravagante; en gaspillant.

extreme *adj* extrême; suprême; ultime; * *n* extrême *m*; ~ly *adv* extrêmement.

extremist *adj n* extrémiste *mf*.

extremity *n* extrémité *f*.

extricate *vt* extirper, démêler.

extrinsic(al) *adj* extrinsèque.

extrovert *adj n* extraverti *m* -e *f*.

exuberance *n* exubérance *f*.

exuberant *adj* exubérant; ~ly *adv* avec exubérance.

exude *vi* exsuder.

exult *vi* exulter, triompher.

exultation *n* exultation *f*.

eye *n* œil *m*; * *vt* regarder, observer; lorgner.

eyeball *n* globe oculaire *m*.

eyebrow *n* sourcil *m*.

eyelash *n* cil *m*.

eyelid *n* paupière *f*.

eyesight *n* vue *f*.

eyesore *n* monstruosité *f*.

eyetooth *n* canine *f*.

eyewitness *n* témoin oculaire *m*.

eyrie *n* aire *f*, nid *m* d'aigle.

F

fable *n* fable *f*; légende *f*.

fabric *n* tissu *m*.

fabricate *vt* fabriquer; inventer.

fabrication *n* fabrication *f*; invention *f*.

fabulous *adj* fabuleux; ~ly *adv* fabuleusement.

facade *n* façade *f*.

face *n* visage *m*, figure *f*; surface *f*; façade *f*; mine *f*; apparence *f*; * *vt* faire face à; affronter; ~ **up to** faire face à.

face cream *n* crème pour le visage *f*.

face-lift *n* lifting *m*.

face powder *n* poudre de riz *f*.

facet *n* facette *f*.

facetious *adj* facétieux, plaisant, spirituel; ~ly *adv* facétieusement.

face value *n* valeur nominale *f*.

facial *adj* facial.

facile *adj* facile; superficiel.

facilitate *vt* faciliter.

facility *n* facilité *f*; équipement *m*, infrastructure *f*.

facing *n* revers *m*; * *prep* en face de.

facsimile *n* fac-similé *m*.

fact *n* fait *m*; réalité *f*; in ~ en fait.

faction *n* faction *f*; dissension *f*.

factor *n* facteur *m*.

factory *n* usine *f*.

factual *adj* factuel, basé sur les faits.

faculty *n* faculté *f*; le corps enseignant *m*.

fad *n* engouement *m*.

fade *vi* se faner; perdre son éclat.

fail *vt* échouer à; omettre; manquer à ses engagements envers; * *vi* échouer; faiblir; manquer.

failing *n* défaut *m*.

failure *n* échec *m*; panne *f*;

raté *m*; faillite *f*; manque*··* *n*t *m*.

faint *vi* s'évanouir, défaillir; * *n* évanouissement *m*; * *adj* faible; ~**ly** *adv* faiblement.

fainthearted *adj* timide, timoré, pusillanime.

faintness *n* faiblesse *f*; légèreté *f*.

fair *adj* beau; blond; clair; favorable; juste, équitable; considérable; passable; * *adv* loyalement; * *n* foire *f*.

fairly *adv* équitablement; absolument.

fairness *n* beauté *f*; justice *f*.

fair play *n* fair-play, franc-jeu *m*.

fairy *n* fée *f*.

fairy tale *n* conte de fées *m*.

faith *n* foi *f*; croyance *f*; fidélité *f*.

faithful *adj* fidèle, loyal; ~**ly** *adv* fidèlement.

faithfulness *n* fidélité, loyauté *f*.

fake *n* falsification *f*; imposteur *m*; * *adj* faux; * *vt* feindre; falsifier.

falcon *n* faucon *m*.

falconry *n* fauconnerie *f*.

fall *vi* tomber; s'effondrer; diminuer, baisser; ~ **asleep** s'endormir; ~ **back** reculer; ~ **back on** avoir recours à; ~ **behind** être à la traîne; ~ **down** tomber; ~ **for** se faire avoir; tomber amoureux de; ~ **in** s'effondrer; ~ **short** échouer; ~ **sick** tomber malade; ~ **in love** tomber amoureux; ~ **off** tomber; diminuer; ~ **out** se produire; se quereller; * *n* chute *f*; automne *m*.

fallacious *adj* fallacieux, trompeur; ~**ly** *adv* d'une manière fallacieuse.

fallacy *n* erreur *f*; sophisme *m*; tromperie *f*.

fallibility *n* faillibilité *f*.

fallible *adj* faillible.

fallout *n* retombées *fpl*.

fallout shelter *n* abri antiatomique *m*.

fallow *adj* en jachère; ~ **deer** *n* daim *m*.

false *adj* faux; ~**ly** *adv* faussement.

false alarm *n* fausse alerte *f*.

falsehood, falseness *n* mensonge *m*; fausseté *f*.

falsify *vt* falsifier.

falsity *n* fausseté *f*.

falter *vi* vaciller; faiblir.

faltering *adj* chancelant.

fame *n* réputation *f*; renommée, notoriété *f*.

famed *adj* célèbre.

familiar *adj* familier; domestique; ~ly *adv* familièrement.

familiarity *n* familiarité *f*.

familiarize *vt* familiariser.

family *n* famille *f*.

family business *n* affaire de famille *f*.

family doctor *n* médecin de famille *m*.

famine *n* famine *f*; disette *f*.

famished *adj* affamé.

famous *adj* célèbre, fameux; ~ly *adv* fameusement.

fan *n* éventail *m*; ventilateur *m*; jeune admirateur *m* -trice *f*; * *vt* éventer; attiser.

fanatic *adj n* fanatique *mf*.

fanaticism *n* fanatisme *m*.

fan belt *n* courroie de ventilateur *f*.

fanciful *adj* fantasque, capricieux; ~ly *adv* capricieusement.

fancy *n* fantaisie, imagination *f*; caprice *m*; * *vt* avoir envie de; s'imaginer.

fancydress ball *n* bal masqué *m*.

fancy goods *npl* nouveautés *fpl*.

fanfare *n* (*mus*) fanfare *f*.

fang *n* croc *m*.

fantastic *adj* fantastique; excentrique; ~ally *adv* fantastiquement.

fantasy *n* imagination *f*.

far *adv* loin; * *adj* lointain, éloigné; ~ and away de très loin; ~ off lointain.

faraway *adj* lointain.

farce *n* farce *f*.

farcical *adj* grotèsque.

fare *n* prix (du voyage) *m*; tarif *m*; nourriture *f*; voyageur *m* -euse *f*; client *m* -e *f*.

farewell *n* adieu *m*; ~! *excl* adieu!

farm *n* ferme *f*, exploitation agricole *f*; * *vt* cultiver.

farmer *n* fermier *m*; agriculteur *m*.

farmhand *n* ouvrier agricole *m*.

farmhouse *n* ferme *f*.

farming *n* agriculture *f*.

farmland *n* terres arables *fpl*.

farmyard *n* cour de ferme *f*.

far-reaching *adj* d'une grande portée, considérable.

fart n (sl) pet; * vi péter.

farther adv plus loin; * adj plus éloigné.

farthest adv le plus lointain; le plus loin; au plus.

fascinate vt fasciner, captiver.

fascinating adj fascinant.

fascination n fascination f; charme m.

fascism n fascisme.

fashion n manière, façon f; forme f; coutume f; mode f; style m; **people of ~** personnes élégantes fpl; * vt façonner, confectionner.

fashionable adj à la mode; chic; **the ~ world** le beau monde; **~bly** adv à la mode.

fashion show n défilé de mode m.

fast vi jeûner; * n jeûne m; * adj rapide; ferme, stable; * adv rapidement; fermement; solidement.

fasten vt attacher; fixer; attribuer; * vi se fixer, s'attacher.

fastener, fastening n attache f; fermoir m.

fast food n restauration rapide f.

fastidious adj minutieux, méticuleux; **~ly** adv minutieusement.

fat adj gros, gras; * n graisse f.

fatal adj mortel; néfaste; **~ly** adv mortellement.

fatalism n fatalisme m.

fatalist n fataliste mf.

fatality n accident mortel m, fatalité f.

fate n destin, sort m.

fateful adj fatidique.

father n père m.

fatherhood n paternité f.

father-in-law n beau-père m.

fatherland n patrie f.

fatherly adj (adv) paternel(lement).

fathom n brasse (mesure) f; * vt sonder; pénétrer.

fatigue n fatigue f; * vt fatiguer, lasser.

fatten vt vi engraisser.

fatty adj gras, graisseux.

fatuous adj imbécile, stupide, niais.

faucet n (US) robinet m.

fault n défaut m, faute f; délit m; faille f.

faultfinder n chicaneur m -euse f.

faultless adj irréprochable.

faulty adj défectueux.

fauna n faune f.

faux pas n impair m.

favour n faveur f; approbation f; avantage m; * vt favoriser, préférer.

favourable adj favorable, propice; ~**bly** adv favorablement.

favoured adj favorisé.

favourite n favori m; * adj favori.

favouritism n favoritisme m.

fawn n faon m; * vi flatter servilement.

fawningly adv d'une flatterie servile.

fax n télécopieur, fax m; télécopie f, fax m; * vt envoyer par fax, télécopier.

fear vt craindre; * n crainte f.

fearful adj effrayant; craintif, peureux; ~**ly** adv terriblement; craintivement.

fearless adj intrépide, courageux; ~**ly** adv courageusement.

fearlessness n intrépidité f.

feasibility n faisabilité f.

feasible adj faisable, réalisable.

feast n festin, banquet m; fête f; * vi banqueter.

feat n exploit m; prouesse f.

feather n plume f;.

feather bed n lit de plumes m.

feature n caractéristique f; trait m; * vi figurer.

feature film n long métrage m.

February n février m.

federal adj fédéral.

federalist n fédéraliste mf.

federate vt fédérer; * vi se fédérer.

federation n fédération f.

fed-up adj: to be ~ en avoir marre.

fee n honoraires mpl; frais mpl.

feeble adj faible, frêle.

feebleness n faiblesse f.

feebly adv faiblement.

feed vt nourrir; alimenter; ~ **on** se nourrir de; * vi manger; se nourrir; * n nourriture f; alimentation f.

feedback n réaction f, répercussion f.

feel vt sentir; toucher; croire; ~ **around** tâtonner, fouiller; * n sensation f; toucher m.

feeler n antenne f; (fig) tentative f.

feeling n sensation f; sentiment m.

feelingly *adv* avec émotion.

feign *vt* inventer; feindre, simuler.

feline *adj* félin.

fellow *n* homme, type *m*; membre *m*.

fellow citizen *n* concitoyen *m* -enne *f*.

fellow countryman *n* compatriote *m*.

fellow feeling *n* sympathie *f*.

fellow men *npl* semblables *mpl*.

fellowship *n* camaraderie *f*; association *f*.

fellow student *n* copain (copine) de fac *m(f)*.

fellow traveller *n* compagnon (compagne) de voyage *m(f)*.

felon *n* criminel *m* -le *f*.

felony *n* crime *m*.

felt *n* feutre *m*.

felt-tip pen *n* feutre *m*.

female *n* femelle *f*; * *adj* de sexe féminin, femelle.

feminine *adj* féminin.

feminist *n* féministe *mf*.

fen *n* marais *m*.

fence *n* barrière *f*; clôture *f*; * *vt* clôturer; * *vi* faire de l'escrime.

fencing *n* escrime *f*.

fender *n* pare-chocs *m invar*.

fennel *n* (*bot*) fenouil *m*.

ferment *n* agitation *f*; * *vi* fermenter.

fern *n* (*bot*) fougère *f*.

ferocious *adj* féroce; ~ly *adv* férocement.

ferocity *n* férocité *f*.

ferret *n* furet *m*; * *vt* fureter; ~ out découvrir, dénicher.

ferry *n* bac *m*; ferry *m*; * *vt* transporter.

fertile *adj* fertile, fécond.

fertility *n* fertilité, fécondité *f*.

fertilize *vt* fertiliser.

fertilizer *n* engrais *m*.

fervent *adj* fervent; ardent; ~ly *adv* avec ferveur.

fervid *adj* ardent, véhément.

fervour *n* ferveur, ardeur *f*.

fester *vi* suppurer; s'envenimer.

festival *n* fête *f*; festival *m*

festive *adj* de fête.

festivity *n* fête *f*, réjouissances *fpl*.

fetch *vt* aller chercher.

fetching *adj* charmant, séduisant.

fête *n* fête *f*.

fetid *adj* fétide, nauséabond.

fetus *n* fœtus *m*.

feud *n* rivalité *f*, dissension *f*.
feudal *adj* féodal.
feudalism *n* féodalité *f*.
fever *n* fièvre *f*.
feverish *adj* fiévreux.
few *adj* peu; a ~ quelques; ~ and far between rares.
fewer *adj* moins (de); * *adv* moins.
fewest *adj* le moins (de).
fiancé *n* fiancé *m*.
fiancée *n* fiancée *f*.
fib *n* bobard *m*; * *vi* raconter des bobards.
fibre *n* fibre *f*.
fibreglass *n* fibre de verre *f*.
fickle *adj* volage, inconstant.
fiction *n* fiction *f*; invention *f*.
fictional *adj* fictif.
fictitious *adj* fictif, imaginaire; feint; ~ly *adv* fictivement.
fiddle *n* violon *m*; combine *f*; * *vi* jouer du violon.
fiddler *n* violoneux *m*.
fidelity *n* fidélité, loyauté *f*.
fidget *vi* s'agiter, s'impatienter.
fidgety *adj* agité, remuant.
field *n* champ *m*; étendue *f*; domaine *m*.
field day *n* (*mil*) jour de grandes manœuvres *m*.
fieldmouse *n* mulot *m*.

fieldwork *n* recherches sur le terrain *fpl*.
fiend *n* démon *m*; mordu *m*.
fiendish *adj* diabolique.
fierce *adj* féroce, violent; acharné, furieux; ~ly *adv* férocement.
fierceness *n* férocité, fureur *f*.
fiery *adj* ardent; fougueux.
fifteen *adj n* quinze *m*.
fifteenth *adj n* quinzième *mf*.
fifth *adj n* cinquième *mf*; ~ly *adv* cinquièmement.
fiftieth *adj n* cinquantième *mf*.
fifty *adj n* cinquante *m*.
fig *n* figue *f*.
fight *vt vi* se battre (contre); combattre; lutter; * *n* bataille *f*; combat *m*; lutte *f*.
fighter *n* combattant *m*; lutteur *m*; chasseur *m*.
fighting *n* combat *m*.
fig-leaf *n* feuille de figuier *f*.
fig tree *n* figuier *m*.
figurative *adj* figuratif; ~ly *adv* figurativement.
figure *n* figure *f*; forme, silhouette *f*; image *f*; chiffre *m*; * *vi* figurer; avoir du sens; ~ out comprendre.
figurehead *n* figure de proue *f*.

filament n filament m; fibre f.

filch vt chiper.

filcher n voleur m -euse f.

file n file f; liste f; (mil) colonne, rangée f; lime f; dossier m; fichier m; * vt enregistrer; limer; classer; déposer; * vi ~ in/out entrer/sortir en file; ~ past défiler devant.

filing cabinet n classeur (meuble) m.

fill vt remplir; ~ in remplir; ~ up remplir (jusqu'au bord).

fillet n filet m.

fillet steak n filet de bœuf m.

filling station n station-service f.

fillip n (fig) coup de fouet m.

filly n pouliche f.

film n pellicule f; film m; cellophane m; * vt filmer; * vi s'embuer.

film star n vedette de cinéma f.

filmstrip n film m.

filter n filtre m; * vt filtrer.

filter-tipped adj à bout filtre.

filth(iness) n immondice, ordure f; saleté, crasse f.

filthy adj crasseux, dégoûtant.

fin n nageoire f.

final adj dernier; définitif; ~ly adv finalement.

finale n finale m.

finalist n finaliste mf.

finalize vt parachever, rendre définitif.

finance n finance f.

financial adj financier.

financier n financier m.

find vt trouver, découvrir; ~ out découvrir; démasquer; ~ o.s. se retrouver; * n trouvaille f.

findings npl résultats mpl, conclusions fpl; verdict m.

fine adj fin; pur; aigu; raffiné; beau, f belle; délicat; subtil; élégant; * n amende f; * vt infliger une amende à.

fine arts npl beaux arts mpl.

finely adv magnifiquement.

finery n parure f.

finesse n finesse, subtilité f.

finger n doigt m; * vt toucher, manier.

fingernail n ongle m.

fingerprint n empreinte digitale f.

fingertip n bout du doigt m.

finicky adj pointilleux, difficile.

finish vt finir, terminer,

achever; ~ **off** finir; ~ **up** terminer; * *vi*: ~ **up** se retrouver.

finishing line *n* ligne d'arrivée *f*.

finishing school *n* école privée (pour jeunes filles) *f*.

finite *adj* fini.

fir *n* sapin *m*

fire *n* feu *m*; incendie *m*; * *vt* mettre le feu à; incendier; tirer; * *vi* s'enflammer, faire feu.

fire alarm *n* alarme d'incendie *f*.

firearm *n* arme à feu *f*.

fireball *n* boule de feu *f*.

fire department *n* pompiers *mpl*.

fire engine *n* voiture de pompiers *f*.

fire escape *n* escalier de secours *m*.

fire extinguisher *n* extincteur *m*.

firefly *n* luciole *f*.

fireman *n* pompier *m*.

fireplace *n* cheminée *f*, foyer *m*.

fireproof *adj* ignifugé.

fireside *n* coin du feu *m*.

fire station *n* caserne de pompiers *f*.

firewater *n* eau de vie *f*.

firewood *n* bois de chauffage *m*.

fireworks *npl* feu d'artifice *m*.

firing *n* fusillade *f*.

firing squad *n* peloton d'exécution *m*.

firm *adj* ferme, solide; constant; * *n* (*com*) compagnie *f*; ~**ly** *adv* fermement.

firmament *n* firmament *m*.

firmness *n* fermeté *f*; résolution *f*.

first *adj* premier; * *adv* premièrement; at ~ d'abord; ~**ly** *adv* en premier lieu.

first aid *n* premiers secours *mpl*.

first-aid kit *n* trousse de premiers secours *f*.

first-class *adj* de première classe, de première catégorie.

first-hand *adj* de première main.

First Lady *n* (US) première dame, femme du président d'un pays *f*.

first name *n* prénom *m*.

first-rate *adj* de première qualité.

fiscal *adj* fiscal.

fish *n* poisson *m*; * *vi* pêcher.

fishbone *n* arête *f*.

fisherman *n* pêcheur *m*.

fish farm n entreprise de pisciculture f.

fishing n pêche f.

fishing line n ligne de pêche f.

fishing rod n canne à pêche f.

fishing tackle n attirail de pêche m.

fish market n marché au poisson m.

fishseller n poissonnier m -ière f.

fishstore n poissonnerie f.

fishy adj (fig) suspect.

fissure n fissure, crevasse f.

fist n poing m.

fit n accès m, attaque f; crise f; * adj en forme; capable; adapté à, qui convient; * vt aller à; ajuster, adapter; ~ out équiper; * vi (bien) aller; ~ in s'accorder avec; être en harmonie avec.

fitment n meuble encastré m.

fitness n forme physique f; aptitude f.

fitted carpet n moquette f.

fitted kitchen n cuisine encastrée f.

fitter n monteur m.

fitting adj qui convient, approprié, juste; * n accessoire m; ~s pl installations fpl.

five adj n cinq m.

five spot n (sl) (US) billet m de cinq dollars.

fix vt fixer, établir; ~ up arranger.

fixation n obsession f.

fixed adj fixe.

fixings npl garniture f; accessoires mpl.

fixture n (sport) rencontre f.

fizz vi pétiller.

fizzy adj gazeux.

flabbergasted adj abasourdi.

flabby adj mou, f molle, flasque.

flaccid adj flasque, mou, f molle.

flag n drapeau m; (bot) iris m; * vi s'affaiblir.

flagpole n mât m de drapeau.

flagrant adj flagrant.

flagship n vaisseau amiral m.

flagstop n (US) arrêt m facultatif.

flair n flair m; talent m.

flak n tir antiaérien m; critiques fpl.

flake n flocon m; paillette f; * vi s'effriter, s'écailler.

flaky adj floconneux; friable.

flamboyant adj flamboyant; ostentatoire.

flame n flamme f; ardeur f.

flamingo n flamant m.

flammable adj inflammable.

flank n flanc m; (also mil); * vt flanquer.

flannel n flanelle f.

flap n battement m; rabat m; * vt vi battre.

flare vi luire, briller; ~ up s'embraser; se mettre en colère; éclater; * n flamme f.

flash n éclat m; éclair m; * vt faire briller; allumer.

flashbulb n ampoule de flash f.

flash cube n cube de flash m.

flashlight n lampe f de poche.

flashy adj tape-à-l'œil, voyant.

flask n flasque f; flacon m.

flat adj plat; uniforme; insipide; * n plaine f; plat m; (mus) bémol m; ~ly adv h o r i z o n t a l e m e n t ; platement; également; catégoriquement.

flatness n égalité f; monotonie f.

flatten vt aplanir; aplatir.

flatter vt flatter.

flattering adj flatteur.

flattery n flatterie f.

flatulence n (med) flatulence f.

flaunt vt étaler, afficher.

flavour n saveur m; * vt parfumer; assaisonner.

flavoured adj savoureux; parfumé.

flavourless adj insipide.

flaw n défaut m; imperfection f.

flawless adj parfait.

flax n lin m.

flea n puce f.

flea bite n piqûre de puce f.

fleck n petite tache f; particule f.

flee vt fuir de; * vi s'enfuir; fuir.

fleece n toison f; * vt (sl) tondre.

fleet n flotte f; (autos) parc m.

fleeting adj fugace, fugitif.

flesh n chair f.

flesh wound n blessure superficielle f.

fleshy adj charnu.

flex n cordon m; * vt fléchir.

flexibility n flexibilité f.

flexible adj flexible, souple.

flick n petit coup m; * vt donner un petit coup à.

flicker vt vaciller; trembloter.

flier n aviateur m -trice f.

flight n vol m; fuite f; volée f; (fig) envolée f.

flight attendant *n* steward *m*, hôtesse de l'air *f*.

flight deck *n* cabine de pilotage *f*.

flimsy *adj* léger; fragile.

flinch *vi* sourciller.

fling *vt* lancer, jeter.

flint *n* silex *m*.

flip *vt* lancer.

flippant *adj* désinvolte, cavalier.

flipper *n* nageoire *f*.

flirt *vi* flirter; * *n* charmeur *m* -euse *f*.

flirtation *n* flirt *f*.

flit *vi* voler, voleter.

float *vt* faire flotter; lancer; * *vi* flotter; * *n* flotteur *m*; char (de carnaval) *m*; provision *f*.

flock *n* troupeau *m*; volée *f*; foule *f*; * *vi* affluer.

flog *vt* fustiger.

flogging *n* fustigation, flagellation *f*.

flood *n* inondation *f*; marée haute *f*; déluge *m*; * *vt* inonder.

flooding *n* inondation *f*.

floodlight *n* projecteur *m*.

floor *n* sol *m*; plancher *m*; étage *m*; * *vt* parqueter; déconcerter.

floorboard *n* planche *f*.

floor lamp *n* lampadaire *m*.

floor show *n* spectacle de cabaret *m*.

flop *n* four, fiasco *m*.

floppy *adj* lâche; * *n* disquette *f*.

flora *n* flore *f*.

floral *adj* floral.

florescence *n* floraison *f*.

florid *adj* fleuri.

florist *n* fleuriste *mf*.

florist's (shop) *n* boutique de fleuriste *f*.

flotilla *n* (*mar*) flotille *f*.

flounder *n* flet *m*; * *vi* patauger.

flour *n* farine *f*.

flourish *vi* fleurir; prospérer; * *n* fioriture *f*; (*mus*) fioriture *f*.

flourishing *adj* florissant.

flout *vt* mépriser, se moquer de.

flow *vi* couler; circuler; monter (marée); ondoyer; * *n* flux *m*; écoulement *m*; flot *m*.

flow chart *n* organigramme *m*.

flower *n* fleur *f*; * *vi* fleurir.

flowerbed *n* parterre de fleurs *m*.

flowerpot *n* pot de fleurs *m*.

flowery *adj* fleuri.

flower show *n* exposition de fleurs *f*.

fluctuate *vi* fluctuer.

fluctuation *n* fluctuation *f*.

fluency *n* aisance *f*.

fluent *adj* coulant; facile; ~ly *adv* couramment.

fluff *n* peluche *f*; ~y *adj* duveteux.

fluid *adj n* fluide *m*.

fluidity *n* fluidité *f*.

fluke *n* (*sl*) veine *f*.

fluoride *n* fluorure *m*.

flurry *n* rafale *f*; agitation *f*.

flush *vt*: to ~ out nettoyer à grande eau; * *vi* rougir; * *n* rougeur *f*; éclat *m*.

flushed *adj* rouge.

fluster *vt* énerver.

flustered *adj* énervé.

flute *n* flûte *f*.

flutter *vi* voleter; s'agiter; * *n* agitation *f*; émoi *m*.

flux *n* flux *m*.

fly *vt* piloter; transporter par avion; * *vi* voler; fuir; ~ away/off s'envoler; * *n* mouche *f*; braguette *f*.

flying *n* aviation *f*.

flying saucer *n* soucoupe volante *f*.

flypast *n* défilé aérien *m*.

flysheet *n* feuille volante *f*.

foal *n* poulain *m*.

foam *n* écume *f*; * *vi* écumer.

foam rubber *n* caoutchouc mousse *m*.

foamy *adj* écumeux.

focus *n* foyer *m*; centre *m*.

fodder *n* fourrage *m*.

foe *n* ennemi *m* -e *f*, adversaire *mf*.

fog *n* brouillard *m*.

foggy *adj* brumeux.

fog light *n* feu de brouillard *m*.

foible *n* point faible *m*.

foil *vt* déjouer; * *n* papier d'aluminium *m*; fleuret *m*.

fold *n* pli *m*; parc à moutons *m*; * *vt* plier; ~ up faire faillite; * *vi*: ~ up plier, replier.

folder *n* chemise *f*; dépliant *m*.

folding *adj* pliant.

folding chair *n* chaise pliante *f*.

foliage *n* feuillage *m*.

folio *n* folio *m*.

folk *n* gens *mpl*.

folklore *n* folklore *m*.

folk song *n* chant folklorique *m*.

follow *vt* suivre; ~ up suivre;

exploiter; * *vi* suivre, s'ensuivre, résulter.

follower *n* serviteur *m*; disciple *mf*, partisan *m* -e *f*; adhérent *m* -e *f*; admirateur *m* -trice *f*.

following *adj* suivant; * *n* partisans *mpl*.

folly *n* folie, extravagance *f*.

foment *vt* fomenter.

fond *adj* affectueux; **to be ~ of** aimer; **~ly** *adv* affectueusement.

fondle *vt* caresser.

fondness *n* prédilection *f*; affection *f*.

font *n* fonts baptismaux *mpl*.

food *n* nourriture *f*.

food mixer *n* mixer *m*.

food poisoning *n* intoxication alimentaire *f*.

food processor *n* robot *m* ménager.

foodstuffs *npl* denrées alimentaires *fpl*.

fool *n* imbécile *mf*, idiot *m* -e *f*; * *vt* duper.

foolhardy *adj* téméraire.

foolish *adj* idiot, insensé; **~ly** *adv* bêtement.

foolproof *adj* infaillible.

foolscap *n* papier ministre *m*.

foot *n* pied *m*; patte *f*; **on** *or* **by ~** à pied.

footage *n* métrage *m*.

football *n* football *m*; ballon de football *m*.

footballer *n* footballeur *m* -euse *f*.

footbrake *n* frein à pied *m*.

footbridge *n* passerelle *f*.

foothills *npl* contreforts *mpl*.

foothold *n* prise (pour le pied) *f*.

footing *n* prise (pour le pied) *f*; statut *m*; situation *f*; plan *m*.

footlights *npl* feux de la rampe *mpl*.

footman *n* valet de pied *m*; soldat d'infanterie *m*.

footnote *n* note (de bas de page) *f*.

footpath *n* sentier *m*.

footprint *n* empreinte (de pas) *f*.

footsore *adj* aux pieds endoloris.

footstep *n* pas *m*.

footwear *n* chaussures *fpl*.

for *prep* pour; en raison de; pendant; * *conj* car; **as ~ me** quant à moi; **what ~?** pourquoi?; pourquoi faire?

forage *n* fourrage *m*; * *vt* fourrager; fouiller.

foray *n* incursion *f*.

forbid *vt* interdire, défendre; empêcher; **God** ~! pourvu que non!

forbidding *adj* menaçant; sévère.

force *n* force *f*; puissance, vigueur *f*; violence *f*; ~s *pl* forces armées *fpl*; * *vt* forcer, obliger, contraindre; imposer.

forced *adj* forcé.

forced march *n* (*mil*) marche forcée *f*.

forceful *adj* énergique.

forceps *n* forceps *m*.

forcible *adj* énergique, vigoureux, puissant; ~**bly** *adv* énergiquement, avec véhémence.

ford *n* gué *m*; * *vt* passer à gué.

fore *n*: **to the** ~ en évidence.

forearm *n* avant-bras *m*.

foreboding *n* pressentiment *m*.

forecast *vt* prévoir; * *n* prévision *f*.

forecourt *n* avant-cour *f*.

forefather *n* aïeul, ancêtre *m*.

forefinger *n* index *m*.

forefront *n*: **in the** ~ **of** au premier plan de.

forego *vt* renoncer à, s'abstenir de.

foregone *adj* passé; anticipé.

foreground *n* premier plan *m*.

forehead *n* front *m*.

foreign *adj* étranger.

foreigner *n* étranger *m* -ère *f*.

foreign exchange *n* devises *fpl*.

foreleg *n* patte de devant *f*.

foreman *n* contremaître *m*; (*law*) premier juré *m*.

foremost *adj* principal.

forenoon *n* matinée *f*.

forensic *adj* médico-légal.

forerunner *n* précurseur *m*; signe avant-coureur *m*.

foresee *vt* prévoir.

foreshadow *vt* présager.

foresight *n* prévoyance *f*; prescience *f*.

forest *n* forêt *f*.

forestall *vt* anticiper; prévenir.

forester *n* garde forestier *m*.

forestry *n* sylviculture *f*.

foretaste *n* avant-goût *m*.

foretell *vt* prédire.

forethought *n* prévoyance *f*; préméditation *f*.

forever *adv* toujours; un temps infini.

forewarn *vt* avertir, prévenir.

foreword n préface f.

forfeit n amende f; confiscation f; * vt perdre.

forge n forge f; usine métallurgique f; * vt forger; contrefaire; * vi: ~ ahead aller de l'avant.

forger n faussaire mf.

forgery n contrefaçon f.

forget vt vi oublier.

forgetful adj étourdi; négligent.

forgetfulness n étourderie f; négligence f.

forget-me-not n (bot) myosotis m.

forgive vt pardonner.

forgiveness n pardon m; indulgence f.

fork n fourchette f; fourche f; * vi bifurquer; ~ out (sl) casquer.

forked adj fourchu.

fork-lift truck n chariot élévateur m.

forlorn adj malheureux, abandonné.

form n forme f; formule f; formulaire m; formalité f; moule m; * vt former.

formal adj formel; méthodique; cérémonieux; ~ly adv formellement.

formality n formalité f; cérémonie f.

format n format m; * vt formater.

formation n formation f.

formative adj formateur m -trice f.

former adj précédent, ancien; ~ly adv autrefois, jadis.

formidable adj effrayant, terrible.

formula n formule f.

formulate vt formuler.

forsake vt abandonner, renoncer à.

fort n fort m.

forte n fort m.

forthcoming adj prochain; sociable.

forthright adj franc.

forthwith adv immédiatement, tout de suite.

fortieth adj n quarantième mf.

fortification n fortification f.

fortify vt fortifier, renforcer.

fortitude n stoïcisme m; courage m.

fortnight n quinze jours mpl; deux semaines fpl; * adj ~ly bimensuel; * adv ~ly tous les quinze jours.

fortress *n* (*mil*) forteresse *f*.

fortuitous *adj* fortuit; imprévu; ~**ly** *adv* fortuitement.

fortunate *adj* chanceux; ~**ly** *adv* heureusement.

fortune *n* chance *f*, sort *m*; fortune *f*.

fortune-teller *n* diseuse de bonne aventure *f*.

forty *adj n* quarante *m*.

forum *n* forum *m*, tribune *f*.

forward *adj* avancé; précoce; présompteux; ~(**s**) *adv* en avant, vers l'avant; * *vt* transmettre; promouvoir; expédier.

forwardness *n* précocité *f*; effronterie *f*.

fossil *adj* fossilisé; * *n* fossile *m*.

foster *vt* encourager.

foster child *n* enfant adoptif *m*.

foster father *n* père adoptif *m*.

foster mother *n* mère adoptive *f*.

foul *adj* infect, ignoble; vil, déloyal; ~ **copy** *n* copie illisible *f*; ~**ly** *adv* salement; ignoblement; * *vt* polluer.

foul play *n* jeu déloyal *m*; meurtre *m*.

found *vt* fonder, créer; établir, édifier; fondre.

foundation *n* foundation *f*; fondement *m*.

founder *n* fondateur *m* -trice *f*; fondeur *m*; * *vi* (*mar*) couler.

foundling *n* enfant trouvé(e) *mf*.

foundry *n* fonderie *f*.

fount, fountain *n* fontaine *f*.

fountainhead *n* source, origine *f*.

four *adj n* quatre *m*.

fourfold *adj* quadruple.

four-poster (bed) *n* lit à baldaquin *m*.

foursome *n* groupe de quatre personnes *m*.

fourteen *adj n* quatorze *m*.

fourteenth *adj n* quatorzième *mf*.

fourth *adj n* quatrième *mf*; * *n* quart *m*; ~**ly** *adv* quatrièmement.

fowl *n* volaille *f*.

fox *n* renard *f*; (*fig*) rusé *m*.

foyer *n* vestibule *m*.

fracas *n* rixe *f*.

fraction *n* fraction *f*.

fracture *n* fracture *f*; * *vt* fracturer.

fragile *adj* fragile; frêle.

fragility *n* fragilité *f*; faiblesse, délicatesse *f*.

fragment *n* fragment *m*.

fragmentary *adj* fragmentaire.

fragrance *n* parfum *m*.

fragrant *adj* parfumé, odorant; ~ly *adv* en exhalant un parfum.

frail *adj* frêle, fragile.

frailty *n* fragilité *f*; faiblesse *f*.

frame *n* charpente *f*; châssis *m*, armature *f*; cadre *m*; structure *f*; monture *f*; * *vt* encadrer; concevoir; construire; former.

frame of mind *n* état d'esprit *m*.

framework *n* charpente *f*; structure *f*, cadre *m*.

franchise *n* droit de vote *m*; franchise *f*.

frank *adj* franc, direct.

frankly *adv* franchement.

frankness *n* franchise *f*.

frantic *adj* frénétique, effréné.

fraternal *adj* ~ly *adv* fraternel(lement).

fraternity *n* fraternité *f*.

fraternize *vi* fraterniser.

fratricide *n* fratricide *mf*.

fraud *n* fraude, tromperie *f*.

fraudulence *n* caractère frauduleux *m*.

fraudulent *adj* frauduleux; ~ly *adv* frauduleusement.

fraught *adj* accablé, tendu.

fray *n* rixe, bagarre, querelle *f*.

freak *n* caprice *m*; phénomène *m*.

freckle *n* tache de rousseur *f*.

freckled *adj* couvert de taches de rousseur.

free *adj* libre; autonome; gratuit; dégagé; * *vt* affranchir; libérer; débarrasser.

freedom *n* liberté *f*.

free-for-all *n* mêlée générale *f*.

free gift *n* prime *f*.

freehold *n* propriété libre *f*.

free kick *n* coup franc *m*.

freelance *adj* indépendant; * *adv* en indépendant.

freely *adv* librement; franchement; libéralement.

freemason *n* franc-maçon *m*.

freemasonry *n* franc-maçonnerie *f*.

freepost *n* port payé *m*.

free-range *adj* de plein air.

freethinker n libre-penseur m -euse f.

freethinking n libre pensée f.

free trade n libre échange m.

freeway n (US) autoroute f.

freewheel vi rouler en roue libre.

free will n libre arbitre m.

freeze vi geler; * vt congeler; geler.

freeze-dried adj lyophilisé.

freezer n congélateur m.

freezing adj gelé.

freezing point n point de congélation m.

freight n cargaison f; fret m.

freighter n affréteur m.

freight train n train de marchandises m.

French bean n haricot vert m.

French fries npl frites fpl.

French window n porte-fenêtre f.

frenzied adj fou, frénétique.

frenzy n frénésie f; folie f.

frequency n fréquence f.

frequent adj fréquent; ~ly adv fréquemment; * vt fréquenter.

fresco n fresque f.

fresh adj frais; nouveau, récent; ~ water n eau douce f.

freshen vt rafraîchir; * vi se rafraîchir.

freshly adv nouvellement; récemment.

freshman n nouveau m, nouvelle f.

freshness n fraîcheur f.

freshwater adj d'eau douce.

fret vi s'agiter, se tracasser.

friar n moine m.

friction n friction f.

Friday n vendredi m; **Good** ~ Vendredi Saint m.

friend n ami m -e f.

friendless adj sans amis.

friendliness n amitié, bienveillance f.

friendly adj amical.

friendship n amitié f.

frieze n frise f.

frigate n (mar) frégate f.

fright n peur, frayeur f.

frighten vt effrayer.

frightened adj effrayé, apeuré.

frightening adj effrayant.

frightful adj épouvantable, effroyable; ~ly adv affreusement, effroyablement.

frigid adj froid, glacé; frigide; ~ly adv froidement.

fringe n frange f.

fringe benefits npl avantages mpl en nature.

frisk *vt* fouiller.

frisky *adj* vif, fringant.

fritter *vt*: to ~ away gaspiller.

frivolity *n* frivolité *f*.

frivolous *adj* frivole, léger.

frizz *vt* friser.

frizzle *vt vi* grésiller.

frizzy *adj* frisé.

fro *adv*: to go to and ~ aller et venir.

frock *n* robe *f*.

frog *n* grenouille *f*.

frolic *vi* folâtrer, gambader.

frolicsome *adj* folâtre, gai.

from *prep* de; depuis; à partir de.

front *n* avant, devant *m*; façade *f*; front *m*; * *adj* de devant; premier.

frontal *adj* de front.

front door *n* porte d'entrée *f*.

frontier *n* frontière *f*.

front page *n* première page *f*.

front-wheel drive *n* (*auto*) traction avant *f*.

frost *n* gel *m*; gelée *f*; * *vt* geler.

frostbite *n* engelure *f*.

frostbitten *adj* gelé.

frosted *adj* gelé, givré.

frosty *adj* glacial; givré.

froth *n* écume *f*; * *vi* écumer.

frothy *adj* mousseux, écumeux.

frown *vt* froncer les sourcils; * *n* froncement de sourcils *m*.

frozen *adj* gelé.

frugal *adj* frugal; économique; simple; ~ly *adv* frugalement.

fruit *n* fruit *m*.

fruiterer *n* fruitier *m* -ière *f*.

fruiterer's (shop) *n* fruiterie *f*.

fruitful *adj* fécond, fertile; fructueux, utile; ~ly *adv* fructueusement.

fruitfulness *n* fertilité *f*; caractère fructueux *m*.

fruition *n* réalisation *f*.

fruit juice *n* jus de fruit *m*.

fruitless *adj* stérile; infécond; ~ly *adv* vainement, inutilement.

fruit salad *n* salade de fruits *f*.

fruit tree *n* arbre fruitier *m*.

frustrate *vt* contrecarrer; frustrer; énerver.

frustrated *adj* frustré.

frustration *n* frustration *f*.

fry *vt* frire.

frying pan *n* poêle *f*.

fuchsia *n* (*bot*) fuchsia *m*.

fudge *n* caramel *m* mou.

fuel *n* combustible, carburant *m*.

fuel tank *n* réservoir à carburant *m*.

fugitive *adj n* fugitif *m* -ive *f*.

fugue *n* (*mus*) fugue *f*.

fulcrum *n* pivot *m*.

fulfil *vt* accomplir; réaliser.

fulfilment *n* accomplissement *m*.

full *adj* plein, rempli; complet; * *adv* pleinement, entièrement.

full-blown *adj* complet.

full-length *adj* en pied; de long métrage.

full moon *n* pleine lune *f*.

fullness *n* plénitude *f*; abondance *f*.

full-scale *adj* grandeur nature; total, complet.

full-time *adj* à plein temps.

fully *adv* pleinement, entièrement.

fully fledged *adj* diplômé, qualifié.

fulsome *adj* exagéré.

fumble *vi* manier gauchement; farfouiller.

fume *vi* exhaler des vapeurs; rager, fumer; * ~s *npl* exhalaisons *fpl*.

fumigate *vt* fumiger.

fun *n* amusement *m*; plaisir *m*; **to have** ~ (bien) s'amuser.

function *n* fonction *f*.

functional *adj* fonctionnel.

fund *n* fonds *m*; * *vt* financer.

fundamental *adj* fondamental; ~ly *adv* fondamentalement.

funeral *n* enterrement *m*.

funeral service *n* service *m* funèbre.

funereal *adj* funèbre, lugubre.

fungus *n* champignon *m*; moisissure *f*.

funnel *n* entonnoir *m*; cheminée *f*.

funny *adj* amusant; curieux.

fur *n* fourrure *f*.

fur coat *n* manteau de fourrure *m*.

furious *adj* furieux; déchaîné; ~ly *adv* furieusement.

furlong *n* mesure de longueur (220 yards = 201 mètres), furlong *m*.

furnace *n* fourneau *m*; chaudière *f*.

furnish *vt* meubler; fournir; pourvoir.

furnishings *npl* ameublement *m*.

furniture *n* meubles *mpl*.

furrow *n* sillon *m*; * *vt* sillonner; rider.

furry *adj* à poil.

further *adj* supplémentaire; plus lointain; * *adv* plus loin, plus avant; en outre; de plus; * *vt* faire avancer; favoriser; promouvoir.

further education *n* formation *f* postscolaire.

furthermore *adv* de plus.

furthest *adv* le plus loin, le plus éloigné.

furtive *adj* furtif; secret; **~ly** *adv* furtivement.

fury *n* fureur *f*; furie *f*; colère *f*.

fuse *vt* fondre; faire sauter; * *vi* fondre, sauter; * *n* fusible *m*; amorce *f*.

fuse box *n* boîte à fusibles *f*.

fusion *n* fusion *f*.

fuss *n* tapage *m*; histoires *fpl*.

fussy *adj* tatillon, chipoteur.

futile *adj* futile, vain.

futility *n* futilité *f*.

future *adj* futur; * *n* futur *m*; avenir *m*.

fuzzy *adj* flou, confus; crépu.

gab *n* (*fam*) bavardage *m*.

gabble *vi* baragouiner; * *n* charabia *m*.

gable *n* pignon *m*.

gadget *n* gadget *m*.

gaffe *n* gaffe *f*, bévue *f*.

gag *n* bâillon *m*; blague *f*; * *vt* bâillonner.

gaiety *n* gaieté *f*.

gaily *adv* gaiement.

gain *n* gain *m*; bénéfice *m*; * *vt* gagner; atteindre.

gait *n* démarche *f*; maintien *m*.

gala *n* gala *m*.

galaxy *n* galaxie *f*.

gale *n* grand vent *m*.

gall *n* bile *f*; fiel *m*.

gallant *adj* galant.

gall bladder *n* vésicule biliaire *f*.

gallery *n* galerie *f*.

galley *n* galère *f*; (*mar*) cuisine *f*.

gallon *n* gallon *m* (mesure).

gallop *n* galop *m*; * *vi* galoper.

gallows *n* potence *f*.

gallstone *n* calcul biliaire *m*.

galore *adv* en abondance.

galvanize *vt* galvaniser.

gambit *n* stratagème *m*.

gamble *vi* jouer; spéculer; * *n* risque *m*; pari *m*.

gambler *n* joueur *m* -euse *f*.

gambling *n* jeu *m* (d'argent).

game *n* jeu *m*; divertissement *m*; partie *f*; gibier *m*; * *vi* jouer.

gamekeeper *n* garde-chasse *m*.

gaming *n* jeu *m* (d'argent).

gammon *n* jambon *m*.

gamut *n* (*mus*) gamme *f*.

gander *n* jars *m*.

gang *n* gang *m*, bande *f*.

gangrene *n* gangrène *f*.

gangster *n* gangster *m*.

gangway *n* passerelle *f*.

gap *n* trou *m*; vide *m*; intervalle, écart *m*.

gape *vi* être bouche bée; bâiller.

gaping *adj* béant.

garage *n* garage *m*.

garbage *n* ordures *fpl*.

garbage can *n* poubelle *f*.

garbage man *n* éboueur *m*.

garbled *adj* confus.

garden *n* jardin *m*.

garden hose *n* tuyau d'arrosage *m*.

gardener *n* jardinier *m* -ière *f*.

gardening *n* jardinage *m*.

gargle *vi* se gargariser.

gargoyle *n* gargouille *f*.

garish *adj* tapageur.

garland *n* guirlande *f*.

garlic *n* ail *m*.

garment *n* vêtement *m*.

garnish *vt* garnir, décorer; * *n* garniture *f*.

garret *n* mansarde *f*.

garrison *n* (*mil*) garnison *f*; * *vt* (*mil*) mettre en garnison; protéger d'une garnison.

garrote *vt* étrangler, garrotter.

garrulous *adj* locace, bavard.

garter *n* jarretelle *f*.

gas *n* gaz *m*; essence *f*.

gas burner *n* brûleur à gaz *m*.

gas cylinder *n* bouteille de gaz *f*.

gaseous *adj* gazeux.

gas fire *n* radiateur à gaz *m*.

gash *n* entaille *f*; fente *f*; * *vt* entailler.

gasket *n* joint d'étanchéité *m*.

gasp *vi* haleter; * *n* halètements *mpl*.

gas mask *n* masque à gaz *m*.

gas meter *n* compteur à gaz *m*.

gasoline *n* (US) essence *f*.

gas pedal *n* (US) accélérateur *m*.

gas ring *n* brûleur à gaz *m*.

gas station *n* (US) poste d'essence *m*.

gassy *adj* gazeux.

gas tap *n* robinet de gaz *m*.

gastric *adj* gastrique.

gastronomic *adj* gastronomique.

gasworks *npl* usine à gaz *f*.

gate *n* porte *f*; portail *m*.

gateway *n* porte *f*.

gather *vt* rassembler; ramasser; comprendre; * *vi* se rassembler.

gathering *n* réunion *f*; récolte *f*.

gauche *adj* gauche, maladroit.

gaudy *adj* criard.

gauge *n* calibre *m*; écartement *m*; * *vt* mesurer; calibrer.

gaunt *adj* décharné.

gauze *n* gaze *f*.

gay *adj* gai; vif; homosexuel.

gaze *vi* contempler, considérer; * *n* regard *m*.

gazelle *n* gazelle *f*.

gazette *n* gazette *f*.

gazetteer *n* répertoire géographique *m*.

gear *n* équipement *m*, matériel *m*; appareil *m*; affaires *fpl*; vitesse *f*.

gearbox *n* boîte de vitesses *f*.

gear shift *n* levier de vitesse *m*.

gear wheel *n* roue d'engrenage *f*.

gel *n* gel *m*.

gelatin(e) *n* gélatine *f*.

gelignite *n* gélignite *f*.

gem *n* pierre précieuse *f*; perle *f*.

Gemini *n* Gémeaux *mpl* (signe du zodiaque).

gender *n* genre *m*.

gene *n* gène *m*.

genealogical *adj* généalogique.

genealogy *n* généalogie *f*.

general *adj* général; commun, usuel; in ~ en général; ~ly *adv* généralement; * *n* général *m*; générale *f*.

general delivery *n* (US) poste restante *f*.

general election *n* élections générales *fpl*.

generality *n* généralité; majeure partie *f*.

generalization *n* généralisation *f*.

generalize *vt* généraliser.

generate *vt* engendrer; produire; causer.

generation *n* génération *f*.

generator *n* générateur *m*.

generic *adj* générique.

generosity *n* générosité, libéralité *f*.

generous *adj* généreux.

genetics *npl* génétique *f*.

genial *adj* cordial; doux.

genitals *npl* organes génitaux *mpl*.

genitive n (gr) génitif m.

genius n génie m.

genteel adj distingué.

gentle adj doux, f douce, modéré.

gentleman n gentleman m.

gentleness n douceur f.

gently adv doucement.

gentry n aristocratie f.

gents n toilettes pour hommes fpl.

genuflexion n génuflexion f.

genuine adj authentique; sincère; ~ly adv authentiquement; sincèrement.

genus n genre m.

geographer n géographe mf.

geographical adj géographique.

geography n géographie f.

geological adj géologique.

geologist n géologue mf.

geology n géologie f.

geometric(al) adj géométrique.

geometry n géométrie f.

geranium n (bot) géranium m.

geriatric n malade gériatrique mf; * adj gériatrique.

germ n (bot) germe m.

germinate vi germer.

gesticulate vi gesticuler.

gesture n geste m.

get vt avoir; obtenir; atteindre; gagner; attraper; * vi devenir; aller; ~ the better avoir l'avantage, surpasser.

geyser n geyser m; chauffe-eau m invar.

ghastly adj affreux; sinistre.

gherkin n cornichon m.

ghost n fantôme, spectre m.

ghostly adj spectral.

giant n géant m - e f.

gibberish n charabia m; sornettes fpl.

gibe vi se moquer; * n moquerie f.

giblets npl abattis (de volaille) mpl.

giddiness n vertige m.

giddy adj vertigineux.

gift n cadeau m; don m; talent m.

gifted adj talentueux; doué.

gift voucher n bon-cadeau m.

gigantic adj gigantesque.

giggle vi rire bêtement.

gild vt dorer.

gilding, gilt n dorure f.

gill n quart de pinte m; ~s pl branchies fpl.

gilt-edged adj de premier ordre.

gimmick n truc m.

gin *n* gin *m*.

ginger *n* gingembre *m*.

gingerbread *n* pain d'épice *m*.

ginger-haired *adj* roux, *f* rousse.

giraffe *n* girafe *f*.

girder *n* poutre *f*.

girdle *n* gaine *f*; ceinture *f*.

girl *n* fille *f*.

girlfriend *n* amie *f*; petite amie *f*.

girlish *adj* de fille.

giro *n* virement *m*.

girth *n* sangle *f*; circonférence *f*.

gist *n* essence *f*.

give *vt* donner; offrir; prononcer, faire; consacrer; ~ **away** offrir; trahir; révéler; ~ **back** rendre; ~ **in** *vi* céder; *vt* remettre; ~ **off** dégager; ~ **out** distribuer; ~ **up** *vi* abandonner; *vt* renoncer à.

gizzard *n* gésier *m*.

glacial *adj* glacial.

glacier *n* glacier *m*.

glad *adj* joyeux, content; I am ~ **to** see that je me réjouis de voir que; ~ly *adv* avec joie, avec plaisir.

gladden *vt* réjouir.

gladiator *n* gladiateur *m*.

glamorous *adj* attrayant, séduisant.

glamour *n* attrait *m*, séduction *f*.

glance *n* regard *m*; * *vi* regarder; jeter un coup d'œil.

glancing *adj* oblique.

gland *n* glande *f*.

glare *n* éclat *m*; regard féroce *m*; * *vi* éblouir, briller; lancer des regards indignés.

glaring *adj* éclatant; évident; furieux.

glass *n* verre *m*; longue-vue *f*; miroir *m*; ~es *pl* lunettes *fpl*; * *adj* en verre.

glassware *n* verrerie *f*.

glassy *adj* vitreux, cristallin.

glaze *vt* vitrer; vernisser.

glazier *n* vitrier *m*.

gleam *n* rayon *m*; * *vi* rayonner, briller.

gleaming *adj* brillant.

glean *vt* glaner.

glee *n* joie *f*; exultation *f*.

glen *n* vallée *f*.

glib *adj* facile; volubile; ~ly *adv* facilement; volubilement.

glide *vi* glisser; planer.

gliding *n* vol plané *m*.

glimmer *n* lueur *f*; * *vi* luire.

glimpse *n* aperçu *m*; vision *f*; * *vt* entrevoir.

glint *vi* briller, scintiller.

glisten, glitter *vi* luire, briller.

gloat *vi* exulter.

global *adj* global; mondial.

globe *n* globe *m*; sphère *f*.

gloom, gloominess *n* obscurité *f*; mélancolie, tristesse *f*; ~**ily** *adv* sombrement; tristement.

gloomy *adj* sombre, obscur; triste, mélancolique.

glorification *n* glorification *f*.

glorify *vt* glorifier, célébrer.

glorious *adj* glorieux, illustre; ~**ly** *adv* glorieusement.

glory *n* gloire, célébrité *f*.

gloss *n* glose *f*; lustre *m*; * *vt* gloser, interpréter; lustrer; ~ **over** passer sur.

glossary *n* glossaire *m*.

glossy *adj* lustré, brillant.

glove *n* gant *m*.

glove compartment *n* boîte à gants *f*.

glow *vi* rougeoyer; rayonner; * *n* rougeoiement *m*; éclat *m*; feu *m*.

glower *vi* lancer des regards noirs.

glue *n* colle *f*; * *vt* coller.

gluey *adj* gluant, visqueux.

glum *adj* abattu, triste.

glut *n* surabondance *f*.

glutinous *adj* glutineux.

glutton *n* glouton *m* -ne *f*.

gluttony *n* gloutonnerie *f*.

glycerine *n* glycérine *f*.

gnarled *adj* noueux.

gnash *vt*: to ~ one's teeth grincer des dents.

gnat *n* moucheron *m*.

gnaw *vt* ronger.

gnome *n* gnome *m*.

go *vi* aller; s'en aller, partir; disparaître; se perdre; ~ ahead continuer; ~ away s'en aller; ~ back repartir; ~ by passer; ~ for *vt* se lancer sur; aimer; ~ in entrer; ~ off s'en aller, partir; se passer; se gâter; ~ on continuer; se passer; ~ out sortir; s'éteindre; ~ up monter.

goad *n* aiguillon *m*; * *vt* aiguillonner; stimuler.

go-ahead *adj* entreprenant; * *n* feu vert *m*.

goal *n* but, objectif *m*.

goalkeeper *n* gardien de but *m*.

goalpost *n* poteau de but *m*.

goatherd *n* chevrier *m* -ière *f*.

gobble *vt* engloutir, avaler.

go-between *n* intermédiaire *mf*.

goblet *n* coupe *f*.

goblin *n* lutin *m*.

God *n* Dieu *m*.

godchild *n* filleul *m* -e *f*.

goddaughter *n* filleule *f*.

goddess *n* déesse *f*.

godfather *n* parrain *m*.

godforsaken *adj* perdu.

godhead *n* divinité *f*.

godless *adj* impie, athée.

godlike *adj* divin.

godliness *n* piété, dévotion, sainteté *f*.

godly *adj* pieux, dévot, religieux; droit.

godmother *n* marraine *f*.

godsend *n* don du ciel *m*.

godson *n* filleul *m*.

goggle-eyed *adj* aux yeux exorbités de surprise.

goggles *npl* lunettes *fpl*; lunettes de plongée *fpl*.

going *n* départ *m*; sortie *f*; progrès *m*.

gold *n* or *m*.

golden *adj* doré; d'or; excellent; ~ **rule** *n* règle d'or *f*.

goldfish *n* poisson rouge *m*.

gold-plated *adj* plaqué or.

goldsmith *n* orfèvre *m*.

golf *n* golf *m*.

golf ball *n* balle de golf *f*.

golf club *n* club de golf *m*.

golf course *n* terrain de golf *m*.

golfer *n* golfeur *m* -euse *f*.

gondolier *n* gondolier *m*.

gone *adj* parti; perdu; passé; fini; mort, disparu.

gong *n* gong *m*.

good *adj* bon; bienveillant; favorable; valable; * *adv* bien; * *n* bien *m*; avantage *m*; ~**s** *pl* biens *mpl*; marchandises *fpl*.

goodbye ! *excl* au revoir!

Good Friday *n* Vendredi Saint *m*.

goodies *npl* gourmandises *fpl*.

good-looking *adj* beau.

good nature *n* bon caractère *m*.

good-natured *adj* qui a bon caractère.

goodness *n* bonté *f*; qualité *f*.

goodwill *n* bienveillance *f*.

goose *n* oie *f*.

gooseberry *n* groseille à maquereau *f*.

goosebumps *npl* chair de poule *f*.

goose-step *n* pas de l'oie *m*.

gore *n* sang *m*; * *vt* blesser d'un coup de corne.

gorge *n* (*geogr*) gorge *f*; * *vt* engloutir, avaler.

gorgeous *adj* merveilleux.

gorilla *n* gorille *m*.

gorse *n* ajonc *m*.

gory *adj* sanglant.

goshawk *n* autour *m*.

gospel *n* évangile *m*.

gossamer *n* gaze *f*; toile d'araignée *f*.

gossip *n* commérages, cancans *mpl*; * *vi* cancaner, faire des commérages.

gothic *adj* gothique.

gout *n* goutte *f* (maladie).

govern *vt* gouverner, diriger.

governess *n* gouvernante *f*.

government *n* gouvernement *m*; administration publique *f*.

governor *n* gouverneur *m*.

gown *n* toge *f*; robe *f*; robe de chambre *f*.

grab *vt* saisir.

grace *n* grâce *f*; faveur *f*; pardon *m*; grâces *fpl*; **to say ~** dire le bénédicité; * *vt* orner; honorer.

graceful *adj* gracieux; **~ly** *adv* gracieusement.

gracious *adj* gracieux; favorable; **~ly** *adv* gracieusement.

gradation *n* gradation *f*.

grade *n* grade *m*; degré *m*; classe *f*.

grade crossing *n* (US) passage à niveau *m*.

grade school *n* (US) école primaire *f*.

gradient *n* (*rail*) rampe *f*.

gradual *adj* graduel; **~ly** *adv* graduellement.

graduate *vi* obtenir son diplôme.

graduation *n* remise des diplômes *f*.

graffiti *n* graffiti *mpl*.

graft *n* greffe *f*; * *vt* greffer.

grain *n* grain *m*; graine *f*; céréales *fpl*.

gram *n* gramme *m*.

grammar *n* grammaire *f*.

grammatical *adj* **~ly** *adv* grammatical(lement).

granary *n* grenier *m*.

grand *adj* grandiose; magnifique.

grandchild *n* petit-fils *m*; petite-fille *f*; **grandchildren** *pl* petits-enfants *mpl*.

grandad *n* pépé *m*.

granddaughter *n* petite-fille *f*; **great~** arrière-petite-fille *f*.

grandeur *n* grandeur *f*; pompe *f*.

grandfather *n* grand-père *m*; **great~** arrière-grand-père *m*.

grandiose *adj* grandiose.

grandma *n* mémé *f*.

grandmother *n* grand-mère *f*; **great~** arrière-grand-mère *f*.

grandparents *npl* grands-parents *mpl*.

grand piano *n* piano à queue *m*.

grandson *n* petit-fils *m*; **great~** arrière-petit-fils *m*.

grandstand *n* tribune *f*.

granite *n* granit *m*.

granny *n* mamie *f*.

grant *vt* accorder; **to take for ~ed** considérer comme acquis; * *n* bourse *f*; allocation *f*.

granulate *vt* granuler.

granule *n* granule *m*.

grape *n* grain *m* de raisin; **bunch of ~s** grappe *f* de raisin.

grapefruit *n* pamplemousse *m*.

graph *n* graphe, graphique *m*.

graphic(al) *adj* graphique; pittoresque; **~ally** *adv* graphiquement.

graphics *n* art graphique *m*; graphiques *mpl*.

grapnel *n* (*mar*) grappin *m*.

grasp *vt* saisir, empoigner; comprendre; * *n* poigne *f*; compréhension *f*; prise *f*.

grasping *adj* avide.

grass *n* herbe *f*.

grasshopper *n* sauterelle *f*.

grassland *n* prés *mpl*.

grass-roots *adj* populaire; de base.

grass snake *n* couleuvre *f*.

grassy *adj* herbeux.

grate *n* grille *f*; * *vt* râper; grincer (des dents); * *vi* grincer.

grateful *adj* reconnaissant; **~ly** *adv* avec reconnaissance.

gratefulness *n* gratitude, reconnaissance *f*.

gratification *n* satisfaction *f*.

gratify *vt* satisfaire; faire plaisir à.

gratifying *adj* réjouissant.

grating *n* grillage *m*; grincement *m*; * *adj* grinçant; énervant.

gratis *adv* gratis, gratuitement.

gratitude *n* gratitude, reconnaissance *f*.

gratuitous *adj* gratuit; volontaire; **~ly** *adv* gratuitement.

gratuity *n* gratification *f*.

grave *n* tombe *f*; * *adj* grave, sérieux; ~**ly** *adv* gravement, sérieusement.

grave digger *n* fossoyeur *m*.

gravel *n* gravier *m*.

gravestone *n* pierre tombale *f*.

graveyard *n* cimetière *m*.

gravitate *vi* graviter.

gravitation *n* gravitation *f*.

gravity *n* gravité *f*.

gravy *n* jus de viande *m*; sauce *f*.

graze *vt* paître; effleurer; * *vi* paître.

grease *n* graisse *f*; * *vt* graisser.

greaseproof *adj* (papier) sulfurisé.

greasy *adj* gras.

great *adj* grand; important; fort; ~**ly** *adv* énormément.

greatcoat *n* pardessus *m*.

greatness *n* grandeur *f*; importance *f*; pouvoir *m*; noblesse *f*.

greedily *adv* avidement.

greediness, greed *n* avidité *f*; gloutonnerie *f*.

greedy *adj* avide; glouton.

Greek *n* grec *m*; Grec *m*; Grecque *f*.

green *adj* vert; inexpérimenté;

* *n* vert *m*; verdure *f*; ~**s** *npl* légumes verts *mpl*.

greenback *n* (US) billet *m*.

green belt *n* zone verte *f*.

green card *n* carte verte *f*; (US) permis de travail *m*.

greenery *n* verdure *f*.

greengrocer *n* marchand(e) de fruits et légumes *m(f)*.

greenhouse *n* serre *f*.

greenish *adj* verdâtre.

greenness *n* verdure *f*; manque d'expérience *m*.

green room *n* foyer des artistes *m*.

greet *vt* saluer; accueillir.

greeting *n* salutation *f*; accueil *m*.

greeting(s) card *n* carte de vœux *f*.

grenade *n* (mil) grenade *f*.

grenadier *n* grenadier *m*.

grey *adj* gris; * *n* gris *m*.

grey-haired *adj* aux cheveux gris.

greyhound *n* lévrier *m*.

greyish *adj* grisâtre; grisonnant.

greyness *n* couleur grise *f*; grisaille *f*.

grid *n* grille *f*; réseau *m*.

gridiron *n* gril *m*; terrain de football américain *m*.

grief n chagrin m, douleur, peine f.

grievance n grief m; doléance f; différend m; injustice f; tort m.

grieve vt peiner, affliger; * vi se chagriner, s'affliger.

grievous adj douloureux; grave, atroce; ~ly adv douloureusement; cruellement.

griffin n griffon m.

grill n gril m; grillade f; * vt faire griller; interroger, cuisiner.

grille n grille f.

grim adj peu engageant; sinistre.

grimace n grimace f; moue f.

grime n saleté f.

grimy adj crasseux.

grin n grimace f; sourire m; * vi grimacer; sourire.

grind vt moudre; piler, broyer; affûter, aiguiser; * vi grincer.

grinder n moulin m; rémouleur m; molaire f.

grip n prise f; poignée f; sac m de voyage; * vt saisir, agripper.

gripping adj passionnant.

grisly adj horrible; sinistre.

gristle n cartilage m.

gristly adj cartilagineux.

grit n gravillon m; cran m.

groan vi gémir; grogner; * n gémissement m; grognement m.

grocer n épicier m -ière f.

groceries npl épicerie f, provisions fpl.

grocer's (shop) n épicerie f.

groggy adj sonné, étourdi.

groin n aine f.

groom n palefrenier m; valet m; marié m; * vt panser; préparer.

groove n rainure f.

grope vt chercher à tâtons; * vi tâtonner.

gross adj gros, corpulent; épais; grossier; brut; ~ly adv énormément.

grotesque adj grotesque.

grotto n grotte f.

ground n terre f, sol m; terrain, territoire m; fondement m; raison fondamentale f; fond m; * vt retenir au sol; fonder; mettre une prise de terre à.

ground floor n rez-de-chaussée m.

grounding n connaissances de base fpl.

groundless adj sans

fondement; ~ly *adv* sans fondement.

ground staff *n* personnel au sol *m*.

groundwork *n* travaux de préparation *mpl*.

group *n* groupe *m*; * *vt* regrouper.

grouse *n* grouse *f*, coq de bruyère *m*; * *vi* grogner.

grove *n* bosquet *m*.

grovel *vi* se traîner; ramper.

grow *vt* cultiver; faire pousser; * *vi* pousser; grandir; augmenter; ~ **up** grandir.

grower *n* cultivateur *m* -trice *f*; producteur *m* -trice *f*.

growing *adj* croissant; grandissant.

growl *vi* grogner; * *n* grognement *m*.

grown-up *n* adulte *mf*.

growth *n* croissance *f*; augmentation *f*; poussée *f*.

grub *n* asticot *m*.

grubby *adj* sale.

grudge *n* rancune *f*; * *vt* accorder à contrecœur; *vi* avoir de la rancune.

grudgingly *adv* à contrecœur.

gruelling *adj* difficile, pénible.

gruesome *adj* horrible.

gruff *adj* brusque; ~ly *adv* brusquement.

gruffness *n* brusquerie *f*.

grumble *vi* grogner; grommeler.

grumpy *adj* ronchon, grincheux.

grunt *vi* grogner; * *n* grognement *m*.

G-string *n* cache-sexe *m*.

guarantee *n* garantie *f*; * *vt* garantir.

guard *n* garde *f*; garde *m*; * *vt* garder; défendre.

guarded *adj* prudent; surveillé.

guardroom *n* (*mil*) corps de garde *m*.

guardian *n* tuteur *m* -trice *f*; gardien *m* -ne *f*.

guardianship *n* tutelle *f*.

guerrilla *n* guérillero *m*.

guerrilla warfare *n* guérilla *f*.

guess *vt* deviner; supposer; * *vi* deviner; * *n* conjecture *f*.

guesswork *n* conjectures *fpl*.

guest *n* invité *m* -ée *f*; client *m* -e *f*.

guest room *n* chambre d'amis *f*.

guffaw *n* éclat de rire *m*.

guidance *n* guidage *m*; direction *f*.

guide *vt* guider, diriger; * *n* guide *m*.

guidebook *n* guide *m*.

guide dog *n* chien d'aveugle *m*.

guidelines *npl* directives *fpl*.

guild *n* association *f*; corporation *f*.

guile *n* astuce *f*.

guillotine *n* guillotine *f*; * *vt* guillotiner.

guilt *n* culpabilité *f*.

guiltless *adj* innocent.

guilty *adj* coupable.

guinea pig *n* cochon d'Inde, cobaye *m*.

guise *n* apparence *f*.

guitar *n* guitare *f*.

gulf *n* golfe *m*; abîme *m*.

gull *n* mouette *f*.

gullet *n* œsophage *m*.

gullibility *n* crédulité *f*.

gullible *adj* crédule.

gully *n* ravine *f*.

gulp *n* gorgée *f*; * *vt vi* avaler.

gum *n* gomme *f*; gencive *f*; chewing-gum *m*; * *vt* coller.

gum tree *n* gommier *m*.

gun *n* pistolet *m*; fusil *m*.

gunboat *n* canonnière *f*.

gun carriage *n* affût de canon *m*.

gunfire *n* coups de feu *mpl*.

gunman *n* homme armé *m*.

gunmetal *n* bronze à canon *m*.

gunner *n* artilleur *m*.

gunnery *n* artillerie *f*.

gunpoint *n*: at ~ sous la menace d'une arme à feu.

gunpowder *n* poudre à canon *f*.

gunshot *n* coup de feu *m*.

gunsmith *n* armurier *m*.

gurgle *vi* gargouiller.

guru *n* gourou *m*.

gush *vi* jaillir; bouillonner; * *n* jaillissement *m*.

gushing *adj* jaillissant; très exubérant.

gusset *n* soufflet *m*.

gust *n* rafale *f*; bouffée *f*.

gusto *n* plaisir *m*, délectation *f*.

gusty *adj* venteux.

gut *n* intestin *m*; ~s *npl* cœur au ventre *m*; * *vt* vider.

gutter *n* gouttière *f*; caniveau *m*.

guttural *adj* guttural.

guy *n* mec, type *m*.

guzzle *vt* bouffer, engloutir; avaler.

gym(nasium) *n* gymnase *m*.

gymnast *n* gymnaste *mf*.

gymnastic *adj* gymnastique; ~s *npl* gymnastique *f*.

gynaecologist *n* gynécologue *mf*.

gypsy *n* gitan *m* -e *f*.

gyrate *vi* tourner.

H

haberdasher *n* mercier *m* -ière *f*.

haberdashery *n* mercerie *f*.

habit *n* habitude *f*.

habitable *adj* habitable.

habitat *n* habitat *m*.

habitual *adj* habituel; ~ly *adv* d'habitude, habituellement.

hack *n* coupure, entaille *f*; * *vt* entailler, couper.

hackneyed *adj* rebattu.

haddock *n* aiglefin *m*.

haemorrhage *n* hémorragie *f*.

haemorrhoids *npl* hémorroïdes *fpl*.

hag *n* sorcière *f*.

haggard *adj* exténué; défait.

haggle *vi* marchander.

hail *n* grêle *f*; * *vt* saluer; * *vi* grêler.

hailstone *n* grêlon *m*.

hair *n* cheveux *mpl*; poil *m*.

hairbrush *n* brosse à cheveux *f*.

haircut *n* coupe de cheveux *f*.

hairdresser *n* coiffeur *m* -euse *f*.

hairdryer *n* séchoir à cheveux *m*.

hairless *adj* chauve; sans poils.

hairnet *n* filet à cheveux *m*.

hairpin *n* épingle à cheveux *f*.

hairpin bend *n* virage en épingle à cheveux *m*.

hair remover *n* crème dépilatoire *f*.

hairspray *n* laque à cheveux *f*.

hairstyle *n* coiffure *f*.

hairy *adj* chevelu; poilu.

hale *adj* vigoureux.

half *n* moitié *f*; * *adj* demi; * *adv* à moitié.

half-caste *adj* métis.

half-hearted *adj* peu enthousiaste.

half-hour *n* demi-heure *f*.

half-moon *n* demi-lune *f*.

half-price *adj* à moitié prix.

half-time *n* mi-temps *f*.

halfway *adv* à mi-chemin.

hall *n* vestibule *m*.

hallmark *n* marque *f*.

hallow *vt* consacrer, sanctifier.

hallucination *n* hallucination *f*.

halo *n* halo *m*.

halt *vi* s'arrêter; * *n* arrêt *m*; halte *f*.

halve *vt* couper en deux.

ham *n* jambon *m*.

hamlet *n* hameau *m*.

hammer *n* marteau *m*; * *vt* marteler.

hammock *n* hamac *m*.

hamper *n* panier *m*; * *vt* embarrasser, entraver.

hamstring *vt* couper les jarrets à.

hand *n* main *f*; ouvrier *m* -ière *f*; aiguille *f*; at ~ à portée de main; * *vt* donner, passer.

handbag *n* sac à main *m*.

handbell *n* sonnette *f*.

handbook *n* manuel *m*.

handbrake *n* frein à main *m*.

handcuff *n* menotte *f*.

handful *n* poignée *f*.

handicap *n* handicap *m*.

handicapped *adj* handicapé.

handicraft *n* artisanat *m*.

handiwork *n* travail manuel *m*.

handkerchief *n* mouchoir *m*.

handle *n* manche *m*, queue *f*; anse *f*; poignée *f*; * *vt* manier; traiter, prendre.

handlebars *npl* guidon *m*.

handling *n* maniement *m*; traitement *m*.

handrail *n* garde-fou *m*.

handshake *n* poignée de mains *f*.

handsome *adj* beau; ~ly *adv* élégamment.

handwriting *n* écriture *f*.

handy *adj* pratique; adroit.

hang *vt* accrocher; pendre; * *vi* pendre, être accroché; être pendu.

hanger *n* cintre *m*.

hanger-on *n* parasite *m*.

hangings *npl* tapisserie *f*.

hangman *n* bourreau *m*.

hangover *n* gueule de bois *f*.

hang-up *n* complexe *m*.

hanker *vi* avoir envie.

haphazard *adj* fortuit.

hapless *adj* malheureux.

happen *vi* se passer; I ~ to have one il se trouve que j'en ai un.

happening *n* événement *m*.

happily *adv* heureusement; gaiement.

happiness *n* bonheur *m*.

happy *adj* heureux.

harangue *n* harangue *f*; * *vt* haranguer.

harass *vt* harceler; tourmenter.

harbinger *n* précurseur *m*.

harbour *n* port *m*; * *vt* héberger; entretenir, nourrir.

hard *adj* dur; pénible; sévère, rigide; ~ of hearing dur d'oreille; ~ by tout près.

harden *vt vi* durcir.

hard-headed *adj* réaliste.

hard-hearted *adj* au cœur dur, insensible.

hardiness *n* robustesse *f*.

hardly *adv* à peine; ~ ever presque jamais.

hardness *n* dureté *f*; difficulté *f*; sévérité *f*.

hardship *n* épreuve(s) *f(pl)*.

hard-up *adj* fauché, sans le sou.

hardware *n* matériel *m*; quincaillerie *f*.

hardwearing *adj* résistant.

hardy *adj* fort, robuste; résistant.

hare *n* lièvre *m*.

hare-brained *adj* écervelé.

hare-lipped *adj* qui a un bec de lièvre.

haricot *n* haricot blanc *m*.

harlequin *n* arlequin *m*.

harm *n* mal *m*; tort *m*; * *vt* faire du mal à; nuire à.

harmful *adj* nuisible.

harmless *adj* inoffensif.

harmonic *adj* harmonique.

harmonious *adj* harmonieux; ~ly *adv* harmonieusement.

harmonize *vt* harmoniser.

harmony *n* harmonie *f*.

harness *n* harnais *m*; * *vt* harnacher.

harp *n* harpe *f*.

harpist *n* harpiste *mf*.

harpoon *n* harpon *m*.

harpsichord *n* clavecin *m*.

harrow *n* herse *f*.

harry *vt* harceler; dévaster.

harsh *adj* dur; austère; rude; ~ly *adv* sévèrement; durement.

harshness *n* aspérité, dureté *f*; austérité *f*.

harvest *n* récolte *f*; moisson *f*; * *vt* récolter; moissonner.

harvester *n* moissonneur *m* -euse *f*; moissonneuse *f* (machine).

hash *n* hachis *m*; gâchis *m*.

hassock *n* agenouilloir *m*.

haste *n* hâte *f*; to be in ~ être pressé.

hasten *vt* accélérer, hâter; * *vi* se dépêcher.

hastily *adv* à la hâte, précipitamment.

hastiness *n* précipitation *f*.

hasty *adj* hâtif; irréfléchi.

hat *n* chapeau *m*.

hatbox *n* carton à chapeau *m*.

hatch *vt* couver; faire éclore; tramer; * *n* écoutille *f*.

hatchback *n* (*auto*) voiture à hayon arrière *f*.

hatchet *n* hachette *f*.

hatchway *n* (*mar*) écoutille *f*.

hate *n* haine *f*; * *vt* haïr, détester.

hateful *adj* odieux, détestable.

hatred *n* haine *f*.

hatter *n* chapelier *m* -ière *f*.

haughtily *adv* hautainement.

haughtiness *n* orgueil *m*; hauteur *f*.

haughty *adj* hautain, orgueilleux.

haul *vt* tirer; * *n* prise *f*; butin *m*.

haulier *n* camionneur *m*.

haunch *n* hanche *f*.

haunt *vt* hanter; fréquenter; * *n* repaire *m*.

have *vt* avoir; posséder.

haven *n* refuge *m*.

haversack *n* sac à dos *m*.

havoc *n* ravages *mpl*.

hawk *n* faucon *m*; * *vi* chasser au faucon.

hawthorn *n* aubépine *f*.

hay *n* foin *m*.

hay fever *n* rhume des foins *m*.

hayloft *n* fenil *m*.

hayrick, haystack *n* meule de foin *f*.

hazard *n* risque, danger *m*; * *vt* risquer.

hazardous *adj* risqué, dangereux.

haze *n* brume *f*.

hazel *n* noisetier *m*; * *adj* noisette.

hazelnut *n* noisette *f*.

hazy *adj* brumeux.

he *pn* il.

head *n* tête *f*; chef *m*; esprit *m*; * *vt* conduire; ~ for se diriger vers.

headache *n* mal de tête *m*.

headdress *n* coiffe *f*.

headland *n* promontoire *m*.

headlight *n* phare *m*.

headline *n* titre *m*.

headlong *adv* à toute allure.

headmaster *n* directeur *m*.

head office *n* siège social *m*.

headphones *npl* écouteurs *mpl*.

headquarters *npl* (*mil*) quartier général *m*; siège social *m*.

headroom *n* hauteur *f*.

headstrong *adj* têtu.

headwaiter *n* maître d'hôtel *m*.

headway *n* progrès *m*(*pl*).

heady *adj* capiteux.

heal vt vi guérir.

health n santé f.

healthiness n bonne santé f.

healthy adj en bonne santé; sain.

heap n tas m; * vt entasser.

hear vt entendre; écouter; * vi entendre; avoir des nouvelles.

hearing n ouïe f.

hearing aid n audiophone m.

hearsay n rumeur f.

hearse n corbillard m.

heart n cœur m; by ~ par cœur; with all my ~ de tout cœur.

heart attack n crise cardiaque f.

heartbreaking adj à fendre le cœur.

heartburn n acidité f gastrique.

heart failure n arrêt cardiaque m.

heartfelt adj sincère.

hearth n foyer m.

heartily adv sincèrement, cordialement.

heartiness n cordialité, sincérité f.

heartless adj cruel; ~ly adv cruellement.

hearty adj cordial.

heat n chaleur f; * vt chauffer.

heater n radiateur m.

heather n (bot) bruyère f.

heathen n païen m, païenne f; ~ish adj sauvage, barbare.

heating n chauffage m.

heatwave n onde de chaleur f.

heave vt lever; tirer; * n effort m.

heaven n ciel m.

heavenly adj divin.

heavily adv lourdement.

heaviness n lourdeur f.

heavy adj lourd, pesant; considérable.

Hebrew n hébreu m (langue).

heckle vt interrompre.

hectic adj agité.

hedge n haie f; * vt entourer d'une haie.

hedgehog n hérisson m.

heed vt tenir compte de; * n soin m; attention f.

heedless adj inattentif, étourdi; ~ly adv étourdiment.

heel n talon m; to take to one's ~s prendre ses jambes à son cou.

hefty adj costaud, puissant.

heifer n génisse f.

height n hauteur f; altitude f.

heighten vt rehausser; augmenter; intensifier.

heinous *adj* atroce.

heir *n* héritier *m*; ~ **apparent** héritier présomptif *m*.

heiress *n* héritière *f*.

heirloom *n* héritage *m*.

helicopter *n* hélicoptère *m*.

hell *n* enfer *m*.

hellish *adj* infernal.

helm *n* (*mar*) barre *f*.

helmet *n* casque *m*.

help *vt* aider, secourir; **I cannot ~ it** je n'y peux rien; je ne peux pas m'en empêcher; * *n* aide *f*; secours *m*.

helper *n* aide *mf*.

helpful *adj* utile; qui rend service.

helping *n* portion *f*.

helpless *adj* impuissant; ~**ly** *adv* désespérément; sans pouvoir rien faire.

helter-skelter *adv* n'importe comment, en désordre.

hem *n* ourlet *m*; * *vt* ourler.

he-man *n* dur, mâle *m*.

hemisphere *n* hémisphère *m*.

hemp *n* chanvre *m*.

hen *n* poule *f*.

henchman *n* acolyte *m*.

henceforth, henceforward *adv* dorénavant.

hen-house *n* poulailler *m*.

hepatitis *n* hépatite *f*.

her *pn* son, sa, ses; elle; la; lui.

herald *n* héraut *m*.

heraldry *n* héraldique *f*.

herb *n* herbe *f*; ~**s** *pl* fines herbes *fpl*.

herbaceous *adj* herbacé.

herbalist *n* herboriste *mf*.

herbivorous *adj* herbivore.

herd *n* troupeau *m*.

here *adv* ici.

hereabout(s) *adv* dans les environs.

hereafter *adv* plus tard; ci-après.

hereby *adv* par la présente.

hereditary *adj* héréditaire.

heredity *n* hérédité *f*.

heresy *n* hérésie *f*.

heretic *n*, *adj* hérétique *mf*.

herewith *adv* avec ceci.

heritage *n* patrimoine, héritage *m*.

hermetic *adj* hermétique; ~**ly** *adv* hermétiquement.

hermit *n* ermite *m*.

hermitage *n* ermitage *m*.

hernia *n* hernie *f*.

hero *n* héros *m*.

heroic *adj* héroïque; ~**ally** *adv* héroïquement.

heroine *n* héroïne *f*.

heroism n héroïsme m.

heron n héron m.

herring n hareng m.

hers pn le sien, la sienne, le(s) sien(ne)s, à elle.

herself pn elle-même.

hesitant adj hésitant.

hesitate vi hésiter.

hesitation n hésitation f.

heterogeneous adj hétérogène.

heterosexual adj n hétérosexuel m -le f.

hew vt tailler; couper.

heyday n apogée m.

hi excl salut!

hiatus n (gr) hiatus m.

hibernate vi hiberner.

hiccup n hoquet m; * vi avoir le hoquet.

hickory n noyer d'Amérique m.

hide vt cacher; * n cuir m; peau f.

hideaway n cachette f.

hideous adj hideux; horrible; ~ly adv horriblement.

hiding-place n cachette f.

hierarchy n hiérarchie f.

hieroglyphic adj hiéroglyphique; * n hiéroglyphe m.

hi-fi n hi-fi f invar.

higgledy-piggledy adv pêle-mêle.

high adj haut; élevé.

high altar n maître-autel m.

high chair n chaise haute f.

high-handed adj tyrannique.

highlands npl terres montagneuses fpl.

highlight n point fort m.

highly adv extrêmement, hautement.

highness n hauteur f; altesse f.

high school n lycée m.

high-strung adj nerveux, tendu.

high water n marée haute f.

highway n grande route f.

hike vi faire une randonnée.

hijack vt détourner.

hijacker n pirate de l'air m.

hilarious adj hilarant; hilare.

hill n colline f.

hillock n petite colline f.

hillside n coteau m.

hilly adj montagneux.

hilt n poignée f.

him pn lui; le.

himself pn lui-même; soi.

hind adj derrière; * n biche f.

hinder vt gêner, entraver.

hindrance n gêne f, obstacle m.

hindmost adj dernier.

hindquarter n arrière-train m.

hindsight n: with ~ rétrospectivement.

hinge *n* charnière *f*; gond *m*.

hint *n* allusion *f*; insinuation *f*; * *vt* insinuer; suggérer.

hip *n* hanche *f*.

hippopotamus *n* hippopotame *m*.

hire *vt* louer; * *n* location *f*.

his *pn* son, sa, ses; le sien, la sienne, les sien(ne)s; à lui.

Hispanic *adj* hispanique.

hiss *vt vi* siffler.

historian *n* historien *m* -ne *f*.

historic(al) *adj* historique; ~ally *adv* historiquement.

history *n* histoire *f*.

histrionic *adj* théâtral.

hit *vt* frapper; atteindre; heurter; * *n* coup *m*; succès *m*.

hitch *vt* accrocher; * *n* nœud *m*; anicroche *f*.

hitchhike *vi* faire du stop.

hitherto *adv* jusqu'à présent, jusqu'ici.

hive *n* ruche *f*.

hoard *n* stock *m*; trésor caché *m*; * *vt* accumuler, amasser.

hoarfrost *n* givre *m*.

hoarse *adj* rauque; ~ly *adv* d'une voix rauque.

hoarseness *n* voix rauque *f*.

hoax *n* canular *m*; * *vt* faire un canular à.

hobble *vi* boitiller.

hobby *n* passe-temps *m invar*.

hobbyhorse *n* cheval de bataille *m*.

hobo *n* vagabond *m*.

hockey *n* hockey *m*.

hodge-podge *n* confusion *f*.

hoe *n* binette *f*; * *vt* biner.

hog *n* porc *m*.

hoist *vt* hisser; * *n* grue *f*.

hold *vt* tenir; détenir; contenir; ~ on to se tenir à; * *vi* valoir; * *n* prise *f*; pouvoir *m*.

holder *n* détenteur *m* -trice *f*; titulaire *mf*.

holding *n* possession *f*.

holdup *n* hold-up *m*; retard *m*.

hole *n* trou *m*.

holiday *n* jour de congé *m*; jour férié *m*; ~s *pl* vacances *fpl*.

holiness *n* sainteté *f*.

hollow *adj* creux; * *n* creux *m*; * *vt* creuser, vider.

holly *n* (*bot*) houx *m*.

hollyhock *n* rose trémière *f*.

holocaust *n* holocauste *m*.

holster *n* étui de révolver *m*.

holy *adj* saint; bénit; sacré.

holy water *n* eau bénite *f*.

holy week *n* semaine sainte *f*.

homage *n* hommage *m*.

home *n* maison *f*; patrie *f*; domicile *m*; ~**ly** *adj* simple.

home address *n* domicile *m*.

homeless *adj* sans abri.

homeliness *n* simplicité *f*.

home-made *adj* fait maison.

homesick *adj* nostalgique, qui a le mal du pays.

homesickness *n* nostalgie *f*, mal du pays *m*.

hometown *n* ville natale *f*.

homeward *adj* vers chez soi; vers son pays.

homework *n* devoirs *mpl*.

homicidal *adj* homicide.

homicide *n* homicide *m*; homicide *mf*.

homoeopathist *n* homéopathe *mf*.

homoeopathy *n* homéopathie *f*.

homogeneous *adj* homogène.

homosexual *adj n* homosexuel *m* -le *f*.

honest *adj* honnête; ~**ly** *adv* honnêtement.

honesty *n* honnêteté *f*.

honey *n* miel *m*.

honeycomb *n* rayon de miel *m*.

honeymoon *n* lune de miel *f*.

honeysuckle *n* (*bot*) chèvrefeuille *m*.

honorary *adj* honoraire.

honour *n* honneur *m*; * *vt* honorer.

honourable *adj* honorable.

honourably *adv* honorablement.

hood *n* capot *m*; capuche *f*.

hoodlum *n* truand *m*.

hoof *n* sabot *m*.

hook *n* crochet *m*; hameçon *m*; by ~ or by crook coûte que coûte; * *vt* accrocher.

hooked *adj* crochu.

hooligan *n* vandale *m*.

hoop *n* cerceau *m*.

hooter *n* sirène *f*.

hop *n* (*bot*) houblon *m*; saut *m*; * *vi* sauter.

hope *n* espoir *m*, espérance *f*; * *vi* espérer.

hopeful *adj* plein d'espoir; prometteur; ~**ly** *adv* avec espoir.

hopefulness *n* bon espoir *m*.

hopeless *adj* désespéré; ~**ly** *adv* désespérément.

horde *n* horde *f*.

horizon *n* horizon *m*.

horizontal *adj* horizontal; ~**ly** *adv* horizontalement.

hormone *n* hormone *f*.

horn *n* corne *f*.

horned *adj* à cornes.

hornet *n* frelon *m*.

horny *adj* calleux.

horoscope *n* horoscope *m*.

horrendous *adj* horrible.

horrible *adj* horrible.

horribly *adv* horriblement; énormément.

horrid *adj* horrible.

horrific *adj* horrible, affreux.

horrify *vt* horrifier.

horror *n* horreur *f*.

horror film *n* film d'horreur *m*.

hors d'oeuvre *n* hors-d'œuvre *m invar*.

horse *n* cheval *m*.

horseback *adv*: on ~ à cheval.

horse-breaker *n* dresseur(-euse) de chevaux *m(f)*.

horse chestnut *n* marron d'Inde *m*.

horsefly *n* taon *m*.

horseman *n* cavalier *m*.

horsemanship *n* équitation *f*.

horsepower *n* cheval-vapeur *m*; puissance en chevaux *f*.

horse race *n* course de chevaux *f*.

horseradish *n* raifort *m*.

horseshoe *n* fer à cheval *m*.

horsewoman *n* cavalière *f*.

horticulture *n* horticulture *f*.

horticulturist *n* horticulteur *m* -trice *f*.

hose-pipe *n* tuyau *m*.

hosiery *n* bonneterie *f*.

hospitable *adj* hospitalier.

hospitably *adv* avec hospitalité.

hospital *n* hôpital *m*.

hospitality *n* hospitalité *f*.

host *n* hôte *m*; hostie *f*.

hostage *n* otage *m*.

hostess *n* hôtesse *f*.

hostile *adj* hostile.

hostility *n* hostilité *f*.

hot *adj* chaud; épicé.

hotbed *n* foyer *m*.

hotdog *n* hot-dog *m*.

hotel *n* hôtel *m*.

hotelier *n* hôtelier *m* -ière *f*.

hotheaded *adj* exalté.

hothouse *n* serre *f*.

hotline *n* téléphone rouge *m*.

hotplate *n* plaque chauffante *f*.

hotly *adv* violemment.

hound *n* chien de chasse *m*.

hour *n* heure *f*.

hourglass *n* sablier *m*.

hourly *adv* toutes les heures.

house *n* maison *f*; maisonnée *f*; * *vt* loger.

houseboat *n* péniche *f*.

housebreaker *n* cambrioleur *m*.

housebreaking *n* cambriolage *m*.

household *n* famille *f*, ménage *m*.

householder *n* propriétaire *mf*; chef de famille *m*.

housekeeper *n* gouvernante *f*.

housekeeping *n* travaux ménagers *mpl*.

houseless *adv* sans abri.

house-warming party *n* pendaison de crémaillère *f*.

housewife *n* ménagère *f*.

housework *n* travaux ménagers *mpl*.

housing *n* logement *m*.

housing development *n* urbanisation *f*.

hovel *n* taudis *m*.

hover *vi* planer.

how *adv* comme; comment; ~ do you do! enchanté.

however *adv* de quelque manière que; cependant, néanmoins.

howl *vi* hurler; * *n* hurlement *m*.

hub *n* centre *m*; moyeu *m*.

hubbub *n* vacarme *m*.

hubcap *n* enjoliveur *m*.

hue *n* teinte *f*; nuance *f*.

huff *n*: in a ~ fâché.

hug *vt* étreindre; * *n* étreinte *f*.

huge *adj* énorme; ~ly *adv* énormément.

hulk *n* (*mar*) carcasse *f*; ponton *m*.

hull *n* (*mar*) coque *f*.

hum *vi* chantonner.

human *adj* humain.

humane *adj* humain; ~ly *adv* humainement.

humanist *n* humaniste *mf*.

humanitarian *adj* humanitaire.

humanity *n* humanité *f*.

humanize *vt* humaniser.

humanly *adv* humainement.

humble *adj* humble, modeste; * *vt* humilier.

humbleness *n* humilité *f*.

humbly *adv* humblement.

humbug *n* blagues *fpl*.

humdrum *adj* monotone.

humid *adj* humide.

humidity *n* humidité *f*.

humiliate *vt* humilier.

humiliation *n* humiliation *f*.

humility *n* humilité *f*.

hummingbird *n* colibri *m*.

humorist *n* humoriste *mf*.

humorous *adj* humoristique; ~ly *adv* avec humour.

humour *n* sens de l'humour *m*, humour *m*; * *vt* complaire à.

hump *n* bosse *f*.

hunch n intuition f; ~backed adj bossu.

hundred adj cent; * n centaine f.

hundredth adj centième.

hundredweight n quintal m.

hunger n faim f; * vi avoir faim.

hunger strike n grève de la faim f.

hungrily adv avidement.

hungry adj qui a faim, affamé.

hunt vt chasser; poursuivre; chercher; * vi chasser; * n chasse f.

hunter n chasseur m.

hunting n chasse f.

huntsman n chasseur m.

hurdle n haie f.

hurl vt lancer avec violence, jeter.

hurricane n ouragan m.

hurried adj fait à la hâte; précipité; ~ly adv hâtivement; précipitamment.

hurry vt presser; * vi se presser, se dépêcher; * n hâte f.

hurt vt faire mal à; blesser; * n mal m.

hurtful adj blessant; ~ly adv de manière blessante.

husband n mari m.

husbandry n agriculture f.

hush! chut!, silence!; * vt faire taire; * vi se taire.

husk n coque f (graine).

huskiness n voix rauque f.

husky adj rauque.

hustings n plate-forme électorale f.

hustle vt pousser avec force, bousculer.

hut n cabane, hutte f.

hutch n clapier m.

hyacinth n jacinthe f.

hydrant n bouche d'incendie f.

hydraulic adj hydraulique; ~s npl hydraulique f.

hydroelectric adj hydroélectrique.

hydrofoil n hydroptère m.

hydrogen n hydrogène m.

hydrophobia n hydrophobie f.

hyena n hyène f.

hygiene n hygiène f.

hygienic adj hygiénique.

hymn n hymne m.

hyperbole n hyperbole f.

hypermarket n hypermarché m.

hyphen n (gr) trait d'union m.

hypochondria n hypocondrie f.

hypochondriac adj n hypocondriaque mf.

hypocrisy n hypocrisie f.

hypocrite *n* hypocrite *mf*.
hypocritical *adj* hypocrite.
hypothesis *n* hypothèse *f*.
hypothetical *adj* ~ly *adv*

hypothétique(ment).
hysterical *adj* hystérique.
hysterics *npl* hystérie *f*; crise
de nerfs *f*.

I

I *pn* je, j'; moi

ice *n* glace *f*; * *vt* glacer; geler.

ice-axe *n* piolet *m*.

iceberg *n* iceberg *m*.

ice-bound *adj* fermé par les glaces.

icebox *n* glacière *f*.

ice cream *n* glace *f*.

ice rink *n* patinoire *f*.

ice skating *n* patinage sur glace *m*.

icicle *n* stalactite *f*, glaçon *m*.

iconoclast *n* iconoclaste *mf*.

icy *adj* glacé.

idea *n* idée *f*.

ideal *adj* idéal; ~ly *adv* idéalement.

idealist *n* idéaliste *mf*.

identical *adj* identique.

identification *n* identification *f*.

identify *vt* identifier.

identity *n* identité *f*.

ideology *n* idéologie *f*.

idiom *n* expression idiomatique *f*.

idiomatic *adj* idiomatique.

idiosyncrasy *n* idiosyncrasie *f*.

idiot *n* imbécile *mf*.

idiotic *adj* idiot, bête.

idle *adj* désœuvré; au repos; inutile.

idleness *n* paresse *f*; oisiveté *f*.

idler *n* paresseux *m* -euse *f*.

idly *adv* oisivement; paresseusement; vainement.

idol *n* idole *f*.

idolatry *n* idôlatrie *f*.

idolize *vt* idôlatrer.

idyllic *adj* idyllique.

i.e. *adv* c.-à-d., c'est-à-dire.

if *conj* si; ~ not sinon.

ignite *vt* allumer, enflammer.

ignition *n* (*chem*) ignition *f*; allumage *m*.

ignition key *n* clé de contact *f*.

ignoble *adj* infâme; bas.

ignominious *adj* ignominieux; ~ly *adv* ignominieusement.

ignominy *n* ignominie, infamie *f*.

ignoramus *n* ignorant *m* -e *f*.

ignorance *n* ignorance *f*.

ignorant *adj* ignorant; ~**ly** *adv* par ignorance.

ignore *vt* ne pas tenir compte de.

ill *adj* malade; * *n* mal *m*; dommage *m*; * *adv* mal.

ill-advised *adj* malavisé.

illegal *adj* ~**ly** *adv* illégal(ement).

illegality *n* illégalité *f*.

illegible *adj* illisible.

illegibly *adv* illisiblement.

illegitimacy *n* illégitimité *f*.

illegitimate *adj* illégitime; ~**ly** *adv* illégitimement.

ill feeling *n* rancœur *f*.

illicit *adj* illicite.

illiterate *adj* analphabète, illettré.

illness *n* maladie *f*.

illogical *adj* illogique.

ill-timed *adj* inopportun.

ill-treat *vt* maltraiter.

illuminate *vt* illuminer.

illumination *n* illumination *f*.

illusion *n* illusion *f*.

illusory *adj* illusoire.

illustrate *vt* illustrer.

illustration *n* illustration *f*.

illustrative *adj* qui illustre.

illustrious *adj* illustre.

ill-will *n* malveillance *f*.

image *n* image *f*.

imagery *n* images *fpl*.

imaginable *adj* imaginable.

imaginary *adj* imaginaire.

imagination *n* imagination *f*.

imaginative *adj* imaginatif.

imagine *vt* imaginer.

imbalance *n* déséquilibre *m*.

imbecile *adj* imbécile, idiot.

imbibe *vt* boire; imbiber; absorber.

imbue *vt* imprégner.

imitate *vt* imiter.

imitation *n* imitation *f*.

imitative *adj* imitatif.

immaculate *adj* immaculé.

immaterial *adj* insignifiant.

immature *adj* pas mûr.

immeasurable *adj* incommensurable.

immeasurably *adv* immensément.

immediate *adj* immédiat; ~**ly** *adv* immédiatement.

immense *adj* immense; énorme; ~**ly** *adv* immensément.

immensity *n* immensité *f*.

immerse *vt* immerger.

immersion *n* immersion *f*.

immigrant *n* immigrant *m* -e *f*.

immigration *n* immigration *f*.

imminent *adj* imminent.

immobile *adj* immobile.

immobility *n* immobilité *f*.

immoderate *adj* immodéré, excessif; ~ly *adv* immodérément.

immodest *adj* immodeste.

immoral *adj* immoral.

immorality *n* immoralité *f*.

immortal *adj* immortel.

immortality *n* immortalité *f*.

immortalize *vt* immortaliser.

immune *adj* immunisé.

immunity *n* immunité *f*.

immunize *vt* immuniser.

immutable *adj* immuable.

imp *n* lutin *m*.

impact *n* impact *m*.

impair *vt* diminuer; affaiblir.

impale *vt* empaler.

impalpable *adj* impalpable.

impart *vt* communiquer.

impartial *adj* ~ly *adv* impartial(ement).

impartiality *n* impartialité *f*.

impassable *adj* impraticable; infranchissable.

impasse *n* impasse *f*.

impassive *adj* impassible.

impatience *n* impatience *f*.

impatient *adj* impatient; ~ly *adv* impatiemment.

impeach *vt* (*law*) mettre en accusation.

impeccable *adj* impeccable.

impecunious *adj* impécunieux.

impede *vt* empêcher; entraver.

impediment *n* obstacle *m*.

impel *vt* pousser.

impending *adj* imminent.

impenetrable *adj* impénétrable.

imperative *adj* impératif.

imperceptible *adj* imperceptible.

imperceptibly *adv* imperceptiblement.

imperfect *adj* ~ly imparfait(ement); * *n* (*gr*) imparfait *m*.

imperfection *n* imperfection *f*; défaut *m*.

imperial *adj* impérial.

imperialism *n* impérialisme *m*.

imperious *adj* impérieux; ~ly *adv* impérieusement.

impermeable *adj* imperméable.

impersonal *adj* ~ly *adv* impersonel(lement).

impersonate *vt* se faire passer pour; imiter.

impertinence *n* impertinence *f*.

impertinent *adj* impertinent;
~**ly** *adv* impertinemment.
imperturbable *adj* imperturbable.
impervious *adj*
imperméable; indifférent.
impetuosity *n* impétuosité *f*.
impetuous *adj* impétueux;
~**ly** *adv* impétueusement.
impetus *n* élan *m*.
impiety *n* impiété *f*.
impinge (on) *vi* affecter;
empiéter (sur).
impious *adj* impie.
implacable *adj* implacable.
implacably *adv* implacablement.
implant *vt* implanter.
implement *n* outil *m*;
ustensile *m*.
implicate *vt* impliquer.
implication *n* implication *f*.
implicit *adj* implicite; ~**ly** *adv*
implicitement.
implore *vt* supplier.
imply *vt* supposer.
impolite *adj* impoli.
impoliteness *n* impolitesse *f*.
impolitic *adj* maladroit;
impolitique.
import *vt* importer; * *n* importation *f*.
importance *n* importance *f*.
important *adj* important.

importation *n* importation *f*.
importer *n* importateur *m*
-trice *f*.
importunate *adj* importun.
importune *vt* importuner.
importunity *n* importunité *f*.
impose *vt* imposer.
imposing *adj* imposant.
imposition *n* imposition *f*.
impossibility *n* impossibilité *f*.
impossible *adj* impossible.
impostor *n* imposteur *m*.
impotence *n* impotence *f*.
impotent *adj* impotent; ~**ly**
adv faiblement.
impound *vt* confisquer.
impoverish *vt* appauvrir.
impoverished *adj* appauvri.
impoverishment *n*
appauvrissement *m*.
impracticability *n* impraticabilité
f.
impracticable *adj* impraticable.
impractical *adj* peu pratique.
imprecation *n* imprécation,
malédiction *f*.
imprecise *adj* imprécis.
impregnable *adj* inexpugnable.
impregnate *vt* imprégner;
féconder.
impregnation *n* fécondation
f; imprégnation *f*.
impress *vt* impressionner.

impression *n* impression *f*; édition *f*.

impressionable *adj* impressionnable.

impressive *adj* impressionnant.

imprint *n* empreinte *f*; * *vt* imprimer; marquer.

imprison *vt* emprisonner.

imprisonment *n* emprisonnement *m*.

improbability *n* improbabilité *f*.

improbable *adj* improbable.

impromptu *adj* impromptu.

improper *adj* indécent; déplacé; impropre; ~ly *adv* indécemment; de manière déplacée; improprement.

impropriety *n* impropriété *f*; inconvenance *f*.

improve *vt* améliorer; * *vi* s'améliorer.

improvement *n* amélioration *f*.

improvident *adj* imprévoyant.

improvise *vt* improviser.

imprudence *n* imprudence *f*.

imprudent *adj* imprudent.

impudence *n* impudence *f*.

impudent *adj* impudent; ~ly *adv* impudemment.

impugn *vt* attaquer, contester.

impulse *n* impulsion *f*.

impulsive *adj* impulsif.

impunity *n* impunité *f*.

impure *adj* impur; ~ly *adv* impurement.

impurity *n* impureté *f*.

in *prep* dans; en.

inability *n* incapacité *f*.

inaccessible *adj* inaccessible.

inaccuracy *n* inexactitude *f*.

inaccurate *adj* inexact.

inaction *n* inaction *f*.

inactive *adj* inactif.

inactivity *n* inactivité *f*.

inadequate *adj* inadéquat.

inadmissible *adj* inadmissible.

inadvertently *adv* par inadvertance.

inalienable *adj* inaliénable.

inane *adj* inepte.

inanimate *adj* inanimé.

inapplicable *adj* inapplicable.

inappropriate *adj* impropre.

inasmuch *adv* attendu que.

inattentive *adj* inattentif.

inaudible *adj* inaudible.

inaugural *adj* inaugural.

inaugurate *vt* inaugurer.

inauguration *n* inauguration *f*.

inauspicious *adj* peu propice.

in-between *adj* intermédiaire.

inborn, inbred *adj* inné.

incalculable *adj* incalculable.

incandescent *adj* incandescent.

incantation *n* incantation *f*.

incapable *adj* incapable.

incapacitate *vt* mettre dans l'incapacité.

incapacity *n* incapacité *f*.

incarcerate *vt* incarcérer.

incarnate *adj* incarné.

incarnation *n* incarnation *f*.

incautious *adj* imprudent; ~ly *adv* imprudemment.

incendiary *n* bombe incendiaire *f*; incendiaire *mf*

incense *n* encens *m*; * *vt* exaspérer.

incentive *n* stimulant *m*; prime, aide *f*

inception *n* commencement *m*.

incessant *adj* incessant, continuel; ~ly *adv* continuellement.

incest *n* inceste *m*.

incestuous *adj* incestueux.

inch *n* pouce *m*; ~ by ~ petit à petit.

incidence *n* fréquence *f*.

incident *n* incident *m*.

incidental *adj* fortuit; ~ly *adv* incidemment.

incinerator *n* incinérateur *m*.

incipient *adj* naissant.

incise *vt* inciser.

incision *n* incision *f*.

incisive *adj* incisif.

incisor *n* incisive *f*.

incite *vt* inciter, encourager.

inclement *adj* inclément.

inclination *n* inclination, propension *f*.

incline *vt* incliner; * *vi* s'incliner.

include *vt* inclure, comprendre.

including *prep* inclus, y compris.

inclusion *n* inclusion *f*.

inclusive *adj* inclus; tout compris.

incognito *adv* incognito.

incoherence *n* incohérence *f*.

incoherent *adj* incohérent; ~ly *adv* d'une manière incohérente.

income *n* revenu *m*; recettes *fpl*.

income tax *n* impôt sur le revenu *m*.

incoming *adj* entrant; nouveau.

incomparable *adj* incomparable.

incomparably *adv* incomparablement.

incompatibility *n* incompatibilité *f*.

incompatible *adj* incompatible.

incompetence *n* incompétence *f*.

incompetent *adj* incompétent; **~ly** *adv* de manière incompétente.

incomplete *adj* incomplet.

incomprehensibility *n* incompréhensibilité *f.*

incomprehensible *adj* incompréhensible.

inconceivable *adj* inconcevable.

inconclusive *adj* peu concluant; * *adv* d'une manière peu concluante.

incongruity *n* incongruité *f.*

incongruous *adj* incongru; **~ly** *adv* incongrûment.

inconsequential *adj* inconséquent.

inconsiderate *adj* sans considération; inconsidéré; **~ly** *adv* sans considération.

inconsistency *n* inconsistance *f.*

inconsistent *adj* inconsistant.

inconsolable *adj* inconsolable.

inconspicuous *adj* discret.

incontinence *n* incontinence *f.*

incontinent *adj* incontinent.

incontrovertible *adj* indéniable.

inconvenience *n* inconvénient, désagrément *m*; * *vt* incommoder.

inconvenient *adj* incommode; **~ly** *adv* incommodément.

incorporate *vt* incorporer; * *vi* s'incorporer.

incorporated company *n* société constituée *f.*

incorporation *n* incorporation *f.*

incorrect *adj* incorrect, inexact; **~ly** *adv* incorrectement.

incorrigible *adj* incorrigible.

incorruptibility *n* incorruptibilité *f.*

incorruptible *adj* incorruptible.

increase *vt vi* augmenter; * *n* augmentation *f.*

increasing *adj* croissant; *adv* **~ly** de plus en plus.

incredible *adj* incroyable.

incredulity *n* incrédulité *f.*

incredulous *adj* incrédule.

increment *n* augmentation *f.*

incriminate *vt* incriminer.

incrust *vt* incruster.

incubate *vi* couver.

incubator *n* couveuse *f.*

inculcate *vt* inculquer.

incumbent *adj* en exercice; * *n* titulaire *mf.*

incur *vt* encourir.

incurability *n* incurabilité *f.*

incurable *adj* incurable.

incursion *n* incursion *f.*

indebted *adj* endetté; redevable.

indecency *n* indécence *f.*

indecent *adj* indécent; ~ly *adv* indécemment.

indecision *n* indécision, irrésolution *f.*

indecisive *adj* indécis, irrésolu.

indecorous *adj* inconvenant.

indeed *adv* vraiment.

indefatigable *adj* infatigable.

indefinite *adj* ~ly *adv* indéfini(ment).

indelible *adj* indélébile.

indelicacy *n* indélicatesse *f.*

indelicate *adj* peu délicat.

indemnify *vt* indemniser.

indemnity *n* indemnité *f.*

indent *vt* bosseler; renfoncer.

independence *n* indépendance *f.*

independent *adj* indépendant; ~ly *adv* indépendamment.

indescribable *adj* indescriptible.

indestructible *adj* indestructible.

indeterminate *adj* indéterminé.

index *n* (*math*) indice *m*; index *m.*

index card *n* fiche *f.*

indexed *adj* indexé.

index finger *n* index *m.*

indicate *vt* indiquer.

indication *n* indication *f*; indice *m.*

indicative *adj n* (*gr*) indicatif *m.*

indicator *n* indicateur *m.*

indict *vt* accuser.

indictment *n* accusation *f.*

indifference *n* indifférence *f.*

indifferent *adj* indifférent; ~ly *adv* indifféremment.

indigenous *adj* indigène.

indigent *adj* indigent.

indigestible *adj* indigeste.

indigestion *n* indigestion *f.*

indignant *adj* indigné.

indignation *n* indignation *f.*

indignity *n* indignité *f.*

indigo *n* indigo *m.*

indirect *adj* indirect; ~ly *adv* indirectement.

indiscreet *adj* indiscret; ~ly *adv* indiscrètement.

indiscretion *n* indiscrétion *f.*

indiscriminate *adj* ~ly *adv* sans discernement.

indispensable *adj* indispensable.

indisposed *adj* indisposé.

indisposition *n* indisposition *f.*

indisputable *adj* indiscutable.

indisputably *adv* indiscutablement.

indistinct *adj* indistinct, confus; ~ly *adv* indistinctement.

indistinguishable *adj* indiscernable.

individual *adj* ~ly *adv* individuel(lement); * *n* individu *m*.

individuality *n* individualité *f*.

indivisible *adj* ~bly *adv* indivisible(ment).

indoctrinate *vt* endoctriner.

indoctrination *n* endoctrinement *m*.

indolence *n* indolence *f*.

indolent *adj* indolent; ~ly *adv* indolemment.

indomitable *adj* indomptable.

indoors *adv* à l'intérieur.

indubitably *adv* indubitablement.

induce *vt* persuader; causer, provoquer.

inducement *n* encouragement *m*; incitation *f*.

induction *n* induction *f*.

indulge *vt* céder à; *vi* se permettre, se laisser aller.

indulgence *n* indulgence *f*.

indulgent *adj* indulgent; ~ly *adv* avec indulgence.

industrial *adj* industriel.

industrialist *n* industriel *m*.

industrialize *vt* industrialiser.

industrial park *n* zone industrielle *f*.

industrious *adj* travailleur.

industry *n* industrie *f*.

inebriated *vt* ivre.

inebriation *n* ivresse *f*.

inedible *adj* non comestible.

ineffable *adj* ineffable.

ineffective, ineffectual *adj* inefficace; ~ly *adv* inefficacement.

inefficiency *n* inefficacité *f*.

inefficient *adj* inefficace.

ineligible *adj* inéligible.

inept *adj* inepte; déplacé.

ineptitude *n* ineptie *f*; manque d'à-propos *m*.

inequality *n* inégalité *f*.

inert *adj* inerte.

inertia *n* inertie *f*.

inescapable *adj* inévitable.

inestimable *adj* inestimable.

inevitable *adj* inévitable.

inevitably *adv* inévitablement.

inexcusable *adj* inexcusable.

inexhaustible *adj* inépuisable.

inexorable *adj* inexorable.

inexpedient *adj* imprudent, inopportun.

inexpensive *adj* bon marché.

inexperience *n* inexpérience *f*.

inexperienced *adj* inexpérimenté.

inexpert *adj* néophyte.

inexplicable *adj* inexplicable.

inexpressible *adj* indicible; inexprimable.

inextricably *adv* inextricablement.

infallibility *n* infaillibilité *f*.

infallible *adj* infaillible.

infamous *adj* vil, infâme; ~ly *adv* vilement.

infamy *n* infamie *f*.

infancy *n* enfance *f*.

infant *n* bébé *m*; enfant *mf*.

infanticide *n* infanticide *mf*.

infantile *adj* infantile.

infantry *n* infanterie *f*.

infatuated *adj* fou.

infatuation *n* folie *f*; obsession *f*.

infect *vt* infecter.

infection *n* infection *f*.

infectious *adj* contagieux; infectieux.

infer *vt* inférer.

inference *n* inférence *f*.

inferior *adj* inférieur; * *n* subordonné *m* -e *f*.

inferiority *n* infériorité *f*.

infernal *adj* infernal.

inferno *n* enfer *m*.

infest *vt* infester.

infidel *n* infidèle *mf*.

infidelity *n* infidélité *f*.

infiltrate *vi* s'infiltrer.

infinite *adj* ~ly *adv* infini(ment).

infinitive *n* (*gr*) infinitif *m*.

infinity *n* infini *m*; infinité *f*.

infirm *adj* infirme.

infirmary *n* infirmerie *f*.

infirmity *n* infirmité *f*.

inflame *vt* enflammer; * *vi* s'enflammer.

inflammation *n* inflammation *f*.

inflammatory *adj* inflammatoire.

inflatable *adj* gonflable.

inflate *vt* gonfler.

inflation *n* inflation *f*.

inflection *n* inflexion *f*.

inflexibility *n* inflexibilité *f*.

inflexible *adj* inflexible.

inflexibly *adv* inflexiblement.

inflict *vt* infliger.

influence *n* influence *f*; * *vt* influencer.

influential *adj* influent.

influenza *n* grippe *f*.

influx *n* afflux *m*.

inform *vt* informer.

informal *adj* informel; simple; familier.

informality *n* simplicité *f*.

informant *n* informateur *m* -trice *f*.

information *n* information *f*.

infraction *n* infraction *f*.

infrared *adj* infrarouge.

infrastructure *n* infrastructure *f*.

infrequent *adj* ~ly *adv* rare(ment).

infringe *vt* enfreindre.

infringement *n* infraction *f*.

infuriate *vt* rendre furieux.

infuse *vt* infuser.

infusion *n* infusion *f*.

ingenious *adj* ingénieux; ~ly *adv* ingénieusement.

ingenuity *n* ingéniosité *f*.

ingenuous *adj* ~ly *adv* ingénu(ment); sincère(ment).

inglorious *adj* infamant; ~ly *adv* honteusement.

ingot *n* lingot *m*.

ingrained *adj* invétéré.

ingratiate *vi*: ~ with sb chercher à entrer dans les bonnes grâces de qn.

ingratitude *n* ingratitude *f*.

ingredient *n* ingrédient *m*.

inhabit *vt vi* habiter.

inhabitable *adj* habitable.

inhabitant *n* habitant *m* -e *f*.

inhale *vt* inhaler.

inherent *adj* inhérent.

inherit *vt* hériter.

inheritance *n* héritage *m*.

inheritor *n* héritier *m* -ière *f*.

inhibit *vt* inhiber.

inhibited *adj* inhibé.

inhibition *n* inhibition *f*.

inhospitable *adj* inhospitalier.

inhospitality *n* inhospitalité *f*.

inhuman *adj* inhumain; ~ly *adv* inhumainement.

inhumanity *n* inhumanité, cruauté *f*.

inimical *adj* hostile, ennemi.

inimitable *adj* inimitable.

iniquitous *adj* inique, injuste.

iniquity *n* iniquité, injustice *f*.

initial *adj* initial; * *n* initiale *f*.

initially *adv* au début.

initiate *vt* commencer; initier.

initiation *n* début, commencement *m*; initiation *f*.

initiative *n* initiative *f*.

inject *vt* injecter.

injection *n* injection *f*.

injudicious *adj* peu judicieux.

injunction *n* injonction *f*; ordre *m*.

injure *vt* blesser.

injury *n* blessure *f*; tort *m*.

injury time *n* arrêts de jeu *mpl*.

injustice *n* injustice *f*.

ink *n* encre *f*.

inkling *n* soupçon *m*.

inkstand *n* encrier *m*.

inlaid *adj* incrusté.

inland *adj* intérieur; * *adv* vers l'intérieur, dans les terres.

in-laws *npl* belle-famille *f*.

inlay *vt* incruster.

inlet *n* entrée *f*; bras de mer *m*.

inmate *n* détenu *m* -e *f*.

inmost *adj* le plus profond.

inn *n* auberge *f*; hôtel *m*.

innate *adj* inné.

inner *adj* intérieur.

innermost *adj* le plus profond.

inner tube *n* chambre à air *f*.

innkeeper *n* aubergiste *mf*, hôtelier *m* -ière *f*.

innocence *n* innocence *f*.

innocent *adj* innocent; ~ly *adv* innocemment.

innocuous *adj* inoffensif; ~ly *adv* de manière inoffensive.

innovate *vt* innover.

innovation *n* innovation *f*.

innuendo *n* allusion *f*; insinuation *f*.

innumerable *adj* innombrable.

inoculate *vt* inoculer.

inoculation *n* inoculation *f*.

inoffensive *adj* inoffensif.

inopportune *adj* inopportun.

inordinately *adv* démesurément.

inorganic *adj* inorganique.

in-patient *n* patient(e) hospitalisé(e) *m(f)*.

input *n* entrée *f*; consommation *f*.

inquest *n* enquête *f*.

inquire *vti* demander; ~ **about** s'informer de; ~ **after** *vt* demander des nouvelles de; ~ **into** *vt* faire des recherches sur; enquêter sur.

inquiry *n* demande de renseignements *f*; enquête *f*.

inquisition *n* investigation *f*.

inquisitive *adj* curieux.

inroad *n* incursion *f*.

insane *adj* fou, *f* folle.

insanity *n* folie *f*.

insatiable *adj* insatiable.

inscribe *vt* inscrire; dédier.

inscription *n* inscription *f*; dédicace *f*.

inscrutable *adj* impénétrable.

insect *n* insecte *m*.

insecticide *n* insecticide *m*.

insecure *adj* peu assuré.

insecurity *n* insécurité *f*.

insemination *n* insémination *f*.

insensible *adj* inconscient; insensible.

insensitive *adj* insensible.

inseparable *adj* inséparable.

insert *vt* introduire, insérer.

insertion n insertion f.

inshore adj côtier.

inside n intérieur m; * adv à l'intérieur.

inside out adv à l'envers; à fond.

insidious adj insidieux; ~ly insidieusement.

insight n perspicacité f.

insignia npl insignes mpl.

insignificant adj insignifiant.

insincere adj peu sincère.

insincerity n manque de sincérité m.

insinuate vt insinuer.

insinuation n insinuation f.

insipid adj insipide.

insist vi insister.

insistence n insistance f.

insistent adj insistant.

insole n semelle intérieure f.

insolence n insolence f.

insolent adj insolent; ~ly adv insolemment.

insoluble adj insoluble.

insolvency n insolvabilité f.

insolvent adj insolvable.

insomnia n insomnie f.

insomuch conj à tel point.

inspect vt examiner, inspecter.

inspection n inspection f.

inspector n inspecteur m -trice f.

inspiration n inspiration f.

inspire vt inspirer.

instability n instabilité f.

instal vt installer.

installation n installation f.

instalment n installation f; versement m.

instalment plan n plan de vente à tempérament m.

instance n exemple m; for ~ par exemple.

instant adj instantané; ~ly adv immédiatement; * n instant, moment m.

instantaneous adj ~ly adv instantané(ment).

instead (of) pr au lieu, à la place (de).

instep n cou-de-pied m.

instigate vt inciter; susciter.

instigation n incitation f.

instil vt instiller; inspirer.

instinct n instinct m.

instinctive adj instinctif; ~ly adv instinctivement, d'instinct.

institute vt instituer; * n institut m.

institution n institution f.

instruct vt instruire.

instruction n instruction f.

instructive adj instructif.

instructor n professeur m; moniteur m -trice f.

instrument *n* instrument *m*.

instrumental *adj* instrumental.

insubordinate *adj* insubordonné.

insubordination *n* insubordination *f*.

insufferable *adj* insupportable.

insufferably *adv* insupportablement.

insufficiency *n* insuffisance *f*.

insufficient *adj* insuffisant; ~ly *adv* insuffisamment.

insular *adj* insulaire; borné.

insulate *vt* isoler; insonoriser.

insulating tape *n* ruban isolant *m*.

insulation *n* isolation *f*; insonorisation *f*.

insulin *n* insuline *f*.

insult *vt* insulter; * *n* insulte *f*.

insulting *adj* insultant.

insuperable *adj* insurmontable.

insurance *n* (com) assurance *f*.

insurance policy *n* police d'assurance *f*.

insure *vt* assurer.

insurgent *n* insurgé, rebelle *m*.

insurmountable *adj* insurmontable.

insurrection *n* insurrection *f*.

intact *adj* intact.

intake *n* admission *f*; consommation *f*.

integral *adj* intégrant; (*chem*) intégral; * *n* intégrale *f*.

integrate *vt* intégrer.

integration *n* intégration *f*.

integrity *n* intégrité *f*.

intellect *n* intellect *m*.

intellectual *adj* intellectuel.

intelligence *n* intelligence *f*.

intelligent *adj* intelligent.

intelligentsia *n* intelligentsia *f*.

intelligible *adj* intelligible.

intelligibly *adv* intelligiblement.

intemperate *adj* ~ly *adv* immodéré(ment).

intend *vt* avoir l'intention de.

intendant *n* intendant *m* -e *f*.

intended *adj* voulu.

intense *adj* intense; ~ly *adv* intensément.

intensify *vt* intensifier.

intensity *n* intensité *f*.

intensive *adj* intensif.

intensive care unit *n* service de soins intensifs *m*.

intent *adj* résolu; attentif; ~ly *adv* attentivement; * *n* intention *f*, dessein *m*.

intention *n* intention *f*, dessein *m*.

intentional *adj* intentionnel;

~ly *adv* à dessein, intentionnellement.

inter *vt* enterrer.

interaction *n* interaction *f*.

intercede *vi* intercéder.

intercept *vt* intercepter.

intercession *n* intercession *f*.

interchange *n* échange *m*.

intercom *n* interphone *m*.

intercourse *n* relations sexuelles *fpl*.

interest *vt* intéresser; * *n* intérêt *m*.

interesting *adj* intéressant.

interest rate *n* taux d'intérêt *m*.

interfere *vi* s'ingérer.

interference *n* ingérence *f*; interférence *f*.

interim *adj* intérimaire.

interior *adj* intérieur.

interior designer *n* d(écorateur(-trice) d'intérieur *m(f)*.

interjection *n* (*gr*) interjection *f*.

interlock *vi* s'entremêler.

interlocutor *n* interlocuteur *m* -trice *f*.

interloper *n* intrus *m* -e *f*.

interlude *n* intermède *m*.

intermarriage *n* intermariage *m*.

intermediary *n* intermédiaire *mf*.

intermediate *adj* intermédiaire.

interment *n* enterrement *m*.

interminable *adj* interminable.

intermingle *vt* entremêler; * *vi* s'entremêler.

intermission *n* entracte *m*; interruption *f*.

intermittent *adj* intermittent.

intern *n* interne *mf*.

internal *adj* intérieur; interne; ~ly *adv* intérieurement.

international *adj* international.

interplay *n* interaction *f*.

interpose *vt* interposer.

interpret *vt* interpréter.

interpretation *n* interprétation *f*.

interpreter *n* interprète *mf*.

interregnum *n* interrègne *m*.

interrelated *adj* en corrélation.

interrogate *vt* interroger.

interrogation *n* interrogatoire *m*.

interrogative *adj* interrogatif.

interrupt *vt* interrompre.

interruption *n* interruption *f*.

intersect *vi* se croiser.

intersection *n* croisement *m*.

intersperse *vt* parsemer.

intertwine *vt* entrelacer.

interval *n* intervalle *m*; mi-temps *f*.

intervene *vi* intervenir.

intervention *n* intervention *f*.

interview *n* entrevue *f*; interview *f*; * *vt* faire passer une entrevue à; interviewer.

interviewer *n* interviewer *m*.

interweave *vt* entrelacer.

intestate *adj* intestat.

intestinal *adj* intestinal.

intestine *n* intestin *m*.

intimacy *n* intimité *f*.

intimate *n* intime *mf*; * *adj* ~ly *adv* intime(ment); * *vt* insinuer, laisser entendre.

intimidate *vt* intimider.

into *prep* dans, en.

intolerable *adj* intolérable.

intolerably *adv* intolérablement.

intolerance *n* intolérance *f*.

intolerant *adj* intolérant.

intonation *n* intonation *f*.

intoxicate *vt* enivrer.

intoxication *n* ivresse *f*.

intractable *adj* intraitable.

intransitive *adj* (*gr*) intransitif.

intravenous *adj* intraveineux.

in-tray *n* courrier à l'arrivée *m*.

intrepid *adj* intrépide; ~ly *adv* intrépidement.

intrepidity *n* intrépidité *f*.

intricacy *n* complexité *f*.

intricate *adj* complexe, compliqué; ~ly *adv* de manière compliquée.

intrigue *n* intrigue *f*; * *vi* intriguer.

intriguing *adj* intrigant.

intrinsic *adj* ~ally *adv* intrinsèque(ment).

introduce *vt* introduire.

introduction *n* introduction *f*.

introductory *adj* d'introduction.

introspection *n* introspection *f*.

introvert *n* introverti *m* -ie *f*.

intrude *vi* s'ingérer, s'immiscer.

intruder *n* intrus *m* -e *f*.

intrusion *n* intrusion *f*.

intuition *n* intuition *f*.

intuitive *adj* intuitif.

inundate *vt* inonder.

inundation *n* inondation *f*.

inure *vt* endurcir.

invade *vt* envahir.

invader *n* envahisseur *m* -euse *f*.

invalid *adj* invalide; * *n* invalide *mf*.

invalidate *vt* invalider, annuler.

invaluable *adj* inappréciable.

invariable *adj* invariable.

invariably *adv* invariablement.

invasion *n* invasion *f*.

invective *n* invective *f*.

inveigle *vt* persuader, entraîner.

invent *vt* inventer.

invention *n* invention *f*.

inventive *adj* inventif.

inventor *n* inventeur *m* -trice *f*.

inventory *n* inventaire *m*.

inverse *adj* inverse.

inversion *n* inversion *f*.

invert *vt* inverser.

invest *vt* investir.

investigate *vt* faire des recherches sur; examiner.

investigation *n* investigation *f*; recherches *fpl*.

investigator *n* investigateur *m* -trice *f*; chercheur *m* -euse *f*.

investment *n* investissement *m*.

inveterate *adj* invétéré.

invidious *adj* odieux; désobligeant.

invigilate *vt* surveiller.

invigorating *adj* vivifiant.

invincible *adj* invincible.

invincibly *adv* invinciblement.

inviolable *adj* inviolable.

invisible *adj* invisible.

invisibly *adv* invisiblement.

invitation *n* invitation *f*.

invite *vt* inviter.

inviting *adj* attrayant, tentant.

invoice *n* (*com*) facture *f*.

invoke *vt* invoquer.

involuntarily *adv* involontairement.

involuntary *adj* involontaire.

involve *vt* impliquer, entraîner.

involved *adj* compliqué; impliqué.

involvement *n* implication *f*; confusion *f*.

invulnerable *adj* invulnérable.

inward *adj* intérieur; intime; ~, ~s *adv* vers l'intérieur.

iodine *n* (*chem*) iode *m*.

IOU (I owe you) *n* reçu *m*.

irascible *adj* irascible.

irate, ireful *adj* irrité.

iris *n* iris *m*.

irksome *adj* fastidieux, ennuyeux.

iron *n* fer *m*; * *adj* de fer; * *vt* repasser.

ironic *adj* ~ally *adv* ironique(ment).

ironing *n* repassage *m*.

ironing board *n* table *f* à repasser.

iron ore *n* minerai de fer *m*.

ironwork *n* ferronnerie *f*; ~s *pl* ferronneries *fpl*.

irony *n* ironie *f*.

irradiate *vt* irradier.

irrational *adj* irrationnel.

irreconcilable *adj* irréconciliable; inconciliable.

irregular *adj* irrégulier; ~ly *adv* irrégulièrement.

irregularity *n* irrégularité *f*.

irrelevant *adj* hors de propos.

irreligious *adj* irréligieux.

irreparable *adj* irréparable.

irreplaceable *adj* irremplaçable.

irrepressible *adj* irrépressible.

irreproachable *adj* irréprochable.

irresistible *adj* irrésistible.

irresolute *adj* ~ly *adv* irrésolu(ment).

irresponsible *adj* irresponsable.

irretrievably *adv* irréparablement.

irreverence *n* irrévérence *f*.

irreverent *adj* irrévérencieux; ~ly *adv* irrévérencieusement.

irrigate *vt* irriguer.

irrigation *n* irrigation *f*.

irritability *n* irritabilité *f*.

irritable *adj* irritable.

irritant *n* (*med*) irritant *m*.

irritate *vt* irriter.

irritating *adj* irritant.

irritation *n* irritation *f*.

Islam *n* Islam *m*.

island *n* île *f*.

islander *n* insulaire *mf*.

isle *n* île *f*.

isolate *vt* isoler.

isolation *n* isolement *m*.

issue *n* sujet *m*, question *f*; * *vt* publier; distribuer; fournir.

isthmus *n* isthme *m*.

it *pn* il, elle; le, la; cela, ça, ce, c'.

italic *n* italique *m*.

itch *n* démangeaison *f*; * *vi* avoir des démangeaisons.

item *n* article *m*.

itemize *vt* détailler.

itinerant *adj* ambulant, itinérant.

itinerary *n* itinéraire *m*.

its *pn* son, sa, ses.

itself *pn* lui-même, elle-même.

ivory *n* ivoire *m*.

ivy *n* lierre *m*.

J

jab *vt* planter, enfoncer.

jabber *vi* baragouiner.

jack *n* cric *m*; valet *m*.

jackal *n* chacal *m*.

jackboots *npl* bottes de militaire *fpl*.

jackdaw *n* choucas *m*.

jacket *n* veste *f*; couverture *f*.

jackknife *vi* se mettre en travers.

jack plug *n* prise à fiche *f*.

jackpot *n* gros lot *m*.

jade *n* jade *m*.

jagged *adj* dentelé.

jaguar *n* jaguar *m*.

jail *n* prison *f*.

jailbird *n* prisonnier *m* -ière *f*.

jailer *n* geôlier *m* -ière *f*.

jam *n* confiture *f*; embouteillage *m*.

jangle *vi* cliqueter.

janitor *n* portier *m*.

January *n* janvier *m*.

jar *vi* se heurter; (*mus*) détonner; grincer; * *n* pot *m*.

jargon *n* jargon *m*.

jasmine *n* jasmin *m*.

jaundice *n* jaunisse *f*.

jaunt *n* promenade *f*.

jaunty *adj* enjoué.

javelin *n* javelot *m*.

jaw *n* mâchoire *f*.

jay *n* geai *m*.

jealous *adj* jaloux.

jealousy *n* jalousie *f*.

jeans *npl* jean *m*.

jeer *vi* se moquer, railler; * *n* raillerie, moquerie *f*.

jelly *n* gelée *f*.

jellyfish *n* méduse *f*.

jeopardize *vt* risquer, mettre en péril.

jerk *n* secousse *f*; * *vt* donner une secousse à.

jerky *adj* saccadé.

jersey *n* jersey *m*, tricot *m*.

jest *n* blague, plaisanterie *f*.

jester *n* bouffon *m*.

jestingly *adv* en plaisantant.

Jesuit *n* jésuite *m*.

Jesus *n* Jésus *m*.

jet *n* avion à réaction *m*; jet *m*; gicleur *m*.

jet engine *n* moteur à réaction *m*.

jettison *vt* se défaire de.

jetty *n* jetée *f*.

Jew *n* Juif *m*.

jewel *n* bijou *m*.

jeweller *n* bijoutier *m* -ière *f*.

jewellery *n* bijoux *mpl*.

jewellery store *n* bijouterie *f*.

Jewess *n* Juive *f*.

Jewish *adj* juif.

jib *n* (*mar*) foc *m*.

jibe *n* raillerie, moquerie *f*.

jig *n* gigue *f*.

jigsaw *n* puzzle *m*.

jilt *vt* laisser tomber.

jinx *n* porte-malheur *m invar*.

job *n* travail *m*.

jockey *n* jockey *m*.

jocular *adj* joyeux; facétieux.

jog *vi* faire du jogging.

join *vt* joindre, unir; ~ in participer à; * *vi* se réunir; se joindre.

joiner *n* menuisier *m*.

joinery *n* menuiserie *f*.

joint *n* articulation *f*; * *adj* commun.

jointly *adv* conjointement.

joint-stock company *n* (*com*) société par actions *f*.

joke *n* blague, plaisanterie *f*; * *vi* blaguer, plaisanter.

joker *n* blagueur *m* -euse *f*.

jollity *n* gaieté *f*.

jolly *adj* gai, joyeux.

jolt *vt* secouer; * *n* secousse *f*.

jostle *vt* bousculer.

journal *n* revue *f*.

journalism *n* journalisme *m*.

journalist *n* journaliste *mf*.

journey *n* voyage *m*; * *vi* voyager.

jovial *adj* jovial, gai; ~ly *adv* jovialement.

joy *n* joie *f*.

joyful, joyous *adj* joyeux, gai; ~ly *adv* joyeusement.

joystick *n* manche à balai *m*.

jubilant *adj* réjoui.

jubilation *n* jubilation *f*.

jubilee *n* jubilé *m*.

Judaism *n* judaïsme *m*.

judge *n* juge *m*; * *vt* juger.

judgment *n* jugement *m*.

judicial *adj* ~ly *adv* judiciaire(ment).

judiciary *n* pouvoir judiciaire *m*.

judicious *adj* judicieux.

judo *n* judo *m*.

jug *n* cruche *f*.

juggle *vi* jongler.

juggler *n* jongleur *m* -euse *f*.

juice n jus m; suc m.

juicy adj juteux.

jukebox n juke-box m.

July n juillet m.

jumble vt mélanger; * n mélange m; fouillis m.

jump vi sauter; * n saut m.

jumper n pull m; sauteur m -euse f.

jumpy adj nerveux.

juncture n joncture f.

June n juin m.

jungle n jungle f.

junior adj plus jeune

juniper n (bot) genièvre m.

junk n cochonnerie f; bric-à-brac m invar.

junta n junte f.

jurisdiction n juridiction f.

jurisprudence n jurisprudence f.

jurist n juriste mf.

juror, juryman n juré m.

jury n jury m.

just adj juste; * adv justement, exactement; ~ as juste quand; ~ now tout de suite.

justice n justice f.

justifiably adv légitimement.

justification n justification f.

justify vt justifier.

justly adv justement.

justness n justesse f.

jut vi: to ~ out faire saillie, dépasser.

jute n jute m.

juvenile adj juvénile; pour enfants.

juxtaposition n juxtaposition f.

K

kaleidoscope *n* kaléidoscope *m*.

kangaroo *n* kangourou *m*.

karate *n* karaté *m*.

kebab *n* brochette *f*.

keel *n* (*mar*) quille *f*.

keen *adj* aiguisé; vif; enthousiaste.

keenness *n* enthousiasme *m*.

keep *vt* garder, conserver; tenir.

keeper *n* gardien *m* -ne *f*.

keepsake *n* souvenir *m*.

keg *n* baril *m*.

kennel *n* niche *f*.

kernel *n* amande *f*; noyau *m*.

kerosene *n* kérosène *m*.

kettle *n* bouilloire *f*.

kettledrum n timbale *f*.

key *n* clé, clef *f*; (*mus*) ton *m*; touche *f*.

keyboard *n* clavier *m*.

keyhole *n* trou de la serrure *m*.

keynote *n* (*mus*) tonique *f*.

key ring *n* porte-clefs *m invar*.

keystone *n* clef de voûte *f*.

khaki *n* kaki *m*.

kick *vi* (*vt*) donner un coup de pied (à); * *n* coup de pied *m*; plaisir *m*.

kid *n* gamin *m* -e *f*.

kidnap *vt* kidnapper.

kidnapper *n* kidnappeur *m* -euse *f*.

kidnapping *n* kidnapping *m*.

kidney *n* rein *m*; rognon *m*.

killer *n* assassin *m*.

killing *n* assassinat *m*.

kiln *n* four *m*.

kilo *n* kilo *m*.

kilobyte *n* kilo-octet *m*.

kilogram *n* kilogramme *m*.

kilometre *n* kilomètre *m*.

kin *n* parents *mpl*; next of ~ parent proche *m*.

kind *adj* gentil; * *n* genre *m*, sorte *f*.

kindergarten *n* jardin d'enfants *m*.

kind-hearted *adj* bon.

kindle *vt* allumer; * *vi* s'allumer.

kindliness *n* gentillesse, bonté *f*.

kindly *adj* bon, bienveillant.

kindness *n* bonté *f*.

kindred *adj* apparenté.

kinetic *adj* cinétique.

king *n* roi *m*.

kingdom *n* royaume *m*.

kingfisher *n* martin-pêcheur *m*.

kiosk *n* kiosque *m*.

kiss *n* baiser *m*; * *vt* embrasser.

kissing *n* baisers *mpl*.

kit *n* équipement *m*.

kitchen *n* cuisine *f*.

kitchen garden *n* potager *m*.

kite *n* cerf-volant *m*.

kitten *n* chaton *m*.

knack *n* don, chic *m*.

knapsack *n* sac à dos *m*.

knave *n* fripouille *f*; (*cards*) valet *m*.

knead *vt* pétrir.

knee *n* genou *m*.

knee-deep *adj* jusqu'aux genoux.

kneel *vi* s'agenouiller.

knell *n* glas *m*.

knife *n* couteau *m*.

knight *n* chevalier *m*.

knit *vt vi* tricoter; ~ **the brows** froncer les sourcils.

knitter *n* tricoteur *m* -euse *f*.

knitting pin *n* aiguille à tricoter *f*.

knitwear *n* tricots *mpl*.

knob *n* bouton *m*; nœud *m* (du bois).

knock *vt vi* cogner, frapper; ~ **down** abattre; * *n* coup *m*.

knocker *n* heurtoir *m*.

knock-kneed *adj* aux genoux cagneux.

knock-out *n* knock-out *m*.

knoll *n* butte *f*.

knot *n* nœud *m*; * *vt* nouer.

knotty *adj* emmêlé; épineux.

know *vt vi* savoir; connaître.

know-all *n* je-sais-tout *m*.

know-how *n* savoir-faire *m*.

knowing *adj* entendu; ~**ly** *adv* en connaissance de cause.

knowledge *n* connaissances *fpl*.

knowledgeable *adj* bien informé.

knuckle *n* articulation *f*.

L

label *n* étiquette *f*.

laboratory *n* laboratoire *m*.

laborious *adj* laborieux; pénible; **~ly** *adv* laborieusement.

labour *n* travail *m*; **to be in ~** être en train d'accoucher; * *vi* travailler.

labourer *n* ouvrier *m*.

labour union *n* syndicat *m*.

labyrinth *n* labyrinthe *m*.

lace *n* lacet *m*; dentelle *f*; * *vt* lacer.

lacerate *vt* lacérer.

lack *vt* manquer de; * *vi* manquer; * *n* manque *m*.

lackadaisical *adj* nonchalant.

lackey *n* laquais *m*.

laconic *adj* laconique.

lacquer *n* laque *f*.

lad *n* garçon *m*.

ladder *n* échelle *f*.

ladle *n* louche *f*.

ladleful *n* louchée *f*.

lady *n* dame *f*.

ladybird *n* coccinelle *f*.

ladykiller *n* bourreau des cœurs *m*.

ladylike *adj* distingué.

ladyship *n* madame *f*.

lag *vi* se laisser distancer.

lager *n* bière blonde *f*.

lagoon *n* lagune *f*.

laidback *adj* décontracté.

lair *n* repaire *m*.

laity *n* laïcat *m*.

lake *n* lac *m*.

lamb *n* agneau *m*; * *vi* agneler.

lambswool *n* laine d'agneau *f*.

lame *adj* boiteux.

lament *vt* se lamenter sur; * *vi* se lamenter; * *n* lamentation *f*.

lamentable *adj* lamentable, déplorable.

lamentation *n* lamentation *f*.

laminated *adj* laminé.

lamp *n* lampe *f*.

lampoon *n* satire *f*.

lampshade *n* abat-jour *m* invar.

lance *n* lance *f*; bistouri *m*; *
vt inciser.

lancet *n* bistouri *m*.

land *n* pays *m*; terre *f*; * *vt*
débarquer; * *vi* atterrir,
débarquer.

land forces *npl* armée de terre
f.

landholder *n* propriétaire
terrien *m*.

landing *n* atterrissage *m*.

landing strip *n* piste
d'atterrissage *f*.

landlady *n* propriétaire *f*.

landlord *n* propriétaire *m*.

landlubber *n* marin d'eau
douce *m*.

landmark *n* point de repère *m*.

landowner *n* propriétaire
terrien *m*.

landscape *n* paysage *m*.

landslide *n* glissement de terrain *m*.

lane *n* allée, ruelle *f*; file *f*.

language *n* langue *f*; langage
m.

languid *adj* languissant; ~ly
adv languissamment.

languish *vi* languir.

lank *adj* raide, plat.

lanky *adj* grand et maigre.

lantern *n* lanterne *f*.

lap *n* genoux *mpl*; * *vt* laper.

lapdog *n* chien *m* de salon.

lapel *n* revers *m*.

lapse *n* laps *m*; défaillance *f*;
* *vi* expirer, se périmer; se
relâcher.

larceny *n* vol *m*.

larch *n* mélèze *m*.

lard *n* saindoux *m*.

larder *n* garde-manger *m*
invar.

large *adj* grand; **at ~** en
liberté; ~ly *adv* en grande
partie.

large-scale *adj* à grande échelle.

largesse *n* largesse *f*.

lark *n* alouette *f*.

larva *n* larve *f*.

laryngitis *n* laryngite *f*.

larynx *n* larynx *m*.

lascivious *adj* lascif; ~ly *adv*
lascivement.

laser *n* laser *m*.

lash *n* coup de fouet *m*; * *vt*
fouetter; attacher.

lasso *n* lasso *m*.

last *adj* dernier; **at ~** enfin;
~ly *adv* finalement; * *n*
dernier *m*, dernière *f*;
forme *f* (de cordonnier); *
vi durer.

last-ditch *adj* ultime.

lasting *adj* ~ly *adv*
durable(ment).

last-minute *adj* de dernière minute.

latch *n* loquet *m*.

latchkey *n* clef de porte d'entrée *f*.

late *adj* en retard; défunt; (*rail*) the train is ten minutes ~ le train a dix minutes de retard; * *adv* tard; ~ly *adv* récemment.

latecomer *n* retardataire *mf*.

latent *adj* latent.

lateral *adj* ~ly *adv* latérale(ment).

lathe *n* tour *m*.

lather *n* mousse *f*.

latitude *n* latitude *f*.

latrine *n* latrine *f*.

latter *adj* dernier; ~ly *adv* récemment.

lattice *n* treillis *m*.

laudable *adj* louable.

laudably *adv* louablement.

laugh *vi* rire; ~ at *vt* rire de, se moquer de; * *n* rire *m*.

laughable *adj* risible; dérisoire.

laughing stock *n* risée *f*.

laughter *n* rires *mpl*.

launch *vt* lancer; * *vi* se lancer; * *n* (*mar*) vedette *f*.

launching *n* lancement *m*.

launching pad *n* rampe de lancement *f*.

launder *vt* laver.

laundrette, laundromat *n* laverie automatique *f*.

laundry *n* lessive *f*.

laurel *n* laurier *m*.

lava *n* lave *f*.

lavatory *n* toilettes *fpl*.

lavender *n* (*bot*) lavande *f*.

lavish *adj* prodigue; ~ly *adv* avec prodigalité; * *vt* prodiguer.

law *n* loi *f*; droit *m*.

law-abiding *adj* respectueux de la loi.

law and order *n* ordre public *m*.

law court *n* tribunal *m*.

lawful *adj* légal; légitime; ~ly *adv* légalement.

lawless *adj* anarchique.

lawlessness *n* anarchie *f*.

lawmaker *n* législateur *m* -trice *f*.

lawn *n* pelouse *f*, gazon *m*.

lawnmower *n* tondeuse à gazon *f*.

law school *n* faculté de droit *f*.

law suit *n* procès *m*.

lawyer *n* avocat *m*; juriste *m*.

lax *adj* relâché.

laxative *n* laxatif *m*.

laxity *n* relâchement *m*; flou *m*.

lay *vt* coucher; mettre; pondre; ~ **claim** réclamer; prétendre (à); * *vi* pondre.

layabout *n* paresseux *m* -euse *f*.

layer *n* couche *f*.

layette *n* layette *f*.

layman *n* laïc *m*.

layout *n* disposition *f*; présentation *f*.

laze *vi* paresser.

lazily *adv* paresseusement.

laziness *n* paresse *f*.

lazy *adj* paresseux.

lead *n* plomb *m*; * *vt vi* conduire, mener.

leader *n* chef *m*.

leadership *n* direction *f*.

leading *adj* principal; premier; ~ **article** *n* article de fond *m*.

leaf *n* feuille *f*.

leaflet *n* feuillet *m*; prospectus *m*.

leafy *adj* feuillu.

league *n* ligue *f*; lieue *f*.

leak *n* fuite *f*; * *vi* (*mar*) faire eau.

leaky *adj* qui fuit.

lean *vt* appuyer; * *vi* s'appuyer; * *adj* maigre.

leap *vi* sauter; * *n* saut *m*.

leapfrog *n* saute-mouton *m*.

leap year *n* année bisextile *f*.

learn *vt vi* apprendre.

learned *adj* instruit.

learner *n* élève *mf*; débutant *m* -e *f*.

learning *n* érudition *f*.

lease *n* bail *m*; * *vt* louer.

leasehold *n* bail *m*.

leash *n* laisse *f*.

least *adj* moindre; **at ~** au moins; **not in the ~** pas du tout.

leather *n* cuir *m*.

leathery *adj* qui a l'aspect du cuir.

leave *n* permission *f*; congé *m*; **to take ~** prendre congé; * *vt* laisser.

leaven *n* levain *m*; * *vt* faire lever.

leavings *npl* restes *mpl*.

lecherous *adj* lascif, lubrique.

lecture *n* conférence *f*; * *vi* faire une conférence.

lecturer *n* conférencier *m* -ière *f*.

ledge *n* rebord *m*.

ledger *n* (*com*) registre *m*.

lee *n* (*mar*) côté sous le vent *m*.

leech *n* sangsue *f*.

leek *n* (*bot*) poireau *m*.

leer *vt* regarder d'un œil lascif.

lees *npl* lie *f*.

leeward *adj* (*mar*) sous le vent.

leeway *n* liberté d'action *f*.

left *adj* gauche; **on the ~** à gauche.

left-handed *adj* gau. .her.

left-luggage office *n* consigne *f*.

leftovers *npl* restes *mpl*.

leg *n* jambe *f*; patte *f*.

legacy *n* héritage, legs *m*.

legal *adj* légal, légitime; **~ly** *adv* légalement.

legal holiday *n* jour férié *m*.

legality *n* légalité, légitimité *f*.

legalize *vt* légaliser.

legal tender *n* monnaie légale *f*.

legate *n* légat *m*.

legatee *n* légataire *mf*.

legation *n* légation *f*.

legend *n* légende *f*.

legendary *adj* légendaire.

legible *adj* lisible.

legibly *adv* lisiblement.

legion *n* légion *f*.

legislate *vt vi* légiférer.

legislation *n* législation *f*.

legislative *adj* législatif.

legislator *n* législateur *m* -trice *f*.

legislature *n* corps législatif *m*.

legitimacy *n* légitimité *f*.

legitimate *adj* légitime; **~ly** *adv* légitimement; * *vt* légitimer.

leisure *n* loisir *m*; **~ly** *adj* tranquille; **at ~** au calme.

lemon *n* citron *m*.

lemonade *n* limonade *f*.

lemon tea *n* thé au citron *m*.

lemon tree *n* citronnier *m*.

lend *vt* prêter.

length *n* longueur *f*; durée *f*; **at ~** longuement; enfin.

lengthen *vt* allonger; * *vi* s'allonger.

lengthways, lengthwise *adv* dans le sens de la longueur.

lengthy *adj* long.

lenient *adj* indulgent.

lens *n* lentille *f* (optique).

Lent *n* Carême *m*.

lentil *n* lentille *f*.

Leo *n* Lion *m* (signe du zodiaque).

leopard *n* léopard *m*.

leotard *n* justaucorps *m*.

leper *n* lépreux *m* -euse *f*.

leprosy *n* lèpre *f*.

lesbian *n* lesbienne *f*.

less *adj* moins; * *adv* moins.

lessen *vt vi* diminuer.

lesser *adj* moindre.

lesson *n* leçon *f*.

lest *conj* de crainte que.

let *vt* laisser, permettre; louer.

lethal *adj* mortel.

lethargic *adj* léthargique.

lethargy *n* léthargie *f*.

letter *n* lettre *f*.

letter bomb *n* lettre piégée *f*.

letter box boite aux lettres *f*.

lettering *n* inscription *f*.

letter of credit *n* lettre de crédit *f*.

lettuce *n* salade *f*.

leukaemia *n* leucémie *f*.

level *adj* plat, égal; à niveau; * *n* niveau *m*; * *vt* niveler.

level-headed *adj* sensé.

lever *n* levier *m*.

leverage *n* effet de levier *m*; prise *f*.

levity *n* légèreté *f*.

levy *n* levée *f*; prélèvement *m*; * *vt* prélever.

lewd *adj* obscène.

lexicon *n* lexique *m*.

liability *n* responsabilité *f*.

liable *adj* sujet (à); responsable.

liaise *vi* effectuer une liaison.

liaison *n* liaison *f*.

liar *n* menteur *m* -euse *f*.

libel *n* diffamation *f*; * *vt* diffamer.

libellous *adj* diffamatoire.

liberal *adj* libéral; généreux; ~**ly** *adv* libéralement.

liberality *n* libéralité, générosité *f*.

liberate *vt* libérer.

liberation *n* libération *f*.

libertine *n* libertin *m* -e *f*.

liberty *n* liberté *f*.

Libra *n* Balance *f* (signe du zodiaque).

librarian *n* bibliothécaire *mf*.

library *n* bibliothèque *f*.

libretto *n* livret *m*.

licence *n* licence *f*; permis *m*; permission *f*.

licentious *adj* licencieux.

lichen *n* (*bot*) lichen *m*.

lick *vt* lécher.

lid *n* couvercle *m*.

lie *n* mensonge *m*; * *vi* mentir; être allongé.

lieu *n*: in ~ of au lieu de.

lieutenant *n* lieutenant *m*.

life *n* vie *f*; **for** ~ pour toute la vie.

life belt *n* gilet de sauvetage *m*.

lifeboat *n* canot de sauvetage *m*.

lifeguard *n* maître nageur *m*; garde du corps *m*.

life jacket *n* gilet de sauvetage *m*.

lifeless *adj* mort; sans vie.

lifelike *adj* naturel.

lifeline *n* bouée de sauvetage *f*.

life sentence *n* condamnation à perpétuité *f*.

life-sized *adj* grandeur nature.

lifespan *n* durée de vie *f*.

lifestyle *n* style de vie *m*.

life-support system *n* système de respiration artificielle *m*.

lifetime *n* vie *f*.

lift *vt* lever.

ligament *n* ligament *m*.

light *n* lumière *f*; * *adj* léger; clair; * *vt* allumer; éclairer.

light bulb *n* ampoule *f*.

lighten *vi* s'éclaircir; * *vt* éclairer; éclaircir; alléger.

lighter *n* briquet *m*.

light-headed *adj* étourdi.

lighthearted *adj* joyeux.

lighthouse *n* (*mar*) phare *m*.

lighting *n* éclairage *m*.

lightly *adv* légèrement.

lightning *n* éclair *m*.

lightning rod *n* paratonnerre *m*.

light pen *n* crayon optique *m*.

lightweight *adj* léger.

light year *n* année-lumière *f*.

ligneous *adj* ligneux.

like *adj* pareil; * *adv* comme; * *vt* *vi* aimer.

likeable *adj* sympathique.

likelihood *n* probabilité *f*.

likely *adj* probable, vraisemblable.

liken *vt* comparer.

likeness *n* ressemblance *f*.

likewise *adv* pareillement.

liking *n* goût *m*.

lilac *n* lilas *m*.

lily *n* lis *m*; ~ **of the valley** muguet *m*.

limb *n* membre *m*.

limber *adj* flexible, souple.

lime *n* chaux *f*; lime *f*; ~ **tree** tilleul *m*.

limestone *n* pierre à chaux *f*.

limit *n* limite *f*; * *vt* limiter.

limitation *n* limitation *f*; restriction *f*.

limitless *adj* illimité.

limo(usine) *n* limousine *f*.

limp *vi* boiter; * *n* boitement *m*; * *adj* mou.

limpet *n* patelle *f*.

limpid *adj* limpide.

line *n* ligne *f*; ride *f*; * *vt* rayer; rider.

lineage *n* lignage *m*.

linear *adj* linéaire.

lined *adj* rayé; ridé.

linen *n* lin *m*; linge *m* de maison.

liner *n* transatlantique *m*.

linesman *n* juge de ligne *m*.

linger *vi* traîner.

lingerie *n* lingerie *f*.

lingering *adj* long.

linguist *n* linguiste *mf*.

linguistic *adj* linguistique.

linguistics *n* linguistique *f*.

liniment *n* liniment *m*.

lining *n* doublure *f*.

link *n* chaînon *m*; * *vt* relier.

linnet *n* linotte *f*.

linoleum *n* linoléum *m*.

linseed *n* graine de lin *f*.

lint *n* peluche *f*.

lintel *n* linteau *m*.

lion *n* lion *m*.

lioness *n* lionne *f*.

lip *n* lèvre *f*; bord *m*.

lip-read *vi* lire sur les lèvres.

lip salve *n* pommade pour les lèvres *f*.

lipstick *n* rouge à lèvres *m*.

liqueur *n* liqueur *f*.

liquid *adj* liquide; * *n* liquide *m*.

liquidate *vt* liquider.

liquidation *n* liquidation *f*.

liquidize *vt* liquéfier.

liquor *n* spiritueux *m*.

liquorice *n* réglisse *m/f*.

liquor store *n* magasin de vins et spiritueux *m*.

lisp *vi* zézayer; * *n* zézaiement *m*.

list *n* liste *f*; * *vt* faire une liste de.

listen *vi* écouter.

listless *adj* indifférent.

litany *n* litanie *f*.

literal *adj* ~ly *adv* littéral(ement).

literary *adj* littéraire.

literate *adj* cultivé.

literature *n* littérature *f*.

lithe *adj* agile.

lithograph *n* lithographie *f*.

lithography *n* lithographie *f*.

litigation *n* litige *m*.

litigious *adj* litigieux.

litre *n* litre *m*.

litter *n* litière *f*; ordures *fpl*; * *vt* recouvrir, joncher.

little *adj* petit; ~ by ~ petit à petit; * *n* peu *m*.

liturgy *n* liturgie *f*.

live *vi* vivre; habiter; ~ on *vt* se nourrir de; ~ up to *vt* faire honneur à; * *adj* vivant.

livelihood *n* moyens de subsistance *mpl*.

liveliness *n* vivacité *f*.

lively *adj* vif.

liven up *vt* animer.

liver *n* foie *m*.

livery *n* livrée *f*.

livestock *n* bétail *m*.

livid *adj* livide; furieux.

living *n* vie *f*; * *adj* vivant.

living room n salle de séjour f.

lizard n lézard m.

load vt charger; * n charge f.

loaded adj chargé.

loaf n pain m.

loafer n paresseux m -euse f.

loam n terreau m.

loan n prêt m.

loathe vt détester.

loathing n aversion f.

loathsome adj répugnant.

lobby n vestibule m.

lobe n lobe m.

lobster n langouste f.

local adj local.

local anaesthetic n anesthésique local m.

local government n administration f municipale, administration f locale.

locality n localité f.

localize vt localiser.

locally adv localement.

locate vt localiser.

location n situation f.

lock n serrure f; * vt fermer à clé.

locker n casier m.

locket n médaillon m.

lockout n grève patronale f.

locksmith n serrurier m.

lock-up n cellule f.

locomotive n locomotive f.

locust n sauterelle f.

lodge n loge du gardien f; * vi se loger.

lodger n locataire mf.

loft n grenier m.

lofty adj haut.

log n bûche f.

logbook n (mar) journal de bord m.

logic n logique f.

logical adj logique.

logo n logo m.

loins npl reins mpl.

loiter vi s'attarder.

loll vi se prélasser.

lollipop n sucette f.

lonely, lonesome adj seul, solitaire.

loneliness n solitude f.

long adj long, f longue; * vi désirer.

long-distance n: ~ **call** appel interurbain m.

longevity n longévité f.

long-haired adj aux cheveux longs.

longing n désir m.

longitude n longitude f.

longitudinal adj longitudinal.

long jump n saut en longueur m.

long-playing record n trente-trois tours m.

long-range adj à longue portée.

long-term *adj* à long terme.

long wave *n* grandes ondes *fpl*.

long-winded *adj* prolixe.

look *vi* regarder; sembler; ~ after *vt* s'occuper de; garder; ~ for *vt* chercher; ~ forward to *vt* attendre avec impatience; ~ out for *vt* guetter; * *n* aspect *m*; regard *m*.

looking glass *n* miroir *m*.

look-out *n* (*mil*) sentinelle *f*; vigie *f*.

loom *n* métier à tisser *m*; * *vi* menacer.

loop *n* boucle *f*.

loophole *n* échappatoire *f*.

loose *adj* lâché; desserré; ~ly *adv* approximativement; ~, **loosen** *vt* lâcher; desserrer.

loot *vt* piller; * *n* butin *m*.

lop *vt* élaguer.

lopsided *adj* de travers; déséquilibré.

loquacious *adj* loquace.

loquacity *n* loquacité *f*.

lord *n* seigneur *m*.

lore *n* savoir *m* (traditionnel).

lose *vt* *vi* perdre.

loss *n* perte *f*; to be at a ~ ne pas savoir que faire.

lost and found *n* objets trouvés *mpl*.

lot *n* sort *f*; lot *m*; a ~ beaucoup.

lotion *n* lotion *f*.

lottery *n* loterie *f*.

loud *adj* fort, bruyant; ~ly *adv* bruyamment; haut.

loudspeaker *n* haut-parleur *m*.

lounge *n* salon *m*.

louse *n* (*pl* lice) pou *m*.

lousy *adj* minable.

lout *n* vaurien *m*.

lovable *adj* sympathique.

love *n* amour *m*; to fall in ~ tomber amoureux; * *vt* aimer.

love letter *n* lettre d'amour *f*.

love life *n* vie sentimentale *f*.

loveliness *n* beauté *f*.

lovely *adj* beau.

lover *n* amant *m*.

love-sick *adj* fou amoureux.

loving *adj* affectueux.

low *adj* bas; * *vi* meugler.

low-cut *adj* décolleté.

lower *adj* plus bas; * *vt* baisser.

lowest *adj* le plus bas.

lowland *n* plaine *f*.

lowliness *n* humilité *f*.

lowly *adj* humble.

low-water *n* basse mer *f*.

loyal *adj* loyal, fidèle; ~ly *adv* loyalement.

loyalty *n* loyauté *f*; fidélité *f*.

lozenge *n* pastille *f*.

lubricant *n* lubrifiant *m*.

lubricate *vt* lubrifier.

lucid *adj* lucide.

luck *n* chance *f*.

luckily *adv* heureusement, par chance.

luckless *adj* malchanceux.

lucky *adj* chanceux, qui a de la chance.

lucrative *adj* lucratif.

ludricrous *adj* absurde.

lug *vt* traîner.

luggage *n* bagages *mpl*.

lugubrious *adj* lugubre, triste.

lukewarm *adj* tiède.

lull *vt* bercer; * *n* répit *m*.

lullaby *n* berceuce *f*.

lumbago *n* lumbago *m*.

lumberjack *n* bûcheron *m*.

lumber room *n* débarras *m*.

luminous *adj* lumineux.

lump *n* bosse *f*; grosseur *f*; morceau *m*; * *vt* réunir.

lump sum *n* somme globale *f*.

lunacy *n* folie *f*.

lunar *adj* lunaire.

lunatic *adj* fou, *f* folle.

lunch, luncheon *n* déjeuner *m*.

lungs *npl* poumons *mpl*.

lurch *n* embardée *f*.

lure *n* leurre *m*; attrait *m*; * *vt* séduire, attirer.

lurid *adj* criard (couleur); horrible.

lurk *vi* être tapi.

luscious *adj* délicieux.

lush *adj* luxuriant.

lust *n* luxure *f*; sensualité *f*; désir *m*; * *vi* désirer; ~ **after** *vt* convoiter.

lustful *adj* luxurieux, voluptueux; ~**ly** *adv* luxurieusement.

lustily *adv* vigoureusement.

lustre *n* lustre *m*.

lusty *adj* fort, vigoureux.

lute *n* luth *m*.

Lutheran *n* luthérien *m* -ne *f*.

luxuriance *n* exubérance, luxuriance *f*.

luxuriant *adj* exubérant, luxuriant.

luxuriate *vi* pousser de manière exubérante.

luxurious *adj* luxueux; ~**ly** *adv* luxueusement.

luxury *n* luxe *m*.

lying *n* mensonges *mpl*.

lymph *n* lymphe *f*.

lynch *vt* lyncher.

lynx *n* linx *m*.

lyrical *adj* lyrique.

lyrics *npl* paroles *fpl*.

M

macaroni *n* macaronis *mpl*.

macaroon *n* macaron *m*.

mace *n* massue *f*; macis *m*.

macerate *vt* macérer.

machination *n* machination *f*.

machine *n* machine *f*.

machine gun *n* mitrailleuse *f*.

machinery *n* machinerie *f*; mécanisme *m*.

mackerel *n* maquereau *m*.

mad *adj* fou, *f* folle; furieux; insensé.

Madam *n* madame *f*.

madden *vt* rendre fou; rendre furieux.

madder *n* (*bot*) garance *f*.

madhouse *n* asile de fous *m*.

madly *adv* à la folie; comme un fou.

madman *n* fou *m*.

madness *n* folie *f*.

magazine *n* magazine *m*, revue *f*; (*mil*) magasin *m*.

maggot *n* asticot *m*.

magic *n* magie *f*; * *adj* ~ally *adv* magique(ment).

magician *n* magicien *m* -ne *f*.

magisterial *adj* ~ly *adv* magistral(ement).

magistracy *n* magistrature *f*.

magistrate *n* magistrat *m*.

magnanimity *n* magnanimité *f*.

magnanimous *adj* ~ly *adv* magnanime(ment).

magnet *n* aimant *m*.

magnetic *adj* magnétique.

magnetism *n* magnétisme *m*.

magnificence *n* magnificence *f*.

magnificent *adj* ~ly *adv* magnifique(ment).

magnify *vt* grossir; exagérer.

magnifying glass *n* loupe *f*.

magnitude *n* magnitude *f*.

magpie *n* pie *f*.

mahogany *n* acajou *m*.

maid *n* bonne *f*.

maiden *n* jeune fille *f*.

maiden name *n* nom de jeune fille *m*.

mail *n* courrier *m*.

mailbox *n* boîte aux lettres *f*.

mail coach *n* malle-poste *f*.

mailing list *n* fichier-clientèle *m*.

mail-order *n* vente par correspondance *f*.

mail train *n* (*rail*) train-poste *m*.

maim *vt* mutiler.

main *adj* principal; essentiel; **in the ~** en général.

mainland *n* continent *m*.

main line *n* (*rail*) grande ligne *f*.

mainly *adv* principalement, essentiellement.

main street *n* rue principale *f*.

maintain *vt* maintenir; soutenir.

maintenance *n* entretien *m*.

maize *n* maïs *m*.

majestic *adj* majestueux; **~ally** *adv* majestueusement.

majesty *n* majesté *f*.

major *adj* majeur; * *n* (*mil*) commandant *m*.

majority *n* majorité *f*.

make *vt* faire; **~ for** se diriger vers; **~ up** inventer; **~ up for** compenser; * *n* marque *f*.

make-believe *n* invention *f*.

makeshift *adj* improvisé, de fortune.

make-up *n* maquillage *m*.

make-up remover *n* démaquillant *m*.

malady *n* maladie *f*.

malaise *n* malaise *m*.

malaria *n* malaria *f*.

malcontent *adj n* mécontent *m* -e *f*.

male *adj* mâle; masculin; * *n* mâle *m*.

malevolence *n* malveillance *f*.

malevolent *adj* malveillant; **~ly** *adv* avec malveillance.

malfunction *n* mauvais fonctionnement *m*.

malice *n* méchanceté *f*.

malicious *adj* méchant; **~ly** *adv* méchamment.

malign *adj* nocif; * *vt* calomnier.

malignant *adj* malfaisant; **~ly** *adv* méchamment.

mall *n* centre commercial *m*.

malleable *adj* malléable.

mallet *n* maillet *m*.

mallow *n* (*bot*) mauve *f*.

malnutrition *n* malnutrition *f*.

malpractice *n* malversations *fpl*.

malt *n* malt *m*.

maltreat *vt* maltraiter.

mammal *n* mammifère *m*.

mammoth *adj* gigantesque.

man *n* homme *m*; * *vt* (*mar*) équiper en personnel.

manacle *n* entrave *f*; **~s** *pl* menottes *fpl*.

manage *vt* diriger; réussir; *
vi réussir.

manageable *adj* maniable.

management *n* direction *f*.

manager *n* directeur *m*.

manageress *n* directrice *f*.

managerial *adj* directorial.

managing director *n* directeur *m* général.

mandarin *n* mandarine *f*; mandarin *m*.

mandate *n* mandat *m*.

mandatory *n* obligatoire.

mane *n* crinière *f*.

manfully *adv* vaillamment.

manger *n* mangeoire *f*.

mangle *n* essoreuse *f*; * *vt* mutiler.

mangy *adj* miteux.

manhandle *vt* maltraiter; manutentionner.

manhood *n* âge d'homme *m*; virilité *f*.

man-hour *n* heure *f* de main d'œuvre.

mania *n* manie *f*.

maniac *n* maniaque *mf*.

manic *adj* obsessionnel.

manicure *n* manucure *f*.

manifest *adj* manifeste; * *vt* manifester.

manifestation *n* manifestation *f*.

manifesto *n* manifeste *m*.

manipulate *vt* manipuler.

manipulation *n* manipulation *f*.

mankind *n* humanité *f*.

manlike *adj* viril; d'homme.

manliness *n* virilité *f*; courage *m*.

manly *adj* viril.

man-made *adj* artificiel.

manner *n* manière *f*; attitude *f*; ~s *pl* manières *fpl*.

manoeuvre *n* manœuvre *f*.

manpower *n* main-d'œuvre *f*.

mansion *n* château *m*.

manslaughter *n* homicide involontaire *m*.

mantelpiece *n* manteau de cheminée *m*.

manual *adj n* manuel *m*.

manufacture *n* fabrication *f*; * *vt* fabriquer.

manufacturer *n* fabricant *m*.

manure *n* fumier *m*; engrais *m*; purin *m*; * *vt* fumer.

manuscript *n* manuscrit *m*.

many *adj* beaucoup de; ~ a time de nombreuses fois; how ~? combien?; as ~ as autant que.

map *n* carte *f*; plan *m*; * *vt* dessiner un plan de; ~ out programmer.

maple *n* érable *m*.

mar *vt* gâter, gâcher.

marathon *n* marathon *m*.

marauder *n* maraudeur *m* -euse *f*.

marble *n* marbre *m*; * *adj* marbré.

March *n* mars *m*.

march *n* marche *f*; * *vi* marcher.

marchpast *n* défilé *m*.

mare *n* jument *f*.

margarine *n* margarine *f*.

margin *n* marge *f*; bord *m*.

marginal *adj* marginal.

marigold *n* (*bot*) calendula *f*, souci *m*.

marijuana *n* marijuana *f*.

marinate *vt* mariner.

marine *adj* marin; * *n* fusilier *m* marin.

mariner *n* marin *m*.

marital *adj* matrimonial.

maritime *adj* maritime.

marjoram *n* marjolaine *f*.

mark *n* marque *f*; signe *m*; * *vt* marquer.

marker *n* marque *f*; marqueur *m*.

market *n* marché *m*.

marketable *adj* vendable.

marketing *n* marketing *m*.

marketplace *n* marché *m*.

market research *n* étude de marché *f*.

market value *n* valeur sur le marché *f*.

marksman *n* tireur d'élite *m*.

marmalade *n* confiture d'oranges *f*.

maroon *adj* marron rouge.

marquee *n* tente *f*.

marriage *n* mariage *m*.

marriageable *adj* mariable.

marriage certificate *n* acte de mariage *m*.

married *adj* marié; conjugal.

marrow *n* moelle *f*.

marry *vi* se marier.

marsh *n* marécage *m*.

marshal *n* maréchal *m*.

marshy *adj* marécageux.

marten *n* martre *f*.

martial *adj* martial; ~ law *n* loi martiale *f*.

martyr *n* martyr *m* -e *f*.

martyrdom *n* martyre *m*.

marvel *n* merveille *f*; * *vi* s'émerveiller.

marvellous *adj* merveilleux; ~ly *adv* merveilleusement.

marzipan *n* massepain *m*, pâte d'amandes *f*.

mascara *n* mascara *m*.

masculine *adj* masculin, viril.

mash *n* bouillie, purée *f*.

mask *n* masque *m*; * *vt* masquer.

masochist *n* masochiste *mf*.

mason *n* maçon *m*.

masonry *n* maçonnerie *f*.

masquerade *n* mascarade *f*.

mass *n* masse *f*; messe *f*; multitude *f*.

massacre *n* massacre *m*; * *vt* massacrer.

massage *n* massage *m*.

masseur *n* masseur *m*.

masseuse *n* masseuse *f*.

massive *adj* énorme.

mass media *npl* média *mpl*.

mast *n* mât *m*.

master *n* maître *m*; * *vt* maîtriser.

masterly *adj* magistral.

mastermind *vt* diriger.

masterpiece *n* chef-d'œuvre *m*.

mastery *n* maîtrise *f*.

masticate *vt* mastiquer.

mastiff *n* mastiff *m*.

mat *n* tapis *m*.

match *n* allumette *f*; match *m*; * *vt* égaler; * *vi* bien aller ensemble.

matchbox *n* boîte d'allumettes *f*.

matchless *adj* incomparable, sans pareil.

matchmaker *n* marieur *m* -euse *f*.

mate *n* camarade *mf*; * *vt* accoupler.

material *adj* ~ly *adv* matériel(lement).

materialism *n* matérialisme *m*.

maternal *adj* maternel.

maternity dress *n* robe de grossesse *f*.

maternity hospital *n* maternité *f*.

mathematical *adj* ~ly *adv* mathématique(ment).

mathematician *n* mathématicien *m* -ne *f*.

mathematics *npl* mathématiques *fpl*.

maths *n* maths *fpl*.

matinee *n* matinée *f*.

mating *n* accouplement *m*.

matins *npl* matines *fpl*.

matriculate *vt* immatriculer.

matriculation *n* immatriculation *f*.

matrimonial *adj* matrimonial.

mat(t) *adj* mat.

matted *adj* emmêlé.

matter *n* matière, substance *f*; sujet *m*; affaire *f*; what is the ~? que se passe-t-il?; a ~ of fact un fait; * *vi* importer.

mattress *n* matelas *m*.

mature *adj* mûr; * *vi* mûrir.

maturity *n* maturité *f*.

maul *vt* meurtrir.

mausoleum *n* mausolée *m*.

mauve *adj* mauve.

maxim *n* maxime *f*.

maximum *n* maximum *m*.

may *v aux* pouvoir; **~be** peut-être.

May *n* mai *m*.

Mayday *n* le Premier Mai *m*.

mayor *n* maire *m*.

mayoress *n* mairesse *f*.

maze *n* labyrinthe *m*.

me *pn* moi; me.

meadow *n* prairie *f*, pré *m*.

meagre *adj* pauvre.

meagreness *n* pauvreté *f*.

meal *n* repas *m*; farine *f*.

mealtime *n* heure du repas *f*.

mean *adj* avare, mesquin; moyen; **in the ~time**, **~while** pendant ce temps-là; **~s** *npl* moyens *mpl*; * *vt vi* signifier.

meander *vi* serpenter.

meaning *n* sens *m*, signification *f*.

meaningful *adj* significatif.

meaningless *adj* vide de sens.

meanness *n* avarice, mesquinerie *f*.

meantime, meanwhile *adv* pendant ce temps-là.

measles *npl* rougeole *f*.

measure *n* mesure *f*; * *vt* mesurer.

measurement *n* mesure *f*.

meat *n* viande *f*.

meatball *n* boulette de viande *f*.

meaty *adj* riche en viande.

mechanic *n* mécanicien *m*.

mechanical *adj* **~ly** *adv* mécanique(ment).

mechanics *npl* mécanique *f*.

mechanism *n* mécanisme *m*.

medal *n* médaille *f*.

medallion *n* médaillon *m*.

medallist *n* médaillé *m* -e *f*.

meddle *vi* se mêler des affaires des autres.

meddler *n* fouineur *m* -euse *f*, indiscret *m* -ète *f*.

media *npl* média *mpl*.

median *n* médiane *f*.

mediate *vi* agir en tant que médiateur.

mediation *n* médiation *f*.

mediator *n* médiateur *m* -trice *f*.

medical *adj* médical.

medicate *vt* traiter.

medicated *adj* médical.

medicinal *adj* médicinal.

medicine *n* médecine *f*; médicament *m*.

medieval *adj* médiéval.

mediocre *adj* médiocre.

mediocrity *n* médiocrité *f*.

meditate *vi* méditer.

meditation *n* méditation *f*.

meditative *adj* méditatif.

Mediterranean *adj* méditerranéen.

medium *n* milieu *m*; médium *m*; * *adj* moyen.

medium wave *n* ondes moyennes *fpl*.

medley *n* mélange *m*.

meek *adj* docile; ~ly *adv* docilement.

meekness *n* docilité *f*.

meet *vt* rencontrer; ~ with retrouver; * *vi* se rencontrer; se retrouver.

meeting *n* réunion *f*; congrès *m*.

megaphone *n* mégaphone *m*.

melancholy *n* mélancolie *f*; * *adj* mélancolique.

mellow *adj* moelleux; doux; * *vi* mûrir.

mellowness *n* moelleux *m*.

melodious *adj* mélodieux; ~ly *adv* mélodieusement.

melody *n* mélodie *f*.

melon *n* melon *m*.

melt *vt* faire fondre; * *vi* fondre.

melting point *n* point de fusion *m*.

member *n* membre *m*.

membership *n* adhésion *f*.

membrane *n* membrane *f*.

memento *n* mémento *m*.

memo *n* note de service *f*.

memoir *n* mémoire *m*.

memorable *adj* mémorable.

memorandum *n* mémorandum *m*; note de service *f*.

memorial *n* monument commémoratif, mémorial *m*.

memorize *vt* mémoriser.

memory *n* mémoire *f*; souvenir *m*.

menace *n* menace *f*; * *vt* menacer.

menacing *adj* menaçant.

menagerie *n* ménagerie *f*.

mend *vt* réparer; raccommoder.

mending *n* réparation *f*; raccommodage *m*.

menial *adj* vil.

meningitis *n* méningite *f*.

menopause *n* ménopause *f*.

menstruation *n* menstruation *f*.

mental *adj* mental.

mentality *n* mentalité *f*.

mentally *adv* mentalement.

mention *n* mention *f*; * *vt* mentionner.

menu *n* menu *m*.

mercantile *adj* commercial.

mercenary *adj n* mercenaire *m*.

merchandise *n* marchandise *f*.

merchant *n* négociant *m* -e *f*.

merchantman *n* navire marchand *m*.

merchant marine *n* marine marchande *f*.

merciful *adj* miséricordieux.

merciless *adj* ~ly *adv* impitoyable(ment).

mercury *n* mercure *m*.

mercy *n* pitié *f*.

mere *adj* ~ly *adv* simple(ment).

merge *vt vi* fusionner.

merger *n* fusion *f*.

meridian *n* méridien *m*.

merit *n* mérite *m*; * *vt* mériter.

meritorious *adj* méritoire.

mermaid *n* sirène *f*.

merrily *adv* joyeusement.

merriment *n* divertissement *m*; réjouissance *f*.

merry *adj* joyeux.

merry-go-round *n* manège *m*.

mesh *n* maille *f*.

mesmerize *vt* hypnotiser.

mess *n* désordre *m*; confusion *f*; (*mil*) mess *m*; ~ up *vt* mettre en désordre.

message *n* message *m*.

messenger *n* messager *m* -ère *f*.

metabolism *n* métabolisme *m*.

metal *n* métal *m*.

metallic *adj* métallique.

metallurgy *n* métallurgie *f*.

metamorphosis *n* métamorphose *f*

metaphor *n* métaphore *f*.

metaphoric(al) *adj* métaphorique.

metaphysical *adj* métaphysique.

metaphysics *npl* métaphysique *f*.

mete (out) *vt* distribuer.

meteor *n* météore *m*.

meteorological *adj* météorologique.

meteorology *n* météorologie *f*.

meter *n* compteur *m*.

method *n* méthode *f*.

methodical *adj* ~ly *adv* méthodique(ment).

Methodist *n* méthodiste *mf*.

metre *n* mètre *m*.

metric *adj* métrique.

metropolis *n* métropole *f*.

metropolitan *adj* métropolitain.

mettle *n* courage *m*.

mettlesome *adj* courageux.

mew *vi* miauler.

mezzanine *n* mezzanine *f*.

microbe *n* microbe *m*.

microphone *n* microphone *m*.

microchip *n* microprocesseur *m*, puce *f*.

microscope *n* microscope *m*.

microscopic *adj* microscopique.

microwave *n* four à micro-ondes *m*.

mid *adj* demi; mi-.

midday *n* midi *m*.

middle *adj* moyen; du milieu; * *n* milieu *m*.

middle name *n* deuxième prénom *m*.

middleweight *n* poids moyen *m*.

middling *adj* moyen, passable.

midge *n* moucheron *m*.

midget *n* nain *m* -e *f*.

midnight *n* minuit *m*.

midriff *n* diaphragme *m*; estomac *m*.

midst *n* milieu *m*.

midsummer *n* milieu de l'été *m*.

midway *adv* à mi-chemin.

midwife *n* sage-femme *f*.

midwifery *n* obstétrique *f*.

might *n* force *f*.

mighty *adj* fort, puissant.

migraine *n* migraine *f*.

migrate *vi* émigrer.

migration *n* émigration *f*.

migratory *adj* migratoire.

mike *n* micro *m*.

mild *adj* doux; modéré; ~ly *adv* doucement.

mildew *n* moisissure *f*; mildiou *m*.

mildness *n* douceur *f*.

mile *n* mile *m*.

mileage *n* kilométrage *m*.

milieu *n* milieu *m*.

militant *adj* militant.

military *adj* militaire.

militate *vi* militer.

militia *n* milice *f*.

milk *n* lait *m*; * *vt* traire; exploiter.

milkshake *n* milk-shake *m*.

milky *adj* laiteux; M~ Way *n* Voie lactée *f*.

mill *n* moulin *m*; * *vt* moudre.

millennium *n* millénaire *m*.

miller *n* meunier *m*.

millet *n* (*bot*) millet *m*.

milligram *n* milligramme *m*.

millilitre *n* millilitre *m*.

millimetre *n* millimètre *m*.

milliner *n* chapelier *m* -ière *f*.

millinery *n* chapellerie *f*.

million *n* million *m*.

millionaire *n* millionaire *mf*.

millionth *adj n* millionième *mf*.

millstone *n* meule *f*.

mime *n* mime *m*.

mimic *vt* mimer.

mimicry *n* mimique *f*.

mince *vt* hacher.

mind *n* esprit *m*; * *vt* prendre soin de; * *vi*: do you ~? est-ce que cela vous dérange?

minded *adj* disposé.

mindful *adj* soucieux; attentif.

mindless *adj* insouciant.

mine *pn* le mien, la mienne, les miens, les miennes; à moi; * *n* mine *f*; * *vi* exploiter la mine.

minefield *n* champ de mines *m*.

miner *n* mineur *m*.

mineral *adj n* minéral *m*.

mineralogy *n* minéralogie *f*.

mineral water *n* eau minérale *f*.

minesweeper *n* dragueur de mines *m*.

mingle *vt* mêler.

miniature *n* miniature *f*.

minimal *adj* minime.

minimize *vt* minimiser.

minimum *n* minimum *m*.

mining *n* exploitation minière *f*.

minion *n* larbin *m*; favorit(te) *m(f)*.

minister *n* ministre *m*; * *vt* servir.

ministerial *adj* ministériel.

ministry *n* ministère *m*.

mink *n* vison *m*.

minnow *n* vairon *m*.

minor *adj* mineur; * *n* mineur *m* -e *f*.

minority *n* minorité *f*.

minstrel *n* ménestrel *m*.

mint *n* (*bot*) menthe *f*; hôtel de la Monnaie *m*; * *vt* frapper la monnaie.

minus *adv* moins.

minute *adj* minuscule; ~ly *adv* minutieusement.

minute *n* minute *f*.

miracle *n* miracle *m*.

miraculous *adj* miraculeux.

mirage *n* mirage *m*.

mire *n* bourbe *f*.

mirky *adj* trouble; ténébreux.

mirror *n* miroir *m*.

mirth *n* allégresse *f*.

mirthful *adj* joyeux.

misadventure *n* mésaventure *f*.

misanthropist *n* misanthrope *mf*.

misapply *vt* mal appliquer.

misapprehension *n* méprise *f*.

misbehave *vi* se conduire mal.

misbehaviour *n* mauvaise conduite *f*.

miscalculate *vt* mal calculer.

miscarriage *n* fausse couche *f*.

miscarry *vi* faire une fausse couche; échouer.

miscellaneous *adj* divers, varié.

miscellany *n* mélange, assortiment *m*.

mischief *n* mal, tort *m*.

mischievous *adj* mauvais; espiègle.

misconception *n* méprise *f*.

misconduct *n* mauvaise conduite *f*.

misconstrue *vt* mal interpréter.

miscount *vt* mal compter.

miscreant *n* scélérat *m*.

misdeed *n* méfait *m*.

misdemeanour *n* délit *m*.

misdirect *vt* mal diriger.

miser *n* avare *mf*.

miserable *adj* malheureux.

miserly *adj* mesquin, avare.

misery *n* malheur *m*; misère *f*.

misfit *n* inadapté *m* -e *f*.

misfortune *n* infortune *f*.

misgiving *n* doute *m*.

misgovern *vt* mal gouverner.

misguided *adj* malencontreux; malavisé.

mishandle *vt* maltraiter; mal s'y prendre avec.

mishap *n* mésaventure *f*.

misinform *vt* mal renseigner.

misinterpret *vt* mal interpréter.

misjudge *vt* méjuger.

mislay *vt* égarer.

mislead *vt* induire en erreur.

mismanage *vt* mal administrer.

mismanagement *n* mauvaise administration *f*.

misnomer *n* (*law*) nom inapproprié *m*.

misogynist *n* misogyne *mf*.

misplace *vt* égarer.

misprint *vt* mal imprimer; * *n* coquille *f*.

misrepresent *vt* mal représenter.

Miss *n* Mlle, Mademoiselle *f*.

miss *vt* rater; s'ennuyer de.

missal *n* missel *m*.

misshapen *adj* déformé.

missile *n* missile *m*.

missing *adj* perdu; absent.

mission *n* mission *f*.

missionary *n* missionnaire *mf*.

misspent *adj* gaspillé.

mist *n* brouillard *m*.

mistake *vt* confondre; * *vi* se tromper; to be mistaken se tromper; * *n* méprise *f*; erreur *f*.

Mister *n* monsieur *m*.

mistletoe *n* (*bot*) gui *m*.

mistress *n* maîtresse *f*.

mistrust *vt* se méfier de; * *n* méfiance *f*.

mistrustful *adj* méfiant.

misty *adj* brumeux.

misunderstand *vt* mal comprendre.

misunderstanding *n* malentendu *m*.

misuse *vt* faire un mauvais usage de; abuser de.

mitigate *vt* atténuer.

mitigation *n* atténuation *f*.

mitre *n* mitre *f*.

mittens *npl* moufles *fpl*.

mix *vt* mélanger.

mixed *adj* mélangé; mixte.

mixed-up *adj* confus.

mixer *n* mixeur *m*.

mixture *n* mélange *m*.

mix-up *n* confusion *f*.

moan *n* gémissement *m*; * *vi* gémir; se plaindre.

moat *n* fossé *m*.

mob *n* foule *f*; masse *f*.

mobile *adj* mobile.

mobile home *n* caravane *f*.

mobility *n* mobilité *f*.

mobilize *vt* (*mil*) mobiliser.

moccasin *n* mocassin *m*.

mock *vt* se moquer de.

mockery *n* moquerie *f*.

mode *n* mode *m*.

model *n* modèle *m*; * *vt* modeler.

moderate *adj* ~ly *adv* modéré(ment); * *vt* modérer.

moderation *n* modération *f*.

modern *adj* moderne.

modernize *vt* moderniser.

modest *adj* ~ly *adv* modeste(ment).

modesty *n* modestie *f*.

modicum *n* minimum *m*.

modification *n* modification *f*.

modify *vt* modifier.

modulate *vt* moduler.

modulation *n* (*mus*) modulation *f*.

module *n* module *m*.

mogul *n* magnat *m*.

mohair *n* mohair *m*.

moist *adj* humide.

moisten *vt* humidifier.

moisture *n* humidité *f*.

molar *n* molaire *f*.

molasses *npl* mélasse *f*.

mole *n* taupe *f*.

molecule *n* molécule *f*.

molehill *n* taupinière *f*.

molest *vt* importuner.

mollify *vt* apaiser.

mollusc *n* mollusque *m*.

mollycoddle *vt* dorloter.

molten *adj* fondu.

mom, mommy *n* maman *f*.

moment *n* moment *m*.

momentarily *adv* momentanément.

momentary *adj* momentané.

momentous *adj* capital.

momentum *n* vitesse *f*; élan *m*.

monarch *n* monarque *m*.

monarchy *n* monarchie *f*.

monastery *n* monastère *m*.

monastic *adj* monastique.

Monday *n* lundi *m*.

monetary *adj* monétaire.

money *n* argent *m*; pièce de monnaie *f*.

money order *n* mandat *m*.

mongol *n* (*med*) mongolien *m* -ne *f*.

mongrel *adj n* bâtard *m* -e *f*.

monitor *n* moniteur *m* -trice *f*.

monk *n* moine *m*.

monkey *n* singe *m*.

monochrome *adj* monochrome.

monocle *n* monocle *m*.

monologue *n* monologue *m*.

monopolize *vt* monopoliser.

monopoly *n* monopole *m*.

monosyllable *n* monosyllabe *m*.

monotonous *adj* monotone.

monotony *n* monotonie *f*.

monsoon *n* mousson *f*.

monster *n* monstre *m*.

monstrosity *n* monstruosité *f*.

monstrous *adj* monstrueux; ~ly *adv* monstrueusement.

montage *n* montage *m*.

month *n* mois *m*.

monthly *adj* mensuel; *adv* mensuellement.

monument *n* monument *m*.

monumental *adj* monumental.

moo *vi* meugler.

mood *n* humeur *f*.

moodiness *n* mauvaise humeur *f*.

moody *adj* de mauvaise humeur; lunatique.

moon *n* lune *f*.

moonbeams *npl* rayons de lune *mpl*.

moonlight *n* clair de lune *m*.

moor *n* lande *f*; * *vt* (*mar*) amarrer.

moorland *n* lande *f*.

moose *n* élan *m*, orignal *m*.

mop *n* lavette *f*; * *vt* éponger.

mope *vi* se morfondre.

moped *n* vélomoteur *m*.

moral *adj* ~ly *adv* moral(ement); ~s *npl* moralité *f*.

morale *n* moral *m*.

moralist *n* moraliste *mf*.

morality *n* moralité *f*.

moralize *vt vi* moraliser.

morass *n* marais *m*.

morbid *adj* morbide.

more *adj adv* plus; never ~ plus jamais; once ~ encore une fois; ~ and ~ de plus en plus; so much the ~ d'autant plus.

moreover *adv* de plus, en outre.

morgue *n* morgue *f*.

morning *n* matin *m*; good ~ bonjour.

moron *n* imbécile *mf*.

morose *adj* morose.

morphine *n* morphine *f*.

morse *n* morse *m*.

morsel *n* bouchée *f*; morceau *m*.

mortal *adj* ~ly *adv* mortel(lement); * *n* mortel *m* -le *f*.

mortality *n* mortalité *f*.

mortar *n* mortier *m*.

mortgage *n* hypothèque *f*; * *vt* hypothéquer.

mortgage company *n* banque de prêts hypothécaires *f*.

mortgager *n* débiteur(-trice) hypothécaire *m(f)*.

mortification *n* mortification *f*.

mortify *vt* mortifier.

mortuary *n* morgue *f*.

mosaic *n* mosaïque *f*.

mosque *n* mosquée *f*.

mosquito *n* moustique *m*.

moss *n* (*bot*) mousse *f*.

mossy *adj* moussu.

most *adj pn* la plupart de; * *adv* extrêmement; at ~ au maximum; ~ly *adv* surtout, essentiellement.

moth *n* papillon de nuit *m*; mite *f*.

mothball *n* boule de naphtaline *f*.

mother *n* mère *f*.

motherhood *n* maternité *f*.

mother-in-law *n* belle-mère *f*.

motherless *adj* sans mère.

motherly *adj* maternel.

mother-of-pearl *n* nacre *f*.

mother-to-be *n* future maman *f*.

mother tongue *n* langue maternelle *f*.

motif *n* (*art, mus*) motif *m*.

motion *n* mouvement *m*.

motionless *adj* immobile.

motion picture *n* film *m*.

motivated *adj* motivé.

motive *n* motif *m*.

motley *adj* bigarré.

motor *n* moteur *m*.

motorbike *n* moto *f*.

motorboat *n* canot à moteur *m*.

motorcycle *n* motocyclette *f*.

motor vehicle *n* automobile *f*.

mottled *adj* marbré, tacheté.

motto *n* devise *f*.

mould *n* moule *m*; * *vt* mouler.

moulder *vi* s'effriter.

mouldy *adj* moisi.

moult *vi* muer.

mound *n* monticule *m*.

mount *n* mont *m*; * *vt* gravir.

mountain *n* montagne *f*.

mountaineer *n* alpiniste *mf*.

mountaineering *n* alpinisme *m*.

mountainous *adj* montagneux.

mourn *vt* pleurer.

mourner *n* personne en deuil *f*.

mournful *adj* ~ly *adv* triste(ment).

mourning *n* deuil *m*.

mouse *n* (*pl* mice) souris *f*.

mouth *n* bouche *f*; embouchure *f*.

mouthful *n* bouchée *f*.

mouth organ *n* harmonica *m*.

mouthpiece *n* bec *m*; microphone *m*.

mouthwash *n* eau dentifrice *f*.

mouthwatering *adj* appétissant.

movable *adj* mobile.

move *vt* déplacer; toucher, émouvoir; * *vi* bouger; * *n* mouvement *m*.

movement *n* mouvement *m*.

movie *n* film *m*.

movie camera *n* caméra *f*.

moving *adj* touchant, émouvant.

mow *vt* tondre.

mower *n* tondeuse *f*.

Mrs *n* Mme, Madame *f*.

much *adj pn* beaucoup; *adv* beaucoup, très.

muck *n* saleté *f*.

mucous *adj* muqueux.

mucus *n* mucus *m*.

mud *n* boue *f*.

muddle *vt* confondre; embrouiller; * *n* confusion *f*; désordre *m*.

muddy *adj* boueux.

mudguard *n* garde-boue *m invar*.

muffle *vt* assourdir.

mug *n* tasse *f*.

muggy *adj* lourd, étouffant.

mulberry *n* mûre *f*; ~ **tree** mûrier *m*.

mule *n* mulet *m*; mule *f*.

mull *vt* méditer.

multifarious *adj* divers.

multiple *adj* multiple.

multiplication *n* multiplication *f*; ~ **table** table de multiplication *f*.

multiply *vt* multiplier.

multitude *n* multitude *f*.

mumble *vt vi* grommeler.

mummy *n* momie *f*.

mumps *npl* oreillons *mpl*.

munch *vt* mâcher.

mundane *adj* banal.

municipal *adj* municipal.

municipality *n* municipalité *f*.

munificence *n* munificence *f*.

munitions *npl* munitions *fpl*.

mural *n* mural *m*.

murder *n* assassinat, meurtre *m*; homicide volontaire *m*; * *vt* assassiner.

murderer *n* assassin, meurtrier *m*.

murderess *n* meurtrière *f*.

murderous *adj* meurtrier.

murky *adj* obscur, glauque.

murmur *n* murmure *m*; * *vt vi* murmurer.

muscle *n* muscle *m*.

muscular *adj* musculaire.

muse *vi* méditer, rêver.

museum *n* musée *m*.

mushroom *n* (*bot*) champignon *m*.

music *n* musique *f*.

musical *adj* musical; mélodieux.

musician *n* musicien *m* -ne *f*.

musk *n* musc *m*.

muslin *n* mousseline *f*.

mussel *n* moule *f*.

must *v aux* devoir.

mustard *n* moutarde *f*.

muster *vt* rassembler.

musty *adj* moisi.

mute *adj* muet, silencieux.

muted *adj* assourdi.

mutilate *vt* mutiler.

mutilation *n* mutilation *f*.

mutiny *n* mutinerie *f*; *vi* se mutiner, se révolter.

mutter *vt vi* grommeler, marmonner; * *n* grommellement *m*.

mutton *n* mouton *m* (viande).

mutual *adj* ~ly *adv* mutuel(lement), réciproque(ment).

muzzle *n* muselière *f*; museau *m*; * *vt* museler.

my *pn* mon, ma, mes.

myriad *n* myriade *f*.

myrrh *n* myrrhe *f*.

myrtle *n* myrte *m*.

myself *pn* moi-même.

mysterious *adj* mystérieux; ~ly *adv* mystérieusement.

mystery *n* mystère *m*.

mystic(al) *adj* mystique.

mystify *vt* mystifier; laisser perplexe.

mystique *n* mystique *f*.

myth *n* mythe *m*.

mythology *n* mythologie *f*.

N

nab *vt* coincer, pincer.

nag *n* bourrin *m*; * *vt* harceler.

nagging *adj* persistant; * *npl* harcèlement *m*.

nail *n* ongle *m*; clou *m*; * *vt* clouer.

nailbrush *n* brosse à ongles *f*.

nailfile *n* lime à ongles *f*.

nail polish *n* vernis à ongles *m*.

nail scissors *npl* ciseaux à ongles *mpl*.

naive *adj* naïf.

naked *adj* nu; dénudé; pur, simple.

name *n* nom *m*; réputation *f*; * *vt* nommer; mentionner.

nameless *adj* anonyme.

namely *adv* à savoir.

namesake *n* homonyme *m*.

nanny *n* nourrice *f*.

nap *n* sieste *f*, somme *m*.

napalm *n* napalm *m*.

nape *n* nuque *f*.

napkin *n* serviette *f*.

narcissus *n* (*bot*) narcisse *m*.

narcotic *adj n* narcotique *m*.

narrate *vt* narrer, raconter.

narrative *adj* narratif; * *n* narration *f*.

narrow *adj* ~ly *adv* étroit(ement); * *vt* resserrer; limiter.

narrow-minded *adj* à l'esprit étroit.

nasal *adj* nasal.

nasty *adj* méchant; mauvais; sale.

natal *adj* natal.

nation *n* nation *f*.

national *adj* ~ly *adv* national(ement).

nationalism *n* nationalisme *m*.

nationalist *adj n* nationaliste *mf*.

nationality *n* nationalité *f*.

nationalize *vt* nationaliser.

nationwide *adj* au niveau national.

native *adj* natal; * *n* autochtone *mf*.

native language *n* langue maternelle *f*.

Nativity n Nativité f.

natural adj ~**ly** adv naturel(lement).

natural gas n gaz naturel m.

naturalist n naturaliste mf.

naturalize vt naturaliser.

nature n nature f; sorte f.

naught n zéro m.

naughty adj méchant.

nausea n nausée, envie de vomir f.

nauseate vt donner des nausées à.

nauseous adj écœurant.

nautic(al), naval adj nautique.

nave n nef (d'église) f.

navel n nombril m.

navigate vi naviguer.

navigation n navigation f.

navy n marine f.

Nazi n nazi m -e f.

near prep près de; * adv près; à côté; * adj proche.

nearby adj proche.

nearly adv presque.

near-sighted adj myope.

neat adj soigné; net, propre; ~**ly** adv proprement; élégamment.

nebulous adj nébuleux.

necessarily adv nécessairement.

necessary adj nécessaire.

necessitate vt nécessiter.

necessity n nécessité f.

neck n cou m; * vi se bécoter.

necklace n collier m.

necktie n cravate f.

nectar n nectar m.

née adj: ~ **Brown** née Brown.

need n besoin m; pauvreté f; * vt avoir besoin de, nécessiter.

needle n aiguille f.

needless adj superflu, inutile.

needlework n couture f.

needy adj nécessiteux, pauvre.

negation n négation f.

negative adj négatif; ~**ly** adv négativement; * n négative f; négation f; négatif m.

neglect vt négliger; * n négligence f.

negligee n négligé, déshabillé m.

negligence n négligence f; manque de soin m.

negligent adj négligent; ~**ly** adv négligemment.

negligible adj négligeable.

negotiate vt vi négocier.

negotiation n négociation f.

Negress n Noire f.

Negro adj noir; * n Noir m.

neigh *vi* hennir; * *n* hennissement *m*.

neighbour *n* voisin *m* -e *f*; * *vt* être voisin de.

neighbourhood *n* voisinage *m*.

neighbouring *adj* voisin.

neighbourly *adj* sociable.

neither *conj* ni; * *pn* aucun(e), ni l'un(e) ni l'autre.

neon *n* néon *m*.

neon light *n* lumière au néon *f*.

nephew *n* neveu *m*.

nepotism *n* népotisme *m*.

nerve *n* nerf *m*; courage *m*; toupet *m*.

nerve-racking *adj* exaspérant.

nervous *adj* nerveux.

nervous breakdown *n* dépression nerveuse *f*.

nest *n* nid *m*; nichée *f*.

nest egg *n* (*fig*) économies *fpl*.

nestle *vt vi* se blottir.

net *n* filet *m*.

net curtain *n* voile *m*.

netting *n* filet *m*.

nettle *n* ortie *f*.

network *n* réseau *f*.

neurosis *n* névrose *f*.

neurotic *adj n* névrosé *m* -e *f*.

neuter *adj* (*gr*) neutre.

neutral *adj* neutre.

neutrality *n* neutralité *f*.

neutralize *vt* neutraliser.

neutron *n* neutron *m*.

neutron bomb *n* bombe à neutrons *f*.

never *adv* jamais; ~ **mind** ça ne fait rien.

never-ending *adj* interminable.

nevertheless *adv* cependant, néanmoins.

new *adj* neuf; nouveau; dernier; ~**ly** *adv* nouvellement.

newborn *adj* nouveau-né, *f* nouvelle-née.

newcomer *n* nouveau venu *m*, nouvelle venue *f*.

new-fangled *adj* moderne.

news *npl* nouvelles, informations *fpl*.

news agency *n* agence de presse *f*.

newscaster *n* présentateur *m* -trice *f*.

newsdealer *n* (US) marchand(e) de journaux *m(f)*.

news flash *n* flash d'information *m*.

newsletter *n* bulletin *m*.

newspaper *n* journal *m*.

newsreel *n* actualités *fpl*.

New Year *n* Nouvel An *m*; ~'s
Day *n* Jour du Nouvel An *m*;
~'s Eve Saint-Sylvestre *f*.

next *adj* prochain; the ~ day
le jour suivant; * *adv*
ensuite, après.

nib *n* pointe *f*; plume *f*.

nibble *vt* mordiller.

nice *adj* gentil(le) *m(f)*;
agréable; joli; ~ly *adv*
gentiment; bien.

nice-looking *adj* beau, *f* belle.

niche *n* niche *f*.

nick *n* entaille *f*; * *vt* (*sl*)
faucher.

nickel *n* nickel *m*; (US) pièce
f de cinq cents.

nickname *n* surnom *m*; * *vt*
surnommer.

niece *n* nièce *f*.

niggling *adj* insignifiant.

night *n* nuit *f*; by ~ de nuit;
good ~ bonne nuit.

nightclub *n* boîte de nuit *f*.

nightfall *n* tombée de la nuit
f.

nightingale *n* rossignol *m*.

nightly *adv* tous les soirs;
toutes les nuits; * *adj* nocturne.

nightmare *n* cauchemar *m*.

night school *n* cours du soir
mpl.

night shift *n* équipe de nuit *f*.

night-time *n* nuit *f*.

nihilist *n* nihiliste *mf*.

nimble *adj* léger; agile,
souple.

nine *adj n* neuf *m*.

nineteen *adj n* dix-neuf *m*.

nineteenth *adj n* dix-neuvième *mf*.

ninetieth *adj n* quatre-vingt-dixième *mf*.

ninety *adj n* quatre-vingt-dix
m.

ninth *adj n* neuvième *mf*.

nip *vt* pincer; mordre.

nipple *n* mamelon *m*; tétine *f*.

nit *n* lente *f*.

nitrogen *n* nitrogène *m*.

no *adv* non; * *adj* aucun; pas
de.

nobility *n* noblesse *f*.

noble *adj* noble; * *n* noble
mf.

nobleman *n* noble *m*.

nobody *pn* personne *f*.

nocturnal *adj* nocturne.

nod *n* signe de tête *m*; * *vi*
faire un signe de la tête;
somnoler.

noise *n* bruit *m*.

noisily *adv* bruyamment.

noisiness *n* bruit, tapage *m*.

noisy *adj* bruyant.

nominal *adj* ~ly *adv* nominal(ement).

nominate *vt* nommer.

nomination *n* nomination *f*.

nominative *n* (*gr*) nominatif *m*.

nominee *n* candidat *m* -e *f*.

nonalcoholic *adj* non alcoolisé.

non-aligned *adj* non-aligné.

nonchalant *adj* nonchalant.

noncommittal *adj* réservé.

nonconformist *n* non-conformiste *mf*.

nondescript *adj* quelconque.

none *pn* aucun; personne.

nonentity *n* nullité *f*.

nonetheless *adv* cependant.

nonexistent *adj* inexistant.

nonfiction *n* ouvrages non romanesques *mpl*.

nonplussed *adj* perplexe.

nonsense *n* absurdité *f*.

nonsensical *adj* absurde.

nonsmoker *n* non-fumeur *m*.

nonstick *adj* anti-adhérent.

nonstop *adj* direct; * *adv* sans s'arrêter.

noodles *npl* nouilles *fpl*.

noon *n* midi *m*.

noose *n* nœud coulant *m*.

nor *conj* ni.

normal *adj* normal.

north *n* nord *m*; * *adj* du nord.

North America *n* Amérique du Nord *f*.

northeast *n* nord-est *m*.

northerly, northern *adj* du nord.

North Pole *n* pôle Nord *m*.

northward(s) *adv* vers le nord.

northwest *n* nord-ouest *m*.

nose *n* nez *m*.

nosebleed *n* saignement de nez *m*.

nosedive *n* piqué *m*.

nostalgia *n* nostalgie *f*.

nostril *n* narine *f*.

not *adv* pas; non.

notable *adj* notable.

notably *adv* notamment.

notary *n* notaire *m*.

notch *n* cran *m*, dent *f*; * *vt* denteler.

note *n* note *f*; billet *m*; mot *m*; marque *f*; * *vt* noter, marquer; remarquer.

notebook *n* carnet *m*.

noted *adj* célèbre, connu.

notepad *n* bloc-notes *m*.

notepaper *n* papier à lettres *m*.

nothing *n* rien *m*; good for ~ bon à rien.

notice *n* notice *f*; avis *m*; * *vt* remarquer.

noticeable *adj* visible.

notification *n* notification *f*.

notify *vt* notifier.

notion *n* notion *f*; opinion *f*; idée *f*.

notoriety *n* notoriété *f*.

notorious *adj* notoire; **~ly** *adv* notoirement.

notwithstanding *conj* quoique.

nougat *n* nougat *m*.

nought *n* zéro *m*.

noun *n* (*gr*) nom, substantif *m*.

nourish *vt* nourrir, alimenter.

nourishing *adj* nourrissant.

nourishment *n* nourriture *f*, aliments *mpl*.

novel *n* roman *m*.

novelist *n* romancier *m* -ière *f*.

novelty *n* nouveauté *f*.

November *n* novembre *m*.

novice *n* novice *mf*, débutant(e) *m(f)*.

now *adv* maintenant; **~ and then** de temps en temps.

nowadays *adv* de nos jours, à l'heure actuelle.

nowhere *adv* nulle part.

noxious *adj* nocif.

nozzle *n* douille *f*.

nuance *n* nuance *f*.

nuclear *adj* nucléaire.

nucleus *n* noyau *m*.

nude *adj* nu.

nudge *vt* donner un coup de coude à.

nudist *n* nudiste *mf*.

nudity *n* nudité *f*.

nuisance *n* ennui *m*; gêne *f*.

nuke *n* (*col*) bombe atomique *f*; * *vt* atomiser.

null *adj* nul.

nullify *vt* annuler; invalider.

numb *adj* engourdi; * *vt* engourdir.

number *n* numéro, nombre *m*; quantité *f*; * *vt* numéroter; compter.

numberplate *n* plaque d'immatriculation *f*.

numbness *n* engourdissement *m*.

numeral *n* chiffre *m*.

numerical *adj* numérique.

numerous *adj* nombreux.

nun *n* religieuse *f*.

nunnery *n* couvent *m*.

nuptial *adj* nuptial; **~s** *npl* noces *fpl*.

nurse *n* infirmière *f*; * *vt* soigner; ménager.

nursery *n* crèche *f*; chambre d'enfant *f*.

nursery rhyme *n* comptine *f*.

nursery school *n* (école) maternelle *f*.

nursing home *n* maison de repos *f*.

nurture *vt* élever, soigner.

nut *n* noix *f*.

nutcrackers *npl* casse-noix *m invar*, casse-noisettes.

nutmeg *n* noix de muscade *f*.

nutritious *adj* nutritif.

nut shell *n* coquille de noix *f*.

nylon *n* nylon *m*; * *adj* en nylon.

O

oak *n* chêne *m*.

oar *n* rame *f*.

oasis *n* oasis *f*.

oat *n* avoine *f*.

oath *n* serment *m*.

oatmeal *n* flocons d'avoine *mpl*.

oats *npl* avoine *f*.

obedience *n* obéissance *f*.

obedient *adj* obéissant; ~ly *adv* avec obéissance.

obese *adj* obèse.

obesity *n* obésité *f*.

obey *vt* obéir à.

obituary *n* nécrologie *f*.

object *n* objet *m*; * *vt* objecter.

objection *n* objection *f*.

objectionable *adj* désagréable.

objective *adj n* objectif *m*.

obligation *n* obligation *f*.

obligatory *adj* obligatoire.

oblige *vt* obliger; rendre service à.

obliging *adj* obligeant.

oblique *adj* oblique; indirect; ~ly *adv* obliquement.

obliterate *vt* effacer.

oblivion *n* oubli *m*.

oblivious *adj* oublieux.

obnoxious *adj* odieux.

oboe *n* hautbois *m*.

obscene *adj* obscène.

obscenity *n* obscénité *f*.

obscure *adj* obscur; ~ly *adv* obscurément; * *vt* obscurcir.

obscurity *n* obscurité *f*.

observance *n* observation *f*; observance *f*.

observant *adj* observateur; respectueux.

observation *n* observation *f*.

observatory *n* observatoire *m*.

observe *vt* observer.

observer *n* observateur *m* -trice *f*.

observingly *adv* attentivement.

obsess *vt* obséder.

obsessive *adj* obsédant.

obsolete *adj* désuet.

obstacle *n* obstacle *m*.

obstinate *adj* obstiné; ~**ly** *adv* obstinément.

obstruct *vt* obstruer; entraver.

obstruction *n* obstruction *f*; encombrement *m*.

obtain *vt* obtenir.

obtainable *adj* disponible.

obtrusive *adj* importun.

obtuse *adj* obtus.

obvious *adj* évident; ~**ly** *adv* évidemment.

occasion *n* occasion *f*; * *vt* occasionner, causer.

occasional *adj* occasionnel; ~**ly** *adv* occasionnellement.

occupant, occupier *n* occupant *m* -e *f*; locataire *mf*.

occupation *n* occupation *f*; emploi *m*.

occupy *vt* occuper.

occur *vi* se produire, arriver.

occurrence *n* incident *m*.

ocean *n* océan *m*.

ocean-going *adj* de haute mer.

oceanic *adj* océanique.

ochre *n* ocre *m*.

octave *n* octave *f*.

October *n* octobre *m*.

octopus *n* poulpe *m*.

odd *adj* impair; étrange; quelconque; ~**ly** *adv* étrangement.

oddity *n* singularité, particularité *f*.

odd jobs *npl* petits travaux *mpl*.

oddness *n* étrangeté *f*; singularité *f*.

odds *npl* chances *fpl*.

odious *adj* odieux.

odometer *n* (US) odomètre *m*.

odorous *adj* odorant.

odour *n* odeur *f*; parfum *m*.

of *prep* de; à.

off *adj* éteint; fermé; annulé; en congé; ~**!** *excl* du vent!

offence *n* offense *f*; injure *f*.

offend *vt* offenser, blesser; choquer; * *vi* pécher.

offender *n* délinquant *m* -e *f*.

offensive *adj* offensant; injurieux; ~**ly** *adv* d'une manière offensante.

offer *vt* offrir; * *n* offre *f*.

offering *n* offrande *f*; offre *f*.

offhand *adj* désinvolte; * *adv* soudainement.

office *n* bureau *m*; poste *m*, fonctions *fpl*; service *m*.

office automation *n* bureautique *f*.

office building *n* immeuble de bureaux *m*.

office hours *npl* heures de bureau *fpl*.

officer *n* officier *m*; fonctionnaire *mf*.

office worker *n* employé(e) de bureau *m(f)*.

official *adj* ~ly *adv* officiel(lement); * *n* employé *m* -e *f*.

officiate *vi* officier.

officious *adj* officieux; ~ly *adv* officieusement.

off-line *adj adv* hors ligne.

off-peak *adj* aux heures creuses.

off-season *adj adv* horssaison.

offset *vt* compenser; décaler.

offshoot *n* ramification *f*.

offshore *adj* côtier.

offside *adj* hors jeu.

offspring *n* progéniture *f*; descendance *f*.

offstage *adv* en coulisses.

off-the-rack *adj* prêt-à-porter.

ogle *vt* lorgner.

oil *n* huile *f*; * *vt* huiler.

oilcan *n* burette d'huile *f*; bidon d'huile *m*.

oilfield *n* gisement pétrolifère *m*.

oil filter *n* filtre à huile *m*.

oil painting *n* peinture à l'huile *f*.

oil rig *n* derrick *m*.

oil tanker *n* pétrolier *m*.

oil well *n* puits pétrolifère *m*.

oily *adj* huileux; gras.

ointment *n* onguent *m*.

OK, okay *excl* O.K., d'accord; * *adj* bien; * *vt* approuver.

old *adj* vieux, *f* vieille.

old age *n* vieillesse *f*.

old-fashioned *adj* démodé.

olive *n* olivier *m*; olive *f*.

olive oil *n* huile d'olive *f*.

omelet(te) *n* omelette *f*.

omen *n* augure, présage *m*.

ominous *adj* menaçant.

omission *n* omission *f*; négligence *f*.

omit *vt* omettre.

omnipotence *n* omnipotence *f*.

omnipotent *adj* omnipotent, tout-puissant.

on *prep* sur, dessus; en; pour; * *adj* allumé, branché; ouvert; de service.

once *adv* une fois; at ~ tout de suite; all at ~ tout d'un coup; ~ more encore une fois.

oncoming *adj* qui arrive.

one *adj* un, une; ~ **by** ~ un par un.

one-day excursion *n* billet d'aller-retour valable une journée *m*.

one-man *adj* individuel.

onerous *adj* lourd; (*law*) dur.

oneself *pn* soi-même.

one-sided *adj* partial.

one-to-one *adj* face à face.

ongoing *adj* continu; en cours.

onion *n* oignon *m*.

on-line *adj adv* en ligne.

onlooker *n* spectateur *m* -trice *f*.

only *adj* seul, unique; * *adv* seulement.

onset, onslaught *n* début *m*; attaque *f*.

onus *n* obligation *f*.

onward(s) *adv* en avant.

ooze *vi* suinter.

opaque *adj* opaque.

open *adj* ouvert; public; déclaré; sincère, franc; ~ly *adv* ouvertement; * *vt* ouvrir; * *vi* s'ouvrir; commencer; ~ **on to** donner sur; ~ **up** *vt* ouvrir; *vi* s'ouvrir.

opening *n* ouverture *f*; (*com*) débouché *m*; inauguration *f*; commencement *m*.

open-minded *adj* aux idées larges.

openness *n* clareté *f*; franchise, sincérité *f*.

opera *n* opéra *m*.

opera house *n* théâtre de l'opéra *m*.

operate *vi* fonctionner; opérer.

operation *n* fonctionnement *m*; opération *f*.

operational *adj* opérationnel.

operative *adj* actif; en vigueur.

operator *n* opérateur *m* -trice *f*; téléphoniste *mf*.

ophthalmic *adj* ophtalmique.

opine *vt* être d'avis (que).

opinion *n* opinion *f*; jugement *m*.

opinionated *adj* entêté.

opinion poll *n* sondage *m*.

opponent *n* opposant *m* -e *f*; adversaire *mf*.

opportune *adj* opportun.

opportunist *n* opportuniste *mf*.

opportunity *n* occasion *f*.

oppose *vt* s'opposer à.

opposing *adj* opposé.

opposite *adj* opposé; contraire; * *adv* en face; *prep* en face de; * *n* contraire *m*.

opposition *n* opposition *f*; résistance *f*.

oppress *vt* opprimer.

oppression *n* oppression *f.*

oppressive *adj* oppressif.

oppressor *n* oppresseur *m.*

optic(al) *adj* optique; ~s *npl* optique *f.*

optician *n* opticien *m* -ne *f.*

optimist *n* optimiste *mf.*

optimistic *adj* optimiste.

option *n* option *f.*

optional *adj* optionnel; facultatif.

opulent *adj* opulent.

or *conj* ou.

oracle *n* oracle *m.*

oral *adj* oral, verbal; ~ly *adv* oralement.

orange *n* orange *f.*

orator *n* orateur *m* -trice *f.*

orbit *n* orbite *f.*

orchard *n* verger *m.*

orchestra *n* orchestre *m.*

orchestral *adj* orchestral.

orchid *n* orchidée *f.*

ordain *vt* ordonner.

ordeal *n* épreuve *f.*

order *n* ordre *m*; commande *f*; mandat *m*; classe *f*; * *vt* ordonner; commander; mettre en ordre.

order form *n* bon de commande *m.*

orderly *adj* ordonné; réglé.

ordinarily *adv* ordinairement.

ordinary *adj* ordinaire.

ordination *n* ordination *f.*

ordnance *n* artillerie *f.*

ore *n* minerai *m.*

organ *n* organe *m*; orgue *m.*

organic *adj* organique.

organism *n* organisme *m.*

organist *n* organiste *mf.*

organization *n* organisation *f.*

organize *vt* organiser.

orgasm *n* orgasme *m.*

orgy *n* orgie *f.*

oriental *adj* oriental.

orifice *n* orifice *m.*

origin *n* origine *f.*

original *adj* original; originel; ~ly *adv* à l'origine; originalement.

originality *n* originalité *f.*

originate *vi* provenir (de); être originaire (de).

ornament *n* ornement *m*; * *vt* ornementer, décorer.

ornamental *adj* ornemental.

ornate *adj* ornementé.

orphan *adj n* orphelin *m* -e *f.*

orphanage *n* orphelinat *m.*

orthodox *adj* orthodoxe.

orthodoxy *n* orthodoxie *f.*

orthography *n* orthographe *f.*

orthopaedic *adj* orthopédique.

oscillate *vi* osciller.

osprey *n* balbuzard pêcheur *m*.

ostensibly *adv* selon les apparences.

ostentatious *adj* ostentatoire.

osteopath *n* ostéopathe *mf*.

ostracize *vt* frapper d'ostracisme.

ostrich *n* autruche *f*.

other *pn* autre.

otherwise *adv* autrement.

otter *n* loutre *f*.

ouch *excl* aïe!

ought *v aux* devoir; falloir.

ounce *n* once *f*.

our *pn* notre, *pl* nos.

ours *pn* le nôtre, la nôtre, les nôtres; à nous.

ourselves *pn pl* nous-mêmes.

oust *vt* évincer; déposséder.

out *adv* dehors; éteint.

outback *n* intérieur *m*.

outboard *adj*: ~ **motor** (moteur) hors-bord *m*.

outbreak *n* éruption *f*; explosion *f*.

outburst *n* explosion *f*.

outcast *n* paria *m*.

outcome *n* résultat *m*.

outcry *n* protestations *fpl*.

outdated *adj* démodé; périmé.

outdo *vt* surpasser.

outdoor *adj* de plein air, ~**s** *adv* à l'extérieur.

outer *adj* extérieur.

outermost *adj* extrême; le plus à l'extérieur.

outer space *n* espace *m*.

outfit *n* tenue *f*; équipement *m*.

outfitter *n* confectionneur *m* -euse *f*.

outgoing *adj* extroverti; sortant.

outgrow *vt* devenir plus grand que.

outhouse *n* dépendances *fpl*.

outing *n* excursion *f*.

outlandish *adj* bizarre.

outlaw *n* hors-la-loi *m*; * *vt* proscrire.

outlay *n* dépenses *fpl*, frais *mpl*.

outlet *n* sortie *f*; débouché *m*.

outline *n* contour *m*; grandes lignes *fpl*.

outlive *vt* survivre à.

outlook *n* perspective *f*.

outlying *adj* distant, éloigné.

outmoded *adj* démodé.

outnumber *vt* être plus nombreux que.

out-of-date *adj* périmé; démodé.

out-patient *n* patient(e) en consultation externe *m(f)*.

outpost *n* avant-poste *m*.

output *n* rendement *m*; sortie *f*.

outrage *n* outrage *m*; * *vt* outrager.

outrageous *adj* outrageant; atroce; **~ly** *adv* outrageusement; atrocement.

outright *adv* absolument, complètement; * *adj* absolu, complet.

outrun *vt* gagner de vitesse, distancer.

outset *n* commencement *m*.

outshine *vt* éclipser.

outside *n* surface *f*; extérieur *m*; apparence *f*; * *adv* dehors; * *prep* en dehors de.

outsider *n* étranger *m* -ère *f*.

outsize *adj* grande taille.

outskirts *npl* périphérie *f*, alentours *mpl*.

outspoken *adj* franc.

outstanding *adj* exceptionnel; en suspens.

outstretch *vi* s'étendre.

outstrip *vt* devancer; surpasser.

out-tray *n* courrier au départ *m*.

outward *adj* extérieur; vers l'extérieur; d'aller; **~ly** *adv* à l'extérieur, extérieurement.

outweigh *vt* peser plus lourd que; l'emporter sur.

outwit *vt* être plus spirituel que.

oval *n*, *adj* ovale *m*.

ovary *n* ovaire *m*.

oven *n* four *m*.

ovenproof *adj* allant au four.

over *prep* sur, dessus; plus de; pendant; all ~ de tous côtés; * *adj* fini; en trop, en plus; ~ **again** à nouveau; ~ **and** ~ de nombreuses fois.

overall *adj* total; * *adv* dans l'ensemble; **~s** *npl* salopette *f*.

overawe *vt* impressionner.

overbalance *vi* perdre l'équilibre.

overbearing *adj* despotique.

overboard *adv* (*mar*) par-dessus bord.

overbook *vt* surréserver.

overcast *adj* couvert.

overcharge *vt* surcharger; faire payer un prix excessif à.

overcoat *n* pardessus *m*.

overcome *vt* vaincre; surmonter.

overconfident *adj* trop confiant.

overcrowded *adj* bondé; surpeuplé.

overdo *vi* exagérer.

overdraft *n* découvert *m*.

overdrawn *adj* à découvert.

overdress *vi* s'habiller trop élégamment.

overdue *adj* en retard; arriéré.

overeat *vi* trop manger.

overestimate *vt* surestimer.

overflow *vt* déborder de; * *vi* déborder; * *n* inondation *f*; surplus *m*.

overgrown *adj* envahi.

overgrowth *n* végétation envahissante *f*.

overhang *vt* surplomber.

overhaul *vt* réviser; * *n* révision *f*.

overhead *adv* en l'air, au-dessus.

overhear *vt* entendre par hasard.

overjoyed *adj* fou de joie.

overkill *n* (*fig*) matraquage *m*.

overland *adj adv* par voie de terre.

overlap *vi* se chevaucher.

overleaf *adv* au dos.

overload *vt* surcharger.

overlook *vt* dominer; donner sur; oublier; laisser passer, tolérer; négliger.

overnight *adv* pendant la nuit; * *adj* de nuit.

overpass *n* pont surélevé *m*.

overpower *vt* dominer, écraser.

overpowering *adj* écrasant.

overrate *vt* surévaluer.

override *vt* outrepasser.

overriding *adj* prédominant.

overrule *vt* rejeter; annuler.

overrun *vt* envahir; infester; dépasser.

overseas *adv* à l'étranger; outre-mer; * *adj* étranger.

oversee *vt* inspecter, surveiller.

overseer *n* contremaître *m*.

overshadow *vt* éclipser.

overshoot *vt* dépasser.

oversight *n* oubli *m*; erreur *f*.

oversleep *vi* se réveiller en retard.

overspill *n* excédent de population *m*.

overstate *vi* exagérer.

overstep *vt* dépasser.

overt *adj* ouvert; public; ~ly *adv* ouvertement.

overtake *vt* doubler.

overthrow *vt* renverser; détruire; * *n* renversement *m*; ruine, déroute *f*.

overtime *n* heures supplémentaires *fpl*.

overtone *n* harmonique *mf*; connotation *f*.

overture *n* ouverture *f*.

overturn *vt* renverser.

overweight *adj* trop lourd.

overwhelm *vt* écraser; submerger.

overwhelming *adj* écrasant; irrésistible.

overwork *vi* se surmener, trop travailler.

owe *vt* devoir; être redevable de.

owing *adj* dû; ~ **to** en raison de.

owl *n* chouette *f*.

own *adj* propre; my ~ mon, ma, mes propre(s); * *vt* posséder; ~ **up** *vi* confesser.

owner *n* propriétaire *mf*.

ownership *n* possession *f*.

ox *n* bœuf *m*; ~**en** *pl* bœufs *mpl*.

oxidize *vt* oxyder.

oxygen *n* oxygène *m*.

oxygen mask *n* masque à oxygène *m*.

oxygen tent *n* tente à oxygène *f*.

oyster *n* huître *f*.

ozone *n* ozone *m*.

P

pa *n* papa *m*.

pace *n* pas *m*; allure *f*; * *vt* arpenter; * *vi* marcher.

pacemaker *n* meneur *m* -euse *f* de train; (*med*) pacemaker *m*.

pacific(al) *adj* pacifique.

pacification *n* pacification *f*.

pacify *vt* pacifier.

pack *n* paquet *m*; jeu de cartes *m*; bande *f*; * *vt* empaqueter; remplier; * *vi* faire ses valises.

package *n* paquet *m*; accord *m*.

package tour *n* voyage organisé *m*.

packet *n* paquet *m*.

packing *n* emballage *m*.

pact *n* pacte *m*.

pad *n* bloc *m*; coussinet, tampon *m*; plateforme *f*; (*sl*) piaule *f*; * *vt* rembourrer.

padding *n* rembourrage *m*.

paddle *vi* ramer; * *n* pagaie *f*.

paddle steamer *n* vapeur à roues *m*.

paddock *n* paddock *m*.

paddy *n* rizière *f*.

paediatrics *n* pédiatrie *f*.

pagan *adj n* païen *m*, païenne *f*.

page *n* page *f*; page *m*.

pageant *n* grand spectacle *m*.

pageantry *n* pompe *f*.

pail *n* seau *m*.

pain *n* douleur *f*; mal *m*; peine *f*; * *vt* peiner.

pained *adj* peiné.

painful *adj* douloureux; pénible; ~ly *adv* douloureusement; péniblement; à grand-peine.

painkiller *n* analgésique *m*.

painless *adj* indolore; sans peine.

painstaking *adj* soigneux.

paint *vt* peindre.

paintbrush *n* pinceau *m*.

painter *n* peintre *m*.

painting *n* peinture *f*; tableau *m*.

paintwork *n* peinture *f*.

pair *n* pair *m*.

pajamas *npl* = pyjamas.

pal *n* copain *m*, copine *f*, pote *m*.

palatable *adj* savoureux.

palate *n* palais *m*.

palatial *adj* grandiose.

palaver *n* discussions *fpl*; situation embrouillée *f*.

pale *adj* pâle; clair.

palette *n* palette *f*.

paling *n* palissade *f*.

pall *n* nuage *m* (de fumée); * *vi* perdre sa saveur.

pallet *n* palette *f*.

palliative *adj n* palliatif *m*.

pallid *adj* pâle.

pallor *n* pâleur *f*.

palm *n* (*bot*) palme *f*, palmier *m*.

palmistry *n* chiromancie *f*.

Palm Sunday *n* Dimanche des Rameaux *m*.

palpable *adj* palpable; évident.

palpitation *n* palpitation *f*.

paltry *adj* dérisoire; mesquin.

pamper *vt* gâter, dorloter.

pamphlet *n* pamphlet *m*; brochure *f*.

pan *n* casserole *f*; poêle *f*.

panacea *n* panacée *f*.

panache *n* panache *m*.

pancake *n* crêpe *f*.

pandemonium *n* pandémonium *m*.

pane *n* vitre *f*.

panel *n* panneau *m*; comité *m*.

panelling *n* lambrissage *m*.

pang *n* angoisse *f*; tourment *m*.

panic *adj n* (de) panique *f*.

panicky *adj* paniqué, affolé.

panic-stricken *adj* pris de panique.

pansy *n* (*bot*) pensée *f*.

pant *vi* haleter.

panther *n* panthère *f*.

panties *npl* (petite) culotte *f*.

pantihose *n* collant *m*.

pantry *n* placard *m*.

pants *npl* slip *m*; pantalon *m*.

papacy *n* papauté *f*.

papal *adj* papal.

paper *n* papier *m*; journal *m*; épreuve *f* d'examen; exposé *m*, étude *f*; ~s *pl* documents *mpl*; (*com*) fonds *mpl*; * *adj* en papier; * *vt* garnir de papier; tapisser.

paperback *n* livre de poche *m*.

paper bag *n* sac en papier *m*.

paper clip *n* trombone *m*.

paperweight *n* presse-papiers *m*.

paperwork *n* paperasserie *f*.

paprika *n* paprika *m*.

par *n* équivalence *f*; égalité *f*; pair *m*; at ~ *(com)* au pair.

parable *n* parabole *f*.

parachute *n* parachute *m*; * *vi* sauter en parachute.

parade *n* parade *f*; *(mil)* défilé *m*; * *vt* faire défiler, faire parader; * *vi* défiler, parader; se pavaner.

paradise *n* paradis *m*.

paradox *n* paradoxe *m*.

paradoxical *adj* paradoxal.

paragon *n* modèle absolu *m*.

paragraph *n* paragraphe *m*.

parallel *adj* parallèle; * *n* parallèle *f*; * *vt* mettre en parallèle; comparer.

paralyse *vt* paralyser.

paralysis *n* paralysie *f*.

paralytic(al) *adj* paralytique.

paramedic *n* auxiliaire médical(e) *m(f)*.

paramount *adj* suprême, supérieur.

paranoid *adj* paranoïaque.

paraphernalia *n* affaires *fpl*; attirail *m*.

parasite *n* parasite *m*.

parasol *n* parasol *m*.

paratrooper *n* parachutiste *m*.

parcel *n* paquet *m*; parcelle *f*; * *vt* empaqueter, emballer.

parch *vt* dessécher.

parched *adj* desséché.

parchment *n* parchemin *m*.

pardon *n* pardon *m*; * *vt* pardonner.

parent *n* parent *m* -e *f*; ~s parents *mpl*.

parentage *n* parenté *f*; origine *f*.

parental *adj* parental.

parenthesis *n* parenthèse *f*.

parish *n* paroisse *f*; * *adj* paroissial.

parishioner *n* paroissien *m* -ne *f*.

parity *n* parité *f*.

park *n* parc *m*; * *vt* garer; *vi* se garer.

parking *n* stationnement *m*.

parking lot *n* parking *m*.

parking meter *n* parcomètre *m*.

parking ticket *n* amende pour stationnement interdit *f*.

parlance *n* langage *m*.

parliament *n* parlement *m*.

parliamentary *adj* parlementaire.

parlour *n* parloir *m*; salon *m*.

parody *n* parodie *f*; * *vt* parodier.

parole *n*: on ~ sur parole.

parricide *n* parricide *m*; parricide *mf*.

parrot *n* perroquet *m*.

parry *vt* parer.

parsley *n* (*bot*) persil *m*.

parsnip *n* (*bot*) navet *m*.

part *n* partie *f*; part *f*; rôle (d'acteur) *m*; raie *f*; ~s *pl* parties *fpl*; parages *mpl*; * *vt* séparer; diviser; * *vi* se séparer; se diviser; ~ **with** céder; se défaire de; donner; ~ly *adv* en partie.

partial *adj* partial; ~ly *adv* avec partialité; partiellement.

participant *n* participant *m* -e *f*.

participate *vi* participer (à).

participation *n* participation *f*.

participle *n* (*gr*) participe *m*.

particle *n* particule *f*.

particular *adj* particulier, singulier; ~ly *adv* particulièrement; * *n* particulier *m*; particularité *f*.

parting *n* séparation *f*; raie (dans les cheveux) *f*.

partisan *n* partisan *m* -e *f*.

partition *n* partition, séparation *f*; * *vt* diviser en plusieurs parties, partager;

partner *n* associé *m* -e *f*.

partnership *n* association *f*; société *f*.

partridge *n* perdrix *f*.

party *n* parti *m*; fête *f*.

pass *vt* passer; dépasser; adopter; être admis à; * *vi* passer; * *n* permis *m*; passage *m*; ~ **away** *vi* mourir; ~ **by** *vi* passer; *vt* négliger, oublier; ~ **on** *vt* transmettre; passer.

passable *adj* passable; praticable.

passage *n* passage *m*; traversée *f*; couloir *m*.

passbook *n* livret *m* (bancaire).

passenger *n* passager *m* -ère *f*.

passer-by *n* passant *m* -e *f*.

passing *adj* passager.

passion *n* passion *f*; amour *m*; emportement *m*.

passionate *adj* passionné; ~ly *adv* passionnément; ardemment.

passive *adj* passif; ~ly *adv* passivement.

passkey *n* passe-partout *m invar*.

Passover *n* Pâque *f* juive.

passport *n* passeport *m*.

passport control *n* contrôle des passeports *m*.

password n mot de passe m.

past adj passé; * n (gr) prétérit m; passé m; * prep au-delà de; après.

pasta n pâtes fpl.

paste n pâte f; colle f; * vt coller.

pasteurized adj pasteurisé.

pastime n passe-temps m invar; divertissement m.

pastor n pasteur m.

pastoral adj pastoral.

pastry n pâtisserie f.

pasture n pâture f.

pasty adj pâteux; pâle.

pat vt tapoter.

patch n pièce f; tache f; terrain m; * vt rapiécer; ~ **up** réparer; se réconcilier.

pâté n pâté m.

patent adj breveté; évident; * n brevet m; * vt faire breveter.

patentee n détenteur d'un brevet m.

patent leather n cuir verni m.

paternal adj paternel.

paternity n paternité f.

path n chemin, sentier m.

pathetic adj ~ally adv pathétique(ment); lamentable(ment).

pathological adj pathologique.

pathology n pathologie f.

pathos n pathétique m.

pathway n sentier m.

patience n patience f.

patient adj patient; ~ly adv patiemment; * n patient m -e f.

patio n patio m.

patriarch m patriarche m.

patriot n patriote mf.

patriotic adj patriotique.

patriotism n patriotisme m.

patrol n patrouille f; * vi patrouiller.

patrol car n voiture de patrouille f.

patrolman n agent de police m.

patron n protecteur m; client m -e f.

patronage n patronage m; clientèle f.

patronize vt patronner, protéger.

patter n trottinement m; bavardage m; * vi trottiner.

pattern n motif m; modèle m.

paunch n panse f; ventre m.

pauper n pauvre mf.

pause n pause f; * vi faire une pause; hésiter.

pave vt paver; carreler.

pavement n trottoir m.

pavilion n pavillon m.

paving stone n pavé m.

paw n patte f; * vt tripoter.

pawn n pion m; gage m; * vt engager.

pawn broker n prêteur(-euse) sur gages m(f).

pawnshop n mont-de-piété m.

pay vt payer; ~ **back** vt rembourser; ~ **for** payer; ~ **off** vt liquider; vi payer; rapporter; * n paie f; salaire m.

payable adj payable:

pay day n jour de paie m.

payee n bénéficiaire mf.

pay envelope n enveloppe de paie f.

paymaster n caissier m.

payment n paiement m.

pay-phone n téléphone public m.

payroll n liste des employés f.

pea n pois m.

peace n paix f.

peaceful adj paisible; pacifique.

peach n pêche f.

peacock n paon m.

peak n pic m; maximum m.

peak hours, peak period n heures de pointe fpl.

peal n carillon m; grondement m.

peanut n cacahuète f.

pear n poire f.

pearl n perle f.

peasant n paysan m -ne f.

peat n tourbe f.

pebble n caillou m; galet m.

peck n coup de bec m; * vt picoter.

pecking order n hiérarchie f.

peculiar adj étrange, singulier; ~**ly** adv étrangement.

peculiarity n particularité, singularité f.

pedal n pédale f; * vi pédaler.

pedant n pédant m -e f.

pedantic adj pédant.

peddler n colporteur m.

pedestal n piédestal m.

pedestrian n piéton m -ne f; * adj pédestre.

pediatrics n (US) pédiatrie f.

pedigree n généalogie f; pedigree m; * adj de race.

peek vi regarder à la dérobée.

peel vt peler; éplucher; * vi peler; * n peau f; pelure f.

peer n pair m.

peerless adj incomparable.

peeved adj fâché.

peevish adj maussade, ronchon (fam).

peg n cheville f; piquet m; *
vt cheviller.

pelican n pélican m.

pellet n boulette f.

pelt n fourrure f; * vt arroser;
* vi pleuvoir à verse.

pen n stylo m; plume f; enclos
m.

penal adj pénal.

penalty n peine f; sanction f;
amende f.

penance n pénitence f.

pence n = pl of penny.

pencil n crayon m.

pencil case n trousse f.

pendant n pendentif m.

pending adj pendant.

pendulum n pendule m.

penetrate vt pénétrer (dans).

penguin n pingouin m.

penicillin n pénicilline f.

peninsula n péninsule f.

penis n pénis m.

penitence n pénitence f.

penitent adj n pénitent m -e
f.

penitentiary n pénitencier m.

penknife n canif m.

pennant n fanion m.

penniless adj sans le sou.

penny n penny m.

penpal n correspondant m
-e f.

pension n pension f; * vt
pensionner.

pensive adj pensif; ~ly adv
pensivement.

pentagon n: the P~ le
Pentagone.

Pentecost n la Pentecôte f.

penthouse n appartement
situé sur le toit d'un
immeuble m.

pent-up adj reprimé, refoulé.

penultimate adj pénultième,
avant-dernier.

penury n pénurie f.

people n peuple m; nation f;
gens mpl; * vt peupler.

pep n énergie f; ~ up vt
animer.

pepper n poivre m; * vt
poivrer.

peppermint n menthe
poivrée f.

per prep par.

per annum adv par an.

per capita adj adv par
habitant.

perceive vt percevoir.

percentage n pourcentage m.

perception n perception f;
notion f.

perch n perche f.

perchance adv par hasard.

percolate vt filtrer.

percolator *n* percolateur *m*.

percussion *n* percussion *f*.

perdition *n* perte, ruine *f*.

peremptory *adj* péremptoire; décisif.

perennial *adj* perpétuel.

perfect *adj* parfait; idéal; ~ly *adv* parfaitement; * *vt* parfaire, perfectionner.

perfection *n* perfection *f*.

perforate *vt* perforer.

perforation *n* perforation *f*.

perform *vt* exécuter; effectuer; * *vi* donner une représentation, tenir un rôle.

performance *n* exécution *f*; accomplissement *m*; rendement *m*; représentation *f*.

performer *n* exécutant *m* -e *f*; acteur *m* -trice *f*.

perfume *n* parfum *m*; * *vt* parfumer.

perhaps *adv* peut-être.

peril *n* péril, danger *m*.

perilous *adj* dangereux; ~ly *adv* dangereusement.

perimeter *n* périmètre *m*.

period *n* période *f*; époque *f*; règles *fpl*.

periodic(al) *adj* périodique; ~ally *adv* périodiquement.

periodical *n* journal *m*.

peripheral *adj* périphérique; * *n* unité périphérique *f*.

perish *vi* périr.

perishable *adj* périssable.

perjure *vt* parjurer.

perjury *n* parjure *m*.

perk *n* extra, à-côté *m*.

perky *adj* animé, plein d'entrain.

perm *n* permanente *f*.

permanent *adj* permanent; ~ly *adv* en permanence.

permeate *vt* pénétrer, traverser.

permissible *adj* permis.

permission *n* permission *f*.

permissive *adj* permissif.

permit *vt* permettre; * *n* permis *m*.

permutation *n* permutation *f*.

perpendicular *adj* ~ly *adv* perpendiculaire(ment); * *n* perpendiculaire *f*.

perpetrate *vt* perpétrer, commettre.

perpetual *adj* perpétuel; ~ly *adv* perpétuellement.

perpetuate *vt* perpétuer, éterniser.

perplex *vt* confondre, laisser perrplexe.

persecute *vt* persécuter; importuner.

persecution *n* persécution *f*.

perseverance *n* persévérance *f*.

persevere *vi* persévérer.

persist *vi* persister.

persistence *n* persistance *f*.

persistent *adj* persistant.

person *n* personne *f*.

personable *adj* attrayant.

personage *n* personnage *m*.

personal *adj* ~ly *adv* personnel(lement).

personal assistant *n* secrétaire *mf* de direction.

personal column *n* annonces personnelles *fpl*.

personal computer *n* ordinateur individuel *m*.

personality *n* personnalité *f*.

personification *n* personnification *f*.

personify *vt* personnifier.

personnel *n* personnel *m*.

perspective *n* perspective *f*.

perspiration *n* transpiration *f*.

perspire *vi* transpirer.

persuade *vt* persuader.

persuasion *n* persuasion *f*.

persuasive *adj* persuasif; ~ly *adv* de manière persuasive.

pert *adj* plein d'entrain.

pertaining: ~ to *prep* relatif à.

pertinent *adj* pertinent; ~ly *adv* de manière pertinente.

pertness *n* impertinence *f*; entrain *m*.

perturb *vt* perturber.

perusal *n* lecture *f*.

peruse *vt* lire; examiner attentivement.

pervade *vt* pénétrer, traverser.

perverse *adj* pervers, dépravé; ~ly *adv* perversement.

pervert *vt* pervertir, corrompre.

pessimist *n* pessimiste *mf*.

pest *n* insecte nuisible *m*; (*fam*) casse-pieds *mf invar*.

pester *vt* importuner, fatiguer.

pestilence *n* peste *f*.

pet *n* animal domestique *m*; préféré *m* -e *f*; * *vt* gâter; * *vi* (*fam*) se peloter.

petal *n* (*bot*) pétale *m*.

petite *adj* menue.

petition *n* pétition *f*; * *vt* présenter une pétition à; supplier.

petrified *adj* pétrifié.

petroleum *n* pétrole *m*.

petticoat *n* jupon *m*.

pettiness *n* insignifiance *f*.

petty *adj* mesquin; insignifiant.

petty cash *n* argent destiné aux dépenses courantes *m*.

petty officer *n* second maître *m*.

petulant *adj* pétulant.

pew *n* banc *m*.

pewter *n* étain *m*.

phantom *n* fantôme *m*.

Pharisee *n* Pharisien *m*.

pharmaceutic(al) *adj* pharmaceutique.

pharmacist *n* pharmacien *m* -ienne *f*.

pharmacy *n* pharmacie *f*.

phase *n* phase *f*.

pheasant *n* faisan *m*.

phenomenal *adj* phénoménal.

phenomenon *n* phénomène *m*.

phial *n* fiole *f*.

philanthropic *adj* philanthropique.

philanthropist *n* philanthrope *mf*.

philanthropy *n* philanthropie *f*.

philologist *n* philologue *mf*.

philology *n* philologie *f*.

philosopher *n* philosophe *mf*.

philosophical(ly) *adj* (*adv*) philosophique(ment).

philosophize *vi* philosopher.

philosophy *n* philosophie *f*; natural ~ physique *f*.

phlegm *n* flegme *m*.

phlegmatic(al) *adj* flegmatique.

phobia *n* phobie *f*.

phone *n* téléphone *m*; * *vt* téléphoner à; ~ back *vt vi* rappeler; ~ up *vt* appeler au téléphone.

phone book *n* annuaire *m*.

phone box, phone booth *n* cabine téléphonique *f*.

phone call *n* coup de téléphone *m*.

phosphorus *n* phosphore *m*.

photocopier *n* photocopieuse *f*.

photocopy *n* photocopie *f*.

photograph *n* photo(graphie) *f*; * *vt* photographier.

photographer *n* photographe *mf*.

photographic *adj* photographique.

photography *n* photo(graphie) *f*.

phrase *n* phrase *f*; locution *f*; * *vt* exprimer.

phrase book *n* guide de conversation *m*.

physical *adj* ~ly *adv* physique(ment).

physical education *n* éducation physique *f*.

physician *n* médecin *m*.

physicist *n* physicien *m* -ne *f*.

physiological   *adj*
  physiologique.

physiologist *n* physiologiste,
  physiologue *mf*.

physiology *n* physiologie *f*.

physiotherapy   *n*
  physiothérapie *f*.

physique *n* physique *m*.

pianist *n* pianiste *mf*.

pick *vt* choisir; cueillir;
  gratter; ~ on *vt* s'en prendre à; ~ out *vt* choisir; ~ up
  vi s'améliorer; se remettre;
  * *vt* ramasser; décrocher;
  arrêter; acheter; * *n* pic *m*;
  choix *m*.

pickaxe *n* pic *m*.

picket *n* piquet *m*.

pickle *n* saumure *f*; * *vt*
  saumurer.

pickpocket *n* pickpocket *m*.

pickup *n* (*auto*) fourgonnette *f*.

picnic *n* pique-nique *m*.

pictorial *adj* pictural; illustré.

picture *n* image *f*; peinture *f*;
  photo *f*; * *vt* dépeindre; se
  figurer.

picture book *n* livre d'images
  m.

picturesque *adj* pittoresque.

pie *n* gâteau *m*; tarte *f*; pâté
  en croûte *m*.

piece *n* morceau *m*; pièce *f*;
  tranche *f*; * *vt* raccommoder.

piecemeal *adv* petit à petit; *
  adj partiel.

piecework *n* travail à la pièce
  m.

pier *n* jetée *f*.

pierce *vt* percer, transpercer.

piercing *adj* perçant.

piety *n* piété, dévotion *f*.

pig *n* cochon *m*.

pigeon *n* pigeon *m*.

pigeonhole *n* casier *m*.

piggy bank *n* tirelire *f*.

pigheaded *adj* têtu.

pigsty *n* porcherie *f*.

pigtail *n* natte *f*.

pike *n* brochet *m*; pique *f*.

pile *n* tas *m*; pile *f*; amas *m*;
  poil *m*; ~s *pl* hémorroïdes
  fpl; * *vt* entasser, empiler.

pile-up *n* carambolage *m*.

pilfer *vt* chaparder.

pilgrim *n* pèlerin *m*.

pilgrimage *n* pèlerinage *m*.

pill *n* pilule *f*.

pillage *vt* piller, mettre à sac.

pillar *n* pilier *m*.

pillion *n* siège arrière *m*.

pillow *n* oreiller *m*.

pillow case *n* taie d'oreiller *f*.

pilot *n* pilote *m*; * *vt* piloter;
  (*fig*) mener.

pilot light *n* témoin *m*.

pimp *n* proxénète, maquereau (*fam*) *m*.

pimple *n* bouton *m*.

pin *n* épingle *f*; goupille *f*; ~s and needles *npl* fourmis *fpl*; * *vt* épingler; goupiller.

pinafore *n* tablier *m*.

pinball *n* flipper *m*.

pincers *n* tenailles *fpl*.

pinch *vt* pincer; (*sl*) piquer, faucher; * *vi* serrer; * *n* pincement *m*; pincée *f*.

pincushion *n* pelote à épingles *f*.

pine *n* (*bot*) pin *m*; * *vi* languir.

pineapple *n* ananas *m*.

ping *n* tintement *m*.

pink *adj n* rose *m*.

pinnacle *n* sommet *m*.

pinpoint *vt* préciser; souligner.

pint *n* pinte *f*.

pioneer *n* pionnier *m*.

pious *adj* pieux, dévot; ~ly *adv* pieusement.

pip *n* pépin *m*.

pipe *n* tube, tuyau *m*; pipe *f*; ~s tuyauterie *f*.

pipe cleaner *n* cure-pipe *m*.

pipe dream *n* rêve impossible *m*.

pipeline *n* canalisation *f*; oléoduc *m*; gazoduc *m*.

piper *n* joueur de cornemuse *m*.

piping *adj* bouillant; aigu, *f* aiguë.

pique *n* pique *f*; dépit *m*.

piracy *n* piraterie *f*.

pirate *n* pirate *m*.

pirouette *n* pirouette *f*; *vi* pirouetter.

Pisces *n* Poissons *mpl* (signe du zodiaque).

piss *n* (*sl*) pisse *f*; * *vi* pisser.

pistol *n* pistolet *m*.

piston *n* piston *m*.

pit *n* noyau *m*; mine *f*; fosse *f*.

pitch *n* lancement *m*; ton *m*; * *vt* lancer, jeter; * *vi* tomber; piquer du nez.

pitchblack *adj* noir comme dans un four.

pitcher *n* cruche *f*.

pitchfork *n* fourche *f*.

pitfall *n* piège *m*.

pithy *adj* moelleux; vigoureux.

pitiable *adj* pitoyable; déplorable.

pitiful *adj* pitoyable; lamentable; ~ly *adv* pitoyablement.

pittance *n* salaire de misère *m*; pitance *f*.

pity *n* pitié *f*; * *vt* avoir pitié de.

pivot *n* pivot, axe *m*.

pizza *n* pizza *f*.

placard *n* affiche *f*.

placate *vt* apaiser.

place *n* endroit, lieu *m*; place *f*; * *vt* placer; mettre.

placid *adj* placide, calme; **~ly** *adv* placidement.

plagiarism *n* plagiat *m*.

plague *n* peste *f*; * *vt* tourmenter; infester.

plaice *n* carrelet *m*.

plaid *n* tartan *m*; plaid *m*.

plain *adj* uni; simple; clair, sincère; commun; évident; **~ly** *adv* simplement; clairement; * *n* plaine *f*.

plaintiff *n* (*law*) plaignant *m* -e *f*.

plait *n* tresse *f*; * *vt* tresser.

plan *n* plan *m*; projet *m*; * *vt* projeter.

plane *n* avion *m*; plan *m*; rabot *m*; * *vt* aplanir; raboter.

planet *n* planète *f*.

planetary *adj* planétaire.

plank *n* planche *f*.

planner *n* planificateur *m* -trice *f*.

planning *n* planification *f*.

plant *n* plante *f*; usine *f*; machinerie *f*; * *vt* planter.

plantation *n* plantation *f*.

plaque *n* plaque *f*.

plaster *n* plâtre *m*; emplâtre *m*; * *vt* plâtrer; emplâtrer.

plastered *adj* (*sl*) bourré, soûl.

plasterer *n* plâtrier *m*.

plastic *adj* plastique.

plastic surgery *n* chirurgie esthétique *f*.

plate *n* assiette *f*; plaque *f*; lame *f*.

plateau *n* (*geol*) plateau *m*.

plate glass *n* vitre *f*.

platform *n* plateforme *f*.

platinum *n* platine *m*.

platitude *n* platitude *f*.

platoon *n* (*mil*) peloton *m*.

platter *n* écuelle *f*; plat *m*.

plaudit *n* applaudissement *m*.

plausible *adj* plausible.

play *n* jeu *m*; pièce de théâtre *f*; * *vt vi* jouer; (*also mus*) **~ down** *vt* rabaisser; minimiser.

playboy *n* playboy *m*.

player *n* joueur *m* -euse *f*; acteur *m* -trice *f*.

playful *adj* enjoué, amusé; **~ly** *adv* d'une manière enjouée; pour s'amuser.

playmate *n* camarade de jeu *mf*.

playground *n* cour de récréation *f*; jardin d'enfants *m*.

playgroup *n* halte-garderie *f*.

play-off *n* prolongation *f* (match).

playpen *n* parc pour enfant *m*.

plaything *n* jouet *m*.

playwright *n* dramaturge *mf*.

plea *n* appel *m*; excuse *f*, prétexte *m*.

plead *vt* plaider; prétexter.

pleasant *adj* agréable; plaisant; aimable; ~ly *adv* agréablement.

please *vt* faire plaisir à.

pleased *adj* content.

pleasing *adj* agréable, plaisant.

pleasure *n* plaisir *m*; gré *m*, volonté *f*.

pleat *n* pli *m*.

pledge *n* promesse *f*; gage *m*; * *vt* engager; promettre.

plentiful *adj* copieux; abondant.

plenty *n* abondance *f*; ~ of beaucoup de.

plethora *n* pléthore *f*.

pleurisy *n* pleurésie *f*.

pliable, pliant *adj* pliable, pliant; souple.

pliers *npl* pinces *fpl*.

plight *n* épreuve *f*; situation difficile *f*.

plinth *n* plinthe *f*.

plod *vi* se traîner, avancer péniblement.

plot *n* petit morceau de terrain *m*; complot *m*; intrigue *f*; * *vt* tracer; comploter; conspirer.

plough *n* charrue *f*; * *vt* labourer; ~ **back** *vt* réinvestir; ~ **through** *vi* se faire un chemin; avancer péniblement.

ploy *n* truc *m*.

pluck *vt* tirer; arracher; déplumer; * *n* courage *m*.

plucky *adj* courageux.

plug *n* tampon *m*; bouchon *m*; bougie *f*; prise *f*; * *vt* boucher.

plum *n* prune *f*.

plumage *n* plumage *m*.

plumb *n* aplomb *m*; * *adv* d'aplomb; * *vt* plomber; sonder.

plumber *n* plombier *m*.

plume *n* plume *f*, panache *m*.

plump *adj* rondouillet, dodu.

plum tree *n* prunier *m*.

plunder *vt* mettre à sac, piller; * *n* pillage *m*; butin *m*.

plunge *vi* plonger; s'élancer.

plunger *n* piston *m*.

pluperfect *n* (*gr*) plus-que-parfait *m*.

plural *adj n* pluriel *m*.

plurality *n* pluralité *f*.

plus *n* signe plus *m*; * *prep* plus.

plush *adj* en peluche.

plutonium *n* plutonium *m*.

ply *vt* manier avec vigueur; * *vi* s'appliquer; (*mar*) faire la navette.

plywood *n* contreplaqué *m*.

pneumatic *adj* pneumatique.

pneumatic drill *n* marteau pneumatique *m*.

pneumonia *n* pneumonie *f*.

poach *vt* pocher; braconner; *vi* braconner.

poached *adj* poché.

poacher *n* braconnier *m*.

poaching *n* braconnage *m*.

pocket *n* poche *f*; * *vt* empocher.

pocketbook *n* portefeuille *m*.

pocket money *n* argent de poche *m*.

pod *n* cosse *f*.

podgy *adj* boudiné.

poem *n* poème *m*.

poet *n* poète *m*.

poetess *n* poétesse *f*.

poetic *adj* poétique.

poetry *n* poésie *f*.

poignant *adj* poignant.

point *n* pointe *f*; point *m*; promontoire *m*; ~ **of view** *n* point de vue *m*; * *vt* pointer; tailler en pointe; indiquer.

point-blank *adv* à bout portant; directement.

pointed *adj* pointu; acéré; ~**ly** *adv* subtilement.

pointer *n* auguille *f*; pointer *m*.

pointless *adj* inutile.

poise *n* attitude *f*; équilibre *m*.

poison *n* poison *m*; * *vt* empoisonner.

poisoning *n* empoisonnement *m*.

poisonous *adj* vénéneux.

poke *vt* attiser; donner un coup de coude à; pousser du doigt.

poker *n* tison *m*; poker *m*.

poker-faced *adj* au visage impassible.

poky *adj* exigu, *f* exiguë.

polar *adj* polaire.

pole *n* pôle *m*; mât *m*; perche *f*.

pole bean *n* haricot en rames *m*.

pole vault *n* saut à la perche *m*.

police *n* police *f*.

police car *n* voiture de police *f*.

policeman *n* agent de police *m*.

police state *n* état policier *m*.

police station *n* commissariat *m*.

policewoman *n* femme agent de police *f*.

policy *n* politique *f*; police d'assurance *f*.

polio *n* polio *f*.

polish *vt* polir; cirer; ~ **off** *vt* parachever; expédier; * *n* poli *m*.

polished *adj* poli; ciré; élégant.

polite *adj* ~**ly** *adv* poli(ment), courtois(-ement).

politeness *n* politesse, courtoisie *f*.

politic *adj* politique; rusé.

political *adj* politique.

politician *n* homme (femme) politique *m(f)*.

politics *npl* politique *f*.

polka *n* polka *f*; ~ **dot** *n* pois *m*.

poll *n* liste électorale *f*; vote *m*; sondage *m*.

pollen *n* (*bot*) pollen *m*.

pollute *vt* polluer; corrompre.

pollution *n* pollution, contamination *f*.

polyester *n* polyester *m*.

polyethylene *n* polyéthylène *m*.

polygamy *n* polygamie *f*.

polystyrene *n* polystyrène *m*.

polytechnic *n* école d'enseignement technique *f*.

pomegranate *n* grenade *f*.

pomp *n* pompe *f*; splendeur *f*.

pompom *n* pompon *m*.

pompous *adj* pompeux.

pond *n* mare *f*; étang *m*.

ponder *vt* considérer; réfléchir à.

ponderous *adj* lourd, pesant.

pontiff *n* pontife *m*.

pontoon *n* ponton *m*.

pony *n* poney *m*.

ponytail *n* queue de cheval *f*.

pool *n* flaque d'eau *f*; piscine *f*; * *vt* grouper.

poor *adj* pauvre; mauvais; ~**ly** *adv* pauvrement; **the** ~ *n* les pauvres *mpl*.

pop *n* pop *m*; papa *m*; boisson gazeuse *f*; éclatement *m*; * ~ **in/out** *vi* entrer/sortir un instant.

pop concert *n* concert de musique pop *m*.

popcorn *n* popcorn *m*.

Pope n pape m.

poplar n peuplier m.

poppy n (bot) pavot m.

popsicle n (US) sucette f glacée.

populace n populace f.

popular adj ~ly adv populaire(ment).

popularity n popularité f.

popularize vt populariser.

populate vi peupler.

population n population f.

populous adj populeux.

porcelain n porcelaine f.

porch n porche m.

porcupine n porc-épic m.

pore n pore m.

pork n porc m (viande).

pornography n pornographie f.

porous adj poreux.

porpoise n marsouin m.

porridge n porridge m, flocons d'avoine mpl.

port n port m; (mar) sabord m; babord m; porto (vin) m.

portable adj portable, portatif.

portal n portail m.

porter n portier m; garçon m.

portfolio n serviette f; carton m; portefeuille m.

porthole n hublot m.

portico n portique m.

portion n portion, part f.

portly adj corpulent.

portrait n portrait m.

portray vt faire le portrait de; dépeindre.

pose n posture f; pose f; * vt vi poser.

posh adj chic; bourgeois.

position n position f; situation f; * vt mettre en position.

positive adj positif; réel; favorable; ~ly adv positivement; assurément.

posse n peloton m, détachement m.

possess vt posséder.

possession n possession f.

possessive adj possessif.

possibility n possibilité f.

possible adj possible; ~ly adv peut-être.

post n courrier m; poste f; emploi m; poste m; pieu m; * vt poster; fixer.

postage n affranchissement m.

postage stamp n timbre m.

postcard n carte postale f.

postdate vt postdater.

posterior n postérieur m.

posterity n postérité f.

postgraduate n licencié m -e f.

posthumous adj posthume.

postman n facteur m.

postmark n cachet de la poste m.

postmaster n receveur des postes m.

post office n poste f, bureau de poste m.

postpone vt remettre; différer.

postscript n post-scriptum m.

posture n posture f.

postwar adj d'après-guerre.

posy n petit bouquet de fleurs m.

pot n pot m; marmite f; (sl) marijuana f; * vt empoter; mettre en pot.

potato n pomme de terre, patate (fam) f.

potato peeler n couteau éplucheur m.

potbellied adj ventru.

potent adj puissant.

potential adj potentiel.

pothole n trou m.

potion n potion f.

potted adj en pot.

potter n potier m.

pottery n poterie f.

potty adj insignifiant; (sl) fou, maboul.

pouch n sac m.

poultice n cataplasme m.

poultry n volaille f.

pound n livre f; livre sterling f; fourrière f; * vt concasser; * vi taper fort.

pour vt verser; servir; * vi couler; pleuvoir à verse.

pout vi faire la moue.

poverty n pauvreté f.

powder n poudre f; * vt saupoudrer.

powder compact n poudrier m.

powdered milk n lait en poudre m.

powder puff n houppette f.

powder room n toilettes fpl.

powdery adj poudreux.

power n pouvoir m; puissance f; empire m; autorité f; force f; * vt propulser.

powerful adj puissant; ~ly adv puissamment; avec force.

powerless adj impuissant.

power station n centrale électrique f.

practicable adj praticable; faisable.

practical adj ~ly adv pratique(ment).

practicality n faisabilité f.

practical joke n farce f.

practice n pratique f; usage m; entraînement m; ~s pl agissements mpl.

practise *vt* pratiquer, exercer; * *vi* s'exercer, s'entraîner.

practitioner *n* médecin *m*.

pragmatic *adj* pragmatique.

prairie *n* prairie *f*.

praise *n* éloge *m*; louange *f*; * *vt* louer.

praiseworthy *adj* digne d'éloges.

prance *vi* cabrioler.

prank *n* folie, extravagance *f*.

prattle *vi* jacasser; * *n* jacasserie *f*.

prawn *n* crevette *f*.

pray *vi* prier.

prayer *n* prière *f*.

prayer book *n* livre de messe *m*.

preach *vt* prêcher.

preacher *n* prédicateur *m*.

preamble *n* préambule *m*.

precarious *adj* précaire, incertain; ~**ly** *adv* précairement.

precaution *n* précaution *f*.

precautionary *adj* préventif.

precede *vt* précéder.

precedence *n* précédence *f*.

precedent *adj n* précédent *m*.

precinct *n* limite *f*; enceinte *f*; circonscription *f*.

precious *adj* précieux.

precipice *n* (*fig*) précipice *m*.

precipitate *vt* précipiter; * *adj* précipité.

precise *n* précis, exact; ~**ly** *adv* précisément, exactement.

precision *n* précision, exactitude *f*.

preclude *vt* exclure, empêcher.

precocious *adj* précoce, prématuré.

preconceive *vt* préconcevoir.

preconception *n* préjugé *m*; idée préconçue *f*.

precondition *n* condition préalable *f*.

precursor *n* précurseur *m*.

predator *n* prédateur *m*.

predecessor *n* prédécesseur *m*.

predestination *n* prédestination *f*.

predicament *n* situation difficile *f*.

predict *vt* prédire.

predictable *adj* prévisible.

prediction *n* prédiction *f*.

predilection *n* prédilection *f*.

predominant *adj* prédominant.

predominate *vt* prédominer.

preen *vt* nettoyer (ses plumes).

prefab *n* maison préfabriquée *f*.

preface *n* préface *f*.

prefer *vt* préférer.

preferable *adj* préférable.

preferably *adv* de préférence.

preference *n* préférence *f*.

preferential *adj* préférentiel.

preferment *n* promotion *f*; préférence *f*.

prefix *vt* préfixer; * *n* (*gr*) préfixe *m*.

pregnancy *n* grossesse *f*.

pregnant *adj* enceinte.

prehistoric *adj* préhistorique.

prejudice *n* (*law*) préjudice, tort *m*; préjugé *m*; * *vt* préjudicier à, faire du tort à.

prejudiced *adj* qui a des préjugés; partial.

prejudicial *adj* préjudiciable.

preliminary *adj* préliminaire.

prelude *n* prélude *m*.

premarital *adj* préconjugal.

premature *adj* ~ly *adv* prématuré(ment).

premeditation *n* préméditation *f*.

premier *n* premier ministre *m*.

première *n* (*thea*) première *f*.

premise *n* prémisse *f*.

premises *npl* locaux *mpl*.

premium *n* prix *m*; indemnité *f*; prime *f*.

premonition *n* pressentiment *m*, prémonition *f*.

preoccupied *adj* préoccupé; absorbé.

prepaid *adj* port payé.

preparation *n* préparation *f*.

preparatory *adj* préparatoire.

prepare *vt* préparer; * *vi* se préparer.

preponderance *n* prépondérance *f*.

preposition *n* préposition *f*.

preposterous *adj* ridicule, absurde.

prerequisite *n* condition requise *f*.

prerogative *n* prérogative *f*.

prescribe *vt* prescrire.

prescription *n* prescription *f*; ordonnance *f*.

presence *n* présence *f*.

present *n* cadeau *m*; * *adj* présent; actuel; ~ly *adv* actuellement; * *vt* offrir, donner; présenter.

presentable *adj* présentable.

presentation *n* présentation *f*.

present-day *adj* actuel.

presenter *n* présentateur *m* -trice *f*.

presentiment *n* pressentiment *m*, prémonition *f*.

preservation *n* préservation *f*.

preservative *n* préservatif *m*.

preserve *vt* préserver; conserver; faire des conserves de; * *n* conserve *f*; confiture *f*.

preside *vi* présider; diriger.

presidency *n* présidence *f*.

president *n* président *m*.

presidential *adj* présidentiel.

press *vt* appuyer sur; serrer; pressurer; * *vi* se presser; * *n* presse *f*; pressoir *m*; pression *f*.

press agency *n* agence de presse *f*.

press conference *n* conférence de presse *f*.

pressing *adj* pressant; urgent; ~ly *adv* de manière pressante; d'urgence.

pressure *n* pression *f*.

pressure cooker *n* autocuiseur *m*.

pressure group *n* groupe de pression *m*.

pressurized *adj* pressurisé.

prestige *n* prestige *m*.

presumable *adj* vraisemblable.

presumably *adv* vraisemblablement.

presume *vt* présumer, supposer.

presumption *n* présomption *f*.

presumptuous *adj* présomptueux.

presuppose *vt* présupposer.

pretence *n* prétexte *m*; simulation *f*; prétention *f*.

pretend *vi* prétendre; faire semblant.

pretender *n* prétendant *m*.

pretension *n* prétention *f*.

pretentious *adj* prétentieux.

preterite *n* prétérit *m*.

pretext *n* prétexte *m*.

pretty *adj* joli, mignon; * *adv* assez; plutôt.

prevail *vi* prévaloir; prédominer.

prevailing *adj* dominant.

prevalent *adj* prédominant.

prevent *vt* prévenir; empêcher; éviter.

prevention *n* prévention *f*.

preventive *adj* préventif.

preview *n* avant-première *f*.

previous *adj* précédent; antérieur; ~ly *adv* auparavant.

prewar *adj* d'avant-guerre.

prey *n* proie *f*.

price *n* prix *m*.

priceless *adj* inappréciable.

price list *n* tarif *m*.

prick *vt* piquer; exciter; * *n* piqûre *f*; pointe *f*.

prickle *n* picotement *m*; épine *f*.

prickly *adj* épineux.

pride *n* orgueil *m*; vanité *f*; fierté *f*.

priest *n* prêtre *m*.

priestess *n* prêtresse *f*.

priesthood *n* sacerdoce *m*, prêtrise *f*.

priestly *adj* sacerdotal.

priggish *adj* affecté, bégueule.

prim *adj* prude, affecté.

primacy *n* primauté *f*.

primarily *adv* principalement, surtout.

primary *adj* primaire; principal, premier.

primate *n* primate *m*.

prime *n* (*fig*) fleur *f*; commencement *m*; * *adj* premier; principal; excellent; * *vt* amorcer.

prime minister *n* premier ministre *m*.

primeval *adj* primitif.

priming *n* amorçage *m*.

primitive *adj* primitif; ~ly *adv* primitivement.

primrose *n* (*bot*) primevère *f*.

prince *n* prince *m*.

princess *n* princesse *f*.

principal *adj* ~ly *adv* principal(ement); * *n* principal *m*.

principality *n* principauté *f*.

principle *n* principe *m*.

print *vt* imprimer; * *n* impression *f*; estampe *f*; caractères imprimés *mpl*; **out of ~** épuisé (livres).

printed matter *n* imprimés *mpl*.

printer *n* imprimeur *m*; imprimante *f*.

printing *n* impression *f*.

prior *adj* antérieur, précédent; * *n* prieur *m*.

priority *n* priorité *f*.

priory *n* prieuré *m*.

prise *vt*: **to ~ open** ouvrir par la force, forcer.

prism *n* prisme *m*.

prison *n* prison *f*.

prisoner *n* prisonnier *m* -ière *f*.

pristine *adj* d'origine; intact.

privacy *n* intimité *f*.

private *adj* privé; secret; particulier; **~ soldier** *n* simple soldat *m*; **~ly** *adv* en privé.

private eye *n* détective privé *m*.

privet *n* troène *m*.

privilege *n* privilège *m*.

prize *n* prix *m*; * *vt* apprécier, évaluer.

prize-giving *n* distribution des prix *f*.

prizewinner *n* gagnant *m* -e *f*.

pro *prep* pour.

probability *n* probabilité *f*; vraisemblance *f*.

probable *adj* probable, vraisemblable; ~bly *adv* probablement.

probation *n* essai *m*; probation *f*.

probationary *adj* d'essai.

probe *n* sonde *f*; enquête *f*; * *vt* sonder; * *vi* faire des recherches.

problem *n* problème *m*.

problematical *adj* ~ly *adv* problématique(ment).

procedure *n* procédure *f*.

proceed *vi* procéder; provenir; poursuivre; ~s *npl* produit *m*; montant *m*; gross ~s bénéfices bruts *mpl*; net ~s benéfices nets *mpl*.

proceedings *n* procédure *f*; procédé *m*; procès *m*.

process *n* processus *m*; procédé *m*.

procession *n* procession *f*.

proclaim *vt* proclamer; promulguer.

proclamation *n* proclamation *f*; décret *m*.

procrastinate *vt* différer, retarder.

proctor *n* censeur *m*.

procure *vt* procurer.

procurement *n* obtention *f*.

prod *vt* pousser.

prodigal *adj* prodigue.

prodigious *adj* prodigieux; ~ly *adv* prodigieusement.

prodigy *n* prodige *m*.

produce *vt* produire; créer; fabriquer; * *n* produit *m*.

produce dealer *n* revendeur *m* -euse *f*.

producer *n* producteur *m* -trice *f*.

product *n* produit *m*; œuvre *f*; fruit *m*.

production *n* production *f*; produit *m*.

production line *n* chaîne *f* de fabrication.

productive *adj* productif.

productivity *n* productivité *f*.

profane *adj* profane.

profess *vt* professer; exercer; déclarer.

profession *n* profession *f*.

professional *adj* professionnel.

professor *n* professeur *m*.

proficiency *n* capacité *f*.

proficient *adj* compétent.

profile *n* profil *m*.

profit *n* bénéfice, profit *m*; avantage *m*; * *vi* profiter (de).

profitability *n* rentabilité *f*.

profitable *adj* profitable, avantageux.

profiteering *n* exploitation *f*, mercantilisme *m*.

profound *adj* ~ly *adv* profond(ément).

profuse *adj* profus; prodigue; ~ly *adv* à profusion.

program(me) *n* programme *m*.

programming *n* programmation *f*.

programmer *n* programmeur *m* -euse *f*.

progress *n* progrès *m*; cours *m*; * *vi* progresser.

progression *n* progression *f*; avance *f*.

progressive *adj* progressif; ~ly *adv* progressivement.

prohibit *vt* prohiber; défendre.

prohibition *n* prohibition *f*.

project *vt* projeter; * *n* projet *m*.

projectile *n* projectile *m*.

projection *n* projection *f*.

projector *n* projecteur *m*.

proletarian *adj* prolétaire.

proletariat *n* prolétariat *m*.

prolific *adj* prolifique, fécond.

prolix *adj* prolixe.

prologue *n* prologue *m*.

prolong *vt* prolonger.

prom *n* bal *m*; concert-promenade *m*.

promenade *n* promenade *f*.

prominence *n* proéminence *f*; éminence *f*.

prominent *adj* proéminent.

promiscuous *adj* immoral, débauché.

promise *n* promesse *f*; * *vt* promettre.

promising *adj* prometteur.

promontory *n* promontoire *m*.

promote *vt* promouvoir.

promoter *n* promoteur *m*.

promotion *n* promotion *f*.

prompt *adj* ~ly *adv* prompt(ement); * *vt* suggérer; inciter; souffler (au théâtre).

prompter *n* souffleur *m* -euse *f*.

prone *adj* enclin (à).

prong *n* dent *f* (fourchette).

pronoun *n* pronom *m*.

pronounce *vt* prononcer; déclarer.

pronounced *adj* marqué, prononcé.

pronouncement *n* déclaration *f*.

pronunciation *n* prononciation *f*.

proof *n* preuve *f*; * *adj* imperméable; résistant.

prop *vt* soutenir; * *n* appui, soutien *m*; tuteur *m*.

propaganda *n* propagande *f*.

propel *vt* propulser.

propeller *n* hélice *f*.

propensity *n* propension, tendance *f*.

proper *adj* propre; convenable; exact; approprié; ~ly *adv* convenablement; correctement.

property *n* propriété *f*.

prophecy *n* prophétie *f*.

prophesy *vt* prophétiser, prédire.

prophet *n* prophète *m*.

prophetic *adj* prophétique.

proportion *n* proportion *f*; symétrie *f*.

proportional *adj* proportionnel.

proportionate *adj* proportionné.

proposal *n* proposition *f*; offre *f*.

propose *vt* proposer.

proposition *n* proposition *f*.

proprietor *n* propriétaire *mf*.

propriety *n* propriété *f*.

pro rata *adv* au prorata.

prosaic *adj* prosaïque.

prose *n* prose *f*.

prosecute *vt* poursuivre en justice.

prosecution *n* poursuites *fpl*; accusation *f*.

prosecutor *n* (*law*) procureur *m*.

prospect *n* perspective *f*; espoir *m*; * *vt vi* prospecter.

prospecting *n* prospection *f*.

prospective *adj* probable; futur.

prospector *n* prospecteur *m* -trice *f*.

prospectus *n* prospectus *m*.

prosper *vi* prospérer.

prosperity *n* prospérité *f*.

prosperous *adj* prospère.

prostitute *n* prostituée *f*.

prostitution *n* prostitution *f*.

prostrate *adj* prostré.

protagonist *n* protagoniste *mf*.

protect *vt* protéger; abriter.

protection *n* protection *f*.

protective *adj* protecteur.

protector *n* protecteur *m* -trice *f*.

protégé *n* protégé *m* -e *f*.

protein *n* protéine *f*.

protest *vi* protester; * *n* protestation *f*.

Protestant *n* protestant *m* -e *f*.

protester *n* manifestant *m* -e *f*; protestataire *mf*.

protocol *n* protocole *m*.

prototype *n* prototype *m*.

protracted *adj* prolongé.

protrude *vi* déborder, ressortir.

proud *adj* fier, orgueilleux; ~ly *adv* fièrement.

prove *vt* prouver; justifier; * *vi* s'avérer; se révéler.

proverb *n* proverbe *m*.

proverbial *adj* ~ly *adv* proverbial(ement).

provide *vt* fournir; ~ for pourvoir aux besoins de; prévoir.

provided *conj*: ~ that pourvu que.

providence *n* providence *f*.

province *n* province *f*; compétence *f*.

provincial *adj n* provincial *m* -e *f*.

provision *n* provision *f*; disposition *f*.

provisional *adj* ~ly *adv* provisoire(ment).

proviso *n* stipulation *f*.

provocation *n* provocation *f*.

provocative *adj* provocateur.

provoke *vt* provoquer.

prow *n* (*mar*) proue *f*.

prowess *n* prouesse *f*.

prowl *vi* rôder.

prowler *n* rôdeur *m* -euse *f*.

proximity *n* proximité *f*.

proxy *n* procuration *f*; délégué *m* -e *f*.

prudence *n* prudence *f*.

prudent *adj* prudent, circonspect; ~ly *adv* prudemment.

prudish *adj* prude.

prune *vt* tailler; * *n* pruneau *m*.

prussic acid *n* acide prussique *m*.

pry *vi* espionner; ~ open *vt* (US) forcer.

psalm *n* psaume *m*.

pseudonym *n* pseudonyme *m*.

psyche *n* psyché *f*.

psychiatric *adj* psychiatrique.

psychiatrist *n* psychiatre *mf*.

psychiatry *n* psychiatrie *f*.

psychic *adj* psychique.

psychoanalysis *n* psychanalyse *f*.

psychoanalyst *n* psychanaliste *mf*.

psychological *adj* psychologique.

psychologist *n* psychologue *mf*.

psychology *n* psychologie *f*.

puberty *n* puberté *f*.

public *adj* public; commun; ~ly *adv* publiquement; * *n* public *m*.

public address system *n* sonorisation *f*.

publican *n* patron(ne) de pub *m(f)*.

publication *n* publication *f*; édition *f*.

publicity *n* publicité *f*.

publicize *vt* faire de la publicité pour.

public opinion *n* opinion publique *f*.

public school *n* école privée *f*.

publish *vt* publier.

publisher *n* éditeur *m* -trice *f*.

publishing *n* édition *f*.

pucker *vt* plisser.

pudding *n* pudding *m*; dessert *m*.

puddle *n* flaque d'eau *f*.

puerile *adj* puéril.

puff *n* souffle *m*; bouffée *f*; * *vt* souffler; dégager; * *vi* souffler; bouffer.

puff pastry *n* pâte feuilletée *f*.

puffy *adj* bouffi, gonflé.

pull *vt* tirer; arracher; ~ **down** faire descendre; abattre; ~ **in** *vi* s'arrêter; entrer en gare; ~ **off** enlever; ~ **out** *vi* partir; * *vt* arracher; ~ **through** *vi* s'en sortir; se remettre; ~ **up** *vi* s'arrêter; * *vt* arracher; arrêter; * *n* tirage *m*; secousse *f*.

pulley *n* poulie *f*.

pulp *n* pulpe *f*.

pulpit *n* chaire *f*.

pulsate *vi* palpiter.

pulse *n* pouls *m*; légumes *mpl* secs.

pulverize *vt* pulvériser.

pumice *n* pierre ponce *f*.

pummel *vt* marteler.

pump *n* pompe *f*; * *vt* pomper; puiser.

pumpkin *n* citrouille *f*.

pun *n* jeu de mots *m*; * *vi* faire des jeux de mots.

punch *n* coup de poing *m*; poinçon *m*; punch *m*; * *vt* cogner; perforer; poinçonner.

punctual *adj* ponctuel, exact; ~ly *adv* ponctuellement.

punctuate *vt* ponctuer.

punctuation *n* ponctuation *f*.

pundit *n* expert *m*.

pungent *adj* piquant, âcre; mordant.

punish *vt* punir.

punishment *n* châtiment *m*, punition *f*; peine *f*.

punk *n* punk *mf*; minable *mf*; ~ (music) punk *m*.

punt *n* bateau plat *m*.

puny *adj* chétif, maigrelet.

pup, puppy *n* chiot *m*; * *vi* avoir des chiots, mettre bas.

pupil *n* élève *mf*; pupille *mf*.

puppet *n* marionnette *f*.

purchase *vt* acheter; * *n* achat *m*; acquisition *f*.

purchaser *n* acheteur *m* -euse *f*.

pure *adj* pur; ~ly *adv* purement.

purée *n* purée *f*.

purge *vt* purger.

purification *n* purification *f*.

purify *vt* purifier.

purist *n* puriste *mf*.

puritan *n* puritain *m* -e *f*.

purity *n* pureté *f*.

purl *n* maille à l'envers *f*.

purple *adj n* pourpre, violet *m*.

purport *vt*: to ~ to prétendre.

purpose *n* intention *f*; but, dessein *m*; to the ~ à propos; to no ~ en vain; on ~ exprès, à dessein.

purposeful *adj* résolu.

purr *vi* ronronner.

purse *n* sac à main *m*; porte-monnaie *m invar*.

purser *n* commissaire *m* de bord.

pursue *vi* poursuivre; suivre.

pursuit *n* poursuite *f*; occupation *f*.

purveyor *n* fournisseur *m* -euse *f*.

push *vt* pousser; presser; ~ aside écarter; ~ off *vi* (*sl*) se casser; ~ on *vi* continuer; * *n* poussée *f*; impulsion *f*; effort *m*; énergie *f*.

pusher *n* trafiquant de drogues *m*.

push-up *n* (*gymn*) pompe *f*.

put *vt* mettre, poser; proposer; obliger; ~ away ranger; ~ down poser par terre; rabaisser; attribuer; ~ forward avancer; ~ off remettre; décourager; ~ on mettre; allumer; prendre; affecter; ~ out éteindre;

faire sortir; déranger; ~ up lever; augmenter; loger.

putrid *adj* putride.

putt *n* putt *m*;* *vt* *vi* putter.

putty *n* mastic *m*.

puzzle *n* énigme *f*; casse-tête *m* *invar*.

puzzling *adj* étrange, mystérieux.

pyjamas *npl* pyjama *m*.

pylon *n* pylône *m*.

pyramid *n* pyramide *f*.

python *n* python *m*.

quack *vi* cancaner; * *n* canard *m*; (*sl*) charlatan *m*.

quadrangle *n* quadrilatère *m*.

quadrant *n* quadrant *m*.

quadrilateral *adj* quadrilatéral.

quadruped *n* quadrupède *m*.

quadruple *adj* quadruple.

quadruplet *n* quadruplé *m* -e *f*.

quagmire *n* marécage *m*.

quail *n* caille *f*.

quaint *adj* désuet; bizarre.

quake *vi* trembler.

Quaker *n* quaker *m*.

qualification *n* qualification *f*; diplôme *m*.

qualified *adj* qualifié; diplômé.

qualify *vt* qualifier; modérer; * *vi* se qualifier.

quality *n* qualité *f*.

qualm *n* scrupule *m*.

quandary *n* incertitude *f*, doute *m*.

quantitative *adj* quantitatif.

quantity *n* quantité *f*.

quarantine *n* quarantaine *f*.

quarrel *n* dispute, querelle *f*; * *vi* se disputer, se quereller.

quarrelsome *adj* querelleur.

quarry *n* carrière *f*.

quarter *n* quart *m*; a ~ of an hour un quart d'heure; * *vt* diviser en quatre.

quarterly *adj* trimestriel; * *adv* tous les trimestres.

quartermaster *n* (*mil*) intendant *m*.

quartet *n* (*mus*) quartette *m*; quatuor *m*.

quartz *n* (*min*) quartz *m*.

quash *vt* écraser; annuler.

quay *n* quai *m*.

queasy *adj* qui a des nausées; écœurant.

queen *n* reine *f*; dame *f* (cartes).

queer *adj* extrange; (*sl*) pédale *f*.

quell *vt* étouffer; apaiser.

quench *vt* assouvir; éteindre.

query *n* question *f*; * *vt* demander.

quest *n* recherche *f*.

question *n* question *f*; sujet *m*; doute *m*; * *vt* douter de; mettre en question; questionner.

questionable *adj* discutable; douteux.

questioner *n* interrogateur *m*.

question mark *n* point d'interrogation *m*.

questionnaire *n* questionnaire *m*.

quibble *vi* chicaner.

quick *adj* rapide; vif; prompt; ~ly *adv* rapidement, vite.

quicken *vt* presser; accélérer; * *vi* s'accélérer.

quicksand *n* sables mouvants *mpl*.

quicksilver *n* mercure *m*.

quick-witted *adj* à l'esprit vif.

quiet *adj* calme; silencieux; ~ly *adv* calmement.

quietness *n* calme *m*, tranquillité *f*; silence *m*.

quinine *n* quinine *f*.

quintet *n* (*mus*) quintette *m*.

quintuple *adj* quintuple.

quintuplet *n* quintuplé *m* -e *f*.

quip *n* sarcasme *m*; * *vt* railler.

quirk *n* particularité *f*.

quit *vt* arrêter de; quitter; * *vi* abandonner; démissionner; * *adj* quitte.

quite *adv* assez; complètement, absolument.

quits *adj* quitte.

quiver *vi* trembler.

quixotic *adj* donquichottesque.

quiz *n* concours *m*; examen *m*; * *vt* interroger.

quizzical *adj* railleur.

quota *n* quota *m*.

quotation *n* citation *f*.

quotation marks *npl* guillemets *mpl*.

quote *vt* citer.

quotient *n* quotient *m*.

R

rabbi *n* rabbi, rabbin *m*.

rabbit *n* lapin *m*.

rabbit hutch *n* clapier *m*.

rabble *n* cohue *f*.

rabid *adj* forcené, enragé.

rabies *n* rage *f*.

race *n* course *f*; race *f*; * *vt* faire une course avec; * *vi* courir; faire une course; aller très vite; foncer.

racer *n* cheval de course *m*.

racial *adj* racial; ~ist *adj n* raciste *mf*.

raciness *n* vivacité *f*.

racing *n* courses *fpl*.

rack *n* casier *m*; étagère *f*; * *vt* soumettre au supplice du chevalet; tourmenter.

racket *n* vacarme *m*; raquette *f*.

rack-rent *n* loyer démesuré *m*.

racy *adj* piquant, plein de verve.

radiance *n* rayonnement *m*, éclat *m*.

radiant *adj* rayonnant, radieux.

radiate *vt vi* rayonner, irradier.

radiation *n* irradiation *f*.

radiator *n* radiateur *m*.

radical(ly) *adj* (*adv*) radical(ement).

radicalism *n* radicalisme *m*.

radio *n* radio *f*.

radioactive *adj* radioactif.

radish *n* radis *m*.

radius *n* radius *m*.

raffle *n* tombola *f*; * *vt* mettre en tombola.

raft *n* radeau, train de flottage *m*.

rafter *n* chevron *m*.

rag *n* lambeau *m*, loque *f*.

ragamuffin *n* va-nu-pieds *m invar*; galopin *m*.

rage *n* rage *f*; fureur *f*; * *vi* être furieux; faire rage.

ragged *adj* déguenillé.

raging *adj* furieux, déchaîné, enragé.

ragman, ~ picker *n* chiffonnier *m*.

raid *n* raid *m*; * *vt* faire un raid sur.

raider *n* raider *m*, pillard *m*.

rail *n* rambarde *f*, garde-fou *m*; (*rail*) rail, chemin de fer *m*; * *vt* entourer d'une barrière.

raillery *n* taquinerie *f*.

railroad, railway *n* chemin de fer *m*.

raiment *n* vêtements *mpl*.

rain *n* pluie *f*; * *vi* pleuvoir.

rainbow *n* arc-en-ciel *m*.

rainwater *n* eau de pluie *f*.

rainy *adj* pluvieux.

raise *vt* lever, soulever; ériger, édifier; élever.

raisin *n* raisin sec *m*.

rake *n* râteau *m*; libertin *m*; * *vt* ratisser.

rakish *adj* libertin, débauché.

rally *vt* (*mil*) rallier; * *vi* se rallier.

ram *n* bélier *m*; navire bélier *m*; * *vt* enfoncer.

ramble *vi* errer; faire une randonnée; * *n* excursion à pied, randonnée *f*.

rambler *n* excursionniste *mf*.

ramification *n* ramification *f*.

ramify *vi* se ramifier.

ramp *n* rampe *f*.

rampant *adj* exubérant.

rampart *n* terre-plein *m*; (*mil*) rempart *m*.

ramrod *n* baguette *f*; refouloir *m*.

ramshackle *adj* délabré.

ranch *n* ranch *m*.

rancid *adj* rance.

rancour *n* rancœur *f*.

random *adj* fortuit, fait au hasard; **at ~** au hasard.

range *vt* ranger, classer; * *vi* s'étendre; * *n* rangée *f*; ordre *m*; portée *f*; chaîne *f*; champ de tir *m*; fourneau de cuisine *m*.

ranger *n* garde forestier *m*.

rank *adj* exubérant; fétide; flagrant; * *n* rang *m*, classe *f*, grade *m*.

rankle *vi* rester sur le cœur.

rankness *n* exubérance *f*; odeur rance *f*.

ransack *vt* saccager, piller.

ransom *n* rançon *f*.

rant *vi* déclamer.

rap *vi* donner un coup sec; * *n* petit coup sec *m*.

rapacious *adj* rapace; **~ly** *adv* avec rapacité.

rapacity *n* rapacité *f*.

rape *n* viol *m*; rapt *m*; (*bot*) colza *m*; * *vt* violer.

rapid *adj* ~**ly** *adv* rapide(ment).

rapidity *n* rapidité *f*.

rapier *n* rapière *f*.

rapist *n* violeur *m*.

rapt *adj* extasié; absorbé.

rapture *n* ravissement *m*; extase *f*.

rapturous *adj* de ravissement.

rare *adj* ~**ly** *adv* rare(ment).

rarity *n* rareté *f*.

rascal *n* vaurien *m*.

rash *adj* imprudent, téméraire; ~**ly** *adv* sans réfléchir; * *n* vague *f*; éruption (cutanée) *f*.

rashness *n* imprudence *f*.

rasp *n* râpe *f*; * *vt* râper.

raspberry *n* framboise *f*; ~ **bush** framboisier *m*.

rat *n* rat *m*.

rate *n* taux, prix, cours *m*; classe *f*; vitesse *f*; * *vt* estimer, évaluer.

rather *adv* plutôt; quelque peu.

ratification *n* ratification *f*.

ratify *vt* ratifier.

rating *n* estimation *f*; classement *m*; indice *m*.

ratio *n* rapport *m*.

ration *n* ration *f*; (*mil*) vivres *mpl*.

rational *adj* rationnel; raisonnable; ~**ly** *adv* rationnellement.

rationality *n* rationalité *f*.

rattan *n* (*bot*) rotin *m*.

rattle *vi* s'entrechoquer; cliqueter * *vt* faire s'entrechoquer; * *n* fracas *m*; cliquetis *m*.

rattlesnake *n* serpent à sonnettes *m*.

ravage *vt* ravager, piller; dévaster; * *n* ravage *m*.

rave *vi* délirer.

raven *n* corbeau *m*.

ravenous *adj* ~**ly** *adv* vorace(ment).

ravine *n* ravin *m*.

ravish *vt* enchanter; ravir.

ravishing *adj* enchanteur.

raw *adj* cru; brut; novice.

rawboned *adj* décharné; maigre.

rawness *n* crudité *f*; inexpérience *f*.

ray *n* rayon *m*; (*fish*) raie *f*.

raze *vt* raser.

razor *n* rasoir *m*.

reach *vt* atteindre; arriver à; * *vi* s'étendre, porter; * *n* portée *f*.

react *vi* réagir.

reaction *n* réaction *f*.

read *vt vi* lire.

readable *adj* lisible.

reader *n* lecteur *m* -trice *f*.

readily *adv* volontiers; facilement.

readiness *n* bonne volonté *f*; empressement *m*.

reading *n* lecture *f*.

reading room *n* salle de lecture *f*.

readjust *vt* réajuster, réadapter.

ready *adj* prêt; enclin; disposé.

real *adj* réel, vrai; ~ly *adv* vraiment.

realization *n* réalisation *f*.

realize *vt* se rendre compte de; réaliser.

reality *n* réalité *f*.

realm *n* royaume *m*.

ream *n* rame *f* de papier.

reap *vt* moissonner.

reaper *n* moissonneuse *f* (machine).

reappear *vi* réapparaître.

rear *n* arrière *m*; derrière *m*; * *vt* élever, dresser.

rearmament *n* réarmement *m*.

reason *n* raison *f*; cause *f*; * *vt vi* raisonner.

reasonable *adj* raisonnable.

reasonableness *n* bon sens *m*, sagesse *f*.

reasonably *adv* raisonnablement.

reasoning *n* raisonnement *m*.

reassure *vt* rassurer; (*com*) réassurer.

rebel *n* rebelle *mf*; * *vi* se rebeller.

rebellion *n* rébellion *f*.

rebellious *adj* rebelle.

rebound *vi* rebondir.

rebuff *n* rebuffade *f*; * *vt* repousser.

rebuild *vt* reconstruire.

rebuke *vt* réprimander; * *n* réprimande *f*.

rebut *vt* réfuter.

recalcitrant *adj* récalcitrant.

recall *vt* (se) rappeler; retirer; * *n* retrait *m*.

recant *vt* rétracter, désavouer.

recantation *n* rétractation *f*.

recapitulate *vt vi* récapituler.

recapitulation *n* récapitulation *f*.

recapture *n* reprise *f*.

recede *vi* reculer.

receipt *n* reçu *m*; réception *f*; ~s *npl* recettes *fpl*.

receivable *adj* recevable.

receive *vt* recevoir; accueillir.

recent *adj* récent, neuf; ~ly *adv* récemment.

receptacle *n* récipient *m*.

reception *n* réception *f*.

recess n (*law*) vacance f;
renfoncement m; recoin m.

recession n recul m; (*com*)
récession f.

recipe n recette f.

recipient n destinataire mf.

reciprocal adj ~**ly** adv
réciproque(ment).

reciprocate vi rendre la
pareille.

reciprocity n réciprocité f.

recital n récit m; récital m.

recite vt réciter; exposer,
énumérer.

reckless adj téméraire; ~**ly**
adv imprudemment.

reckon vt compter, calculer;
* vi calculer.

reckoning n compte m; calcul
m.

reclaim vt assainir; récupérer.

reclaimable adj remboursable;
récupérable.

recline vt reposer; * vi être
allongé.

recluse n reclus m -e f.

recognition n reconnaissance
f.

recognize vt reconnaître.

recoil vi reculer.

recollect vt se rappeler, se
souvenir de.

recollection n souvenir m.

recommence vt recommencer.

recommend vt recommander.

recommendation n
recommandation f.

recompense n récompense f;
* vt récompenser.

reconcilable adj conciliable.

reconcile vt réconcilier.

reconciliation n
réconciliation f.

recondite adj abstrus, obscur.

reconnoitre vt (*mil*)
reconnaître.

reconsider vt reconsidérer.

reconstruct vt reconstruire.

record vt enregistrer; consigner par écrit; * n rapport m, registre m; disque
m; record m; ~**s** pl archives
fpl.

recorder n magnétophone m,
archiviste mf; (*mus*) flûte à
bec f.

recount vt raconter.

recourse n recours m.

recover vt retrouver; reprendre;
récupérer; * vi se remettre,
se rétablir.

recoverable adj récupérable.

recovery n guérison f; reprise
f.

recreation n détente f;
récréation f.

recriminate vi récriminer.

recrimination n récrimination f.

recruit vt recruter; * n (mil) recrue f.

recruiting n recrutement m.

rectangle n rectangle m.

rectangular adj rectangulaire.

rectification n rectification f.

rectify vt rectifier.

rectilinear adj rectiligne.

rectitude n rectitude f.

rector n pasteur m.

recumbent adj couché, étendu.

recur vi se reproduire.

recurrence n répétition f.

recurrent adj répétitif.

red adj rouge; * n rouge m.

redden vt vi rougir.

reddish adj rougeâtre.

redeem vt racheter, rembourser.

redeemable adj rachetable.

Redeemer n Rédempteur m.

redemption n rachat m.

redeploy vt réaffecter.

redhanded adj: to catch sb ~ prendre quelqu'un la main dans le sac.

redhot adj brûlant, ardent.

red-letter day n jour à marquer d'une pierre blanche m.

redness n rougeur, rousseur f.

redolent adj parfumé, odorant.

redouble vt vi redoubler.

redress vt réparer; corriger; redresser; * n réparation f, redressement m.

redskin n Peau-Rouge mf.

red tape n (fig) paperasserie f.

reduce vt réduire; diminuer; abaisser.

reducible adj réductible.

reduction n réduction f; baisse f.

redundancy n licenciement m.

redundant adj superflu; licencié.

reed n roseau m.

reedy adj couvert de roseaux.

reef n (mar) ris m; récif m.

reek n puanteur f; * vi empester; puer.

reel n bobine f; bande f; dévidoir m; * vi chanceler.

re-election n réélection f.

re-engage vt rengager.

re-enter vt rentrer.

re-establish vt rétablir; réhabiliter.

re-establishment n rétablissement m; restauration f.

refectory *n* réfectoire *m*.

refer *vt* soumettre, renvoyer; se référer à; * *vi* se référer.

referee *n* arbitre *m*.

reference *n* référence, allusion *f*.

refine *vt* raffiner, affiner.

refinement *n* raffinement *m*; raffinerie *f*; culture *f*.

refinery *n* raffinerie *f*.

refit *vt* réparer (*also mar*).

reflect *vt* réfléchir, refléter; * *vi* réfléchir.

reflection *n* réflexion, pensée *f*.

reflector *n* réflecteur *m*; cataphote *m*.

reflex *adj* réflexe.

reform *vt* réformer; * *vi* se réformer.

reform, reformation *n* réforme *f*.

reformer *n* réformateur *m* -trice *f*.

reformist *n* réformiste *mf*.

refract *vt* réfracter.

refraction *n* réfraction *f*.

refrain *vi*: **to ~ from sth** s'abstenir de qch.

refresh *vt* rafraîchir.

refreshment *n* rafraîchissement *m*.

refrigerator *n* glacière *f*; réfrigérateur *m*.

refuel *vi* se ravitailler (en carburant).

refuge *n* refuge, asile *m*.

refugee *n* réfugié *m* -e *f*.

refund *vt* rembourser; * *n* remboursement *m*.

refurbish *vt* rénover.

refusal *n* refus *m*.

refuse *vt* refuser; * *n* déchets *mpl*.

refute *vt* réfuter.

regain *vt* recouvrer, reprendre.

regal *adj* royal.

regale *vt* régaler.

regalia *n* insignes *mpl*.

regard *vt* considérer; * *n* considération *f*; respect *m*.

regarding *pr* en ce qui concerne.

regardless *adv* quand même, malgré tout.

regatta *n* régate *f*.

regency *n* régence *f*.

regenerate *vt* régénérer; * *adj* régénéré.

regeneration *n* régénération *f*.

regent *n* régent *m*.

regime *n* régime *m*.

regiment *n* régiment *m*.

region *n* région *f*.

register *n* registre *m*; * *vt* enregistrer; **~ed letter** *n* lettre recommandée *f*.

registrar n officier d'état civil m.

registration n enregistrement m.

registry n enregistrement m.

regressive adj régressif.

regret n regret m * vt regretter.

regretful adj plein de regrets.

regular adj régulier; ordinaire; ~ly adv régulièrement; * n habitué m -e f.

regularity n régularité f.

regulate vt régler, réglementer.

regulation n règlement m; réglementation f.

regulator n régulateur m.

rehabilitate vt réhabiliter.

rehabilitation n réhabilitation f.

rehearsal n répétition f.

rehearse vt répéter; raconter.

reign n règne m; * vi régner.

reimburse vt rembourser.

reimbursement n remboursement m.

rein n rêne f; * vt ~ in (fig) contenir.

reindeer n renne m.

reinforce vt renforcer.

reinstate vt réintégrer.

reinsure vt (com) réassurer.

reissue n réédition f.

reiterate vt réitérer.

reiteration n réitération, répétition f.

reject vt rejeter.

rejection n refus, rejet m.

rejoice vt réjouir; * vi se réjouir.

rejoicing n réjouissance f.

relapse vi retomber; * n rechute f.

relate vt relater; rapprocher; * vi se rapporter.

related adj apparenté.

relation n rapport m; parent m.

relationship n lien de parenté m; relation f; rapport m.

relative adj relatif; ~ly adv relativement; * n parent m -e f.

relax vt relâcher; détendre; * vi se relâcher; se détendre.

relaxation n relâchement m; détente f.

relay n relais m; * vt retransmettre.

release vt libérer, relâcher; * n libération f; décharge f.

relegate vt reléguer.

relegation n relégation f.

relent vi s'adoucir.

relentless *adj* implacable.

relevant *adj* pertinent.

reliable *adj* fiable, digne de confiance.

reliance *n* confiance *f*.

relic *n* relique *f*.

relief *n* soulagement *m*; secours *m*.

relieve *vt* soulager, alléger; secourir.

religion *n* religion *f*.

religious *adj* religieux; ~ly *adv* religieusement.

relinquish *vt* abandonner, renoncer à.

relish *n* saveur *f*; goût *m*; attrait *m*; * *vt* savourer, se délecter de.

reluctance *n* répugnance *f*.

reluctant *adj* peu disposé.

rely *vi* compter sur, avoir confiance en.

remain *vi* rester, demeurer.

remainder *n* reste, restant *m*.

remains *npl* restes, vestiges *mpl*; dépouille *f*.

remand *vt*: to ~ in custody mettre en détention préventive.

remark *n* remarque, observation *f*; * *vt* (faire) remarquer, (faire) observer.

remarkable *adj* remarquable, notable.

remarkably *adv* remarquablement.

remarry *vi* se remarier.

remedial *adj* de rattrapage.

remedy *n* remède, recours *m*; * *vt* remédier à.

remember *vt* se souvenir de; se rappeler.

remembrance *n* mémoire *f*; souvenir *m*.

remind *vt* rappeler.

reminiscence *n* réminiscence *f*.

remiss *adj* négligent.

remission *n* rémission *f*.

remit *vt* remettre, pardonner; * *vi* diminuer.

remittance *n* remise *f*.

remnant *n* reste, restant *m*.

remodel *vt* remodeler.

remonstrate *vi* protester.

remorse *n* remords *m*.

remorseless *adj* implacable.

remote *adj* lointain, éloigné; ~ly *adv* au loin, de loin.

remoteness *n* éloignement *m*; isolement *m*.

removable *adj* amovible.

removal *n* suppression *f*; déménagement *m*.

remove *vt* enlever; * *vi* déménager.

remunerate *vt* rémunérer.

remuneration *n* rémunération *f*.

render *vt* rendre, remettre; traduire; (*law*) rendre.

rendezvous *n* rendez-vous *m*; point de ralliement *m*.

renegade *n* renégat *m* -e *f*.

renew *vt* renouveler.

renewal *n* renouvellement *m*.

rennet *n* présure *f*.

renounce *vt* renoncer à.

renovate *vt* rénover.

renovation *n* rénovation *f*.

renown *n* renommée *f*; célébrité *f*.

renowned *adj* célèbre, renommé.

rent *n* loyer *m*; location *f*; * *vt* louer.

rental *n* loyer *m*.

renunciation *n* renonciation *f*.

reopen *vt* rouvrir.

reorganization *n* réorganisation *f*.

reorganize *vt* réorganiser.

repair *vt* réparer; * *n* réparation *f*.

repairable *adj* réparable.

reparation *n* réparation *f*.

repartee *n* répartie, réplique *f*.

repatriate *vt* rapatrier.

repay *vt* rembourser; rendre, récompenser.

repayment *n* remboursement *m*.

repeal *vt* abroger, annuler; * *n* abrogation, annulation *f*.

repeat *vt* répéter.

repeatedly *adv* à plusieurs reprises.

repeater *n* montre à répétition *f*.

repel *vt* repousser, rebuter.

repent *vi* se repentir.

repentance *n* repentir *m*.

repentant *adj* repentant.

repertory *n* répertoire *m*.

repetition *n* répétition, réitération *f*.

replace *vt* replacer; remplacer.

replant *vt* replanter.

replenish *vt* remplir de nouveau.

replete *adj* rempli, rassasié.

reply *n* réponse *f*; * *vi* répondre.

report *vt* rapporter, relater; rendre compte de; * *n* rapport *m*; compte rendu *m*; rumeur *f*.

reporter *n* journaliste *mf*.

repose *vi* (se) reposer; * *n* repos *m*.

repository *n* dépôt *m*.

repossess *vt* reprendre possession de.

reprehend *vt* condamner.

reprehensible *adj* répréhensible.

represent *vt* représenter.

representation *n* représentation *f*.

representative *adj* représentatif; * *n* représentant(e) *m(f)*.

repress *vt* réprimer, contenir.

repression *n* répression *f*.

repressive *adj* répressif.

reprieve *vt* accorder un sursis *ou* un répit à; * *n* sursis *m*.

reprimand *vt* réprimander, blâmer; * *n* blâme *m*; réprimande *f*.

reprint *vt* réimprimer.

reprisal *n* représailles *fpl*.

reproach *n* reproche, opprobre *m*; * *vt* reprocher.

reproachful *adj* réprobateur; ~ly *adv* d'un air de reproche.

reproduce *vt* reproduire.

reproduction *n* reproduction *f*.

reptile *n* reptile *m*.

republic *n* république *f*.

republican *adj n* républicain *m* -e *f*.

republicanism *n* républicanisme *m*.

repudiate *vt* renier.

repugnance *n* répugnance f, dégoût *m*.

repugnant *adj* répugnant; ~ly *adv* avec répugnance.

repulse *vt* repousser, rejeter; * *n* rebuffade *f*; refus *m*.

repulsion *n* répulsion *f*.

repulsive *adj* répulsif.

reputable *adj* honorable.

reputation *n* réputation *f*.

repute *n* renom *m*.

request *n* demande, requête *f*; * *vt* demander.

require *vt* demander, nécessiter.

requirement *n* besoin *m*; exigence *f*.

requisite *adj* nécessaire, indispensable; * *n* objet(s) nécessaire(s) *m(pl)*.

requisition *n* demande; *(mil)* réquisition *f*.

requite *vt* rembourser.

rescind *vt* annuler, abroger.

rescue *vt* sauver, secourir; * *n* secours *m*, délivrance *f*.

research *vt* faire des/de la recherche(s); * *n* recherche(s) *f(pl)*.

resemblance *n* ressemblance *f*.

resemble *vt* ressembler à.

resent *vt* être contrarié/irrité par.

resentful *adj* plein de

ressentiment; amer; ~ly *adv* avec ressentiment.

resentment *n* ressentiment *m*.

reservation *n* réserve *f*; réservation *f*.

reserve *vt* réserver; * *n* réserve *f*.

reservedly *adv* avec réserve.

reservoir *n* réservoir *m*.

reside *vi* résider.

residence *n* résidence *f*; séjour *m*.

resident *adj* résidant; * *n* résident *m* -e *f*.

residuary *adj* restant; ~ **legatee** *n* (*law*) légataire universel *m*.

residue *n* reste, résidu *m*.

residuum *n* (*chem*) résidu *m*.

resign *vt* démissionner de, renoncer à, céder; se résigner à; * *vi* démissionner.

resignation *n* démission *f*.

resin *n* résine *f*.

resinous *adj* résineux.

resist *vt* résister, s'opposer.

resistance *n* résistance *f*.

resolute *adj* ~**ly** *adv* résolu(ment).

resolution *n* résolution *f*.

resolve *vt* résoudre; * *vi* (se) résoudre, (se) décider.

resonance *n* résonance *f*.

resonant *adj* résonant.

resort *vi* recourir; * *n* lieu de vacances *m*; recours *m*.

resound *vi* résonner.

resource *n* ressource(s) *f(pl)*; expédient *m*.

respect *n* respect *m*; égard *m*; rapport *m*; ~**s** *pl* respects *mpl*; * *vt* respecter.

respectability *n* respectabilité *f*.

respectable *adj* respectable; considérable; ~**bly** *adv* convenablement.

respectful *adj* respectueux; ~**ly** *adv* respectueusement.

respecting *prep* en ce qui concerne.

respective *adj* respectif; ~**ly** *adv* respectivement.

respirator *n* respirateur *m*.

respiratory *adj* respiratoire.

respite *n* répit *m*; (*law*) sursis *m*; * *vt* repousser, différer.

resplendence *n* resplendissement *m*, splendeur *f*.

resplendent *adj* resplendissant.

respond *vi* répondre; réagir.

respondent *n* (*law*) défendeur *m* -deresse *f*.

response *n* réponse, réaction *f*.

responsibility *n* responsabilité *f*.

responsible *adj* responsable.

responsive *adj* sensible à, réceptif.

rest *n* repos *m*; (*mus*) pause *f*; reste, restant *m*; * *vt* faire *or* laisser reposer; appuyer; * *vi* se reposer, reposer.

resting place *n* lieu de repos *m*.

restitution *n* restitution *f*.

restive *adj* rétif, récalcitrant; agité.

restless *adj* agité; instable.

restoration *n* restauration *f*.

restorative *adj* fortifiant.

restore *vt* restituer, restaurer.

restrain *vt* retenir, contenir.

restraint *n* contrainte, entrave *f*.

restrict *vt* restreindre, limiter.

restriction *n* restriction *f*.

restrictive *adj* restrictif.

rest room *n* (US) toilettes *fpl*.

result *vi* résulter; * *n* résultat *m*.

resume *vt* reprendre.

resurrection *n* résurrection *f*.

resuscitate *vt* réanimer.

retail *vt* vendre au détail, détailler; * *n* vente au détail *f*.

retain *vt* retenir, conserver.

retainer *n* serviteur *m*; ~s *pl* arrhes *fpl*; suite *f*.

retake *vt* reprendre.

retaliate *vi* se venger.

retaliation *n* représailles *fpl*.

retardation *n* retard *m*.

retarded *adj* retardé.

retch *vi* avoir des haut-le-cœur.

retention *n* rétention *f*.

retentive *adj* qui retient bien.

reticence *n* réticence *f*.

reticule *n* réticule m.

retina *n* rétine *f*.

retire *vt* mettre à la retraite; * *vi* se retirer; prendre sa retraite.

retired *adj* retraité, à la retraite.

retirement *n* isolement *m*; retraite *f*.

retort *vt* rétorquer; * *n* réplique *f*.

retouch *vt* retoucher.

retrace *vt* retracer.

retract *vt* rétracter; retirer.

retrain *vt* recycler.

retraining *n* recyclage *m*.

retreat *n* repli *m*; * *vi* se retirer.

retribution *n* châtiment *m*; récompense *f*.

retrievable *adj* récupérable; réparable.

retrieve *vt* récupérer, recouvrer.

retriever *n* chien d'arrêt *m*.

retrograde *adj* rétrograde.

retrospect, retrospection *n* regard rétrospectif *m*.

retrospective *adj* rétrospectif.

return *vt* rendre; restituer; renvoyer; * *n* retour *m*; renvoi *m*; récompense *f*; revenu *m*; remboursement *m*.

reunion *n* réunion *f*.

reunite *vt* réunir; * *vi* se réunir.

reveal *vt* révéler.

revel *vi* faire la fête.

revelation *n* révélation *f*.

reveller *n* fêtard *m*.

revelry *n* fête *f*.

revenge *vt* venger; * *n* vengeance *f*.

revengeful *adj* vindicatif.

revenue *n* revenu *m*; rente *f*.

reverberate *vt* réverbérer; * *vi* résonner, retentir; se réverbérer.

reverberation *n* répercussion *f*; réverbération *f*.

revere *vt* révérer, vénérer.

reverence *n* vénération *f*; * *vt* révérer.

reverend *adj* révérend; vénérable; * *n* curé *m*.

reverent, reverential *adj* révérenciel, respectueux.

reversal *n* renversement *m*; annulation *f*.

reverse *vt* renverser; annuler; * *vi* faire marche arrière; * *n* inverse *m*; contraire *m*; revers *m*.

reversible *adj* révocable; réversible.

reversion *n* retour *m*; réversion *f*.

revert *vi* revenir; retourner.

review *vt* revoir; (*mil*) passer en revue; * *n* revue *f*; examen *m*.

reviewer *n* critique *m*.

revile *vt* vilipender.

revise *vt* réviser; mettre à jour.

reviser *n* réviseur *m*.

revision *n* révision *f*.

revisit *vt* retourner voir.

revival *n* reprise *f*; renouveau *m*.

revive *vt* ranimer; raviver; * *vi* reprendre connaissance; reprendre.

revocation *n* révocation *f*.

revoke *vt* révoquer, annuler.

revolt *vi* se révolter; * *n* révolte *f*.

revolting *adj* exécrable.

revolution *n* révolution *f*.

revolutionary *adj* *n* révolutionnaire *mf*.

revolve *vt* (re)tourner; * *vi* tourner.

revolving *adj* tournant.

revue *n* revue *f*.

revulsion *n* écœurement *m*.

reward *n* récompense *f*; * *vt* récompenser.

rhapsody *n* r(h)apsodie *f*.

rhetoric *n* rhétorique *f*.

rhetorical *adj* rhétorique.

rheumatic *adj* rhumatisant.

rheumatism *n* rhumatisme *m*.

rhinoceros *n* rhinocéros *m*.

rhombus *n* rhombe *m*.

rhomboid *n* rhomboïd *m*.

rhubarb *n* rhubarbe *f*.

rhyme *n* rime *f*; vers *mpl*; * *vi* rimer.

rhythm *n* rythme *m*.

rhythmical *adj* rythmique.

rib *n* côte *f*.

ribald *adj* paillard.

ribbon *n* ruban *m*; lambeaux *mpl*.

rice *n* riz *m*.

rich *adj* riche; somptueux; abondant; ~ly *adv* richement.

riches *npl* richesse *f*.

richness *n* richesse *f*; abondance *f*.

rickets *n* rachitisme *m*.

rickety *adj* rachitique.

rid *vt* débarrasser; se débarrasser de.

riddance *n*: good ~! bon débarras!

riddle *n* énigme *f*; crible *m*; * *vt* cribler.

ride *vi* monter à cheval; aller en voiture; * *n* promenade à cheval *ou* en voiture *f*.

rider *n* cavalier *m* -ière *f*.

ridge *n* arête, crête *f*; chaîne *f*; * *vt* rider, strier.

ridicule *n* ridicule *m*; raillerie *f*; * *vt* ridiculiser.

ridiculous *adj* ~ly *adv* ridicule(ment).

riding *n* équitation *f*; monte *f*.

riding habit *n* tenue d'amazone *f*.

riding school *n* manège *m*.

rife *adj* répandu, abondant.

riffraff *n* racaille *f*.

rifle *vt* dévaliser, piller; strier, rayer; * *n* fusil *m*.

rifleman *n* fusilier *m*.

rig *vt* équiper; truquer; (*mar*) gréer; * *n* gréement *m*; plateforme de forage *f*.

rigging *n* (*mar*) gréement *m*.

right *adj* droit, bien; juste; équitable; ~! bien!, bon!; ~ly *adv* bien; correctement;

à juste titre; * *n* justice *f*; raison *f*; droit *m*; droite *f*; * *vt* redresser.

righteous *adj* droit, vertueux; ~**ly** *adv* vertueusement.

righteousness *n* droiture *f*; vertu *f*.

rigid *adj* rigide; sévère, strict; ~**ly** *adv* rigidement.

rigidity *n* rigidité *f*; sévérité *f*.

rigmarole *n* galimatias *m*.

rigorous *adj* rigoureux; ~**ly** *adv* rigoureusement.

rigour *n* rigueur *f*; sévérité *f*.

rim *n* bord *m*, monture *f*.

rind *n* peau, écorce *f*.

ring *n* anneau, cercle, rond *m*; bague *f*; tintement *m* de cloche; * *vt* sonner; * *vi* sonner, retentir; ~ **the bell** sonner.

ringer *n* carillonneur *m*.

ringleader *n* meneur *m*.

ringlet *n* anglaise *f*.

ringworm *n* (*med*) teigne *f*.

rink *n* (*also* ice ~) patinoire *f*.

rinse *vt* rincer.

riot *n* émeute *f*; * *vi* se livrer à une émeute.

rioter *n* émeutier *m*, -ière *f*.

riotous *adj* séditieux; dissolu; ~**ly** *adv* de façon tapageuse.

rip *vt* déchirer, fendre.

ripe *adj* mûr.

ripen *vt* *vi* mûrir.

ripeness *n* maturité *f*.

rip-off *n* (*sl*): **it's a** ~! c'est du vol!

ripple *vt* rider; * *vi* se rider; * *n* ondulation *f*, ride *f*.

rise *vi* se lever; naître; se soulever; monter; provenir de; s'élever; croître; ressusciter; * *n* hausse *f*; augmentation *f*; montée *f*; lever *m*; source *f*.

rising *n* insurrection *f*; levée, clôture *f*.

risk *n* risque, danger *m*; * *vt* risquer.

risky *adj* risqué.

rissole *n* rissole *f*.

rite *n* rite *m*.

ritual *adj n* rituel *m*.

rival *adj* rival; * *n* rival *m* -e *f*; * *vt* rivaliser avec, concurrencer.

rivalry *n* rivalité *f*.

river *n* rivière *f*.

rivet *n* rivet *m*; * *vt* riveter, river.

rivulet *n* petit ruisseau *m*.

roach *n* blatte *f*.

road *n* route *f*.

roadsign *n* panneau de signalisation *m*.

roadstead n (*mar*) rade *f*.

roadworks *npl* travaux routiers *mpl*.

roam *vt* parcourir; errer dans; * *vi* errer.

roan *adj* rouan.

roar *vi* hurler, rugir; mugir; * *n* hurlement *m*; rugissement, mugissement*m*; grondement *m*.

roast *vt* rôtir; griller.

roast beef *n* rôti de bœuf *m*.

rob *vt* voler.

robber *n* voleur *m* -euse *f*.

robbery *n* vol *m*.

robe *n* robe (de cérémonie) *f*; peignoir de bain *m*; * *vt* revêtir d'une robe de cérémonie.

robin (redbreast) *n* rouge-gorge *m*.

robust *adj* robuste.

robustness *n* robustesse *f*.

rock *n* roche *f*; rocher *m*; roc *m*; * *vt* bercer; balancer; ébranler; * *vi* (se) balancer.

rock and roll *n* rock (and roll) *m*.

rock crystal *n* cristal de roche *m*.

rocket *n* fusée *f*.

rocking chair *n* fauteuil à bas-cule *m*.

rock salt *n* sel gemme *m*.

rocky *adj* rocheux.

rod *n* baguette, tringle, canne *f*.

rodent *n* rongeur *m*.

roe *n* chevreuil *m*; œufs *mpl* de poisson.

roebuck *n* chevreuil (mâle) *m*.

rogation *n* rogations *fpl*.

rogue *n* coquin, polisson *m*; gredin *m*.

roguish *adj* coquin.

roll *vt* rouler; étendre; enrouler; * *vi* (se) rouler; * *n* roulement *m*; rouleau *m*; liste *f*; catalogue *m*; liasse *f*; petit pain *m*.

roller *n* rouleau, cylindre *m*.

roller skates *npl* patins à roulettes *mpl*.

rolling pin *n* rouleau à pâtisserie *m*.

Roman Catholic *adj* *n* catholique *mf*.

romance *n* romance *f*; roman *m*; conte *m*; fable *f*.

romantic *adj* romantique.

romp *vi* jouer bruyamment.

roof *n* toit *m*; voûte *f*; * *vt* couvrir.

roofing *n* toiture *f*.

rook *n* freux *m*; tour *f* (*aux échecs*).

room *n* pièce, salle *f*; place *f*; espace *m*; chambre *f*.

roominess *n* grande envergure *f*.

rooming house *n* pension *f*.

roomy *adj* spacieux.

roost *n* perchoir *m*; * *vi* se percher.

root *n* racine *f*; origine *f*; * *vt vi* ~ out extirper; dénicher.

rooted *adj* enraciné; ancré.

rope *n* corde *f*; cordage *m*; * *vi* attacher.

ropemaker *n* cordier *m*.

rosary *n* rosaire *m*.

rose *n* rose *f*.

rosebed *n* massif de roses *m*.

rosebud *n* bouton de rose *m*.

rosebush *n* rosier *m*.

rosemary *n* (*bot*) romarin *m*.

rosette *n* rosette *f*.

rosé wine *n* (vin) rosé *m*.

rosewood *n* bois de rose *m*.

rosiness *n* couleur rosée *f*.

rosy *adj* rosé.

rot *vi* pourrir; * *n* pourriture *f*.

rotate *vt* faire tourner; * *vi* tourner.

rotation *n* rotation *f*.

rote *n*: by ~ par cœur.

rotten *adj* pourri; corrompu.

rottenness *n* pourriture *f*.

rotund *adj* rond, replet, arrondi.

rouble *n* rouble *m*.

rouge *n* rouge (à joues) *m*.

rough *adj* accidenté, inégal, rugueux; rude, brutal, brusque; houleux; ~ly *adv* rudement.

roughcast *n* crépi *m*.

roughen *vt* rendre rugueux.

roughness *n* rugosité *f*; rudesse, brusquerie *f*; agitation *f*.

round *adj* rond, circulaire; rondelet; franc; * *n* cercle *m*; rond *m*; tour *m*; tournée *f*; partie *f*; ronde *f*; canon *m*; série *f*; * *adv* autour de; environ; ~ly *adv* rondement; franchement; * *vt* contourner; arrondir.

roundabout *adj* détourné, indirect; * *n* rond-point *m*.

roundness *n* rondeur *f*.

rouse *vt* réveiller; exciter.

rout *n* déroute, débâcle *f*; * *vt* mettre en déroute.

route *n* itinéraire *m*; route *f*.

routine *adj* habituel; * *n* routine *f*; numéro *m*.

rove *vi* vagabonder, errer.

rover *n* vagabond *m* -e *f*; pirate *m*.

row *n* querelle *f*; vacarme *m*.

row n rangée, file f; * vt (mar) ramer.

rowdy n hooligan, voyou m.

rower n rameur m -euse f.

royal adj royal; princier; ~ly adv royalement.

royalist n royaliste mf.

royalty n royauté f; droits d'auteur mpl; royalties fpl; redevance f; membres de la famille royale mpl.

rub vt frotter; irriter; * n frottement m; (fig) ennui m; difficulté f.

rubber n caoutchouc m, gomme f; préservatif m.

rubber band n élastique m.

rubbish n détritus mpl; ordures fpl; bêtises fpl; décombres mpl.

rubric n rubrique f.

ruby n rubis m.

rucksack n sac à dos m.

rudder n gouvernail m.

ruddiness n teint vif m, rougeur f.

ruddy adj coloré, rouge.

rude adj impoli, rude, brusque; grossier, primitif; ~ly adv impoliment, grossièrement.

rudeness n impolitesse f; rudesse, insolence f.

rudiment n rudiments mpl.

rue vt regretter amèrement; * n (bot) rue f.

rueful adj triste.

ruffian n voyou m, brute f; * adj brutal.

ruffle vt ébouriffer, déranger; rider.

rug n tapis m, carpette f.

rugged adj accidenté, déchiqueté; rude; robuste.

ruin n ruine f; perte f; ruines fpl; * vt ruiner; détruire.

ruinous adj ruineux.

rule n règle f; règlement m; pouvoir m; domination f; * vt gouverner, dominer; décider, régler, diriger.

ruler n dirigeant m -e f; règle f.

rum n rhum m.

rumble vi gronder, tonner.

ruminate vt ruminer.

rummage vi fouiller.

rumour n rumeur f; * vt faire courir le bruit.

rump n croupe f.

run vt diriger; organiser; faire couler; passer; ~ the risk courir le risque; * vi courir; fuir, se sauver; filer; fonctionner; aller; couler; concourir; * n course, compétition *f*; parcours *m*; cours *m*; série *f*; mode *f*; ruée *f*.

runaway *n* fugitif *m* -ive *f*, fuyard *m*.

rung *n* barreau, échelon *m*.

runner *n* coureur *m*; concurrent *m* -e *f*; messager *m*.

running *n* course *f*; direction *f*.

runway *n* piste de décollage *f*.

rupture *n* rupture *f*; hernie *f*; * *vt* rompre; * *vi* se rompre.

rural *adj* rural, champêtre.

ruse *n* ruse *f*, stratagème m.

rush *n* jonc *m*; ruée *f*; hâte *f*; * *vt* pousser vivement; * *vi* se précipiter, s'élancer.

rusk *n* biscotte *f*.

russet *adj* roux.

rust *n* rouille *f*; * *vi* se rouiller.

rustic *adj* rustique; * *n* paysan, rustaud *m*.

rustiness *n* rouille *f*.

rustle *vi* bruire; * *vt* faire bruire; froisser.

rustling *n* vol de bétail *m*; bruissement *m*.

rusty *adj* rouillé; roux.

rut *n* (*zool*) rut *m*; ornière *f*.

ruthless *adj* cruel, impitoyable; ~ly *adv* sans pitié.

rye *n* (*bot*) seigle *m*.

S

Sabbath *n* sabbat *m*; dimanche *m*.

sable *n* zibeline *f*.

sabotage *n* sabotage *m*.

sabre *n* sabre *m*.

saccharin *n* saccharine *f*.

sack *n* sac *m*; * *vt* mettre à sac; renvoyer.

sacrament *n* sacrement *m*; Eucharistie *f*.

sacramental *adj* sacramentel.

sacred *adj* saint, sacré; inviolable.

sacredness *n* (caractère) sacré *m*.

sacrifice *n* sacrifice *m*; * *vt* sacrifier.

sacrificial *adj* sacrificiel.

sacrilege *n* sacrilège *m*.

sacrilegious *adj* sacrilège.

sad *adj* triste, déprimé; attristant; regrettable; ~ly *adv* tristement.

sadden *vt* attrister.

saddle *n* selle *f*; col *m*; * *vt* seller.

saddlebag *n* sacoche de selle *f*.

saddler *n* sellier *m*.

sadness *n* tristesse *f*.

safe *adj* sûr; en sécurité; hors de danger; sans danger; ~ly *adv* sans accident; ~ and sound sain et sauf; * *n* coffre-fort *m*.

safe-conduct *n* sauf-conduit *m*.

safeguard *n* sauvegarde *f*; * *vt* sauvegarder, protéger.

safety *n* sécurité *f*; sûreté *f*.

safety belt *n* ceinture de sécurité *f*.

safety pin *n* épingle de nourrice *f*.

saffron *n* safran *m*.

sage *n* (*bot*) sauge *f*; sage *m*; * *adj* sage; ~ly *adv* avec sagesse.

Sagittarius *n* Sagittaire *m* (signe du zodiaque).

sago *n* (*bot*) sagou *m*.

sail *n* voile *f*; * *vt* piloter; * *vi* aller à la voile, naviguer.

sailing *n* navigation *f*.

sailor *n* marin *m*.

saint *n* saint *m* -e *f*.

sainted, saintly *adj* saint.

sake *n* bien *m*, égard *m*; for God's ~ pour l'amour de Dieu.

salad *n* salade *f*.

salad bowl *n* saladier *m*.

salad dressing *n* vinaigrette *f*.

salad oil *n* huile de table *f*.

salamander *n* salamandre *f*.

salary *n* salaire *m*.

sale *n* vente *f*; solde *m*.

saleable *adj* vendable.

salesman *n* vendeur *m*.

saleswoman *n* vendeuse *f*.

salient *adj* saillant.

saline *adj* salin.

saliva *n* salive *f*.

sallow *adj* jaunâtre, cireux.

sally *n* (*mil*) sortie, saillie *f*; * *vi* saillir.

salmon *n* saumon *m*.

salmon trout *n* truite saumonée *f*.

saloon *n* bar *m*.

salt *n* sel *m*; * *vt* saler.

salt cellar *n* salière *f*.

saltness *n* salinité *f*.

saltpetre *n* salpêtre *m*.

saltworks *npl* salines *fpl*.

salubrious *adj* salubre, sain.

salubrity *n* salubrité *f*.

salutary *adj* salutaire.

salutation *n* salutation(s) *f(pl)*.

salute *vt* saluer; * *n* salut *m*.

salvage *n* (*mar*) droit de sauvetage *m*.

salvation *n* salut *m*.

salve *n* baume, onguent *m*.

salver *n* plateau *m*.

salvo *n* salve *f*.

same *adj* même, identique.

sameness *n* monotonie *f*.

sample *n* échantillon *m*; prélèvement *m*; * *vt* goûter.

sampler *n* échantillonneur *m* -euse *f*; modèle *m*.

sanatorium *n* sanatorium *m*.

sanctify *vt* sanctifier.

sanctimonious *adj* cagot.

sanction *n* sanction *f*; * *vt* sanctionner.

sanctity *n* sainteté *f*.

sanctuary *n* sanctuaire *m*; asile *m*.

sand *n* sable *m*; * *vt* sabler.

sandal *n* sandale *f*.

sandbag *n* (*mil*) sac *m* de sable.

sandpit *n* carrière de sable *f*.

sandstone *n* grès *m*.

sandy *adj* sablonneux, sableux.

sane *adj* sain.

sanguinary *adj* sanguinaire, sanglant.

sanguine *adj* sanguin.

sanitary towel *n* serviette *f* hygiénique.

sanity *n* santé mentale, raison *f*.

sap *n* sève *f*; * *vt* miner.

sapient *adj* sage, prudent.

sapling *n* jeune arbre *m*.

sapphire *n* saphir *m*.

sarcasm *n* sarcasme *m*.

sarcastic *adj* sarcastique, caustique; ~ally *adv* d'une manière sarcastique.

sarcophagus *n* sarcophage *m*.

sardine *n* sardine *f*.

sash *n* écharpe *f*; ceinture *f*.

sash window *n* fenêtre à guillotine *f*.

sassy *adj* (US) insolent.

Satan *n* Satan *m*.

satanic(al) *adj* satanique.

satchel *n* cartable *m*.

satellite *n* satellite *m*.

satiate, sate *vt* rassasier, assouvir.

satin *n* satin *m*; * *adj* en *ou* de satin.

satire *n* satire *f*.

satirical *adj* satirique; ~ly *adv* d'une manière satirique.

satirist *n* écrivain satirique *m*.

satirize *vt* faire la satire de.

satisfaction *n* satisfaction *f*.

satisfactorily *adv* d'une manière satisfaisante.

satisfactory *adj* satisfaisant.

satisfy *vt* satisfaire; convaincre.

saturate *vt* saturer.

Saturday *n* samedi *m*.

saturnine *adj* saturnien, sombre.

satyr *n* satyre *m*.

sauce *n* sauce *f*; assaisonnement *m*; * *vt* assaisonner.

saucepan *n* casserole *f*.

saucer *n* soucoupe *f*.

saucily *adv* avec impertinence.

sauciness *n* impertinence, insolence *f*.

saucy *adj* impertinent.

saunter *vi* flâner, se balader.

sausage *n* saucisse *f*.

savage *adj* sauvage, barbare; ~ly *adv* sauvagement; * *n* sauvage *mf*.

savageness *n* sauvagerie *f*; barbarie *f*.

savagery *n* sauvagerie, barbarie *f*.

savannah *n* savane *f*.

save *vt* sauver; économiser; épargner; éviter; conserver; * *adv* sauf, à l'exception de; * *n* (*sport*) arrêt *m*.

saveloy *n* cervelas *m*.

saver *n* libérateur *m* -trice *f*; épargnant *m* -e *f*.

saving *adj* économique, économe; * *prep* sauf, à l'exception de; * *n* sauvetage *m*; ~s *pl* économies *fpl*, épargne *f*.

savings account *n* compte d'épargne *m*.

savings and loan association *n* (US) organisme *m* de crédit immobilier.

savings bank *n* caisse d'épargne *f*.

Saviour *n* Sauveur *m*.

savour *n* saveur *f*; goût *m*; * *vt* déguster, savourer.

savouriness *n* goût *m*; saveur *f*.

savoury *adj* savoureux.

saw *n* scie *f*; * *vt* scier.

sawdust *n* sciure *f*.

sawfish *n* poisson scie *m*.

sawmill *n* scierie *f*.

sawyer *n* scieur *m*.

saxophone *n* saxophone *m*.

say *vt* dire.

saying *n* dicton, proverbe *m*.

scab *n* gale *f*; croûte *f*.

scabbard *n* gaine *f*; fourreau *m*.

scabby *adj* galeux.

scaffold *n* échafaud *m*; échafaudage *m*.

scaffolding *n* échafaudage *m*.

scald *vt* échauder; * *n* brûlure *f*.

scale *n* balance *f*; échelle *f*; gamme *f*; écaille *f*; * *vt* escalader; écailler.

scallion *n* échalote *f*.

scallop *n* feston *m*; coquille *f* St Jacques; * *vt* festonner.

scalp *n* cuir chevelu *m*; * *vt* scalper.

scamp *n* coquin *m*.

scamper *vi* galoper.

scampi *npl* langoustines *fpl*.

scan *vt* scruter; explorer; scander.

scandal *n* scandale *m*; infamie *f*.

scandalize *vt* scandaliser.

scandalous *adj* scandaleux; ~ly *adv* scandaleusement.

scant, scanty *adj* rare, insuffisant.

scantily *adv* pauvrement, insuffisamment.

scantiness *n* insuffisance, pauvreté *f*.

scapegoat *n* bouc émissaire *m*.

scar *n* cicatrice *f*; ** vt* marquer d'une cicatrice.

scarce *adj* rare; ~**ly** *adv* à peine.

scarcity *n* rareté *f*; pénurie *f*.

scare *vt* effrayer; ** n* peur; panique *f*.

scarecrow *n* épouvantail *m*.

scarf *n* écharpe *f*.

scarlatina *n* scarlatine *f*.

scarlet *n* écarlate *f*; ** adj* écarlate.

scarp *n* escarpement *m*.

scat *interj* (*sl*) ouste!

scatter *vt* éparpiller; disperser.

scavenger *n* charognard *m*; éboueur *m*.

scenario *n* scénario *m*; (*also fig*).

scene *n* scène *f*; lieu *m*; spectacle *m*, vue *f*.

scenery *n* vue *f*; décor (de théâtre) *m*.

scenic *adj* scénique.

scent *n* parfum *m*, odeur *f*; odorat *m*; piste *f*; ** vt* parfumer.

scent bottle *n* flacon à parfum *m*.

scentless *adj* sans odeur, inodore.

sceptic *n* sceptique *mf*.

sceptic(al) *adj* sceptique.

scepticism *n* scepticisme *m*.

sceptre *n* sceptre *m*.

schedule *n* horaire *m*; programme *m*; liste *f*.

scheme *n* projet, plan *m*; schéma *m*; système *m*; machination *f*; ** vt* machiner; ** vi* intriguer.

schemer *n* conspirateur *m* -trice *f*, intrigant *m* -e *f*.

schism *n* schisme *m*.

schismatic *n* schismatique *mf*.

scholar *n* élève *mf*; érudit *m* -e *f*.

scholarship *n* savoir *m*, science *f*; bourse (d'études) *f*.

scholastic *adj* scolaire.

school *n* école *f*; ** vt* instruire.

schoolboy *n* écolier, élève *m*.

schoolgirl *n* écolière, élève *f*.

schooling *n* instruction, éducation *f*.

schoolmaster *n* instituteur, maître (d'école) *m*.

schoolmistress *n* institutrice, maîtresse (d'école) *f*.

schoolteacher *n* instituteur *m* -trice *f*; professeur *mf*.

schooner *n* (*mar*) goélette *f*.

sciatica *n* sciatique *f*.

science *n* science *f*.

scientific *adj* ~ally *adv* scientifique(ment).

scientist *n* scientifique *mf*.

scimitar *n* cimeterre *m*.

scintillate *vi* scintiller, étinceler.

scintillating *adj* brillant, scintillant.

scission *n* scission, division *f*.

scissors *npl* ciseaux *mpl*.

scoff *vi* se moquer.

scold *vt* réprimander; * *vi* grogner.

scoop *n* louche *f*; pelle *f*; exclusivité *f*; * *vt* évider; écoper.

scooter *n* scooter *m*; trottinette *f*.

scope *n* portée, envergure, étendue *f*; zone de compétence *f*; liberté d'action *f*.

scorch *vt* brûler; roussir, griller; * *vi* se brûler, roussir.

score *n* score *m*; marque *f*; entaille, rayure *f*; titre, égard *m*; compte *m*; (*mus*) partition *f*; vingtaine *f*; * *vt* marquer; souligner; * *vi* marquer un/des point(s).

scoreboard *n* tableau (d'affichage) *m*.

scorn *vt* mépriser; dédaigner; * *n* dédain, mépris *m*.

scornful *adj* dédaigneux; ~ly *adv* avec mépris.

Scorpio *n* Scorpion *m* (signe du zodiaque).

scorpion *n* scorpion *m*.

scotch *vt* contrecarrer.

Scotch *n* whisky *m*.

Scotch tape *n* scotch *m*.

scoundrel *n* vaurien *m*.

scour *vt* récurer, frotter; nettoyer; * *vi* battre la campagne.

scourge *n* fouet *m*; châtiment *m*; * *vt* fouetter; châtier.

scout *n* (*mil*) éclaireur *m* -euse *f*; guetteur *m*; reconnaissance *f*; * *vi* aller en reconnaissance.

scowl *vi* se renfrogner; * *n* mine renfrognée *f*.

scragginess *n* décharnement *m*, maigreur extrême *f*; rugosité *f*.

scraggy *adj* rugueux; famélique.

scramble *vi* avancer à quatre pattes; grimper; se battre, se disputer; * *n* bousculade, ruée *f*; ascension *f*.

scrap *n* bout *m*; restes *mpl*;

petit morceau *m*; bagarre *f*; ferraille *f*.

scrape *vt vi* racler, gratter; * *vt* érafler; * *n* embarras *m*, ennui *m*.

scraper *n* racloir *m*.

scratch *vt* griffer, égratigner; gratter, griffonner; * *n* égratignure *f*.

scrawl *vt vi* gribouiller; * *n* griffonnage *m*.

scream, **screech** *vi* hurler, pousser des cris; * *n* cri perçant, hurlement *m*.

screen *n* écran *m*; paravent *m*; rideau *m*; écran de cheminée *m*; * *vt* abriter, cacher; projeter; passer au crible, sélectionner.

screenplay *n* scénario *m*.

screw *n* vis *f*; * *vt* visser; extorquer, soutirer.

screwdriver *n* tournevis *m*.

scribble *vt* gribouiller; * *n* gribouillage *m*.

scribe *n* scribe *m*.

scrimmage *n* mêlée *f*.

script *n* scénario *m*; script *m*.

scriptural *adj* biblique.

Scripture *n* Écriture *f* sainte.

scroll *n* rouleau (de papier *ou* parchemin) *m*.

scrub *vt* nettoyer à la brosse, récurer; annuler; * *n* broussailles *fpl*.

scruffy *adj* mal soigné.

scruple *n* scrupule *m*.

scrupulous *adj* scrupuleux; ~**ly** *adv* scrupuleusement.

scrutinize *vt* étudier minutieusement, examiner.

scrutiny *n* examen minutieux *m*.

scuffle *n* échauffourée, rixe *f*; * *vi* se bagarrer.

scull *n* aviron *m*.

scullery *n* arrière-cuisine *f*.

sculptor *n* sculpteur *m* -trice *f*.

sculpture *n* sculpture *f*; * *vt* sculpter.

scum *n* écume *f*; crasse *f*; rebut *m*.

scurrilous *adj* injurieux; vil, ignoble; ~**ly** *adv* injurieusement.

scurvy *n* scorbut *m*; * *adj* vil, mesquin.

scuttle *n* corbeille *f*; * *vi* courir précipitamment.

scythe *n* faux *f*.

sea *n* mer *f*; * *adj* marin; heavy ~ mer houleuse *f*.

sea breeze *n* brise de mer *f*.

sea coast *n* côte *f*.

sea fight n combat naval m.

seafood n fruits de mer mpl.

sea front n bord de mer m.

seagreen adj vert glauque.

seagull n mouette f.

sea horse n hippocampe m.

seal n sceau m; phoque m; * vt sceller.

sealing wax n cire à cacheter f.

seam n couture f; * vt faire une couture.

seaman n marin m.

seamanship n habileté à naviguer f.

seamstress n couturière f.

seamy adj sordide.

sea plane n hydravion m.

seaport n port de mer m.

sear vt cautériser.

search vt fouiller; inspecter; examiner; scruter, sonder; * n fouille f; recherche f; perquisition f.

searchlight n projecteur m.

seashore n rivage m, bord de mer m.

seasick adj sujet au mal de mer.

seasickness n mal de mer m.

seaside n bord de mer m.

season n saison f; moment opportun m; assaisonnement m; * vt assaisonner; dessécher.

seasonable adj opportun, à propos.

seasonably adv de façon opportune, à propos.

seasoning n assaisonnement m.

season ticket n carte d'abonnement f.

seat n siège m; place f; derrière m; fond m; * vt (faire) asseoir; placer.

seat belt n ceinture de sécurité f.

seaward adj du large; ~s adv vers le large.

seaweed n algue f.

seaworthy adj en état de naviguer.

secede vi faire sécession, se séparer.

secession n sécession f; séparation f.

seclude vt éloigner, isoler.

seclusion n solitude f; isolement m.

second adj ~(ly) adv deuxième(ment); * n second m; seconde f; (mus) seconde f; * vt aider; seconder.

secondary adj secondaire.

secondary school n collège d'enseignement secondaire m.

secondhand *adj* d'occasion.

secrecy *n* secret *m*; discrétion *f*.

secret *adj n* secret *m*; ~ly *adv* secrètement.

secretary *n* secrétaire *mf*.

secrete *vt* cacher; (*med*) sécréter.

secretion *n* sécrétion *f*.

secretive *adj* secret, dissimulé.

sect *n* secte *f*.

sectarian *n* sectaire *mf*.

section *n* section *f*.

sector *n* secteur *m*.

secular *adj* séculaire.

secularize *vt* séculariser.

secure *adj* sûr; en sûreté; ~ly *adv* en sécurité; * *vt* mettre en sûreté; assurer.

security *n* sécurité *f*; sûreté *f*; protection *f*; caution *f*.

sedan *n* (US) berline *f*.

sedan chair *n* chaise à porteurs *f*.

sedate *adj* ~ly *adv* calme(ment), posé(ment).

sedateness *n* calme *m*.

sedative *n* sédatif *m*.

sedentary *adj* sédentaire.

sedge *n* (*bot*) carex *m*.

sediment *n* sédiment *m*; lie *f*; dépôt *m*.

sedition *n* sédition *f*.

seditious *adj* séditieux.

seduce *vt* séduire; corrompre.

seducer *n* séducteur *m* -trice *f*.

seduction *n* séduction *f*.

seductive *adj* séduisant.

sedulous *adj* assidu; ~ly *adv* assidûment.

see *vt* voir, remarquer, découvrir; connaître; juger; comprendre; * *vi* voir; comprendre; ~! regarde!; tu vois!

seed *n* graine, semence *f*; * *vi* monter en graine.

seedling *n* semis *m*.

seedsman *n* grainetier *m*.

seed time *n* (époque des) semailles *f(pl)*.

seedy *adj* minable.

seeing *conj*: ~ **that** vu que.

seek *vt* chercher; demander.

seem *vi* paraître, sembler.

seeming *n* apparence *f*; ~ly *adv* apparemment.

seemliness *n* bienséance *f*.

seemly *adj* convenable, bienséant.

seer *n* prophète *m*.

seesaw *n* bascule *f*; * *vi* osciller.

seethe *vi* bouillir, bouillonner.

segment *n* segment *m*.

seize *vt* saisir, attraper; opérer la saisie de.

seizure *n* capture *f*; saisie *f*.

seldom *adv* rarement, peu souvent.

select *vt* sélectionner, choisir; * *adj* choisi, sélectionné.

selection *n* sélection *f*.

self *n* soi-même; the ~ le moi; * *pref* auto-.

self-command *n* maîtrise de soi *f*.

self-conceit *n* vanité *f*.

self-confident *adj* sûr de soi.

self-defence *n* autodéfense *f*.

self-denial *n* abnégation de soi *f*.

self-employed *adj* indépendant.

self-evident *adj* évident, qui va de soi.

self-governing *adj* autonome.

self-interest *n* intérêt personnel *m*.

selfish *adj* ~ly *adv* égoïste(ment).

selfishness *n* égoïsme *m*.

self-pity *n* apitoiement sur soi-même *m*.

self-portrait *n* autoportrait *m*.

self-possession *n* sang-froid *m*, assurance *f*.

self-reliant *adj* indépendant.

self-respect *n* respect de soi *m*.

selfsame *adj* exactement le même, identique.

self-satisfied *adj* suffisant.

self-seeking *adj* égoïste.

self-service *adj* libre-service.

self-styled *adj* autoproclamé.

self-sufficient *adj* autosuffisant.

self-taught *adj* autodidacte.

self-willed *adj* obstiné, volontaire.

sell *vt* vendre; attraper; * *vi* se vendre.

seller *n* vendeur *m* -euse *f*.

selling-off *n* liquidation *f*.

semblance *n* semblant *m*, apparence *f*.

semen *n* sperme *m*.

semester *n* semestre *m*.

semicircle *n* demi-cercle *m*.

semicircular *adj* semi-circulaire.

semicolon *n* point-virgule *m*.

semiconductor *n* semi-conducteur *m*.

seminary *n* séminaire *m*.

semitone *n* (*mus*) demi-ton *m*.

senate *n* sénat *m*.

senator *n* sénateur *m* -trice *f*.

senatorial *adj* sénatorial.

send *vt* envoyer, expédier, adresser; émettre; pousser.

sender *n* expéditeur *m* -trice *f*.

senile *adj* sénile.

senility *n* sénilité *f*.

senior *n* aîné *m* -e *f*; * *adj* aîné; supérieur.

seniority *n* ancienneté *f*.

senna *n* (*bot*) séné *m*.

sensation *n* sensation *f*.

sense *n* sens *m*; sensation *f*; raison *f*; bon sens *m*; sentiment *m*.

senseless *adj* insensé; sans connaissance; ~ly *adv* stupidement.

senselessness *n* manque de bon sens *m*; absurdité *f*.

sensibility *n* sensibilité *f*.

sensible *adj* sensé, raisonnable; sensible.

sensibly *adv* raisonnablement.

sensitive *adj* sensible.

sensual, sensuous *adj* ~ly *adv* sensuelle(ment).

sensuality *n* sensualité *f*.

sentence *n* phrase *f*; condamnation *f*; * *vt* condamner, prononcer une sentence contre.

sententious *adj* sentencieux; ~ly *adv* sentencieusement.

sentient *adj* sensible.

sentiment *n* sentiment *m*; opinion *f*.

sentimental *adj* sentimental.

sentinel, sentry *n* sentinelle *f*.

sentry box *n* guérite *f*.

separable *adj* séparable.

separate *vt* séparer; * *vi* se séparer; * *adj* séparé; distinct; ~ly *adv* séparément.

separation *n* séparation *f*.

September *n* septembre *m*.

septennial *adj* septennal.

septuagenarian *n* septuagénaire *m*.

sepulchre *n* sépulcre *m*.

sequel *n* conséquence *f*; suite *f*.

sequence *n* ordre *m*, série *f*.

sequester, sequestrate *vt* séquestrer.

sequestration *n* séquestration *f*.

seraglio *n* sérail *m*.

seraph *n* séraphin *m*.

serenade *n* sérénade *f*; * *vt* jouer une sérénade pour.

serene *adj* serein; ~ly *adv* sereinement.

serenity *n* sérénité *f*.

serf *n* serf *m*, serve *f*.

serge *n* serge *f*.

sergeant *n* sergent *m*; (US) caporal-chef *m*; brigadier *m*.

serial *adj* de/en série; * *n* feuilleton *m*; téléroman *m*.

series *n* série *f*.

serious *adj* sérieux, grave; ~ly *adv* sérieusement.

sermon *n* sermon *m*.

serous *adj* séreux.

serpent *n* serpent *m*.

serpentine *adj* sinueux; * *n* (chem) serpentine *f*.

serrated *adj* en dents de scie.

serum *n* sérum *m*.

servant *n* domestique *mf*.

servant-girl *n* servante, bonne *f*.

serve *vt* servir; desservir; faire; accomplir; * *vi* servir; être utile; ~ a warrant remettre un mandat.

service *n* service *m*; office *m*; entretien *m*; * *vt* entretenir; réviser.

serviceable *adj* utilisable; pratique.

service station *n* station-service *f*.

servile *adj* servile.

servitude *n* servitude *f*, esclavage *m*.

session *n* séance, session *f*; réunion *f*.

set *vt* mettre, poser, placer; fixer, déterminer; * *vi* se coucher (soleil); se figer; se mettre; * *n* jeu *m*; service *m*; ensemble *m*; (cine) plateau *m*; set *m*; groupe *m*, bande *f*; * *adj* fixe, figé; prêt; déterminé.

settee *n* canapé *m*.

setting *n* disposition *f*; cadre *m*; monture *f*; ~ of the sun coucher du soleil *m*.

settle *vt* poser, installer, arranger; régler; calmer; * *vi* se poser; s'installer; se calmer.

settlement *n* règlement *m*; établissement *m*; accord *m*; résolution *f*; colonie *f*; colonisation *f*.

settler *n* colon *m*, colonisateur *m* -trice *f*.

set-to *n* lutte *f*; combat *m*.

seven *adj n* sept *m*.

seventeen *adj n* dix-sept *m*.

seventeenth *adj n* dix-septième *mf*.

seventh *adj n* septième *mf*.

seventieth *adj n* soixante-dixième *mf*.

seventy *adj n* soixante-dix *m*.

sever vt séparer.

several adj pn plusieurs.

severance n séparation f.

severe adj sévère, rigoureux, austère, dur; ~ly adv sévèrement.

severity n sévérité f.

sew vt vi coudre.

sewer n égout m.

sewerage n (système d') égouts mpl; eaux d'égout fpl.

sewing machine n machine à coudre f.

sex n sexe m.

sexist adj n sexiste mf.

sextant n sextant m.

sexton n sacristain m.

sexual adj sexuel.

sexy adj sexy.

shabbily adv petitement, mesquinement.

shabbiness n aspect décrépit ou miteux m.

shabby adj miteux.

shackle vt enchaîner; ~s npl chaînes fpl.

shade n ombre, obscurité f; nuance f; abat-jour m; * vt ombrager; abriter; atténuer.

shadiness n ombre f; ombrage m.

shadow n ombre f.

shadowy adj ombragé; sombre; indistinct.

shady adj ombreux, ombragé; sombre.

shaft n flèche f; fût m; puits m; (tech) arbre m; rayon m.

shag n tabac m; cormoran huppé m.

shaggy adj hirsute.

shake vt secouer; agiter; * vi trembler; chanceler; ~ hands se serrer la main; * n secousse f; tremblement m.

shaking adj tremblant.

shaky adj tremblant.

shallow adj peu profond, superficiel; futile.

shallowness n manque de profondeur m; futilité f.

sham vt feindre; * n imitation f; imposture f; * adj feint, simulé.

shambles npl désordre m.

shame n honte f; * vt faire honte à, déshonorer.

shamefaced adj honteux, confus.

shameful adj honteux; scandaleux; ~ly adv honteusement.

shameless adj ~ly adv effronté(ment).

shamelessness *n* effronterie, impudeur *f*.

shammy *n* (peau de) chamois *m*.

shampoo *vt* faire un shampooing à; * *n* shampooing *m*.

shamrock *n* trèfle *m*.

shank *n* jambe *f*; hampe *f*; tuyau (de pipe) *m*; canon *m*.

shanty *n* baraque *f*.

shanty town *n* bidonville *m*.

shape *vt* former; façonner; modeler; * *vi* prendre forme; * *n* forme, figure *f*; modèle *m*.

shapeless *adj* informe.

shapely *adj* bien proportionné.

share *n* part, portion *f*; (*com*) action *f*; soc (de charrue) *m*; * *vt* partager; répartir; * *vi* partager.

sharer *n* participant *m*.

shark *n* requin *m*.

sharp *adj* aigu, acéré; malin; fin; pénétrant; âpre, mordant, cinglant; perçant; vif, violent; * *n* (*mus*) dièse *m*; * *adv* pile.

sharpen *vt* aiguiser, affûter.

sharply *adv* brusquement; sévèrement; vivement; nettement.

sharpness *n* tranchant *m*; finesse, acuité *f*; aigreur *f*.

shatter *vt* fracasser, détruire; * *vi* se fracasser.

shave *vt* raser, raboter; * *vi* se raser; *n* rasage *m*.

shaver *n* rasoir électrique *m*.

shaving *n* rasage *m*.

shaving brush *n* blaireau *m*.

shaving cream *n* crème à raser *f*.

shawl *n* châle *m*.

she *pn* elle.

sheaf *n* gerbe *f*; liasse *f*.

shear *vt* tondre; ~s *npl* cisailles *fpl*.

sheath *n* fourreau *m*.

shed *vt* verser, répandre; perdre; * *n* hangar *m*; cabane *f*.

sheen *n* lustre *m*.

sheep *n* mouton *m*.

sheepfold *n* parc à moutons *m*.

sheepish *adj* penaud; timide.

sheepishness *n* timidité *f*, air penaud *m*.

sheep-run *n* pâturage pour moutons *m*.

sheepskin *n* peau de mouton *f*.

sheer *adj* pur, absolu, véritable; abrupt; * *adv* abruptement.

sheet *n* drap *m*; plaque *f*; feuille (de papier) *f*; (*mar*) écoute *f*.

sheet anchor *n* ancre de veille *f*.

sheeting *n* toile pour draps *f*.

sheet iron *n* tôle *f*.

sheet lightning *n* éclairs en nappes *mpl*.

shelf *n* étagère *f*; (*mar*) écueil *m*; saillie *f*; on the ~ au rancart.

shell *n* coquille *f*; carcasse *f*; écorce *f*; obus *m*; * *vt* écosser, décortiquer; bombarder; * *vi* se décortiquer.

shellfish *npl invar* crustacé *m*; fruits de mer *mpl*.

shelter *n* abri *m*; asile, refuge *m*; * *vt* abriter; protéger; * *vi* s'abriter.

shelve *vt* mettre au rancart.

shelving *n* rayonnage *m*.

shepherd *n* berger *m*.

shepherdess *n* bergère *f*.

sherbet *n* sorbet *m*.

sheriff *n* shérif *m*.

sherry *n* xérès *m*.

shield *n* bouclier *m*; écran protecteur *m*; * *vt* protéger.

shift *vi* changer; se déplacer; * *vt* changer, bouger;

transférer; * *n* changement *m*; roulement *m*.

shinbone *n* tibia *m*.

shine *vi* briller, reluire, illuminer; * *vt* cirer; * *n* éclat *m*.

shingle *n* galets *mpl*; ~s *pl* (*med*) zona *m*.

shining *adj* resplendissant; * *n* éclat *m*.

shiny *adj* brillant, reluisant.

ship *n* bateau *m*; navire *m*; bâtiment *m*; * *vt* embarquer; transporter.

shipbuilding *n* construction navale *f*.

shipmate *n* (*mar*) camarade de bord *m*.

shipment *n* cargaison *f*.

shipowner *n* armateur *m*.

shipwreck *n* naufrage *m*.

shirt *n* chemise *f*.

shit *excl* (*sl*) merde!

shiver *vi* frissonner.

shoal *n* banc *m* (de poissons).

shock *n* choc *m*; décharge *f*; coup *m*; * *vt* bouleverser; choquer.

shock absorber *n* amortisseur *m*.

shoddy *adj* de mauvaise qualité.

shoe *n* chaussure *f*; fer (à

cheval) *m*; * *vt* chausser; ferrer (un cheval).

shoeblack *n* cireur de chaussures *m*.

shoehorn *n* chausse-pied *m*.

shoelace *n* lacet de chaussure *m*.

shoemaker *n* cordonnier *m*.

shoestring *n* lacet de chaussure *m*.

shoot *vt* tirer, lancer, décocher; * *vi* pousser, bourgeonner; passer en flèche; s'élancer; * *n* pousse *f*.

shooter *n* tireur *m* -euse *f*.

shooting *n* fusillade *f*; tir *m*.

shop *n* magasin *m*; atelier *m*.

shopfront *n* devanture *f*.

shoplifter *n* voleur(-euse) à l'étalage *m(f)*.

shopper *n* acheteur *m* -euse *f*.

shopping *n* courses *fpl*.

shopping centre *n* centre commercial *m*.

shore *n* rivage, bord *m*, côte *f*.

short *adj* court, bref, succinct, concis; ~ly *adv* brièvement; rapidement.

shortcoming *n* insuffisance *f*; défaut *m*.

shorten *vt* raccourcir; abréger.

shortness *n* petitesse *f*; brièveté *f*.

short-sighted *adj* myope.

short-sightedness *n* myopie *f*.

shortwave *n* ondes courtes *fpl*.

shot *n* coup *m*; décharge *f*; plomb *m*; tentative *f*; prise *f*.

shotgun *n* fusil de chasse *m*.

shoulder *n* épaule *f*; accotement *m*; * *vt* charger sur son épaule.

shout *vi* crier; * *vt* crier; * *n* cri *m*, acclamation *f*.

shouting *n* cris *mpl*.

shove *vt vi* pousser; * *n* poussée *f*.

shovel *n* pelle *f*; * *vt* pelleter.

show *vt* montrer; faire voir, présenter; prouver; expliquer; * *vi* se voir; * *n* exposition *f*; spectacle *m*; manifestation *f*; salon *m*.

show business *n* monde du spectacle *m*.

shower *n* averse *f*; douche *f*; (*fig*) torrent *m*; * *vi* pleuvoir.

showery *adj* pluvieux.

showroom *n* salle d'exposition *f*.

showy *adj* voyant, ostentatoire.

shred *n* lambeau *m*, parcelle *f*; * *vt* mettre en lambeaux.

shrew *n* mégère *f*; musaraigne *f*.

shrewd *adj* astucieux; perspicace; ~ly *adv* astucieusement.

shrewdness *n* astuce *f*.

shriek *vt vi* hurler; * *n* hurlement *m*.

shrill *adj* aigu, strident.

shrillness *n* ton aigu *m*.

shrimp *n* crevette *f*; nabot *m* -e *f*, avorton *m*.

shrine *n* lieu saint *m*.

shrink *vi* rétrécir; se réduire, rapetisser.

shrivel *vi* se ratatiner, se flétrir; * *vt* ratatiner.

shroud *n* voile *m*; linceul *m*; * *vt* envelopper, voiler; ensevelir.

Shrove Tuesday *n* Mardi gras *m*.

shrub *n* arbuste *m*.

shrubbery *n* massif d'arbustes *m*.

shrug *vt* hausser les épaules; * *n* haussement d'épaules *m*.

shudder *vi* frissonner; * *n* frisson *m*.

shuffle *vt* mélanger; battre.

shun *vt* fuir, éviter.

shunt *vt* (*rail*) aiguiller.

shut *vt* fermer; *vi* (se) fermer.

shutter *n* volet *m*.

shuttle *n* navette *f*.

shuttlecock *n* volant *m*.

shy *adj* timide; réservé; embarrassé, gauche; ~ly *adv* timidement.

shyness *n* timidité *f*.

sibling *n*: ~s enfants de mêmes parents *mpl*.

sibyl *n* sibylle *f*.

sick *adj* malade; écœuré.

sicken *vt* rendre malade; * *vi* tomber malade.

sickle *n* faucille *f*.

sick leave *n* congé de maladie *m*.

sickliness *n* état maladif *m*.

sickly *adj* maladif.

sickness *n* maladie *f*.

sick pay *n* indemnité de maladie *f*.

side *n* côté *m*; flanc *m*; camp *m*; parti *m*; * *adj* latéral; secondaire; * *vi* se ranger du côté de.

sideboard *n* buffet *m*.

sidelight *n* veilleuse *f*.

sidelong *adj* oblique.

sideways *adv* de côté, obliquement.

siding n (rail) voie de garage f.

sidle vi avancer de côté; avancer furtivement.

siege n (mil) siège m.

sieve n tamis m; crible m; passoire f; * vt tamiser.

sift vt tamiser; passer au crible; dégager.

sigh vi soupirer, gémir; * n soupir m.

sight n vue f; mire f; spectacle m.

sightless adj aveugle.

sightly adj agréable à regarder; séduisant.

sightseeing n tourisme m.

sign n signe m, indication f; panneau m; geste m; trace f; * vt signer.

signal n signal m; * adj insigne, remarquable.

signalize vt signaler.

signal lamp n (rail) lampe de signalisation f.

signalman n (rail) aiguilleur m.

signature n signature f.

signet n sceau m.

significance n importance f.

significant adj considérable.

signify vt signifier.

signpost n poteau indicateur m.

silence n silence m; * vt imposer le silence à.

silent adj silencieux; ~ly adv silencieusement.

silex n silex m.

silicon chip n puce f électronique.

silk n soie f.

silken adj soyeux; satiné.

silkiness n soyeux m.

silkworm n ver à soie m.

silky adj soyeux; satiné.

sill n rebord m; seuil m.

silliness n stupidité, bêtise, niaiserie f.

silly adj bête, stupide.

silver n argent m; * adj en argent.

silversmith n orfèvre m.

silvery adj argenté.

similar adj semblable; similaire; ~ly adv de la même façon.

similarity n ressemblance f.

simile n comparaison f.

simmer vi cuire à feu doux, mijoter.

simony n simonie f.

simper vi minauder; * n sourire affecté m.

simple adj simple; naïf.

simpleton n nigaud m -e f.

simplicity n simplicité f; naïveté f.

simplification *n* simplification *f*.

simplify *vt* simplifier.

simply *adv* simplement; seulement.

simulate *vt* simuler, feindre.

simulation *n* simulation *f*.

simultaneous *adj* simultané.

sin *n* péché *m*; * *vi* pécher.

since *adv* depuis; * *prep* depuis; * *conj* depuis que; puisque.

sincere *adj* ~**ly** *adv* sincère(ment); **yours** ~**ly** veuillez agréer, Monsieur/ Madame, l'expression de mes salutations distinguées.

sincerity *n* sincérité *f*.

sinecure *n* sinécure *f*.

sinew *n* tendon *m*.

sinewy *adj* musclé; tendineux.

sinful *adj* coupable, honteux; ~**ly** *adv* honteusement.

sinfulness *n* corruption *f*, péché *m*.

sing *vt vi* chanter; (*poet*) *vt* célébrer.

singe *vt* roussir.

singer *n* chanteur *m* -euse *f*.

singing *n* chant *m*.

single *adj* seul, unique, simple; célibataire; * *n* aller simple *m*; 45 tours *m*; * *vt* distinguer; séparer.

singly *adv* séparément.

singular *adj* singulier, rare; * *n* singulier *m*; ~**ly** *adv* singulièrement.

singularity *n* singularité *f*.

sinister *adj* sinistre; de mauvais augure, funeste.

sink *vi* couler; sombrer; s'affaisser; tomber très bas, baisser; * *vt* couler, faire sombrer; ruiner; * *n* évier *m*.

sinking fund *n* fonds d'amortissement *m*.

sinner *n* pécheur *m*; pécheresse *f*.

sinuosity *n* sinuosité *f*.

sinuous *adj* sinueux.

sinus *n* sinus *m*.

sip *vt* boire à petites gorgées; * *n* petite gorgée *f*.

siphon *n* siphon *m*.

sir *n* monsieur *m*.

sire *n* étalon *m*.

siren *n* sirène *f*.

sirloin *n* aloyau (de bœuf) *m*.

sister *n* sœur *f*.

sisterhood *n* solidarité féminine *f*.

sister-in-law *n* belle-sœur *f*.

sisterly *adj* de sœur.

sit *vi* s'asseoir; se trouver; *
vt se présenter à.

site *n* emplacement *m*; site *m*.

sit-in *n* sit-in *m*, manifestation avec occupation de lieux publics *f*.

sitting *n* séance, réunion *f*; position assise *f*.

sitting room *n* salle de séjour *f*.

situated *adj* situé.

situation *n* situation *f*.

six *adj n* six *m*.

sixteen *adj n* seize *m*.

sixteenth *adj n* seizième *mf*.

sixth *adj n* sixième *mf*.

sixtieth *adj n* soixantième *mf*.

sixty *adj n* soixante *m*.

size *n* taille, grandeur *f*; volume *m*; dimension *f*; ampleur *f*; étendue *f*.

sizeable *adj* assez grand.

skate *n* patin *m*; * *vi* patiner.

skateboard *n* planche à roulettes *f*, skateboard *m*.

skating *n* patinage *m*.

skating rink *n* patinoire *f*.

skein *n* écheveau *m*.

skeleton *n* squelette *m*.

skeleton key *n* passe(-partout) *m*.

sketch *n* croquis *m*; esquisse *f*; * *vt* equisser, faire un croquis de.

skewer *n* broche *f*; brochette *f*; * *vt* embrocher.

ski *n* ski *m*; * *vi* skier.

ski boot *n* chaussure de ski *f*.

skid *n* dérapage *m*; * *vi* déraper.

skier *n* skieur *m* -euse *f*.

skiing *n* ski *m*.

skilful *adj* ~ly *adv* adroit(ement), habile(ment).

skilfulness *n* habileté *f*.

skill *n* habileté, adresse, dextérité *f*.

skilled *adj* adroit; qualifié.

skim *vt* écrémer; effleurer.

skimmed milk *n* lait écrémé *m*.

skimmer *n* écumoire *f*.

skin *n* peau *f*; * *vt* écorcher.

skin diving *n* plongée sous-marine *f*.

skinned *adj* dépouillé.

skinny *adj* maigre, efflanqué.

skip *vi* sautiller, gambader; * *vt* sauter, passer; * *n* saut, bond *m*; benne *f*.

ski pants *npl* fuseau (de ski) *m*.

skipper *n* capitaine *m*.

skirmish *n* escarmouche *f*; * *vi* s'engager dans une escarmouche.

skirt n jupe f; bordure f; * vt contourner.

skit n parodie, satire f.

skittish adj espiègle, fantasque; coquet; inconstant; ~ly adv d'une manière espiègle.

skittle n quille f.

skulk vi se cacher, rôder furtivement.

skull n crâne m.

skullcap n calotte f.

sky n ciel m.

skylight n lucarne f.

skyrocket n fusée f.

skyscraper n gratte-ciel m invar.

slab n dalle f.

slack adj lâche, mou, indolent, négligent.

slack(en) vt relâcher; ralentir; diminuer; * vi se relâcher; ralentir.

slackness n manque d'énergie, ralentissement m; laisser-aller m.

slag n scories fpl.

slam vt claquer violemment; * vi se refermer en claquant.

slander vt calomnier, dire du mal de; * n calomnie f.

slanderer n calomniateur m -trice f.

slanderous adj calomnieux; ~ly adv calomnieusement.

slang n argot m.

slant vi pencher; être incliné; * n inclinaison f; point de vue m.

slanting adj en pente, incliné.

slap n claque f; (on the face) gifle f; * adv en plein; * vt donner une claque à, gifler.

slash vt entailler; * n entaille f.

slate n ardoise f.

slater n ardoisier m.

slating n recouvrement en ardoises m.

slaughter n carnage, massacre m; * vt abattre; massacrer.

slaughterer n tueur, meurtrier m.

slaughterhouse n abattoir m.

slave n esclave mf; * vi travailler comme un nègre.

slaver n bave f; * vi baver.

slavery n esclavage m.

slavish adj servile, d'esclave; ~ly adv servilement.

slavishness n servilité f.

slay vt tuer.

slayer n tueur m -euse f.

sleazy adj louche, sordide.

sledge, sleigh n traîneau m.

sledgehammer n marteau de forgeron m.

sleek adj lisse et brillant, luisant.

sleep vi dormir; * n sommeil m.

sleeper n dormeur m -euse f.

sleepily adv d'un air endormi.

sleepiness n envie de dormir f.

sleeping bag n sac de couchage m.

sleeping pill n somnifère m.

sleepless adj sans sommeil.

sleepwalking n somnambulisme m.

sleepy adj qui a envie de dormir; endormi.

sleet n neige fondue f.

sleeve n manche f.

sleight n: ~ of hand tour de passe-passe m.

slender adj svelte, mince, élancé; faible; ~ly adv faiblement.

slenderness n sveltesse f, minceur f; faiblesse f.

slice n tranche f; spatule f; * vt couper (en tranches).

slide vi glisser; faire des glissades; * n glissade f; coulisse f; diapositive f; toboggan m.

sliding adj glissant; coulissant.

slight adj léger, mince, petit; * n affront m; * vt manquer d'égards pour.

slightly adv légèrement.

slightness n fragilité f; insignifiance f.

slim adj mince; * vi maigrir.

slime n vase f; dépôt visqueux m.

sliminess n viscosité f.

slimming n amaigrissement m.

slimy adj visqueux, gluant.

sling n fronde f; écharpe f; * vt lancer.

slink vi s'en aller furtivement; s'éclipser.

slip vi (se) glisser, se faufiler; * vt glisser; * n glissade f; faux pas m; oubli m; fiche f.

slipper n pantoufle f.

slippery adj glissant.

slipshod adj négligé.

slipway n (mar) cale f.

slit vt fendre, inciser; * n fente, incision f.

slobber n bave f.

sloe n (bot) prunelle f.

slogan n slogan m.

sloop n (mar) sloop m.

slop n fange f; bouillon m; ~s pl eaux sales fpl.

slope n inclinaison f; pente f; déclivité f; versant m; * vt incliner.

sloping adj en pente; incliné.

sloppy adj négligé; peu soigné.

sloth n paresse f.

slouch vi manquer de tenue; se tenir d'une façon négligée.

slovenliness n négligence f; manque de soin m.

slovenly adj négligé, sale, débraillé.

slow adj lent; lourd; ennuyeux; ~ly adv lentement.

slowness n lenteur, lourdeur f, manque d'intérêt m.

slow worm n orvet m.

slug n lingot m; limace f; jeton m; coup m.

sluggish adj paresseux; léthargique; ~ly adv paresseusement.

sluggishness n paresse, mollesse f.

sluice n écluse f; * vt lâcher les vannes.

slum n taudis m; quartier pauvre m.

slumber vi dormir paisiblement; * n sommeil paisible m.

slump n effondrement m.

slur vt dénigrer; calomnier; mal articuler; * n calomnie f.

slush n neige fondante f.

slut n traînée f.

sly adj rusé; ~ly adv de façon rusée.

slyness n ruse, finesse f.

smack n léger goût m; claque f; gros baiser retentissant m; * vi sentir; embrasser bruyamment; * vt donner une claque à.

small adj petit, menu.

smallish adj assez petit.

smallness n petitesse f.

smallpox n variole f.

smalltalk n conversation f banale.

smart adj élégant; rapide; astucieux; vif; * vi brûler.

smartly adv astucieusement, vivement; avec élégance; habilement.

smartness n astuce, vivacité, finesse f.

smash vt casser, briser; détruire; * vi se briser (en mille morceaux), se fracasser; * *n* fracas *m*; coup violent *m*.

smattering *n* connaissances superficielles *fpl*.

smear *n* (*med*) frottis *m*; * *vt* enduire; salir.

smell *vt vi* sentir; * *n* odorat *m*; odeur *f*; mauvaise odeur *f*.

smelly *adj* malodorant.

smelt *n* éperlan *m*; * *vt* fondre.

smelter *n* fondeur *m*.

smile *vi* sourire; * *n* sourire *m*.

smirk *vi* sourire d'un air affecté.

smite *vt* frapper.

smith *n* forgeron *m*.

smithy *n* forge *f*.

smock *n* blouse *f*.

smoke *n* fumée *f*; vapeur *f*; * *vt vi* fumer.

smokeless *adj* sans fumée.

smoker *n* fumeur *m* -euse *f*.

smoke shop *n* (US) bureau de tabac *m*.

smoking: 'no ~' 'interdiction de fumer'.

smoky *adj* enfumé; qui fume.

smooth *adj* lisse, uni, égal; doucereux, mielleux; * *vt* lisser; aplanir; adoucir.

smoothly *adv* facilement; doucement.

smoothness *n* douceur *f*; aspect lisse *m*; air doucereux *m*.

smother *vt* étouffer; réprimer.

smoulder *vi* couver, se consumer.

smudge *vt* étaler; * *n* tache *f*.

smug *adj* suffisant.

smuggle *vt* passer en contrebande.

smuggler *n* contrebandier *m* -ière *f*.

smuggling *n* contrebande *f*.

smut *n* saleté *f*; trace de suie *f*.

smuttiness *n* suie *f*; obscénité *f*.

smutty *adj* noirci; obscène.

snack *n* collation *f*.

snack bar *n* snack-bar *m*.

snag *n* obstacle *m*.

snail *n* escargot *m*.

snake *n* serpent *m*.

snaky *adj* sinueux.

snap *vt* casser net; * *vi* se casser net; claquer; mordre; parler sèchement; **~ one's fingers** faire claquer ses doigts; * *n* claquement *m*; photographie *f*.

snapdragon *n* (*bot*) gueule-de-loup *f*.

snap fastener n bouton-pression m.

snare n piège m; collet m.

snarl vi gronder férocement.

snatch vt saisir; s'emparer de; * n geste vif m; vol m; fragment m.

sneak vi se glisser furtivement; * n faux-jeton m.

sneakers npl chaussures de basket fpl.

sneer vi parler d'un ton méprisant; ricaner.

sneeringly adv d'un ton méprisant.

sneeze vi éternuer.

sniff vt renifler; * vi renifler.

snigger vi ricaner.

snip vt donner de petits coups de ciseaux dans; * n petit coup de ciseaux m; petit bout m.

snipe n bécassine f.

sniper n franc-tireur m.

snivel n pleurnicherie f; * vi pleurnicher.

sniveller n pleurnicheur m -euse f.

snobbish adj snob.

snooze n petit somme m; * vi faire un somme.

snore vi ronfler.

snorkel n tube respiratoire m.

snort vi renifler fortement.

snout n museau m; groin m.

snow n neige f; * vi neiger.

snowball n boule de neige f.

snowdrop n (bot) perce-neige m invar.

snowman n bonhomme de neige m.

snowplough n chasse-neige m invar.

snowy adj neigeux; enneigé.

snub vt repousser, rejeter.

snub-nosed adj au nez retroussé.

snuff n tabac à priser m.

snuffbox n tabatière f.

snuffle vi parler d'une voix nasillarde, nasiller; renifler.

snug adj confortable, douillet; bien abrité.

so adv si, tellement, aussi; ainsi.

soak vi tremper; * vt faire tremper.

soap n savon m; * vt savonner.

soap bubble n bulle de savon f.

soap opera n feuilleton à l'eau de rose m.

soap powder n lessive f.

soapsuds n mousse de savon f.

soapy *adj* savonneux.

soar *vi* monter en flèche.

sob *n* sanglot *m*; * *vi* sangloter.

sober *adj* sobre; sérieux; ~ly *adv* sobrement; sérieusement.

sobriety *n* sobriété *f*; sérieux, calme *m*.

soccer *n* football *m*.

sociability *n* sociabilité *f*.

sociable *adj* sociable, liant.

sociably *adv* sociablement.

social *adj* social, sociable; ~ly *adv* socialement.

socialism *n* socialisme *m*.

socialist *n* socialiste *mf*.

social work *n* assistance sociale *f*.

social worker *n* assistant(e) social(e) *m(f)*.

society *n* société *f*; compagnie *f*.

sociologist *n* sociologue *mf*.

sociology *n* sociologie *f*.

sock *n* chaussette *f*.

socket *n* prise de courant *f*.

sod *n* gazon *m*.

soda *n* soude *f*; eau *f* de Seltz, soda *m*.

soft *adj* doux, moelleux; aimable, gentil; ~ly *adv* doucement; tendrement.

soften *vt* (r)amollir, adoucir; atténuer.

soft-hearted *adj* compatissant.

softness *n* douceur, mollesse *f*.

soft-spoken *adj* à la voix douce.

software *n* logiciel *m*.

soil *vt* salir, souiller; * *n* salissure, souillure *f*; sol *m*; terre *f*.

sojourn *vi* séjourner; * *n* séjour *m*.

solace *vt* consoler, soulager; * *n* consolation *f*.

solar *adj* solaire.

solder *vt* souder; * *n* soudure *f*.

soldier *n* soldat *m*.

soldierly *adj* militaire.

sole *n* plante du pied *f*; semelle (de chaussure) *f*; sole *f*; * *adj* seul, unique.

solecism *n* (*gr*) solécisme *m*.

solemn *adj* ~ly *adv* solennel(lement).

solemnity *n* solennité *f*.

solemnize *vt* solenniser.

solicit *vt* solliciter; quémander.

solicitation *n* sollicitation *f*.

solicitor *n* notaire *m*.

solicitous *adj* plein de sollicitude; ~ly *adv* avec sollicitude.

solicitude *n* sollicitude *f*.

solid *adj* solide, compact; *
n solide *m*; **~ly** *adv*
solidement.

solidify *vt* solidifier.

solidity *n* solidité *f*.

soliloquy *n* soliloque *m*.

solitaire *n* solitaire *m* (jeu).

solitary *adj* solitaire, retiré;
* *n* anachorète *m*.

solitude *n* solitude *f*.

solo *n* (*mus*) solo *m*.

solstice *n* solstice *m*.

soluble *adj* soluble.

solution *n* solution *f*.

solve *vt* résoudre.

solvency *n* solvabilité *f*.

solvent *adj* solvable; *n*
(*chem*) solvant *m*.

some *adj* du, de la, de l', des;
quelques; quelconque;
certain(e)s; quelque.

somebody *pn* quelqu'un.

somehow *adv* d'une façon
ou d'une autre.

someplace *adv* quelque part.

something *pn* quelque chose.

sometime *adv* au cours de,
un jour ou l'autre.

sometimes *adv* quelquefois,
parfois.

somewhat *adv* quelque peu.

somewhere *adv* quelque
part.

somnambulism *n*
somnambulisme *m*.

somnambulist *n* somnambule
mf.

somnolence *n* somnolence *f*.

somnolent *adj* somnolent.

son *n* fils *m*.

sonata *n* (*mus*) sonate *f*.

song *n* chanson *f*.

son-in-law *n* gendre *m*.

sonnet *n* sonnet *m*.

sonorous *adj* sonore.

soon *adv* bientôt; **as ~ as** dès
que.

sooner *adv* plus tôt; plutôt.

soot *n* suie *f*.

soothe *vt* calmer, apaiser; flatter.

soothsayer *n* devin *m*.

sop *n* pain trempé *m*.

sophism *n* sophisme *m*.

sophist *n* sophiste *mf*.

sophistical *adj* sophistiqué.

sophisticate *vt* falsifier;
sophistiquer.

sophisticated *adj*
sophistiqué.

sophistry *n* sophistique *f*.

sophomore *n* (US)
étudiant(e) *m(f)* de
seconde année.

soporific *adj* soporifique.

sorcerer *n* sorcier *m*.

sorceress n sorcière f.

sorcery n sorcellerie f.

sordid adj sordide, sale.

sordidness n bassesse f, saleté f.

sore n plaie, blessure f; * adj douloureux, sensible; contrarié; ~ly adv fortement.

sorrel n (bot) oseille f; * adj alezan, roux.

sorrow n peine f; chagrin m; * vi se lamenter.

sorrowful adj triste, affligé; ~ly adv tristement.

sorry adj désolé, navré; déplorable; I am ~ je suis désolé.

sort n sorte f; genre m; espèce f; race f; manière f; * vt classer; trier.

soul n âme f; essence f; personne f.

sound adj sain; solide; valide; ~ly adv sainement, solidement; * n son m; bruit m; * vt sonner (de); * vi sonner, retentir; ressembler; sembler.

sound effects npl bruitage m.

sounding board n table d'harmonie f; abat-voix m.

soundings npl (mar) sondages mpl; (mar) fonds mpl.

soundness n santé f; solidité f.

soundtrack n bande sonore f.

soup n soupe f.

sour adj aigre, acide; acerbe; revêche; ~ly adv aigrement; * vt aigrir, faire tourner; * vi s'aigrir; tourner.

source n source f; origine f.

sourness n acidité, aigreur f; acrimonie f.

souse n (sl) soûlard m -e f; * vt mariner; faire tremper.

south n sud m; * adj sud, du sud, au sud; * adv au sud; vers le sud.

southerly, southern adj du sud, sud, méridional.

southward(s) adv vers le sud.

southwester n (mar) vent du sud-ouest m; suroît m.

sovereign adj n souverain m -e f.

sovereignty n souveraineté f.

sow n truie f.

sow vt semer; disperser.

sowing time n époque des semailles f.

soy n soja m.

space n espace m; intervalle m; * vt espacer.

spacecraft *n* vaisseau spatial *m*.

spaceman/woman *n* astronaute *mf*.

spacious *adj* spacieux, ample; ~ly *adv* spacieusement.

spaciousness *n* dimensions spacieuses *fpl*, espace *m*.

spade *n* bêche *f*; pique *m* (carte).

span *n* envergure *f*; * *vt* enjamber; embrasser.

spangle *n* paillette *f*; * *vt* orner de paillettes.

spaniel *n* épagneul *m*.

Spanish *adj* espagnol; * *n* espagnol *m*; Espagnol *m* -e *f*.

spar *n* (*mar*) espar *m*; * *vi* s'entraîner.

spare *vt vi* épargner; ménager; éviter; se passer de; * *adj* de trop; de réserve.

sparing *adj* limité, modéré, économe; ~ly *adv* frugalement, avec modération.

spark *n* étincelle *f*.

sparkle *n* scintillement *m*, étincelle *f*; * *vi* étinceler; briller.

spark plug *n* bougie *f*.

sparrow *n* moineau *m*.

sparrowhawk *n* épervier *m*.

sparse *adj* clairsemé; épars; ~ly *adv* faiblement.

spasm *n* spasme *m*.

spasmodic *adj* spasmodique.

spatter *vt* éclabousser; * *vi* gicler.

spatula *n* spatule *f*.

spawn *n* frai *m*; * *vt* pondre; engendrer.

spawning *n* frai *m*.

speak *vt* parler; dire; * *vi* parler, s'entretenir; prendre la parole.

speaker *n* haut-parleur m; interlocuteur *m* -trice *f*; orateur *m*.

spear *n* lance *f*; harpon *m*; * *vt* transpercer d'un coup de lance.

special *adj* spécial, particulier; ~ly *adv* spécialement.

speciality *n* spécialité *f*.

species *n* espèce *f*.

specific *adj* spécifique; * *n* remède spécifique *m*.

specifically *adv* spécifiquement; explicitement.

specification *n* spécification *f*.

specify *vt* spécifier.

specimen *n* spécimen *m*; exemple *m*.

specious *adj* spécieux.

speck(le) *n* grain, tache *f*; * *vt* tacheter, moucheter.

spectacle *n* spectacle *m*.

spectator *n* spectateur *m* -trice *f*.

spectral *adj* spectral; ~ analysis *n* analyse spectrale *f*.

spectre *n* spectre *m*.

speculate *vi* spéculer; méditer.

speculation *n* spéculation *f*; conjecture *f*; méditation *f*.

speculative *adj* spéculatif, méditatif.

speculum *n* spéculum *m*.

speech *n* parole *f*; discours *m*; langage *m*; élocution *f*.

speechify *vi* discourir, pérorer.

speechless *adj* muet.

speed *n* vitesse *f*; rapidité *f*; * *vt* presser; accélérer; * *vi* se presser.

speedboat *n* vedette *f*.

speedily *adv* rapidement, vite.

speediness *n* rapidité, promptitude, célérité *f*.

speed limit *n* limitation de vitesse *f*.

speedometer *n* compteur de vitesse *m*.

speedway *n* piste de course *f*.

speedy *adj* rapide, prompt.

spell *n* charme, sortilège *m*; période *f*; * *vt* écrire; épeler; ensorceler, envoûter; * s'écrire; s'épeler.

spelling *n* ortographe *f*.

spend *vt* dépenser; passer; épuiser; gaspiller.

spendthrift *n* dépensier *m* -ière *f*.

spent *adj* épuisé.

sperm *n* sperme *m*.

spermaceti *n* spermaceti *m*.

spew *vi* (*sl*) vomir.

sphere *n* sphère *f*.

spherical *adj* sphérique; ~ly *adv* de forme sphérique.

spice *n* épice *f*; * *vt* épicer.

spick-and-span *adj* impeccable; tiré à quatre épingles.

spicy *adj* épicé.

spider *n* araignée *f*.

spigot *n* clef de robinet *f*.

spike *n* pointe *f*; clou *m*; * *vt* clouter.

spill *vt* renverser, répandre; * *vi* se répandre.

spin *vt* filer; inventer, fabriquer; faire tourner; * *vi* tourner; * *n* tournoiement *m*; tour (en voiture) *m*.

spinach n épinard m.

spinal adj spinal.

spindle n fuseau m; broche f.

spine n colonne vertébrale, épine dorsale f.

spinet n (mus) épinette f.

spinner n fileur m; fileuse f.

spinning wheel n rouet m.

spin-off n sous-produit m.

spinster n célibataire f.

spiral adj ~ly adv en spirale.

spire n flèche f; aiguille f; tige f.

spirit n esprit m; âme f; caractère m, disposition f; courage m; humeur f; * vt encourager; animer; ~ away faire disparaître comme par enchantement.

spirited adj vif, fougueux; ~ly adv fougueusement.

spirit lamp n lampe à alcool f.

spiritless adj sans entrain, abattu.

spiritual adj ~ly adv spirituel(lement).

spiritualist n spiritualiste mf.

spirituality n spiritualité f.

spit n crachat m; salive f; * vt vi cracher; crépiter.

spite n dépit m, rancune f; in ~ of en dépit de, malgré; * vt vexer.

spiteful adj rancunier, malveillant; ~ly adv par méchanceté, par rancune.

spitefulness n méchanceté f; rancune f.

spittle n salive f; crachat m.

splash vt éclabousser, faire gicler; * vi barboter; * n éclaboussure f; tache f.

spleen n rate f; spleen m.

splendid adj splendide, magnifique; ~ly adv splendidement.

splendour n splendeur f; magnificence f.

splice vt (mar) épisser, abouter.

splint n éclisse f.

splinter n éclat m; esquille f; écharde f; * vt (vi) (se) fendre en éclats.

split n fente f; rupture f; * vt fendre, diviser; * vi se fendre.

spoil vt abîmer; gâter; gâcher.

spoiled adj abîmé; gâté.

spoke n rayon (de roue) m.

spokesman/woman n porte-parole mf.

sponge n éponge f; * vt éponger; * vi être un parasite.

sponger n parasite m.

sponginess *n* spongiosité *f*.

spongy *adj* spongieux.

sponsor *n* caution *m*; parrain *m*; marraine *f*.

sponsorship *n* parrainage *m*.

spontaneity *n* spontanéité *f*.

spontaneous *adj* ~ly *adv* spontané(ment).

spool *n* bobine *f*; rouleau *m*.

spoon *n* cuiller *f*.

spoonful *n* cuillerée *f*.

sporadic(al) *adj* sporadique.

sport *n* sport *m*; jeu *m*; divertissement, amusement *m*.

sports car *n* voiture de sport *f*.

sports jacket *n* veste sport *f*.

sportsman/woman *n* sportif *m* -ive *f*.

sportswear *n* vêtements de sport *mpl*.

spot *n* tache *f*; point *m*; endroit *m*; pois *m*; * *vt* apercevoir; tacher.

spotless *adj* impeccable, immaculé.

spotlight *n* feu de projecteur *m*.

spotted, spotty *adj* tacheté; à pois.

spouse *n* époux *m*, épouse *f*.

spout *vi* jaillir; gicler; déblatérer; * *vt* faire jaillir; * *n* bec *m*; gargouille *f*; jet *m*.

sprain *vt* fouler; * *n* entorse *f*.

sprawl *vi* s'étaler.

spray *n* spray *m*; pulvérisation *f*; embruns *mpl*.

spread *vt* étendre, étaler; répandre, propager; * *vi* s'étendre, se répandre; * *n* propagation, diffusion *f*.

spree *n* fête *f*.

sprig *n* brin *m*.

sprightliness *n* vivacité *f*, entrain *m*.

sprightly *adj* alerte, vif, fringant.

spring *vi* bondir, sauter; provenir, découler; émaner, naître; * *n* printemps *m*; élasticité *f*; ressort *m*; saut *m*; source *f*.

springiness *n* élasticité *f*.

springtime *n* printemps *m*.

springwater *n* eau de source *f*.

springy *adj* élastique.

sprinkle *vt* arroser.

sprinkling *n* arrosage *m*.

sprout *n* pousse *f*, germe *m*; ~s *npl* choux de Bruxelles *mpl*; * *vi* germer.

spruce *adj* net, impeccable; ~ly *adv* tiré à quatre épingles; * *vi* se mettre sur son trente-et-un.

spruceness n élégance f.

spur n éperon m; ergot (coq) m; stimulant m; * vt éperonner; stimuler.

spurious adj faux, feint; falsifié, de contrefaçon.

spurn vt repousser avec mépris.

sputter vi postillonner; bredouiller; bafouiller.

spy n espion m -ne f; * vt apercevoir; espionner; vi espionner.

squabble vi se disputer, se quereller; * n querelle, dispute f.

squad n escouade f; brigade f; équipe f.

squadron n (mil) escadron m.

squalid adj misérable, sordide.

squall n rafale f; bourrasque f; * vi brailler.

squally adj qui souffle en rafales.

squalor n saleté f; misère f.

squander vt gaspiller, dilapider.

square adj carré; catégorique; honnête; * n carré m; place f; équerre f; * vt cadrer; mettre en ordre, régler; * vi cadrer.

squareness n forme carrée f.

squash vt écraser; * n squash m.

squat vi s'accroupir; * adj accroupi; trapu, courtaud.

squaw n squaw, femme peau-rouge f.

squeak vi grincer, crier; * n cri, couinement m.

squeal vi pousser un cri aigu, couiner.

squeamish adj impressionable; délicat.

squeeze vt presser, tordre; comprimer; * n pression f; serrement de main m; cohue f.

squid n calmar m.

squint adj atteint de strabisme; * vi loucher; * n strabisme.

squirrel n écureuil m.

squirt vt faire gicler; * n giclée f; jet m.

stab vt poignarder; * n coup de couteau m.

stability n stabilité, solidité f.

stable n écurie f; * vt mettre à l'écurie; * adj stable.

stack n pile f; * vt empiler.

staff n personnel m; bâton m; soutien m.

stag n cerf m.

stage *n* étape *f*; scène *f*; échafaudage *m*; théâtre *m*; stade *m*; estrade *f*.

stagger *vi* vaciller, tituber; hésiter; * *vt* stupéfier; échelonner.

stagnation *n* stagnation *f*.

stagnant *adj* stagnant.

stagnate *vi* stagner.

staid *adj* posé, sérieux, guindé.

stain *vt* tacher; ternir; * *n* tache *f*.

stainless *adj* sans tache; immaculé.

stair *n* marche *f*; ~s *pl* escalier *m*.

staircase *n* escalier *m*.

stake *n* pieu *m*; enjeu *m*; * *vt* marquer; délimiter.

stale *adj* rassis, rance.

staleness *n* manque de fraîcheur *m*; rance *m*.

stalk *vi* avancer d'un air majestueux; * *n* tige, queue *f*, trognon *m*.

stall *n* stalle *f*; stand, étalage *m*; (fauteuil d') orchestre *m*; emplacement *m*; * *vt* caler; * *vi* caler; atermoyer.

stallion *n* étalon *m*.

stalwart *n* partisan fidèle *m*.

stamen *n* étamine *f*.

stamina *n* résistance *f*.

stammer *vi* bégayer; * *n* bégaiement *m*.

stamp *vt* trépigner; timbrer; affranchir; tamponner; * *vi* trépigner; * *n* timbre *m*; cachet *m*; tampon *m*; empreinte *f*; estampille *f*.

stampede *n* débandade *f*.

stand *vi* être debout, se tenir; se maintenir; résister; être situé, se trouver; rester, durer; s'arrêter, faire halte; * *vt* poser; résister; soutenir, supporter; * *n* position, prise de position *f*; pied, support *m*; étalage *m*; état *m*; tribune *f*; stand *m*.

standard *n* étendard *m*; modèle *m*; étalon *m*; norme *f*; * *adj* normal.

standing *adj* permanent, fixe, établi; en pied; * *n* durée *f*; importance *f*; rang *m*.

standstill *n* arrêt *m*; immobilisation *f*.

staple *n* agrafe *f*; * *adj* principal, de base; * *vt* agrafer.

star *n* étoile *f*; astérisque *m*.

starboard *n* tribord *m*.

starch *n* amidon *m*; * *vt* amidonner.

stare *vi*: to ~ at regarder

fixement; * *n* regard fixe *m*.

stark *adj* raide, rigide; cru; * *adv* complètement.

starling *n* étourneau *m*.

starry *adj* étoilé.

start *vi* commencer, débuter; sursauter, tressaillir; démarrer, se mettre en route; * *vt* commencer; amorcer; lancer; mettre en marche; * *n* début *m*; ouverture *f*; sursaut *m*; départ *m*; avance *f*.

starter *n* starter, démarreur *m*.

starting point *n* point de départ *m*.

startle *vt* faire sursauter.

startling *adj* surprenant, alarmant.

starvation *n* inanition, faim *f*.

starve *vi* mourir de faim.

state *n* état *m*; condition *f*; pompe *f*, apparat *m*; **the S~s** les Etats-Unis *mpl*; * *vt* déclarer; exposer.

stateliness *n* majesté, grandeur *f*.

stately *adj* majestueux, imposant.

statement *n* déclaration, affirmation *f*.

statesman *n* homme d'État *m*.

statesmanship *n* qualité d'homme politique *f*.

static *adj* statique; * *n* parasites *mpl*.

station *n* station *f*; place, position *f*; condition *f*, rang *m*; situation *f*; condition *f*; (*rail*) gare *f*; * *vt* placer.

stationary *adj* stationnaire, immobile.

stationer *n* papetier *m*-ière *f*.

stationery *n* papeterie *f*.

station wagon *n* (US) break *m*.

statistical *adj* statistique.

statistics *npl* statistiques *fpl*.

statuary *n* statuaire *f*.

statue *n* statue *f*.

stature *n* stature, taille *f*.

statute *n* statut *m*; loi *f*.

stay *n* séjour *m*; ~**s** *npl* corset *m*; * *vi* rester, demeurer; tenir; loger; ~ **in** rester à la maison; ~ **on** rester encore quelque temps; ~ **up** ne pas se coucher.

stead *n* place *f*, lieu *m*.

steadfast *adj* ferme, résolu, inébranlable; ~**ly** *adv* fermement, résolument.

steadily *adv* fermement; régulièrement.

steadiness *n* fermeté, stabilité *f*.

steady *adj* stable, solide; ** vt* affermir.

steak *n* bifteck *m*; steak *m*.

steal *vt vi* voler.

stealth *n* discrétion *f*; **by ~** à la dérobée.

stealthily *adv* furtivement.

stealthy *adj* furtif.

steam *n* vapeur *f*; buée *f*; ** vt* cuire à la vapeur; ** vi* fumer.

steam engine *n* locomotive à vapeur *f*.

steamer, steamboat *n* (bateau à) vapeur, paquebot *m*.

steel *n* acier *m*; ** adj* d'acier.

steelyard *n* balance romaine *f*.

steep *adj* abrupt; excessif; ** vt* tremper.

steeple *n* clocher *m*; flèche *f*.

steeplechase *n* steeple (course) *m*.

steepness *n* raideur *f*; escarpement *m*.

steer *n* bouvillon *m*; ** vt* conduire; diriger; gouverner; ** vi* tenir le gouvernail.

steering *n* direction *f*.

steering wheel *n* volant *m*.

stellar *adj* stellaire.

stem *n* tige *f*, tronc *m*; souche *f*; pied *m*; tuyau *m*; ** vt* endiguer.

stench *n* odeur fétide *f*.

stencil *n* stencil *m*, pochoir *m*.

stenographer *n* sténographe *mf*.

stenography *n* sténographie *f*.

step *n* pas *m*, marche *f*; trace *f*; ** vi* faire un pas; marcher.

stepbrother *n* demi-frère *m*.

stepdaughter *n* belle-fille *f*.

stepfather *n* beau-père *m*.

stepmother *n* belle-mère *f*.

stepping stone *n* pierre de gué *f*.

stepsister *n* demi-sœur *f*.

stepson *n* beau-fils *m*.

stereo *n* stéréo *f*.

stereotype *n* stéréotype *m*; ** vt* stéréotyper.

sterile *adj* stérile.

sterility *n* stérilité *f*.

sterling *adj* de bon aloi, vrai, véritable; ** n* livres sterling *fpl*.

stern *adj* sévère, rigide, strict; ** n* (*mar*) poupe *f*; *~ly adv* sévèrement.

stethoscope *n* (*med*) stéthoscope *m*.

stevedore *n* (*mar*) docker *m*.

stew *vt* faire cuire à l'étouffée; ** n* ragoût *m*.

steward *n* intendant *m*; (*mar*) steward *m*.

stewardess *n* hôtesse de l'air *f*.

stewardship *n* intendance *f*.

stick *n* bâton *m*; canne *f*; baguette *f*; * *vt* coller; piquer, planter; supporter; * *vi* tenir; se planter; rester fidèle.

stickiness *n* viscosité *f*.

stick-up *n* braquage *m*, hold-up *m*.

sticky *adj* collant, poisseux.

stiff *adj* raide, rigide; inflexible; dur; entêté; ~ly *adv* raidement; obstinément.

stiffen *vt* raidir, renforcer; * *vi* se raidir.

stiff neck *n* torticolis *m*.

stiffness *n* raideur, rigidité *f*; opiniâtreté *f*.

stifle *vt* étouffer.

stifling *adj* suffocant.

stigma *n* stigmate *m*.

stigmatize *vt* stigmatiser.

stile *n* tourniquet *m*.

stiletto *n* stylet *m*; talon aiguille *m*.

still *vt* calmer, apaiser; faire taire; * *adj* silencieux, calme; * *n* alambic *m*; * *adv* encore; toujours; quand même, tout de même.

stillborn *adj* mort-né.

stillness *n* calme *m*, tranquillité *f*.

stilts *npl* échasses *fpl*.

stimulant *n* stimulant *m*.

stimulate *vt* stimuler.

stimulation *n* stimulant *m*; stimulation *f*.

stimulus *n* stimulant *m*.

sting *vt* piquer; * *vi* brûler; * *n* dard *m*; piqûre *f*; aiguillon *m*.

stingily *adv* avec avarice.

stinginess *n* mesquinerie, avarice *f*.

stingy *adj* mesquin, avare, pingre.

stink *vi* puer; * *n* puanteur *f*.

stint *n* tâche assignée *f*.

stipulate *vt* stipuler.

stipulation *n* stipulation *f*.

stir *vt* remuer; agiter; exciter; * *vi* remuer, bouger; * *n* agitation *f*; émoi *m*.

stirrup *n* étrier *m*.

stitch *vt* coudre; * *n* point *m*; point de suture *m*.

stoat *n* hermine *f*.

stock *n* réserve *f*; provision *f*; bouillon *m*; souche *f*; lignée *f*; capital *m*; fonds *mpl*; ~s *pl* valeurs mobilières *fpl*; * *vt* approvisionner, stocker.

stockade *n* prison militaire *f*.

stockbroker *n* agent de change *m*.

stock exchange n Bourse f.

stockholder n actionnaire mf.

stocking n bas m.

stock market n Bourse f.

stoic n stoïque mf.

stoical adj ~**ly** adv stoïque(ment).

stoicism n stoïcisme m.

stole n étole f.

stomach n estomac m; ventre m; * vt digérer; endurer.

stone n pierre f; caillou m; noyau m; * adj de pierre; * vt lancer des pierres sur; dénoyauter; empierrer.

stone deaf adj sourd comme un pot.

stoning n empierrement m.

stony adj pierreux, rocailleux; dur.

stool n tabouret m; rebord, appui m.

stoop vi se baisser, se pencher; * n inclination en avant f.

stop vt arrêter, interrompre; boucher; * vi s'arrêter, cesser; * n arrêt m; halte f; pause f; point m.

stopover n escale; étape f.

stoppage, stopping n obstruction f; engorgement m; (rail) suppression f.

stopwatch n chronomètre m.

storage n emmagasinage m; entreposage m.

store n provision f; réserve f; entrepôt m, magasin m; * vt mettre en réserve, accumuler, emmagasiner.

storekeeper n marchand m -e f.

storey n (UK) étage m.

stork n cigogne f.

storm n tempête f, orage m; assaut m; * vt prendre d'assaut; * vi faire rage.

stormily adv violemment.

stormy adj orageux; houleux.

story n histoire f; récit m; (US) étage m.

stout adj corpulent, robuste, vigoureux; solide; ~**ly** adv solidement; vaillamment; résolument.

stoutness n vigueur f; puissance f; corpulence f.

stove n poêle m; cuisinière f.

stow vt ranger, mettre en place; (mar) arrimer.

straggle vi être disséminé.

straggler n traînard m -e f.

straight adj droit; direct; franc; * adv droit; directement.

straightaway *adv* tout de suite, immédiatement

straighten *vt* redresser.

straightforward *adj* honnête; franc; direct.

straightforwardness *n* honnêteté *f*.

strain *vt* tendre; fouler; forcer; mettre à l'épreuve; * *vi* peiner; * *n* tension *f*; effort *m*; entorse *f*; contrainte *f*; lignée *f*; accent *m*; ton *m*.

strainer *n* passoire *f*.

strait *n* détroit *m*; embarras *m*; situation critique *f*.

strait-jacket *n* camisole de force *f*.

strand *n* brin *m*; rivage *m*, rive *f*.

strange *adj* inconnu; étrange; ~ly *adv* étrangement, curieusement.

strangeness *n* étrangeté *f*; nouveauté *f*.

stranger *n* inconnu(e) *m(f)*, étranger *m* -ère *f*.

strangle *vt* étrangler.

strangulation *n* strangulation *f*.

strap *n* lanière, sangle *f*; courroie *f*; * *vt* attacher avec une courroie.

strapping *adj* robuste, charpenté.

stratagem *n* stratagème *m*.

strategic *adj* stratégique *m*.

strategy *n* stratégie *f*.

stratum *n* strate *f*.

straw *n* paille *f*.

strawberry *n* fraise *f*.

stray *vi* s'égarer; vagabonder; * *adj* perdu; errant.

streak *n* raie, bande *f*; filet *m*; * *vt* strier.

stream *n* ruisseau *m*, rivière *f*; torrent *m*; * *vi* ruisseler.

streamer *n* serpentin *m*.

street *n* rue *f*.

streetcar *n* tramway *m*.

strength *n* force, puissance *f*; vigueur *f*; robustesse *f*.

strengthen *vt* fortifier; confirmer, renforcer.

strenuous *adj* ardu; vigoureux.

stress *n* pression *f*; stress *m*; tension *f*; contrainte *f*; importance *f*; accent *m*; * *vt* souligner; accentuer.

stretch *vt* étendre, étirer; élargir; forcer; * *vi* s'étendre, s'étirer; * *n* extension *f*; étendue *f*; période *f*.

stretcher *n* brancard *m*.

strew *vt* éparpiller; semer.

strict *adj* strict, sévère; exact, rigoureux, précis; ~ly *adv* strictement, sévèrement.

strictness *n* sévérité *f*; rigueur *f*.

stride *n* grand pas *m*; * *vi* marcher à grandes enjambées.

strife *n* conflit *m*, lutte *f*.

strike *vt* frapper; heurter; attaquer; rayer; * *vi* frapper; se mettre en grève; sonner; * *n* coup *m*; grève *f*; découverte *f*.

striker *n* gréviste *mf*.

striking *adj* frappant; saisissant; ~ly *adv* remarquablement.

string *n* ficelle *f*; corde *f*; cordon *m*; rang *m*; fibre *f*; * *vt* munir d'une corde; enfiler; suspendre.

stringent *adj* rigoureux.

stringy *adj* filandreux.

strip *vt* déshabiller, dévêtir; * *vi* se déshabiller; * *n* bande *f*; langue *f*; bandelette *f*.

stripe *n* raie, rayure *f*; coup de fouet *m*; * *vt* rayer.

strive *vi* s'efforcer; s'évertuer; lutter, se battre.

stroke *n* coup *m*; trait *m*; course *f*; caresse *f*; apoplexie *f*; * *vt* caresser.

stroll *n* petit tour; * *vi* flâner.

strong *adj* fort, vigoureux, robuste; puissant; intense; ~ly *adv* fortement, énergiquement.

strongbox *n* coffre-fort *m*.

stronghold *n* forteresse *f*.

strophe *n* strophe *f*.

structure *n* structure *f*; construction *f*.

struggle *vi* lutter; se battre; se démener; * *n* lutte *f*.

strum *vt* (*mus*) tapoter de.

strut *vi* se pavaner; * *n* démarche affectée *f*.

stub *n* souche *f*; bout *m*; talon *m*.

stubble *n* chaume *m*; barbe de plusieurs jours *f*.

stubborn *adj* entêté, obstiné; ~ly *adv* obstinément.

stubbornness *n* entêtement *m*, obstination *f*.

stucco *n* stuc *m*.

stud *n* clou *m*; crampon *m*; écurie *f*.

student *n, adj* étudiant *m* -e *f*.

stud horse *n* étalon *m*.

studio *n* studio, atelier *m*.

studio apartment *n* studio *m*.

studious *adj* studieux; sérieux;
  ~ly *adv* studieusement,
  sérieusement.

study *n* étude *f*; études *fpl*;
  méditation *f*; * *vt* étudier;
  observer; * *vi* étudier; faire
  des études.

stuff *n* matière *f*; matériaux
  mpl; étoffe *f*; * *vt*
  (rem)bourrer, remplir;
  empailler.

stuffing *n* rembourrage *m*.

stuffy *adj* mal aéré; collet
  monté.

stumble *vi* trébucher; * *n* faux
  pas, trébuchement *m*.

stumbling block *n* hésitation
  f; pierre d'achoppement *f*.

stump *n* souche *f*; moignon
  m; bout *m*.

stun *vt* étourdir; stupéfier.

stunner *n* personne *ou* chose
  extraordinaire *f*.

stunt *n* cascade *f*; coup de
  publicité *m*; * *vt* empêcher
  de croître.

stuntman *n* cascadeur *m*.

stupefy *vt* hébéter; stupéfier.

stupendous *adj* prodigieux,
  remarquable.

stupid *adj* ~ly *adv*
  stupide(ment).

stupidity *n* stupidité *f*.

stupor *n* stupeur *f*.

sturdily *adv* fortement.

sturdiness *n* force, robustesse
  f; résolution *f*.

sturdy *adj* vigoureux,
  robuste, fort; hardi, résolu.

sturgeon *n* esturgeon *m*.

stutter *vi* bégayer.

sty *n* porcherie *f*; taudis *m*.

stye *n* orgelet *m*.

style *n* style *m*; mode *f*; * *vt*
  appeler, dénommer; créer,
  dessiner.

stylish *adj* élégant, qui a du
  chic.

suave *adj* suave.

subdivide *vt* subdiviser.

subdivision *n* subdivision *f*.

subdue *vt* subjuguer, assujettir;
  contenir, réfréner; adoucir.

subject *adj* soumis; sujet à; *
  n sujet *m*; thème *m*; * *vt*
  soumettre; exposer.

subjection *n* sujétion *f*.

subjugate *vt* subjuguer,
  assujettir.

subjugation *n* subjugation *f*.

subjunctive *n* subjonctif *m*.

sublet *vt* sous-louer.

sublimate *vt* sublimer.

sublime *adj* sublime, suprême;
  ~ly *adv* sublimement; * *n*
  sublime *m*.

sublimity *n* sublimité *f*.

submachine gun *n* mitraillette *f*.

submarine *adj n* sous-marin *m*.

submerge *vt* submerger.

submersion *n* submersion *f*.

submission *n* soumission *f*.

submissive *adj* soumis, docile; ~ly *adv* avec soumission.

submissiveness *n* docilité *f*; soumission *f*.

submit *vt* soumettre; * *vi* se soumettre.

subordinate *adj* subalterne, inférieur; * *vt* subordonner.

subordination *n* subordination *f*.

subpoena *n* assignation *f* à comparaître; * *vt* assigner.

subscribe *vi* souscrire; * *vt* apposer; signer.

subscriber *n* souscripteur *m* -trice *f*.

subscription *n* souscription *f*.

subsequent *adj* ~ly *adv* ultérieur(ement).

subservient *adj* subordonné; utile.

subside *vi* s'affaisser, baisser.

subsidence *n* affaissement *m*.

subsidiary *adj* subsidiaire.

subsidize *vt* subventionner, fournir des subsides à.

subsidy *n* subvention *f*; subside *m*.

subsist *vi* subsister; exister.

subsistence *n* existence *f*; subsistance *f*.

substance *n* substance *f*; fond *m*; essentiel *m*.

substantial *adj* considérable; réel, substantiel; solide; ~ly *adv* considérablement.

substantiate *vt* justifier.

substantive *n* substantif *m*.

substitute *vt* substituer; * *n* remplaçant *m* -e *f*.

substitution *n* substitution *f*.

substratum *n* substrat *m*.

subterfuge *n* subterfuge *m*; faux-fuyant *m*.

subterranean *adj* souterrain.

subtitle *n* sous-titre *m*.

subtle *adj* subtile.

subtlety *n* subtilité *f*.

subtly *adv* subtilement.

subtract *vt* (*math*) soustraire.

suburb *n* banlieue *f*.

suburban *adj* de banlieue.

subversion *n* subversion *f*.

subversive *adj* subversif.

subvert *vt* subvertir, renverser.

subway *n* (US) métro *m*.

succeed *vi* réussir; succéder; avoir du succès; * *vt* succéder à, suivre.

success n succès m.

successful adj couronné de succès, qui réussit; ~ly adv avec succès.

succession n succession f.

successive adj successif; ~ly adv successivement.

successor n successeur m.

succinct adj succinct, concis; ~ly adv succinctement.

succulent adj succulent.

succumb vi succomber.

such adj tel, pareil; ~ as tel que.

suck vt vi sucer; vi téter.

suckle vt allaiter.

suckling n nourrisson m.

suction n succion f.

sudden adj ~ly adv soudain (ement), subit(ement).

suddenness n soudaineté f.

suds npl mousse de savon f.

sue vt poursuivre en justice; supplier.

suede n daim m.

suet n graisse de rognon f de bœuf.

suffer vt souffrir, subir; tolérer, endurer; * vi souffrir.

suffering n souffrance f; douleur f.

suffice vi suffire, être suffisant.

sufficiency n quantité suffisante f; aisance f.

sufficient adj suffisant; ~ly adv suffisamment.

suffocate vt vi étouffer.

suffocation n suffocation f.

suffrage n suffrage, vote m.

suffuse vt baigner, se répandre sur.

sugar n sucre m; * vt sucrer.

sugar beet n betterave à sucre f.

sugar cane n canne à sucre f.

sugar loaf n pain de sucre m.

sugar plum n bonbon m.

sugary adj sucré.

suggest vt suggérer.

suggestion n suggestion f.

suicidal adj suicidaire.

suicide n suicide m; suicidé m -e f.

suit n procès m; pétition f; costume m; tailleur m; requête f; * vt convenir à; aller à; arranger, adapter.

suitable adj qui convient, approprié.

suitably adv convenablement.

suitcase n valise f.

suite n suite f; escorte f; mobilier m; cortège m.

suitor n plaideur m; prétendant m.

sulkiness *n* bouderie *f*.

sulky *adj* boudeur, maussade.

sullen *adj* maussade; sombre; **~ly** *adv* d'un air maussade; de mauvaise grâce.

sullenness *n* maussaderie *f*; silence *m*.

sulphur *n* soufre *m*.

sulphurous *adj* sulfureux.

sultan *n* sultan *m*.

sultana *n* sultane *f*; raisin sec *m*.

sultry *adj* étouffant; chaud.

sum *n* somme *f*; total *m*; **~ up** *vt* résumer; récapituler; * *vi* résumer.

summarily *adv* sommairement.

summary *adj n* résumé *m*.

summer *n* été *m*.

summerhouse *n* gloriette *f*, pavillon de jardin *m*.

summit *n* sommet *m*; cime *f*.

summon *vt* convoquer, citer à comparaître; sommer; (*mil*) sommer de se rendre.

summons *n* convocation *f*; sommation *f*.

sumptuous *adj* somptueux; **~ly** *adv* somptueusement.

sun *n* soleil *m*.

sunbathe *vi* prendre un bain de soleil, se faire bronzer.

sunburnt *adj* bronzé, hâlé.

Sunday *n* dimanche *m*.

sundial *n* cadran solaire *m*.

sundry *adj* divers, différent.

sunflower *n* tournesol *m*.

sunglasses *npl* lunettes de soleil *fpl*.

sunless *adj* sans soleil.

sunlight *n* lumière du soleil *f*.

sunny *adj* ensoleillé; radieux.

sunrise *n* lever de soleil *m*.

sun roof *n* toit ouvrant *m*.

sunset *n* coucher de soleil *m*.

sunshade *n* parasol *m*.

sunshine *n* (lumière du) soleil *m*; ensoleillement *m*.

sunstroke *n* insolation *f*.

suntan *n* bronzage *m*.

suntan oil *n* huile solaire *f*.

super *adj* (*fam*) sensationnel.

superannuated *adj* en retraite.

superannuation *n* retraite, pension de retraite *f*.

superb *adj* **~ly** *adv* superbe(ment).

supercargo *n* (*mar*) subrécargue *m*.

supercilious *adj* hautain, dédaigneux; **~ly** *adv* avec dédain.

superficial *adj* **~ly** *adv* superficiel(lement).

superfluity *n* surabondance, superfluité *f*.

superfluous *adj* superflu.

superhuman *adj* surhumain.

superintendent *n* directeur *m* -trice *f*.

superior *adj n* supérieur *m* -e *f*.

superiority *n* supériorité *f*.

superlative *adj n* superlatif *m*; ~ly *adv* extrêmement, au suprême degré.

supermarket *n* supermarché *m*.

supernatural *n* surnaturel.

supernumerary *adj* surnuméraire.

superpower *n* superpuissance *f*.

supersede *vt* remplacer; supplanter.

supersonic *adj* supersonique.

superstition *n* superstition *f*.

superstitious *adj* superstitieux; ~ly *adv* superstitieusement.

superstructure *n* superstructure *f*.

supertanker *n* gros pétrolier, supertanker *m*.

supervene *vi* survenir.

supervise *vt* surveiller, superviser.

supervision *n* surveillance *f*.

supervisor *n* surveillant *m* -e *f*.

supine *adj* couché, étendu sur le dos; indolent.

supper *n* dîner *m*.

supplant *vt* supplanter.

supple *adj* souple, flexible; obséquieux.

supplement *n* supplément *m*.

supplementary *adj* supplémentaire.

suppleness *n* souplesse *f*.

suppli(c)ant *n* suppliant *m* -e *f*.

supplicate *vt* supplier.

supplication *n* supplique, supplication *f*.

supplier *n* fournisseur *m*.

supply *vt* fournir, approvisionner; suppléer à, remédier à; * *n* approvisionnement *m*; provision *f*.

support *vt* soutenir; supporter, appuyer; * *n* appui *m*.

supportable *adj* supportable.

supporter *n* partisan *m*; supporter *m*, adepte *mf*.

suppose *vt vi* supposer.

supposition *n* supposition *f*.

suppress *vt* supprimer.

suppression *n* suppression *f*.

supremacy *n* suprématie *f*.

supreme *adj* ~ly *adv* suprême(ment).

surcharge *vt* surcharger; * *n* surtaxe *f*.

sure *adj* sûr, certain; infaillible; **to be ~** certainement; **~ly** *adv* sûrement, certainement, sans doute.

sureness *n* certitude, sûreté *f*.

surety *n* certitude *f*; caution *f*.

surf *n* (*mar*) ressac *m*.

surface *n* surface *f*; * *vt* revêtir; * *vi* remonter à la surface.

surfboard *n* planche (de surf) *f*.

surfeit *n* excès *m*.

surge *n* vague, montée *f*; * *vi* déferler.

surgeon *n* chirurgien *m*.

surgery *n* chirurgie *m*.

surgical *adj* chirurgical.

surliness *n* air revêche, bourru *m*.

surly *adj* revêche, bourru.

surmise *vt* conjecturer; * *n* conjecture *f*.

surmount *vt* surmonter.

surmountable *adj* surmontable.

surname *n* nom de famille *m*.

surpass *vt* surpasser, dépasser.

surpassing *adj* sans pareil, incomparable.

surplice *n* surplis *m*.

surplus *n* excédent *m*; surplus *m*; * *adj* en surplus.

surprise *vt* surprendre; * *n* surprise *f*.

surprising *adj* surprenant.

surrender *vt* rendre; céder; * *vi* se rendre; * *n* reddition *f*.

surreptitious *adj* **~ly** *adv* subreptice(ment).

surrogate *vt* remplacer; * *n* substitut *m*.

surrogate mother *n* mère porteuse *f*.

surround *vt* entourer, cerner, encercler.

survey *vt* examiner, inspecter; faire le relevé de; * *n* enquête *f*; relevé (des plans) *m*.

survive *vi* survivre; * *vt* survivre à.

survivor *n* survivant *m* -e *f*.

susceptibility *n* sensibilité *f*.

susceptible *adj* sensible.

suspect *vt* soupçonner; * *n* suspect *m* -e *f*.

suspend *vt* suspendre.

suspense *n* incertitude *f*; suspense *m*.

suspension *n* suspension *f*.

suspension bridge *n* pont suspendu *m*.

suspicion *n* soupçon *m*.

suspicious *adj* soupçonneux; ~ly *adv* soupçonneusement.

suspiciousness *n* caractère soupçonneux *m*.

sustain *vt* soutenir, supporter, maintenir; subir.

sustenance *n* (moyens de) subsistance *f*.

suture *n* suture *f*.

swab *n* tampon *m*; prélèvement *m*.

swaddle *vt* emmailloter.

swaddling clothes *npl* langes *mpl*.

swagger *vi* plastronner.

swallow *n* hirondelle *f*; * *vt* avaler.

swamp *n* marais *m*.

swampy *adj* marécageux.

swan *n* cygne *m*.

swap *vt* échanger; * *n* échange *m*.

swarm *n* essaim *m*; grouillement *m*; nuée *f*; * *vi* fourmiller; grouiller de monde; pulluler.

swarthy *adj* basané.

swarthiness *n* teint basané *m*.

swashbuckling *adj* fanfaron.

swath *n* andain *m*.

swathe *vt* emmailloter; * *n* bande *f*.

sway *vt* balancer; * *vi* se balancer, osciller; * *n* balancement *m*; emprise, domination, puissance *f*.

swear *vt* jurer; faire prêter serment; * *vi* jurer.

sweat *n* sueur *f*; * *vi* suer, transpirer.

sweater, sweatshirt *n* pullover *m*.

sweep *vt* balayer; ramoner; * *vi* s'étendre; avancer rapidement, majestueusement; * *n* coup de balai *m*; grand geste *m*; champ *m*.

sweeping *adj* rapide; ~s *pl* balayures *fpl*.

sweepstake *n* sweepstake *m*.

sweet *adj* sucré, doux, agréable; suave; gentil; mélodieux; adorable; * *adv* doux; sucré; * *n* bonbon *m*.

sweetbread *n* ris de veau *m*.

sweeten *vt* sucrer; adoucir; assainir; purifier.

sweetener *n* édulcorant *m*.

sweetheart *n* petit(e) ami(e) *m(f)*; chéri *m* -e *f*.

sweetmeats *npl* sucreries *fpl*.

sweetness *n* goût sucré *m*, douceur *f*.

swell *vi* gonfler; enfler; augmenter; * *vt* gonfler,

enfler, grossir; * *n* houle *f*;
* *adj* (*fam*) génial, épatant.

swelling *n* gonflement *m*;
boursouflure, tuméfaction *f*.

swelter *vi* étouffer de
chaleur.

swerve *vi* faire un écart; * *vt*
dévier.

swift *adj* rapide, prompt, vif;
* *n* martinet *m*.

swiftly *adv* rapidement.

swiftness *n* rapidité, promptitude *f*.

swill *vt* boire avidemment; *
n pâtée *f*.

swim *vi* nager; * *vt* traverser
à la nage; * *n* baignade *f*.

swimming *n* natation *f*, nage
f; vertige *m*.

swimming pool *n* piscine *f*.

swimsuit *n* maillot de bain
m.

swindle *vt* escroquer.

swindler *n* escroc *m*.

swine *n* pourceau, porc *m*.

swing *vi* se balancer, osciller;
virer; * *vt* balancer; faire
tourner; influencer; * *n*
balancement *m*; rythme *m*.

swinging *adj* (*fam*) rythmé.

swinging door *n* porte
battante *f*.

swirl *n* tourbillon.

switch *n* baguette *f*;
interrupteur *m*; (*rail*)
aiguille *f*; * *vt* changer de;
~ **off** éteindre; ~ **on**
allumer.

switchboard *n* standard
(téléphonique) *m*.

swivel *vt* faire pivoter.

swoon *vi* s'évanouir; * *n*
évanouissement *m*,
défaillance *f*.

swoop *vi* fondre sur; * *n*
descente en piqué *f*;
descente, rafle *f*; **in one** ~
d'un seul coup.

sword *n* épée *f*.

swordfish *n* espadon *m*.

swordsman *n* tireur d'épée
m.

sycamore *n* sycomore *m*.

sycophant *n* sycophante *mf*.

syllabic *adj* syllabique.

syllable *n* syllabe *f*.

syllabus *n* programme *m*
(d'un cours).

syllogism *n* syllogisme *m*.

sylph *n* sylphe *m*; sylphide *f*.

symbol *n* symbole *m*.

symbolic(al) *adj* symbolique.

symbolize *vt* symboliser.

symmetrical *adj* ~**ly** *adv*
symétrique(ment).

symmetry *n* symétrie *f*.

sympathetic *adj* compatissant;
   ~**ally** *adv* avec compassion.
sympathize *vi* compatir.
sympathy *n* compassion *f*.
symphony *n* symphonie *f*.
symptom *n* symptôme *m*.
synagogue *n* synagogue *f*.
synchronism *n* synchronisme
   m.
syndicate *n* syndicat *m*.
syndrome *n* syndrome *m*.
synod *n* synode *m*.
synonym *n* synonyme *m*.
synonymous *adj* synonyme;

~**ly** *adv* de façon synonyme.
synopsis *n* synopsis *f*; résumé
   m.
synoptical *adj* synoptique.
syntax *n* syntaxe *f*.
synthesis *n* synthèse *f*.
syringe *n* seringue *f*; * *vt*
   seringuer.
system *n* système *m*.
systematic *adj* ~**ally** *adv*
   systématique(ment).
systems analyst *n* analyste de
   systèmes *mf*.

T

tab *n* patte *f*; étiquette *f*.

tabernacle *n* tabernacle *m*.

table *n* table *f*; * *vt* mettre en forme de tableau; ajourner; ~ d'hôte repas à prix fixe *m*.

tablecloth *n* nappe *f*.

tablespoon *n* grande cuiller *f*.

tablet *n* tablette *f*; comprimé *m*.

table tennis *n* ping-pong *m*.

taboo *adj n* tabou *m*; * *vt* proscrire.

tabular *adj* tabulaire.

tacit *adj* ~ly *adv* tacite(ment).

taciturn *adj* taciturne.

tack *n* broquette *f*; bordée *f*; * *vt* clouer; * *vi* tirer des bordées.

tackle *n* attirail, équipement, matériel *m*; plaquage *m*; (*mar*) appareil de levage *m*, apparaux *mpl*.

tactician *n* tacticien *m*.

tactics *npl* tactique *f*.

tadpole *n* têtard *m*.

taffeta *n* taffetas *m*.

tag *n* ferret *m*; étiquette *f*; * *vt* ferrer.

tail *n* queue *f*; basque *f*; * *vt* suivre, filer.

tailgate *n* hayon arrière *m*.

tailor *n* tailleur *m*.

tailoring *n* métier de tailleur *m*.

tailor-made *adj* fait sur mesure.

tailwind *n* vent arrière *m*.

taint *vt* infecter, polluer; vicier; * *n* tache, souillure *f*.

tainted *adj* infecté; souillé.

take *vt* prendre, saisir; apporter, emporter; conduire; enlever, retirer; passer; * *vi* prendre; ~ away *vt* enlever; emporter; ~ back *vt* reprendre; raccompagner; ~ down *vt* descendre; prendre (notes); ~ in *vt* saisir, comprendre; recevoir; ~ off *vi* décoller; *vt* enlever; imiter; ~ on *vt* accepter; engager; s'attaquer à;

~ **out** *vt* sortir; enlever; ~ **to** *vt* se prendre d'amitié pour; ~ **up** *vt* monter; occuper; se mettre à; * *n* prise *f*.

takeoff *n* décollage *m*.

takeover *n* prise *f* de contrôle.

takings *npl* recette *f*.

talent *n* talent *m*; don *m*.

talented *adj* talentueux.

talisman *n* talisman *m*.

talk *vi* parler, bavarder; causer; * *n* conversation *f*; discussion *f*; entretien *m*.

talkative *adj* loquace.

talk show *n* débat télévisé *m*.

tall *adj* grand, élevé; incroyable.

tally *vi* correspondre.

talon *n* serre *f*.

tambourine *n* tambourin *m*.

tame *adj* apprivoisé, domestiqué; **~ly** *adv* docilement; fadement; * *vt* apprivoiser, domestiquer.

tameness *n* nature apprivoisée *f*; soumission *f*.

tamper *vi* tripoter.

tampon *n* tampon *m*.

tan *vt vi* bronzer; * *n* bronzage *m*.

tang *n* saveur forte *f*.

tangent *n* tangente *f*.

tangerine *n* mandarine *f*.

tangible *adj* tangible.

tangle *vt* enchevêtrer, embrouiller.

tank *n* réservoir *m*; citerne *f*.

tanker *n* pétrolier *m*; camion-citerne *m*.

tanned *adj* bronzé.

tantalizing *adj* tentant.

tantamount *adj* équivalent (à).

tantrum *n* accès de colère *m*.

tap *vt* taper doucement; exploiter; inciser; * *n* petite tape *f*; robinet *m*.

tape *n* ruban *m*; * *vt* enregistrer.

tape measure *n* mètre à ruban *m*.

taper *n* cierge *m*.

tape recorder *n* magnétophone *m*.

tapestry *n* tapisserie *f*.

tar *n* goudron *m*.

target *n* cible *f*.

tariff *n* tarif *m*.

tarmac *n* piste *f* (d'aéroport).

tarnish *vt* ternir.

tarpaulin *n* bâche (goudronnée) *f*.

tarragon *n* (*bot*) estragon *m*.

tart *adj* acidulé; * *n* tarte, tartelette *f*.

tartar *n* tartre *m*.

task *n* tâche *f*.

tassel *n* gland *m* (décoration).

taste *n* goût *m*; saveur *f*; pincée *f*; penchant *m*; * *vt* sentir le goût de; goûter à; déguster; savourer; * *vi* avoir du goût.

tasteful *adj* de bon goût; ~ly *adv* avec goût.

tasteless *adj* insipide, sans goût.

tasty *adj* savoureux.

tattoo *n* tatouage *m*; * *vt* tatouer.

taunt *vt* railler; accabler de sarcasmes; * *n* raillerie *f*, sarcasme *m*.

Taurus *n* Taureau *m* (signe du zodiaque).

taut *adj* tendu.

tautological *adj* tautologique.

tautology *n* tautologie *f*.

tawdry *adj* tapageur, voyant, clinquant.

tax *n* impôt *m*; contribution *f*; * *vt* imposer; mettre à l'épreuve.

taxable *adj* imposable.

taxation *n* imposition *f*.

tax collector *n* percepteur *m*.

tax-free *adj* exonéré d'impôts.

taxi *n* taxi *m*; * *vi* rouler sur la piste.

taxi driver *n* chauffeur de taxi *m*.

taxi stand *n* station de taxis *f*.

tax payer *n* contribuable *mf*.

tax relief *n* dégrèvement fiscal *m*.

tax return *n* déclaration d'impôts *f*.

tea *n* thé *m*.

teach *vt* enseigner, apprendre; * *vi* enseigner.

teacher *n* professeur *m*; instituteur *m* -trice *f*.

teaching *n* enseignement *m*.

teacup *n* tasse à thé *f*.

teak *n* teck *m*.

team *n* équipe *f*.

teamster *n* (US) routier *m*.

teamwork *n* travail d'équipe *m*.

teapot *n* théière *f*.

tear *vt* déchirer; ~ up mettre en morceaux.

tear *n* larme *f*.

tearful *adj* larmoyant; ~ly *adv* en pleurant.

tear gas *n* gaz lacrymogène *m*.

tease *vt* taquiner.

tea-service, tea-set *n* service à thé *m*.

teaspoon *n* petite cuiller *f*.

teat *n* tétine *f*, mamelon *m*.

technical *adj* technique.

technicality *n* technicité *f*.

technician *n* technicien *m* -ne *f*.

technique *n* technique *f*.

technological *adj* technologique.

technology *n* technologie *f*.

teddy (bear) *n* ours en peluche *m*.

tedious *adj* ennuyeux, fastidieux; ~ly *adv* fastidieusement.

tedium *n* ennui, manque d'intérêt *m*.

teem *vi* grouiller (de).

teenage *adj* adolescent; ~r *n* adolescent(e) *m(f)*.

teens *npl* adolescence (de 13 à 20 ans) *f*.

tee-shirt *n* T-shirt *m*.

teeth *npl* de tooth.

teethe *vi* faire ses premières dents.

teetotal *adj* antialcoolique, qui ne boit jamais d'alcool.

teetotaller *n* personne qui ne boit jamais d'alcool *f*.

telegram *n* télégramme *m*.

telegraph *n* télégraphe *m*.

telegraphic *adj* télégraphique.

telegraphy *n* télégraphie *f*.

telepathy *n* télépathie *f*.

telephone *n* téléphone *m*.

telephone booth *n* cabine téléphonique *f*.

telephone call *n* appel téléphonique *m*.

telephone directory *n* annuaire *m*.

telephone number *n* numéro de téléphone *m*.

telescope *n* télescope *m*.

telescopic *adj* télescopique.

televise *vt* téléviser.

television *n* télévision *f*.

television set *n* téléviseur, poste de télévision *m*.

telex *n* télex *m*; *vt* envoyer par télex.

tell *vt* dire; raconter.

teller *n* (banque) caissier *m* -ière *f*.

telling *adj* révélateur.

telltale *adj* dénonciateur.

temper *vt* tempérer, modérer; * *n* colère *f*.

temperament *n* tempérament *m*.

temperance *n* tempérance, modération *f*.

temperate *adj* tempéré, modéré, mesuré.

temperature *n* température *f*.

tempest *n* tempête *f*.

tempestuous *adj* de tempête.

template *n* gabarit *m*.

temple *n* temple *m*; tempe *f*.

temporarily *adv* temporairement.

temporary *adj* temporaire.

tempt *vt* tenter.

temptation *n* tentation *f.*

tempting *adj* tentant.

ten *adj n* dix *m.*

tenable *adj* défendable.

tenacious *adj* tenace, ~ly *adv* avec ténacité.

tenacity *n* ténacité *f.*

tenancy *n* location *f.*

tenant *n* locataire *mf.*

tend *vt* garder, surveiller; * *vi* avoir tendance (à).

tendency *n* tendance *f.*

tender *adj* tendre, délicat; sensible; ~ly *adv* tendrement; * *n* offre *f*; * *vt* offrir.

tenderness *n* tendresse *f.*

tendon *n* tendon *m.*

tenement *n* appartement *m.*

tenet *n* doctrine *f*; principe *m.*

tennis court *n* court *ou* terrain de tennis *m.*

tennis player *n* joueur(-euse) de tennis *m(f).*

tennis racket *n* raquette de tennis *f.*

tennis shoes *npl* chaussures de tennis *fpl.*

tenor *n* (*mus*) ténor *m*; sens *m*; substance *f.*

tense *adj* tendu; * *n* (*gr*) temps *m.*

tension *n* tension *f.*

tent *n* tente *f.*

tentacle *n* tentacule *m.*

tentative *adj* timide, hésitant; ~ly *adv* à titre d'essai.

tenth *adj n* dixième *mf.*

tenuous *adj* ténu.

tenure *n* titularisation *f.*

tepid *adj* tiède.

term *n* terme *m*; trimestre *m*; mot *m*; condition, clause *f*; * *vt* appeler, nommer.

terminal *adj* terminal; * *n* aérogare *f*; terminal *m.*

terminate *vt* terminer.

termination *n* fin, conclusion *f.*

terrace *n* terrace *f.*

terrain *n* (*mil*) terrain *m.*

terrestrial *adj* terrestre.

terrible *adj* terrible.

terribly *adv* terriblement.

terrier *n* terrier *m* (chien).

terrific *adj* terrifiant; fantastique.

terrify *vt* terrifier, épouvanter.

territorial *adj* territorial.

territory *n* territoire *m.*

terror *n* terreur *f.*

terrorism *n* terrorisme *m.*

terrorist *n* terroriste *mf.*

terrorize *vt* terroriser.

terse *adj* concis, net.

test *n* essai *m*; épreuve *f*; * *vt* essayer; examiner.

testament *n* testament *m*.

tester *n* contrôleur *m* -euse *f*.

testicles *npl* testicules *mpl*.

testify *vt* témoigner, déclarer sous serment.

testimonial *n* certificat *m*.

testimony *n* témoignage *m*.

test pilot *n* pilote d'essai *m*.

test tube *n* éprouvette *f*.

testy *adj* irritable.

tetanus *n* tétanos *m*.

tether *vt* attacher.

text *n* texte *m*.

textbook *n* manuel *m*.

textiles *npl* textile *m*.

textual *adj* textuel.

texture *n* texture *f*; (*med*) tissu *m*.

than *adv* que; de.

thank *vt* remercier, dire merci à.

thankful *adj* reconnaissant; ~**ly** *adv* avec reconnaissance.

thankfulness *n* reconnaissance *f*.

thankless *adj* ingrat.

thanks *npl* remerciement(s) *m*(*pl*).

thanksgiving *n* action de grâce *f*.

that *pn* cela, ça, ce; qui, que; celui-là; * *conj* que; afin que; **so** ~ pour que.

thatch *n* chaume *m*; * *vt* couvrir de chaume.

thaw *n* dégel *m*; * *vi* fondre, dégeler.

the *art* le, la, l', les.

theatre *n* théâtre *m*.

theatre-goer *n* habitué(e) du théâtre *m*(*f*).

theatrical *adj* théâtral.

theft *n* vol *m*.

their *pn* leur(s); ~**s** le leur; la leur; les leurs; à elles; à eux.

them *pn* les; leur.

theme *n* thème *m*.

themselves *pn pl* eux-mêmes *mpl*, elles-mêmes *fpl*; se.

then *adv* alors, à cette époque-là; ensuite; en ce cas; * *conj* donc; en ce cas; * *adj* d'alors; **now and** ~ de temps en temps.

theological *adj* théologique.

theologian *n* théologien *m* -ne *f*.

theology *n* théologie *f*.

theorem *n* théorème *m*.

theoretical *adj* ~**ly** *adv* théorique(ment).

theorize *vt* théoriser.

theorist *n* théoricien *m* -ne *f*.

theory *n* théorie *f*.

therapeutics *n* thérapeutique *f*.

therapist *n* thérapeute *mf*.

therapy *n* thérapie *f*.

there *adv* y, là.

thereabout(s) *adv* par là, près de là.

thereafter *adv* par la suite; après.

thereby *adv* de cette façon.

therefore *adv* donc, par conséquent.

thermal *adj* thermal.

thermal printer *n* imprimante thermique *f*.

thermometer *n* thermomètre *m*.

thermostat *n* thermostat *m*.

thesaurus *n* trésor *m*; dictionnaire de synonymes *m*.

these *pn pl* ceux-ci, celles-ci.

thesis *n* thèse *f*.

they *pn pl* ils, elles.

thick *adj* épais, gros; dense; obtus.

thicken *vi* (s')épaissir, grossir.

thicket *n* fourré *m*.

thickness *n* épaisseur *f*.

thickset *adj* trapu; râblé.

thick-skinned *adj* endurci, blindé.

thief *n* voleur *m* -euse *f*.

thigh *n* cuisse *f*.

thimble *n* dé (à coudre) *m*.

thin *adj* mince, fin, maigre; clair; * *vt* amincir; délayer; éclaircir.

thing *n* chose *f*; objet *m*; truc *m*.

think *vi* penser, réfléchir, imaginer; * *vt* penser, croire, juger; ~ **over** *vt* réfléchir à; ~ **up** *vt* imaginer.

thinker *n* penseur *m* -euse *f*.

thinking *n* pensée *f*; réflexion *f*; opinion *f*.

third *adj* troisième; * *n* troisième *mf*; tiers *m*; ~**ly** *adv* troisièmement.

third rate *adj* médiocre, de mauvaise qualité.

thirst *n* soif *f*.

thirsty *adj* assoiffé.

thirteen *adj n* treize *m*.

thirteenth *adj n* treizième *mf*.

thirtieth *adj n* trentième *mf*.

thirty *adj n* trente *m*.

this *adj* ce, cet, cette, ces; * *pn* ceci, ce.

thistle *n* chardon *m*.

thorn *n* épine *f*; aubépine *f*.

thorny *adj* épineux.

thorough *adj* consciencieux,

approfondi; ~ly *adv* minutieusement, à fond.

thoroughbred *adj* pur-sang, de race.

thoroughfare *n* rue, artère *f*.

those *pn pl* ceux-là, celles-la; * *adj* ces, ces... là.

though *conj* bien que, malgré le fait que; * *adv* pourtant.

thought *n* pensée, réflexion *f*; opinion *f*; intention *f*.

thoughtful *adj* pensif.

thoughtless *adj* étourdi; irréfléchi; ~ly *adv* étourdiment, à la légère.

thousand *adj n* mille *m*.

thousandth *adj n* millième *mf*.

thrash *vt* battre; rouer de coups.

thread *n* fil *m*; filetage *m*; * *vt* enfiler.

threadbare *adj* râpé, élimé.

threat *n* menace *f*.

threaten *vt* menacer.

three *adj n* trois *m*.

three-dimensional *adj* à trois dimensions, tridimensionnel.

three-ply *adj* à trois fils *ou* épaisseurs.

threshold *n* seuil *m*.

thrifty *adj* économe.

thrill *vt* faire frissonner; * *n* frisson *m*.

thriller *n* film *ou* roman à suspense *m*.

thrive *vi* prospérer; bien se développer.

throat *n* gorge *f*.

throb *vi* palpiter; vibrer; lanciner.

throne *n* trône *m*.

throng *n* foule *f*; * *vi* affluer.

throttle *n* accélérateur *m*; * *vt* étrangler.

through *prep* à travers; pendant; par, grâce à; * *adj* direct; * *adv* complètement.

throughout *prep* partout dans; * *adv* partout.

throw *vt* jeter, lancer, projeter; * *n* jet *m*; lancement *m*; ~ **away** *vt* jeter; ~ **off** *vt* rejeter; ~ **out** *vt* jeter dehors; ~ **up** *vt vi* vomir.

throwaway *adj* jetable.

thru (US) = **through**.

thrush *n* grive *f*.

thrust *vt* pousser violemment; enfoncer; * *n* poussée *f*.

thud *n* bruit sourd *m*.

thug *n* voyou *m*.

thumb *n* pouce *m*.

thumbtack *n* punaise *f*.

thump *n* coup de poing *m*; *

vi frapper, cogner; * *vt* cogner à.

thunder *n* tonnerre *m*; * *vi* tonner.

thunderbolt *n* foudre *f*.

thunderclap *n* coup de tonnerre *m*.

thunderstorm *n* orage *m*.

thundery *adj* orageux.

Thursday *n* jeudi *m*.

thus *adv* ainsi, de cette manière.

thwart *vt* contrecarrer.

thyme *n* (*bot*) thym *m*.

thyroid *n* thyroïde *f*.

tiara *n* tiare *f*.

tic *n* tic *m*.

tick *n* tic-tac *m*; instant *m*; * *vt* cocher; ~ **over** *vi* tourner au ralenti; aller doucement.

ticket *n* billet, ticket *m*; étiquette *f*; carte *f*.

ticket collector *n* (*rail*) contrôleur *m* -euse *f*.

ticket office *n* guichet *m*.

tickle *vt* chatouiller.

ticklish *adj* chatouilleux.

tidal *adj* (*mar*) de la marée.

tidal wave *n* raz-de-marée *m*.

tide *n* marée *f*; (*fig*) afflux *m*, cours *m*.

tidy *adj* rangé, en ordre; ordonné; soigné.

tie *vt* attacher, nouer; * *vi* se nouer; ~ **up** *vt* ficeler; attacher; amarrer; conclure; * *n* attache *f*; lacet *m*; égalité *f*.

tier *n* gradin *m*; étage *m*.

tiger *n* tigre *m*.

tight *adj* raide, tendu; serré; hermétique; * *adv* très fort.

tighten *vt* (re)serrer, tendre.

tightfisted *adj* avare.

tightly *adv* très fort.

tightrope *n* corde raide *f*.

tigress *n* tigresse *f*.

tile *n* tuile *f*; carreau *m*; * *vt* couvrir de tuiles.

tiled *adj* en tuiles, carrelé.

till *n* caisse *f*; * *vt* labourer, cultiver.

tiller *n* barre du gouvernail *f*.

tilt *vt* pencher; * *vi* s'incliner.

timber *n* bois de construction *m*; arbres *mpl*.

time *n* temps *m*; période *f*; heure *f*; moment *m*; (*mus*) mesure *f*; in ~ à temps; from ~ to ~ de temps en temps; * *vt* fixer; chronométrer.

time bomb *n* bombe à retardement *f*.

time lag *n* décalage *m*.

timeless *adj* éternel.

timely *adj* opportun.

time off *n* temps libre *m*.

timer *n* sablier *m*; minuteur *m*.

time scale *n* durée *f*.

time zone *n* fuseau horaire *m*.

timid *adj* timide, timoré; ~ly *adv* timidement.

timidity *n* timidité *f*.

timing *n* chronométrage *m*.

tin *n* étain *m*; boîte (de conserve) *f*.

tinfoil *n* papier d'aluminium *m*.

tinge *n* teinte *f*.

tingle *vi* picoter; vibrer, frissonner.

tingling *n* picotement *m*; frisson *m*.

tinker *n* rétameur *m*.

tinkle *vi* tinter.

tinplate *n* fer-blanc *m*.

tinsel *n* guirlande *f*.

tint *n* teinte *f*; * *vt* teinter.

tinted *adj* teinté; fumé.

tiny *adj* minuscule, tout petit.

tip *n* pointe *f*, bout *m*; pourboire *m*; conseil, tuyau *m*; * *vt* donner un pourboire à; pencher; effleurer.

tip-off *n* avertissement *m*.

tipsy *adj* gai, éméché.

tiptop *adj* excellent, de premier ordre.

tirade *n* diatribe *f*.

tire *n* (US) pneu *m*; * *vt* fatiguer; * *vi* se fatiguer; se lasser.

tireless *adj* infatigable.

tire pressure *n* (US) pression *f* des pneus.

tiresome *adj* ennuyeux, fatigant.

tiring *adj* fatigant.

tissue *n* (US) tissu *m*(*bot*); mouchoir *m* en papier.

tissue paper *n* papier *m* de soie.

titbit *n* friandise *f*; bon morceau *m*.

titillate *vt* titiller.

title *n* titre *m*.

title deed *n* titre de propriété *m*.

title page *n* page de titre *f*.

titter *vi* rire sottement; * *n* petit rire sot *m*.

titular *adj* titulaire.

to *prep* à; vers; en; chez; moins; de.

toad *n* crapaud *m*.

toadstool *n* (*bot*) champignon vénéneux *m*.

toast *vt* (faire) griller; porter

un toast à la santé de; * *n* toast *m*.

toaster *n* grille-pain *m invar*.

tobacco *n* tabac *m*.

tobacconist *n* marchand(e) de tabac *m(f)*.

tobacco pouch *n* blague à tabac *f*.

tobacco shop *n* bureau de tabac *m*.

toboggan *n* toboggan *m*, luge *f*.

today *adv* aujourd'hui.

toddler *n* enfant qui commence à marcher *m*.

toddy *n* grog *m*.

toe *n* orteil *m*; pointe *f*.

together *adv* ensemble; en même temps.

toil *vi* travailler dur, peiner; se donner du mal; * *n* dur travail *m*; labeur *m*; peine *f*.

toilet *n* toilette *f*; toilettes *fpl*; * *adj* de toilette.

toilet bag *n* trousse de toilette *f*.

toilet bowl *n* cuvette des toilettes *f*.

toilet paper *n* papier hygiénique *m*.

toiletries *npl* articles de toilette *mpl*.

token *n* signe *m*; marque *f*; souvenir *m*; bon *m*; jeton *m*.

tolerable *adj* tolérable; passable.

tolerance *n* tolérance *f*.

tolerant *adj* tolérant.

tolerate *vt* tolérer.

toll *n* péage *m*; nombre de victimes *m*; * *vi* sonner le glas.

tomato *n* tomate *f*.

tomb *n* tombeau *m*; tombe *f*.

tomboy *n* garçon manqué *m*.

tombstone *n* pierre tombale *f*.

tomcat *n* matou *m*.

tomorrow *adv, n* demain *m*.

ton *n* tonne *f*.

tone *n* ton *m*; tonalité *f*; * *vi* s'harmoniser; ~ **down** *vt* adoucir.

tone-deaf *adj* qui n'a pas l'oreille musicale.

tongs *npl* pinces *fpl*.

tongue *n* langue *f*.

tongue-tied *adj* muet.

tongue-twister *n* phrase difficile à prononcer *f*.

tonic *n* (*med*) tonique *m*.

tonight *adv, n* ce soir (*m*).

tonnage *n* tonnage *m*.

tonsil *n* amygdale *f*.

tonsure *n* tonsure *f.*

too *adv* aussi; trop.

tool *n* outil *m*; ustensile *m.*

tool box *n* caisse à outils *f.*

toot *vi* klaxonner.

tooth *n* dent *f.*

toothache *n* rage de dents *f.*

toothbrush *n* brosse à dents *f.*

toothless *adj* édenté.

toothpaste *n* dentifrice *m.*

toothpick *n* cure-dent *m.*

top *n* sommet *m*, cime *f*; haut *m*; tête *f*; dessus *m*; couvercle *m*; étage supérieur *m*; * *adj* du haut; premier; * *vt* dépasser; être au sommet de; ~ **off** couronner.

topaz *n* topaze *f.*

top floor *n* dernier étage *m.*

top-heavy *adj* instable, déséquilibré.

topic *n* sujet *m*; ~**al** *adj* d'actualité.

topless *adj* torse nu, aux seins nus.

top-level *adj* au plus haut niveau.

topmost *adj* le plus haut.

topographic(al) *adj* topographique.

topography *n* topographie *f.*

topple *vt* renverser; * *vi* basculer.

top-secret *adj* ultra-secret.

topsy-turvy *adv* sens dessus dessous.

torch *n* torche *f.*

torment *vt* tourmenter; * *n* tourment *m.*

tornado *n* tornade *f.*

torrent *n* torrent *m.*

torrid *adj* torride.

tortoise *n* tortue *f.*

tortoiseshell *adj* en écaille de tortue.

tortuous *adj* tortueux, sinueux.

torture *n* torture *f*; * *vt* torturer.

toss *vt* lancer, jeter; agiter, secouer.

total *adj* total, global; ~**ly** *adv* totalement.

totalitarian *adj* totalitaire.

totality *n* totalité *f.*

totter *vi* chanceler.

touch *vt* toucher; ~ **on** effleurer; ~ **up** retoucher; * *n* toucher *m*; contact *m*; touche *f.*

touch-and-go *adj* incertain, précaire.

touchdown *n* atterrissage *m*; but *m.*

touched *adj* touché; timbré.

touching *adj* touchant, attendrissant.

touchstone *n* pierre de touche *f*.

touchwood *n* amadou *m*.

touchy *adj* susceptible.

tough *adj* dur; pénible; résistant; fort; * *n* dur *m*.

toughen *vt* durcir.

toupee *n* postiche *m*.

tour *n* voyage *m*; visite *f*; * *vt* visiter.

touring *n* tourisme *m*.

tourism *n* tourisme *m*.

tourist *n* touriste *mf*.

tourist office *n* office de tourisme *m*.

tournament *n* tournoi *m*.

tow *n* remorquage *m*; * *vt* remorquer.

toward(s) *prep* vers, dans la direction de; envers, à l'égard de.

towel *n* serviette *f*.

towelling *n* tissu éponge *m*.

towel rack *n* porte-serviette *m invar*.

tower *n* tour *f*.

towering *adj* imposant.

town *n* ville *f*.

town clerk *n* secrétaire de mairie *mf*.

town hall *n* mairie *f*.

towrope *n* câble de remorquage *m*.

toy *n* jouet *m*.

toyshop *n* magasin de jouets *m*.

trace *n* trace, piste *f*; * *vt* tracer, esquisser; retrouver.

track *n* trace *f*; empreinte *f*; chemin *m*; voie *f*; piste *f*; * *vt* suivre à la trace.

tracksuit *n* survêtement *m*.

tract *n* étendue *f*, région *f*; brochure *f*.

traction *n* traction *f*.

trade *n* commerce *m*, affaires *fpl*; échange *m*; métier *m*; * *vi* faire le commerce (de), commercer.

trade fair *n* foire commerciale *f*.

trademark *n* marque de fabrique *f*.

trade name *n* raison commerciale *f*.

trader *n* négociant *m* -e *f*.

tradesman *n* fournisseur, commerçant *m*.

trade(s) union *n* syndicat *m*.

trade unionist *n* syndicaliste *mf*.

trading *n* commerce *m*; * *adj* commercial.

tradition n tradition f

traditional adj traditionnel.

traffic n circulation f; négoce m; * vi faire le commerce (de).

traffic circle n (US) rond-point m.

traffic jam n embouteillage m.

trafficker n trafiquant m -e f.

traffic lights npl feux de signalisation mpl.

tragedy n tragédie f.

tragic adj ~ally adv tragique(ment).

tragicomedy n tragi-comédie f.

trail vt suivre la piste de; traîner; vi traîner; * n traînée f; trace f; queue f.

trailer n remorque f; caravane f; bande-annonce f.

train vt entraîner; former; * n train m; traîne f; file f.

trained adj qualifié; diplômé.

trainee n stagiaire mf.

trainer n entraîneur m.

training n formation f; entraînement m.

trait n trait m.

traitor n traître m.

tramp n clochard m -e f; (sl) putain f; * vi marcher d'un pas lourd; * vt piétiner.

trample vt piétiner.

trampoline n trampoline m.

trance n transe f; extase f.

tranquil adj tranquille.

tranquillize vt tranquilliser.

tranquillizer n tranquillisant m.

transact vt traiter.

transaction n transaction f; opération f.

transatlantic adj transatlantique.

transcend vt transcender, dépasser; surpasser.

transcription n transcription f; copie f.

transfer vt transférer, déplacer; * n transfert m; mutation f; décalcomanie f.

transform vt transformer.

transformation n transformation f.

transfusion n transfusion f.

transient adj transitoire, passager.

transit n transit m.

transition n transition f; passage m.

transitional adj de transition.

transitive adj transitif.

translate vt traduire.

translation *n* traduction *f*.

translator *n* traducteur *m* -trice *f*.

transmission *n* transmision *f*.

transmit *vt* transmettre.

transmitter *n* transmetteur *m*; émetteur *m*.

transparency *n* transparence *f*; diapositive *f*.

transparent *adj* transparent.

transpire *vi* transpirer; arriver.

transplant *vt* transplanter; * *n* transplantation *f*.

transport *vt* transporter; * *n* transport *m*.

transportation *n* moyen de transport *m*.

trap *n* piège *m*; * *vt* prendre au piège; bloquer.

trap door *n* trappe *f*.

trapeze *n* trapèze *m*.

trappings *npl* ornements *mpl*.

trash *n* camelote *f*; inepties *fpl*.

trash can *n* poubelle *f*.

trashy *adj* sans valeur, de mauvaise qualité.

travel *vi* voyager; * *vt* parcourir; * *n* voyage *m*.

travel agency *n* agence de voyages *f*.

travel agent *n* agent de voyages *m*.

traveller *n* voyageur *m* -euse *f*.

traveller's cheque *n* chèque de voyage *m*.

travelling *n* voyages *mpl*.

travel sickness *n* mal de mer/ de l'air *m*.

travesty *n* parodie *f*.

trawler *n* chalutier *m*.

tray *n* plateau *m*; tiroir *m*.

treacherous *adj* traître, perfide.

treachery *n* traîtrise *f*.

tread *vi* marcher; écraser; * *n* pas *m*; bruit de pas *m*; bande de roulement *f*.

treason *n* trahison *f*; high ~ haute trahison *f*.

treasure *n* trésor *m*; * *vt* conserver précieusement.

treasurer *n* trésorier *m* -ière *f*.

treat *vt* traiter; offrir; * *n* cadeau *m*; plaisir *m*.

treatise *n* traité *m*.

treatment *n* traitement *m*.

treaty *n* traité *m*.

treble *adj* triple; * *vt vi* tripler; * *n* (*mus*) soprano *m*.

treble clef *n* clef de sol *f*.

tree *n* arbre *m*.

trek *n* randonnée *f*.

trellis *n* treillis *m*.

tremble *vi* trembler.

trembling *n* tremblement *m*; frisson *m*.

tremendous *adj* terrible; énorme; formidable.

tremor *n* tremblement *m*.

trench *n* fossé *m*; (*mil*) tranchée *f*.

trend *n* tendance *f*; direction *f*; mode *f*.

trendy *adj* dernier cri.

trepidation *n* vive inquiétude *f*.

trespass *vt* transgresser, violer.

tress *n* boucle de cheveu *f*; ~es chevelure *f*.

trestle *n* tréteau, chevalet *m*.

trial *n* procès *m*; épreuve *f*; essai *m*; peine *f*.

triangle *n* triangle *m*.

triangular *adj* triangulaire.

tribal *adj* tribal.

tribe *n* tribu *f*.

tribulation *n* tribulation *f*.

tribunal *n* tribunal *m*.

tributary *adj n* tributaire *m*.

tribute *n* tribut *m*.

trice *n* instant *m*.

trick *n* ruse, astuce *f*, tour *m*; blague *f*; pli *m*; * *vt* attraper.

trickery *n* supercherie *f*.

trickle *vi* couler goutte à goutte; * *n* filet *m*.

tricky *adj* délicat; difficile.

tricycle *n* tricycle *m*.

trifle *n* bagatelle, vétille *f*; * *vi* jouer; badiner.

trifling *adj* futile, insignifiant.

trigger *n* gâchette *f*; ~ **off** *vt* déclencher.

trigonometry *n* trigonométrie *f*.

trill *n* trille *f*; * *vi* triller.

trim *adj* net, soigné; bien tenu; en parfait état; * *vt* arranger; tailler; orner.

trimmings *npl* ornements *mpl*.

Trinity *n* Trinité *f*.

trinket *n* bibelot *m*, babiole *f*; colifichet *m*.

trio *n* (*mus*) trio *m*.

trip *vt* faire trébucher; * *vi* trébucher; faire un faux pas; ~ **up** *vi* trébucher; *vt* faire trébucher; * *n* faux pas *m*; voyage *m*.

tripe *n* tripes *fpl*; bêtises *fpl*.

triple *adj* triple; * *vt vi* tripler.

triplets *npl* triplés *mpl*.

triplicate *n* copie en trois exemplaires *f*.

tripod n trépied m.

trite adj banal; usé.

triumph n triomphe m; * vi triompher.

triumphal adj triomphal.

triumphant adj triomphant; victorieux; ~ly adv triomphalement.

trivia npl futilités fpl.

trivial adj insignifiant, sans importance; ~ly adv banalement.

triviality n banalité f.

trolley n chariot m.

trombone n trombone m.

troop n bande f; ~s npl troupes fpl.

trooper n soldat de cavalerie m.

trophy n trophée m.

tropical adj tropical.

trot n trot m; * vi trotter.

trouble vt affliger; tourmenter; * n problème m; ennui m; difficulté f; affliction, peine f.

troubled adj inquiet; agité.

troublemaker n agitateur m -trice f.

troubleshooter n médiateur m.

troublesome adj pénible.

trough n abreuvoir m; auge f.

troupe n troupe f.

trousers npl pantalon m.

trout n truite f.

trowel n truelle f.

truce n trêve f.

truck n camion m; wagon m.

truck driver n routier m.

truck farm n jardin maraîcher m.

truculent adj brutal, agressif.

trudge vi marcher lourdement.

true adj vrai, véritable; sincère; exact.

truelove n bien-aimé m -e f.

truffle n truffe f.

truly adv vraiment; sincèrement.

trump n atout m.

trumpet n trompette f.

trunk n malle f, coffre m; trompe f.

truss n botte f; * vt botteler; trousser.

trust n confiance f; trust m; fidéicommis m; * vt avoir confiance en; confier à.

trusted adj de confiance.

trustee n fidéicommissaire m, curateur m -trice f.

trustful adj confiant.

trustily adv fidèlement.

trusting adj confiant.

trustworthy adj digne de confiance.

trusty *adj* fidèle, loyal; sûr.

truth *n* vérité *f*; in ~ en vérité.

truthful *adj* véridique; qui dit la vérité.

truthfulness *n* véracité *f*.

try *vt* essayer, tâcher, chercher à; expérimenter; mettre à l'épreuve; tenter; juger; * *vi* essayer; ~ **on** *vt* essayer; ~ **out** *vt* essayer; * *n* tentative *f*; essai *m*.

trying *adj* pénible; fatigant.

tub *n* cuve *f*, bac *m*; baignoire *f*.

tuba *n* tuba *m*.

tube *n* tube *m*; métro *m*.

tuberculosis *n* tuberculose *f*.

tubing *n* tuyaux *mpl*.

tuck *n* pli *m*; * *vt* mettre.

tucker *vt* (US) fatiguer.

Tuesday *n* mardi *m*.

tuft *n* touffe *f*; houppe *f*.

tug *vt* remorquer; * *n* remorqueur *m*.

tuition *n* cours, enseignement *m*.

tulip *n* tulipe *f*.

tumble *vi* tomber, faire une chute; se jeter; * *vt* renverser; culbuter; * *n* chute *f*; culbute *f*.

tumbledown *adj* délabré.

tumbler *n* verre *m*.

tummy *n* ventre *m*.

tumour *n* tumeur *f*.

tumultuous *adj* tumultueux.

tuna *n* thon *m*.

tune *n* air *m*; accord *m*; harmonie *f*; * *vt* accorder; syntoniser.

tuneful *adj* mélodieux, harmonieux.

tuner *n* syntoniseur *m*.

tunic *n* tunique *f*.

tuning fork *n* (*mus*) diapason *m*.

tunnel *n* tunnel *m*; * *vt* creuser un tunnel dans.

turban *n* turban *m*.

turbine *n* turbine *f*.

turbulence *n* turbulence, agitation *f*.

turbulent *adj* turbulent, agité.

tureen *n* soupière *f*.

turf *n* gazon *m*; * *vt* gazonner.

turgid *adj* gonflé.

turkey *n* dinde *f*.

turmoil *n* agitation *f*; trouble *m*.

turn *vi* (se) tourner; devenir; changer; se retourner; se changer; se transformer; ~ **around** se retourner; tourner; ~ **back** revenir; ~ **down** *vt* rejeter; rabattre; ~

in aller se coucher; ~ **off** *vi* tourner; *vt* éteindre; fermer; ~ **on** *vt* allumer; ouvrir; ~ **out** s'avérer; ~ **over** *vi* se retourner; *vt* tourner; ~ **up** *vi* arriver; se présenter; *vt* monter; * *n* tour *m*; tournure *f*; virage *m*; tendance *f*.

turncoat *n* renégat *m*.

turning *n* embranchement *m*.

turnip *n* navet *m*.

turn-off *n* sortie (d'autoroute) *f*; embranchement *m*.

turnout *n* production *f*.

turnover *n* chiffre d'affaires *m*.

turnpike *n* barrière *f* de péage.

turnstile *n* tourniquet *m*.

turntable *n* platine *f*.

turpentine *n* (essence de) térébenthine *f*.

turquoise *n* turquoise *f*.

turret *n* tourelle *f*.

turtle *n* tortue marine *f*.

turtledove *n* tourterelle *f*.

tusk *n* défense *f*.

tussle *n* lutte *f*.

tutor *n* professeur particulier *m*; directeur d'études *m*; * *vt* enseigner, donner des cours particuliers à.

tuxedo *n* smoking *m*.

twang *n* vibration *f*; ton nasillard *m*.

tweezers *npl* pince à épiler *f*.

twelfth *adj* douzième *mf*.

twelve *adj n* douze *m*.

twentieth *adj n* vingtième *mf*.

twenty *adj n* vingt *m*.

twice *adv* deux fois.

twig *n* brindille *f*; * *vi* piger.

twilight *n* crépuscule *m*.

twin *n* jumeau *m* -elle *f*.

twine *vi* s'enrouler; serpenter; * *n* ficelle *f*.

twinge *vt* élancer; * *n* élancement *m*; remords *m*.

twinkle *vi* scintiller; clignoter.

twirl *vt* faire tournoyer; * *vi* tournoyer; * *n* tournoiement *m*.

twist *vt* tordre, tortiller; entortiller; * *vi* serpenter; * *n* torsion *f*; tournant *m*; rouleau *m*.

twit *n* (*sl*) crétin *m* -e *f*.

twitch *vi* avoir un mouvement nerveux; * *n* tic *m*.

twitter *vi* gazouiller; * *n* gazouillis *m*.

two *adj n* deux *m*.

two-door *adj* à deux portes.

two-faced *adj* hypocrite.

twofold *adj* double; * *adv* au double.

two-seater *n* voiture/avion à deux places *f/m*.

twosome *n* paire *f*; couple *m*.

tycoon *n* magnat *m*.

type *n* type *m*; caractère *m*; exemple *m*; * *vi* taper à la machine.

typecast *adj* enfermé dans un rôle.

typeface *n* police *f* de caractère.

typescript *n* texte dactylographié *m*.

typewriter *n* machine à écrire *f*.

typewritten *adj* dactylographié.

typical *adj* typique.

tyrannical *adj* tyrannique.

tyranny *n* tyrannie *f*.

tyrant *n* tyran *m*.

tyre *n* pneu *m*.

tyre pressure *n* pression *f* des pneus.

U

ubiquitous *adj* doué d'ubiquité.

udder *n* pis *m*.

ugh *excl* pouah!, berk!

ugliness *n* laideur *f*.

ugly *adj* laid; inquiétant.

ulcer *n* ulcère *m*.

ulterior *adj* ultérieur.

ultimate *adj* final; ~ly *adv* finalement; à la fin.

ultimatum *n* ultimatum *m*.

ultramarine *n*, *adj* outremer *m*.

ultrasound *n* ultrason *m*.

umbilical cord *n* cordon ombilical *m*.

umbrella *n* parapluie *m*.

umpire *n* arbitre *m*.

umpteen *adj* un très grand nombre de, beaucoup de.

unable *adj* incapable.

unaccompanied *adj* non accompagné, seul.

unaccomplished *adj* inaccompli, inachevé.

unaccountable *adj* inexplicable.

unaccountably *adv* inexplicablement.

unaccustomed *adj* inaccoutumé, inhabituel.

unacknowledged *adj* non reconnu; (resté) sans réponse.

unacquainted *adj* qui ignore, qui n'a pas connaissance de.

unadorned *adj* sans ornement.

unadulterated *adj* pur; sans mélange.

unaffected *adj* sincère; non affecté.

unaided *adj* sans aide.

unaltered *adj* inchangé.

unambitious *adj* sans ambition.

unanimity *n* unanimité *f*.

unanimous *adj* ~ly *adv* unanime(ment).

unanswerable *adj* incontestable.

unanswered *adj* sans réponse.

unapproachable *adj* inaccessible.

unarmed *adj* non armé, désarmé.

unassuming *adj* sans prétention, modeste.

unattached *adj* indépendant; libre.

unattainable *adj* inaccessible.

unattended *adj* sans surveillance.

unauthorized *adj* sans autorisation.

unavoidable *adj* inévitable.

unavoidably *adv* inévitablement.

unaware *adj* ignorant; inconscient.

unawares *adv* à l'improviste; par mégarde.

unbalanced *adj* déséquilibré; non soldé.

unbearable *adj* insupportable.

unbecoming *adj* malséant, déplacé, peu seyant.

unbelievable *adj* incroyable.

unbend *vi* se détendre; * *vt* redresser.

unbiased *adj* impartial.

unblemished *adj* sans tache, sans défaut.

unborn *adj* à naître, pas encore né.

unbreakable *adj* incassable.

unbroken *adj* non brisé; intact; ininterrompu; indompté.

unbutton *vt* déboutonner.

uncalled-for *adj* injustifié.

uncanny *adj* mystérieux.

unceasing *adj* incessant, continu.

unceremonious *adj* brusque.

uncertain *adj* incertain, douteux.

uncertainty *n* incertitude *f*.

unchangeable *adj* immuable.

unchanged *adj* inchangé.

unchanging *adj* invariable, immuable.

uncharitable *adj* peu charitable.

unchecked *adj* non maîtrisé.

unchristian *adj* peu chrétien.

uncivil *adj* impoli, grossier.

uncivilized *adj* barbare, non civilisé.

uncle *n* oncle *m*.

uncomfortable *adj* inconfortable; incommode; désagréable.

uncomfortably *adv* inconfortablement; mal; désagréablement.

uncommon *adj* rare, extraordinaire.

uncompromising *adj* intransigeant.

unconcerned *adj* indifférent.

unconditional *adj* inconditionnel, absolu.

unconfined *adj* illimité, sans bornes.

unconfirmed *adj* non confirmé.

unconnected *adj* sans rapport.

unconquerable *adj* invincible, insurmontable.

unconscious *adj* inconscient; ~ly *adv* inconsciemment, sans s'en rendre compte.

unconstrained *adj* non contraint, libre.

uncontrollable *adj* irrésistible; qui ne peut être maîtrisé.

unconventional *adj* peu conventionnel.

unconvincing *adj* peu convaincant.

uncork *vt* déboucher.

uncorrected *adj* non corrigé.

uncouth *adj* grossier.

uncover *vt* découvrir.

uncultivated *adj* inculte.

uncut *adj* non taillé, intégral.

undamaged *adj* non endommagé, indemne.

undaunted *adj* intrépide.

undecided *adj* indécis.

undefiled *adj* pur, immaculé.

undeniable *adj* indéniable, incontestable; ~bly *adv* incontestablement.

under *prep* sous; dessous; moins de; selon; * *adv* au-dessous, en-dessous.

under-age *adj* mineur.

undercharge *vt* ne pas faire payer assez.

underclothing *n* sous-vêtements *mpl*.

undercoat *n* première couche *f*.

undercover *adj* secret, clandestin.

undercurrent *n* courant sous-marin *m*.

undercut *vt* vendre moins cher que.

underdeveloped *adj* sous-développé, insuffisamment développé.

underdog *n* opprimé *m* -e *f*.

underdone *adj* pas assez cuit.

underestimate *vt* sous-estimer.

undergo *vt* subir; supporter.

undergraduate *n* étudiant(e) en licence *m(f)*.

underground *n* mouvement clandestin *m*.

undergrowth *n* broussailles *fpl*, sous-bois *m*.

underhand *adv* en cachette; * *adj* secret, clandestin.

underlie *vi* être à la base de.

underline *vt* souligner.

undermine *vt* saper.

underneath *adv* (en) dessous; * *prep* sous, au-dessous de.

underpaid *adj* sous-payé.

underprivileged *adj* défavorisé.

underrate *vt* sous-estimer.

undersecretary *n* sous-secrétaire *mf*.

undershirt *n* (US) maillot de corps *m*.

undershorts *npl* (US) caleçon *m*.

underside *n* dessous *m*.

understand *vt* comprendre.

understandable *adj* compréhensible.

understanding *n* compréhension *f*; intelligence *f*; entendement *m*; accord *m*; * *adj* compréhensif.

understatement *n* affirmation en dessous de la vérité *f*.

undertake *vt* entreprendre.

undertaking *n* entreprise *f*; engagement *m*.

undervalue *vt* sous-estimer.

underwater *adj* sous-marin; * *adv* sous l'eau.

underwear *n* sous-vêtements *mpl*, dessous *mpl*.

underworld *n* pègre *f*.

underwrite *vt* souscrire à; assurer contre.

underwriter *n* assureur *m*.

undeserved *adj* immérité; ~ly *adv* à tort, indûment.

undeserving *adj* peu méritant.

undesirable *adj* peu souhaitable.

undetermined *adj* indéterminé; indécis.

undigested *adj* non digéré.

undiminished *adj* non diminué.

undisciplined *adj* indiscipliné.

undisguised *adj* non déguisé.

undismayed *adj* non découragé.

undisputed *adj* incontesté.

undisturbed *adj* non dérangé, paisible.

undivided *adj* indivisé, entier.

undo *vt* défaire; détruire.

undoing *n* ruine *f*.

undoubted *adj* ~ly *adv* indubitable(ment).

undress *vi* se déshabiller.

undue *adj* excessif; injuste.

undulating *adj* ondulant.

unduly *adv* trop, excessivement.

undying *adj* éternel.

unearth *vt* déterrer.

unearthly *adj* surnaturel.

uneasy *adj* inquiet; troublé, gêné.

uneducated *adj* sans instruction.

unemployed *adj* au chômage.

unemployment *n* chômage *m*.

unending *adj* interminable.

unenlightened *adj* peu éclairé.

unenviable *adj* peu enviable.

unequal *adj* ~ly *adv* inégal(ement).

unequalled *adj* inégalé.

unerring *adj* ~ly *adv* infaillible(ment).

uneven *adj* inégal; impair; ~ly *adv* inégalement.

unexpected *adj* inattendu; inopiné; ~ly *adv* de manière inattendue; inopinément.

unexplored *adj* inexploré.

unfailing *adj* infaillible, certain.

unfair *adj* injuste; inéquitable; ~ly *adv* injustement.

unfaithful *adj* infidèle.

unfaithfulness *n* infidélité *f*.

unfaltering *adj* ferme, assuré.

unfamiliar *adj* peu familier, peu connu.

unfashionable *adj* démodé; ~bly *adv* sans se préoccuper de la mode.

unfasten *vt* détacher, défaire.

unfathomable *adj* insondable, impénétrable.

unfavourable *adj* défavorable.

unfeeling *adj* insensible, impitoyable.

unfinished *adj* inachevé, incomplet.

unfit *adj* inapte; impropre.

unfold *vt* déplier; révéler; * *vi* s'ouvrir.

unforeseen *adj* imprévu.

unforgettable *adj* inoubliable.

unforgivable *adj* impardonnable.

unforgiving *adj* implacable.

unfortunate *adj* malheureux, malchanceux; ~ly *adv* malheureusement, par malheur.

unfounded *adj* sans fondement.

unfriendly *adj* inamical.

unfruitful *adj* stérile; infructueux.

unfurnished *adj* non meublé.

ungainly *adj* gauche.

ungentlemanly *adj* peu galant.

ungovernable *adj* ingouvernable, indomptable.

ungrateful *adj* ingrat; peu reconnaissant; ~ly *adv* avec ingratitude.

ungrounded *adj* infondé.

unhappily *adv* malheureusemnt.

unhappiness *n* tristesse *f*.

unhappy *adj* malheureux.

unharmed *adj* indemne, sain et sauf.

unhealthy *adj* malsain; maladif.

unheard-of *adj* inédit, sans précédent.

unheeding *adj* insouciant; distrait.

unhook *vt* décrocher; dégrafer.

unhoped(-for) *adj* inespéré.

unhurt *adj* indemne.

unicorn *n* licorne *f*.

uniform *adj* uniforme; ~ly *adv* uniformément; * *n* uniforme *m*.

uniformity *n* uniformité *f*.

unify *vt* unifier.

unimaginable *adj* inimaginable.

unimpaired *adj* non diminué, intact.

unimportant *adj* sans importance.

uninformed *adj* mal informé.

uninhabitable *adj* inhabitable.

uninhabited *adj* inhabité, désert.

uninjured *adj* indemne, sain et sauf.

unintelligible *adj* inintelligible.

unintelligibly *adv* inintelligiblement.

unintentional *adj* involontaire.

uninterested *adj* indifférent.

uninteresting *adj* inintéressant.

uninterrupted *adj* ininterrompu, continu.

uninvited *adj* sans être invité.

union *n* union *f*; syndicat *m*.

unionist *n* syndicaliste *mf*.

unique *adj* unique, exceptionnel.

unison *n* unisson *m*.

unit *n* unité *f*.

unitarian *n* unitarien *m* -ne *f*.

unite *vt* unir; * *vi* s'unir.

unitedly *adv* conjointement, ensemble.

United States (of America) *npl* États-Unis *mpl*.

unity *n* unité, harmonie *f*, accord *m*.

universal *adj* ~ly *adv* universel(lement).

universe *n* univers *m*.

university *n* université *f*.

unjust *adj* ~ly *adv* injuste(ment).

unkempt *adj* négligé; débraillé.

unkind *adj* peu aimable; méchant.

unknowingly *adv* inconsciemment.

unknown *adj* inconnu.

unlawful *adj* illégal, illicite; ~ly *adv* illégalement.

unlawfulness *n* illégalité *f*.

unleash *vt* lâcher, déchaîner.

unless *conj* à moins que/de, sauf.

unlicensed *adj* illicite.

unlike *adj* différent, dissemblable.

unlikelihood *n* improbabilité *f*.

unlikely *adj* improbable; invraisemblable; *adv* improbablement.

unlimited *adj* illimité.

unlisted *adj* ne figurant pas sur une liste/sur l'annuaire.

unload *vt* décharger.

unlock *vt* ouvrir, déverrouiller.

unluckily *adv* malheureusement.

unlucky *adj* malchanceux.

unmanageable *adj* difficile, peu maniable, impossible.

unmannered *adj* mal élevé, impoli.

unmannerly *adj* rustre.

unmarried *adj* célibataire, qui n'est pas marié.

unmask *vt* démasquer.

unmentionable *adj* qu'il ne faut pas mentionner.

unmerited *adj* immérité.

unmindful *adj* oublieux, indifférent.

unmistakable *adj* indubitable; ~ly *adv* sans aucun doute.

unmitigated *adj* absolu.

unmoved *adj* insensible, impassible.

unnatural *adj* non naturel; pervers; affecté.

unnecessary *adj* inutile, superflu.

unneighbourly *adj* peu aimable avec ses voisins, peu sociable.

unnoticed *adj* inaperçu.

unnumbered *adj* innombrable.

unobserved *adj* inaperçu.

unobtainable *adj* impossible à obtenir; introuvable.

unobtrusive *adj* discret.

unoccupied *adj* inoccupé.

unoffending *adj* inoffensif, innocent.

unofficial *adj* non officiel.

unorthodox *adj* hétérodoxe; peu orthodoxe.

unpack *vt* défaire; déballer.

unpaid *adj* non payé.

unpalatable *adj* désagréable au goût.

unparalleled *adj* incomparable; sans pareil.

unpleasant *adj* ~ly *adv* désagréable(ment).

unpleasantness *n* caractère désagréable *m*.

unplug *vt* débrancher.

unpolished *adj* non ciré; fruste, rude.

unpopular *adj* impopulaire.

unpractised *adj* inexpérimenté, inexercé.

unprecedented *adj* sans précédent.

unpredictable *adj* imprévisible.

unprejudiced *adj* impartial.

unprepared *adj* qui n'est pas préparé.

unprofitable *adj* inutile; peu rentable.

unprotected *adj* sans protection; exposé.

unpublished *adj* inédit.

unpunished *adj* impuni.

unqualified *adj* non qualifié; inconditionnel.

unquestionable *adj* incontestable, indiscutable; ~ly *adv* indiscutablement, sans conteste.

unquestioned *adj* incontesté, indiscuté.

unravel *vt* débrouiller.

unread *adj* qui n'a pas été lu; inculte.

unreal *adj* irréel.

unrealistic *adj* irréaliste.

unreasonable *adj* déraisonnable.

unreasonably *adv* déraisonnablement.

unregarded *adj* négligé; dont on fait peu de cas.

unrelated *adj* sans rapport; sans lien de parenté.

unrelenting *adj* implacable.

unreliable *adj* peu fiable.

unremitting *adj* inlassable, constant.

unrepentant *adj* impénitent.

unreserved *adj* sans réserve; franc; ~ly *adv* sans réserve.

unrest *n* agitation *f*; troubles *mpl*.

unrestrained *adj* non contenu; non réprimé.

unripe *adj* vert, pas mûr.

unrivalled *adj* sans égal, sans pareil.

unroll *vt* dérouler.

unruliness *n* indiscipline *f*; turbulence *f*.

unruly *adj* indiscipliné.

unsafe *adj* dangereux, peu sûr.

unsatisfactory *adj* peu satisfaisant.

unsavoury *adj* désagréable, insipide.

unscathed *adj* indemne.

unscrew *vt* dévisser.

unscrupulous *adj* sans scrupules.

unseasonable *adj* hors de saison, inopportun.

unseemly *adj* inconvenant.

unseen *adj* invisible; inaperçu.

unselfish *adj* généreux.

unsettle *vt* perturber.

unsettled *adj* perturbé; instable; variable.

unshaken *adj* inébranlable, ferme.

unshaven *adj* non rasé.

unsightly *adj* disgracieux, laid.

unskilful *adj* maladroit, malhabile.

unskilled *adj* inexpérimenté.

unsociable *adj* insociable, sauvage.

unspeakable *adj* ineffable, indicible.

unstable *adj* instable.

unsteadily *adv* d'un pas chancelant; d'une manière mal assurée.

unsteady *adj* instable.

unstudied *adj* naturel; spontané.

unsuccessful *adj* infructueux, vain; ~**ly** *adv* sans succès.

unsuitable *adj* peu approprié; inopportun.

unsure *adj* peu sûr.

unsympathetic *adj* peu compatissant.

untamed *adj* sauvage.

untapped *adj* non exploité.

untenable *adj* insoutenable.

unthinkable *adj* inconcevable.

unthinking *adj* irréfléchi, étourdi.

untidiness *n* désordre *m*.

untidy *adj* en désordre; peu soigné.

untie *vt* dénouer, défaire.

until *prep* jusqu'à; * *conj* jusqu'à ce que.

untimely *adj* intempestif.

untiring *adj* infatigable.

untold *adj* jamais révélé;
   indicible; incalculable.

untouched *adj* intact.

untoward *adj* fâcheux;
   inconvenant.

untried *adj* qui n'a pas été
   essayé *ou* mis à l'épreuve.

untroubled *adj* tranquille,
   paisible.

untrue *adj* faux.

untrustworthy *adj* indigne de
   confiance.

untruth *n* mensonge *m*,
   fausseté *f*.

unused *adj* neuf, inutilisé.

unusual *adj* inhabituel,
   exceptionnel; **~ly** *adv*
   exceptionnellement,
   rarement.

unveil *vt* dévoiler.

unwavering *adj* inébranlable.

unwelcome *adj* importun.

unwell *adj* indisposé,
   souffrant.

unwieldy *adj* peu maniable.

unwilling *adj* peu disposé;
   ~ly *adv* de mauvaise grâce.

unwillingness *n* mauvaise
   grâce, mauvaise volonté *f*.

unwind *vt* dérouler; * *vi* se
   détendre.

unwise *adj* imprudent.

unwitting *adj* involontaire.

unworkable *adj* impraticable.

unworthy *adj* indigne.

unwrap *vt* défaire.

unwritten *adj* non écrit.

up *adv* en haut, en l'air; levé;
   * *prep* au haut de; plus loin.

upbringing *n* éducation *f*.

update *vt* mettre à jour.

upheaval *n* bouleversement *m*.

uphill *adj* difficile, pénible; *
   adv en montant.

uphold *vt* soutenir.

upholstery *n* tapisserie *f*.

upkeep *n* entretien *m*.

uplift *vt* élever.

upon *prep* sur.

upper *adj* supérieur; (plus)
   élevé.

upper-class *adj* aristocratique.

upper-hand *n* (*fig*) dessus *m*.

uppermost *adj* le plus haut,
   le plus élevé; **to be ~**
   prédominer.

upright *adj* droit, vertical;
   droit, honnête.

uprising *n* soulèvement *m*.

uproar *n* tumulte, vacarme *m*.

uproot *vt* déraciner.

upset *vt* renverser; déranger,
   bouleverser; * *n* désordre
   m; bouleversement *m*; *
   adj vexé; bouleversé.

upshot *n* résultat *m*; aboutissement *m*; conclusion *f*.

upside-down *adv* sens dessus dessous.

upstairs *adv* en haut (d'un escalier).

upstart *n* parvenu *m* -e *f*.

uptight *adj* très tendu.

up-to-date *adj* à jour.

upturn *n* amélioration *f*.

upward *adj* ascendant; ~s *adv* vers le haut; en montant.

urban *adj* urbain.

urbane *adj* courtois.

urchin *n* gamin *m*; **sea ~** oursin *m*.

urge *vt* pousser; * *n* impulsion *f*; désir ardent *m*.

urgency *n* urgence *f*.

urgent *adj* urgent.

urinal *n* urinoir *m*.

urinate *vi* uriner.

urine *n* urine *f*.

urn *n* urne *f*.

us *pn* nous.

usage *n* utilisation *f*; usage *m*.

use *n* usage *m*; utilisation *f*, emploi *m*; * *vt* se servir de, utiliser.

used *adj* usagé.

useful *adj* ~ly *adv* utile(ment).

usefulness *n* utilité *f*.

useless *adj* ~ly *adv* inutile(ment).

uselessness *n* inutilité *f*.

user-friendly *adj* facile à utiliser.

usher *n* huissier *m*; placeur *m*.

usherette *n* ouvreuse *f*.

usual *adj* habituel, courant; ~ly *adv* habituellement.

usurer *n* usurier *m* -ière *f*.

usurp *vt* usurper.

usury *n* usure *f*.

utensil *n* ustensile *m*.

uterus *n* utérus *m*.

utility *n* utilité *f*.

utilize *vt* utiliser.

utmost *adj* extrême, le plus grand; dernier.

utter *adj* complet; absolu; total; * *vt* prononcer; proférer; émettre.

utterance *n* expression *f*.

utterly *adv* complètement, tout à fait.

V

vacancy *n* chambre libre *f*.

vacant *adj* vacant; inoccupé; libre.

vacant lot *n* (US) terrain vague *m*.

vacate *vt* quitter; démissionner.

vacation *n* vacances *fpl*.

vacationer *n* vacancier *m* -ière *f*.

vaccinate *vt* vacciner.

vaccination *n* vaccination *f*.

vaccine *n* vaccin *f*.

vacuous *adj* vide.

vacuum *n* vide *m*.

vacuum bottle *n* thermos *m*.

vagina *n* vagin *m*.

vagrant *n* vagabond *m* -e *f*.

vague *adj* ~ly *adv* vague(ment).

vain *adj* vain, inutile; vaniteux.

valet *n* valet de chambre *m*.

valiant *adj* courageux, brave.

valid *adj* valide, valable.

valley *n* vallée *f*.

valour *n* courage *m*, bravoure *f*.

valuable *adj* précieux, de valeur; ~s *npl* objets de valeur *mpl*.

valuation *n* évaluation, estimation *f*.

value *n* valeur *f*; * *vt* évaluer; tenir à, apprécier.

valued *adj* précieux, estimé.

valve *n* soupape *f*.

vampire *n* vampire *m*.

van *n* camionnette *f*.

vandal *n* vandale *mf*.

vandalism *n* vandalisme *m*.

vandalize *vt* saccager.

vanguard *n* avant-garde *f*.

vanilla *n* vanille *f*.

vanish *vi* disparaître, se dissiper.

vanity *n* vanité *f*.

vanity case *n* vanity-case *m*.

vanquish *vt* vaincre.

vantage point *n* position avantageuse *f*.

vapour *n* vapeur *f*.

variable *adj* variable; changeant.

variance *n* désaccord, différend *m*.

variation *n* variation *f*.

varicose vein *n* varice *f*.

varied *adj* varié.

variety *n* variété *f*.

variety show *n* spectacle de variétés *m*.

various *adj* divers, différent.

varnish *n* vernis *m*; * *vt* vernir.

vary *vt vi* varier; *vi* changer.

vase *n* vase *m*.

vast *adj* vaste; immense.

vat *n* cuve *f*.

vault *n* voûte *f*; cave *f*, caveau *m*; saut *m*; * *vi* sauter.

veal *n* veau *m*.

veer *vi* (*mar*) virer.

vegetable *adj* végétal; * *n* végétal *m*; ~s *pl* légumes *mpl*.

vegetable garden *n* (jardin) potager *m*.

vegetarian *n* végétarien *m* -ne *f*.

vegetate *vi* végéter.

vegetation *n* végétation *f*.

vehemence *n* véhémence, fougue *f*.

vehement *adj* véhément, violent; ~ly *adv* avec véhémence.

vehicle *n* véhicule *m*.

veil *n* voile *m*; * *vt* voiler, dissimuler.

vein *n* veine *f*; nervure *f*; disposition *f*.

velocity *n* vitesse *f*.

velvet *n* velours *m*.

vending machine *n* distributeur automatique *m*.

vendor *n* vendeur *m*.

veneer *n* placage *m*; vernis *m*.

venerable *adj* vénérable.

venerate *vt* vénérer.

veneration *n* vénération *f*.

venereal *adj* vénérien.

vengeance *n* vengeance *f*.

venial *adj* véniel.

venison *n* venaison *f*.

venom *n* venin *m*.

venomous *adj* vénéneux; ~ly *adv* avec animosité.

vent *n* orifice *m*; conduit *m*; * *vt* (*fig*) décharger.

ventilate *vt* aérer.

ventilation *n* ventilation, aération *f*.

ventilator *n* ventilateur *m*.

ventriloquist *n* ventriloque *mf*.

venture *n* entreprise *f*; * *vi* s'aventurer; * *vt* risquer, hasarder.

venue *n* lieu *m* (de réunion).

veranda(h) *n* véranda *f*.

verb *n* (*gr*) verbe *m*.

verbal *adj* verbal, oral; ~**ly** *adv* verbalement.

verbatim *adv* textuellement, mot pour mot.

verbose *adj* verbeux.

verdant *adj* verdoyant.

verdict *n* (*law*) verdict *m*; jugement *m*.

verification *n* vérification *f*.

verify *vt* vérifier.

veritable *adj* véritable.

vermin *n* vermine *f*.

vermouth *n* vermout(h) *m*.

versatile *adj* doué de talents multiples; versatile.

verse *n* vers *m*; verset *m*.

versed *adj* versé.

version *n* version *f*.

versus *prep* contre.

vertebra *n* vertèbre *f*.

vertebral *adj* vertébral.

vertebrate *adj n* vertébré *m*.

vertex *n* sommet *m*.

vertical *adj* ~**ly** *adv* vertical(ement).

vertigo *n* vertige *m*.

verve *n* verve *f*, brio *m*.

very *adj* vrai, véritable; exactement, même; * *adv* très, fort, bien.

vessel *n* récipient *m*; vase *m*; navire *m*.

vest *n* gilet *m*.

vestibule *n* vestibule *m*.

vestige *n* vestige *m*.

vestment *n* vêtement de cérémonie *m*; chasuble *f*.

vestry *n* sacristie *f*.

veteran *adj n* vétéran *m*.

veterinarian *n* vétérinaire *mf*.

veterinary *adj* vétérinaire.

veto *n* véto *m*; * *vt* opposer son véto à.

vex *vt* contrarier.

vexed *adj* contrarié.

via *prep* via, par.

viaduct *n* viaduc *m*.

vial *n* fiole, ampoule *f*.

vibrate *vi* vibrer.

vibration *n* vibration *f*.

vicarious *adj* par personne interposée.

vice *n* vice *m*; défaut *m*; étau *m*.

vice-chairman *n* vice-président *m*.

vice versa *adv* vice versa.

vicinity *n* voisinage *m*, proximité *f*.

vicious *adj* méchant; ~**ly** *adv* méchamment.

victim *n* victime *f*.

victimize *vt* prendre pour victime.

victor *n* vainqueur *m*.

victorious *adj* victorieux.

victory *n* victoire *f*.

video *n* vidéo *f*; vidéocassette *f*; magnétoscope *m*.

video tape *n* bande vidéo *f*.

viewer *n* téléspectateur *m* -trice *f*.

vie *vi* rivaliser.

view *n* vue *f*; perspective *f*; opinion *f*; panorama *m*; * *vt* voir; examiner.

viewfinder *n* viseur *m*.

viewpoint *n* point de vue *m*.

vigil *n* veille *f*; vigile *f*.

vigilance *n* vigilance *f*.

vigilant *adj* vigilant, attentif.

vigorous *adj* vigoureux; ~ly *adv* vigoureusement.

vigour *n* vigueur *f*; énergie *f*.

vile *adj* vil, infâme; exécrable.

vilify *vt* diffamer.

villa *n* pavillon *m*; maison de campagne *f*.

village *n* village *m*.

villager *n* villageois *m* -e *f*.

villain *n* scélérat *m*.

vindicate *vt* venger, défendre.

vindication *n* défense *f*; justification *f*.

vindictive *adj* vindicatif.

vine *n* vigne *f*.

vinegar *n* vinaigre *m*.

vineyard *n* vignoble *m*.

vintage *n* millésime *m*; époque *f*.

vinyl *n* vinyle *m*.

viola *n* (*mus*) viole *f*.

violate *vt* violer.

violation *n* violation *f*.

violence *n* violence *f*.

violent *adj* violent; ~ly *adv* violemment.

violet *n* (*bot*) violette *f*.

violin *n* (*mus*) violon *m*.

violinist *n* violiniste *mf*.

violoncello *n* (*mus*) violoncelle *m*.

viper *n* vipère *f*.

virgin *n*, *adj* vierge *f*.

virginity *n* virginité *f*.

Virgo *n* Vierge *f* (signe du zodiaque).

virile *adj* viril.

virility *n* virilité *f*.

virtual *adj* virtuel; quasiment; ~ly *adv* de fait, pratiquement.

virtue *n* vertu *f*.

virtuous *adj* vertueux.

virulent *adj* virulent.

virus *n* virus *m*.

vis-à-vis *prep* vis-à-vis.

viscous *adj* visqueux, gluant.

visibility *n* visibilité *f*.

visible *adj* visible.

visibly *adv* visiblement.

vision *n* vision *f*; vue *f*.

visit *vt* visiter; * *n* visite *f*.

visitation *n* visite *f*.

visiting hours *npl* heures *fpl* de visite.

visitor *n* visiteur *m* -euse *f*; touriste *mf*.

visor *n* visière *f*.

vista *n* vue, perspective *f*.

visual *adj* visuel.

visual aid *n* support visuel *m*.

visualize *vt* s'imaginer.

vital *adj* vital; essentiel; indispensable; ~ly *adv* vitalement; ~s *npl* organes vitaux *mpl*.

vitality *n* vitalité *f*.

vital statistics *npl* statistiques démographiques *fpl*.

vitamin *n* vitamine *f*.

vitiate *vt* vicier.

vivacious *adj* vif.

vivid *adj* vif; vivant; frappant; ~ly *adv* de façon éclatante; de façon frappante.

vivisection *n* vivisection *f*.

vocabulary *n* vocabulaire *m*.

vocal *adj* vocal.

vocation *n* vocation *f*; profession *f*, métier *m*; ~al *adj* professionnel.

vocative *n* vocatif *m*.

vociferous *adj* bruyant.

vogue *n* vogue *f*; mode *f*.

voice *n* voix *f*; * *vt* exprimer.

void *adj* vide; * *n* vide *m*.

volatile *adj* volatile; versatile.

volcanic *adj* volcanique.

volcano *n* volcan *m*.

volition *n* volonté *f*.

volley *n* volée *f*; salve *f*; grêle *f*.

volleyball *n* volley-ball *m*.

voltage *n* voltage *m*.

voluble *adj* volubile, loquace.

volume *n* volume *m*.

voluntarily *adv* volontairement.

voluntary *adj* volontaire.

volunteer *n* volontaire *mf*; * *vi* se porter volontaire.

voluptuous *adj* voluptueux.

vomit *vt* *vi* vomir; * *n* vomissement *m*.

voracious *adj* ~ly *adv* vorace(ment).

vortex *n* tourbillon *m*.

vote *n* vote, suffrage *m*; voix *f*; * *vt* voter.

voter *n* électeur *m* -trice *f*.

voting *n* vote *m*.

voucher *n* bon *m*.

vow *n* vœu *m*; * *vt* jurer.
vowel *n* voyelle *f*.
voyage *n* voyage par mer *m*; traversée *f*.
vulgar *adj* vulgaire; grossier.

vulgarity *n* grossièreté *f*; vulgarité *m*.
vulnerable *adj* vulnérable.
vulture *n* vautour *m*.

W

wad n tampon m; bouchon m, liasse f.

waddle vi se dandiner.

wade vi patauger.

wading pool n petit bassin (pour enfants) m.

wafer n gaufrette f; plaque f.

waffle n gaufre f.

waft vt porter, apporter; * vi flotter.

wag vt vi remuer.

wage n salaire m.

wage earner n salarié m -e f.

wager n pari m; * vt parier.

wages npl salaire m.

waggle vt remuer.

waggon n chariot m; (rail) wagon m.

wail n gémissement m, plainte f; * vi gémir.

waist n taille f.

waistline n taille f.

wait vi attendre; * n attente f; arrêt m.

waiter n serveur m.

waiting list n liste d'attente f.

waiting room n salle d'attente f.

waive vt renoncer à.

wake vi se réveiller; * vt réveiller; * n veillée f; (mar) sillage m.

waken vt réveiller; * vi se réveiller.

walk vi marcher, aller à pied; * vt parcourir; * n promenade f; marche f.

walker n marcheur m -euse f.

walkie-talkie n talkie-walkie m.

walking n marche à pied f.

walking stick n canne f.

walkout n grève f surprise.

walkover n (sl) victoire facile f, gâteau m.

walkway n passage pour piétons m.

wall n mur m; muraille f; paroi f.

walled adj muré.

wallet n portefeuille m.

wallflower n (bot) giroflée f.

wallow vi se vautrer.

wallpaper *n* papier peint *m*.

walnut *n* noix *f*; noyer *m*.

walrus *n* morse *m*.

waltz *n* valse *f*.

wan *adj* pâle.

wand *n* baguette (magique) *f*.

wander *vi* errer; aller sans but.

wane *vi* décroître.

want *vt* vouloir; demander; * *vi* manquer; * *n* besoin *m*; manque *m*.

wanting *adj* manquant, qui manque, qui fait défaut.

wanton *adj* lascif; capricieux.

war *n* guerre *f*.

ward *n* salle *f*; pupille *mf*.

wardrobe *n* garde-robe *f*, penderie *f*.

warehouse *n* entrepôt *m*.

warfare *n* guerre *f*.

warhead *n* ogive *f*.

warily *adv* avec circonspection.

wariness *n* circonspection, prudence *f*.

warm *adj* chaud; chaleureux; * *vt* réchauffer; ~ **up** *vi* se réchauffer; s'échauffer; s'animer; *vt* réchauffer.

warm-hearted *adj* affectueux.

warmly *adv* chaudement, chaleureusement.

warmth *n* chaleur *f*.

warn *vt* prévenir; avertir.

warning *n* avertissement *m*.

warning light *n* voyant lumineux *m*.

warp *vi* se voiler; * *vt* voiler; fausser.

warrant *n* garantie *f*; mandat *m*.

warranty *n* garantie *f*.

warren *n* terrier *m*.

warrior *n* guerrier *m* -ière *f*.

warship *n* navire de guerre *m*.

wart *n* verrue *f*.

wary *adj* prudent, circonspect.

wash *vt* laver; * *vi* se laver; * *n* lavage *m*; lessive *f*.

washable *adj* lavable.

washbowl *n* lavabo *m*.

washcloth *n* gant de toilette *m*.

washer *n* rondelle *f*.

washing *n* linge à laver *m*; lessive *f*.

washing machine *n* machine à laver *f*.

washing-up *n* vaisselle *f*.

wash-out *n* (*sl*) fiasco *m*.

washroom *n* toilettes *fpl*.

wasp *n* guêpe *f*.

wastage *n* gaspillage *m*; perte *f*.

waste *vt* gaspiller; dévaster,

saccager; perdre; * *vi* se perdre; * *n* gaspillage *m*; détérioration *f*; terre inculte *f*; déchets *mpl*.

wasteful *adj* gaspilleur; prodigue; ~ly *adv* avec prodigalité.

waste paper *n* vieux papiers *mpl*.

waste pipe *n* tuyau d'échappement *m*.

watch *n* montre *f*; surveillance *f*; garde *f*; * *vt* regarder; observer; surveiller; faire attention à; * *vi* regarder; monter la garde.

watchdog *n* chien de garde *m*.

watchful *adj* vigilant; ~ly *adv* avec vigilance.

watchmaker *n* horloger *m*.

watchman *n* veilleur de nuit *m*; gardien *m*.

watchtower *n* tour de guet *f*.

watchword *n* mot de passe *m*; mot d'ordre *m*.

water *n* eau *f*; * *vt* arroser, mouiller; * *vi* pleurer, larmoyer.

water closet *n* W.C. *mpl*.

watercolour *n* aquarelle *f*.

waterfall *n* cascade *f*.

water heater *n* chauffe-eau *m invar*.

watering-can *n* arrosoir *m*.

water level *n* niveau de l'eau *m*.

waterlily *n* nénuphar *m*.

water line *n* ligne de flottaison *f*.

waterlogged *adj* imprégné d'eau.

water main *n* conduite principale d'eau *f*.

watermark *n* filigrane *m*.

watermelon *n* pastèque *f*.

watershed *n* (*fig*) moment *m* critique.

watertight *adj* étanche.

waterworks *npl* usine hydraulique *f*.

watery *adj* aqueux; détrempé; délavé.

wave *n* vague *f*; lame *f*; onde *f*; * *vi* faire signe de la main; onduler; * *vt* agiter.

wavelength *n* longueur d'ondes *f*.

waver *vi* vaciller, osciller.

wavering *adj* hésitant.

wavy *adj* ondulé.

wax *n* cire *f*; * *vt* cirer; * *vi* croître.

wax paper *n* papier paraffiné *m*.

waxworks *n* musée de cire *m*.

way *n* chemin *m*; voie *f*; route *f*; manière *f*; direction *f*; **to give ~** céder.

waylay *vt* attaquer, arrêter au passage.

wayward *adj* capricieux.

we *pn* nous.

weak *adj* **~ly** *adv* faible(ment).

weaken *vt* affaiblir.

weakling *n* personne faible *f*.

weak-minded *adj* faible d'esprit.

weakness *n* faiblesse *f*; point faible *m*.

wealth *n* richesse *f*; abondance *f*.

wealthy *adj* riche.

wean *vt* sevrer.

weapon *n* arme *f*.

wear *vt* porter; user; * *vi* s'user; **~ away** *vt* user; *vi* s'user; **~ down** *vt* user; épuiser; **~ off** *vi* s'effacer; **~ out** *vi* s'user; s'épuiser; *vt* user; * *n* usage *m*; usure *f*.

weariness *n* lassitude *f*; fatigue *f*; ennui *m*.

wearisome *adj* fatigant.

weary *adj* las, fatigué; ennuyeux.

weasel *n* belette *f*.

weather *n* temps *m*; * *vt* surmonter.

weather-beaten *adj* ayant souffert des intempéries.

weathercock *n* girouette *f*.

weather forecast *n* prévisions météorologiques *fpl*.

weave *vt* tisser; entrelacer.

weaving *n* tissage *m*.

web *n* tissu *m*; toile *f* d'araignée; palmure *f*.

wed *vt* épouser; * *vi* se marier.

wedding *n* mariage *m*; noces *fpl*.

wedding day *n* jour du mariage *m*.

wedding dress *n* robe de mariée *f*.

wedding present *n* cadeau de mariage *m*.

wedding ring *n* alliance *f*.

wedge *n* cale *f*; * *vt* caler; enfoncer.

wedlock *n* mariage *m*.

Wednesday *n* mercredi *m*.

wee *adj* petit.

weed *n* mauvaise herbe *f*; * *vt* désherber.

weedkiller *n* désherbant *m*.

weedy *adj* envahi par les mauvaises herbes.

week n semaine f; tomorrow ~ demain en huit; yesterday ~ il y a eu une semaine hier.

weekday n jour de semaine, jour ouvrable m.

weekend n week-end m, fin de semaine f.

weekly adj de la semaine, hebdomadaire; * adv chaque semaine, par semaine.

weep vt vi pleurer.

weeping willow n saule pleureur m.

weigh vt vi peser.

weight n poids m.

weightily adv pesamment.

weightlifter n haltérophile m.

weighty adj lourd; important.

welcome adj opportun; ~! bienvenue !; * n accueil m; * vt accueillir.

weld vt souder; * n soudure f.

welfare n bien-être m; assistance sociale f.

welfare state n État-providence m.

well n source f; fontaine f; puits m; * adj bien, bon; * adv bien; as ~ as aussi bien que, en plus de, comme.

well-behaved adj bien élevé, sage.

well-being n bien-être m.

well-bred adj bien élevé.

well-built adj bien bâti, solide.

well-deserved adj bien mérité.

well-dressed adj bien habillé.

well-known adj connu, célèbre.

well-mannered adj poli, bien élevé.

well-meaning adj bien intentionné.

well-off adj aisé, dans l'aisance.

well-to-do adj aisé, riche.

well-wisher n admirateur m -trice f.

wench n jeune fille, jeune femme f.

west n ouest, Occident m; * adj ouest, de/à l'ouest; * adv vers/à l'ouest.

westerly, western adj (d')ouest.

westward adv vers l'ouest.

wet adj mouillé, humide; * n humidité f; * vt mouiller.

wetnurse n nourrice f.

wet suit n combinaison de plongée f.

whack *vt* donner un grand coup à; * *n* grand coup *m*.

whale *n* baleine *f*.

wharf *n* quai *m*.

what *pn* qu'est-ce qui, (qu'est-ce) que, quoi; que, qui; ce qui, ce que; quel(le), que; * *adj* quel(s), quelle(s); * *excl* quoi! comment!.

whatever *pn* quoi que; tout; n'importe quoi.

wheat *n* blé *m*.

wheedle *vt* cajoler, câliner.

wheel *n* roue *f*; volant *m*; gouvernail *m*; * *vt* tourner; pousser, rouler; * *vi* tourner en rond, tournoyer.

wheelbarrow *n* brouette *f*.

wheelchair *n* fauteuil roulant *m*.

wheelclamp *n* sabot *m*.

wheeze *vi* respirer bruyamment.

when *adv*, *conj* quand.

whenever *adv* quand; chaque fois que.

where *adv* où; * *conj* où; any~ n'importe où; every~ partout.

whereabout(s) *adv* où.

whereas *conj* tandis que; attendu que.

whereby *pn* par lequel (laquelle), au moyen duquel (de laquelle).

wherever *adv* où que.

whereupon *conj* sur quoi; après quoi.

wherewithal *npl* ressources *fpl*.

whet *vt* aiguiser.

whether *conj* si.

which *pn* lequel, laquelle; celui/celle(s)/ceux que, celui/celle(s)/ceux qui; ce qui, ce que; quoi, ce dont * *adj* quel(s), quelle(s).

whiff *n* bouffée, odeur *f*.

while *n* moment *m*; a ~ quelque temps; * *conj* pendant que; alors que; quoique.

whim *n* caprice *m*.

whimper *vi* gémir, pleurnicher.

whimsical *adj* capricieux, fantasque.

whine *vi* gémir, se plaindre; * *n* gémissement *m*, plainte *f*.

whinny *vi* hennir.

whip *n* fouet *m*; cravache *f*; * *vt* fouetter; battre.

whipped cream *n* crème fouettée *f*.

whirl *vi* tourbillonner, tournoyer; aller à toute allure; * *vt* faire tourbillonner, faire tournoyer.

whirlpool *n* tourbillon *m*.

whirlwind *n* tornade *f*.

whisper *vi* chuchoter; murmurer.

whispering *n* chuchotement *m*; murmure *m*.

whistle *vi* siffler; * *n* sifflement *m*.

white *adj* blanc; pâle; * *n* blanc *m*; blanc d'œuf *m*.

white elephant *n* bibelot *m*.

white-hot *adj* chauffé à blanc.

white lie *n* petit mensonge, mensonge innocent *m*.

whiten *vt vi* blanchir.

whiteness *n* blancheur *f*; pâleur *f*.

whitewash *n* blanc de chaux *m*; * *vt* blanchir à la chaux; disculper.

whiting *n* merlan *m*.

whitish *adj* blanchâtre.

who *pn* qui.

whoever *pn* quiconque, qui que ce soit, quel(le) que soit.

whole *adj* tout, entier; intact, complet; sain; * *n* tout *m*; ensemble *m*.

wholehearted *adj* sincère.

wholemeal *adj* complet.

wholesale *n* vente en gros *f*.

wholesome *adj* sain, salubre.

wholewheat *adj* complet.

wholly *adv* complètement.

whom *pn* qui; que.

whooping cough *n* coqueluche *f*.

whore *n* putain *f*.

why *n* pourquoi *m*; * *conj* pourquoi; * *excl* eh bien!, tiens!

wick *n* mèche *f*.

wicked *adj* méchant, mauvais; ~ly *adv* méchamment.

wickedness *n* méchanceté, perversité *f*.

wicker *n* osier *m*; * *adj* en osier.

wide *adj* large, ample; grand; ~ly *adv* partout; far and ~ de tous côtés.

wide-awake *adj* bien réveillé.

widen *vt* élargir, agrandir.

wide open *adj* grand ouvert.

widespread *adj* très répandu.

widow *n* veuve *f*.

widower *n* veuf *m*.

width *n* largeur *f*.

wield *vt* manier, brandir.

wife *n* femme *f*; épouse *f*.

wig *n* perruque *f*.

wiggle *vt* agiter; * *vi* s'agiter.

wild *adj* sauvage, féroce; désert; fou; furieux; ~ly *adv* violemment; furieusement; follement.

wilderness *n* étendue déserte *f*.

wild life *n* faune *f*.

wilful *adj* délibéré; entêté.

wilfulness *n* obstination *f*.

wiliness *n* ruse, astuce *f*.

will *n* volonté *f*; testament *m*; * *vt* vouloir.

willing *adj* prêt, disposé; ~ly *adv* volontiers, de bon cœur.

willingness *n* bonne volonté *f*, empressement *m*.

willow *n* saule *m*.

willpower *n* volonté *f*.

wilt *vi* se fâner.

wily *adj* astucieux.

win *vt* gagner, conquérir; remporter.

wince *vi* tressaillir.

winch *n* treuil *m*.

wind *n* vent *m*; souffle *m*; gaz *mpl*.

wind *vt* enrouler; envelopper; donner un tour de; * *vi* serpenter.

windfall *n* fruit abattu par le vent *m*; (*fig*) aubaine *f*.

winding *adj* tortueux.

windmill *n* moulin à vent *m*.

window *n* fenêtre *f*.

window box *n* jardinière *f*.

window cleaner *n* laveur(-euse) *m(f)* de carreaux.

window ledge *n* appui *m* de fenêtre.

window pane *n* carreau *m*.

window sill *n* rebord *m* de fenêtre.

windpipe *n* trachée *f* artère.

windscreen *n* pare-brise *m invar*.

windscreen washer *n* lave-glace *m invar*.

windscreen wiper *n* essuie-glace *m invar*.

windy *adj* venteux.

wine *n* vin *m*.

wine cellar *n* cave (à vin) *f*.

wine glass *n* verre à vin *m*.

wine list *n* carte des vins *f*.

wine merchant *n* négociant en vins *m*.

wine tasting *n* dégustation de vins *f*.

wing *n* aile *f*.

winged *adj* ailé.

winger *n* ailier *m*.

wink *vi* faire un clin d'œil; * *n* clin d'œil *m*; clignement *m*.

winner *n* gagnant *m* -e *f*; vainqueur *m*.

winning post *n* poteau d'arrivée *m*.

winter *n* hiver *m*; * *vi* hiverner.

winter sports *npl* sports d'hiver *mpl*.

wintry *adj* d'hiver, hivernal.

wipe *vt* essuyer; effacer.

wire *n* fil *m*; télégramme *m*; * *vt* installer des fils électriques à; télégraphier.

wiring *n* installation électrique *f*.

wiry *adj* effilé et nerveux.

wisdom *n* sagesse, prudence *f*.

wisdom teeth *npl* dents de sagesse *fpl*.

wise *adj* sage, avisé, judicieux, prudent.

wisecrack *n* bon mot *m*, plaisanterie *f*.

wish *vt* souhaiter, désirer; * *n* souhait, désir *m*.

wishful *adj* désireux.

wisp *n* brin *m*; mince volute *f*.

wistful *adj* nostalgique, rêveur.

wit *n* esprit *m*, intelligence *f*.

witch *n* sorcière *f*.

witchcraft *n* sorcellerie *f*.

with *prep* avec; à; de; contre.

withdraw *vt* retirer; rappeler; annuler; * *vi* se retirer.

withdrawal *n* retrait *m*.

withdrawn *adj* réservé.

wither *vi* se flétrir, se faner.

withhold *vt* détenir, retenir, empêcher.

within *prep* à l'intérieur de; * *adv* dedans; à l'intérieur.

without *prep* sans.

withstand *vt* résister à.

witless *adj* sot, stupide.

witness *n* témoin *m*; témoignage *m*; * *vt* être témoin de; attester.

witness stand *n* barre des témoins *f*.

witticism *n* mot d'esprit *m*.

wittily *adv* spirituellement.

wittingly *adv* sciemment, à dessein.

witty *adj* spirituel, plein d'esprit.

wizard *n* sorcier, magicien *m*.

wobble *vi* trembler.

woe *n* malheur *m*; affliction *f*.

woeful *adj* triste, malheureux; ~ly *adv* tristement.

wolf *n* loup *m*; she ~ louve *f*.

woman *n* femme *f*.

womanish *adj* de femme.

womanly *adj* féminin, de femme.

womb *n* utérus *m*.

women's lib *n* mouvement de libération de la femme *m*.

wonder *n* merveille *f*; miracle *m*; émerveillement *m*; * *vi* s'émerveiller.

wonderful *adj* merveilleux; ~ly *adv* merveilleusement.

wondrous *adj* merveilleux.

won't *abrev* de will not.

wont *n* coutume *f*.

woo *vt* faire la cour à.

wood *n* bois *m*.

wood alcohol *n* alcool méthylique *m*.

wood carving *n* sculpture sur bois *f*.

woodcut *n* gravure sur bois *f*.

woodcutter *n* bûcheron *m*.

wooded *adj* boisé.

wooden *adj* de bois, en bois.

woodland *n* région boisée *f*.

woodlouse *n* cloporte *m*.

woodman *n* forestier *m*; garde-forestier *m*.

woodpecker *n* pic *m*.

woodwind *n* (*mus*) bois *mpl*.

woodwork *n* menuiserie *f*.

woodworm *n* ver du bois *m*.

wool *n* laine *f*.

woollen *adj* de laine.

woollens *npl* lainages *mpl*.

woolly *adj* laineux, de laine.

word *n* mot *m*; parole *f*; * *vt* exprimer; rédiger.

wordiness *n* verbosité *f*.

wording *n* formulation *f*.

word processing *n* traitement *m* de texte.

word processor *n* machine *f* à traitement de texte.

wordy *adj* verbeux.

work *vi* travailler; opérer; fonctionner; fermenter; * *vt* (faire) travailler, faire fonctionner; façonner; * ~ out *vi* marcher; * *vt* résoudre; * *n* travail *m*; œuvre *f*; ouvrage *m*; emploi *m*.

workable *adj* exploitable.

workaholic *n* drogué du travail *m*.

worker *n* travailleur *m* -euse *f*; ouvrier *m* -ère *f*.

workforce *n* main-d'œuvre *f*.

working-class *adj* ouvrier.

workman *n* ouvrier, artisan *m*.

workmanship *n* exécution *f*; qualité du travail *f*.

workmate *n* camarade de travail *mf*.

workshop *n* atelier *m*.

world n monde m; * adj du monde; mondial.

worldliness n mondanité f; attachement aux choses matrielles m.

worldly adj mondain; terrestre.

worldwide adj mondial.

worm n ver m.

worn-out adj épuisé; usé.

worried adj inquiet.

worry vt inquiéter; n souci m.

worrying adj inquiétant.

worse adj adv pire; * n le pire.

worship n culte m; adoration f; **your ~** Monsieur le Maire, Monsieur le Juge; * vt adorer, vénérer.

worst adj le pire; * adv le plus mal; * n le pire m.

worth n valeur f, prix m; mérite m.

worthily adv dignement, à juste titre.

worthless adj sans valeur; inutile.

worthwhile adj qui vaut la peine; louable.

worthy adj digne; louable.

would-be adj soi-disant.

wound n blessure f; * vt blesser.

wrangle vi se disputer; * n dispute f.

wrap vt envelopper.

wrath n colère f.

wreath n couronne, guirlande f.

wreck n naufrage m; ruines fpl; destruction f; épave f; * vt causer le naufrage de; démolir.

wreckage n naufrage m; épave f, débris mpl.

wren n roitelet m.

wrench vt tordre; forcer; tourner violemment; * n clé f; torsion violente f.

wrest vt arracher.

wrestle vi lutter.

wrestling n lutte f.

wretched adj malheureux, misérable.

wriggle vi remuer, se tortiller.

wring vt tordre; essorer; arracher.

wrinkle n ride f; * vt rider; * vi se rider.

wrist n poignet m.

wristband n manchette de chemise f.

wristwatch n montre-bracelet f.

writ n écriture f; assignation f; acte judiciaire m.

write *vt* écrire; composer; ~ **down** consigner par écrit; ~ **off** annuler; réduire; ~ **up** rédiger.

write-off *n* perte *f*.

writer *n* écrivain *m*; auteur *m*.

writhe *vi* se tordre.

writing *n* écriture *f*; œuvres *fpl*; écrit *m*.

writing desk *n* bureau *m*.

writing paper *n* papier à lettres *m*.

wrong *n* mal *m*; injustice *f*; tort *m*; injure *f*; * *adj* mauvais, mal; injuste; inopportun; faux, erroné; * *adv* mal, inexactement; * *vt* faire du tort à, léser.

wrongful *adj* injuste.

wrongly *adv* injustement.

wry *adj* ironique, narquois.

XYZ

xenon *n* xénon *m*.

xenophobe *n* xénophobe *mf*.

xenophobia *n* xénophobie *f*.

xenophobic *adj* xénophobique.

Xmas *abbr* Noël *m*.

X-ray *n* rayon X *m*.

xylophone *n* xylophone *m*.

yacht *n* yacht *m*.

yachting *n* navigation de plaisance *f*.

Yankee *n* yankee *m*.

yard *n* yard (0.914 m) *m*; cour *f*.

yardstick *n* critère d'évaluation *m*.

yarn *n* longue histoire *f*; fil *m*.

yawn *vi* bâiller; * *n* bâillement *m*.

yawning *adj* béant.

yeah *adv* (*fam*) oui, ouais.

year *n* année *f*.

yearbook *n* annuaire *m*.

yearling *n* animal âgé d'un an *m*.

yearly *adj adv* annuel(lement).

yearn *vi* languir.

yearning *n* désir ardent *m*.

yeast *n* levure *f*.

yell *vi* hurler; * *n* hurlement *m*.

yellow *adj n* jaune *m*.

yellowish *adj* jaunâtre.

yelp *vi* japper, glapir; * *n* jappement *m*.

yes *adv*, *n* oui *m*.

yesterday *adv*, *n* hier (*m*).

yet *conj* pourtant; cependant; * *adv* encore.

yew *n* if *m*.

yield *vt* donner, produire; rapporter; * *vi* se rendre; céder; * *n* production *f*; récolte *f*; rendement *m*.

yoga *n* yoga *m*.

yog(h)urt *n* yaourt *m*.

yoke *n* joug *m*.

yolk *n* jaune d'œuf *m*.

yonder *adv* là-bas.

you *pn* vous; tu; te; toi.

young *adj* jeune; ~er *adj* plus jeune.

youngster *n* jeune *mf*.

your(s) *pn* ton, ta, tes; votre, vos; le tien, la tienne, les tiens, les tiennes; le/la vôtre, les vôtres; **sincerely ~s** je vous prie d'agréer, Monsieur/Madame, l'expression de mes sentiments les meilleurs.

yourself *pn* toi-même; vous-même(s).

youth *n* jeunesse, adolescence *f*; jeune homme *m*.

youthful *adj* jeune.

youthfulness *n* jeunesse *f*.

yuppie (*adj*) *n* (de) jeune cadre dynamique *m*.

zany *adj* farfelu.

zap *vt* flinguer.

zeal *n* zèle *m*; ardeur *f*.

zealous *adj* zélé.

zebra *n* zèbre *m*.

zenith *n* zénith *m*.

zero *n* zéro *m*.

zest *n* enthousiasme *m*.

zigzag *n* zigzag *m*.

zinc *n* zinc *m*.

zip, zipper *n* fermeture éclair *f*.

zip code *n* code postal *m*.

zodiac *n* zodiaque *m*.

zone *n* zone *f*; secteur *m*.

zoo *n* zoo *m*.

zoological *adj* zoologique.

zoologist *n* zoologiste *mf*.

zoology *n* zoologie *f*.

zoom *vi* vrombir.

zoom lens *n* zoom *m*.

Verbs

Verbes Irréguliers en Anglais

Verbe	*Prétérit*	*Participe passé*
arise	arose	arisen
awake	awoke	awaked, awoke
be	[I am, you/we/they are, he/she/it is, *gérondif* being] was, were	been
bear	bore	borne
beat	beat	beaten
become	became	become
begin	began	begun
behold	beheld	beheld
bend	bent	bent
beseech	besought, beseeched	besought, beseeched
beset	beset	beset
bet	bet, betted	bet, betted
bid	bade, bid	bid, bidden
bite	bit	bitten
bleed	bled	bled
bless	blessed, blest	blessed, blest
blow	blew	blown
break	broke	broken
breed	bred	bred
bring	brought	brought
build	built	built
burn	burnt, burned	burnt, burned
burst	burst	burst
buy	bought	bought

Verbs

Verbe	Prétérit	Participe passé
can	could	(been able)
cast	cast	cast
catch	caught	caught
choose	chose	chosen
cling	clung	clung
come	came	come
cost	cost	cost
creep	crept	crept
cut	cut	cut
deal	dealt	dealt
dig	dug	dug
do	[he/she/it does] did	done
draw	drew	drawn
dream	dreamed, dreamt	dreamed, dreamt
drink	drank	drunk
drive	drove	driven
dwell	dwelt, dwelled	dwelt, dwelled
eat	ate	eaten
fall	fell	fallen
feed	fed	fed
feel	felt	felt
fight	fought	fought
find	found	found
flee	fled	fled
fling	flung	flung
fly	[he/she/it flies] flew	flown
forbid	forbade	forbidden
forecast	forecast	forecast
forget	forgot	forgotten
forgive	forgave	forgiven
forsake	forsook	forsaken
forsee	foresaw	foreseen
freeze	froze	frozen

Verbe	*Prétérit*	*Participe passé*
get	got	got, (US) gotten
give	gave	given
go	[he/she/it goes]	
	went	gone
grind	ground	ground
grow	grew	grown
hang	hung, hanged	hung, hanged
have	[I/you/we/they have, he/she/it has, *gérondif* having]	
	had	had
hear	heard	heard
hide	hid	hidden
hit	hit	hit
hold	held	held
hurt	hurt	hurt
keep	kept	kept
kneel	knelt	knelt
know	knew	known
lay	laid	laid
lead	led	led
lean	leant, leaned	leant, leaned
leap	leapt, leaped	leapt, leaped
learn	learnt, learned	learnt, learned
leave	left	left
lend	lent	lent
let	let	let
lie	[*gérondif* lying]	
	lay	lain
light	lighted, lit	lighted, lit
lose	lost	lost
make	made	made
may	might	—
mean	meant	meant
meet	met	met
mistake	mistook	mistaken

Verbs

Verbe	Prétérit	Participe passé
mow	mowed	mowed, mown
must	(had to)	(had to)
overcome	overcame	overcome
pay	paid	paid
put	put	put
quit	quit, quitted	quit, quitted
read	read	read
rid	rid	rid
ride	rode	ridden
ring	rang	rung
rise	rose	risen
run	ran	run
saw	sawed	sawn, sawed
say	said	said
see	saw	seen
seek	sought	sought
sell	sold	sold
send	sent	sent
set	set	set
sew	sewed	sewn, sewed
shake	shook	shaken
shall	should	—
shear	sheared	sheared, shorn
shed	shed	shed
shine	shone	shone
shoot	shot	shot
show	showd	shown, showed
shrink	shrank	shrunk
shut	shut	shut
sing	sang	sung
sink	sank	sunk
sit	sat	sat
slay	slew	slain
sleep	slept	slept
slide	slid	slid

Verbe	Prétérit	Participe passé
sling	slung	slung
smell	smelt, smelled	smelt, smelled
sow	sowed	sown, sowed
speak	spoke	spoken
speed	sped, speeded	sped, speeded
spell	spelt, spelled	spelt, spelled
spend	spent	spent
spill	spilt, spilled	spilt, spilled
spin	spun	spun
spit	spat	spat
split	split	split
spoil	spoilt	spoilt
spread	spread	spread
spring	sprang	sprung
stand	stood	stood
steal	stole	stolen
stick	stuck	stuck
sting	stung	stung
stink	stank	stunk
stride	strode	stridden
strike	struck	struck
strive	strove	striven
swear	swore	sworn
sweep	swept	swept
swell	swelled	swelled, swollen
swim	swam	swum
swing	swung	swung
take	took	taken
teach	taught	taught
tear	tore	torn
tell	told	told
think	thought	thought
throw	threw	thrown
thrust	thrust	thrust
tread	trod	trodden, trod

Verbs

Verbe	*Prétérit*	*Participe passé*
understand	understood	understood
upset	upset	upset
wake	woke	woken
wear	wore	worn
weave	wove,	wove, woven
wed	wedded	wed, wedded
weep	wept	wept
win	won	won
wind	wound	wound
withdraw	withdrew	withdrawn
withhold	withheld	withheld
withstand	withstood	withstood
wring	wrung	wrung
write	wrote	written

French Verbs

Regular Verbs

infinitive	**donner**	**finir**	**vendre**
	to give	*to finish*	*to sell*
present participle	donn**ant**	finiss**ant**	vend**ant**
past participle	donn**é**	fin**i**	vend**u**
present	je donn**e**	je fin**is**	je vend**s**
	tu donn**es**	tu fin**is**	tu vend**s**
	il donn**e**	il fin**it**	il vend
	nous donn**ons**	nous fin**issons**	nous vend**ons**
	vous donn**ez**	vous fin**issez**	vous vend**ez**
	ils donn**ent**	ils fin**issent**	ils vend**ent**
imperfect	je donn**ais**	je fin**issais**	je vend**ais**
	tu donn**ais**	tu fin**issais**	tu vend**ais**
	il donn**ait**	il fin**issait**	il vend**ait**
	nous donn**ions**	nous fin**issions**	nous vend**ions**
	vous donn**iez**	vous fin**issiez**	vous vend**iez**
	ils donn**aient**	ils fin**issaient**	ils vend**aient**
future	je donn**erai**	je fin**irai**	je vend**rai**
	tu donn**eras**	tu fin**iras**	tu vend**ras**
	il donn**era**	il fin**ira**	il vend**ra**
	nous donn**erons**	nous fin**irons**	nous vend**rons**
	vous donn**erez**	vous fin**irez**	vous vend**rez**
	ils donn**eront**	ils fin**iront**	ils vend**ront**
conditional	je donn**erais**	je fin**irais**	je vend**rais**
	tu donn**erais**	tu fin**irais**	tu vend**rais**
	il donn**erait**	il fin**irait**	il vend**rait**
	nous donn**erions**	nous fin**irions**	nous vend**rions**

	vous donn**eriez**	vous fin**iriez**	vous vend**riez**
	ils donn**eraient**	ils fin**iraient**	ils vend**raient**
past historic	je donn**ai**	je fin**is**	je vend**is**
	tu donn**as**	tu fin**is**	tu vend**is**
	il donn**a**	il fin**it**	il vend**it**
	nous donn**âmes**	nous fin**îmes**	nous vend**îmes**
	vous donn**âtes**	vous fin**îtes**	vous vend**îtes**
	ils donn**èrent**	ils fin**irent**	ils vend**irent**
present	je donn**e**	je fin**isse**	je vend**e**
subjunctive	tu donn**es**	tu fin**isses**	tu vend**es**
	il donn**e**	il fin**isse**	il vend**e**
	nous donn**ions**	nous fin**issions**	nous vend**ions**
	vous donn**iez**	vous fin**issiez**	vous vend**iez**
	ils donn**ent**	ils fin**issent**	ils vend**ent**
imperfect	je donn**asse**	je fin**isse**	je vend**isse**
subjunctive	tu donn**asses**	tu fin**isses**	tu vend**isses**
	il donn**ât**	il fin**ît**	il vend**ît**
	nous donn**assions**	nous fin**issions**	nous vend**issions**
	vous donn**assiez**	vous fin**issiez**	vous vend**issiez**
	ils donn**assent**	ils fin**issent**	ils vend**issent**

Auxiliary Verbs

	être	**avoir**
infinitive	to be	to have
present participle	étant	ayant
past participle	été	eu
present	je suis	j'ai
	tu es	tu as
	il est	il a
	nous sommes	nous avons
	vous êtes	vous avez
	ils sont	ils ont
imperfect	j'étais	j'avais
	tu étais	tu avais
	il était	il avait
	nous étions	nous avions

	vous étiez	vous aviez
	ils étaient	ils avaient
future	je serai	j' aurai
	tu seras	tu auras
	il sera	il aura
	nous serons	nous aurons
	vous serez	vous aurez
	ils seront	ils auront
conditional	je serais	je aurais
	tu serais	tu aurais
	il serait	il aurait
	nous serions	nous aurions
	vous seriez	vous auriez
	ils seraient	ils auraient
past historic	je fus	j'eus
	tu fus	tu eus
	il fut	il eut
	nous fûmes	nous eûmes
	vous fûtes	vous eûtes
	ils furent	ils eurent
present subjunctive	je sois	j'aie
	tu sois	tu aies
	il soit	il ait
	nous soyons	nous ayons
	vous soyez	vous ayez
	ils soient	ils aient
imperfect subjunctive	je fusse	j'eusse
	tu fusses	tu eusses
	il fût	il eût
	nous fussions	nous eussions
	vous fussiez	vous eussiez
	ils fussent	ils eussent

Irregular Verbs

	acheter	**acquérir**	**aller**	**appeler**
	to buy	*to acquire*	*to go*	*to call*
present	achète	acquiers	vais	appelle
	achètes	acquiers	vas	appelles
	achète	acquiert	va	appelle
	achetons	acquérons	allons	appelons
	achetez	acquérez	allez	appelez
	achètent	acquièrent	vont	appellent
imperfect	achetais	acquérais	allais	appelais
	achetais	acquérais	allais	appelais
	achetait	acquérait	allait	appelait
	achetions	acquérions	allions	appelions
	achetiez	acquériez	alliez	appeliez
	achetaient	acquéraient	allaient	appelaient
future	achèterai	acquerrai	irai	appellerai
	achèteras	acquerras	iras	appelleras
	achètera	acquerra	ira	appellera
	achèterons	acquerrons	irons	appellerons
	achèterez	acquerrez	irez	appellerez
	achèteront	acquerront	iront	appelleront
conditional	achèterais	acquerrais	irais	appellerais
	achèterais	acquerrais	irais	appellerais
	achèterait	acquerrait	irait	appellerait
	achèterions	acquerrions	irions	appellerions
	achèteriez	acquerriez	iriez	appelleriez
	achèteraient	acquerraient	iraient	appelleraient
past historic	achetai	acquis	allai	appelai
	achetas	acquis	allas	appelas
	acheta	acquit	alla	appela
	achetâmes	acquîmes	allâmes	appelâmes
	achetâtes	acquîtes	allâtes	appelâtes
	achetèrent	acquirent	allèrent	appelèrent
present	achète	acquière	aille	appelle
subjunctive	achètes	acquières	ailles	appelles

	achète	acquière	aille	appelle
	achetions	acquérions	allions	appelions
	achetiez	acquériez	alliez	appeliez
	achètent	acquièrent	aillent	appellent
imperfect	achetasse	acquisse	allasse	appelasse
subjunctive	achetasses	acquisses	allasses	appelasses
	achetât	acquît	allât	appelât
	achetassions	acquissions	allassions	appelassions
	achetassiez	acquissiez	allassiez	appelassiez
	achetassent	acquissent	allassent	appelassent
	appuyer	**s'asseoir**	**battre**	**boire**
	to lean	*to sit down*	*to hit*	*to drink*
present	appuie	m'assieds	bats	bois
	appuies	t'assieds	bats	bois
	appuie	s'assied	bat	boit
	appuyons	nous asseyons	battons	buvons
	appuyez	vous asseyez	battez	buvez
	appuient	s'asseyent	battent	boivent
imperfect	appuyais	m'asseyais	battais	buvais
	appuyais	t'asseyais	battais	buvais
	appuyait	s'asseyait	battait	buvait
	appuyions	nous asseyions	battions	buvions
	appuyiez	vous asseyiez	battiez	buviez
	appuient	s'asseyaient	battaient	buvaient
future	appuierai	m'assiérai	battrai	boirai
	appuieras	t'assiéras	battras	boiras
	appuiera	s'assiéra	battra	boira
	appuierons	nous assiérons	battrons	boirons
	appuierez	vous assiérez	battrez	boirez
	appuieront	s'assiéront	battront	boiront
conditional	appuierais	m'assiérais	battrais	boirais
	appuierais	t'assiérais	battrais	boirais
	appuierait	s'assiérait	battrait	boirait
	appuierions	nous assiérions	battrions	boirions
	appuieriez	vous assiériez	battriez	boiriez
	appuieraient	s'assiéraient	battraient	boiraient
past historic	appuyai	m'assis	battis	bus

	appuyas	t'assis	battis	bus
	appuya	s'assit	battit	but
	appuyâmes	nous assîmes	battîmes	bûmes
	appuyâtes	vous assîtes	battîtes	bûtes
	appuyèrent	s'assirent	battirent	burent
present subjunctive	appuie	m'asseye	batte	boive
	appuies	t'asseyes	battes	boives
	appuie	s'asseye	batte	boive
	appuyions	nous asseyions	battions	buvions
	appuyiez	vous asseyiez	battiez	buviez
	appuient	s'asseyent	battent	boivent
imperfect subjunctive	appuyasse	m'assisse	battisse	busse
	appuyasses	t'assisses	battisses	busses
	appuyât	s'assît	battît	bût
	appuyassions	nous assissions	battissions	bussions
	appuyassiez	vous assissiez	battissiez	bussiez
	appuyassent	s'assissent	battissent	bussent

	commencer	**conduire**	**connaître**	**courir**
	to begin	*to drive*	*to know*	*to run*
present	commence	conduis	connais	cours
	commences	conduis	connais	cours
	commence	conduit	connaît	court
	commençons	conduisons	connaissons	courons
	commencez	conduisez	connaissez	courez
	commencent	conduisent	connaissent	courent
imperfect	commençais	conduisais	connaissais	courais
	commençais	conduisais	connaissais	courais
	commençait	conduisait	connaissait	courait
	commencions	conduisions	connaissions	courions
	commenciez	conduisiez	connaissiez	couriez
	commençaient	conduisaient	connaissaient	couraient
future	commencerai	conduirai	connaîtrai	courrai
	commenceras	conduiras	connaîtras	courras
	commencera	conduira	connaîtra	courra
	commencerons	conduirons	connaîtrons	courrons
	commencerez	conduirez	connaîtrez	courrez
	commenceront	conduiront	connaîtront	courront

conditional	commencerais	conduirais	connaîtrais	courrais
	commencerais	conduirais	connaîtrais	courrais
	commencerait	conduirait	connaîtrait	courrait
	commencerions	conduirions	connaîtrions	courrions
	commenceriez	conduiriez	connaîtriez	courriez
	commenceraient	conduiraient	connaîtraient	courraient
past historic	commençai	conduisis	connus	courus
	commenças	conduisis	connus	courus
	commença	conduisit	connut	courut
	commençâmes	conduisîmes	connûmes	courûmes
	commençâtes	conduisîtes	connûtes	courûtes
	commencèrent	conduisirent	connurent	coururent
present	commence	conduise	connaisse	coure
subjunctive	commences	conduises	connaisses	coures
	commence	conduise	connaisse	coure
	commencions	conduisions	connaissions	courions
	commenciez	conduisiez	connaissiez	couriez
	commencent	conduisent	connaissent	courent
imperfect	commençasse	conduisisse	connusse	courusse
subjunctive	commençasses	conduisisses	connusses	courusses
	commençât	conduisît	connût	courût
	commençassions	conduisissions	connussions	courussions
	commençassiez	conduisissiez	connussiez	courussiez
	commençassent	conduisissent	connussent	courussent

	couvrir	**craindre**	**croire**	**devoir**
	to cover	_to fear_	_to believe_	_to owe, to have to_
present	couvre	crains	crois	dois
	couvres	crains	crois	dois
	couvre	craint	croit	doit
	couvrons	craignons	croyons	devons
	couvrez	craignez	croyez	devez
	couvrent	craignent	croient	doivent
imperfect	couvrais	craignais	croyais	devais
	couvrais	craignais	croyais	devais
	couvrait	craignait	croyait	devait
	couvrions	craignions	croyions	devions
	couvriez	craigniez	croyiez	deviez

Verms

	couvraient	craignaient	croyaient	devaient
future	couvrirai	craindrai	croirai	devrai
	couvriras	craindras	croiras	devras
	couvrira	craindra	croira	devra
	couvrirons	craindrons	croirons	devrons
	couvrirez	craindrez	croirez	devrez
	couvriront	craindront	croiront	devront
conditional	couvrirais	craindrais	croirais	devrais
	couvrirais	craindrais	croirais	devrais
	couvrirait	craindrait	croirait	devrait
	couvririons	craindrions	croirions	devrions
	couvririez	craindriez	croiriez	devriez
	couvriraient	craindraient	croiraient	devraient
past historic	couvris	craignis	crus	dus
	couvris	craignis	crus	dus
	couvrit	craignit	crut	dut
	couvrîmes	craignîmes	crûmes	dûmes
	couvrîtes	craignîtes	crûtes	dûtes
	couvrirent	craignirent	crurent	durent
present	couvre	craigne	croie	doive
subjunctive	couvres	craignes	croies	doives
	couvre	craigne	croie	doive
	couvrions	craignions	croyions	devions
	couvriez	craigniez	croyiez	deviez
	couvrent	craignent	croient	doivent
imperfect	couvrisse	craignisse	crusse	dusse
subjunctive	couvrisses	craignisses	crusses	dusses
	couvrît	craignît	crût	dût
	couvrissions	craignissions	crussions	dussions
	couvrissiez	craignissiez	crussiez	dussiez
	couvrissent	craignissent	crussent	dussent
	dire	**écrire**	**envoyer**	**faire**
	to say	*to write*	*to send*	*to do; to make*
present	dis	écris	envoie	fais
	dis	écris	envoies	fais
	dit	écrit	envoie	fait
	disons	écrivons	envoyons	faisons

	dites	écrivez	envoyez	faites
	disent	écrivent	envoient	font
imperfect	disais	écrivais	envoyais	faisais
	disais	écrivais	envoyais	faisais
	disait	écrivait	envoyait	faisait
	disions	écrivions	envoyions	faisions
	disiez	écriviez	envoyiez	faisiez
	disaient	écrivaient	envoyaient	faisaient
future	dirai	écrirai	enverrai	ferai
	diras	écriras	enverras	feras
	dira	écrira	enverra	fera
	dirons	écrirons	enverrons	ferons
	direz	écrirez	enverrez	ferez
	diront	écriront	enverront	feront
conditional	dirais	écrirais	enverrais	ferais
	dirais	écrirais	enverrais	ferais
	dirait	écrirait	enverrait	ferait
	dirions	écririons	enverrions	ferions
	diriez	écririez	enverriez	feriez
	diraient	écriraient	enverraient	feraient
past historic	dis	écrivis	envoyai	fis
	dis	écrivis	envoyas	fis
	dit	écrivit	envoya	fit
	dîmes	écrivîmes	envoyâmes	fîmes
	dîtes	écrivîtes	envoyâtes	fîtes
	dirent	écrivirent	envoyèrent	firent
present subjunctive	dise	écrive	envoie	fasse
	dises	écrives	envoies	fasses
	dise	écrive	envoie	fasse
	disions	écrivions	envoyions	fassions
	disiez	écriviez	envoyiez	fassiez
	disent	écrivent	envoient	fassent
imperfect subjunctive	disse	écrivisse	envoyasse	fisse
	disses	écrivisses	envoyasses	fisses
	dît	écrivît	envoyât	fît
	dissions	écrivissions	envoyassions	fissions
	dissiez	écrivissiez	envoyassiez	fissiez

Verbs

	dissent	écrivissent	envoyassent	fissent
	fuir	**haïr**	**jeter**	**lire**
	to flee	to hate	to throw	to read
present	fuis	hais	jette	lis
	fuis	hais	jettes	lis
	fuit	hait	jette	lit
	fuyons	haïssons	jetons	lisons
	fuyez	haïssez	jetez	lisez
	fuient	haïssent	jettent	lisent
imperfect	fuyais	haïssais	jetais	lisais
	fuyais	haïssais	jetais	lisais
	fuyait	haïssait	jetait	lisait
	fuyions	haïssions	jetions	lisions
	fuyiez	haïssiez	jetiez	lisiez
	fuyaient	haïssaient	jetaient	lisaient
future	fuirai	haïrai	jetterai	lirai
	fuiras	haïras	jetteras	liras
	fuira	haïra	jettera	lira
	fuirons	haïrons	jetterons	lirons
	fuirez	haïrez	jetterez	lirez
	fuiront	haïront	jetteront	liront
conditional	fuirais	haïrais	jetterais	lirais
	fuirais	haïrais	jetterais	lirais
	fuirait	haïrait	jetterait	lirait
	fuirions	haïrions	jetterions	lirions
	fuiriez	haïriez	jetteriez	liriez
	fuiraient	haïraient	jetteraient	liraient
past historic	fuis	haïs	jetai	lus
	fuis	haïs	jetas	lus
	fuit	haït	jeta	lut
	fuîmes	haïmes	jetâmes	lûmes
	fuîtes	haïtes	jetâtes	lûtes
	fuirent	haïrent	jetèrent	lurent
present	fuie	haïsse	jette	lise
subjunctive	fuies	haïsses	jettes	lises
	fuie	haïsse	jette	lise
	fuyions	haïssions	jetions	lisions

	fuyiez	haïssiez	jetiez	lisiez
	fuient	haïssent	jettent	lisent
imperfect	fuisse	haïsse	jetasse	lusse
subjunctive	fuisses	haïsses	jetasses	lusses
	fuît	haït	jetât	lût
	fuissions	haïssions	jetassions	lussions
	fuissiez	haïssiez	jetassiez	lussiez
	fuissent	haïssent	jetassent	lussent
	manger	**mettre**	**mourir**	**mouvoir**
	to eat	*to put*	*to die*	*to drive, to move*
present	mange	mets	meurs	meus
	manges	mets	meurs	meus
	mange	met	meurt	meut
	mangeons	mettons	mourons	mouvons
	mangez	mettez	mourez	mouvez
	mangent	mettent	meurent	meuvent
imperfect	mangeais	mettais	mourais	mouvais
	mangeais	mettais	mourais	mouvais
	mangeait	mettait	mourait	mouvait
	mangions	mettions	mourions	mouvions
	mangiez	mettiez	mouriez	mouviez
	mangeaient	mettaient	mouraient	mouvaient
future	mangerai	mettrai	mourrai	mouvrai
	mangeras	mettras	mourras	mouvras
	mangera	mettra	mourra	mouvra
	mangerons	mettrons	mourrons	mouvrons
	mangerez	mettrez	mourrez	mouvrez
	mangeront	mettront	mourront	mouvront
conditional	mangerais	mettrais	mourrais	mouvrais
	mangerais	mettrais	mourrais	mouvrais
	mangerait	mettrait	mourrait	mouvrait
	mangerions	mettrions	mourrions	mouvrions
	mangeriez	mettriez	mourriez	mouvriez
	mangeraient	mettraient	mourraient	mouvraient
past historic	mangeai	mis	mourus	mus
	mangeas	mis	mourus	mus
	mangea	mit	mourut	mut

Verbs

	mangeâmes	mîmes	mourûmes	mûmes
	mangeâtes	mîtes	mourûtes	mûtes
	mangèrent	mirent	moururent	murent
present	mange	mette	meure	meuve
subjunctive	manges	mettes	meures	meuves
	mange	mette	meure	meuve
	mangions	mettions	mourions	mouvions
	mangiez	mettiez	mouriez	mouviez
	mangent	mettent	meurent	meuvent
imperfect	mangeasse	misse	mourusse	musse
subjunctive	mangeasses	misses	mourusses	musses
	mangeât	mît	mourût	mût
	mangeassions	missions	mourussions	mussions
	mangeassiez	missiez	mourussiez	mussiez
	mangeassent	missent	mourussent	mussent
	naître	**partir**	**plaire**	**pouvoir**
	to be born	*to leave*	*to please*	*to be able; can*
present	nais	pars	plais	peux
	nais	pars	plais	peux
	naît	part	plaît	peut
	naissons	partons	plaisons	pouvons
	naissez	partez	plaisez	pouvez
	naissent	partent	plaisent	peuvent
imperfect	naissais	partais	plaisais	pouvais
	naissais	partais	plaisais	pouvais
	naissait	partait	plaisait	pouvait
	naissions	partions	plaisions	pouvions
	naissiez	partiez	plaisiez	pouviez
	naissaient	partaient	plaisaient	pouvaient
future	naîtrai	partirai	plairai	pourrai
	naîtras	partiras	plairas	pourras
	naîtra	partira	plaira	pourra
	naîtrons	partirons	plairons	pourrons
	naîtrez	partirez	plairez	pourrez
	naîtront	partiront	plairont	pourront
conditional	naîtrais	partirais	plairais	pourrais
	naîtrais	partirais	plairais	pourrais

	naîtrait	partirait	plairait	pourrait
	naîtrions	partirions	plairions	pourrions
	naîtriez	partiriez	plairiez	pourriez
	naîtraient	partiraient	plairaient	pourraient
past historic	naquis	partis	plus	pus
	naquis	partis	plus	pus
	naquit	partit	plut	put
	naquîmes	partîmes	plûmes	pûmes
	naquîtes	partîtes	plûtes	pûtes
	naquirent	partirent	plurent	purent
present subjunctive	naisse	parte	plaise	puisse
	naisses	partes	plaises	puisses
	naisse	parte	plaise	puisse
	naissions	partions	plaisions	puissions
	naissiez	partiez	plaisiez	puissiez
	naissent	partent	plaisent	puissent
imperfect subjunctive	naquisse	partisse	plusse	pusse
	naquisses	partisses	plusses	pusses
	naquît	partît	plût	pût
	naquissions	partissions	plussions	pussions
	naquissiez	partissiez	plussiez	pussiez
	naquissent	partissent	plussent	pussent
	préférer	**prendre**	**recevoir**	**rire**
	to prefer	*to take*	*to receive*	*to laugh*
present	préfère	prends	reçois	ris
	préfères	prends	reçois	ris
	préfère	prend	reçoit	rit
	préférons	prenons	recevons	rions
	préférez	prenez	recevez	riez
	préfèrent	prennent	reçoivent	rient
imperfect	préférais	prenais	recevais	riais
	préférais	prenais	recevais	riais
	préférait	prenait	recevait	riait
	préférions	prenions	recevions	riions
	préfériez	preniez	receviez	riiez
	préféraient	prenaient	recevaient	riaient
future	préférerai	prendrai	recevrai	rirai

	préférer	prendre	recevoir	rire
	préféreras	prendras	recevras	riras
	préférera	prendra	recevra	rira
	préférerons	prendrons	recevrons	rirons
	préférerez	prendrez	recevrez	rirez
	préféreront	prendront	recevront	riront
conditional	préférerais	prendrais	recevrais	rirais
	préférerais	prendrais	recevrais	rirais
	préférerait	prendrait	recevrait	rirait
	préférerions	prendrions	recevrions	ririons
	préféreriez	prendriez	recevriez	ririez
	préféreraient	prendraient	recevraient	riraient
past historic	préférai	pris	reçus	ris
	préféras	pris	reçus	ris
	préféra	prit	reçut	rit
	préférâmes	prîmes	reçûmes	rîmes
	préférâtes	prîtes	reçûtes	rîtes
	préférèrent	prirent	reçurent	rirent
present subjunctive	préfère	prenne	reçoive	rie
	préfères	prennes	reçoives	ries
	préfère	prenne	reçoive	rie
	préférions	prenions	recevions	riions
	préfériez	preniez	receviez	riiez
	préfèrent	prennent	reçoivent	rient
imperfect subjunctive	préférasse	prisse	reçusse	risse
	préférasses	prisses	reçusses	risses
	préférât	prît	reçût	rît
	préférassions	prissions	reçussions	rissions
	préférassiez	prissiez	reçussiez	rissiez
	préférassent	prissent	reçussent	rissent
	savoir	**suffire**	**suivre**	**tenir**
	to know	*to be enough*	*to follow*	*to hold*
present	sais	suffis	suis	tiens
	sais	suffis	suis	tiens
	sait	suffit	suit	tient
	savons	suffisons	suivons	tenons
	savez	suffisez	suivez	tenez
	savent	suffisent	suivent	tiennent

imperfect	savais	suffisais	suivais	tenais
	savais	suffisais	suivais	tenais
	savait	suffisait	suivait	tenait
	savions	suffisions	suivions	tenions
	saviez	suffisiez	suiviez	teniez
	savaient	suffisaient	suivaient	tenaient
future	saurai	suffirai	suivrai	tiendrai
	sauras	suffiras	suivras	tiendras
	saura	suffira	suivra	tiendra
	saurons	suffirons	suivrons	tiendrons
	saurez	suffirez	suivrez	tiendrez
	sauront	suffiront	suivront	tiendront
conditional	saurais	suffirais	suivrais	tiendrais
	saurais	suffirais	suivrais	tiendrais
	saurait	suffirait	suivrait	tiendrait
	saurions	suffirions	suivrions	tiendrions
	sauriez	suffiriez	suivriez	tiendriez
	sauraient	suffiraient	suivraient	tiendraient
past historic	sus	suffis	suivis	tins
	sus	suffis	suivis	tins
	sut	suffit	suivit	tint
	sûmes	suffîmes	suivîmes	tînmes
	sûtes	suffîtes	suivîtes	tîntes
	surent	suffirent	suivirent	tinrent
present subjunctive	sache	suffise	suive	tienne
	saches	suffises	suives	tiennes
	sache	suffise	suive	tienne
	sachions	suffisions	suivions	tenions
	sachiez	suffisiez	suiviez	teniez
	sachent	suffisent	suivent	tiennent
imperfect subjunctive	susse	suffisse	suivisse	tinsse
	susses	suffisses	suivisse	tinsses
	sût	suffît	suivît	tînt
	sussions	suffissions	suivissions	tinssions
	sussiez	suffissiez	suivissiez	tinssiez
	sussent	suffissent	suivissent	tinssent

Verbs

	valoir	**venir**	**vivre**	**voir**
	to be worth	*to come*	*to live*	*to see*
present	vaux	viens	vis	vois
	vaux	viens	vis	vois
	vaut	vient	vit	voit
	valons	venons	vivons	voyons
	valez	venez	vivez	voyez
	valent	viennent	vivent	voient
imperfect	valais	venais	vivais	voyais
	valais	venais	vivais	voyais
	valait	venait	vivait	voyait
	valions	venions	vivions	voyions
	valiez	veniez	viviez	voyiez
	valaient	venaient	vivaient	voyaient
future	vaudrai	viendrai	vivrai	verrai
	vaudras	viendras	vivras	verras
	vaudra	viendra	vivra	verra
	vaudrons	viendrons	vivrons	verrons
	vaudrez	viendrez	vivrez	verrez
	vaudront	viendront	vivront	verront
conditional	vaudrais	viendrais	vivrais	verrais
	vaudrais	viendrais	vivrais	verrais
	vaudrait	viendrait	vivrait	verrait
	vaudrions	viendrions	vivrions	verrions
	vaudriez	viendriez	vivriez	verriez
	vaudraient	viendraient	vivraient	verraient
past historic	valus	vins	vécus	vis
	valus	vins	vécus	vis
	valut	vint	vécut	vit
	valûmes	vînmes	vécûmes	vîmes
	valûtes	vîntes	vécûtes	vîtes
	valurent	vinrent	vécurent	virent
present subjunctive	vaille	vienne	vive	voie
	vailles	viennes	vives	voies
	vaille	vienne	vive	voie
	valions	venions	vivions	voyions
	valiez	veniez	viviez	voyiez

	vaillent	viennent	vivent	voient
imperfect	valusse	vinsse	vécusse	visse
subjunctive	valusses	vinsses	vécusses	visses
	valût	vînt	vécût	vît
	valussions	vinssions	vécussions	vissions
	valussiez	vinssiez	vécussiez	vissiez
	valussent	vinssent	vécussent	vissent

Everyday Phrases

Key to Pronunciation

Guide to French pronunciation scheme

ah	as in b<u>a</u>d, f<u>ar</u>, f<u>a</u>ther
ai	as in m<u>e</u>t, <u>e</u>xcuse, w<u>e</u>ll, m<u>e</u>rcy
ay	as in ob<u>ey</u>, d<u>ay</u>
aw	as in h<u>o</u>t, bl<u>o</u>t, f<u>ough</u>t
ee	as in m<u>ea</u>l, f<u>ee</u>l, souven<u>i</u>r
er	as in th<u>e</u>, t<u>i</u>ck, speak<u>er</u>
ew	as in b<u>eau</u>tiful*
oo	as in tr<u>ue</u>, bl<u>ue</u>, gl<u>ue</u>
oh	as in n<u>o</u>te, b<u>oa</u>t

* There is no exact equivalent in English for the French 'closed' oo sound. Try with your lips to make the oo shape, while saying the ee sound through them.

The other area of French pronunciation without exact equivalents in English is the ng sounds, reduced here for simplicity to two:

an as in French compr<u>end</u> (sounds like ong, as in s<u>ong</u>)

ern as in French bien (sounds like ang, as in b<u>ang</u>)

French consonants are pronounced much as in English.

Everyday Words and Phrases

Yes
Oui
wee

No
Non
non

Please
S'il vous plaît
seel voo play

Yes, please
Oui, s'il vous plaît
wee, seel voo play

No, thank you
Non, merci
non, mair-see

Thank you
Merci
mair-see

Good
Bien
byern

OK
Ça va
sah vah

Excuse me
Excusez-moi
aiks-kew-say-mwah

I am very sorry
Je suis désolé
jer swee day-soh-lay

Being Understood

I do not understand
Je ne comprends pas
jer ner kohm-pran pah

I understand
Je comprends
jer kohm-pran

Do you understand?
Comprenez-vous?
kohm-prer-nay-voo?

I do not speak French
Je ne parle pas français
jer ner pahrl pah fran-say

Do you speak English?
Parlez-vous anglais?
par-lay-voo zan-glay

Can you help me, please?
Pouvez-vous m'aider, s'il vous plaît?
poo-vay-voo may-day, seel voo play

Could you repeat that?
Pourriez-vous répétez, s'il vous plaît?
poo-ryay-voo ray-pay-tay, seel voo play

Please repeat that slowly
Répétez lentement, s'il vous plaît
ray-pay-tay lan-ter-man, seel voo play

Everyday Phrases

Please write it down
Notez-le, s'il vous plaît
noh-tay-ler, seel voo play

Can you translate this for me?
Pouvez-vous me traduire ceci?
poo-vay-voo me trah-dweer ser-see

Is there someone who speaks English?
Y a-t-il quelqu'un qui parle anglais?
ee-ah-teel kail-kern kee pahrl an-glay

Please point to the phrase in the book
Montrez-moi la phrase dans le livre, s'il vous plaît
mon-tray mwah la frahz dan ler leevr, seel voo play

It does not matter
Ce n'est rien
ser nai ryern

I do not mind
Ça ne me dérange pas
sa ner mer day-ranj pah

Greetings and Exchanges

Hello
Bonjour
bon-joor

Hi
Salut
sah-lew

Good morning
Bonjour
bon-joor

Good evening
Bonsoir
bon-swahr

How are you?
Comment allez-vous?
koh-man tah-lay voo

I am very well, thank you
Très bien, merci
trai byern, mair-see

It is good to see you
Je suis heureux de vous voir
jer swee zer-rer der voo vwahr

It is nice to meet you
Heureux de faire votre connaissance
her-rer der fair vohtr koh-nay-sans

That is very kind of you
Vous êtes très aimable
voo zait trai zai-mahbl

You are very kind
Vous êtes bien aimable
voo zait byern ay-mahbl

You are very welcome
Je vous en prie
jer voo zan pree

Good night
Bonne nuit
bohner nwee

Goodbye
Au revoir
oh rer-vwahr

See you soon
A bientôt
ah byern-toh

My name is...
Je m'appelle...
jer mah-pail

What is your name?
Comment vous appelez-vous?
koh-man voo zah-play voo

Here is my son
Voici mon fils
vwah-see mon fees

This is	— my daughter
Voici	— ma fille
vwah-see	— *mah fee*
	— **my husband**
	— mon mari
	— *mon mah-ree*
	— **my wife**
	— ma femme
	— *mah fahm*

I am on holiday
Je suis en vacances
jer swee zan vah-kans

I am a student
Je suis étudiant
jer swee zay-tew-dyan

I live in London
J'habite à Londres
jah-beet ah londr

I am from	— **Britain**
Je suis	— Britannique
jer swee	— *bree-tah-neek*
	— **England**
	— Anglais
	— *ang-lay*
	— **Scotland**
	— Ecossais
	— *zay-koh-say*
I am from	— **Wales**
Je suis	— Gallois
jer swee	— *gahl-wah*
	— **Ireland**
	— Irlandais
	— *zeer-lan-day*
	— **America**
	— Américain
	— *zah-may-reek-ern*
	— **Australia**
	— Australien
	— *zoh-strah-lyern*
	— **South Africa**
	— Sud-Africain
	— *sewd-ahf-ree-kern*
	— **New Zealand**
	— Néo-Zélandais
	— *nayoh-zay-lan-day*

Common Questions

Where?
Où?
oo

Where is...?
Où se trouve...?
oo ser troov...

Where are...?
Où se trouvent...?
oo ser troov...

When?
Quand?
kan

Everyday Phrases

What?
Quoi/Comment?
kwah/koh-mon

How?
Comment?
koh-man

How much?
Combien?
kohm-byern

Who?
Qui?
kee

Why?
Pourquoi?
poor-kwah

Which?
Lequel?
ler-kail

Have you got any change?
Avez-vous de la monnaie?
ahvay voo der lah moh-nay

How long will it take?
Il y en a pour combien de temps?
eel-yohn-ah poor kohm-byern der tan

How much do I have to pay?
Combien dois-je payer?
kohm-byern dwah-jer pay-yay

What do you call this in French?
Comment appelez-vous ceci en français?
koh-man tah-play voo ser-see an fran-say

What does this mean?
Que veut dire ceci?
ker ver deer ser-see

What is the problem?
Quel est le problème?
kail ai ler proh-blaim

What is this?
Qu'est-ce que c'est?
kais-ker say

What is wrong?
Qu'est-ce qui ne va pas?
kais-kee ner vah pah

What time do you close?
A quelle heure fermez-vous?
ah kail err fair-may voo

Where can I change my clothes?
Où puis-je me changer?
oo pwee-jer mer shan-gay

Who did this?
Qui a fait cela?
kee ah fay ser-lah

Who should I see about this?
A qui puis-je m'adresser?
ah kee pwee-jer mah-drai-say

Where can I buy a postcard?
Où puis-je acheter une carte postale?
oo pwee-jer ahsh-tay ewn kahrt pohs-tahl

Do you know a good restaurant?
Connaissez-vous un bon restaurant?
koh-nai-say voo zern bon rais-toh-ran

Do you mind if I...?
Est-ce que ça vous dérange si...?
ais-ker sah voo day-ranj see...

Asking the Time

What time is it?
Quelle heure est-il?
kail err ay-teel

It is...
Il est...
eel ai

a quarter past ten
dix heures et quart
dee-zerr ay kahr

a quarter to eleven
onze heures moins le quart
on-zerr mwan ler kahr

after three o'clock
après trois heures
ah-prai trwah zerr

at about one o'clock
vers une heure
vair ewn err

at half past six
à six heures et demie
ah see-zerr ay der-mee

at night
la nuit
lah nwee

before midnight
avant minuit
ah-van mee-nwee

early
de bonne heure
der bohn err

eleven o'clock
onze heures
onz err

five past ten
dix heures cinq
deez err sank

five to eleven
onze heures moins cinq
onz err mwan sank

half past eight exactly
huit heures et demie pile
weet err zai der-mee peel

half past ten
dix heures et demie
deez err zai der-mee

in an hour's time
dans une heure
dan zewn err

in half an hour
dans une demi-heure
dan zewn der-mee err

late
tard
tahr

midnight
minuit
mee-nwee

nearly five o'clock
presque cinq heures
praisk sank err

soon
bientôt
byern-toh

ten o'clock
dix heures
dee zerr

ten past ten
dix heures dix
dee zerr dees

ten to eleven
onze heures moins dix
on zerr mwan dees

this afternoon
cet après-midi
sait ah-prai mee-dee

this evening
ce soir
ser swahr

this morning
ce matin
ser mahtern

tonight
cette nuit
sait nwee

twelve o'clock (midday)
midi
mee-dee

twenty-five past ten
dix heures vingt-cinq
dee zerr vern-sank

twenty to eleven
onze heures moins vingt
onz err mwan vern

two hours ago
il y a deux heures
eel ee ah derr zerr

Common Problems

I have no currency
Je n'ai pas d'argent liquide
jer nay pah dahr-jan lee-keed

I have dropped a contact lens
J'ai laissé tomber une lentille
jay lay-say tohm-bay ewn lan-tee

I cannot find my driving licence
Je ne trouve pas mon permis de conduire
jer ner troov pah mon pair-mee der kon-dweer

I have lost my credit cards
J'ai perdu mes cartes de crédit
jay pair-dew may kahrt der kray-dee

I must see a lawyer
Je veux voir un avocat
jer ver vwahr ern ah-voh-kah

My car has been stolen
On m'a volé ma voiture
on mah voh-lay mah vwah-tewr

My handbag has been stolen
On m'a volé mon sac
on mah voh-lay mon sahk

My wallet has been stolen
On m'a volé mon portefeuille
on mah voh-lay mon pohrt-fery